The Eighteenth-Century British Novel and Its Background:

an annotated bibliography and guide to topics

by
H. GEORGE HAHN
and
CARL BEHM III

The Scarecrow Press, Inc.
Metuchen, N.J., & London
1985

Library of Congress Cataloging in Publication Data

Hahn, H. George (Henry George), 1942–
    The eighteenth-century British novel and its
background.

    Includes index.
    1. English fiction--18th century--History and
criticism--Bibliography. I. Behm, Carl, 1942–
II. Title.
Z2014.F4H33 1985   [PR851] 016.823'5'09   85–1745
ISBN 0–8108–1786–1

CONTENTS

Acknowledgments   v

Preface   vii

PART I: A GUIDE TO TOPICS: AN INDEX OF SUBJECTS,
            THEMES, AND CRITICAL ISSUES   1

PART II: BIBLIOGRAPHIES AND SURVEYS OF CRITICISM   49

PART III: STUDIES OF EIGHTEENTH-CENTURY LIFE:
            BACKGROUNDS OF THE NOVEL   57

PART IV: GENERAL CRITICISM OF THE EIGHTEENTH-
            CENTURY BRITISH NOVEL AND RELATED
            STUDIES   115

PART V: MAJOR NOVELISTS   153

                Daniel Defoe   153
                Henry Fielding   175
                Samuel Richardson   206
                Tobias Smollett   229
                Laurence Sterne   245

PART VI: MINOR NOVELISTS   269

                Penelope Aubin   269
                Robert Bage   270
                Jane Barker   271
                William Beckford   271
                Arthur Blackamore   275
                Frances Moore Brooke   276
                Henry Brooke   277
                Fanny Burney, Mme. d'Arblay   278
                John Cleland   282
                Francis Coventry   284
                Richard Cumberland   285
                Mary Davys   285

Thomas Day   286
Sarah Fielding   287
William Godwin   288
Oliver Goldsmith   294
Richard Graves   301
John Hawkesworth   302
Mary Hays   302
Eliza Haywood   303
Thomas Holcroft   304
Elizabeth Inchbald   305
Charles Johnstone   307
Sophia Lee   307
Charlotte Ramsay Lennox   308
Matthew Gregory Lewis   309
Henry Mackenzie   311
Delarivière Manley   313
John Moore   314
Ann Radcliffe   315
Clara Reeve   318
Mary Darby Robinson   319
Elizabeth Singer Rowe   320
Sarah Scott   321
Frances Sheridan   322
Charlotte Turner Smith   322
George Walker   324
Horace Walpole   324
Mary Wollstonecraft   328

PART VII: "NEAR" NOVELISTS   331

           Samuel Johnson   331
           Jonathan Swift   346

Index of Critics and Scholars   373

iv

ACKNOWLEDGMENTS

Primary thanks must go to the Faculty Development Committee of Towson State University, whose commitment to scholarship and generous help in the form of two grants fueled this project to its completion.

Appreciation is due to our students and research aides, Alicia Driesen, Gary Gura, Kerri Roberts, Christopher Scharpf, and Halaine Silberg, whose checking and rechecking, in monklike mien, tested our accuracy.

Special gratitude goes to the staff of Cook Library at Towson, particularly to Librarian Thomas Strader, who provided office space, and to Reference Librarian Marcella Fultz, who filled those offices with interlibrary loans.

Praise is due also to the word-processing staff at Towson. Without the assistance of Alcie Cooper and Tammy Boyce this book would not have been possible.

Finally, citations for patience go to Cynthia, Susan, Jennifer, and Justin, who never failed to keep this project in proper critical perspective.

PREFACE

Notes on Using This Guide

The eighteenth century did not suffer criticism lightly. To Steele, "Of all mortals, a critic is the silliest." To Fielding, critics are "clerks who have assumed dictatorial powers." And to Sterne, "Of all the cants which are canted in this canting world ... the cant of criticism is the most tormenting."

This checklist of modern criticism of the Georgian novel prefers to regard critics as expert witnesses ready for trial duty to explain a novel, to validate a line of argument in a research paper, or to support a position in a seminar exchange. Much as the lawyer has access to catalogues of experts offering authoritative evidence, the users of this bibliography--advanced undergraduate and graduate students, their professors, and their reference librarians--will find here a directory of authorities on specific issues recurrent to the eighteenth-century British novel.

THE GUIDE TO TOPICS

The key to effective use of this book is Part I: A Guide to Topics. It is helpful in three main ways.

As a Topic Finder. Nothing is more important for the student than settling on an appropriate topic. The "Guide to Topics" lists more than eight hundred themes, subjects, and critical issues. It is meant for browsing, for suggesting possibilities that range from "Bildungsroman" to "Novel of sensibility," from "Autobiographical elements in the novel" to "Personality of novelist," from "The Church" to "The Navy." And the student of a nautical turn of mind who fixes on "The Navy" will be directed not only to critics who have written on the naval aspects of Roderick Random, but also to historians of the Royal Navy in the eighteenth century whose work deepens our understanding of the background of Smollett's novel.

An additional value of the topic index is that it encourages the student to connect issues. The student drawn to "The Navy" will discover a further entry, "The Sailor," which may suggest an essay on Smollett's characterization. Juxtaposing "The Sailor" with "The Pirate" raises other possibilities. The student who questions whether the depiction of sailors in Smollett is more or less realistic than the depiction of pirates in Defoe has taken the first step towards a thesis. And it is then that the authorities listed in this bibliography may be called upon to offer their testimony.

As an Evidence Finder. More than 3,000 books, parts of books, and articles are listed and annotated topically in this bibliography. The student who uses the "Guide to Topics" will be directed to those works, and only those works, which pointedly treat his or her subject. An examination of titles and annotations in the body of the bibliography will quickly provide a manageable but authoritative checklist of pertinent criticism, the best that has been written on the chosen topic. Hence there lies the value of the "Guide to Topics" to the reference librarian as well, who typically must field such questions as, "I've got to do a paper on Richardson's use of setting. Where can I find information on it?"

The "Guide to Topics" underlines the numbers of books and articles of the highest scholarly caliber to direct the user to the best and the brightest criticism on a particular topic. And accordingly any research paper that has not engaged these authorities is deficient in its use of expert evidence, an objection the professor or research librarian can quickly raise.

It is important to note, though, that the topic index does not attempt an exhaustive listing of relevant sources under every topic. Especially in the case of highly restrictive or duplicative topics, only one or two model essays might be cited. The user must seek out related headings, a task which carries with it the benefit of expanding his or her perspective on the subject. Under "Chastity," for example, the researcher will find an essay precisely on that topic. But to expand the checklist the user must move beyond that single model essay and call for additional expert testimony by examining those titles listed under such related topics as "Sex," "Virtue," "Morality," and "Women."

As a Pedagogical Tool. The "Guide to Topics" offers a valuable survey of recurring ideas of the Georgian novelists and their critics. Additionally, lengthy lists of character types, sub-genres, and specific subjects will be found under such broad headings as "Characterization," "Novel," and "Religion."

The "Guide to Topics" also permits the student or professor to see at a glance how much or how little attention has been paid to a particular novelist on a given subject since the section of the bibliography in which an entry is to be found follows each topic. For example, the entries for "The Rake" are "Background: 406; Fielding: 1632; Richardson: 1681, 1733, 1840, 1852." Immediately apparent are the possibilities for a truly pioneering thesis using the topic on another author, perhaps on a minor novelist like Goldsmith or Lewis.

Finally, the professor will find it a useful guide for students seeking ancillary reading on assigned novels. Or prepping a class or seminar for next week's lecture on sentiment versus satire in The Vicar of Wakefield, the professor can alert students to the crucial criticism under these two topic headings; then insight and evidence will replace hazy impressions and generalizations, with a better class discussion the result.

THE BIBLIOGRAPHY

This bibliography ranges broadly across the terrain of the Georgian novel and its background, but it is selective. To use the book efficiently, the user must be aware of this selectivity.

Authors Included. This bibliography encompasses the main twentieth-century critical and biographical scholarship on the major novelists (Defoe, Richardson, Fielding, Smollett, and Sterne); the "near novelists" (Frederick Karl's phrase, which we have limited to refer to Johnson and Swift); and thirty-nine minor novelists (e.g., Penelope Aubin, Eliza Haywood, Henry Mackenzie). The criteria for inclusion among this last group are two: first, the author must have published a novel between 1700 and 1799, and second, the author must have a recognized reputation as a novelist or have been the subject of a critical or scholarly work within the past twenty-five years.

Entries of Exceptional Importance. Entries marked with a bullet (•) represent books of distinguished caliber. Those marked with a solid box (■) are articles and parts of books of exceptional value. The entries so designated include not only seminal studies with a well-deserved reputation, but also recent books and articles that offer new insights or chart new courses in the criticism of the eighteenth-century novel.

Exclusions. This bibliography excludes brief notes, dissertations, foreign language items, introductions to the novels, recorded criticism, outdated and superseded criticism, factual biographical notes the substance of which has been incorporated into full-scale biographies, "popular" criticism, book reviews, and review articles. There will, of course, be exceptions; those are made stipulatively at the authors' judgment.

Terminal Date. The bibliography is inclusive through 1981 and is as thorough as possible through 1984. To bring this register of literary scholarship down to date, the researcher should begin with the 1982 MLA International Bibliography, now topically annotated itself.

PART I: A GUIDE TO TOPICS

An Index of Subjects, Themes, and Critical Issues

ABSURD, THE
   Sterne: 2165, 2252.
ACHIEVEMENT AND REPUTATION
   Fielding: 1388. Richardson: 1728, 1800. Smollett: 1877,
   1906. Goldsmith: 2515. Lewis: 2614. Johnson: 2768.
ADDISON AND STEELE
   Novel: 888. Swift: 3015.
ADOLESCENT, THE
   Novel: 855, 1052, 1060.
ADULTERY. See also SEX.
   Background: 641. Fielding: 1510.
AESTHETIC DISTANCE
   Fielding: 1374. Smollett: 1943.
AESTHETIC THEORY AND BACKGROUND
   Bibliographies: 25. Background: 80, 101, 157, 160, 178, 179,
   217, 260, 262, 279, 321, 354, 355, 389, 425, 426, 452, 465, 468,
   513, 520, 525, 543, 601, 640, 663, 741. Novel: 927, 956, 1006.
AFRICA
   Defoe: 1242.
AGGRESSION. See also VIOLENCE.
   Defoe: 1201.
AGRICULTURAL REVOLUTION. See also AGRICULTURE.
   Background: 171, 462, 483.
AGRICULTURE. See also COUNTRY LIFE.
   Background: 221, 253, 255, 266, 359, 374, 377, 397, 402, 676.
ALE
   Background: 319.
ALLEGORY
   Novel: 764. Defoe. 1131, 1141, 1190, 1192, 1195, 1276, 1298,
   1310, 1314, 1340. Fielding: 1406, 1558, 1594, 1603, 1614, 1651.
   Richardson: 1704, 1706, 1791, 1869. Johnson: 2790, 2793,
   2814, 2826, 2844. Swift: 2985, 3001, 3002, 3030, 3058, 3067,
   3110, 3124, 3167, 3185.
ALLUSION. See also CLASSICAL ALLUSIONS AND BIBLICAL ALLU-
      SIONS.
   Novel: 834, 875, 1303. Fielding: 1508. Richardson: 1702.
AMBIGUITY
   Defoe: 1144. Fielding: 1380, 1570. Sterne: 2094. Gold-
   smith: 2538, 2551. Radcliffe: 2665. Johnson: 2854, 2860,

2890. Swift: 3033.
AMBIVALENCE
  Defoe: 1171. Lewis: 2611. Radcliffe: 2650.
AMERICA
  Bibliographies: 38, 59. Richardson: 1689, 1732. Sterne:
  2076, 2131, 2224.
AMERICAN, THE
  Novel: 865.
AMERICAN REVOLUTION
  Background: 239, 507, 584. Novel: 865.
"AMIABLE HUMORIST." See also BENEVOLENCE and "GOOD-
  NATURED MAN."
  Novel: 1077. Sterne: 2257.
AMUSEMENTS. See SPORT AND RECREATION.
ANALOGUES. See SOURCES, ANALOGUES, AND INFLUENCES.
ANCIENTS VS. MODERNS
  Swift: 2942.
ANDROGYNY
  Defoe: 1154.
ANGELOLOGY
  Defoe: 1135.
ANGLICANISM
  Background: 102, 107, 208, 219, 312, 519. Fielding: 1392.
  F. Brooke: 2333. Johnson: 2784, 2868.
ANTI-CLERICALISM. See also THE CLERGY.
  Background: 256.
ANTI-HERO. See also HERO/HEROINE.
  Novel: 743.
ANTI-REVOLUTIONARY NOVEL. See also CONSERVATISM and
  JACOBIN NOVEL.
  Walker: 2702.
ANTI-SLAVERY FICTION
  Novel. 1075.
ANXIETY
  Defoe: 1184, 1275. Burney: 2382.
APOLOGUE. See also DIDACTICISM; EXEMPLUM; and FABLE.
  Johnson: 2836, 2878.
APPEARANCE VS. REALITY
  Smollett: 1915, 1944, 1946. Burney: 2364. Goldsmith: 2504.
APPRENTICE, THE
  Background: 537.
ARCHITECTURE. See also LITERATURE AND THE OTHER ARTS.
  Background: 89, 101, 167, 178, 189, 215, 227, 231, 260, 349,
  387, 414, 459, 577, 578, 579, 651, 652, 676, 729, 736. Novel:
  917, 937, 1049, 1072. Smollett: 2015. Beckford: 2302, 2307,
  2328. Walpole: 2706, 2724, 2735.
ARISTOCRACY, THE. See also "BOURGEOIS ARISTOCRACY" and
  SOCIAL STRUCTURE.
  Background: 316, 362, 481, 558, 648a, 659, 672, 722.
ARISTOTLE
  Defoe: 1337. Fielding: 1577.

ARMY, THE
Background: 268, 290, 343, 363, 577, 676.
ART. See also LITERATURE AND THE OTHER ARTS.
Background: 80, 86, 106, 158, 179, 185, 247, 260, 281, 309,
348, 383, 427, 446, 459, 468, 533, 536, 538, 577, 599, 631, 676,
700, 729, 741. Novel: 762, 766, 1011. Fielding: 1596.
Sterne: 2072, 2141.
ARTISTIC DECLINE. See also DEFECTS IN THE NOVEL.
Beckford: 2299. Burney: 2353, 2366.
ARTISTIC DEVELOPMENT
Defoe: 1211, 1353. Fielding: 1384, 1418, 1423, 1475, 1480,
1495, 1560, 1572, 1600. Richardson: 1674, 1715, 1728, 1777,
1794, 1831. Smollett: 1893, 1895, 1939, 2037. Burney: 2356.
Godwin: 2438, 2478. Graves: 2556. Holcroft: 2577.
ASSOCIATIONISM. See also JOHN LOCKE.
Background: 110, 349. Sterne: 2054, 2060, 2080, 2158.
AUGUSTANISM
Novel: 831.
AUGUSTINIANISM
Background: 254, 310.
AUTHOR-READER RELATIONSHIP [includes reader-response criti-
cism]
Novel: 766, 778, 942, 1002, 1032, 1092. Defoe: 1281, 1341.
Fielding: 1395, 1419, 1435, 1460, 1481, 1530, 1532, 1537, 1544,
1549, 1563, 1590, 1598, 1617, 1620, 1636. Richardson: 1696,
1744, 1783, 1820, 1852, 1855, 1863, 1865. Smollett: 1968, 1991.
Sterne: 2053, 2055, 2065, 2100, 2145, 2193, 2201, 2205, 2208,
2268, 2270. Godwin: 2486. Lewis: 2611. Johnson: 2897,
2898, 2907. Swift: 2960a, 2984, 3031, 3033, 3046, 3087, 3100,
3105, 3117, 3133, 3142a, 3168, 3169.
AUTHORITY
Background: 207. Defoe: 1260. Fielding: 1369, 1641.
Richardson: 1717. Swift: 3127.
AUTOBIOGRAPHICAL ELEMENTS IN THE NOVEL
Novel: 1055. Defoe: 1204, 1276, 1322, 1339. Fielding: 1379,
1451a, 1470, 1611, 1643, 1658. Richardson: 1813. Smollett:
1900, 1961, 1966, 1978. Sterne: 2113, 2117, 2135, 2147, 2219,
2247. Beckford: 2317. Burney: 2353, 2382. Goldsmith:
2513. Smith: 2698. Walpole: 2716. Johnson: 2792, 2818,
2827. Swift: 2958, 2985, 3018, 3043, 3123, 3142, 3165.
AUTOBIOGRAPHICAL FAÇADE
Defoe: 1191. Johnson: 2847, 2863.
AUTOBIOGRAPHY
Defoe: 1158.

BAROQUE
Background: 414.
BASTARDY
Background: 437, 583. Novel: 833. Smollett: 1908.
BATH

Background: 180, 200, 278, 510, 591, 692. Smollett: 1931.
BEAUTY, OR THE BEAUTIFUL. See THE SUBLIME AND THE
  BEAUTIFUL.
BEDLAM. See also INSANITY.
  Background: 271. Mackenzie: 2622.
BENEVOLENCE
  Background: 382, 586. Novel: 751. Fielding: 1458, 1607,
  1652. Richardson: 1751. Sterne: 2278. Goldsmith: 2536.
BERKELEY, GEORGE. See also INTELLECTUAL BACKGROUND.
  Richardson: 1862.
BEST SELLERS. See also BOOK TRADE and READING PUBLIC.
  Novel: 934, 953, 954. Moore: 2639.
BIBLICAL ALLUSIONS
  Fielding: 1402, 1485, 1558, 1579, 1594. Richardson: 1694.
  Sterne: 2236. Godwin: 2476. Goldsmith: 2499, 2523, 2533.
  Johnson: 2789, 2865. Swift: 2939, 3006, 3088, 3159, 3183.
BIBLIOGRAPHY OF BIBLIOGRAPHIES
  Bibliographies: 39.
BIBLIOGRAPHY OF BOOK REVIEWS
  Bibliographies: 15, 20, 22, 40, 42, 74.
BIBLIOGRAPHY OF CRITICISM
  Bibliographies: 1, 2, 5, 6, 9, 10, 13, 14, 18, 24, 27, 28, 29,
  34, 35, 36, 46, 47, 51, 52, 55, 63, 67, 68, 72, 77. Defoe:
  1121, 1123, 1124. Fielding: 1356, 1358, 1362, 1363. Richard-
  son: 1667, 1669. Smollett: 1879, 1880, 1881, 1883, 1884a.
  Sterne: 2042, 2043, 2047. Aubin: 2283. Bage: 2286, 2287.
  Barker: 2294. Beckford: 2298. H. Brooke: 2341. Burney:
  2346, 2347. Cleland: 2389. Davys: 2412. Day: 2414. S.
  Fielding: 2419, 2420. Godwin: 2425. Graves: 2554. Hays:
  2560. Haywood: 2563, 2564. Holcroft: 2569. Inchbald:
  2580. Lennox: 2591, 2592. Lewis: 2600, 2601. Mackenzie:
  2618. Manley: 2630, 2631. Radcliffe: 2640, 2641, 2642.
  Reeve: 2674, 2675. Robinson: 2678. Rowe: 2681. Scott:
  2686. Sheridan: 2689. Smith: 2693, 2694, 2695. Walpole:
  2703, 2705. Wollstonecraft: 2738, 2739. Johnson: 2754.
  Swift: 2918, 2925, 2926, 2928a, 2931, 2932.
BIBLIOGRAPHY OF HISTORICAL STUDIES
  Bibliographies: 17, 30, 50, 56, 61.
BIBLIOGRAPHY OF PRIMARY SOURCES
  Bibliographies: 4, 8, 9, 11, 12, 14, 21, 23, 25, 31, 32, 33, 35,
  36, 38, 44, 45, 46, 48, 49, 52, 53, 54, 59, 66, 69, 71. Backgrounds: 246. Novel: 817, 933, 1071. Defoe: 1120. Fielding: 1362. Richardson: 1670. Smollett: 1880, 1884a. Bage:
  2287. Beckford: 2296, 2297, 2298. Burney: 2347. Cleland:
  2390. Godwin: 2424. Goldsmith: 2491, 2492. Holcroft:
  2570. Inchbald: 2581. Lennox: 2592. Lewis: 2601. Radcliffe: 2642. Reeve: 2675. Smith: 2695. Walpole: 2704,
  2705. Johnson: 2755, 2757. Swift: 2932.
BIBLIOGRAPHY OF SCIENCE
  Bibliographies: 26.
BILDUNGSROMAN. See also INITIATION.

Smollett: 1995. Godwin: 2476.
BIOGRAPHY. See also PERSONAL RELATIONS BETWEEN AUTHORS.
Novel: 879, 926, 992, 1060a. Defoe: 1137, 1178, 1250, 1274,
1275, 1334. Fielding: 1381, 1387, 1420, 1429, 1485, 1566, 1584.
Richardson: 1716, 1728, 1800, 1832, 1878. Smollett: 1902,
1959, 1962, 1965. Sterne: 2058, 2079, 2086, 2090, 2091, 2097,
2117, 2126, 2132, 2134, 2191, 2213, 2235, 2258, 2281, 2282.
Beckford: 2300, 2303, 2304, 2318, 2325. F. Brooke: 2333.
H. Brooke: 2344. Burney: 2353, 2362, 2365, 2368, 2370,
2377. Cleland: 2395. Day: 2415, 2418. S. Fielding: 2421.
Godwin: 2431, 2436, 2441, 2446, 2457, 2489. Goldsmith: 2521,
2534, 2536, 2549, 2550, 2552. Graves: 2556. Hawkesworth:
2559a. Hays: 2562. Haywood: 2568. Holcroft: 2576. Inchbald: 2584, 2588. Lennox: 2596, 2597, 2598. Lewis: 2613.
Mackenzie: 2629. Manley: 2634, 2638. Radcliffe: 2651.
Robinson: 2680. Rowe: 2682, 2684. Sheridan: 2692. Smith:
2700. Walpole: 2712, 2721, 2723, 2725. Wollstonecraft: 2741,
2742, 2743, 2747, 2749, 2752, 2753. Johnson: 2770, 2772,
2782, 2785, 2787, 2820, 2840, 2869, 2904. Swift: 2965, 2975,
2988, 3013, 3015, 3028, 3039, 3057, 3058, 3059, 3064, 3090.
BLACKS. See also ANTI-SLAVERY FICTION; RACISM; and SLAV-
    ERY.
Background: 201, 626, 693. Novel: 828, 862, 936. Defoe:
1242.
BLUESTOCKING, THE. See also WOMEN and WOMEN NOVELISTS.
Background: 130, 546, 620. Novel: 856. Sterne: 2126.
BOOK CLUBS
Background: 411.
BOOK TRADE. See also BEST SELLERS; MINERVA PRESS; and
    READING PUBLIC.
Bibliographies: 16. Background: 125, 127, 196, 198, 246,
280, 284, 551, 585, 684, 837. Novel: 953, 954, 1073, 1088.
Cleland: 2396. Goldsmith: 2531.
BOOKSELLERS
Background: 676.
BOSWELL, JAMES
Fielding: 1611.
"BOURGEOIS ARISTOCRACY." See also THE MIDDLE CLASS.
Richardson: 1740.
BOURGEOIS IDEOLOGY. See also THE MIDDLE CLASS.
Novel: 905. Fielding: 1541. Richardson: 1722, 1834. Bur-
ney: 2381.
BOW STREET RUNNERS. See also CRIME AND PUNISHMENT.
Background: 204.
BRIDGES
Background: 706.
BRITISH EMPIRE
Background: 295. Novel: 892a.
BROBDINGNAGIANS, THE
Swift: 3071.
BUNBURY, HENRY WILLIAM

Walpole: 2729.
BUNYAN'S THE PILGRIM'S PROGRESS
Johnson: 2790.
BURKE, EDMUND
Novel: 887. Godwin: 2430, 2432, 2458, 2460. Radcliffe:
2670. Walpole: 2720.
BURLESQUE NOVEL. See also PARODY and SATIRE.
Novel: 1037. Richardson: 1836. Smollett: 1888.
BURTON, ROBERT
Sterne: 2146.
BYRON, LORD
Novel: 870, 1081. Beckford: 2309, 2331.
BYRONIC HERO. See GOTHIC HERO.

CAD, THE. See also THE RAKE.
Richardson: 1756.
CALVINISM
Defoe: 1332.
CAMBRIDGE UNIVERSITY. See also THE UNDERGRADUATE and
THE PROFESSOR.
Background: 401, 635, 648, 733, 734. Novel: 1007. Johnson:
2910.
CANADA
F. Brooke: 2333, 2334, 2335, 2338, 2340.
CANALS
Background: 320.
CANNIBALS
Defoe: 1277.
CAPITALISM. See also ECONOMICS and MERCANTILISM.
Background: 299, 645. Novel: 905, 946. Defoe: 1167, 1200.
Smollett: 1993. Cleland: 2393, 2405.
CARICATURE. See also ILLUSTRATION and SATIRE.
Background: 98, 99, 100, 286, 287, 342, 530. Fielding: 1539.
Smollett: 1911, 1954, 1970, 1975. Walpole: 2729.
CASUISTRY
Defoe: 1325.
CATHOLICISM
Background: 134. Novel: 1063, 1076. Sterne: 2166. Aubin:
2284.
CENSORSHIP
Richardson: 1841. Cleland: 2401.
CERVANTES, MIGUEL DE. See also DON QUIXOTE.
Novel: 1059. Sterne: 2254.
CHANCE. See also FORTUNE and PROVIDENCE.
Sterne: 2230.
CHARACTERIZATION. See also NAMES OF CHARACTERS; PHYSI-
OGNOMY; PHYSIOLOGY; PSYCHOLOGY OF CHARACTERS;
GESTURES AND MANNERISMS; and SPEECH AND DIALOGUE.
Background: 194. Novel: 744, 746, 750, 764, 844, 850, 858,
900, 902, 919, 932, 941, 1035, 1038, 1077, 1084, 1101. Defoe:

1143, 1151, 1153, 1156, 1157, 1168, 1169, 1170, 1176, 1181,
1182, 1193, 1196, 1198, 1205, 1218, 1219, 1224, 1228, 1232,
1239, 1249, 1254, 1255, 1282, 1288, 1290, 1292, 1293, 1297,
1301, 1311, 1320, 1322, 1328, 1331, 1332, 1344, 1350, 1352,
1355. Fielding: 1364, 1365, 1369, 1396, 1397, 1418, 1425, 1434,
1446, 1447, 1459, 1466, 1485, 1496, 1502, 1511, 1513, 1517,
1527, 1534, 1537, 1539, 1539a, 1542, 1565, 1570, 1578, 1589,
1591, 1594, 1602, 1603, 1610, 1622, 1623, 1627, 1641, 1645,
1652, 1659, 1663. Richardson: 1676, 1677, 1678, 1679, 1683,
1690, 1693, 1694, 1701, 1702, 1703, 1707, 1708, 1712, 1713,
1715, 1733, 1740, 1741, 1746, 1749, 1752, 1756, 1758, 1767,
1777, 1780, 1792, 1793, 1806, 1810, 1813, 1816, 1817, 1821,
1822, 1828, 1835, 1839, 1843, 1849, 1850, 1852, 1859, 1860,
1871, 1872, 1873, 1874. Smollett: 1887, 1912, 1919, 1947, 1952,
1955, 1957, 1973, 1974, 1975, 1982, 1983, 1984, 1988, 1989,
1992, 1997, 2003, 2013, 2014, 2016, 2017, 2041. Sterne: 2056,
2088, 2093, 2106, 2111, 2115, 2124, 2128, 2141, 2150, 2155,
2164, 2167, 2169, 2173, 2175, 2184, 2185, 2194, 2205, 2215,
2218, 2227, 2228, 2239, 2242, 2249, 2253, 2260, 2261, 2263,
2269. Aubin: 2284. Burney: 2350, 2360, 2364, 2380, 2385,
2386, 2388. Cleland: 2397, 2406, 2408. Godwin: 2427, 2428,
2448, 2461, 2463, 2464, 2465, 2474, 2480, 2483, 2487. Goldsmith: 2497, 2505, 2508, 2509, 2523, 2524, 2542. Haywood:
2567. Inchbald: 2585, 2587. Johnstone: 2589. Lennox:
2599. Lewis: 2607, 2610. Radcliffe: 2650. Reeve: 2676.
Smith: 2701. Walpole: 2714. Johnson: 2837, 2847, 2891,
2911. Swift: 2941, 2955, 2956, 2980, 3007, 3011, 3019, 3045,
3051, 3053, 3062, 3079, 3088, 3108, 3118, 3119, 3122, 3126,
3132, 3143, 3150, 3153, 3154, 3157, 3161, 3188.
CHARITY. See also BENEVOLENCE and PHILANTHROPY.
Background: 403. Fielding: 1438, 1606, 1651. Goldsmith:
2508. Johnson: 2868, 2901. Swift: 3057.
CHARITY SCHOOL
Background: 407.
CHASTITY. See also SEX.
Fielding: 1647.
CHEYNE, GEORGE
Background: 421.
CHILD, THE
Novel: 806.
CHILD OF NATURE. See also NOBLE SAVAGE.
Novel: 1081.
CHILDREN
Background: 114, 484, 550, 557, 672. Novel: 986.
CHILDREN'S LITERATURE
Novel: 758, 759, 905, 922, 985, 992, 993. Day: 2415.
CHRISTIANITY. See also specific denominations.
Background: 105, 223, 248, 254, 289, 339, 650. Novel: 761,
964, 1000. Defoe: 1141, 1155, 1190, 1195, 1216, 1248, 1298,
1306b, 1325. Fielding: 1364, 1382, 1513, 1589, 1662. Richard-
son: 1680, 1703, 1718, 1720, 1735, 1782a, 1811, 1835. Sterne:

2129, 2189. Goldsmith: 2499. Rowe: 2683. Walpole: 2711.
Johnson: 2779, 2782, 2784, 2804, 2810, 2826, 2849, 2860, 2864,
2868, 2876, 2887. Swift: 2935, 3006, 3026, 3040, 3041, 3058,
3076, 3083, 3086, 3088, 3116, 3121, 3153, 3167, 3174, 3184, 3188.
CHRONOLOGY. See TIME.
CHURCH, THE
    Background: 90, 163, 206, 223, 284, 577, 607, 635, 638, 655,
    676. Goldsmith: 2509. Swift: 3059.
CIBBER, COLLEY
    Fielding:: 1628. Sterne: 2186.
CICERO
    Swift: 3155.
CINDERELLA
    Richardson: 1788.
CIRCULATING LIBRARIES
    Background: 127, 326, 412, 490, 684. Novel: 1073, 1078.
CITY LIFE. See also LONDON.
    Background: 83, 113, 155, 186, 288, 450, 607, 619a. Novel:
    833. Defoe: 1184, 1316. Richardson: 1776.
CIVIL SERVANT, THE
    Background: 363.
CLASSICAL ALLUSIONS
    Novel: 845, 1091. Defoe: 1233. Fielding: 1402, 1453, 1550,
    1558, 1561, 1586, 1595, 1600. Richardson: 1694. Johnson:
    2789. Swift: 3024, 3032, 3050, 3073.
CLERGY, THE. See also ANTI-CLERICALISM; THE PARSON; and
    THE ORDINARY.
    Background: 107, 185, 284, 315, 363, 479, 655, 841. Fielding:
    1382, 1661. Goldsmith: 2509, 2546.
"CLOCKWORK" ANALOGY
    Novel: 820, 923. S. Fielding: 2422.
CLOSURE
    Novel: 952. Defoe: 1209. Fielding: 1425, 1539a, 1542.
    Richardson: 1713. Smollett: 1922. Sterne: 2050, 2064, 2130.
    Godwin: 2428, 2437. Johnson: 2837, 2895, 2903.
CLOTHING [as imagery]
    Fielding: 1446. Richardson: 1795. Swift: 2953, 3066.
CLUBS. See also COFFEE HOUSES.
    Background: 81, 406, 485, 486.
COACHING. See also TRANSPORTATION.
    Background: 117, 682. Novel: 744.
COFFEE HOUSES. See also CLUBS.
    Background: 249, 356, 448.
COLONIALISM. See also BRITISH EMPIRE and IMPERIALISM.
    Defoe: 1200, 1266.
COMEDY [includes humor, wit]
    Novel: 751, 788, 914, 930, 974, 1058, 1077, 1112. Fielding:
    1399, 1421, 1426, 1430, 1455, 1470, 1480, 1491, 1492, 1512,
    1545, 1550, 1591, 1614, 1632, 1663. Richardson: 1715, 1852.
    Smollett: 1900, 1916, 1990, 2024, 2025. Sterne: 2054, 2059,
    2068, 2071, 2082, 2092, 2097, 2102, 2110, 2121, 2139, 2140,

2148, 2150, 2157, 2159, 2162, 2163, 2164, 2216, 2249, 2250, 2252, 2255, 2257, 2261, 2274. Cleland: 2391. Goldsmith: 2543. Graves: 2555. Johnson: 2769, 2780, 2896, 2912, 2915. Swift: 2946, 2986, 2989, 3045, 3130, 3132, 3149.
COMMON SENSE. See also SCOTTISH "COMMON SENSE SCHOOL." Novel: 996. Beckford: 2318a. Johnson: 2845a.
COMMUNICATIONS
  Background: 676.
COMMUNION
  Sterne: 2061.
COMPARISON OF NOVELISTS. See also RASSELAS-CANDIDE COMPARISON.
  Novel: 763, 800, 818, 820, 898, 932, 1012, 1051. Defoe: 1173, 1183, 1251, 1291, 1300, 1338, 1342, 1351. Fielding: 1399, 1401, 1405, 1412, 1431, 1448, 1458, 1471, 1472, 1483, 1494, 1504, 1518, 1538, 1548, 1559, 1569, 1583, 1635, 1640, 1649, 1660. Richardson: 1672, 1687, 1700, 1705, 1728, 1730, 1751, 1761, 1762, 1774, 1776, 1803, 1804, 1815, 1819, 1825, 1854, 1857, 1876. Smollett: 1942, 1947, 1964, 1981, 2009, 2033, 2036. Sterne: 2062, 2067, 2068, 2074, 2087, 2114, 2189, 2226, 2266, 2267. Beckford: 2318a, 2320. H. Brooke: 2343. Burney: 2350, 2363, 2369. Cleland: 2394, 2406. Cumberland: 2411. Day: 2416, 2417. S. Fielding: 2422. Godwin: 2427, 2470, 2471. Goldsmith: 2502, 2542. Haywood: 2565. Lennox: 2595. Mackenzie: 2621. Radcliffe: 2654. Johnson: 2819, 2845a, 2848, 2859, 2876. Swift: 2975, 3079, 3103, 3131.
COMPOSITION OF THE NOVEL
  Defoe: 1174, 1267. Richardson: 1677, 1694, 1725, 1727, 1750, 1755, 1775, 1800, 1818, 1829, 1860, 1861. Smollett: 1904. Sterne: 2050, 2064, 2073, 2081, 2190, 2206, 2211. Beckford: 2311, 2314, 2327. Burney: 2352. Coventry: 2410. Godwin: 2437. Goldsmith: 2511, 2516, 2518, 2535, 2546. Lennox: 2594. Lewis: 2602. Johnson: 2799, 2833, 2840, 2846, 2848, 2908, 2915, 2916. Swift: 2985, 3089.
COMPROMISE
  Swift: 3179.
CONCORDANCE
  Fielding: 1441, 1442.
CONDUCT BOOKS
  Richardson: 1757.
CONFESSIONAL NOVEL
  Defoe: 1177. Godwin: 2442.
CONGREGATIONALISM
  Background: 408, 475.
CONGREVE, WILLIAM
  Novel: 974.
CONSERVATISM
  Background: 147, 842. Fielding: 1666. Smollett: 2000. Radcliffe: 2647, 2650. Walker: 2702. Johnson: 2778, 2796.
"CONSPICUOUS CONSUMPTION." See also LUXURY.
  Background: 686.

CONSTABLE, JOHN
  Background: 427, 535.
CONSTITUTION OF GREAT BRITAIN
  Background: 725.
CONTEMPTUS MUNDI
  Mackenzie: 2625.
CONTRAST AS TECHNIQUE
  Background: 260, 525. Novel: 928. Fielding: 1445, 1492,
  1496, 1514, 1520, 1591, 1626, 1633, 1638. Richardson: 1673,
  1852. Smollett: 1912. Sterne: 2092, 2116, 2152, 2175, 2259.
  F. Brooke: 2336. Mackenzie: 2623. Johnson: 2862. Swift:
  3051, 3104, 3173.
CONVENTIONS OF THE GEORGIAN NOVEL. See also THEORY AND
  PRACTICE OF THE NOVEL and specific conventions (e.g.,
  AUTOBIOGRAPHICAL FAÇADE).
  Novel: 781a, 795, 886, 979, 998, 1030, 1038, 1082. Defoe:
  1151. Richardson: 1705, 1846. Smollett: 1999. Sterne:
  2067, 2149, 2197, 2249, 2262. Cleland: 2391, 2394.
CONVERSATION
  Background: 699a.
CONVERSION AND REPENTANCE
  Defoe: 1196, 1198, 1210, 1249, 1283, 1301. Richardson: 1805.
  Johnson: 2868. Swift: 3184.
COQUETTE, THE
  Novel: 1033.
"COSMIC TORYISM." See also INTELLECTUAL BACKGROUND.
  Background: 723.
COUNTRY HOUSE, THE
  Background: 387. Novel: 824, 892a.
COUNTRY LIFE. See also RETIREMENT; RURAL IDEAL; and VIL-
  LAGES.
  Background: 106, 115, 135, 169, 180, 222, 256, 275, 276, 317,
  331, 337, 369, 374, 377, 387, 423, 462, 483, 494, 495, 502, 503,
  532, 546, 656, 676, 719. Novel: 824, 1047.
COUNTRY VS. CITY
  Background: 168, 728, 1086. Novel: 1056a. Fielding: 1475.
  Smollett: 2003. Goldsmith: 2498, 2522.
COURAGE
  Defoe: 1262.
COURT, THE. See also ARISTOCRACY.
  Background: 119, 418, 526.
COURTESY BOOKS
  Burney: 2367.
COZENS, ALEXANDER
  Beckford: 2329.
CRIME AND PUNISHMENT. See also LAW; PRISONS; and NEWGATE.
  Background: 118, 120, 121, 145, 190, 202, 204, 284, 290, 341,
  351, 373, 392, 419, 451, 480, 544, 546, 572, 625, 665, 676, 689.
  Novel: 833, 978. Defoe: 1134, 1259, 1270, 1301, 1316. Field-
  ing: 1368, 1566, 1666.
CRIMINAL, THE

Background: 537. Novel: 814. Defoe: 1246, 1315.
CRIMINAL BIOGRAPHY. See also NEWGATE CALENDAR.
    Background: 351, 373, 451, 763. Novel: 1015. Defoe: 1270.
CRITICAL REVALUATION
    Novel: 778, 802, 829, 851, 878, 908, 1028, 1034, 1099, 1100.
    Defoe: 1122, 1220, 1306b. Fielding: 1365, 1468, 1474, 1598,
    1627, 1666. Richardson: 1771, 1863, 1869. Smollett: 1882,
    1892a, 1910, 1996. Sterne: 2188, 2226. Bage: 2293. Mac-
    kenzie: 2627. Johnson: 2793, 2806, 2841. Swift: 2946, 3008,
    3030.
CRITICISM. See EIGHTEENTH-CENTURY CRITICISM AND REVIEWS
    OF THE NOVEL; SURVEY OF CRITICISM; and BIBLIOGRAPHY
    OF CRITICISM.
CRUSOISM
    Novel: 1020.
CRYPTONYMY
    Novel: 868.
CURLL, EDMUND
    Barker: 2295.
CUSTOMS. See also MANNERS; PROPRIETY; and SOCIAL BACK-
    GROUND.
    Background: 301, 319, 463.

DEATH
    Background: 182. Novel: 1029. Richardson: 1715, 1717,
    1782a, 1833. Rowe: 2683. Johnson: 2782, 2810.
DECEIT
    Fielding: 1526.
DEFECTS IN THE NOVEL. See also ARTISTIC DECLINE and
    DICHOTOMY OF INTENTION.
    Defoe: 1204, 1220. Fielding: 1452, 1474, 1500, 1547, 1599,
    1658. Richardson: 1788. Smollett: 1922, 1956, 2039, 2040.
    Beckford: 2327. Godwin: 2438, 2450. Goldsmith: 2507, 2538.
    Radcliffe: 2662. Scott: 2687. Swift: 3031, 3037。
DEGENERATION
    Swift: 2946.
DEISM
    Background: 282, 455, 467, 836。 Swift: 3041, 3184.
DELUSION
    Novel: 912。 Johnson: 2763.
DEMOCRACY
    Background: 303. Fielding: 1597. Holcroft: 2579.
DEMOGRAPHY. See also POPULATION.
    Background: 168, 182, 296, 318, 362, 429, 498.
DESIRE
    Novel: 867.
DETECTIVE, THE
    Novel: 978. Godwin: 2464.
DIALECT. See SPEECH AND DIALOGUE.
DIALOGUE. See SPEECH AND DIALOGUE.

DIARY, THE
  Background: 270. Novel: 1050.
DICHOTOMY OF INTENTION [uncertain purpose of novelist]. See
  also DEFECTS IN THE NOVEL.
  Fielding: 1478. Richardson: 1704. Godwin: 2463. Gold-
  smith: 2551. Lewis: 2611. Radcliffe: 2665. Wollstonecraft:
  2746.
DIDACTICISM. See also APOLOGUE and NOVEL OF DOCTRINE.
  Novel: 881, 913, 995, 1015, 1032, 1088. Defoe: 1179. Rich-
  ardson: 1676, 1688, 1690, 1746, 1752, 1875a. Goldsmith:
  2545. Mackenzie: 2623. Reeve: 2676. Rowe: 2683. Woll-
  stonecraft: 2751. Johnson: 2817, 2830. Swift: 3044.
DIDEROT, DENIS
  Sterne: 2114.
DIGRESSIONS AND INTERPOLATED STORIES. See also POINT OF
  VIEW AND NARRATOR and PLOT, STRUCTURE, AND DE-
  SIGN.
  Novel: 778, 1032. Fielding: 1386, 1404, 1408, 1411, 1428,
  1445, 1449, 1454, 1485, 1490, 1514, 1520, 1533, 1582, 1592,
  1593, 1626, 1640, 1647, 1649. Smollett: 2036. Sterne: 2116,
  2176, 2195, 2204, 2222, 2276. Goldsmith: 2527.
DIPLOMACY
  Background: 367, 368, 432.
DISCOVERY
  Fielding: 1527. Swift: 3011.
DISEASE. See also MEDICINE.
  Background: 155, 182, 203. Defoe: 1261.
DISGUISE
  Defoe: 1218. Goldsmith: 2504.
DISPLACEMENT. See ESTRANGEMENT.
DISSENTERS [religious]
  Background: 137, 449, 581, 585, 701.
DISSENTING ACADEMIES
  Background: 528. Defoe: 1189.
DIVERSIFICATION
  Johnson: 2831.
DOMESTIC LIFE
  Background: 116, 138, 159, 276, 345, 443, 546, 579, 676, 736.
  Defoe: 1295.
DOMINANCE
  Richardson: 1740, 1849.
DON QUIXOTE. See also MIGUEL DE CERVANTES.
  Fielding: 1428, 1449, 1454, 1551, 1557.
DRAMATIC CONVENTIONS IN THE NOVEL
  Novel: 789, 975. Fielding: 1391, 1424, 1434. Richardson:
  1721, 1759, 1777, 1780, 1813, 1830, 1838. Smollett: 1989.
  Sterne: 2084, 2125, 2133. Goldsmith: 2497. Walpole: 2714.
DRAPER, ELIZABETH
  Sterne: 2281.
DREAD
  Defoe: 1184.

DREAMS
Novel: 822, 969. Richardson: 1697, 1875. Godwin: 2447.
DRESS AND FASHION. See also CLOTHING [as imagery].
Background: 154, 218, 276, 439, 450, 568, 676.
DUTCH, THE
Swift: 2960, 3069.

"ECONOMIC INDIVIDUALISM"
Defoe: 1257.
ECONOMICS
Background: 94, 95, 122, 170, 183, 185, 188, 193, 205, 229,
234, 266, 317, 338, 352, 359, 371, 397, 402, 443, 453, 478, 504,
515, 540, 607, 638, 681, 686, 688, 702, 710, 731, 732, 737.
Novel: 865, 946. Defoe: 1178, 1266, 1271. Swift: 3056,
3060.
EDUCATION. See also DISSENTING ACADEMIES; CHARITY
SCHOOL; GRAMMAR SCHOOL; CAMBRIDGE UNIVERSITY; GLAS-
GOW UNIVERSITY; and OXFORD UNIVERSITY.
Bibliographies: 62. Background: 78, 92, 130, 181, 209, 284,
333, 377, 407, 512, 528, 531, 557, 575, 610, 632, 647, 667, 676,
681, 687. Novel: 909. Defoe: 1162, 1189, 1227. Fielding:
1401, 1501. Richardson: 1749. Sterne: 2074. Godwin: 2454,
2467, 2489. Manley: 2636. Johnson: 2761, 2773, 2788, 2798,
2849, 2910.
EIGHTEENTH-CENTURY CRITICISM AND REVIEWS OF THE NOVEL.
See also NOVELISTS ON THE NOVEL and THEORY AND
PRACTICE OF THE NOVEL.
Bibliographies: 41, 42, 51, 57, 74, 76. Novel: 853, 857,
1024, 1078, 1111. Defoe: 1264, 1296. Fielding: 1357, 1448,
1472, 1538, 1556, 1657. Richardson: 1728, 1761, 1804, 1829,
1877. Smollett: 1958. Sterne: 2046, 2143, 2257. Coventry:
2410. Goldsmith: 2503, 2515, 2547. Lewis: 2612. Radcliffe:
2657. Johnson: 2756, 2760, 2775, 2839, 2855. Swift: 3017,
3022, 3182.
ELITE, THE
Background: 541, 546.
EMBLEM
Fielding: 1380.
EMOTION. See SENSIBILITY.
EMPIRICISM
Background: 310. Johnson: 2901.
ENCLOSURES. See also AGRICULTURE.
Background: 135, 255, 331, 483, 548, 656, 677.
ENGLISHMAN, THE
Novel: 796.
ENLIGHTENMENT, THE. See also INTELLECTUAL BACKGROUND.
Background: 166, 250, 283.
ENTHUSIASM
Background: 482, 673.
EPIC

Background: 629. Novel: 928, 1085. Defoe: 1340, 1346. Fielding: 1450, 1491, 1510, 1522, 1545, 1561, 1600, 1615, 1630, 1631, 1644. Richardson: 1864. Swift: 3072.
EPISTEMOLOGY. See also PHILOSOPHY OF NOVELIST.
Novel: 826, 869, 999, 1027, 1068, 1092, 1116. Defoe: 1143. Fielding: 1400, 1488, 1532, 1587, 1616, 1620, 1640. Richardson: 1717, 1719. Smollett: 1969, 2004, 2036. Sterne: 2083, 2101, 2109, 2113, 2122, 2179, 2225, 2264. Godwin: 2477. Goldsmith: 2507. Johnson: 2774, 2875. Swift: 2997, 3071.
EPISTOLARY NOVEL
Bibliographies: 11, 23, 66. Novel: 746, 747a, 772, 816, 817, 872, 1044. Richardson: 1676, 1682, 1688, 1707, 1742, 1763, 1769, 1796. Smollett: 1947. Burney: 2369.
EQUIPOISE
Johnson: 2898.
EROTICISM. See also SEX.
Cleland: 2399.
ESTATE AGENT, THE
Background: 375.
ESTRANGEMENT [and displacement]
Defoe: 1310. Richardson: 1820. Sterne: 2061. Swift: 3121.
ETHICS. See also MORALITY.
Background: 175, 214, 310, 840. Fielding: 1392.
EVANGELICAL FICTION
Novel: 965.
EVANGELICALISM
Background: 219, 248, 635.
EVIL
Background: 488. Novel: 910. Fielding: 1416, 1622. Richardson: 1679, 1870. Lewis: 2607. Johnson: 2776, 2882. Swift: 2986, 3099.
EXEMPLUM. See also APOLOGUE; DIDACTICISM; and FABLE.
Fielding: 1560. Richardson: 1746.
EXILE, THE. See also FLIGHT.
Defoe: 1310.
EXISTENTIALISM
Johnson: 2844, 2860, 2864. Swift: 3099.
EXOTIC, THE
Beckford: 2316.
EXPLORATION
Background: 676.

FABLE. See also APOLOGUE; DIDACTICISM; and EXEMPLUM.
Novel: 809, 967. Johnson: 2774. Swift: 2969, 3149.
FAIRY TALE
Novel: 758. Richardson: 1733, 1788, 1807, 1875. Burney: 2353.
"FALLEN WOMAN," THE
Novel: 893.
FAMILY

Background: 437, 516, 537, 646, 672. Novel: 833. Defoe:
1289. Fielding: 1555. Richardson: 1718a, 1754, 1806, 1847,
1859. Smollett: 1913, 1980. Burney: 2375, 2376, 2378.
Goldsmith: 2513. Inchbald: 2586. Johnson: 2809.
FAMINE
    Background: 182.
FASHION. See DRESS AND FASHION.
FATHERHOOD
    Smollett: 1977. Goldsmith: 2523.
FEAR
    Novel: 914.
FEELING. See SENSIBILITY and "MAN OF FEELING."
"FEMALE QUIXOTE"
    Novel: 1048.
FEMINISM
    Background: 126, 130, 593. Novel: 848, 871, 1064. Defoe:
    1228, 1286, 1294. Richardson: 1823. F. Brooke: 2337.
    Burney: 2358, 2359, 2374. Wollstonecraft: 2743.
FEMININITY
    Defoe: 1201.
FIELDING, SIR JOHN
    Fielding: 1566.
FILM AND THE NOVEL
    Novel: 897. Fielding: 1383, 1390.
FINANCE
    Background: 378.
FIRE SCENES
    Richardson: 1745. Smollett: 1936.
FLIGHT. See also THE EXILE and ESTRANGEMENT.
    Novel: 797.
FOLKLORE. See also SUPERSTITIONS.
    Background: 300.
FONTHILL. See also ARCHITECTURE.
    Beckford: 2301, 2302, 2306, 2307, 2328.
FOOL, THE
    Swift: 3153, 3162.
FORBIDDEN KNOWLEDGE
    Swift: 3121.
FOREIGN LITERATURE IN ENGLISH TRANSLATION
    Bibliographies: 48.
FOREIGN POLICY
    Background: 368, 432.
FOREIGN RECEPTION. See INFLUENCE AND REPUTATION ABROAD.
"FORMAL REALISM." See also REALISM.
    Novel: 1099.
FORTITUDE
    Goldsmith: 2495.
"FORTUNATE FALL," THE
    Fielding: 1416.
FORTUNE. See also CHANCE; PROVIDENCE; CHRISTIANITY; and
    PHILOSOPHY OF NOVELIST.

Novel: 1056a. Fielding: 1489, 1629.
FORTY-FIVE, THE. See REBELLION OF 1745.
FOURTH VOYAGE ISSUES [nature of man, meaning of Houyhnhnms,
    Swift's intentions]. See also HOUYHNHNMS; YAHOOS; and
    GULLIVER-SWIFT RELATIONSHIP.
Swift: 2919, 2920, 2921, 2924, 2938, 2946, 2968, 2969, 2977,
    2983, 2984, 2985, 2990, 2992, 2996, 3006, 3012, 3024, 3025,
    3027, 3034, 3040, 3041, 3045, 3046, 3050, 3051, 3054, 3076,
    3083, 3096, 3098, 3099, 3105, 3111, 3114, 3128, 3130, 3141,
    3149, 3150a, 3167, 3174, 3175, 3178, 3180, 3184, 3186.
FOX HUNTING
    Background: 164, 391.
FRANCE
    Bibliographies: 69. Novel: 931, 1071.
FREE THINKING. See also DEISM.
    Swift: 2936.
FRENCH REVOLUTION. See also JACOBIN NOVEL and JACOBIN-
    ISM.
    Background: 151, 461, 538, 569. Novel: 852, 988. Bage:
    2291. Holcroft: 2572. Inchbald: 2582. Smith: 2699. Wal-
    pole: 2733.
FREUD, SIGMUND
    Novel: 887.
"FRIEND OF MANKIND." See also BENEVOLENCE; CHARITY; and
    PHILANTHROPY.
    Background: 382.
FUNERALS
    Background: 274.

GAMEKEEPER, THE. See also POACHING.
    Background: 502.
GAMES. See SPORT AND RECREATION.
GARRICK, DAVID
    Sterne: 2125.
GAZETTEER. See also PLACES IN THE NOVEL and GEOGRAPHY.
    Background: 264.
GENEROSITY
    Goldsmith: 2539.
GENTILITY
    Defoe: 1312, 1344.
GENTLEMAN, THE
    Background: 139, 294, 476. Novel: 1040. Defoe: 1148, 1238,
    1312. Richardson: 1715, 1840. Smollett: 2003, 2019.
    Sterne: 2237.
GENTRY. See also THE SQUIRE and THE ARISTOCRACY.
    Background: 450, 495, 496, 517a, 558, 648a. Fielding: 1625.
    Smollett: 1918.
GEOGRAPHY. See also GAZETTEER; MAPS; and PLACES IN THE
    NOVEL.
    Background: 221, 264. Johnson: 2802. Swift: 3085.

GERMANY
  Bibliographies: 48. Novel: 832, 1005. Sterne: 2108. Lewis:
  2604.
GESTURES AND MANNERISMS
  Fielding: 1434. Richardson: 1839. Sterne: 2242. Swift:
  3138.
GILPIN, WILLIAM
  Background: 262.
GLASGOW UNIVERSITY
  Background: 477.
GODWIN, WILLIAM [as subject]
  Holcroft: 2576, 2579. Walker: 2702.
GOOD BREEDING. See also GENTILITY and THE GENTLEMAN.
  Background: 140. Fielding: 1572.
"GOOD MAN"
  Novel: 1106. Fielding: 1496, 1658.
"GOOD-NATURED MAN." See also "AMIABLE HUMORIST."
  Background: 624. Novel: 1077. Fielding: 1459.
GOOD SAMARITAN, THE
  Background: 537.
GOOD WILL
  Fielding: 1576.
GOODNESS VS. GREATNESS
  Fielding: 1479, 1496, 1570, 1572.
"GOTHIC" [the word]
  Background: 358, 454.
GOTHIC BACKGROUND
  Background: 101, 124, 178, 227, 231, 425, 455, 459, 468.
  Novel: 925, 934, 963, 1011.
GOTHIC HERO
  Novel: 750, 910, 1001, 1081.
GOTHIC NOVEL. See also GOTHIC HERO and HORROR AND TER-
  ROR.
  Bibliographies: 34, 46, 67, 71. Background: 142, 538.
  Novel: 748, 755, 762, 770, 776, 804, 822, 843, 859, 860, 868,
  869, 872, 878, 885, 887, 890, 896, 910, 912, 913, 914, 915, 917,
  919, 968, 972, 988, 1010, 1035, 1070, 1073, 1076, 1088, 1089,
  1095. Richardson: 1736. Godwin: 2440. Lee: 2590. Lewis:
  2603, 2608, 2615, 2617. Radcliffe: 2646, 2649, 2653, 2658,
  2665, 2668. Smith: 2696. Walpole: 2727, 2735, 2737.
GOUT. See also DISEASE and MEDICINE.
  Background: 203.
GOVERNESS, THE
  Background: 546.
GOVERNMENT. See POLITICS; PARLIAMENT; HOUSE OF LORDS;
  HOUSE OF COMMONS; and THE COURT.
GRAMMAR. See also PUNCTUATION and SYNTAX.
  Sterne: 2253.
GRAMMAR SCHOOLS
  Background: 667, 687.
GRAMMAPHOBIA

Swift: 2958.
GRAND TOUR. See also TRAVEL.
  Background: 350, 424, 668, 713. Moore: 2639.
"GREAT CHAIN OF BEING"
  Background: 456.
"GREAT MAN," THE
  Fielding: 1608.
GREEK REVIVAL. See also NEOCLASSICISM.
  Background: 215.
GROTESQUE, THE
  Background: 104. Novel: 860, 972. Smollett: 1941. Sterne:
  2118. Beckford: 2313. Walpole: 2732. Swift: 2963, 3148.
GROTTOES
  Background: 101.
GRUB STREET. See also CITY LIFE; LONDON; and THE WRITER
  IN SOCIETY.
  Background: 284, 595. Johnson: 2772.
"GUIDE" TRADITION
  Defoe: 1210.
GUILT
  Godwin: 2484.
GULLIVER-SWIFT RELATIONSHIP
  Swift: 2979, 2992, 3030, 3045, 3083, 3084, 3113, 3130, 3149.

HAPPINESS
  Background: 306, 716. Johnson: 2831, 2836, 2845, 2854,
  2865, 2866, 2886, 2906, 2911, 2913.
"HAPPY MAN"
  Background: 600.
HARTLEY, DAVID. See also INTELLECTUAL BACKGROUND.
  Sterne: 2158.
HEALTH. See also MEDICINE; HOSPITALS; and THE PHYSICIAN.
  Smollett: 1997, 2016.
HELL-FIRE CLUB, THE. See also CLUBS.
  Background: 485.
HERMENEUTICS
  Novel: 1003.
HERO/HEROINE. See also ANTI-HERO; GOTHIC HERO; QUIXOTIC
  HERO; and ROGUE HERO.
  Background: 398. Novel: 744, 828, 844, 900, 941, 951. De-
  foe: 1344. Fielding: 1473, 1518. Richardson: 1790. Smol-
  lett: 1964.
HIERARCHY
  Godwin: 2432.
HISTORICAL FAÇADE [in the novel]
  Novel: 773, 813, 879, 906, 1069. Fielding: 1642.
HISTORICAL NOVEL
  Defoe: 1164. Godwin: 2439.
HISTORIOGRAPHY
  Background: 561. Novel: 785, 1003. Defoe: 1270. Fielding:

1400, 1407, 1552, 1621. Sterne: 2136. Goldsmith: 2537.
Swift: 3038.
HISTORY
Background: 146, 295, 309, 394, 498, 507, 508, 521, 638, 669,
702, 724. Novel: 833, 1056a. Fielding: 1619. Swift: 3152.
HISTORY OF THE NOVEL
Novel: 753, 754, 755, 781, 791, 819, 847, 894, 1020, 1034,
1050, 1066, 1099. Defoe: 1221, 1223.
HOBBES, THOMAS. See also INTELLECTUAL BACKGROUND.
Defoe: 1190. Sterne: 2092. Swift: 3004, 3135.
HOBBYHORSE
Sterne: 2128, 2256.
HOGARTH, WILLIAM
Background: 86, 87, 287, 534, 537, 611, 663, 698. Novel:
959, 989. Fielding: 1422, 1487, 1539, 1554, 1596. Smollett:
1970. Sterne: 2072, 2141. Mackenzie: 2622.
HOLCROFT, THOMAS [as subject]
Godwin: 2482.
HOMER
Background: 629. Defoe: 1346. Richardson: 1864. Swift:
3073.
HOMUNCULUS, THE
Sterne: 2160, 2245.
HORACE
Novel: 845.
HORROR AND TERROR. See also GOTHIC NOVEL.
Background: 142. Novel: 860, 878, 887, 915, 968, 1000, 1010,
1070. Defoe: 1273. Lewis: 2603, 2617. Radcliffe: 2659,
2668, 2669.
HOSPITALS
Background: 172, 220.
HOUSE OF COMMONS. See also PARLIAMENT.
Background: 418, 509, 564, 621, 660.
HOUSE OF LORDS. See also PARLIAMENT.
Background: 675.
HOUSEWIFE, THE
Background: 138.
HOUYHNHNMS, THE
Swift: 2934, 2938, 2967, 2968, 3005, 3025, 3041, 3050, 3053,
3071, 3087, 3100, 3116, 3120, 3141, 3149, 3150, 3167, 3180,
3183, 3096.
HOWARD, JOHN. See also PRISONS and CRIME AND PUNISHMENT.
Background: 707.
HUMANISM
Background: 334, 410. Novel: 792, 840. Goldsmith: 2533.
Johnson: 2791, 2812, 2844, 2909.
HUMANITARIANISM
Background: 261.
HUMANITIES, THE
Background: 209.
HUME, DAVID. See also INTELLECTUAL BACKGROUND.

Background: 334. Fielding: 1624. Johnson: 2917.
HUMOR. See COMEDY.
HUMORS, THE
    Fielding: 1502. Smollett: 2034. Swift: 3045.
HYMNS
    Background: 475.
HYPOCHONDRIA
    Smollett: 1973.
HYSTERIA
    Background: 271. Smollett: 2017.

IDEALISM
    Swift: 3081.
ILLUSTRATION
    Background: 327. Novel: 1114. Richardson: 1671, 1724.
    Sterne: 2103. Burney: 2361. Goldsmith: 2526. Swift:
    2981.
IMAGERY. See also SYMBOLISM.
    Background: 430. Novel: 792, 812, 822, 840, 1029, 1035,
    1067, 1068. Defoe: 1180, 1329, 1343. Fielding: 1377, 1446,
    1447, 1463, 1485, 1568. Richardson: 1681, 1715, 1737, 1768,
    1792, 1809. Smollett: 1946, 1948, 1969, 1976, 2011, 2020,
    2027. Sterne: 2109, 2141, 2195, 2244. Beckford: 2323. Cle-
    land: 2405. Goldsmith: 2516, 2534. Mackenzie: 2626. Rad-
    cliffe: 2643, 2644, 2664, 2667. Johnson: 2777, 2797, 2805,
    2870. Swift: 2950, 2951, 3035, 3051, 3066, 3099, 3179, 3183.
IMAGINARY VOYAGE
    Bibliographies: 36. Background: 272. Swift: 2983.
IMAGINATION
    Background: 298, 604. Novel: 762, 821. Smollett: 1913.
    Sterne: 2169. Radcliffe: 2646. Johnson: 2764, 2765, 2768,
    2816, 2874.
IMMORTALITY
    Sterne: 2141. Johnson: 2832, 2888, 2905. Swift: 2936, 3116.
IMPERIALISM. See also BRITISH EMPIRE and COLONIALISM.
    Defoe: 1192, 1194.
IMPOSTURE
    Swift: 3188.
IMPOTENCE
    Novel: 1053. Richardson: 1872. Sterne: 2248.
IMPRISONMENT
    Background: 247. Novel: 776, 793, 797, 1506. Richardson:
    1738. Godwin: 2476. Johnson: 2850. Swift: 3137.
INCEST
    Novel: 1113. Fielding: 1381, 1398, 1457, 1550. S. Fielding:
    2421.
INDIAN, THE. See also NOBLE SAVAGE; PRIMITIVISM; and STATE
    OF NATURE
    Novel: 771. Smollett: 1987.
INDIVIDUALISM

Defoe: 1200, 1349, 1350. Fielding: 1648.
INDUSTRIAL REVOLUTION
Background: 96, 228, 266, 328, 435, 466, 478, 511, 540, 549,
562, 566, 904.
INDUSTRIALIST, THE
Background: 265.
INDUSTRY AND TRADE
Background: 136, 189, 221, 225, 226, 232, 266, 314, 328, 338,
359, 377, 450, 478, 487, 492, 505, 540, 577, 676, 710. Defoe:
1130, 1175, 1243. Smollett: 1931. Swift: 3125.
INFLUENCE AND IMITATION
Novel: 782, 823, 1041, 1093. Defoe: 1126, 1132, 1302. Rich-
ardson: 1723, 1728, 1736, 1749, 1782, 1856. Sterne: 2098,
2192, 2197. Barker: 2295. Beckford: 2309, 2331. H.
Brooke: 2343. Burney: 2351. Godwin: 2473. Lewis: 2612.
Mackenzie: 2620. Radcliffe: 2645. Sheridan: 2690. Smith:
2697. Walpole: 2727. Johnson: 2783. Swift: 2983, 3103.
INFLUENCE AND REPUTATION ABROAD
Bibliographies: 59, 69. Novel: 832, 931, 1005, 1043, 1071.
Richardson: 1689, 1732. Sterne: 2049, 2076, 2108, 2131,
2151, 2161, 2209, 2224, 2238. Goldsmith: 2503.
INFORMATION THEORY
Sterne: 2178.
INITIATION. See also MATURATION.
Richardson: 1686, 1719, 1802, 1811. Burney: 2385. Godwin:
2483. Lennox: 2595.
INNOCENCE
Richardson: 1802.
INNOVATION
Novel: 763, 847, 886, 979. Fielding: 1388, 1615. Richardson:
1760, 1767, 1780. Smollett: 1890, 2022. Sterne: 2067, 2149,
2193, 2249. Barker: 2295. Beckford: 2313. Burney: 2363.
Godwin: 2474. Holcroft: 2577. Lewis: 2608. Radcliffe:
2653, 2654, 2657, 2667. Smith: 2700.
INNS
Background: 319, 580. Novel: 744.
INSANITY. See also SUICIDE; MELANCHOLY; HYPOCHONDRIA;
MADHOUSES; and BEDLAM.
Background: 271, 405, 529, 565, 604. Novel: 793, 794, 1031.
Defoe: 1170, 1186, 1330. Sterne: 2173. Mackenzie: 2622.
Johnson: 2791, 2803, 2809. Swift: 2977, 3150.
INTELLECTUAL BACKGROUND. See also PHILOSOPHY OF NOVEL-
IST.
Background: 91, 110, 123, 129, 141, 142, 143, 153, 166, 209,
214, 250, 272, 283, 293, 305, 309, 310, 313, 334, 371, 381, 399,
409, 415, 425, 456, 467, 499, 518, 567, 574, 585, 602, 662, 664,
685, 723, 738. Novel: 807, 924, 1006. Defoe: 1227, 1262,
1272, 1325. Fielding: 1384, 1459. Sterne: 2180. Goldsmith:
2506. Mackenzie: 2628. Johnson: 2832, 2838, 2868, 2882,
2905. Swift: 2942, 2968, 2990, 3052, 3092, 3111, 3115, 3174,
3175, 3181.

INTELLECTUAL ELITE
  Godwin: 2467.
"INTELLECTUAL REALISM."   See also REALISM.
  Novel: 753.
INTELLIGENCE
  Johnson: 2763.
INTERIOR DESIGN
  Background: 577, 676, 729.
INTERTEXTUALITY
  Defoe: 1302.
INTRODUCTORY GUIDE
  Background: 309, 335, 381. Novel: 827, 944, 945, 1046, 1065.
  Defoe: 1206, 1240, 1333, 1335. Fielding: 1432, 1516, 1519,
  1528, 1571. Richardson: 1682, 1772, 1773, 1799. Smollett:
  1906, 1967, 2023. Sterne: 2174, 2196, 2205, 2214, 2279. Au-
  bin: 2885. Bage: 2289, 2290. Beckford: 2308. Blackamore:
  2332. F. Brooke: 2335, 2340. H. Brooke: 2342, 2345. Bur-
  ney: 2348, 2355, 2371, 2373, 2384, 2387. Cumberland: 2411.
  Davys: 2413. Godwin: 2442, 2444, 2481, 2488. Goldsmith:
  2508, 2510, 2532, 2549. Hays: 2561. Haywood: 2568. Lewis:
  2609. Mackenzie: 2619. Manley: 2633. Radcliffe: 2660,
  2666. Robinson: 2679. Sheridan: 2691. Walpole: 2713,
  2718. Wollstonecraft: 2744. Johnson: 2807, 2892. Swift:
  2975, 2976, 2978, 3036, 3112, 3114, 3146.
IRELAND
  Background: 627. Goldsmith: 2503, 2548. Swift: 2999,
  3021, 3049, 3077, 3078.
IRISH, THE
  Background: 292. Swift: 3160.
IRISH STEREOTYPE
  Swift: 3160.
IRONY
  Novel: 779, 811, 899, 942, 961, 1051, 1098. Defoe: 1122,
  1152, 1201, 1222, 1258, 1265, 1343. Fielding: 1365, 1374,
  1435, 1459, 1465, 1471, 1476, 1507, 1540, 1546, 1549, 1562,
  1563, 1607, 1635. Smollett: 1950. Sterne: 2077, 2088, 2180,
  2217, 2266. Beckford: 2312. Burney: 2379. Godwin: 2472.
  Goldsmith: 2541, 2544. Johnson: 2765, 2906. Swift: 2974,
  2982, 3063, 3097.
IRRATIONALITY
  Background: 149, 417, 598. Lewis: 2606, 2608. Walpole:
  2711. Swift: 2990, 3099.
ISOLATION. See LONELINESS.
ITALIAN, THE
  Novel: 796.
ITALY
  Novel: 929. Sterne: 2151.

JACOBIN NOVEL [Novel of revolution in the 1790s]. See also
  FRENCH REVOLUTION; ANTI-REVOLUTIONARY NOVEL;

RADICALISM; and THE 1790s.
Background: 147. Novel: 852, 891, 892. Bage: 2291, 2292.
Godwin: 2451, 2452. Holcroft: 2571, 2572, 2573, 2574, 2578.
Inchbald: 2582, 2583. Smith: 2699.
JACOBINS [advocates of French Revolution]. See also FRENCH
    REVOLUTION, JACOBIN NOVEL; and THE 1790s.
Background: 199.
JACOBITISM [advocacy of restoration of the Stuart dynasty]. See
    also REBELLION OF 1745.
Background: 273, 396, 404, 444, 491, 542, 666. Defoe: 1148,
1230. Fielding: 1410, 1411.
JAPAN
    Sterne: 2238.
JEW, THE
    Novel: 828, 955, 1026, 1094.
JOHNSON, DR. SAMUEL [as subject]
    Background: 478. Fielding: 1472, 1538. Richardson: 1804.
JOURNALISM
    Background: 144, 433, 450, 457, 643, 721. Defoe: 1157.
    Sterne: 2219.
JOURNEY
    Background: 537. Novel: 989. Defoe: 1299. Fielding:
1475, 1555, 1576. Smollett: 1912, 1976, 1980, 1997, 2041.
Sterne: 2061, 2120. Burney: 2378. Graves: 2556. Inch-
bald: 2586. Johnson: 2777, 2789, 2790, 2802, 2814, 2831,
2895. Swift: 3067.
JUDGMENT
    Fielding: 1511, 1532, 1609.
JUSTICE
    Goldsmith: 2539.

LABOR RELATIONS
    Background: 236.
LABORER, THE
    Background: 276, 329, 330, 331, 549.
LANDSCAPE
    Background: 106, 131, 179, 262, 348, 525, 535. Novel: 972.
    Beckford: 2329. Radcliffe: 2648. Swift: 2997.
LANDSCAPE GARDENING. See also LITERATURE AND THE OTHER
    ARTS.
    Background: 80, 109, 177, 257, 260, 284, 353, 383, 384, 388,
393, 468, 543, 619, 630, 649, 676, 729, 741. Novel: 927.
Beckford: 2306, 2307. Walpole: 2710, 2728.
LANGUAGE. See STYLE AND LANGUAGE.
LAPUTANS, THE
    Swift: 3071, 3080.
LATITUDINARIANISM. See also ANGLICANISM and CHRISTIANITY.
    Background: 219, 311, 655. Fielding: 1382, 1664. Sterne:
2189.
LAW. See also CRIME AND PUNISHMENT and MARRIAGE LAW.

Bibliographies: 43. Background: 145, 244, 245, 290, 308, 341, 360, 403, 423, 503, 544, 572, 641, 676, 681, 705. Novel: 907, 1009. Defoe: 1134. Fielding: 1368, 1397, 1486, 1505, 1531, 1566, 1567, 1618, 1634, 1658, 1665. Smollett: 1937, 1978. Godwin: 2483. Johnson: 2851. Swift: 3005.
LAWYER, THE. See also LAW.
  Background: 363, 588.
LEISURE. See also SPORT AND RECREATION.
  Background: 552.
LETTER-WRITING
  Background: 85, 132, 370, 380, 390. Richardson: 1697, 1733, 1757, 1828. Hays: 2562. Rowe: 2685.
LIBEL
  Novel: 907.
LIBERALISM
  Background: 129. Novel: 833. Godwin: 2441.
LIBERTINISM
  Novel: 837, 971. Cleland: 2408.
LIBERTY
  Background: 247, 609, 662. Fielding: 1436, 1597. Johnson: 2763, 2901.
LIBRARIES. See also CIRCULATING LIBRARIES and LIBRARY OF NOVELIST.
  Background: 413.
LIBRARY OF NOVELIST
  Background: 84. Fielding: 1367. Sterne: 2095. Godwin: 2429. Goldsmith: 2496. Walpole: 2718, 2726. Johnson: 2808. Swift: 3177.
"LIFE AS ART"
  Fielding: 1485. Burney: 2385.
LILLIPUTIANS, THE
  Swift: 3021, 3071.
LITERACY. See also READING PUBLIC.
  Background: 82, 197, 198, 212, 435, 613, 617, 618, 647, 704, 718.
LITERATURE AND THE OTHER ARTS
  Background: 321, 383, 452, 465, 663. Novel: 927. Fielding: 1422.
"LITTLE LANGUAGE" [Swift's invented language in Gulliver's Travels]
  Swift: 2961, 2962, 3094, 3144.
LOCKE, JOHN. See also INTELLECTUAL BACKGROUND.
  Background: 334, 759. Novel: 924, 993. Smollett: 2020. Sterne: 2054, 2057, 2059, 2077, 2080, 2122, 2156, 2170, 2179, 2263, 2264. Johnson: 2763, 2800. Swift: 3115.
LOGIC
  Background: 372.
LONDON. See also CITY LIFE and GRUB STREET.
  Background: 81, 83, 113, 186, 192, 238, 288, 430, 450, 471, 497, 607, 619a, 652, 653, 676, 707, 737. Novel: 792, 1013. Defoe: 1261, 1306. Smollett: 1979.

LONELINESS [and isolation]. See also THE EXILE; FLIGHT; and
  THE WANDERER.
  Novel: 797, 1045. Defoe: 1193, 1262, 1336. Swift: 3011.
LORRAINE, CLAUDE
  Background: 468.
LOVE
  Background: 385. Novel: 787a, 800, 872. Defoe: 1241,
  1262, 1291. Fielding: 1412, 1456, 1492. Richardson: 1680,
  1700, 1715, 1718a, 1732, 1747, 1828, 1858, 1865. Sterne:
  2052, 2127. Cleland: 2404. Godwin: 2443. Mackenzie: 2625.
  Rowe: 2683.
LUGGNAGGIANS
  Swift: 3002.
LUXURY
  Background: 592, 622, 686. Defoe: 1266. Smollett: 2013.
  Goldsmith: 2500. Swift: 3056.

MADHOUSES. See also INSANITY and BEDLAM.
  Background: 271, 405, 529.
MAGAZINES. See NOVEL IN MAGAZINES.
MAIL-COACHMAN, THE. See also POST OFFICE.
  Background: 682.
MALE NOVELIST ASSUMING FEMALE IDENTITY. See also POINT
  OF VIEW AND NARRATOR.
  Defoe: 1293, 1311, 1339. Richardson: 1849. Cleland: 2400.
"MAN OF FEELING." See also SENSIBILITY and SENTIMENTAL
  HERO.
  Background: 210, 237, 311. Novel: 855, 1004, 1081. Smollett:
  1986, 1990. Sterne: 2255. Goldsmith: 2502. Mackenzie:
  2619, 2621, 2625, 2629.
MAN VS. SOCIETY. See also INDIVIDUALISM.
  Background: 185.
MAN VS. WOMAN
  Novel: 752, 1023, 1053. Richardson: 1690, 1714, 1756.
  Sterne: 2248. Burney: 2374.
MANAGEMENT
  Background: 562.
MANDEVILLE, BERNARD. See also INTELLECTUAL BACKGROUND.
  Background: 175, 299, 371, 415, 499, 515, 680. Novel: 768,
  1006, 1092. Defoe: 1253. Fielding: 1606. Richardson: 1862.
MANNERS. See also PROPRIETY; CUSTOMS; and NOVEL OF MAN-
  NERS.
  Background: 140, 301, 385, 636, 676. Novel: 1047.
MAPS. See also GEOGRAPHY.
  Swift: 2944.
MARIVAUX, PIERRE DE
  Richardson: 1808.
MARRIAGE
  Background: 633, 646, 659, 730. Novel: 752. Defoe: 1147,
  1262, 1266, 1279, 1289, 1345. Fielding: 1404, 1605, 1633,

1656. <u>Richardson</u>: 1749, <u>1754</u>, 1782a, 1797, 1806, 1827, 1834, <u>1847</u>, 1865. <u>Burney</u>: 2381. <u>Goldsmith</u>: 2525, 2546. <u>Johnson</u>: 2809.

MARRIAGE LAW
<u>Background</u>: 516. <u>Defoe</u>: 1279. <u>Fielding</u>: 1656. <u>Burney</u>: 2375. <u>Goldsmith</u>: 2525.

MARRIAGE PROPOSAL
<u>Fielding</u>: 1391.

MARVELLOUS, THE. See also THE SUPERNATURAL.
<u>Fielding</u>: 1489, 1630, <u>1653</u>, 1655.

MARYLAND
<u>Defoe</u>: 1188.

MASOCHISM
<u>Richardson</u>: 1789.

MASQUERADE
<u>Background</u>: 166a. <u>Defoe</u>: 1148, 1339. <u>Fielding</u>: 1434, 1445, 1605. <u>Richardson</u>: 1849. <u>Swift</u>: 2996.

MATERIALISM
<u>Background</u>: 738. <u>Defoe</u>: 1190, <u>1343</u>. <u>Cleland</u>: 2392.

MATURATION. See also INITIATION.
<u>Burney</u>: 2360.

MEALS. See also DOMESTIC LIFE.
<u>Background</u>: 276, 676.

MEDICINE
<u>Background</u>: 128, 155, 156, 162, 172, 175, 176, 182, 220, 325, 416, 420, 421, 422, 441, 484, 489, 573, 603, 604, 605, 676, 690, 691. <u>Richardson</u>: 1817. <u>Smollett</u>: 1914, 1952, 1971, 1972, 2006, 2008, 2017, 2031, 2041. <u>Swift</u>: 3055, 3139.

MELANCHOLY
<u>Bibliographies</u>: 65. <u>Background</u>: 142, <u>240</u>, 271, 500, 582, 603. <u>Novel</u>: 794, 958. <u>Defoe</u>: 1330. <u>Johnson</u>: 2762, 2766, 2818.

MEMOIRS
<u>Novel</u>: 926.

MERCANTILISM. See also ECONOMICS.
<u>Background</u>: 157, 346, 371, 714. <u>Defoe</u>: 1130, 1194. <u>Swift</u>: 3056, 3060.

MERCHANT, THE
<u>Background</u>: 450, 493, 556, 727. <u>Novel</u>: 946.

METHODISM
<u>Background</u>: 90, 224, 322, 458, 585, 623, 703. <u>Novel</u>: 1019, 1022, 1036. <u>Smollett</u>: 1930. <u>Graves</u>: 2555, 2556, 2559. <u>Walpole</u>: 2730.

METHODIST FICTION
<u>Novel</u>: 1019.

MICROCOSM, THE
<u>Novel</u>: 938. <u>Smollett</u>: 2038.

MICROSCOPE, THE
<u>Swift</u>: 3091.

MIDDLE CLASS, THE. See also BOURGEOIS IDEOLOGY and SOCIAL STRUCTURE.

Background: 648a, 718, 727. Novel: 874. Defoe: 1312.
Richardson: 1754.
MIDWIFE, THE
Richardson: 1729.
MIDWIFERY. See also PREGNANCY AND CHILDBIRTH.
Background: 615.
MILITIA, THE. See also THE ARMY.
Background: 711.
MILTON, JOHN
Richardson: 1679, 1811. Johnson: 2812, 2829.
MINERVA PRESS. See also BOOK TRADE.
Background: 127. Novel: 872.
MINIATURIZATION
Novel: 1068.
MISANTHROPY
Novel: 1004. Smollett: 1988, 1990. Godwin: 2480. Swift:
3083, 3084, 3130, 3149, 3170.
MISATTRIBUTION
Manley: 2635. Scott: 2688.
MISERY
Novel: 872.
MISOGYNY
Novel: 1023.
MOB, THE. See also CITY LIFE and RIOTS.
Background: 97, 100, 238, 343, 450, 537, 606, 644, 715.
MODERNITY
Sterne: 2094, 2253. Swift: 3121.
MONEY. See also LUXURY and WEALTH.
Background: 478. Novel: 805. Defoe: 1167, 1241, 1292.
Burney: 2356.
MONTAGU, LADY MARY WORTLEY
Novel: 857.
MONTAGU, MRS. EDWARD
Sterne: 2126.
MORALITY. See also ETHICS.
Background: 87, 245, 506, 515, 571, 586. Novel: 777, 782,
870, 994, 995, 1015. Defoe: 1130, 1148, 1149, 1163, 1175,
1179, 1198, 1209, 1241, 1259, 1278, 1301, 1306a, 1325, 1329.
Fielding: 1435, 1437, 1451, 1457, 1458, 1459, 1472, 1478, 1479,
1521, 1545, 1549, 1601, 1602, 1603, 1632, 1635, 1651, 1658,
1662. Richardson: 1676, 1678, 1679, 1688, 1699, 1700, 1733,
1746, 1749, 1751, 1752, 1753, 1754, 1761, 1778, 1868. Smollett:
1900, 1910, 1945, 2012, 2028. Sterne: 2069, 2082, 2085, 2172,
2260. Barker: 2295. Burney: 2367. Cleland: 2399. Godwin: 2462, 2463, 2476, 2483. Goldsmith: 2501, 2519. Radcliffe: 2665. Johnson: 2763, 2767, 2768, 2790, 2819, 2845,
2901, 2906, 2948. Swift: 2972, 3005, 3009, 3032, 3106, 3188.
MORE, SIR THOMAS
Swift: 3081, 3164, 3171.
MOTHER, THE
Defoe: 1167.

MOTIF INDEX
    Novel: 1089.
MOUNTAINS
    Background: 513.
MULSO, HESTER
    Richardson: 1861.
MUSIC. See also LITERATURE AND THE OTHER ARTS.
    Background: 165, 185, 260, 357, 431, 577, 628, 676, 739.
MUSICAL NOVEL
    Sterne: 2066, 2115.
MYSTERY
    Novel: 872, 912. Godwin: 2435a.
MYTH
    Novel: 787a, 1086. Defoe: 1150, 1187, 1217, 1232, 1270, 1348.
    Fielding: 1534. Richardson: 1834, 1859, 1875. Burney:
    2381. Godwin: 2447.

NABOB, THE
    Background: 366.
NAMES OF CHARACTERS. See also CHARACTERIZATION.
    Defoe: 1213, 1347. Fielding: 1485, 1517, 1645. Richardson:
    1866. Sterne: 2241. Godwin: 2469. Swift: 2945, 3047,
    3094, 3144.
NARRATIVE TECHNIQUE
    Background: 698. Novel: 766, 886, 903. Defoe: 1148, 1204,
    1223, 1270, 1299, 1309, 1321, 1322, 1329. Fielding: 1371,
    1460, 1485, 1495, 1582, 1585, 1616, 1639, 1649. Richardson:
    1672, 1673, 1676, 1688, 1715, 1760, 1766, 1767, 1769, 1771,
    1780, 1791. Smollett: 1905. Sterne: 2053, 2109, 2115, 2130,
    2145, 2176, 2201, 2222, 2223, 2232, 2233, 2234, 2243, 2280.
    F. Brooke: 2337. Burney: 2372, 2388. Cleland: 2403.
    Goldsmith: 2497, 2530. Radcliffe: 2652, 2653, 2654, 2671.
    Wollstonecraft: 2746. Johnson: 2871, 2878, 2900. Swift:
    3034, 3061, 3136, 3148.
NARRATOR. See POINT OF VIEW AND NARRATOR.
NASH, "BEAU" RICHARD
    Background: 200, 692.
NATIONAL STEREOTYPES. See also specific types, e.g., THE
    IRISH; THE ITALIAN.
    Background: 342, 582. Novel: 796. Smollett: 2005.
NATURAL LAW. See also INTELLECTUAL BACKGROUND.
    Defoe: 1262.
NATURE
    Background: 101, 334, 455, 513, 640, 662. Novel: 983, 1080.
    Radcliffe: 2648, 2652, 2671. Johnson: 2811, 2828, 2835, 2880.
NATURE VS. ART
    Fielding: 1639. Sterne: 2110, 2210.
NAVAL NOVEL
    Novel: 982, 1021, 1097.
NAVY, THE. See also THE SAILOR.

Background: 111, 213, 332, 363, 416, 447, 469, 470, 577, 676.
Novel: 982. Smollett: 1951, 1960, 1966.
NECESSITY
Novel: 892. Defoe: 1217, 1262, 1269. Godwin: 2451. Holcroft: 2573.
NEOCLASSICAL DECLINE
Background: 263.
NEOCLASSICISM
Background: 110, 215, 279, 399, 400, 455.
NEWGATE [Prison]. See also CRIME AND PUNISHMENT and PRISONS.
Background: 190.
NEWGATE CALENDAR. See also CRIME AND PUNISHMENT and CRIMINAL BIOGRAPHY.
Background: 419, 451. Richardson: 1784.
NEWSPAPERS. See also JOURNALISM.
Background: 173, 211, 676, 717, 719. Fielding: 1495, 1524.
NEWTON, ISAAC
Background: 313.
NOBLE SAVAGE. See also CHILD OF NATURE; PRIMITIVISM; and STATE OF NATURE.
Background: 243, 258. Novel: 828, 973. Defoe: 1249.
NONCONFORMITY [religious]
Background: 122, 137, 230.
NOVEL ABOUT NON-HUMAN CHARACTERS
Novel: 977.
NOVEL AS SUBVERSIVE FORM
Novel: 814, 886.
NOVEL IN MAGAZINES
Bibliographies: 23, 44. Novel: 933, 966.
NOVEL OF DOCTRINE. See also DIDACTICISM.
Novel: 755, 1088, 1090. Godwin: 2459.
NOVEL OF EDUCATION
Novel: 980.
NOVEL OF HUMORS
Smollett: 2034.
NOVEL OF MANNERS
Novel: 893, 960, 990. Richardson: 1709. Goldsmith: 2541.
NOVEL OF SENSIBILITY
Novel: 755, 835. Fielding: 1409. Sterne: 2197. F. Brooke: 2337.
NOVEL OF SINCERITY
Novel: 854.
NOVEL OF TASTE
Radcliffe: 2662.
NOVELISTS ON THE NOVEL. See also EIGHTEENTH-CENTURY CRITICISM AND REVIEWS OF THE NOVEL and THEORY AND PRACTICE OF THE NOVEL.
Novel: 757, 853, 1024. Fielding: 1389, 1394. Richardson: 1726.
NUMEROLOGY. See also PLOT, STRUCTURE, AND DESIGN and

SYMBOLISM.
Novel: 787. Defoe: 1159. Fielding: 1403. Smollett: 1901.
Sterne: 2075.
NURSE, THE
Background: 546.

OBSEQUIOUSNESS
Goldsmith: 2526.
OPTIMISM
Background: 685. Johnson: 2813, 2889.
ORDER
Novel: 761, 1006, 1027. Sterne: 2062. Godwin: 2477. Swift:
2937, 3029.
ORDER VS. DISORDER
Background: 298. Defoe: 1232, 1282. Fielding: 1493, 1572.
Swift: 3104.
ORDINARY, THE. See also THE CLERGY and THE PARSON.
Background: 190, 451.
ORIENTAL NOVEL. See also ORIENTALISM.
Novel: 755, 1102. Beckford: 2305, 2310, 2319, 2321. Hawkes-
worth: 2559a. Johnson: 2792.
ORIENTALISM. See also ORIENTAL NOVEL.
Background: 88, 455, 630. Novel: 790, 803. Beckford:
2308, 2316, 2320. Goldsmith: 2533. Johnson: 2795, 2843,
2848, 2893.
ORPHANS
Background: 437. Novel: 833.
OXFORD UNIVERSITY. See also THE UNDERGRADUATE and THE
PROFESSOR.
Background: 297, 307, 401, 648, 654, 697. Novel: 1007.
Smollett: 2029.

PAGANISM
Background: 467.
PAMELA-SHAMELA
Fielding: 1661. Richardson: 1764, 1782, 1812, 1836.
PARADOX
Swift: 3010.
PARLIAMENT. See also HOUSE OF COMMONS and HOUSE OF
LORDS.
Background: 174, 507.
PARODY. See also SATIRE and BURLESQUE NOVEL.
Novel: 930a, 1024, 1037. Fielding: 1370, 1421, 1427, 1440,
1462, 1479, 1485, 1592, 1595, 1646. Richardson: 1745, 1764,
1782, 1812, 1836. Smollett: 1936. Sterne: 2110, 2157. God-
win: 2472. Johnson: 2815. Swift: 3140.
PARSON, THE. See also THE CLERGY and THE ORDINARY.
Background: 337.
PARTICULAR VS. GENERAL

Beckford: 2329. Johnson: 2797, 2805, 2811, 2815, 2827, 2877, 2907.
PASCAL, BLAISE
    Johnson: 2888.
PASSIONS, THE
    Novel: 943. Fielding: 1526, 1629. Richardson: 1715, 1822.
    Johnson: 2763. Swift: 3096.
PASTORAL NOVEL
    Novel: 1057. Goldsmith: 2540.
PASTORAL TRADITION. See also RURAL IDEAL.
    Novel: 825. Richardson: 1715. Smollett: 1909. Sterne:
    2056. Godwin: 2472.
PATRONAGE. See also THE WRITER IN SOCIETY.
    Background: 196, 198, 269, 284, 428, 634. Fielding: 1415.
PEDAGOGICAL APPROACH
    Background: 184. Novel: 802, 810, 851, 1028. Fielding:
    1596. Sterne: 2107. Swift: 3178, 3187.
"PENNY UNIVERSITIES" [coffee houses]
    Background: 249.
PERFECTIONISM
    Richardson: 1718, 1733.
PERSONAL RELATIONS BETWEEN AUTHORS. See also BIOGRAPHY.
    Fielding: 1529. Richardson: 1726, 1798. Smollett: 2033.
    Sterne: 2267. S. Fielding: 2423. Godwin: 2475. Holcroft:
    2575. Lennox: 2593, 2594. Walpole: 2710. Johnson: 2821.
PERSONALITY OF NOVELIST. See also BIOGRAPHY.
    Defoe: 1142, 1171. Richardson: 1849, 1852. Sterne: 2273.
    Beckford: 2300. Burney: 2354. Goldsmith: 2529. Walpole:
    2716. Johnson: 2766, 2778, 2781, 2820, 2899. Swift: 2985.
PESSIMISM
    Johnson: 2762, 2854, 2871, 3121. Swift: 2947.
PHILANTHROPY
    Background: 382, 407, 460, 590, 676. Richardson: 1718a.
PHILOSOPHIC VOYAGE
    Swift: 2983.
PHILOSOPHICAL NOVEL
    Bage: 2293. Johnson: 2830. Swift: 3044.
PHILOSOPHY. See INTELLECTUAL BACKGROUND.
PHILOSOPHY OF NOVELIST. See also INTELLECTUAL BACK-
    GROUND and EPISTEMOLOGY.
    Novel: 809, 881, 999. Defoe: 1130, 1146, 1153, 1178, 1202,
    1226, 1229, 1246, 1253, 1262, 1298, 1324, 1325, 1337. Fielding:
    1368, 1382, 1384, 1385, 1396, 1416, 1435, 1436, 1451, 1459, 1501,
    1534, 1542, 1548, 1559, 1565, 1572, 1586, 1590, 1598, 1600, 1601,
    1606, 1619, 1622, 1624, 1629, 1636, 1651, 1652, 1658, 1662.
    Richardson: 1678, 1703, 1715, 1720, 1728, 1811, 1815, 1819,
    1848. Smollett: 1893, 1933, 1996, 2002, 2013. Sterne: 2156,
    2172, 2180, 2187, 2188, 2210, 2263, 2278. Beckford: 2312.
    Godwin: 2434, 2441, 2443, 2447, 2457, 2462, 2466, 2467, 2473,
    2479, 2489. Goldsmith: 2506, 2508, 2519, 2522, 2537. Holcroft:
    2571, 2576. Lewis: 2603. Mackenzie: 2628. Radcliffe: 2647,

2661. Wollstonecraft: 2742, 2746, 2752. Johnson: 2763, 2767,
2776, 2796, 2804, 2839, 2841, 2853, 2854, 2864, 2866, 2880,
2881, 2882, 2884, 2889, 2911, 2913, 2917. Swift: 2947, 2948,
2984, 3004, 3009, 3014, 3020, 3075, 3111, 3121, 3127, 3179.
PHYSICIAN, THE. See also MEDICINE.
Background: 152, 325, 363, 517.
PHYSIOGNOMY
Novel: 850, 943, 1038.
PHYSIOLOGY
Novel: 1038. Fielding: 1526. Sterne: 2218.
PICARESQUE NOVEL
Novel: 747, 774, 782, 798, 823, 870, 877, 889, 952, 957, 971,
981, 1014, 1018, 1030, 1042, 1046, 1058, 1079, 1104, 1107,
1108, 1109. Defoe: 1129, 1203, 1269, 1287, 1323. Fielding:
1366. Smollett: 1885, 1892, 1907, 1925, 1932, 1944, 2010,
2025. Swift: 3095.
PICARO. See ROGUE HERO.
PICTURESQUE, THE. See also THE SUBLIME AND THE BEAUTI-
FUL.
Background: 80, 104, 262, 354, 389, 543. Beckford: 2307.
Radcliffe: 2671.
PIETISM
Rowe: 2684.
PILGRIM ALLEGORY. See also JOURNEY.
Defoe: 1210.
PILGRIMAGE. See JOURNEY.
PIRANESI, GIAMBATTISTA
Novel: 748.
PIRATE, THE
Novel: 1015. Defoe: 1134, 1266, 1305.
PLACES IN THE NOVEL. See also GAZETTEER and GEOGRAPHY.
Background: 264. Johnson: 2802, 2824.
PLATO
Swift: 2938, 3120, 3134.
PLOT, STRUCTURE, AND DESIGN. See also UNITY.
Background: 536. Novel: 744, 761, 784, 785, 787, 821, 867,
910, 912, 928, 951, 952, 964, 980, 989, 1012, 1015, 1027, 1030,
1079, 1099. Defoe: 1129, 1145, 1146, 1148, 1159, 1169, 1176,
1179, 1196, 1207, 1209, 1210, 1214, 1225, 1235, 1280, 1281,
1284, 1285, 1287, 1288, 1298, 1306a, 1310, 1318, 1353, 1354.
Fielding: 1365, 1372, 1373, 1382, 1385, 1393, 1400, 1403, 1408,
1416, 1419, 1423, 1424, 1433, 1438, 1440, 1452, 1453, 1468,
1475, 1478, 1485, 1488, 1490, 1491, 1494, 1497, 1498, 1499,
1506, 1510, 1512, 1515, 1522, 1534, 1539a, 1542, 1543, 1551,
1555, 1563, 1565, 1586, 1587, 1588, 1595, 1609, 1638, 1639,
1655, 1663. Richardson: 1676, 1697, 1714, 1741, 1755, 1766,
1767, 1779, 1805, 1809, 1843, 1859, 1871. Smollett: 1893, 1895,
1900, 1901, 1904, 1905, 1908, 1913, 1926, 1928, 1933, 1943,
1946, 1949, 1955, 1980, 1992, 1994, 2002, 2004, 2013, 2030.
Sterne: 2050, 2057, 2062, 2063, 2066, 2069, 2075, 2080, 2110,
2112, 2115, 2124, 2128, 2148, 2167, 2176, 2177, 2204, 2208,

A Guide to Topics 33

2211, 2223, 2225, 2234, 2243, 2244, 2246, 2259, 2262, 2269,
2274. Burney: 2356, 2388. Godwin: 2480. Goldsmith:
2495, 2497, 2504, 2508, 2539, 2543. Inchbald: 2585, 2586.
Lewis: 2605. Mackenzie: 2623, 2624. Johnson: 2792, 2798,
2825, 2836, 2854, 2861, 2862, 2873, 2875, 2883, 2890, 2906,
2912, 2915. Swift: 2937, 2959, 2964, 2966, 3003, 3012, 3023,
3080, 3088, 3089, 3100, 3105, 3122, 3151, 3152, 3157, 3161.
PLUTARCH
Swift: 3023, 3024.
POACHING. See also COUNTRY LIFE and THE GAMEKEEPER.
Background: 135, 423, 503.
POEMS IN THE NOVEL
Goldsmith: 2511, 2527.
POINT OF VIEW AND NARRATOR. See also MALE NOVELIST AS-
SUMING FEMALE IDENTITY.
Novel: 744, 777, 778, 780, 813, 816, 847, 880, 942, 952, 1012,
1018, 1025, 1027, 1039. Defoe: 1138, 1140, 1146, 1151, 1157,
1158, 1164, 1165, 1168, 1172, 1176, 1191, 1212, 1261, 1265,
1268, 1288, 1297, 1300, 1321, 1329, 1341, 1353. Fielding:
1372, 1395, 1400, 1439, 1444, 1452, 1455, 1461, 1485, 1488,
1509, 1530, 1535, 1536, 1572, 1573, 1574, 1587, 1598, 1616,
1620, 1639, 1642, 1663. Richardson: 1672, 1719, 1741, 1765,
1771, 1783, 1826, 1846. Smollett: 1887, 1913, 1981, 1983,
1991, 1992, 2004, 2016. Sterne: 2051, 2053, 2065, 2089,
2113, 2119, 2128, 2135, 2137, 2141, 2163, 2164, 2186, 2194,
2205, 2206, 2225, 2263. Bage: 2293. Godwin: 2433. Goldsmith: 2507, 2520. Wollstonecraft: 2748. Johnson: 2863,
2897. Swift: 2955, 2960a, 2967, 2979, 2992, 2993, 2994, 2996,
3061, 3062, 3081, 3097, 3142, 3148, 3157.
POLITICS [includes government]
Bibliographies: 73. Background: 98, 99, 103, 137, 144, 147,
150, 174, 185, 192, 195, 199, 233, 239, 267, 284, 286, 323,
331, 352, 364, 377, 394, 417, 418, 434, 436, 460, 461, 472,
491, 507, 508, 514, 521, 522, 526, 527, 553, 555, 584, 609,
627, 634, 637, 638, 643, 653, 669, 670, 697, 702, 711, 724.
Novel: 764, 809, 846, 865, 891, 1056a, 1090, 1096. Defoe:
1152, 1229, 1230, 1231, 1260, 1304, 1306b, 1314. Fielding:
1379, 1386, 1387, 1406, 1410, 1414, 1451a, 1454, 1465, 1475,
1482, 1523, 1597, 1650. Smollett: 1921, 1924, 1927, 2003,
2013, 2014, 2021. Sterne: 2091. Bage: 2292. Beckford:
2326. F. Brooke: 2334. Godwin: 2432, 2441, 2442, 2458,
2470, 2471. Goldsmith: 2501, 2548. Holcroft: 2574, 2576,
2578. Inchbald: 2583. Manley: 2637. Smith: 2698. Walpole: 2707, 2714, 2720, 2725, 2731, 2732. Johnson: 2806.
Swift: 2942, 2957, 2965, 2980, 2985, 2997, 2999, 3000, 3001,
3015, 3016, 3029, 3030, 3032, 3049, 3070, 3074, 3086, 3093,
3103, 3110, 3124, 3135, 3145, 3172, 3176.
POOR, THE
Background: 106, 133, 188, 189, 284, 474, 478, 524, 541, 607,
610, 676. Defoe: 1261, 1266. Fielding: 1666. Richardson:
1781.

POOR LAW
    Background: 705.
POPE, ALEXANDER
    Richardson: 1695.
POPULAR CULTURE
    Background: 83, 304, 457, 464, 537, 541, 559, 607, 631, 671, 719.
POPULAR NOVEL
    Novel: 763, 960, 1015, 1034, 1041, 1088, 1105.
POPULATION. See also DEMOGRAPHY.
    Background: 129, 155, 168, 170, 182, 266, 296, 318, 429, 489, 548, 677.
PORNOGRAPHIC NOVEL
    Novel: 837, 918.
PORNOGRAPHY
    Background: 645. Defoe: 1319. Cleland: 2401, 2402, 2403, 2405.
PORTUGAL
    Beckford: 2330.
POST OFFICE
    Background: 523, 587, 682.
POWER
    Richardson: 1809.
PREGNANCY AND CHILDBIRTH. See also THE MIDWIFE and MID-
    WIFERY.
    Background: 583, 672. Richardson: 1817. Smollett: 2008.
    Sterne: 2078, 2168.
PRE-ROMANTIC NOVEL. See also ROMANTIC NOVEL.
    Novel: 836.
PRESBYTERIANISM
    Defoe: 1231.
PREVOST, ABBE
    Novel: 835, 836.
PRIDE
    Background: 455. Swift: 2943, 2990, 3008, 3083.
PRIMITIVISM. See also STATE OF NATURE and NOBLE SAVAGE.
    Background: 243, 662, 1105. Godwin: 2468.
PRINTING. See also BOOK TRADE.
    Background: 148.
PRISONS. See also CRIME AND PUNISHMENT and NEWGATE.
    Background: 145, 202, 392, 707.
PRIVACY
    Richardson: 1739, 1828.
PROBABILITY
    Novel: 902. Defoe: 1128. Sterne: 2223.
PRODIGAL SON MOTIF
    Defoe: 1132.
PROFESSIONS, THE. See also specific types, e.g., THE LAWYER.
    Background: 363, 376, 377. Fielding: 1465.
PROFESSOR, THE
    Background: 363.

PROGRESS [the idea of]
     Background: 208, 714. Novel: 774, 1105. Godwin: 2467,
     2479. Swift: 2943.
PROPAGANDA
     Background: 144.
PROPRIETY. See also MANNERS.
     Background: 520. Novel: 1051. Richardson: 1709, 1749,
     1822. Burney: 2364, 2367. Inchbald: 2587. Lennox: 2599.
     Smith: 2701.
PROSTITUTE, THE. See also PROSTITUTION.
     Novel: 1013, 1015.
PROSTITUTION. See also THE PROSTITUTE.
     Background: 216. Defoe: 1266. Richardson: 1733.
PROTEST. See also THE MOB and RIOTS.
     Background: 608.
PROVIDENCE. See also CHRISTIANITY and PHILOSOPHY OF
     NOVELIST.
     Novel: 964. Defoe: 1210, 1354. Fielding: 1385, 1489, 1559,
     1572, 1652, 1655. Richardson: 1735, 1819. Goldsmith: 2499.
     Reeve: 2676. Walpole: 2714.
PRUDENCE
     Fielding: 1465, 1577. Goldsmith: 2495.
PSYCHOANALYTIC ISSUES [in Gulliver's Travels]
     Swift: 2933, 2949, 2998, 3018, 3042, 3043, 3123.
PSYCHOLOGY OF CHARACTERS. See also CHARACTERIZATION.
     Novel: 797, 1031. Defoe: 1122, 1142, 1166, 1184, 1186, 1201,
     1202, 1211, 1233a, 1272, 1273, 1275, 1277. Fielding: 1451,
     1526. Richardson: 1717, 1719, 1722, 1740, 1778, 1783, 1785,
     1789, 1793, 1847. Smollett: 1977. Sterne: 2060, 2094, 2101,
     2120, 2153, 2198, 2256, 2264. Godwin: 2435, 2443, 2443a,
     2478, 2484, 2486. Goldsmith: 2507. Lee: 2590. Radcliffe:
     2649. Johnson: 2809, 2818, 2830. Swift: 2964, 2998, 3018,
     3044.
PUBLIC OPINION
     Background: 144, 434.
PUBLISHERS. See BOOK TRADE; names of individual publishers
     (e.g., MINERVA PRESS); and BOOKSELLERS.
PUNCTUATION. See also GRAMMAR and SYNTAX.
     Novel: 962. Sterne: 2182.
PURITANISM
     Background: 324, 407, 730, 895. Defoe: 1131, 1180, 1197,
     1210, 1221, 1320, 1324, 1326. Richardson: 1753, 1754, 1778,
     1874.
PURSUIT
     Godwin: 2445.

QUACKERY
     Background: 162. Fielding: 1465.
QUAKERISM
     Background: 314, 450, 683. Defoe: 1237.

QUIXOTIC HERO
  Novel: 1059, 1062, 1103. Fielding: 1557. Smollett: 1974.
QUIXOTIC NOVEL
  Novel: 1014, 1020, 1046. Fielding: 1575. Sterne: 2215.
  Graves: 2556. Lennox: 2598.

RABELAIS, FRANÇOIS
  Novel: 788. Sterne: 2254.
RACISM. See also BLACKS.
  Background: 201, 563. Defoe: 1215.
RADICALISM
  Background: 137, 144, 145, 147, 199, 233, 303, 323, 460, 461,
  581, 593, 607, 608, 740. Novel: 742, 852, 865. Godwin:
  2432, 2456. Hays: 2561. Holcroft: 2578. Robinson: 2679.
  Swift: 3078.
RAKE, THE
  Background: 406. Fielding: 1632. Richardson: 1681, 1733,
  1840, 1852, 1875a.
RAPE
  Richardson: 1668, 1722, 1784.
RASSELAS-CANDIDE COMPARISON
  Novel: 803, 1006, 1106. Johnson: 2786, 2854, 2873, 2889.
READING PUBLIC. See also LITERACY and BEST SELLERS.
  Background: 82, 196, 197, 198, 340, 412, 440, 450, 490, 512,
  585, 684, 704, 718, 720. Novel: 873, 934, 970, 1056a, 1078.
  Richardson: 1801. Burney: 2357.
REALISM. See also "FORMAL REALISM"; "INTELLECTUAL REAL-
  ISM"; and "SOCIAL REALISM"
  Novel: 744, 754, 763, 768, 815, 866, 886, 893, 895, 906, 990,
  1083, 1099, 1116. Defoe: 1179, 1183, 1234, 1261, 1271, 1305,
  1307, 1337, 1349. Fielding: 1478, 1521, 1530, 1612, 1621,
  1624, 1630. Richardson: 1688, 1730, 1787, 1824. Smollett:
  1899, 1900, 1943, 2030, 2032. Sterne: 2051, 2275. Beckford:
  2313. Godwin: 2447. Goldsmith: 2540. Radcliffe: 2646.
  Johnson: 2915.
REALITY
  Johnson: 2765.
REASON
  Background: 207, 334. Novel: 794, 937, 1092. Richardson:
  1855. Sterne: 2121. Cleland: 2404. Godwin: 2467. Woll-
  stonecraft: 2746. Johnson: 2811, 2867, 2901. Swift: 2934,
  3025, 3075, 3179.
REASON VS. IMAGINATION
  Johnson: 2768, 2816.
REBELLION
  Novel: 988. Godwin: 2484. Smith: 2696.
REBELLION OF 1745. See also JACOBITISM and POLITICS.
  Background: 273, 396, 444, 491, 537, 542, 666. Fielding:
  1411, 1482, 1493, 1523, 1552.
REBIRTH

Defoe: 1182.
REFLEXIVITY
Sterne: 2089, 2256.
REFORM
Background: 174, 192, 199, 233, 235, 365, 514. Fielding:
1567, 1665.
RELATIVITY
Swift: 3106, 3173.
RELIGION. See THE CHURCH; THE CLERGY; CHRISTIANITY;
ANGLICANISM; AUGUSTINIANISM; CALVINISM; CATHOLI-
CISM; CONGREGATIONALISM; DEISM; DISSENTERS; EVAN-
GELICALISM; LATITUDINARIANISM; METHODISM; NONCON-
FORMITY; PIETISM; PRESBYTERIANISM; PURITANISM;
QUAKERISM; and UNITARIANISM.
RESSENTIMENT
Richardson: 1793.
RETIREMENT
Background: 619. Novel: 825, 892a, 898, 1086. Defoe:
1150.
REVIEWS, 18TH-CENTURY. See EIGHTEENTH-CENTURY CRITI-
CISM AND REVIEWS OF THE NOVEL.
REVOLUTIONARY NOVEL. See JACOBIN NOVEL.
RHETORIC
Background: 372. Novel: 1112. Defoe: 1152, 1165. Sterne:
2136, 2201, 2202, 2231, 2263. Swift: 2940, 3105.
RHETORICAL NOVEL
Novel: 1032. Johnson: 2873.
RHEUMATISM. See also DISEASE and MEDICINE.
Background: 203.
RHYTHM
Sterne: 2096, 2115, 2246, 2251. Johnson: 2794.
RIDICULE
Background: 293.
RIOTS. See also THE MOB and PROTEST.
Background: 97, 133, 145, 343, 606, 608, 644.
ROCOCO
Background: 612. Fielding: 1582. Sterne: 2265.
ROGUE BIOGRAPHY
Defoe: 1140.
ROGUE HERO
Novel: 747, 774, 952, 957, 981, 1015, 1104. Defoe: 1129,
1139, 1144. Fielding: 1366. Smollett: 1885, 1894, 2025.
ROMANCE [as a literary type]
Novel: 756, 763, 950, 990, 1034, 1109. Fielding: 1375, 1376,
1378, 1417, 1450, 1485, 1524, 1533, 1534, 1553. Richardson:
1711, 1808. Smollett: 1888, 1949, 1999, 2030. Godwin: 2454.
Lewis: 2606. Johnson: 2765.
ROMANTIC NOVEL. See also PRE-ROMANTIC NOVEL.
Novel: 850, 896, 1001. Beckford: 2317. Godwin: 2453.
Lewis: 2610. Radcliffe: 2655. Walpole: 2722.
ROMANTICISM

Background: 110, 124, 217, 279, 455, 599. Novel: 744, 878, 1010, 1011, 1073. Sterne: 2114. Beckford: 2315, 2324. Radcliffe: 2665, 2672. Smith: 2697. Johnson: 2867.
ROMNEY, GEORGE
   Sterne: 2103.
ROSA, SALVATORE
   Background: 468.
ROUSSEAU, JEAN-JACQUES
   Richardson: 1738, 1854. Day: 2416. Godwin: 2449. Wollstonecraft: 2745. Johnson: 2835, 2884, 2885.
ROWLANDSON, THOMAS
   Background: 259, 446, 539. Novel: 1114. Goldsmith: 2526.
RUINS
   Background: 80, 101, 741. Novel: 822.
RURAL IDEAL. See also COUNTRY LIFE; RETIREMENT; and PASTORAL TRADITION.
   Background: 619. Novel: 825, 898, 1086. Fielding: 1382. Smollett: 1918, 1929. Sterne: 2056. Swift: 2997.
RUSSIA
   Novel: 1043. Sterne: 2161.

SADE, MARQUIS DE
   Novel: 1001. Richardson: 1686.
SAILOR, THE. See also THE NAVY.
   Novel: 1017, 1021, 1097. Smollett: 2024.
SALON, THE
   Background: 130, 664. Sterne: 2126.
SATANIC HERO
   Novel: 774.
SATIRE. See also CARICATURE; PARODY; and SOCIAL CRITICISM IN THE NOVEL. Background: 238, 458, 611, 688. Novel: 765, 774, 777, 808, 830, 865, 907, 911, 987, 990, 1004, 1062, 1096. Defoe: 1268. Fielding: 1370, 1392, 1413, 1430, 1443, 1465, 1469, 1479, 1480, 1485, 1487, 1524, 1531, 1553, 1588, 1617, 1634, 1637, 1646, 1650, 1659, 1661. Smollett: 1887, 1888, 1903, 1911, 1919, 1930, 1932, 1963, 1966, 1981, 1983, 1990, 1994, 2000, 2035. Sterne: 2097, 2166, 2188, 2189, 2193, 2199, 2217, 2229, 2233, 2249, 2270, 2271. Beckford: 2305, 2326. Goldsmith: 2512, 2524, 2526, 2527, 2528, 2530, 2551. Graves: 2559. Mackenzie: 2627. Manley: 2637. Walker: 2702. Johnson: 2762, 2769, 2876, 2885, 2890, 2912. Swift: 2943, 2947, 2954, 2955, 2957, 2958, 2972, 2992, 2993, 2995, 3003a, 3040, 3041, 3052, 3055, 3067, 3083, 3094, 3102, 3107, 3110, 3112, 3119, 3125, 3133, 3135, 3136, 3139, 3142, 3148, 3159, 3165, 3167, 3175, 3179, 3184, 3186.
SATIRIC TECHNIQUES. See also BURLESQUE NOVEL; IRONY; and PARODY.
   Fielding: 1553. Smollett: 2038. Swift: 2941, 2952, 2974, 2987, 2992, 2995, 2996, 3023, 3040, 3065, 3077, 3095, 3105, 3106, 3109, 3111, 3113, 3117, 3128, 3130, 3133, 3147, 3150a,

3158, 3165, 3168, 3171.
SCANDAL CHRONICLES
   Novel: 1015.
SCATOLOGY
   Smollett: 1910a, 1911. Swift: 2949, 2997, 3065.
SCHOOLMASTER, THE
   Background: 363.
SCIENCE
   Bibliographies: 75. Background: 161, 189, 478, 504, 505,
   518, 585, 597, 603, 604, 616, 676. Defoe: 1216. Sterne:
   2187. Johnson: 2833, 2841, 2881. Swift: 3052, 3091, 3092,
   3094, 3102, 3159.
SCOTLAND
   Background: 153, 156, 232, 486, 547. Defoe: 1231. Smollett:
   1924, 2005, 2022.
SCOTTISH "COMMON SENSE SCHOOL"
   Background: 305. Smollett: 1933.
SCOTTISH NOVEL
   Novel: 860, 861.
SCULPTURE
   Background: 712.
SEDUCED MAIDEN, THE
   Novel: 1061.
SEDUCTION
   Novel: 1061. Richardson: 1689, 1715, 1732, 1748.
SELF, THE
   Background: 126, 298. Novel: 807, 826, 833, 880, 918, 1054,
   1101. Defoe: 1158, 1180, 1219, 1232, 1288, 1322, 1350, 1353.
   Fielding: 1451, 1611, 1648. Richardson: 1683, 1701, 1708,
   1717, 1719, 1734, 1737, 1739, 1828, 1844, 1867. Sterne: 2247,
   2256, 2277. Burney: 2380, 2382. Godwin: 2448, 2461.
   Swift: 3014.
SELF VS. SOCIETY
   Smollett: 1923. Godwin: 2445, 2488.
SELF-DECEPTION
   Swift: 3154.
SELF-INTEREST
   Background: 371. Fielding: 1606, 1607, 1651.
SELKIRK, ALEXANDER
   Defoe: 1244, 1336.
SEMANTICS
   Background: 191, 231, 252, 358, 454, 673, 674, 735. Novel:
   899.
SENSATIONALISM
   Lewis: 2608. Radcliffe: 2653.
SENSE VS. SENSIBILITY
   Radcliffe: 2663.
SENSIBILITY. See also "MAN OF FEELING" and SENTIMENTALISM.
   Background: 110, 142, 210, 311, 349, 382, 602, 679. Novel:
   769, 806, 807, 836, 839, 844, 1088, 1117. Defoe: 1156.
   Fielding: 1456, 1578. Richardson: 1708, 1747. Smollett:

2028. Sterne: 2069, 2127, 2163, 2172. Goldsmith: 2507.
Mackenzie: 2619. Radcliffe: 2663. Wollstonecraft: 2746.
"SENTIMENTAL" [the word]
Background: 252.
SENTIMENTAL HERO. See also "MAN OF FEELING."
Novel: 1060.
SENTIMENTAL HEROINE
Novel: 1093.
SENTIMENTAL NOVEL
Novel: 755, 784, 786, 1060. Richardson: 1685, 1689, 1830.
Sterne: 2071, 2076, 2149, 2209. Goldsmith: 2502, 2505, 2508.
Mackenzie: 2621, 2629. Smith: 2697, 2698. Wollstonecraft:
2748.
SENTIMENTALISM. See also "MAN OF FEELING" and SENSIBILITY.
Bibliographies: 35. Background: 210, 252, 593, 699. Novel:
769, 786, 801, 836, 838, 848, 939, 984, 990, 1010, 1024, 1115.
Fielding: 1424. Richardson: 1685, 1686, 1732, 1851, 1986.
Sterne: 2082, 2097, 2149, 2165, 2167, 2173, 2192, 2199, 2211,
2212, 2255, 2263. F. Brooke: 2339. Godwin: 2426. Gold-
smith: 2512. Mackenzie: 2619, 2627, 2628. Radcliffe: 2661.
Wollstonecraft: 2748.
SERIALS
Bibliographies: 23.
SERMON, THE
Background: 241, 242, 445. Sterne: 2081, 2129, 2145, 2166,
2189, 2190, 2200, 2222.
SERVANTS. See also DOMESTIC LIFE.
Background: 135, 344, 345, 546. Richardson: 1781, 1785,
1827.
SETTING
Background: 264. Novel: 775, 824, 910, 929, 1080. Defoe:
1127, 1136, 1148, 1149, 1278, 1295, 1306. Fielding: 1438,
1467, 1477, 1510, 1534, 1539. Richardson: 1691, 1734, 1739,
1745, 1749, 1762, 1837. Smollett: 1899, 1936, 1952, 1960, 1984,
2015. Sterne: 2259. Beckford: 2322, 2323, 2329. Goldsmith:
2497. Radcliffe: 2648, 2652, 2667, 2670, 2671. Smith: 2698.
Walpole: 2734. Johnson: 2802, 2849. Swift: 2967, 3085.
1790's, THE. See also JACOBIN NOVEL and FRENCH REVOLUTION.
Background: 98, 235, 251, 303, 323.
SEX
Background: 166a, 385, 437, 442, 569, 633, 642, 646, 730.
Novel: 793, 800, 893, 988, 1004a, 1054. Defoe: 1166, 1273,
1277, 1289. Fielding: 1412, 1456, 1500, 1564, 1568. Richard-
son: 1683, 1684, 1698, 1699, 1700, 1712, 1733, 1747, 1778, 1785,
1789, 1827, 1859, 1865. Sterne: 2052, 2069, 2070, 2085, 2127,
2153, 2195, 2261. Cleland: 2393, 2398, 2404. Lewis: 2608.
Radcliffe: 2649, 2673.
SHAFTESBURY, ANTHONY ASHLEY COOPER, LORD
Background: 334, 482, 678, 679. Novel: 1006. Richardson:
1862.
SHAKESPEARE

Johnson: 2829.
SHAKESPEAREAN INFLUENCE
Novel: 976. Defoe: 1252. Fielding: 1444, 1508, 1594. Richardson: 1721. Smollett: 1917, 1953, 1998. Sterne: 2163, 2181. Walpole: 2708, 2714, 2734.
SHANDYISM
  Sterne: 2088, 2192.
SHELBURNE, WILLIAM
  Background: 514.
SHENSTONE, WILLIAM
  Graves: 2557.
SHEPPARD, JACK
  Background: 351.
SHIPPING
  Background: 226, 492.
SHORT FICTION
  Novel: 781a, 888, 997, 998.
SINCERITY
  Novel: 854.
SKEPTICISM
  Beckford: 2312.
SLAVERY. See also BLACKS and ANTI-SLAVERY FICTION.
  Background: 201, 235, 576, 694, 695. Novel: 864, 1075.
  Swift: 3049.
SLOTH
  Johnson: 2887.
SMELLS
  Novel: 812, 1067.
SMITH, ADAM
  Sterne: 2169.
SNOBBERY
  Swift: 3119.
"SOAP OPERA"
  Defoe: 1126.
SOCIAL BACKGROUND. See also CITY LIFE; COUNTRY LIFE;
    DOMESTIC LIFE; MANNERS; SPORT AND RECREATION; and
    POPULAR CULTURE.
  Background: 112, 113, 136, 139, 166a, 170, 189, 251, 278, 284,
  285, 287, 288, 289, 300, 301, 302, 309, 338, 352, 377, 381, 395,
  411, 438, 471, 472, 473, 497, 530, 537, 570, 577, 580, 589, 594,
  627, 636, 658, 670, 676, 724, 726, 731, 732. Novel: 833, 970,
  1023a, 1096. Fielding: 1475, 1484, 1666. Richardson: 1845.
  Burney: 2349. Godwin: 2446, 2473. Lewis: 2612. Radcliffe:
  2657. Johnson: 2879. Swift: 3125.
SOCIAL CRITICISM IN THE NOVEL. See also SATIRE.
  Novel: 768, 881, 891, 1008, 1056, 1090. Defoe: 1167, 1203,
  1229, 1257, 1316, 1342. Fielding: 1438, 1531, 1542, 1600, 1601,
  1612, 1625, 1654, 1662, 1666. Richardson: 1684, 1777, 1841,
  1857. Smollett: 1894, 1929, 1931, 1932, 1956, 1993, 1994, 2000,
  2003, 2007, 2012, 2013. Bage: 2288. Burney: 2374. Cleland:
  2392. Godwin: 2432, 2434, 2445, 2447, 2455, 2456. Goldsmith:

2500, 2501, 2540, 2548. Holcroft: 2571, 2578, 2579. Macken-
zie: 2625. Manley: 2636. Smith: 2696. Swift: 2970, 2997,
3003, 3078, 3163.
"SOCIAL REALISM." See also REALISM.
  Richardson: 1777.
SOCIAL STRUCTURE. See also ARISTOCRACY; GENTRY; THE
  MIDDLE CLASS; and WORKING CLASSES.
  Background: 250, 284, 294, 335, 369, 435, 478, 479, 495, 507,
  517a, 541, 558, 607, 613, 638, 648a, 702, 722, 727. Novel:
  1056a. Defoe: 1178, 1203, 1312. Fielding: 1415, 1426, 1484,
  1625, 1654. Richardson: 1714, 1754, 1781, 1831, 1850.
  Sterne: 2056. Godwin: 2445, 2487. Goldsmith: 2526. Swift:
  3129.
SOCRATES
  Swift: 3134.
SOURCES, ANALOGUES, AND INFLUENCES
  Novel: 748, 788, 877, 924, 950, 1059, 1073, 1085, 1091. Defoe:
  1131, 1197, 1208, 1210, 1244, 1248, 1256, 1267, 1305, 1308,
  1309, 1321, 1323, 1326, 1336. Fielding: 1413, 1449, 1454,
  1460, 1462, 1522, 1539, 1554, 1557, 1561, 1579, 1630. Richardson: 1715, 1731, 1780, 1786, 1797, 1800, 1808, 1838, 1874.
  Smollett: 1886, 1917, 1933, 1939, 1940, 1960, 1963, 1970, 2035.
  Sterne: 2054, 2057, 2093, 2094, 2109, 2129, 2144, 2146, 2148,
  2154, 2170, 2187, 2191, 2254. Barker: 2295. Beckford: 2310,
  2322. F. Brooke: 2337. Burney: 2367. Coventry: 2409.
  Day: 2416, 2417. Godwin: 2460, 2471, 2482. Goldsmith:
  2497, 2514, 2517, 2518, 2553. Graves: 2557, 2558. Lewis:
  2604, 2616. Radcliffe: 2648, 2656, 2658, 2670. Wollstonecraft:
  2740. Johnson: 2771, 2801, 2812, 2822, 2824, 2833, 2834,
  2835, 2843, 2846, 2849, 2858, 2866, 2893, 2908, 2914. Swift:
  2983, 3023, 3024, 3052, 3098, 3101, 3166, 3171, 3185.
SOUTH SEA BUBBLE
  Background: 205.
SPACE [in the novel]
  Novel: 1099. Defoe: 1142. Richardson: 1692, 1739. Sterne:
  2243, 2244. Johnson: 2777.
SPAIN
  Novel: 877.
SPECTATOR, THE
  Novel: 888.
SPEECH AND DIALOGUE. See also STYLE AND LANGUAGE and
  CHARACTERIZATION.
  Novel: 816, 962, 1060. Fielding: 1391, 1439, 1469, 1503,
  1525, 1535, 1573, 1574, 1613. Smollett: 1889, 1896, 1897, 1898,
  1934, 1938, 2018, 2027, 2032. Sterne: 2093, 2099, 2137, 2200,
  2202, 2220, 2253, 2272. Lennox: 2599. Swift: 3048, 3138.
SPIRITUAL BIOGRAPHY AND AUTOBIOGRAPHY
  Novel: 763. Defoe: 1140, 1210, 1326. Godwin: 2476.
SPORT AND RECREATION
  Background: 83, 166a, 361, 438, 450, 463, 464, 503, 537, 552,
  554, 577, 631, 636, 676, 715. Novel: 1047. Fielding: 1537.

Sterne: 2163. Burney: 2349.
SPY, THE
    Godwin: 2464.
SQUIRE, THE. See also GENTRY.
    Background: 135, 169, 476. Novel: 1047.
STABILITY
    Background: 112, 555.
STANDARD OF LIVING
    Background: 291, 330, 657.
STATE OF NATURE [Man in a]. See also PRIMITIVISM and NOBLE
    SAVAGE.
    Defoe: 1170, 1262, 1272. Johnson: 2885.
STATISTICS
    Background: 197, 437, 478, 498, 732.
"STELLA" [ESTHER JOHNSON]
    Swift: 2973, 3013, 3064.
STEREOTYPES. See CHARACTERIZATION and NATIONAL STEREO-
    TYPES.
STERNE, LYDIA
    Sterne: 2058.
STOICISM
    Background: 237. Johnson: 2804, 2838, 2853, 2902, 2909.
STORMS
    Novel: 1080.
STRAWBERRY HILL. See also ARCHITECTURE.
    Novel: 1072. Walpole: 2706, 2724, 2725.
STRAWBERRY HILL PRESS. See also BOOK TRADE.
    Walpole: 2717.
STRULDBRUGGS, THE
    Swift: 2936, 2943, 3002, 3003a, 3008, 3116.
STYLE AND LANGUAGE
    Background: 191, 252, 501. Novel: 744, 761, 783, 785, 814,
    833, 844, 849, 863, 876, 882, 883, 916, 930a, 940, 948, 949, 952,
    996, 1029, 1074, 1098, 1115. Defoe: 1148, 1193, 1199, 1208,
    1212, 1245, 1263, 1273, 1285, 1303, 1311, 1327, 1355. Fielding:
    1365, 1377, 1391, 1409, 1421, 1439, 1464, 1465, 1469, 1485,
    1491, 1494, 1524, 1534, 1535, 1536, 1569, 1572, 1573, 1574,
    1580, 1598, 1620, 1663. Richardson: 1673, 1675, 1680, 1706,
    1731, 1743, 1760, 1853. Smollett: 1920, 1935, 1937, 1955,
    1965, 1973, 1985, 1996, 2002, 2026, 2027. Sterne: 2052, 2096,
    2099, 2110, 2112, 2119, 2123, 2136, 2137, 2138, 2141, 2142,
    2158, 2162, 2178, 2183, 2185, 2207, 2220, 2231, 2240, 2241,
    2246, 2249, 2251, 2256, 2265, 2274, 2277. Beckford: 2327.
    Burney: 2388. Cleland: 2393, 2397, 2398, 2403. S. Fielding:
    2423. Godwin: 2430, 2448, 2461. Goldsmith: 2508, 2530.
    Johnson: 2794, 2811, 2852, 2872, 2883, 2900, 2916. Swift:
    2962, 2971, 3048, 3068, 3081, 3082, 3100, 3107, 3109, 3144,
    3155, 3156.
SUBJECTIVITY
    Novel: 870, 880. Sterne: 2256.
SUBLIME AND THE BEAUTIFUL, THE. See also THE PICTURESQUE.

Background: 80, 354, 355, 513, 640, 735. Novel: 956. Field-
ing: 1489. Radcliffe: 2670. Johnson: 2811.
SUICIDE. See also INSANITY.
    Background: 108, 639.
SUPERNATURAL. See also THE MARVELLOUS.
    Novel: 972, 1070. Defoe: 1135, 1320. Radcliffe: 2659. Wal-
    pole: 2711, 2736.
SUPERSTITIONS. See also FOLKLORE.
    Background: 302.
SURREALISM
    Sterne: 2221.
SURVEY OF CRITICISM
    Bibliographies: 3, 19, 28, 36, 37, 58, 60, 67, 70. Novel:
    917, 1108. Defoe: 1118, 1119, 1121, 1122, 1125, 1298. Field-
    ing: 1356, 1357, 1359, 1360, 1361. Richardson: 1667, 1668,
    1863. Smollett: 1877, 1881, 1882, 1884. Sterne: 2042, 2043,
    2044, 2045, 2046, 2047, 2048. Goldsmith: 2490, 2493, 2494,
    2515. Manley: 2632. Johnson: 2754, 2758, 2759. Swift:
    2919, 2920, 2921, 2922, 2923, 2924, 2925, 2927, 2928, 2929,
    2930, 2933, 3076.
SURVIVAL
    Defoe: 1234.
SWIFT, JONATHAN [as subject]
    Richardson: 1695.
SYMBOLISM. See also IMAGERY; NUMEROLOGY; and TYPOLOGY.
    Background: 98, 247, 619. Novel: 787, 793, 820, 869, 923,
    1013. Defoe: 1141, 1159, 1182, 1195. Fielding: 1403, 1477,
    1506, 1605, 1608, 1625, 1648. Richardson: 1692a, 1696, 1770,
    1795, 1841, 1859, 1867, 1868, 1871. Smollett: 1901, 1912,
    2015. Sterne: 2075, 2185, 2248, 2271. Goldsmith: 2542.
    Radcliffe: 2644, 2645, 2664. Johnson: 2813. Swift: 2953,
    3006, 3012, 3105, 3126.
SYMPATHY
    Background: 261, 571. Novel: 795, 939. Defoe: 1261.
    Sterne: 2163, 2169, 2193. Mackenzie: 2625.
SYMPATHY VS. JUDGMENT
    Defoe: 1328.
SYNOPSES
    Novel: 884, 1089, 2196.
SYNTAX. See also GRAMMAR and PUNCTUATION.
    Sterne: 2138.

TASTE. See also AESTHETIC THEORY AND BACKGROUND.
    Background: 104, 110, 148, 355, 426, 468, 520, 676. Beck-
    ford: 2301. Radcliffe: 2662.
TAXATION
    Background: 222, 255, 378, 696.
TEXTUAL EDITING
    Bibliographies: 7. Background: 246. Novel: 767. Richard-
    son: 1775, 1818.

"TEXTUALITY"
  Swift: 3033.
THAMES RIVER
  Background: 545.
THEATER, THE
  Background: 577, 676.
THEATER MOTIF
  Novel: 989.
THEORY AND PRACTICE OF THE NOVEL [EiGHTEENTH CENTURY].
  See also CONVENTIONS OF THE GEORGIAN NOVEL.
  Bibliographies: 68. Novel: 757, 853, 938, 999, 1032, 1069,
  1082, 1084, 1110. Defoe: 1264, 1314, 1317. Fielding: 1389,
  1394, 1407, 1448, 1450, 1454, 1485, 1490, 1548, 1575, 1590,
  1604, 1610, 1630, 1644. Richardson: 1676, 1688, 1706, 1800,
  1815, 1865, 1876. Smollett: 1958. Sterne: 2257. Aubin:
  2285. Cleland: 2390. Davys: 2413. Godwin: 2450, 2454,
  2459, 2463, 2485. Goldsmith: 2545. Holcroft: 2577. Radcliffe: 2646. Smith: 2700. Johnson: 2811, 2827, 2854, 2855,
  2856, 2857, 2859, 2916.
THERIOPHILY
  Swift: 3010.
TIME [in the novel]
  Novel: 906, 923, 969, 1099, 1116. Defoe: 1127, 1136, 1149,
  1174, 1183, 1185, 1204, 1207, 1297, 1318. Fielding: 1534,
  1599, 1611, 1612. Richardson: 1692, 1730, 1816. Sterne:
  2057, 2066, 2112, 2115, 2141, 2171, 2177, 2187, 2193, 2230,
  2256, 2275. Johnson: 2777, 2800, 2894. Swift: 3088.
TITHES
  Background: 255, 256.
TOBACCO
  Background: 232. Novel: 935.
TOLERATION
  Background: 105, 282, 347, 701.
TORIES
  Background: 150, 195. Novel: 783. Smollett: 2021. Man-
  ley: 2637. Swift: 2947, 3015.
TOWNS
  Background: 167, 180, 330, 676.
TOWNSHEND, GEORGE
  Background: 99.
TRADESMAN, THE
  Background: 710. Defoe: 1205, 1312.
"TRADING JUSTICE," THE. See also LAW and THE LAWYER.
  Background: 705.
TRAGEDY
  Novel: 975. Fielding: 1444. Richardson: 1715, 1721, 1780,
  1814, 1830. Sterne: 2105. Godwin: 2465.
TRAGIC HERO
  Richardson: 1693.
TRAGICOMEDY
  Johnson: 2780.

TRANSPORTATION. See also CANALS and COACHING.
    Background: 79, 117, 320, 706.
TRAVEL. See also GRAND TOUR.
    Background: 117, 272, 284, 589, 676, 709. Novel: 918. De-
    foe: 1298, 1955. Beckford: 2303. Johnson: 2823.
TRAVEL LITERATURE
    Bibliographies: 3, 21. Novel: 744, 745, 760, 796, 864, 983,
    1015, 1643. Smollett: 1891, 1926. Johnson: 2789.
TURNER, JOSEPH
    Background: 535.
TURNPIKES AND ROADS
    Background: 79, 706.
TYPOGRAPHY
    Sterne: 2142.
TYPOLOGY. See also SYMBOLISM.
    Novel: 901, 903, 1003. Defoe: 1132, 1182.

UNDERGRADUATE, THE
    Background: 401, 478.
"UNIFORMITARIANISM"
    Background: 140.
UNITARIANISM
    Background: 365.
UNITY [formal unity in the novel]. See also PLOT, STRUCTURE,
    AND DESIGN.
    Novel: 908, 1030. Defoe: 1148, 1225, 1235, 1247. Fielding:
    1393, 1419, 1433, 1497, 1640. Richardson: 1871. Smollett:
    1893, 1923, 1928, 1946, 2036. Sterne: 2065, 2115, 2276. God-
    win: 2443a. Goldsmith: 2504. Mackenzie: 2624. Swift:
    3051, 3080, 3151, 3161, 3162, 3172.
UNIVERSITY NOVEL
    Novel: 1007.
UTILITARIANISM
    Godwin: 2466.
UTOPIA
    Background: 93. Defoe: 1271. Johnson: 2876. Swift:
    3005, 3023, 3027, 3081, 3164.
UTOPIAN FICTION
    Defoe: 1187. Swift: 3080.

"VANESSA" [ESTHER VANHOMRIGH]
    Swift: 3028, 3064.
VAUXHALL GARDENS. See also LONDON; CITY LIFE; and SPORT
    AND RECREATION.
    Background: 636.
VIA MEDIA
    Background: 312. Fielding: 1392.
VILLAGES. See also COUNTRY LIFE.
    Background: 277, 331, 532, 656.

VILLAINS
   Novel: 941.
VIOLENCE. See also AGGRESSION.
   Defoe: 1277. Smollett: 1934, 2001.
VIRGIL
   Background: 336. Fielding: 1561.
VIRGINIA
   Blackamore: 2332.
VOLTAIRE. See also RASSELAS-CANDIDE COMPARISON.
   Smollett: 1939.

WAGES
   Background: 291, 657.
WALPOLE, HORACE [as subject]
   Fielding: 1414.
WALPOLE, SIR ROBERT
   Background: 560, 638. Novel: 765, 846. Fielding: 1414,
   1581, 1650. Swift: 3016, 3124.
WANDERER, THE
   Novel: 808, 963. Goldsmith: 2513, 2542. Johnson: 2814.
WANDERING JEW
   Novel: 749.
WAR WITH FRANCE
   Background: 251.
WARBURTON, WILLIAM
   Sterne: 2191.
WEALTH. See also LUXURY and MONEY.
   Goldsmith: 2508.
WESLEY, JOHN. See also METHODISM.
   Background: 102, 592.
WEST INDIES
   Smollett: 1931.
WHIGS
   Background: 137, 150, 313, 426, 724. Novel: 783. Defoe:
   1314. Smollett: 1903. Walpole: 2728. Swift: 3015.
WIDOW, THE
   Sterne: 2227. Reeve: 2677.
WILD, JONATHAN. See also CRIME AND PUNISHMENT.
   Background: 373. Novel: 978.
WILKES, JOHN
   Background: 609.
WILLS [last wills and testaments]
   Richardson: 1779.
WISDOM
   Fielding: 1380.
WIT. See COMEDY.
WOMEN
   Bibliographies: 62, 63, 64, 73. Background: 118, 126, 257,
   275, 308, 377, 386, 412, 442, 450, 506, 516, 546, 549, 575, 583,
   593, 615, 681, 730. Novel: 752, 799, 822, 856, 858, 885, 932,

947, 951, 991, 1001, 1016, 1053, 1054, 1055, 1061, 1078, 1115.
Defoe: 1133, 1161, 1167, 1236, 1339, 1342, 1345. Fielding:
1518, 1583. Richardson: 1684, 1712, 1732, 1733, 1734, 1748,
1753, 1802, 1806, 1817, 1825, 1857, 1859, 1865, 1872. Smollett:
1964. Sterne: 2104. F. Brooke: 2336, 2339. Burney: 2356,
2358, 2359, 2367, 2369, 2375, 2382, 2383. Haywood: 2566,
2567. Lee: 2590. Lennox: 2599. Manley: 2636. Radcliffe:
2661, 2673. Wollstonecraft: 2743, 2746, 2748.
WOMEN NOVELISTS
    Bibliographies: 6, 60. Background: 593, 782, 805, 848, 858.
    Novel: 871, 893, 900, 909, 920, 921, 947, 1088. F. Brooke:
    2336. Inchbald: 2582, 2587. Smith: 2699, 2701. Wollstone-
    craft: 2748.
WOMEN'S FRIENDSHIP
    Novel: 1087. Defoe: 1311. Richardson: 1851. Cleland:
    2407. Wollstonecraft: 2750.
WORK
    Background: 169, 187, 236, 285, 291, 549.
WORKING CLASSES
    Background: 187, 192, 460, 463, 657, 661, 704.
WRITER IN SOCIETY, THE. See also GRUB STREET and PA-
    TRONAGE.
    Background: 185, 189, 196, 198, 595, 596, 614, 664. Novel:
    1056a. Goldsmith: 2514. Inchbald: 2587. Lewis: 2612.
    Smith: 2701. Johnson: 2799, 2879.
WRITING [the act of]
    Richardson: 1722. Burney: 2382.
"WRITING TO THE MOMENT"
    Richardson: 1777, 1839.

YAHOOS, THE
    Swift: 2924, 2968, 3006, 3012, 3071, 3100, 3139, 3160, 3187,
    3096.

PART II: BIBLIOGRAPHIES AND SURVEYS OF CRITICISM

1 Abernethy, Peter L., et al. English Novel Explication: Supplement I [1972-74]. Hamden, Conn.: Shoe String Press, 1976. Continues H. H. Palmer and A. J. Dyson's English Novel Explication: Criticisms to 1972 [see below]; and Inglis F. Bell and Donald Baird's The English Novel 1578-1956: A Checklist of Twentieth-Century Criticisms [see below]. Bibliography of criticism.

2 Abstracts of English Studies. Urbana, Ill.: National Council of Teachers of English, 1958--. Bibliography of criticism [10 yearly; annotated].

3 Adams, Percy G. "Travel Literature of the Seventeenth and Eighteenth Centuries: A Review of Recent Approaches." Texas Studies in Literature and Language, 20 (1978), 488-515. Travel literature. Survey of criticism.

4 Allibone, S. Austin. A Critical Dictionary of English Literature and British and American Authors. 3 vols. Philadelphia: Lippincott, 1871-77. Supplemented by John Foster Kirk's A Supplement to Allibone's "Critical Dictionary." 2 vols. Philadelphia: Lippincott, 1891. Bibliography of primary sources [lists many minor novelists].

5 Annual Bibliography of English Language and Literature ["MHRA"]. Cambridge: Modern Humanities Research Association, 1921 --. Bibliography of criticism [annual].

6 Backscheider, Paula, et al. An Annotated Bibliography of Twentieth-Century Critical Studies of Women and Literature, 1660-1800. New York: Garland, 1977. [British women]. Bibliography of criticism [annotated]. Women novelists.

7 Barnes, Warner. "Eighteenth- and Nineteenth-Century Editorial Problems: A Selective Bibliography." Papers of the Bibliographical Society of America, 62 (1968), 59-67. Textual editing.

8 Beasley, Jerry C. A Check List of Prose Fiction Published in England, 1740-1749. Charlottesville: Univ. Press of Virginia

for the Bibliographical Society of the University of Virginia,
1972. Bibliography of primary sources [annotated].

9 Beasley, Jerry C. English Fiction, 1660-1800: A Guide to Information Sources. Detroit: Gale, 1978. Bibliography of
   primary sources. Bibliography of criticism [annotated].

10 Bell, Inglis F., and Donald Baird. The English Novel, 1578-
   1956: A Checklist of Twentieth-Century Criticisms. Denver:
   Allen Swallow, 1958. [See Abernethy, above]. Bibliography
   of criticism.

11 Black, Frank Gees. The Epistolary Novel in the Late Eighteenth
   Century: A Descriptive and Bibliographical Study. Eugene:
   Univ. of Oregon Press, 1940. [Post-Richardsonian, 1781-1800].
   Epistolary novel. Bibliography of primary sources.

12 Block, Andrew. The English Novel, 1740-1850: A Catalogue.
   2nd ed. London: William Dawson, 1961. Bibliography of
   primary sources.

13 Bond, Donald F. The Eighteenth Century. Goldentree Bibliographies. Northbrook, Ill.: AHM Press, 1975. Bibliography
   of criticism.

14 Bonheim, Helmut W. The English Novel Before Richardson: A
   Checklist of Texts and Criticisms to 1970. Metuchen, N.J.:
   Scarecrow, 1971. Bibliography of primary sources. Bibliog-
   raphy of criticism.

15 Book Review Index. Detroit: Gale, 1965--. Bibliography of
   book reviews.

16 Brack, O M, Jr. "Research Opportunities in the Eighteenth-
   Century Book Trade." Analytical & Enumerative Bibliography,
   3 (1980), 190-200. Book trade.

17 Buttman, William A. "Early Hanoverian England (1714-1760):
   Some Recent Writings." And J. Jean Hecht. "The Reign of
   George III in Recent Historiography." In Changing Views on
   British History: Essays on Historical Writing Since 1939.
   Ed. Elizabeth C. Furber. Cambridge, Mass.: Harvard Univ.
   Press, 1966, pp. 181-205. Bibliography of historical studies.

18 Cambridge Bibliography of English Literature, The. ["CBEL"].
   Vol. II: 1660-1800. Ed. F. W. Bateson. Cambridge: Cambridge Univ. Press, 1941. [See also New Cambridge Bibliography of English Literature, below.] Bibliography of criticism.

19 Clifford, James L. "The Eighteenth Century." Modern Language Quarterly, 26 (1965), 111-34. Survey of criticism.

20 Combined Retrospective Index to Book Reviews in Scholarly Hu-
    manities Journals, 1802-1974. 10 vols. Ed. Evan I. Farber.
    Arlington, Va.: Carrollton Press, 1981. Bibliography of
    book reviews.

21 Cox, Edward Godfrey. A Reference Guide to the Literature of
    Travel. 3 vols. Seattle: Univ. of Washington Press, 1935-
    49. Travel literature. Bibliography of primary sources.

22 Current Book Review Citations. New York: H. W. Wilson,
    1977--. Bibliography of book reviews.

23 Day, Robert Adams. "A Chronological List of English Letter
    Fiction, 1660-1740" and "A List of Letter Fiction in Periodicals."
    In his Told in Letters: Epistolary Fiction Before Richardson.
    Ann Arbor: Univ. of Michigan Press, 1966, pp. 237-58, 267-
    70. Bibliography of primary sources [lists many minor novel-
    ists]. Epistolary novel. Novel in magazines. Serials.

24 Dissertation Abstracts International. Ann Arbor, Mich.: Uni-
    versity Microfilms, 1938--. Bibliography of criticism [anno-
    tated].

25 Draper, John William. Eighteenth-Century English Aesthetics:
    A Bibliography. 1931; rpt. New York: Octagon, 1968. Bib-
    liography of primary sources. Aesthetic theory and back-
    ground.

26 Dudley, Fred Adair. The Relations of Literature and Science:
    A Selected Bibliography, 1930-1967. Ann Arbor, Mich.:
    University Microfilms, 1968. Science.

27 Dunn, Richard J., ed. The English Novel: Twentieth-Century
    Criticism: Vol. I, Defoe Through Hardy. Chicago: Allen
    Swallow, 1976. Bibliography of criticism.

28 Dyson, A. E., ed. The English Novel: Select Bibliographical
    Guides. London: Oxford Univ. Press, 1974. Bibliography
    of criticism. Survey of criticism.

29 Eighteenth Century, The: A Current Bibliography ["ECCB"].
    Continues English Literature, 1660-1800: A Bibliography of
    Modern Studies ["PQ Bibliography"]. New York: AMS
    Press, 1926--. Bibliography of criticism [annual; interdis-
    ciplinary, annotated, and evaluative].

30 Elton, G. R. "The Eighteenth Century (1714-1815)." In his
    Modern Historians on British History, 1485-1945: A Critical
    Bibliography, 1945-1969. Ithaca, N.Y.: Cornell Univ.
    Press, 1970. Bibliography of historical studies.

31 Esdaile, Arundell. A List of English Tales and Prose Romances
    Printed Before 1740. 1912; rpt. New York: Burt Franklin,
    1969. Bibliography of primary sources.

32 Flowering of the Novel, 1740-1775, The: 121 Titles as Original-
    ly Published in 192 Volumes. New York: Garland, n.d.
    [Trade catalogue]. Bibliography of primary sources [mainly
    minor novelists].

33 Foundations of the Novel: Representative Early Eighteenth-
    Century Fiction: A Collection of 101 Rare Titles Reprinted
    in Photofacsimile in 71 Volumes. Compiled and edited by
    Michael F. Shugrue. New York: Garland, n.d. [Trade
    catalogue]. Bibliography of primary sources [mainly minor
    novelists].

34 Frank, Frederick S. "The Gothic Novel: A Checklist of Mod-
    ern Criticism." Bulletin of Bibliography, 30 (1973), 45-54.
    And "The Gothic Novel: A Second Bibliography," ibid., 35
    (1978), 1-14. Gothic novel. Bibliography of criticism.

35 Garmon, Gerald M. "'Tragic Realism' in Sentimental Literature:
    A Bibliography." Bulletin of Bibliography, 33 (1976), 131-
    34, 139, 148. Bibliography of primary sources. Bibliography
    of criticism. Sentimentalism.

36 Gove, Philip B. The Imaginary Voyage in Prose Fiction: A
    History of Its Criticism and a Guide for Its Study with an
    Annotated Check List of 215 Imaginary Voyages from 1700 to
    1800. 1941; rpt. New York: Octagon, 1975. Imaginary
    voyage. Bibliography of primary sources. Bibliography of
    criticism. Survey of criticism.

37 Heidler, Joseph B. The History from 1700 to 1800, of English
    Criticism of Prose Fiction. University of Illinois Studies in
    Language and Literature, 13, No. 2 (1928). Urbana: Univ.
    of Illinois Press, 1928. Survey of criticism.

38 Heilman, Robert Bechtold. "List of Chief Works Consulted:
    Prose Fiction." In his America in English Fiction, 1760-1800:
    The Influences of the American Revolution. 1937; rpt. New
    York: Octagon, 1968, pp. 449-57. Bibliography of primary
    sources [lists many minor novels]. America.

39 Howard-Hill, T. H. Bibliography of British Literary Bibliogra-
    phies. Oxford: Clarendon Press, 1969. Bibliography of
    bibliographies.

40 Index to Book Reviews in the Humanities, An. Williamston,
    Mich.: Phillip Thomson, 1960--. Bibliography of book re-
    views.

41 Jones, Claude E. "The English Novel: A Critical View, 1756-
    85." Modern Language Quarterly, 19 (1958), Pt. I, 147-59;
    Pt. II, 213-24. Eighteenth-century criticism and reviews of
    the novel [survey of articles on fiction in the Critical Re-
    view].

42 Klukoff, Philip J. "Novels Reviewed in the Critical Review,
    1756-1763--Part 1." Bulletin of Bibliography, 28 (1971), 35-
    36. And "Part 2," ibid., 40-41. Bibliography of book re-
    views. Eighteenth-century criticism and reviews of the novel.

43 Maxwell, Leslie F. A Bibliography of English Law from 1651 to
    1800. London: Sweet & Maxwell, 1931. Law.

44 Mayo, Robert D. "A Catalogue of Magazine Novels and Novel-
    ettes." In his The English Novel in the Magazines, 1740-
    1815. With a Catalogue of 1375 Magazine Novels and Novel-
    ettes. Evanston, Ill.: Northwestern Univ. Press, 1962, pp.
    431-620. See also Edward W. Pitcher, "Robert Mayo's The
    English Novel in the Magazines, 1740-1815: New Facts," Li-
    brary, 31 (1976), 20-30. Bibliography of primary sources.
    Novel in magazines.

45 McBurney, William H. A Check List of English Prose Fiction,
    1700-1739. Cambridge, Mass.: Harvard Univ. Press, 1960.
    Bibliography of primary sources.

46 McNutt, Dan J. The Eighteenth-Century Gothic Novel: An
    Annotated Bibliography of Criticism and Selected Texts.
    New York: Garland, 1975. Gothic novel. Bibliography of
    primary sources. Bibliography of criticism [annotated].

47 MLA International Bibliography of Books and Articles on the
    Modern Languages and Literatures. New York: Modern
    Language Association, 1922--. Bibliography of criticism [an-
    nual; annotated beginning in 1981; abstracts of selected arti-
    cles published separately from 1970 to 1975].

48 Morgan, Bayard Quincy. A Critical Bibliography of German
    Literature in English Translation, 1481-1927. 2nd ed. New
    York: Scarecrow, 1965. Foreign literature in English trans-
    lation. Bibliography of primary sources. Germany.

49 Morgan, Charlotte E. "Chronological List of the Prose Fiction
    First Printed in England Between 1600 and 1740." In her
    The Rise of the Novel of Manners: A Study of English Prose
    Fiction Between 1600 and 1740. 1911; rpt. New York: Rus-
    sell & Russell, 1963, pp. 154-233. Bibliography of primary
    sources [lists many minor novelists].

50 Morgan, William Thomas. A Bibliography of British History

(1700-1715): With Special Reference to the Reign of Queen
Anne. Bloomington: Indiana Univ. Press, 1934. For recent
updates see Pat Rogers, "A Bibliography of British History
(1700-1715): Some Additions and Corrections," Publications
of The Bibliographical Society of America, 69 (1975), 226-37;
and "Further Addenda to Morgan's Bibliography of British
History," ibid., 73 (1979), 93-107. Bibliography of historical
studies.

51 Nangle, Benjamin Christie. The Monthly Review: First Series,
    1749-1789. Oxford: Clarendon Press, 1934. And The Month-
    ly Review: Second Series, 1790-1815. Indexes of Contrib-
    utors and Articles. Oxford: Clarendon Press, 1955. Bib-
    liography of criticism. Eighteenth-century criticism and re-
    views of the novel.

52 New Cambridge Bibliography of English Literature, The.
    ["NCBEL"] Vol. II: 1660-1800. Ed. George Watson. Cam-
    bridge: Cambridge Univ. Press, 1971. [See also Cambridge
    Bibliography of English Literature, above.] Bibliography of
    primary sources. Bibliography of criticism.

53 Novel in England, 1700-1775, The: 227 Rare and Important Ti-
    tles Reproduced in Facsimile in 192 Volumes. New York:
    Garland, n.d. [Trade catalogue]. Bibliography of primary
    sources [mainly minor novelists].

54 Novel, 1720-1805, The: Fifteen Important and Influential Titles,
    Reproduced in Facsimile. Selected by Ronald Paulson. New
    Haven, Conn.: Yale Univ. Press, n.d. [Trade catalogue].
    Bibliography of primary sources [minor novelists].

55 Palmer, H. H., and A. J. Dyson. English Novel Explication:
    Criticisms to 1972. Hamden, Conn.: Shoe String Press,
    1973. [See Abernethy, above.]

56 Pargellis, Stanley, and D. J. Medley, eds. Bibliography of
    British History: The Eighteenth Century, 1714-1789. Ox-
    ford: Clarendon Press, 1951. Bibliography of historical
    studies.

57 Park, William. "Change in the Criticism of the Novel After
    1760." Philological Quarterly, 46 (1967), 34-41. Eighteenth-
    century criticism and reviews of the novel.

    "Philological Quarterly Bibliography" ["PQ Bib"]. See Eight-
    eenth Century, The: A Current Bibliography, above.

58 "Recent Studies in the Restoration and Eighteenth Century."
    Studies in English Literature, 1961--. Survey of criticism
    [annually, in the summer number].

59 Rogal, Samuel J. "A Checklist of Eighteenth-Century British
   Literature Published in Eighteenth-Century America." Colby
   Library Quarterly, 10 (1973), 321-56. Influence and repu-
   tation abroad. Bibliography of primary sources. America.

60 Rogers, Katharine M. "Opportunities for Scholarship in Eighteenth-Century British Literature." In Women in Print I.
   Ed. Joan E. Hartman and Ellen Messer-Davidow. New York:
   Modern Language Association, 1982, pp. 187-95. Survey of
   criticism. Women novelists.

61 Royal Historical Society. Writings on British History, 1901-
   1933. Vol. IV: The Eighteenth Century, 1714-1815. New
   York: Barnes & Noble, 1969. Bibliography of historical
   studies.

62 Schnorrenberg, Barbara Brandon. "Education for Women in
   Eighteenth-Century England: An Annotated Bibliography."
   Women & Literature, 4 (1976), 49-55. Education. Women.

63 Schnorrenberg, Barbara Brandon. "Toward a Bibliography of
   Eighteenth-Century Gentlewomen." Eighteenth-Century Life,
   1 (1975), 50-51. Women. Bibliography of criticism.

64 Schnorrenberg, Barbara B., with Jean E. Hunter. "The Eighteenth-Century Englishwoman." In The Women of England
   from Anglo-Saxon Times to the Present: Interpretive Bibliographical Essays. Ed. Barbara Kanner. Hamden, Conn.:
   Shoe String Press, 1979, pp. 183-228. Women.

65 Sena, John F. A Bibliography of Melancholy. London: Nether
   Press, 1970. Melancholy.

66 Singer, Godfrey Frank. "Bibliography." In his The Epistolary
   Novel: Its Origin, Decline, and Residuary Influence. 1933;
   rpt. New York: Russell & Russell, 1963, pp. 217-55, esp.
   221-44. Epistolary novel. Bibliography of primary sources
   [lists many minor epistolary novels].

67 Spector, Robert Donald. The English Gothic: A Bibliographic
   Guide to Writers from Horace Walpole to Mary Shelley. Westport, Conn.: Greenwood Press, 1983. Bibliography of criticism. Survey of criticism. Gothic novel.

68 Stevick, Philip. "Selected Bibliography." In his edition, The
   Theory of the Novel. New York: Free Press, 1967, pp. 407-
   28. Bibliography of criticism. Theory and practice of the
   novel.

69 Streeter, Harold Wade. The Eighteenth-Century English Novel
   in French Translation: Bibliographical Study. 1936; rpt.

New York: Blom, 1970. Influence and reputation abroad.
Bibliography of primary sources. France.

70 "Studies in Eighteenth-Century Fiction." Philological Quarterly,
    1976--. Survey of criticism [annually, in the fall number].

71 Summers, Montague. A Gothic Bibliography. 1941; rpt. New
    York: Russell & Russell, 1964. Gothic novel. Bibliography
    of primary sources.

72 Tobin, James E. Eighteenth-Century Literature and Its Cul-
    tural Background: A Bibliography. New York: Fordham
    Univ. Press, 1939. Bibliography of criticism.

73 Von den Steinen, Karl. "The Discovery of Women in Eight-
    eenth-Century English Political Life." In The Women of Eng-
    land from Anglo-Saxon Times to the Present: Interpretive
    Bibliographical Essays. Ed. Barbara Kanner. Hamden,
    Conn.: Shoe String Press, 1979, pp. 229-58. Women.
    Politics.

74 Ward, William S. Literary Reviews in British Periodicals, 1789-
    1797: A Bibliography with a Supplementary List of General
    (Non-Review) Articles on Literary Subjects. New York:
    Garland, 1979. And Literary Reviews in British Periodicals,
    1798-1820: A Bibliography. 2 vols. New York: Garland,
    1972. Bibliography of book reviews. Eighteenth-century
    criticism and reviews of the novel.

75 Whitrow, Magda, ed. Isis Cumulative Bibliography: A Bibliog-
    raphy of the History of Science Formed from Isis Critical
    Bibliographies 1-90, 1913-1965. 2 vols. London: Mansell,
    1971. Science.

76 Williams, Ioan. Novel and Romance, 1700-1800: A Documentary
    Record. New York: Barnes & Noble, 1970. Eighteenth-
    century criticism and reviews of the novel.

77 Year's Work in English Studies, The. ["YWES"]. London:
    English Association, 1921--. Bibliography of criticism [an-
    nual]. Survey of criticism.

78 Adamson, John William. English Education, 1789-1902. Cambridge: Cambridge Univ. Press, 1930. Education.

79 Albert, William. The Turnpike Road System in England, 1663-1840. Cambridge: Cambridge Univ. Press, 1972. Transportation. Turnpikes and roads.

80 Allen, B. Sprague. Tides in English Taste (1619-1800): A Background for the Study of Literature. 2 vols. 1937; rpt. New York: Pageant, 1958. Aesthetic theory and background. The sublime and the beautiful. The picturesque. Ruins. Art. Landscape gardening.

81 Allen, Robert J. The Clubs of Augustan London. Cambridge, Mass.: Harvard Univ. Press, 1933. London. Clubs.

■82 Altick, Richard D. "The Background: 1477-1800." The English Common Reader: A Social History of the Mass Reading Public, 1800-1900. Chicago: Univ. of Chicago Press, 1957, pp. 30-77. Reading public. Literacy.

83 Altick, Richard D. The Shows of London. Cambridge, Mass.: Belknap Press, 1978. London. Popular culture. Sport and recreation. City life.

84 Amory, Hugh, ed. Sales Catalogues of Libraries of Eminent Persons; Vol. 7: Poets and Men of Letters. London: Mansell Information Publishing, 1973. Library of novelist.

85 Anderson, Howard; Philip B. Daghlian; and Irvin Ehrenpreis, eds. The Familiar Letter in the Eighteenth Century. Lawrence: Univ. of Kansas Press, 1966. [Anthology of criticism]. Letter-writing.

86 Antal, Frederick. Hogarth and His Place in European Art. New York: Basic Books, 1962. Hogarth. Art.

87 Antal, Frederick. "The Moral Purpose of Hogarth's Art." Journal of the Warburg and Courtauld Institute, 15 (1952), 169-97. Hogarth. Morality.

88   Appleton, William W. A Cycle of Cathay: The Chinese Vogue
     in England During the Seventeenth and Eighteenth Cen-
     turies. New York: Columbia Univ. Press, 1951. Oriental-
     ism.

89   Archer, John. "Character in English Architectural Design."
     Eighteenth-Century Studies, 12 (1979), 339-71. Architec-
     ture.

90   Armstrong, Anthony. The Church in England, the Methodists
     and Society, 1700-1850. London: Rowman, 1973. The
     Church. Methodism.

91   Armstrong, Robert L. Metaphysics and British Empiricism.
     Lincoln: Univ. of Nebraska Press, 1970. Intellectual back-
     ground.

92   Armytage, W. H. G. Four Hundred Years of English Education.
     1964. 2nd ed. Cambridge: Cambridge Univ. Press, 1970,
     esp. pp. 27-96. Education.

93   Armytage, W. H. G. Heavens Below: Utopian Experiments in
     England, 1560-1960. London: Routledge & Kegan Paul, 1961.
     Utopia.

94   Ashton, Thomas S. Economic Fluctuations in England, 1700-
     1800. Oxford: Clarendon Press, 1959. Economics.

95   Ashton, Thomas S. An Economic History of England: The
     Eighteenth Century. London: Methuen, 1955. Economics.

96   Ashton, Thomas S. The Industrial Revolution, 1760-1830.
     1948. 2nd ed. London: Oxford, 1968. Industrial Revolu-
     tion.

97   Asquith, Herbert Henry. "Some Popular Frenzies in the Eight-
     eenth Century." In his Studies and Sketches. 2nd ed.
     London: Hutchinson, 1924. The mob [frenzy surrounding
     the celebrity of J. Wesley, Sacheverell, Wilkes, Gordon].
     Riots.

98   Atherton, Herbert M. "The British Defend Their Constitution
     in Political Cartoons and Literature." In Studies in Eight-
     eenth-Century Culture. Vol. 11. Ed. Harry C. Payne.
     Madison: Univ. of Wisconsin Press, 1982, pp. 3-32. Politics.
     Caricature. The 1790s. Symbolism.

99   Atherton, Herbert M. "George Townshend, Caricaturist."
     Eighteenth-Century Studies, 4 (1971), 437-46. George
     Townshend. Caricature. Politics.

100 Atherton, Herbert M. "The 'Mob' in Eighteenth-Century Eng-
     lish Caricature." Eighteenth-Century Studies, 12 (1978),
     47-58. The mob. Caricature.

101 Aubin, Robert A. "Grottoes, Geology, and the Gothic Re-
     vival." Studies in Philology, 31 (1934), 408-16. Aesthetic
     theory and background. Gothic background [related to
     eighteenth-century geological theory]. Ruins. Nature.
     Architecture. Grottoes [symbols of disorder].

102 Baker, Frank. John Wesley and the Church of England.
     London: Abingdon, 1970. John Wesley. Anglicanism.

103 Baker, Norman. "Changing Attitudes Toward Government in
     Eighteenth-Century Britain." In Statesmen, Scholars and
     Merchants: Essays in Eighteenth-Century History Presented
     to Dame Lucy Sutherland. Ed. Anne Whiteman et al. Ox-
     ford: Clarendon Press, 1973, pp. 202-19. Politics.

104 Barasch, Frances K. The Grotesque: A Study in Meanings.
     The Hague: Mouton, 1971, esp. pp. 95-117. The grotesque.
     The picturesque. Taste.

105 Barlow, Richard B. Citizenship and Conscience: A Study in
     the Theory and Practice of Religious Toleration in England
     During the Eighteenth Century. Philadelphia: Univ. of
     Pennsylvania Press, 1962. Christianity. Toleration.

106 Barrell, John. The Dark Side of the Landscape: The Rural
     Poor in English Painting, 1730-1840. Cambridge: Cambridge
     Univ. Press, 1980. Art. Landscape. Country life. The
     poor.

107 Barrow, Andrew. The Flesh Is Weak: An Intimate History of
     the Church of England. London: Hamish Hamilton, 1980.
     Anglicanism. The clergy.

108 Bartel, Roland. "Suicide in Eighteenth-Century England:
     The Myth of a Reputation." Huntington Library Quarterly,
     23 (1960), 145-58. Suicide.

109 Bassin, Joan. "The English Landscape Garden in the Eight-
     eenth Century: The Cultural Importance of an English In-
     stitution." Albion, 11 (1979), 15-32. Landscape gardening.

•110 Bate, W. Jackson. From Classic to Romantic: Premises of
     Taste in Eighteenth-Century England. 1946; rpt. New York:
     Harper & Row, 1961. Taste. Neoclassicism. Romanticism.
     Sensibility. Associationism. Intellectual background.

111 Baugh, Daniel A. British Naval Administration in the Age of

Walpole. Princeton, N.J.: Princeton Univ. Press, 1965.
The navy.

112   Baugh, Daniel A. "Introduction: The Social Basis of Stabil-
      ity." In Aristocratic Government and Society in Eighteenth-
      Century England: The Foundations of Stability. Ed. Daniel
      A. Baugh. New York: New Viewpoints, 1975, pp. 1-28.
      Social background. Stability.

113   Bayne-Powell, Rosamond. Eighteenth-Century London Life.
      New York: Dutton, 1938. London. Social background.
      City life.

114   Bayne-Powell, Rosamond. The English Child in the Eighteenth
      Century. New York: Dutton, 1939. Children.

●115 Bayne-Powell, Rosamond. English Country Life in the Eight-
      eenth Century. London: Murray, 1935. Country life.

116   Bayne-Powell, Rosamond. Housekeeping in the Eighteenth
      Century. London: Murray, 1956. Domestic life.

117   Bayne-Powell, Rosamond. Travellers in Eighteenth-Century
      England. London: Murray, 1951. Travel. Transportation.
      Coaching.

118   Beattie, J. M. "The Criminality of Women in Eighteenth-Cen-
      tury England." Journal of Social History, 8 (1975), 80-116.
      Women. Crime and punishment.

119   Beattie, J. M. The English Court in the Reign of George I.
      Cambridge: Cambridge Univ. Press, 1967. The court.

■120 Beattie, J. M. "The Pattern of Crime in England, 1660-1800."
      Past and Present, No. 62 (1974), pp. 47-95. Crime and
      punishment.

121   Beattie, J. M. "Towards a Study of Crime in 18th-Century
      England: A Note on Indictments." In The Triumph of Cul-
      ture: 18th-Century Perspectives. Ed. Paul S. Fritz and
      David Williams. Toronto: Hakkert, 1972, pp. 299-314.
      Crime and punishment.

122   Bebb, Evelyn D. Nonconformity and Social Economic Life,
      1660-1800. 1935; rpt. Philadelphia: Porcupine Press, 1980.
      Nonconformity. Economics.

●123 Becker, Carl L. The Heavenly City of the Eighteenth-Century
      Philosophers. New Haven, Conn.: Yale Univ. Press, 1932.
      Intellectual background.

124 Beers, Henry A. A History of English Romanticism in the
     Eighteenth Century. 1898; rpt. New York: Henry Holt,
     1926. Romanticism. Gothic background.

125 Belanger, Terry. "From Bookseller to Publisher: Changes
     in the London Book Trade, 1750-1850." In Book Selling
     and Book Buying: Aspects of the Nineteenth-Century Brit-
     ish and North American Book Trade. Ed. Richard G. Lan-
     don. Chicago: American Library Association, 1978, pp.
     7-16. Book trade.

126 Benkovitz, Miriam J. "Some Observations on Woman's Concept
     of Self in the 18th Century." In Woman in the 18th Century
     and Other Essays. Ed. Paul Fritz and Richard Morton.
     Toronto: Hakkert, 1976, pp. 37-54. [Burney]. Women.
     The self. Feminism.

127 Blakey, Dorothy. The Minerva Press, 1790-1820. London:
     Bibliographical Society, 1939. Circulating libraries. Book
     trade. Minerva Press.

128 Blanco, Richard L. "The State of Medicine in 18th-Century
     Britain--An Aspect of the Enlightenment." Enlightenment
     Essays, 3 (1972), 55-63. Medicine.

129 Bland, D. E. "Population and Liberalism, 1770-1817." Journal
     of the History of Ideas, 34 (1973), 113-22. Population.
     Liberalism. Intellectual background.

130 Bodek, Evelyn Gordon. "Salonières and Bluestockings: Edu-
     cated Obsolescence and Germinating Feminism." Feminist
     Studies, 3, No. 3/4 (1976), 185-99. The salon. The blue-
     stocking. Education. Feminism.

131 Boersch, A. "Landscape: Exemplar of Beauty." British Jour-
     nal of Aesthetics, 11 (1971), 81-95. Landscape.

132 Bond, Richmond P. "Eighteenth-Century Correspondence: A
     Survey." Studies in Philology, 33 (1936), 572-86. Letter-
     writing.

133 Booth, Alan. "Food Riots in the North-West of England, 1790-
     1801." Past and Present, No. 77 (1977), pp. 84-107. The
     poor. Riots. The 1790s.

134 Bossy, John. The English Catholic Community, 1570-1850.
     London: Dartman, Longman & Todd, 1975. Catholicism.

•135 Bovill, E. W. English Country Life, 1780-1830. London: Ox-
     ford Univ. Press, 1962. Country life. Enclosures. The
     squire. Poaching. Servants.

136 Bowden, Witt. Industrial Society in England Towards the End
     of the Eighteenth Century. 1925. 2nd ed. London: Cass,
     1965. Industry and trade. Social background.

137 Bradley, James E. "Whigs and Nonconformists: 'Slumbering
     Radicalism' in English Politics, 1739-89." Eighteenth-Century
     Studies, 9 (1975), 1-27. Whigs. Dissenters. Nonconform-
     ity. Politics. Radicalism.

138 Bradley, Rose M. The English Housewife in the Seventeenth
     & Eighteenth Centuries. London: Edward Arnold, 1912.
     Domestic life. The housewife.

139 Brander, Michael. The Georgian Gentleman. Farnborough:
     Saxon House, 1973. The gentleman. Social background.

140 Brauer, George C., Jr. "Good Breeding in the Eighteenth
     Century." Texas University Studies in English, 32 (1953),
     25-44. Good breeding. Manners. "Uniformitarianism."

141 Bredvold, Louis I. The Brave New World of the Enlighten-
     ment. Ann Arbor: Univ. of Michigan Press, 1961. Intel-
     lectual background.

•142 Bredvold, Louis I. The Natural History of Sensibility. De-
     troit: Wayne State Univ. Press, 1962. Sensibility. Intel-
     lectual background. Melancholy. Horror and terror. Gothic
     novel.

143 Bredvold, Louis I. "Some Basic Issues of the Eighteenth Cen-
     tury." Michigan Alumni Quarterly Review, 64 (1957), 45-54.
     Intellectual background.

•144 Brewer, John. Party Ideology and Popular Politics at the Ac-
     cession of George III. Cambridge: Cambridge Univ. Press,
     1976. Politics. Propaganda. Journalism. Radicalism.
     Public opinion.

145 Brewer, John, and John Styles, eds. An Ungovernable Peo-
     ple: The English and Their Law in the Seventeenth and
     Eighteenth Centuries. New Brunswick, N.J.: Rutgers
     Univ. Press, 1980. Law. Crime and punishment. Prisons.
     Riots. Radicalism.

146 Briggs, Asa. The Making of Modern England, 1783-1867.
     1959; rpt. New York: Harper & Row, 1965. History.

147 Brinton, Crane. "Jacobin and Anti-Jacobin." In his The
     Political Ideas of the English Romanticists. 1926; rpt.
     Ann Arbor: Univ. of Michigan Press, 1966. Politics.
     Jacobin novel. Radicalism. Conservatism.

148 Bronson, Bertrand H. "Printing as an Index of Taste in
     Eighteenth-Century England." Bulletin of the New York
     Public Library, 62 (1958), 373-87, 443-62. Taste. Print-
     ing.

149 Bronson, Bertrand H. "The Retreat from Reason." In Studies
     in Eighteenth-Century Culture: Irrationalism in the Eight-
     eenth Century. Vol. 2. Ed. Harold E. Pagliaro. Cleve-
     land: The Press of Case Western Reserve Univ., 1972, pp.
     225-38. Irrationality.

150 Brooke, John. "Party in the Eighteenth Century." In Silver
     Renaissance: Essays in Eighteenth-Century English History.
     Ed. Alex Natan. New York: St. Martin's, 1961, pp. 20-37.
     Politics. Tories. Whigs.

151 Brown, Philip Anthony. The French Revolution in English
     History. 1918; rpt. New York: Barnes & Noble, 1965.
     French Revolution.

152 Brown, Theodore M. "The Changing Self-Concept of the
     Eighteenth-Century London Physician." Eighteenth-Century
     Life, 7 (1982), 31-40. The physician.

153 Bryson, Gladys. Man and Society: The Scottish Inquiry of
     the Eighteenth Century. 1945; rpt. New York: A. M.
     Kelley, 1968. Intellectual background. Scotland.

154 Buck, Anne. Dress in Eighteenth-Century England. New
     York: Holmes & Meier, 1979. Dress and fashion.

155 Buer, M. C. Health, Wealth, and Population in the Early
     Days of the Industrial Revolution. 1926; rpt. New York:
     Fertig, 1968. Medicine. Disease. Population. City life
     [improvement of living conditions].

156 Bullough, Vern, and Bonnie Bullough. "The Causes of the
     Scottish Medical Renaissance of the Eighteenth Century."
     Bulletin of the History of Medicine, 45 (1972), 13-28.
     Medicine. Scotland.

157 Bunn, James H. "The Aesthetics of British Mercantilism."
     New Literary History, 11 (1980), 303-21. Mercantilism.
     Aesthetic theory and background.

158 Burke, Joseph. English Art, 1714-1800. Oxford: Clarendon
     Press, 1976. Art.

159 Burton, Elizabeth. The Georgians at Home, 1714-1830. Dub-
     lin: Longmans, Browne & Nolan, 1967. Domestic life.

160 Butler, Marilyn. "The Arts in an Age of Revolution." In her
     Romantics, Rebels and Reactionaries: English Literature and
     Its Background, 1760-1830. 1981; rpt. New York: Oxford
     Univ. Press, 1982, pp. 11-38. Aesthetic theory and back-
     ground.

•161 Butterfield, Herbert. The Origins of Modern Science, 1300-
     1800. 1949. Rev. ed., New York: Macmillan, 1959. Sci-
     ence.

162 Camp, John. "The Golden Age of Quackery." British History
     Illustrated, June-July 1978, pp. 54-61. Medicine. Quackery.

163 Carpenter, Spencer Cecil. Eighteenth-Century Church and
     People. London: Murray, 1959. The Church.

164 Carr, Raymond. English Fox Hunting: A History. London:
     Weidenfeld & Nelson, 1976. Fox hunting.

165 Carse, Adam. The Orchestra in the XVIIIth Century. Cam-
     bridge: Cambridge Univ. Press, 1940. Music.

•166 Cassirer, Ernst. The Philosophy of the Enlightenment.
     Trans. F. C. A. Koelln and J. P. Pettegrove. Princeton,
     N.J.: Princeton Univ. Press, 1951. [Originally published
     in German in 1932]. Intellectual background. The Enlight-
     enment.

166a Castle, Terry. "Eros and Liberty at the English Masquerade,
     1710-90." Eighteenth-Century Studies, 17 (1983-84), 156-76.
     Masquerade. Sex. Social background. Sport and recrea-
     tion.

167 Chalklin, C. W. The Provincial Towns of Georgian England:
     A Study of the Building Process, 1740-1820. London: Mc-
     Gill-Queens Univ. Press, 1974. Towns. Architecture.

168 Chalklin, C. W., and M. A. Havinden, eds. Rural Change
     and Urban Growth, 1500-1800: Essays in English Regional
     History in Honour of W. G. Hoskins. London: Longman,
     1974. Demography. Population. Country vs. city.

169 Chambers, J. D. Nottinghamshire in the Eighteenth Century:
     A Study of Life and Labour under the Squirearchy. 1932.
     2nd ed. London: Cass, 1966. Country life. Work. The
     squire.

170 Chambers, J. D. Population, Economy, and Society in Pre-
     Industrial England. Oxford: Oxford Univ. Press, 1972.
     Population. Economics. Social background.

•171 Chambers, J. D., and G. E. Mingay. The Agricultural Revo-
      lution, 1750-1880. London: Schocken, 1967. Agricultural
      revolution.

172 Cherry, S. "The Hospitals and Population: The Voluntary
      General Hospitals, Mortality and Local Populations in the
      English Provinces in the Eighteenth and Nineteenth Cen-
      turies." Population Studies, 34 (1980), Part 1, 59-75; Part
      2, 251-65. Hospitals. Medicine.

173 Christie, Ian R. "British Newspapers in the Later Georgian
      Age." In his Myth and Reality in Late-Eighteenth-Century
      British Politics and Other Papers. Berkeley: Univ. of
      California Press, 1970, pp. 311-33. Newspapers.

174 Christie, Ian R. Wilkes, Wyvill and Reform: The Parliamen-
      tary Reform Movement in British Politics, 1760-1785. Lon-
      don: Macmillan, 1962. Reform. Politics. Parliament.

175 Clark, George. "Bernard Mandeville, M.D., and Eighteenth-
      Century Ethics." Bulletin of the History of Medicine, 45
      (1971), 430-43. Medicine. Mandeville. Ethics.

176 Clark, George. A History of the Royal College of Physicians
      of London. Vol. II. Oxford: Clarendon Press, 1964--.
      Medicine.

177 Clark, H. F. The English Landscape Garden. London: Plei-
      ades, 1948. Landscape gardening.

178 Clark, Kenneth. The Gothic Revival: An Essay in the His-
      tory of Taste. 1928; rpt. Harmondsworth: Penguin, 1964.
      Gothic background. Aesthetic theory and background.
      Architecture.

179 Clark, Kenneth. Landscape into Art. 1949; rpt. London:
      Murray, 1966. Aesthetic theory and background. Art.
      Landscape.

180 Clark, Peter, ed. Country Towns in Pre-Industrial England.
      New York: St. Martin's, 1981. Towns. Bath. Country
      life.

181 Clarke, M. L. Classical Education in Britain, 1500-1900.
      Cambridge: Cambridge Univ. Press, 1959. Education.

182 Clarkson, L. A. Death, Disease and Famine in Pre-Industrial
      England. Dublin: Gill & Macmillan, 1975. Demography.
      Population. Medicine. Death. Disease. Famine.

183 Clarkson, L. A. The Pre-Industrial Economy in England, 1500-
      1750. London: Schocken, 1972. Economics.

184 Clifford, James L. "Argument and Understanding: Teaching
     Through Controversy." Eighteenth-Century Life, 5 (1979),
     1-7. Pedagogical approach.

185 Clifford, James L., ed. Man Versus Society in Eighteenth-
     Century Britain: Six Points of View. Cambridge: Cam-
     bridge Univ. Press, 1968. Politics. Economics. The clergy.
     Art. Music. The writer in society. Man vs. society.

186 Clifford, James L. "Some Aspects of London Life in the Mid-
     18th Century." In City & Society in the 18th Century. Ed.
     Paul Fritz and David Williams. Toronto: Hakkert, 1973,
     pp. 19-38. London. City life.

187 Coats, A. W. "Changing Attitudes to Labour in the Mid-
     Eighteenth Century." Economic History Review, 11 (1958),
     35-51. Work. Working classes.

188 Coats, A. W. "Economic Thought and Poor Law Policy in the
     Eighteenth Century." Economic History Review, 13 (1960),
     39-51. Economics. The poor.

189 Cobban, Alfred, ed. The Eighteenth Century: Europe in the
     Age of Enlightenment. New York: McGraw-Hill, 1969.
     Architecture. Science. Industry and trade. The writer in
     society. The poor. Social background.

190 Cockburn, J. S., ed. Crime in England: 1550-1800. Prince-
     ton, N.J.: Princeton Univ. Press, 1977. [Anthology of
     essays]. Crime and punishment [infanticide, poaching].
     Newgate. The ordinary.

191 Cohen, Murray. Sensible Words: Linguistic Practice in Eng-
     land, 1640-1785. Baltimore: The Johns Hopkins Univ.
     Press, 1978. Style and language. Semantics.

192 Cole, G. D. H., and Raymond Postgate. The Common People,
     1746-1946. London: Methuen, 1938. Working classes.
     Politics. London. Reform.

193 Coleman, Donald Cuthbert. The Economy of England, 1450-
     1750. New York: Oxford Univ. Press, 1977. Economics.

194 Coleman, Patrick. "Character in an Eighteenth-Century Con-
     text." The Eighteenth Century: Theory and Interpretation,
     24 (1983), 51-63. Characterization [eighteenth-century con-
     cept of "character"].

195 Colley, Linda. In Defiance of Oligarchy: The Tory Party,
     1714-60. Cambridge: Cambridge Univ. Press, 1982. Tories.
     Politics.

196   Collins, Arthur S.   Authorship in the Days of Johnson: Be-
      ing a Study of the Relation Between Author, Patron, Pub-
      lisher, and Public, 1726-1780.   1927; rpt.   New York:
      Dutton, 1929.   The writer in society.   Reading public.
      Book trade.   Patronage.

197   Collins, Arthur S.   "The Growth of the Reading Public During
      the Eighteenth Century."   Review of English Studies, O.S.
      2 (1926), 284-94, 428-38.   Literacy.   Reading public [its
      growth led to the spread of education].   Statistics.

198   Collins, Arthur S.   The Profession of Letters: A Study in the
      Relation of Author to Patron, Publisher, and Public, 1780-
      1833.   London: Routledge & Kegan Paul, 1928.   The writer
      in society.   Reading public.   Literacy.   Book trade.   Pa-
      tronage.

199   Cone, Carl B.   The English Jacobins: Reformers in Late
      Eighteenth-Century England.   New York: Scribner, 1968.
      Jacobins.   Politics.   Reform.   Radicalism.

200   Connely, Willard.   Beau Nash: Monarch of Bath and Tun-
      bridge Wells.   London: Werner Laurie, 1955.   "Beau" Rich-
      ard Nash.   Bath.

201   Constantine, J. Robert.   "The Ignoble Savage: An Eighteenth-
      Century Stereotype."   Phylon, 27 (1966), 171-79.   Racism.
      Slavery.   Blacks.

202   Cooper, Robert Alan.   "Ideas and Their Execution: English
      Prison Reform."   Eighteenth-Century Studies, 10 (1976),
      73-93.   Crime and punishment.   Prisons.

203   Copeman, W. S. C.   A Short History of the Gout and the
      Rheumatic Diseases.   Berkeley: Univ. of California Press,
      1964.   Gout.   Rheumatism.   Disease.

204   Cowie, Leonard W.   "The Bow Street Runners."   British Heri-
      tage, June-July 1980, pp. 46-57.   Crime and punishment.
      Bow Street Runners.

205   Cowles, Virginia.   The Great Swindle: The Story of the South
      Sea Bubble.   London: Collins, 1960.   South Sea Bubble.
      Economics.

206   Cragg, Gerald R.   The Church and the Age of Reason, 1648-
      1789.   1960; rpt.   Grand Rapids, Mich.:   Wm. B. Eerdmans,
      1967.   The Church.

207   Cragg, Gerald R.   Reason and Authority in the Eighteenth
      Century.   Cambridge: Cambridge Univ. Press, 1964.   Au-
      thority.   Reason.

208 Crane, R. S. "Anglican Apologetics and the Idea of Progress,
     1699-1745." Modern Philology, 31 (1934), 273-306, 349-82.
     Rpt. in his The Idea of the Humanities. Chicago: Univ. of
     Chicago Press, 1967, I, 214-87. Anglicanism. Progress.

209 Crane, R. S. "The Humanities and Themes of Education in
     the Eighteenth Century." In his The Idea of the Humani-
     ties. Chicago: Univ. of Chicago Press, 1967, I, 89-121.
     Intellectual background. Education. The humanities.

■210 Crane, R. S. "Suggestions Toward a Genealogy of the 'Man
     of Feeling.'" ELH: A Journal of English Literary History,
     1 (1934), 205-30. Rpt. in his The Idea of the Humanities.
     Chicago: Univ. of Chicago Press, 1967, I, 188-213. Sen-
     sibility. Sentimentalism. "Man of Feeling."

211 Cranfield, Geoffrey Alan. The Development of the Provincial
     Newspaper, 1700-1760. Oxford: Clarendon Press, 1962.
     Newspapers.

212 Cressey, David. "Levels of Illiteracy in England, 1530-1730."
     Historical Journal, 20 (1977), 1-23. Literacy.

213 Creswell, John. British Admirals of the Eighteenth Century:
     Tactics in Battle. Hamden, Conn.: Archon, 1972. The
     navy.

214 Crocker, Lester G. An Age of Crisis: Man and World in
     Eighteenth-Century Thought. Baltimore: The Johns Hop-
     kins Univ. Press, 1959. Intellectual background. Ethics.

215 Crook, J. Mordaunt. The Greek Revival: Neo-Classical Atti-
     tudes in British Architecture, 1760-1870. London: Murray,
     1972. Greek revival. Architecture. Neoclassicism.

216 Cummings, Dorothea. "Prostitution as Shown in Eighteenth-
     Century Periodicals." Ball State University Forum, 12 (1971),
     44-49. Prostitution.

217 Cummings, Frederick J. "The Problem of Artistic Style as It
     Relates to the Beginnings of Romanticism." In Studies in
     Eighteenth-Century Culture. Vol. 2. Ed. Harold E. Pag-
     liaro. Cleveland: The Press of Case Western Reserve Univ.,
     1972, pp. 143-65. Romanticism. Aesthetic theory and back-
     ground.

218 Cunnington, Cecil W., and Phillis Cunnington. Handbook of
     English Costume in the Eighteenth Century. 1957; rpt.
     Boston: Plays, 1972. Dress and fashion.

219 Curtis, Lewis P. Anglican Moods of the Eighteenth Century.

Hamden, Conn.: Archon, 1966. Anglicanism. Latitudinarianism. Evangelicalism.

220 Dainton, Courtney. "The Age of Hospitals." British History Illustrated, January 1978, pp. 54-64. Medicine. Hospitals.

221 Darby, H. C., ed. A New Historical Geography of England. Cambridge: Cambridge Univ. Press, 1973. Geography. Industry and trade. Agriculture.

222 Davies, E. "The Small Landowner, 1780-1832, in the Light of the Land Tax Assessments." In Essays in Economic History. Ed. E. M. Carus-Wilson. London: Edward Arnold, 1954, I, 270-94. Country life. Taxation.

223 Davies, Horton. Worship and Theology in England. Vol. III: From Watts and Wesley to Maurice, 1690-1850. Princeton, N.J.: Princeton Univ. Press, 1961. Christianity. The Church.

224 Davies, Rupert, and E. G. Rupp, eds. A History of the Methodist Church in Great Britain. Vol. I. London: Epworth Press, 1965. Methodism.

225 Davis, Ralph. A Commercial Revolution: English Overseas Trade in the Seventeenth and Eighteenth Centuries. London: Historical Association, 1967. Industry and trade.

226 Davis, Ralph. The Rise of the English Shipping Industry in the Seventeenth and Eighteenth Centuries. London: Macmillan, 1962. Shipping. Industry and trade.

227 Davis, Terence. The Gothick Taste. Newton Abbot: David & Charles, 1974. Gothic background. Architecture.

228 Deane, Phyllis. The First Industrial Revolution. Cambridge: Cambridge Univ. Press, 1965. Industrial Revolution.

229 Deane, Phyllis, and W. A. Cole. British Economic Growth, 1688-1959: Trends and Structure. 1962; 2nd ed. Cambridge: Cambridge Univ. Press, 1967. Economics.

230 Debb, E. D. Nonconformity and Social and Economic Life, 1600-1800. London: Epworth Press, 1935. Nonconformity [Quakerism, Methodism, Congregationalism].

231 De Beer, E. S. "Gothic: Origin and Diffusion of the Term; The Idea of Style in Architecture." Journal of the Warburg and Courtauld Institute, 11 (1948), 143-62. Gothic background. Architecture. Semantics.

232 Devine, T. M. The Tobacco Lords: A Study of the Tobacco
     Merchants of Glasgow and Their Trading Activities, c. 1740-
     90. Edinburgh: Donald, 1975. Scotland. Tobacco. Indus-
     try and trade.

•233 Dickinson, H. T. Liberty and Property: Political Ideology in
     Eighteenth-Century Britain. New York: Holmes & Meier,
     1977. Politics. Radicalism. Reform.

234 Dickson, P. G. M. The Financial Revolution in England: A
     Study in the Development of Public Credit, 1688-1756. New
     York: St. Martin's, 1967. Economics.

235 Ditchfield, G. M. "Repeal, Abolition, and Reform: A Study
     in the Interaction of Reforming Movements in the Parliament
     of 1790-6." In Anti-Slavery, Religion, and Reform: Essays
     in Memory of Roger Anstey. Ed. Christine Bolt and Seymour
     Drescher. Hamden, Conn.: Archon, 1980, pp. 101-18.
     Slavery. Reform. The 1790s.

236 Dobson, C. R. Masters and Journeymen: A Prehistory of In-
     dustrial Relations, 1717-1800. Totowa, N.J.: Rowman &
     Littlefield, 1980. Labor relations. Work.

237 Donaldson, Ian. "Cato in Tears: Stoical Guises of the Man
     of Feeling." In Studies in the Eighteenth Century: Papers
     Presented at the Second David Nichol Smith Memorial Seminar,
     Canberra, 1970: Vol. 2. Toronto: Univ. of Toronto
     Press, 1973, pp. 377-95. "Man of Feeling." Stoicism.

238 Donaldson, Ian. "The Satirist's London." Essays in Criticism,
     25 (1975), 101-22. The mob. London. Satire.

239 Donoughue, Bernard. British Politics and the American Revo-
     lution: The Path to War, 1773-1775. London: Macmillan,
     1964. American Revolution. Politics.

■240 Doughty, Oswald. "The English Malady of the Eighteenth Cen-
     tury." Review of English Studies, O.S. 2 (1926), 257-69.
     Melancholy [not only a fashionable complaint, but also a
     cause of the modern novel; Fielding and Smollett wrote to
     counteract depression].

241 Downey, James. "Barnabas and Boanerges: Archetypes of
     Eighteenth-Century Preaching." University of Toronto
     Quarterly, 51 (1981), 36-46. The sermon.

242 Downey, James. The Eighteenth-Century Pulpit: A Study of
     the Sermons of Butler, Berkeley, Secker, Sterne, Whitefield
     and Wesley. Oxford: Clarendon Press, 1969. The sermon.

243 Dudley, Edward, and Maximillian E. Novak, eds. The Wild
    Man Within: An Image in Western Thought from the Renais-
    sance to Romanticism. Pittsburgh: Univ. of Pittsburgh
    Press, 1972. Noble savage. Primitivism.

244 Duman, Daniel. The Judicial Bench in England. Atlantic
    Highlands, N.J.: Humanities Press, 1982. Law.

245 Dunham, William Huse, Jr. "'The Wisdom of the Ages': Law
    and Morality in Georgian Britain." Eighteenth-Century Life,
    1 (1975), 77-80. Law. Morality.

246 Eighteenth-Century English Books Considered by Librarians
    and Booksellers, Bibliographers and Collectors. Chicago:
    Association of College & Research Libraries, 1976. [Lec-
    tures]. Book trade. Textual editing. Bibliography of
    primary sources [establishing a short title catalogue, rare
    books].

247 Eitner, Lorenz. "Cages, Prisons, and Captives in Eighteenth-
    Century Art." In Images of Romanticism: Verbal and Visual
    Affinities. Ed. Karl Kroeber and William Walling. New Hav-
    en, Conn.: Yale Univ. Press, 1978, pp. 13-38. Liberty.
    Imprisonment. Symbolism [cages, prisons]. Art.

248 Elliott-Binns, L. E. The Early Evangelicals: A Religious and
    Social Study. London: Lutterworth Press, 1953. Evangeli-
    calism. Christianity.

249 Ellis, Aytoun. The Penny Universities: A History of the
    Coffee-Houses. London: Secker & Warburg, 1956. "Penny
    universities." Coffee houses.

250 Emerson, Roger. "The Enlightenment & Social Structures."
    In City and Society in the 18th Century. Ed. Paul Fritz and
    David Williams. Toronto: Hakkert, 1973, pp. 99-124. So-
    cial structure. Intellectual background. The Enlightenment.

251 Emsley, Clive. British Society and the French Wars, 1793-
    1815. Totowa, N.J.: Rowman & Littlefield, 1979. The
    1790s. Social background. War with France.

252 Erämetsä, Erik. A Study of the Word "Sentimental" and of
    Other Linguistic Characteristics of Eighteenth-Century Senti-
    mentalism in England. Helsinki: Helsingin Liikekirjapaino
    Oy, 1951. Sentimentalism. "Sentimental." Style and lan-
    guage. Semantics.

253 Ernle, Lord. English Farming Past and Present. 1912. 6th
    ed. Chicago: Quadrangle Books, 1961. Agriculture.

254 Erskine-Hill, Howard. "Augustans on Augustinianism: Eng-
     land, 1655-1759." Renaissance and Modern Studies, 11 (1967),
     55-83. Augustinianism. Christianity.

255 Evans, Eric J. The Contentious Tithe: The Tithe Problem
     and English Agriculture, 1750-1850. London: Routledge &
     Kegan Paul, 1976. Agriculture. Tithes. Taxation. En-
     closures.

256 Evans, Eric J. "Some Reasons for the Growth of English Rural
     Anti-Clericalism, c.1750-c.1830." Past and Present, No. 66
     (1975), pp. 84-109. Anti-clericalism. Tithes. Country life.

257 Fabricant, Carole. "Binding and Dressing Nature's Loose
     Tresses: The Ideology of Augustan Landscape Design."
     Studies in the Eighteenth Century. Vol. 8. Ed. Roseann
     Runte. Madison: Univ. of Wisconsin Press, 1979, pp. 109-
     35. Landscape gardening. Women.

258 Fairchild, Hoxie Neale. The Noble Savage: A Study in Ro-
     mantic Naturalism. New York: Columbia Univ. Press, 1928.
     Noble savage.

259 Falk, Bernard. Thomas Rowlandson, His Life and Art: A
     Documentary Record. London: Hutchinson, 1949. Row-
     landson.

260 Fehr, Bernard. "The Antagonism of Forms in the Eighteenth
     Century." English Studies, 18 (1936), 115-21, 193-205; 19
     (1937), 1-3, 49-57. Aesthetic theory and background.
     Architecture. Art. Landscape gardening. Music. Con-
     trast as technique.

261 Fiering, Norman S. "Irresistible Compassion: An Aspect of
     Eighteenth-Century Sympathy and Humanitarianism." Journal
     of the History of Ideas, 37 (1976), 195-218. Sympathy.
     Humanitarianism.

262 Finley, Gerald. "The Encapsulated Landscape: An Aspect of
     Gilpin's Picturesque." In City & Society in the 18th Cen-
     tury. Ed. Paul Fritz and David Williams. Toronto: Hak-
     kert, 1973, pp. 193-213. The picturesque. Aesthetic the-
     ory and background. Landscape. William Gilpin.

263 Fischer, Michael. "The Collapse of English Neoclassicism."
     Centennial Review, 24 (1980), 338-59. Neoclassical decline.

264 Fisher, Lois H. A Literary Gazetteer of England. New York:
     McGraw-Hill, 1980. Places in the novel. Geography. Set-
     ting. Gazetteer.

265 Flinn, Michael W. "The Industrialists." In Silver Renaissance:
    Essays in Eighteenth-Century English History. Ed. Alex
    Natan. New York: St. Martin's, 1961, pp. 57-80. The in-
    dustrialist.

266 Floud, Roderick, and Donald McCloskey, eds. The Economic
    History of Britain since 1700. Volume I: 1700-1860. Cam-
    bridge: Cambridge Univ. Press, 1981. Economics. Popu-
    lation. Agriculture. Industry and trade. Industrial Revo-
    lution.

267 Foord, Archibald S. His Majesty's Opposition, 1714-1830.
    Oxford: Clarendon Press, 1964. Politics.

268 Fortescue, J. W. A History of the British Army. 13 vols.
    London: Macmillan, 1910-35. The army.

269 Foss, Michael. The Age of Patronage: The Arts in England,
    1660-1750. Ithaca, N.Y.: Cornell Univ. Press, 1972. Pa-
    tronage.

270 Fothergill, Robert A. Private Chronicles: A Study of English
    Diaries. London: Oxford Univ. Press, 1974. The diary.

•271 Foucault, Michel. Madness and Civilization: A History of In-
    sanity in the Age of Reason. Trans. Richard Howard.
    New York: Pantheon, 1965. [Originally published in French
    in 1961]. Insanity. Hysteria. Melancholy. Madhouses.
    Bedlam.

272 Frantz, R. W. The English Traveller and the Movement of
    Ideas, 1660-1732. Lincoln: Univ. of Nebraska Press, 1934.
    Imaginary voyage. Travel. Intellectual background.

273 Fritz, Paul S. The English Ministers and Jacobitism Between
    the Rebellions of 1715 and 1745. Toronto: Univ. of Toronto
    Press, 1975. Jacobitism. Rebellion of 1745.

274 Fritz, Paul S. "The Trade in Death: The Royal Funerals in
    England, 1685-1830." Eighteenth-Century Studies, 15 (1982),
    291-316. Funerals.

275 Fussell, G. E. The English Countrywoman: A Farmhouse So-
    cial History. 1953; rpt. New York: Russell & Russell,
    1971. Country life. Women.

276 Fussell, G. E. "Georgian Times." In his The English Rural
    Labourer: His Home, Furniture, Clothing & Food from Tudor
    to Victorian Times. 1949; rpt. Westport, Conn.: Green-
    wood Press, 1975. The laborer. Country life. Domestic
    life. Dress and Fashion. Meals.

•277 Fussell, G. E. Village Life in the Eighteenth Century. Wor-
      cester: Littlebury, 1947. Villages.

278   Gadd, David. Georgian Summer: Bath in the Eighteenth Cen-
      tury. Bath: Adams & Dart, 1971. Bath. Social back-
      ground.

279   Gallaway, Francis. Reason, Rule, and Revolt in English Clas-
      sicism. 1940; rpt. New York: Octagon, 1965. Neoclassi-
      cism. Romanticism. Aesthetic theory and background.

280   Gaskell, Philip. "Eighteenth-Century Press Numbers: Their
      Use and Usefulness." Library, 4 (1950), 249-61. Book
      trade.

•281 Gaunt, William. The Great Century of English Painting: Ho-
      garth to Turner. London: Phaidon, 1971. Art.

282   Gawlick, Günter. "The English Deists' Contribution to the
      Theory of Toleration." In Transactions of the Fourth Inter-
      national Congress on the Enlightenment. Ed. Theodore
      Besterman. Oxford: Voltaire Foundation, 1976, pp. 823-35.
      Deism. Toleration.

•283 Gay, Peter. The Enlightenment: An Interpretation. 2 vols.
      New York: Knopf, 1966-1969. Intellectual background.
      The Enlightenment.

284   George, M. Dorothy, ed. England in Johnson's Day. 1928;
      rpt. Freeport, N.Y.: Books for Libraries Press, 1972.
      [Eighteenth-century comments on the times]. Social back-
      ground. The Church. The clergy. Education. The poor.
      Politics. Patronage. Crime and punishment. Book trade.
      Grub Street. Social structure. Travel. Landscape garden-
      ing. Sport and recreation.

285   George, M. Dorothy. England in Transition: Life and Work
      in the Eighteenth Century. 1931; rpt. London: Penguin,
      1953. Social background. Work.

286   George, M. Dorothy. English Political Caricature: A Study of
      Opinion and Propaganda. 2 vols. Oxford: Clarendon
      Press, 1959. Caricature. Politics.

287   George, M. Dorothy. Hogarth to Cruikshank: Social Change
      in Graphic Satire. New York: Walker, 1967. Caricature.
      Hogarth. Social background.

•288 George, M. Dorothy. London Life in the Eighteenth Century.
      1925; rpt. New York: Harper, 1964. London. Social
      background. City life.

289 Gilbert, Alan D. Religion and Society in Industrial England:
     Church, Chapel and Social Change, 1740-1914. London:
     Longman, 1976. Christianity. Social background.

290 Gilbert, Arthur N. "Military and Civilian Justice in Eight-
     eenth-Century England: An Assessment." Journal of Brit-
     ish Studies, 17, No. 2 (1978), 41-65. Law. Crime and
     punishment. The army.

291 Gilboy, Elizabeth W. Wages in Eighteenth-Century England.
     Cambridge, Mass.: Harvard Univ. Press, 1934. Wages.
     Work. Standard of living.

292 Gilley, Sheridan. "English Attitudes to the Irish in England,
     1780-1900." In Immigrants and Minorities in British Society.
     Ed. Colin Holmes. London: Allen & Unwin, 1978, pp. 81-
     110. The Irish.

293 Gilmore, Thomas B., Jr. The Eighteenth-Century Controversy
     Over Ridicule as a Test of Truth: A Reconsideration. At-
     lanta: Georgia State Univ. Press, 1970. Ridicule. Intel-
     lectual background.

294 Gilmour, Robin. "The Legacy from the Eighteenth Century."
     In his The Idea of the Gentleman in the Victorian Novel.
     London: Allen & Unwin, 1981, pp. 16-36. The gentleman.
     Social structure.

295 Gipson, Lawrence Henry. The British Empire before the Amer-
     ican Revolution. 14 vols. New York: Knopf, 1936-56.
     British Empire. History.

296 Glass, D. V. "Population and Population Movements in England
     and Wales, 1700 to 1850." In Population in History: Essays
     in Historical Demography. Ed. D. V. Glass and D. E. C.
     Eversley. London: Edward Arnold, 1965, pp. 221-46. Popu-
     lation. Demography.

297 Godley, Alfred Denis. Oxford in the Eighteenth Century.
     London: Methuen, 1908. Oxford University.

298 Golden, Morris. "The Imagining Self in the Eighteenth Cen-
     tury." Eighteenth-Century Studies, 3 (1969), 4-27. The
     self. Imagination. Order vs. disorder.

299 Goldsmith, M. M. "Mandeville and the Spirit of Capitalism."
     Journal of British Studies, 17, No. 1 (1977), 63-81. Mande-
     ville. Capitalism.

300 Gomme, George Laurence, ed. English Traditional Lore: The
     Gentleman's Magazine Library. Vol. 4. 1885; rpt. Detroit:
     Singing Tree Press, 1968. Social background. Folklore.

301 Gomme, George Laurence, ed. Manners and Customs: The
     Gentleman's Magazine Library. Vol. 1. 1883; rpt. Detroit:
     Singing Tree Press, 1968. Social background. Manners.
     Customs.

302 Gomme, George Laurence, ed. Popular Superstitions: The
     Gentleman's Magazine Library. Vol. 3. 1884; rpt. Detroit:
     Singing Tree Press, 1968. Social background. Supersti-
     tions.

303 Goodwin, Albert. The Friends of Liberty: The English Demo-
     cratic Movement in the Age of the French Revolution. Cam-
     bridge, Mass.: Harvard Univ. Press, 1979. Radicalism.
     The 1790s. Democracy.

304 Gossman, Lionel. "Literary Scholarship and Popular History."
     Eighteenth-Century Studies, 7 (1974), 133-42. Popular cul-
     ture.

305 Grave, S. A. The Scottish Philosophy of Common Sense.
     Oxford: Oxford Univ. Press, 1960. Intellectual background.
     Scottish Common Sense School.

306 Grave, S. A. "Some Eighteenth-Century Attempts to Use the
     Notion of Happiness." In Studies in the Eighteenth-Century:
     Papers Presented at the David Nichol Smith Memorial Seminar,
     Canberra, 1966. Ed. R. F. Brissenden. Canberra: Aus-
     tralian National Univ. Press, 1968, pp. 155-69. Happiness.

307 Green, V. H. H. A History of Oxford University. London:
     Batsford, 1974. Oxford University.

308 Greenberg, Janelle. "The Legal Status of the English Woman
     in Early Eighteenth-Century Common Law and Equity." In
     Studies in Eighteenth-Century Culture. Vol. 4. Ed. Harold
     E. Pagliaro. Madison: Univ. of Wisconsin Press, 1975, pp.
     171-82. Women. Law [women's legal rights greater than
     conventionally acknowledged].

•309 Greene, Donald. The Age of Exuberance: Backgrounds to
     Eighteenth-Century English Literature. New York: Random
     House, 1970. Introductory guide [excellent account of main
     issues]. Social background. Intellectual background. His-
     tory. Art.

310 Greene, Donald. "Augustinianism and Empiricism: A Note on
     Eighteenth-Century English Intellectual History." Eighteenth-
     Century Studies, 1 (1967), 33-68. Augustinianism. Empiri-
     cism. Intellectual background. Ethics.

311 Greene, Donald. "Latitudinarianism and Sensibility: The

Genealogy of the 'Man of Feeling' Reconsidered." Modern Philology, 75 (1977), 159-83. Latitudinarianism. Sensibility. "Man of Feeling."

312 Greene, Donald. "The Via Media in an Age of Revolution: Anglicanism in the 18th Century." In The Varied Pattern: Studies in the 18th Century. Ed. Peter Hughes and David Williams. Toronto: Hakkert, 1971, pp. 253-67. Anglicanism. Via media.

313 Grinnell, George. "Newton's Principia as Whig Propaganda." In City & Society in the 18th Century. Ed. Paul Fritz and David Williams. Toronto: Hakkert, 1973, pp. 181-92. Intellectual background. Newton. Whigs.

314 Grubb, Isabel. Quakerism and Industry before 1800. London: Williams & Norgate, 1930. Quakerism. Industry and trade.

315 Gury, Jacques. "The Sufferings of the Clergy, 1730-60." Church Quarterly Review, 164 (1962) 44-57. [Fielding, Goldsmith]. The clergy.

■316 Habakkuk, H. J. "England's Nobility." In Aristocratic Government and Society in Eighteenth-Century England: The Foundations of Stability. Ed. Daniel A. Baugh. New York: New Viewpoints, 1975, pp. 97-115. Originally published as "England." In The European Nobility in the Eighteenth Century. Ed. Albert Goodwin. New York: Harper & Row, 1953, pp. 1-21. The aristocracy.

317 Habakkuk, H. J. "English Landownership, 1680-1740." Economic History Review, 10 (1940), 2-17. Country life. Economics.

318 Habakkuk, H. J. "English Population in the Eighteenth Century." Economic History Review, 2nd series, 6 (1953), 117-33. Population. Demography.

319 Hackwood, Frederick W. Inns, Ales, and Drinking Customs of Old England. London: T. Fisher Unwin, 1909. Inns. Ale. Customs.

320 Hadfield, Charles. British Canals: An Illustrated History. 1950. 2nd ed. London: Phoenix House, 1959. Transportation. Canals.

321 Hagstrum, Jean H. The Sister Arts: The Tradition of Literary Pictorialism and English Poetry from Dryden to Gray. Chicago: Univ. of Chicago Press, 1958. Literature and the other arts. Aesthetic theory and background.

322 Halévy, Elie. The Birth of Methodism in England. Trans.
     and ed. by Bernard Semmel. Chicago: Univ. of Chicago
     Press, 1971. Methodism.

323 Hall, Walter Phelps. British Radicalism, 1791-1797. New
     York: Longman, 1912. Politics. Radicalism. The 1790s.

324 Haller, William. The Rise of Puritanism. New York: Harper
     and Row, 1938. Puritanism [sixteenth and seventeenth cen-
     turies].

325 Hamilton, Bernice. "The Medical Profession in the 18th Cen-
     tury." Economic History Review, 2nd series, 4 (1951-2),
     141-69. The physician. Medicine.

326 Hamlyn, Hilda M. "Eighteenth-Century Circulating Libraries
     in England." Library, Series 5, 1 (1946-47), 197-222. Cir-
     culating libraries.

327 Hammelmann, Hanns, and T. S. R. Boase. Book Illustrators
     in Eighteenth-Century England. New Haven, Conn.: Yale
     Univ. Press, 1975. Illustration.

328 Hammond, J. L., and Barbara Hammond. The Rise of Modern
     Industry. 1925; rpt. New York: Harper, 1969. Industry
     and trade. Industrial Revolution.

329 Hammond, J. L., and Barbara Hammond. The Skilled Laborer,
     1760-1832. 1919. 2nd ed. London: Longman, 1927. The
     laborer.

330 Hammond, J. L., and Barbara Hammond. The Town Laborer,
     1760-1832. 2 vols. 1917; rpt. London: British Publishers
     Guild, 1949. The laborer. Towns. Standard of living.

331 Hammond, J. L., and Barbara Hammond. The Village Laborer,
     1760-1832. 1911; rpt. New York: Harper, 1970. The
     laborer. Country life. Politics. Enclosures. Villages.

332 Hannay, David. A Short History of the Royal Navy, 1217-
     1815. London: Methuen, 1909. The navy.

333 Hans, Nicholas. New Trends in Education in the Eighteenth
     Century. London: Routledge & Kegan Paul, 1951. Educa-
     tion.

334 Harris, R. W. Reason and Nature in the Eighteenth Century,
     1714-1780. London: Blandford Press, 1969. [Defoe, Swift,
     Richardson, Fielding, Johnson]. Intellectual background.
     Reason. Nature. Humanism. Locke. Shaftesbury. Hume.

■335 Harrison, John F. C. "Old England: 1714-1760." In his
       The Birth and Growth of Industrial England, 1714-1867.
       New York: Harcourt, 1973, pp. 2-25. Introductory guide.
       Social structure [useful graphs].

336 Harrison, T. W. "English Virgil: The Aeneid in the Eight-
       eenth Century." Philologica Pragensia, 10 (1967), 1-11, 80-
       91. Virgil.

337 Hart, Arthur Tindal. The Eighteenth-Century Country Par-
       son. Shrewsbury: Wilding, 1955. The parson. Country
       life.

338 Hartwell, Ronald M. The Industrial Revolution and Economic
       Growth. London: Methuen, 1971. Industry and trade.
       Economics. Social background.

339 Hassler, Donald M. "Influences on Christian Belief during the
       Enlightenment." Enlightenment Essays, 9 (1978), 3-34.
       Christianity.

340 Hauser, Arnold. "The New Reading Public." In his The So-
       cial History of Art. New York: Vintage Books, n.d., III,
       38-84. Reading public.

341 Hay, Douglas, et al. Albion's Fatal Tree: Crime and Society
       in Eighteenth-Century England. New York: Pantheon, 1975.
       [Anthology of essays]. Crime and punishment [e.g., smug-
       gling, coastal plunder, poaching, forgery]. Law.

342 Hayman, John G. "Notions on National Characters in the
       Eighteenth Century." Huntington Library Quarterly, 35
       (1971), 1-17. National stereotypes. Caricature.

343 Hayter, Tony. The Army and the Crowd in Mid-Georgian Eng-
       land. London: Macmillan, 1978. The army. The mob.
       Riots.

344 Hecht, J. Jean. Continental and Colonial Servants in Eight-
       eenth-Century England. Smith College Studies in History,
       Vol. 40. Northampton, Mass.: Dept. of History of Smith
       College, 1954. Servants.

●345 Hecht, J. Jean. The Domestic Servant Class in Eighteenth-
       Century England. London: Routledge & Kegan Paul, 1956.
       Servants. Domestic life.

346 Heckscher, Eli F. Mercantilism. 2 vols. Trans. Mendel
       Shapiro. Rev. ed. Ed. E. F. Söderlund. London: Allen
       & Unwin, [1962]. Mercantilism.

347 Henriques, Ursula. Religious Toleration in England, 1787-
     1833. London: Routledge & Kegan Paul, 1961. Toleration.

348 Herrmann, Luke. British Landscape Painting of the Eighteenth
     Century. New York: Oxford Univ. Press, 1974. Art.
     Landscape.

349 Hersey, G. L. "Associationism and Sensibility in Eighteenth-
     Century Architecture." Eighteenth-Century Studies, 4
     (1970), 71-89. Architecture. Associationism. Sensibility.

350 Hibbert, Christopher. The Grand Tour. New York: Putnam,
     1969. Grand tour.

351 Hibbert, Christopher. The Road to Tyburn: The Story of
     Jack Sheppard and the Eighteenth-Century Underworld.
     Toronto: Longman, 1957. Crime and punishment. Criminal
     biography. Jack Sheppard.

352 Hill, Christopher. Reformation to Industrial Revolution: The
     Making of Modern English Society, 1530-1780. New York:
     Pantheon, 1967. Economics. Politics. Social background.

353 Hinnant, Charles H. "A Philosophical Origin of the English
     Landscape Garden." Bulletin of Research in the Humanities,
     83 (1980), 292-306. Landscape gardening.

•354 Hipple, Walter J., Jr. The Beautiful, the Sublime, and the
     Picturesque in Eighteenth-Century British Aesthetic Theory.
     Carbondale: Southern Illinois Univ. Press, 1957. Aesthetic
     theory and background. The sublime and the beautiful.
     The picturesque.

355 Hipple, Walter J., Jr. "Philosophical Language and the Theory
     of Beauty in the Eighteenth Century." In Studies in Criti-
     cism and Aesthetics, 1660-1800: Essays in Honor of Samuel
     Holt Monk. Ed. Howard Anderson and John Shea. Minneap-
     olis: Univ. of Minnesota Press, 1967, pp. 213-31. Aesthetic
     theory and background. The Sublime and the beautiful. Taste.

356 Hobson, J. G. S. "The Coffee-House." Blackwood's Magazine,
     234 (1933), 201-17. Coffee houses.

357 Hogwood, Christopher, and Richard Luckett, eds. Music in
     Eighteenth-Century England: Essays in Memory of Charles
     Cudworth. Cambridge: Cambridge Univ. Press, 1983. Mu-
     sic.

358 Holbrook, William C. "The Adjective Gothique in the XVIIIth
     Century." Modern Language Notes, 56 (1941), 498-503.
     "Gothic." Semantics.

359 Holderness, B. A. Pre-Industrial England: Economy and Society, 1500 to 1750. Totowa, N.J.: Rowman & Littlefield, 1976. Economics. Industry and trade. Agriculture.

•360 Holdsworth, William. A History of English Law. Vols. 10, 11, 12. London: Methuen, 1924-38. Law.

361 Hole, Christina. English Sports and Pastimes. London: Batsford, 1949. Sport and recreation.

362 Hollinsworth, T. H. "The Demography of the British Peerage." Population Studies, Supplement to Vol. 18, no. 2 (1964), 3-108. The aristocracy. Demography.

•363 Holmes, Geoffrey. Augustan England: Professions, State and Society, 1680-1730. Boston: Allen & Unwin, 1982. The schoolmaster. The lawyer. The physician. The clergy. The professor. The civil servant. The army. The navy. The professions.

364 Holmes, Geoffrey. British Politics in the Age of Anne. London: Macmillan, 1967. Politics.

365 Holt, R. V. The Unitarian Contribution to Social Progress in England. 1938; 2nd ed. London: Lindsey Press, 1952. Unitarianism. Reform.

366 Holzman, James M. The Nabobs in England: A Study of the Returned Anglo-Indian, 1760-1785. 1926; rpt. New York: Kelly, 1979. The nabob.

367 Horn, David Bayne. The British Diplomatic Service, 1689-1789. Oxford: Clarendon Press, 1961. Diplomacy.

368 Horn, David Bayne. Great Britain and Europe in the Eighteenth Century. Oxford: Clarendon Press, 1967. Diplomacy. Foreign policy.

369 Horn, Pamela. The Rural World, 1780-1850: Social Change in the English Countryside. 1980; rpt. New York: St. Martin's, 1981. Country life. Social structure.

370 Hornbeak, Katherine G. "The Complete Letter Writer in English, 1568-1800." Smith College Studies in Modern Languages, 15 (1934), 1-150. Letter-writing.

371 Horne, Thomas A. The Social Thought of Bernard Mandeville: Virtue and Commerce in Early Eighteenth-Century England. New York: Columbia Univ. Press, 1978. Mandeville. Economics. Self-interest. Mercantilism.

372 Howell, Wilbur Samuel. Eighteenth-Century British Logic and
     Rhetoric. Princeton, N.J.: Princeton Univ. Press, 1971.
     Intellectual background. Logic. Rhetoric.

373 Howson, Gerald. Thief-Taker General: The Rise and Fall of
     Jonathan Wild. London: Hutchinson, 1970. Crime and
     punishment. Jonathan Wild. Criminal biography.

374 Hudson, Kenneth. Patriotism with Profit: British Agricultural
     Societies in the Eighteenth and Nineteenth Centuries. 1972;
     rpt. New York: British Book Centre, 1975. Country life.
     Agriculture.

375 Hughes, E. "The Eighteenth-Century Estate Agent." In Es-
     says in British and Irish History in Honour of James Eadie
     Todd. Ed. H. A. Cronne et al. 1949; rpt. Carby, Pa.:
     Arden Library, 1977. The estate agent.

376 Hughes, E. "The Professions in the Eighteenth Century."
     Durham University Journal, 13 (1952), 46-55. Rpt. in Aris-
     tocratic Government and Society in Eighteenth-Century Eng-
     land: The Foundations of Stability. Ed. Daniel A. Baugh.
     New York: New Viewpoints, 1975, pp. 184-203. The pro-
     fessions.

•377 Hughes, Edward. North Country Life in the Eighteenth Cen-
     tury. 2 vols. London: Oxford Univ. Press, 1952-1965.
     Social background. Country life. Agriculture. Industry
     and trade. Education. The professions. Women. Politics.

378 Hughes, Edward. Studies in Administration and Finance,
     1558-1825. Manchester: Manchester Univ. Press, 1934.
     Finance. Taxation [salt].

379 Hughes, Mary Joe. "Child-Rearing and Social Expectations in
     Eighteenth-Century England: The Case of the Colliers of
     Hastings." In Studies in Eighteenth-Century Culture. Ed.
     O M Brack, Jr. Vol. 13. Madison: Univ. of Wisconsin
     Press, 1984, pp. 79-100. Children. Family.

380 Humiliata, Sister M. "Standards of Taste Advocated for Femi-
     nine Letter Writing, 1640-1797." Huntington Library Quar-
     terly, 13 (1950), 261-77. Letter-writing.

381 Humphreys, A. R. The Augustan World: Society, Thought,
     and Letters in Eighteenth-Century England. 1954; rpt.
     New York: Harper & Row, 1963. Introductory guide. So-
     cial background. Intellectual background.

382 Humphreys, A. R. "'The Friend of Mankind,' 1700-60: An
     Aspect of Eighteenth-Century Sensibility." Review of Eng-

lish Studies, O.S. 24 (1948), 203-18. "Friend of Mankind."
Benevolence. Philanthropy. Sensibility.

383 Hunt, John Dixon. The Figure in the Landscape: Poetry,
     Painting, and Gardening during the Eighteenth Century.
     Baltimore: The Johns Hopkins Univ. Press, 1976. Litera-
     ture and the other arts. Landscape gardening. Art.

•384 Hunt, John Dixon, with Peter Willis. The Genius of the Place:
     The English Landscape Garden, 1620-1820. London: Elek
     Books, 1975. Landscape gardening.

385 Hunt, Morton M. "The Contact of Two Epidermises." In his
     The Natural History of Love. New York: Knopf, 1959, pp.
     255-94. Love. Sex. Manners.

386 Hunter, Jean E. "The 18th-Century Englishwoman: According
     to the Gentleman's Magazine." In Woman in the 18th Century
     and Other Essays. Ed. Paul Fritz and Richard Morton.
     Toronto: Hakkert, 1976, pp. 73-88. Women.

387 Hussey, Christopher. English Country Houses: Early Geor-
     gian, 1715-1760; Mid-Georgian, 1760-1800. 2 vols. London:
     Country Life, 1955-1956. Country house. Architecture.
     Country life.

388 Hussey, Christopher. English Gardens and Landscapes, 1700-
     1750. London: Country Life, 1967. Landscape gardening.

389 Hussey, Christopher. The Picturesque: Studies in a Point
     of View. 1927; rpt. Hamden, Conn.: Archon, 1967.
     Aesthetic theory and background. The picturesque.

390 Irving, William Henry. The Providence of Wit in the English
     Letter Writers. Durham, N.C.: Duke Univ. Press, 1955.
     Letter-writing.

391 Itzkowitz, David. Peculiar Privilege: A Social History of
     English Fox Hunting, 1753-1885. Atlantic Highlands, N.J.:
     Humanities Press, 1977. Fox hunting.

392 Jamison, Ted R. "Prison Reform in the Augustan Age." Brit-
     ish History Illustrated, August-September 1976, pp. 56-65.
     Crime and punishment. Prisons.

393 Jarrett, David. The English Landscape Garden. New York:
     Rizzoli, 1978. Landscape gardening.

394 Jarrett, Derek. Britain, 1688-1815. London: Longman, 1965.
     Politics. History.

395 Jarrett, Derek. England in the Age of Hogarth. New York:
     Viking, 1974. Social background.

396 Jarvis, Rupert C., ed. Collected Papers on the Jacobite Ris-
     ings. 2 vols. Manchester: Manchester Univ. Press, 1971-
     1972. Jacobitism. Rebellion of 1745.

397 John, A. H. "Agricultural Productivity and Economic Growth
     in England, 1700-1760." Journal of Economic History, 25
     (1965), 19-34. Agriculture. Economics.

398 Johnson, James W. "England, 1660-1800: An Age Without a
     Hero?" In The English Hero, 1660-1800. Ed. Robert Folken-
     flik. Newark: Univ. of Delaware Press, 1982, pp. 25-34.
     Hero/heroine [diverse heroes, but disagreement about heroic
     standards].

399 Johnson, James W. The Formation of English Neo-Classical
     Thought. Princeton, N.J.: Princeton Univ. Press, 1967.
     Neoclassicism. Intellectual background.

400 Johnson, James W. "What Was Neo-Classicism?" Journal of
     British Studies, 9, No. 1 (1969), 49-70. For a response,
     see Donald Greene, "What Indeed Was Neo-Classicism? A
     Reply to James William Johnson's 'What Was Neo-Classicism?'"
     ibid., 10, No. 1 (1970), 69-79. Neoclassicism.

401 Johnson, Reginald Brimley, ed. The Undergraduate. London:
     S. Paul, 1928. The undergraduate. Oxford University.
     Cambridge University.

402 Jones, E. L. "Agriculture and Economic Growth in England,
     1660-1750: Agricultural Change." Journal of Economic His-
     tory, 25 (1965), 1-18. Agriculture. Economics.

403 Jones, Gareth. History of the Law of Charity, 1532-1827.
     Cambridge Studies in English Legal History. Cambridge:
     Cambridge Univ. Press, 1969. Charity. Law.

404 Jones, George Hilton. The Main Stream of Jacobitism. Cam-
     bridge, Mass.: Harvard Univ. Press, 1955. Jacobitism.

405 Jones, Kathleen. Lunacy, Law, and Conscience, 1744-1845:
     The Social History of the Care of the Insane. London:
     Routledge & Kegan Paul, 1955. Insanity. Madhouses.

406 Jones, Louis Clark. The Clubs of the Georgian Rakes. New
     York: Columbia Univ. Press, 1942. Clubs. The rake.

407 Jones, Mary G. The Charity School Movement: A Study of
     Eighteenth-Century Puritanism in Action. 1938; rpt. Ham-

den, Conn.:   Archon, 1964.   Charity school.   Education.
Puritanism.   Philanthropy.

408   Jones, R. Tudor.   Congregationalism in England, 1662-1962.
      London: Allenson, 1962.   Congregationalism.

409   Kallich, Martin.   The Association of Ideas and Critical Theory
      in Eighteenth-Century England.   The Hague: Mouton, 1970.
      Intellectual background.

410   Kampf, Louis.   "The Humanist Tradition in Eighteenth-Century
      England--and Today."   In Fearful Joy: Papers from the
      Thomas Gray Bicentenary Conference at Carleton University.
      Ed. James Downey and Ben Jones.   Montreal: McGill-
      Queen's Univ. Press, 1974, pp. 241-55.   Humanism.

411   Kaufman, Paul.   "English Book Clubs and Their Role in Social
      History."   Libri, 14 (1964), 1-31.   Book clubs.   Social back-
      ground.

■412   Kaufman, Paul.   "In Defense of Fair Readers."   Review of
      English Literature, 8, No. 2 (1967), 68-76.   Women [not
      readers of trashy fiction].   Reading public.   Circulating li-
      braries [average library stocked not with fiction but with
      the classics, history, biography, travels, etc.]

413   Kaufman, Paul.   Libraries and Their Users: Collected Papers
      in Library History.   London: The Library Association, 1969.
      Libraries.

414   Kaufmann, Emil.   Architecture in the Age of Reason: Baroque
      and Post-Baroque in England, Italy, and France.   Cambridge,
      Mass.:   Harvard Univ. Press, 1955.   Architecture.   Baroque.

415   Kaye, F. B.   "The Influence of Bernard Mandeville."   Studies
      in Philology, 19 (1922), 83-108.   Rpt. in Studies in the Lit-
      erature of the Augustan Age: Essays Collected in Honor of
      Arthur Ellicott Case.   Ed. Richard C. Boys.   Augustan Re-
      print Society.   Ann Arbor, Mich.:   George Wahr, 1952, pp.
      149-75.   Mandeville.   Intellectual background.

416   Keevil, J. J., et al.   Medicine and the Navy, 1200-1900.
      Volume III, 1714-1815 by Christopher Lloyd and Jack L. S.
      Coulter.   Edinburgh: E. & S. Livingstone, 1957-63.   Medi-
      cine.   The navy.

417   Kelly, George Armstrong.   "Irrationalism and Politics in the
      Eighteenth Century."   In Studies in Eighteenth-Century
      Culture: Irrationalism in the Eighteenth Century.   Vol. 2.
      Ed. Harold E. Pagliaro.   Cleveland: The Press of Case
      Western Reserve Univ., 1972, pp. 239-53.   Irrationality.
      Politics.

418 Kemp, Betty. King and Commons, 1660-1832. New York:
     St. Martin's, 1957. The court. House of Commons. Poli-
     tics.

419 Kerman, Sandra Lee. "Introduction." The Newgate Calendar
     or Malefactor's Bloody Register. New York: Capricorn,
     1962, pp. i-xvii. Crime and punishment. Newgate Calendar.

420 King, Lester S. "Evidence and Its Evaluation in Eighteenth-
     Century Medicine." Bulletin of the History of Medicine, 50
     (1976), 174-90. Medicine.

421 King, Lester S. "George Cheyne, Mirror of Eighteenth-Cen-
     tury Medicine." Bulletin of the History of Medicine, 48
     (1974), 517-39. Medicine. George Cheyne.

422 King, Lester S. The Medical World of the Eighteenth Century.
     Chicago: Univ. of Chicago Press, 1958. Medicine.

423 Kirby, Chester. "The English Game-Law System." American
     Historical Review, 38 (1933), 240-62. Country life. Poach-
     ing. Law.

424 Kirby, Paul F. The Grand Tour in Italy (1700-1800). New
     York: S. F. Vanni, 1952. Grand tour.

425 Kliger, Samuel. The Goths in England: A Study in Seven-
     teenth- and Eighteenth-Century Thought. Cambridge,
     Mass.: Harvard Univ. Press, 1952. Aesthetic theory and
     background. Gothic background. Intellectual background.

■426 Kliger, Samuel. "Whig Aesthetics: A Phase of Eighteenth-
     Century Taste." ELH: A Journal of English Literary His-
     tory, 16 (1949), 135-50. Aesthetic theory and background.
     Taste. Whigs.

427 Knopf, Maria. "John Constable." British History Illustrated.
     August-September, 1976, pp. 34-45. Constable. Art.

428 Korshin, Paul J. "Types of Eighteenth-Century Literary Pa-
     tronage." Eighteenth-Century Studies, 7 (1974), 453-73.
     Patronage.

429 Krause, J. T. "Some Aspects of Population Change, 1690-
     1790." In Land, Labour and Population in the Industrial
     Revolution: Essays Presented to J. D. Chambers. Ed. E. C.
     Jones and G. E. Mingay. 1967; rpt. New York: Barnes &
     Noble, 1968, pp. 187-205. Population. Demography.

430 Landa, Louis A. "London Observed: The Progress of a Sim-
     ile." Philological Quarterly, 54 (1975), 275-88. London.
     Imagery [physiological].

431 Lang, Paul Henry. "The Enlightenment and Music." Eight-
     eenth-Century Studies, 1 (1967), 93-108. Music.

432 Langford, Paul. The Eighteenth Century, 1688-1815. New
     York: St. Martin's, 1976. Foreign policy. Diplomacy.

433 LaPrade, William Thomas. "The Power of the English Press in
     the Eighteenth Century." South Atlantic Quarterly, 27
     (1928) 426-34. Journalism.

434 LaPrade, William Thomas. Public Opinion and Politics in Eight-
     eenth-Century England to the Fall of Walpole. 1936; rpt.
     New York: Octagon, 1977. Politics. Public opinion.

435 Laqueur, Thomas W. "Literacy and Social Mobility in the In-
     dustrial Revolution in England." Past and Present, No. 64
     (1974), pp. 96-107. See also Michael Sanderson, "A Re-
     joinder," ibid., pp. 108-12. Literacy. Social structure.
     Industrial Revolution.

436 Laski, Harold J. Political Thought in England: Locke to
     Bentham. 1920; rpt. London: Oxford Univ. Press, 1961.
     Politics.

437 Laslett, Peter. Family Life and Illicit Love in Earlier Genera-
     tions. Cambridge: Cambridge Univ. Press, 1977. Family.
     Bastardy. Orphans. Statistics. Sex.

438 Laver, James. "Customs and Manners." In Silver Renais-
     sance: Essays in Eighteenth-Century English History. Ed.
     Alex Natan. London: Macmillan, 1961, pp. 102-21. Sport
     and recreation. Social background.

439 Laver, James. English Costume of the Eighteenth Century.
     London: A. & C. Black, 1931. Dress and fashion.

440 Leavis, Q. D. "The Growth of the Reading Public." In her
     Fiction and the Reading Public. 1932; rpt. New York:
     Russell & Russell, 1965, pp. 118-50. Reading public.

441 LeFanu, William R. "The Lost Half-Century in English Medi-
     cine, 1700-1750." Bulletin of the History of Medicine, 46
     (1972), 319-48. Medicine.

442 LeGates, Marlene. "The Cult of Womanhood in Eighteenth-
     Century Thought." Eighteenth-Century Studies, 10 (1976),
     21-39. [Esp. Richardson]. Women [images of chaste maiden
     and obedient wife used to repress woman's insatiable sexual-
     ity]. Sex.

443 Leigh, Agnes. "Domestic Expenses in the Eighteenth Century."

National Review, 91 (1928), 914-21. Domestic life. Economics.

444 Lenman, Bruce. *The Jacobite Risings in Britain, 1689-1746*. London: Methuen, 1980. Rebellion of 1745. Jacobitism.

445 Lessenich, Rolf P. *Elements of Pulpit Oratory in Eighteenth-Century England (1660-1800)*. Cologne: Böhlan Verlag, 1972. The sermon.

446 Levy, Mervyn. "Rowlandson." *British History Illustrated*, October 1974, pp. 16-27. Rowlandson. Art.

447 Lewis, Michael. *A Social History of the Navy, 1793-1815*. London: Allen & Unwin, 1960. The navy.

448 Lillywhite, Bryant. *London Coffee-Houses: A Reference Book*. London: Allen & Unwin, 1963. Coffee houses.

449 Lincoln, Anthony. *Some Political and Social Ideas of English Dissent, 1763-1800*. Cambridge: Cambridge Univ. Press, 1938. Dissenters.

•450 Lindsay, Jack. *The Monster City: Defoe's London, 1688-1730*. New York: St. Martin's, 1978. London. City life. The mob. Reading public. Journalism. Women. Gentry. Quakerism. The merchant. Industry and trade. Sport and recreation. Dress and fashion.

451 Linebaugh, P. "The Ordinary of Newgate and His Account." In *Crime in England, 1550-1800*. Ed. J. S. Cockburn. Princeton, N.J.: Princeton Univ. Press, 1977, pp. 246-69. Criminal biography. Crime and punishment. Newgate Calendar. The ordinary.

452 Lipking, Lawrence. *The Ordering of the Arts in Eighteenth-Century England*. Princeton, N.J.: Princeton Univ. Press, 1970. Aesthetic theory and background. Literature and the other arts.

453 Little, Anthony J. *Deceleration in the Eighteenth-Century British Economy*. London: Croom Helm, 1976. Economics.

■454 Longueil, Alfred E. "The Word 'Gothic' in Eighteenth-Century Criticism." *Modern Language Notes*, 38 (1923), 453-60. "Gothic." Semantics.

•455 Lovejoy, Arthur O. *Essays in the History of Ideas*. Baltimore: The Johns Hopkins Univ. Press, 1948. Gothic background. Nature. Deism. Neoclassicism. Orientalism. Pride [its meanings and importance in eighteenth-century thought]. Romanticism.

•456   Lovejoy, Arthur O.   The Great Chain of Being: A Study in
       the History of an Idea.   Cambridge, Mass.:   Harvard Univ.
       Press, 1936.   Intellectual background.   "Great Chain of Be-
       ing."

457   Lowenthal, Leo, and Marjorie Fiske.   "Reaction to Mass Media
       Growth in Eighteenth-Century England."   Journalism Quar-
       terly, 33 (1956), 442-55.   Popular culture.   Journalism.

458   Lyles, Albert M.   Methodism Mocked: The Satiric Reaction to
       Methodism in the Eighteenth Century.   London: Epworth
       Press, 1960.   Methodism.   Satire.

459   Macaulay, James.   The Gothic Revival, 1745-1845.   Glasgow:
       Blackie, 1975.   Gothic background.   Art.   Architecture.

460   MacCoby, Simon.   English Radicalism, 1762-1785.   London:
       Allen & Unwin, 1955.   Radicalism.   Politics.   Philanthropy.
       Working classes.

461   MacCoby, Simon.   English Radicalism, 1786-1832.   London:
       Allen & Unwin, 1955.   Radicalism.   Politics.   French Revo-
       lution.

462   MacLean, Kenneth.   Agrarian Age: A Background for Words-
       worth.   New Haven, Conn.:   Yale Univ. Press, 1950.   [Later
       eighteenth century].   Country life.   Agricultural revolution.

463   Malcolmson, Robert W.   Life and Labour in England, 1700-1800.
       New York: St. Martin's, 1981.   Work.   Working classes.
       Sport and recreation.   Customs.   Riots.

464   Malcolmson, Robert W.   Popular Recreations in English Society,
       1700-1850.   Cambridge: Cambridge Univ. Press, 1973.
       Sport and recreation.   Popular culture.

465   Malek, James S.   The Arts Compared: An Aspect of Eight-
       eenth-Century British Aesthetics.   Detroit: Wayne State
       Univ. Press, 1974.   Aesthetic theory and background.
       Literature and the other arts.

466   Mantoux, Paul.   The Industrial Revolution in the Eighteenth
       Century: An Outline of the Beginnings of the Modern Fac-
       tory System in England.   1928.   Rev. ed. trans. Marjorie
       Vernon.   London: Jonathan Cape, 1937.   Industrial Revo-
       lution.

467   Manuel, Frank E.   The Eighteenth Century Confronts the Gods.
       Cambridge, Mass.:   Harvard Univ. Press, 1959.   Intellectual
       background.   Paganism.   Deism.

468   Manwaring, Elizabeth Wheeler.   Italian Landscape in Eighteenth-

Century England: A Study Chiefly of the Influence of
Claude Lorrain and Salvator Rosa on English Taste, 1700-
1800. 1925; rpt. New York: Russell & Russell, 1965.
Aesthetic theory and background. Art. Landscape gardening. Taste. Lorrain. Rosa. Gothic background.

469 Marcus, G. J. Heart of Oak: A Survey of British Sea Power
in the Georgian Era. London: Oxford Univ. Press, 1975.
The navy.

470 Marcus, G. J. A Naval History of England: Vol. I, The
Formative Centuries. 1961; rpt. Boston: Little, Brown,
1962. The navy.

471 Marshall, Dorothy. Doctor Johnson's London. London: Wiley,
1968. London. Social background.

472 Marshall, Dorothy. Eighteenth-Century England. New York:
McKay, 1963. Social background. Politics.

473 Marshall, Dorothy. English People in the Eighteenth Century.
1956; rpt. London: Greenwood Press, 1980. Social background.

474 Marshall, Dorothy. The English Poor in the Eighteenth Century, 1662-1782. 1926; rpt. New York: Augustus M. Kelly, 1980. The poor.

475 Marshall, Madeleine Forell, and Janet Todd. English Congre-
gational Hymns in the Eighteenth Century. Lexington:
Univ. Press of Kentucky, 1982. Hymns. Congregationalism.

476 Mason, Philip. The English Gentleman: The Rise and Fall of
an Ideal. New York: Morrow, 1982, esp. pp. 61-69. The
gentleman. The squire.

477 Mathew, W. M. "The Origins and Occupations of Glasgow Students, 1740-1839." Past and Present, No. 33 (1966), pp.
74-94. Glasgow University. The undergraduate.

•478 Mathias, Peter. The Transformation of England: Essays in
the Economic and Social History of England in the Eighteenth
Century. New York: Columbia Univ. Press, 1979. Economics. Science. Industry and trade. Industrial Revolution. Social structure [useful tables]. The poor. Money.
Statistics. Dr. Samuel Johnson [and the business world].

479 Mayo, Charles Herbert. "The Social Status of the Clergy in
the Seventeenth and Eighteenth Centuries." English Historical Review, 37 (1922), 258-66. The clergy. Social structure.

480 McAdoo, William. The Procession to Tyburn: Crime and Pun-
     ishment in the Eighteenth Century. New York: Boni and
     Liveright, 1927. Crime and punishment.

481 McCahill, Michael W. "Peerage Creations and the Changing
     Character of the British Nobility, 1750-1850." English His-
     torical Review, 96 (1981), 259-84. The aristocracy.

482 McCarthy, John A. "Shaftesbury and Wieland: The Question
     of Enthusiasm." In Studies in Eighteenth-Century Culture.
     Vol. 6. Ed. Ronald C. Rosbottom. Madison: Univ. of
     Wisconsin Press, 1977, pp. 79-96. Shaftesbury. Enthusi-
     asm.

483 McCloskey, Donald N. "The Enclosure of Open Fields: Preface
     to a Study of Its Impact on the Efficiency of English Agri-
     culture in the Eighteenth Century." Journal of Economic
     History, 32 (1972), 15-35. Country life. Agricultural revo-
     lution. Enclosures.

484 McClure, Ruth K. "Pediatric Practice at the London Foundling
     Hospital." In Studies in Eighteenth-Century Culture. Vol.
     10. Ed. Harry C. Payne. Madison: Univ. of Wisconsin
     Press, 1981, pp. 361-71. Medicine. Children.

485 McCormick, Donald. The Hell-Fire Club. London: Jarrolds,
     1958. Hell-Fire Club. Clubs.

486 McElroy, David D. Scotland's Age of Improvement: A Survey
     of Eighteenth-Century Literary Clubs and Societies. Pullman:
     Washington State Univ. Press, 1969. Scotland. Clubs.

487 McKendrick, Neil; John Brewer; and J. H. Plumb. The Birth
     of a Consumer Society: The Commercialization of Eighteenth-
     Century England. Bloomington: Indiana Univ. Press, 1982.
     Industry and trade.

488 McKenzie, Alan T. "The Articulated Evil of Augustan Human-
     ism." Modern Language Studies, 9, No. 3 (1979), 150-60.
     Evil.

489 McKeown, Thomas, and R. G. Brown. "Medical Evidence Re-
     lated to English Population Changes in the Eighteenth Cen-
     tury." Population Studies, 9 (1955), 119-41. Population.
     Medicine.

490 McKillop, Alan Dugald. "English Circulating Libraries, 1725-
     1750." The Library, Series 4, 14 (1934), 477-85. Circulat-
     ing libraries. Reading public.

491 McLynn, F. J. "Issues and Motives in the Jacobite Rising of

1745." The Eighteenth Century: Theory and Interpretation,
23 (1982), 97-133. Politics. Jacobitism. Rebellion of 1745.

492   Minchinton, W. E., ed. The Growth of English Overseas Trade
in the Seventeenth and Eighteenth Centuries. London:
Methuen, 1969. Industry and trade. Shipping.

493   Minchinton, W. E. "The Merchants in England in the Eighteenth Century." Explorations in Entrepreneurial History,
O.S. 10 (1957), 62-71. The merchant.

494   Mingay, G. E. "The Agricultural Depression, 1730-1750."
Economic History Review, 2nd series, 8, No. 3 (1956), 323-
38. Country life.

•495   Mingay, G. E. English Landed Society in the Eighteenth Century. London: Routledge & Kegan Paul, 1963. Gentry.
Country life. Social structure.

496   Mingay, G. E. The Gentry: The Rise and Fall of a Ruling
Class. London: Longman, 1976. Gentry.

497   Mingay, G. E. Georgian London. London: Batsford, 1975.
London. Social background.

498   Mitchell, B. R., with Phyllis Deane. Abstract of British Historical Statistics. Cambridge: Cambridge Univ. Press, 1962.
Demography. Statistics. History.

499   Monro, Hector. The Ambivalence of Bernard Mandeville. Oxford: Clarendon Press, 1975. Mandeville. Intellectual background.

500   Moore, Robert Etheridge. "William Hogarth: The Golden
Mean." In The Age of Johnson: Essays Presented to Chauncey Brewster Tinker. Ed. Frederick W. Hilles and Wilmarth
S. Lewis. New Haven, Conn.: Yale Univ. Press, 1949, pp.
385-93. Hogarth.

501   Mullett, Charles F. "Community & Communication." In City
& Society in the 18th Century. Ed. Paul Fritz and David
Williams. Toronto: Hakkert, 1973, pp. 77-97. Style and
language.

502   Munsche, P. B. "The Gamekeeper and English Rural Society."
Journal of British Studies, 20, No. 2 (1981), 82-105. The
gamekeeper. Country life.

503   Munsche, P. B. Gentlemen and Poachers: The English Game
Laws, 1671-1831. Cambridge: Cambridge Univ. Press, 1981.
Country life. Poaching. Law. Sport and recreation.

504   Musson, A. E., ed. Science, Technology, and Economic
      Growth in the Eighteenth Century. London: Methuen, 1972.
      Science. Economics. Industrial Revolution.

505   Musson, A. E., and E. Robinson. "Science and Industry in
      the Late Eighteenth Century." Economic History Review,
      2nd series, 13 (1960), 222-44. Science. Industry and trade.

506   Myers, Mitzi. "Reform or Ruin: 'A Revolution in Female Man-
      ners.'" In Studies in Eighteenth-Century Culture. Vol. 11.
      Ed. Harry C. Payne. Madison: Univ. of Wisconsin Press,
      1982, pp. 199-216. Women. Morality.

●507 Namier, Lewis. England in the Age of the American Revolu-
      tion. 2 vols. 1930. Rev. ed. London: Macmillan, 1961.
      Politics. Social structure. Parliament. American Revolution.
      History.

●508 Namier, Lewis. The Structure of Politics at the Accession of
      George III. 1929. 2nd ed. London: Macmillan, 1957.
      Politics. History.

509   Namier, Lewis, and John Brooke, eds. The History of Parlia-
      ment: The House of Commons, 1754-1790. 3 vols. New
      York: Oxford Univ. Press, 1964. House of Commons.

510   Neale, R. S. "Bath: Ideology and Utopia, 1700-1760."
      Studies in the Eighteenth Century III. Ed. R. F. Brissen-
      den and J. C. Eade. Toronto: Univ. of Toronto Press,
      1976, pp. 37-54. Bath.

511   Nef, John U. "The Industrial Revolution Reconsidered." Jour-
      nal of Economic History, 3, No. 1 (1943), pp. 1-31. Indus-
      trial Revolution.

●512 Neuberg, Victor. Popular Education in the Eighteenth Century:
      A Study in the Origins of the Mass Reading Public. London:
      Woburn Press, 1971. Education. Reading public.

513   Nicolson, Marjorie Hope. Mountain Gloom and Mountain Glory:
      The Development of the Aesthetics of the Infinite. 1959; rpt.
      New York: Norton, 1963. Aesthetic theory and background.
      Nature. The sublime and the beautiful. Mountains.

514   Norris, John M. Shelburne and Reform. London: Macmillan,
      1963. Reform. Politics. William Shelburne.

515   Noxon, James. "Dr. Mandeville: 'A Thinking Man.'" In The
      Varied Pattern: Studies in the 18th Century. Ed. Peter
      Hughes and David Williams. Toronto: Hakkert, 1971, pp.
      233-52. Mandeville. Morality. Economics.

516 Okin, Susan Moller. "Patriarchy and Married Women's Property
     in England: Questions on Some Current Views." Eighteenth-
     Century Studies, 17 (1983-84), 121-38. Marriage law. Wom-
     en. Family.

517 O'Malley, C. D. "The English Physician in the Earlier Eight-
     eenth Century." In England in the Restoration and Early
     Eighteenth Century: Essays on Culture and Society. Ed.
     H. T. Swedenberg, Jr. Berkeley: Univ. of California
     Press, 1970, pp. 145-60. The physician.

517a Osborne, John W. "The Politics of Resentment: Political,
     Economic, and Social Interaction in Eighteenth-Century Eng-
     land." Eighteenth-Century Life, 8, N.S. 3, No. 1 (1983),
     pp. 49-64. Social structure. Gentry [resentment by gentry
     of parvenus].

518 Osler, Margaret J. "Certainty, Scepticism, and Scientific Op-
     timism: The Roots of Eighteenth-Century Attitudes Toward
     Scientific Knowledge." In Probability, Time, and Space in
     Eighteenth-Century Literature. Ed. Paula Backscheider.
     New York: AMS Press, 1979, 3-28. Science. Intellectual
     background.

519 Overton, John H., and Frederic Relton. The English Church
     from the Accession of George I to the End of the Eighteenth
     Century (1714-1800). London: Macmillan, 1906. Anglican-
     ism.

520 Owen, Joan Hildreth. "Philosophy in the Kitchen: Problems
     in Eighteenth-Century Culinary Aesthetics." Eighteenth-
     Century Life, 3 (1977), 77-79. Meals. Propriety. Taste.
     Aesthetic theory and background.

521 Owen, John Beresford. The Eighteenth Century, 1714-1815.
     1974; rpt. New York: Norton, 1976. History. Politics.

522 Owen, John Beresford. The Patterns of Politics in Eighteenth-
     Century England. London: Routledge & Kegan Paul, 1962.
     Politics.

523 Oxley, Geoffrey Frederick. The English Provincial Local
     Posts, 1765-1840. Reigate: Postal History Society, 1973.
     Post Office.

524 Oxley, Geoffrey William. Poor Relief in England and Wales,
     1601-1834. N. Pomfret, Vt.: David & Charles, 1974. The
     poor.

525 Pace, K. Claire. "'Strong Contraries ... Happy Discord':
     Some Eighteenth-Century Discussions About Landscape."

Journal of the History of Ideas, 40 (1979), 141-55. Aesthetic theory and background. Landscape. Contrast as technique.

526 Pares, Richard. King George III and the Politicians. Oxford: Clarendon Press, 1959. [1951-52 lectures]. The court. Politics.

527 Pares, Richard. Limited Monarchy in Great Britain in the Eighteenth Century. London: Routledge & Kegan Paul, 1957. Politics.

528 Parker, Irene. Dissenting Academies in England: Their Rise and Progress and Their Place Among the Educational Systems of the Country. Cambridge: Cambridge Univ. Press, 1914. Dissenting academies. Education.

529 Parry-Jones, William L. The Trade in Lunacy: A Study of Private Madhouses in England in the Eighteenth and Nineteenth Centuries. London: Routledge & Kegan Paul, 1971. Insanity. Madhouses.

530 Paston, George [Emily Morse Symonds]. Social Caricature in the Eighteenth Century. 1905; rpt. New York: Blom, 1968. Social background. Caricature.

531 Paterson, Alice. The Edgeworths: A Study of Later Eighteenth-Century Education. London: W. B. Clive, 1914. Education.

532 Patton, Julia. The English Village: A Literary Study, 1750-1850. New York: Macmillan, 1919. Villages. Country life.

533 Paulson, Ronald. Emblem and Expression: Meaning in English Art of the Eighteenth Century. Cambridge, Mass.: Harvard Univ. Press, 1975. Art.

•534 Paulson, Ronald. Hogarth: His Life, Art, and Times. 2 vols. New Haven, Conn.: Yale Univ. Press, 1971. Hogarth.

535 Paulson, Ronald. Literary Landscape: Turner and Constable. New Haven, Conn.: Yale Univ. Press, 1982. Landscape. Constable. Turner.

536 Paulson, Ronald. "The Pictorial Circuit & Related Structures in 18th-Century England." In The Varied Pattern: Studies in the 18th Century. Ed. Peter Hughes and David Williams. Toronto: Hakkert, 1971, pp. 165-87. Art. Plot, structure, and design.

537 Paulson, Ronald. Popular and Polite Art in the Age of Hogarth

and Fielding. Notre Dame, Ind.: Univ. of Notre Dame
Press, 1979. Popular culture. Hogarth. Social background.
The mob. The criminal. The apprentice. Sport and recre-
ation. Journey. Family. Rebellion of 1745. The Good
Samaritan.

538 Paulson, Ronald. Representations of Revolution (1789-1820).
New Haven, Conn.: Yale Univ. Press, 1982. [Lewis, God-
win]. French Revolution. Art. Gothic novel.

539 Paulson, Ronald. Rowlandson: A New Interpretation. New
York: Oxford Univ. Press, 1972. Rowlandson.

540 Pawson, Eric. The Early Industrial Revolution: Britain in
the Eighteenth Century. New York: Barnes & Noble, 1979.
Economics. Industry and trade. Industrial Revolution.

541 Payne, Harry C. "Elite Versus Popular Mentality in the Eight-
eenth Century." Studies in Eighteenth-Century Culture.
Vol. 8. Ed. Roseann Runte. Madison: Univ. of Wisconsin
Press, 1979, pp. 3-32. Social structure. Popular culture.
The elite. The poor.

542 Petrie, Charles. The Jacobite Movement. 1932. Rev. ed.
London: Eyre & Spottiswoode, 1959. Jacobitism. The Rebellion of 1745.

543 Pevsner, Nikolaus. "The Genesis of the Picturesque." Architectural Review, 96 (1944), 139-46. Aesthetic theory and
background. The picturesque. Landscape gardening.

544 Philips, David. "'A New Engine of Power and Authority':
The Institutionalization of Law-Enforcement in England, 1780-
1830." In Crime and the Law: The Social History of Crime
in Western Europe Since 1500. Ed. V. A. C. Gatrell et al.
London: Europa Publications, 1980, pp. 155-89. Crime and
punishment. Law.

545 Phillips, Hugh. The Thames About 1750. London: Collins,
1952. Thames River.

546 Phillips, M., and W. S. Tomkinson. English Women in Life &
Letters. 1926; rpt. New York: Blom, 1971. Women.
Servants. The bluestocking. The elite. The nurse. The
governess. Crime and punishment. Domestic life. Country
life.

547 Phillipson, Nicholas T., and Rosalind Mitchison, eds. Scotland
in the Age of Improvement. Edinburgh: University Press,
1970. [Anthology of essays]. Scotland.

548 Philpot, Gordon. "Enclosure and Population Growth in Eight-
     eenth-Century England." Explorations in Economic History,
     12 (1975), 29-46. Enclosures. Population.

549 Pinchbeck, Ivy. Women Workers and the Industrial Revolution,
     1750-1850. 1930; rpt. London: Cass, 1977. Women. Work.
     The laborer. Industrial Revolution.

550 Pinchbeck, Ivy, and Margaret Hewitt. Children in English
     Society. 2 vols. London: Routledge & Kegan Paul, 1969.
     Children.

551 Plant, Marjorie. The English Book Trade: An Economic His-
     tory of the Making and Sale of Books. London: Allen &
     Unwin, 1939. Book trade.

552 Plumb, J. H. The Commercialization of Leisure in the Eight-
     eenth Century. Reading: Univ. of Reading Press, 1973.
     Leisure. Sport and recreation.

553 Plumb, J. H. England in the Eighteenth Century, 1714-1815.
     London: Penguin, 1950. Politics.

554 Plumb, J. H. Georgian Delights. Boston: Little, Brown,
     1980. Sport and recreation.

555 Plumb, J. H. The Growth of Political Stability in England,
     1675-1725. London: Macmillan, 1967. Politics. Stability.

556 Plumb, J. H. "The Mercantile Interest: The Rise of the
     British Merchant After 1689." History Today, 5 (1955), 762-
     67. The merchant.

557 Plumb, J. H. "The New World of Children in the Eighteenth
     Century." Past and Present, No. 67 (1975), pp. 64-95.
     Children. Education.

558 Plumb, J. H. "Nobility and Gentry in the Early Eighteenth
     Century." History Today, 5 (1955), 805-17. Social struc-
     ture. The aristocracy. Gentry.

559 Plumb, J. H. "The Public, Literature & the Arts in the 18th
     Century." In The Triumph of Culture: 18th-Century Per-
     spectives. Ed. Paul S. Fritz and David Williams. Toronto:
     Hakkert, 1972, pp. 27-48. Popular culture.

560 Plumb, J. H. Sir Robert Walpole: The Making of a States-
     man. 2 vols. Boston: Houghton Mifflin, 1956, 1961. Sir
     Robert Walpole [the standard biography].

561 Pocock, J. G. A. "Modes of Political and Historical Time in

Early Eighteenth-Century England." In Studies in Eighteenth-Century Culture. Vol. 5. Ed. Ronald C. Rosbottom.
Madison: Univ. of Wisconsin Press, 1976, pp. 87-102. Historiography.

562 Pollard, Sidney. The Genesis of Modern Management: A Study
of the Industrial Revolution in Great Britain. Cambridge,
Mass.: Harvard Univ. Press, 1965. Industrial Revolution.
Management.

563 Popkin, Richard H. "Philosophical Basis of Eighteenth-Century
Racism." In Studies in Eighteenth-Century Culture. Vol.
4. Ed. Harold E. Pagliaro. Madison: Univ. of Wisconsin
Press, 1975, pp. 245-62. Racism.

564 Porritt, Edward, with Annie G. Porritt. The Unreformed
House of Commons. 2 vols. 1903; rpt. New York: Kelley,
1963. House of Commons.

■565 Porter, Roy. "Being Mad in Georgian England." History To-
day, Dec. 1981, pp. 42-48. Insanity.

566 Pressnell, L. S., ed. Studies in the Industrial Revolution
Presented to T. S. Ashton. London: Athlone Press, 1960.
[Anthology of essays]. Industrial Revolution.

567 Price, John Valdimir. "Religion and Ideas." In The Eighteenth Century. Ed. Pat Rogers. New York: Holmes &
Meier, 1978, pp. 120-52. Intellectual background.

568 Price, Julius Mendes. Dame Fashion: Paris-London (1786-
1912). 1912; rpt. New York: Scribner, 1913. Dress and
fashion.

569 Punter, David. "1789: The Sex of Revolution." Criticism,
24 (1982), 201-17. French Revolution. Sex.

570 Quinlan, Maurice J. "The Eighteenth Century." In his Vic-
torian Prelude: A History of English Manners, 1700-1830.
1941; rpt. Hamden, Conn.: Archon, 1965, pp. 7-100.
Social background.

571 Radner, John B. "The Art of Sympathy in Eighteenth-Century
British Moral Thought." In Studies in Eighteenth-Century
Culture. Vol. 9. Ed. Roseann Runte. Madison: Univ. of
Wisconsin Press, 1979, pp. 189-210. Sympathy. Morality.

•572 Radzinowicz, Leon. A History of English Criminal Law and
Its Administration from 1750. 4 vols. London: Stevens,
1948-1968. Law. Crime and punishment.

573 Rather, L. J. Mind and Body in Eighteenth-Century Medicine:
     A Study Based on Jerome Gaub's "De Regimine Mentes."
     Berkeley: Univ. of California Press, 1965. Medicine.

574 Redwood, John. Reason, Ridicule, and Religion: The Age of
     Enlightenment in England, 1660-1750. Cambridge, Mass.:
     Harvard Univ. Press, 1976. Intellectual background.

575 Reynolds, Myra. The Learned Lady in England, 1650-1760.
     Boston: Houghton Mifflin, 1920. Women. Education.

576 Rice, C. Duncan. "Literary Sources and the Revolution in
     British Attitudes to Slavery." In Anti-Slavery, Religion,
     and Reform: Essays in Memory of Roger Anstey. Ed.
     Christine Bolt and Seymour Drescher. Hamden, Conn.:
     Archon, 1980, pp. 319-34. Slavery.

•577 Richardson, Albert E. Georgian England: A Survey of Social
     Life, Trades, Industries & Art from 1700 to 1820. London:
     Batsford, 1931. Social background. Industry and trade.
     Art. Sport and recreation. Architecture. Music. Interior
     design. The navy. The army. The Church. The theater.

578 Richardson, Albert E. An Introduction to Georgian Architec-
     ture. London: Art & Technics, 1949. Architecture.

579 Richardson, Albert E. The Smaller English House of the Later
     Renaissance, 1660-1830. London: Batsford, 1925. Archi-
     tecture. Domestic life.

580 Richardson, Albert E., and H. Donaldson Eberlein. The Eng-
     lish Inn, Past and Present: A Review of Its History and
     Social Life. London: Batsford, 1926. Inns. Social back-
     ground.

581 Richey, Russell E. "The Origins of British Radicalism: The
     Changing Rationale for Dissent." Eighteenth-Century
     Studies, 7 (1973-1974), 179-92. Dissenters. Radicalism.

582 Richmond, William K. The English Disease: A Study in De-
     spondency. London: Redman, 1958. Melancholy. National
     stereotypes.

583 Riley, Madeline. Brought to Bed. New York: A. S. Barnes,
     1968. Pregnancy and childbirth. Women. Bastardy.

584 Ritcheson, Charles R. British Politics and the American Revo-
     lution. Norman: Univ. of Oklahoma Press, 1954. American
     Revolution. Politics.

•585 Rivers, Isabel, ed. Books and Their Readers in Eighteenth-

Century England. New York: St. Martin's, 1982. [Anthology of essays]. Reading public. Book trade. Intellectual background. Methodism. Dissenters. Science.

586 Roberts, T. A. The Concept of Benevolence: Aspects of Eighteenth-Century Moral Philosophy. London: Macmillan, 1973. Benevolence. Morality.

587 Robinson, Howard. The British Post Office: A History. 1948; rpt. Westport, Conn.: Greenwood Press, 1970. Post Office.

588 Robson, Robert. The Attorney in Eighteenth-Century England. Cambridge: Cambridge Univ. Press, 1959. The lawyer.

589 Robson-Scott, W. D. "Foreign Impressions of England in the Eighteenth Century." In Silver Renaissance: Essays in Eighteenth-Century English History. Ed. Alex Natan. London: Macmillan, 1961, pp. 187-205. Travel. Social background.

590 Rodgers, Betsy. Cloak of Clarity: Studies in Eighteenth-Century Philanthropy. London: Methuen, 1949. Philanthropy.

591 Rogal, Samuel J. "Eighteenth-Century Bath: The Sink of Profligacy." Studies in History and Society, 6 (1975), 77-92. Bath.

592 Rogal, Samuel J. "John Wesley and the Attack on Luxury in England." Eighteenth-Century Life, 3 (1977), 91-94. Luxury. John Wesley.

593 Rogers, Katharine M. Feminism in Eighteenth-Century England. Urbana: Univ. of Illinois Press, 1982. Feminism. Women. Sentimentalism. Women novelists. Radicalism.

•594 Rogers, Pat. The Augustan Vision. London: Weidenfeld & Nicolson, 1974. Social background.

•595 Rogers, Pat. Grub Street: Studies in a Subculture. London: Methuen, 1972. Grub Street. The writer in society.

596 Rogers, Pat. "The Writer and Society." In The Eighteenth Century. Ed. Pat Rogers. New York: Holmes & Meier, 1978, pp. 1-80. The writer in society.

597 Ronan, Colin A. "Science in Eighteenth-Century Britain." In Silver Renaissance: Essays in Eighteenth-Century English History. Ed. Alex Natan. London: Macmillan, 1961, pp. 206-19. Science.

598 Rosen, George. "Forms of Irrationality in the Eighteenth Cen-
     tury." In Studies in Eighteenth-Century Culture: Irration-
     alism in the Eighteenth Century. Vol. 2. Ed. Harold E.
     Pagliaro. Cleveland: The Press of Case Western Reserve
     Univ., 1972, pp. 255-88. Irrationality.

599 Rosenblum, Robert. "The Dawn of British Romantic Painting."
     In The Varied Pattern: Studies in the 18th Century. Ed.
     Peter Hughes and David Williams. Toronto: Hakkert, 1971,
     pp. 189-210. Art. Romanticism.

600 Rǿstvig, Maren-Sofie. The Happy Man: Studies in the Meta-
     morphosis of a Classical Ideal. 2 vols. Oslo: University
     Press, 1954-58. "Happy Man."

601 Rothstein, Eric. "'Ideal Presence' and the 'Non Finito' in
     Eighteenth-Century Aesthetics." Eighteenth-Century Studies,
     9 (1976), 307-32. Aesthetic theory and background.

602 Rousseau, George S. "Nerves, Spirits, and Fibres: Towards
     Defining the Origins of Sensibility." In Studies in the
     Eighteenth Century III. Ed. R. F. Brissenden and J. C.
     Eade. Toronto: Univ. of Toronto Press, 1976, pp. 137-57.
     Sensibility. Intellectual background.

603 Rousseau, George S. "Science." In The Eighteenth Century.
     Ed. Pat Rogers. New York: Holmes & Meier, 1978, pp.
     153-207. Science. Medicine. Melancholy.

604 Rousseau, George S. "Science and the Discovery of the
     Imagination in Enlightened England." Eighteenth-Century
     Studies, 3 (1969), 108-35. Science. Imagination. Insanity.
     Medicine.

605 Rousseau, George S. "'Sowing the Wind and Reaping the
     Whirlwind': Aspects of Change in Eighteenth-Century Medi-
     cine." In Studies in Change and Revolution: Aspects of
     English Intellectual History, 1640-1800. Ed. Paul J. Korshin.
     Menston, Yorkshire: Scolar Press, 1972, pp. 129-59. Medi-
     cine.

606 Rudé, George. The Crowd in History: A Study of Popular
     Disturbances in France and England, 1730-1848. London:
     Wiley, 1965. The mob. Riots.

•607 Rudé, George. Hanoverian London, 1714-1808. Berkeley:
     Univ. of California Press, 1971. London. City life. Social
     structure. The poor. The Church. Radicalism. Economics.
     Popular culture.

608 Rudé, George. "Popular Protest in 18th-Century Europe." In

The Triumph of Culture: 18th-Century Perspectives. Ed.
Paul S. Fritz and David Williams. Toronto: Hakkert, 1972,
pp. 277-97. Protest. Riots. Radicalism.

609 Rudé, George. _Wilkes and Liberty: A Social Study of 1763
to 1774_. Oxford: Clarendon Press, 1962. Politics. Liberty. John Wilkes.

610 Salmon, David. "The Education of the Poor in the Eighteenth
Century." _Education Record_, 17 (1906-09), 369-87, 495-512.
Education. The poor.

611 Sampson, H. Grant. "Hogarth and the Traditions of Satire."
Humanities Association Review, 31 (1980), 67-85. Hogarth.
Satire.

612 Sampson, H. Grant. "Rococo in England." _Centennial Review_,
22 (1978), 356-73. Rococo.

613 Sanderson, Michael. "Literacy and Social Mobility in the Industrial Revolution in England." _Past and Present_, No. 56
(1972), pp. 75-103. Literacy. Social structure.

614 Saunders, John W. "The Profession Established" and "The
Romantic Dilemma." In his _The Profession of English Let-
ters_. London: Routledge & Kegan Paul, 1964, pp. 116-73.
The writer in society.

615 Schnorrenberg, Barbara Brandon. "Is Childbirth Any Place
for a Woman? The Decline of Midwifery in Eighteenth-Century England." In _Studies in Eighteenth-Century Culture_.
Vol. 10. Ed. Harry C. Payne. Madison: Univ. of Wisconsin Press, 1981, pp. 393-408. Midwifery. Women.

616 Schofield, Robert E. _Mechanism and Materialism: British Natural Philosophy_. Princeton, N.J.: Princeton Univ. Press,
1970. Science.

617 Schofield, Roger. "Dimensions of Illiteracy, 1750-1850." _Ex-
plorations in Economic History_, 10 (1973), 437-54. Literacy.

618 Schofield, Roger. "The Measurement of Literacy in Pre-Industrial England." In _Literacy in Traditional Societies_. Ed. J.
Goody. Cambridge: Cambridge Univ. Press, 1968. Literacy.

619 Schulz, Max F. "The Circuit Walk of the Eighteenth-Century
Landscape Garden and the Pilgrim's Circuitous Progress."
Eighteenth-Century Studies, 15 (1981), 1-26. Landscape
gardening. Symbolism [return to Eden]. Rural ideal. Retirement.

619a Schwartz, Richard. Daily Life in Johnson's London. Madison:
       Univ. of Wisconsin Press, 1984. City life. London.

620 Scott, Walter S. The Bluestocking Ladies. London: Green,
       1947. [Burney]. The bluestocking.

621 Sedgwick, Romney. The House of Commons, 1715-1754. 2
       vols. New York: Oxford Univ. Press, 1970. House of
       Commons.

•622 Sekora, John. Luxury: The Concept in Western Thought,
       Eden to Smollett. Baltimore: The Johns Hopkins Univ.
       Press, 1977. Luxury [as a seminal eighteenth-century
       theme].

623 Semmel, Bernard. The Methodist Revolution. New York:
       Basic Books, 1973. Methodism.

624 Sheriff, John K. The Good-Natured Man: The Evolution of
       an Ideal, 1660-1800. University: Univ. of Alabama Press,
       1982. "Good-Natured Man."

625 Sherwin, Oscar. "Crime and Punishment in England of the
       Eighteenth Century." American Journal of Economics and
       Sociology, 5 (1946), 169-99. Crime and punishment.

626 Shyllon, Folarin. Black People in Britain, 1555-1833. London:
       Oxford Univ. Press for the Institute of Race Relations, 1977.
       Blacks.

627 Simms, J. G. "Ireland in the Age of Swift." In Jonathan
       Swift, 1667-1967: A Dublin Tercentenary Tribute. Ed. Roger
       McHugh and Philip Edwards. Chester Springs, Pa.: Dufour
       Editions, 1968, pp. 157-75. Ireland. Politics. Social back-
       ground.

628 Simonds, Bruce. "Music in Johnson's London." In The Age of
       Johnson: Essays Presented to Chauncey Brewster Tinker.
       Ed. Frederick W. Hilles and Wilmarth S. Lewis. New Haven,
       Conn.: Yale Univ. Press, 1949, pp. 411-20. Music.

629 Simonsuuri, Kirsti. Homer's Original Genius: Eighteenth-
       Century Notions of the Early Greek Epic (1688-1798). Cam-
       bridge: Cambridge Univ. Press, 1979. Epic. Homer.

630 Sirén, Osvald. China and the Gardens of Europe in the Eight-
       eenth Century. New York: Ronald Press, 1950. Oriental-
       ism. Landscape gardening.

631 Sloan, Kim. "Drawing--A 'Polite Recreation' in Eighteenth-
       Century England." In Studies in Eighteenth-Century Culture.

Vol. 11. Ed. Harry C. Payne. Madison: Univ. of Wisconsin Press, 1982, pp. 217-40. Popular culture. Art. Sport and recreation.

632 Smith, Frank. A History of English Elementary Education, 1760-1902. London: Univ. of London Press, 1931. Education.

633 Smith, Norah. "Sexual Mores in the Eighteenth Century: Robert Wallace's 'Of Venery.'" Journal of the History of Ideas, 39 (1978), 419-33. Sex. Marriage.

634 Smith, Robert A. Eighteenth-Century English Politics: Patrons and Place-Hunters. New York: Holt, Rinehart, Winston, 1972. Politics. Patronage.

635 Smyth, Charles. Simeon and Church Order: A Study of the Origins of the Evangelical Revival in Cambridge in the Eighteenth Century. Cambridge: Cambridge Univ. Press, 1940. The Church. Evangelicalism. Cambridge University.

636 Southworth, James G. Vauxhall Gardens: A Chapter in the Social History of England. New York: Columbia Univ. Press, 1941. Social background. Sport and recreation. Manners. Vauxhall Gardens.

637 Speck, W. A. "Politics." In The Eighteenth Century. Ed. Pat Rogers. New York: Holmes & Meier, 1978, pp. 81-119. Politics.

•638 Speck, W. A. Stability and Strife: England, 1714-1760. Cambridge, Mass.: Harvard Univ. Press, 1977. History. Politics. Economics. Social structure. The Church. Sir Robert Walpole.

639 Sprott, S. E. The English Debate on Suicide from Donne to Hume. La Salle, Ill.: Open Court Publishing Co., 1961. Suicide.

640 Staver, Frederick. "'Sublime' as Applied to Nature." Modern Language Notes, 70 (1955), 484-87. Aesthetic theory and background. The sublime and the beautiful. Nature.

641 Staves, Susan. "Money for Honor: Damages for Criminal Conversation." In Studies in Eighteenth-Century Culture. Vol. 11. Ed. Harry C. Payne. Madison: Univ. of Wisconsin Press, 1982, pp. 279-97. [Smollett, Fielding]. Law. Adultery.

■642 Steeves, Harrison R. "Sex in the Eighteenth-Century Perspective." In his Before Jane Austen: The Shaping of the Eng-

lish Novel in the Eighteenth Century. New York: Holt,
Rinehart, Winston, 1965, pp. 88-102. Sex.

643 Stevens, David Harrison. Party Politics and English Journalism, 1702-1742. Chicago: Univ. of Chicago Libraries, 1916.
Politics. Journalism.

•644 Stevenson, John. Popular Disturbances in England, 1700-1870.
London: Longman, 1979. The mob. Riots.

645 Stewart, Douglas J. "Pornography, Obscenity and Capitalism."
Antioch Review, 35 (1977), 389-98. Pornography. Capitalism.

•646 Stone, Lawrence. The Family, Sex and Marriage in England,
1500-1800. New York: Harper & Row, 1977. Family. Sex.
Marriage.

647 Stone, Lawrence. "Literacy and Education in England, 1640-
1900." Past and Present, No. 42 (1969), pp. 69-139. Literacy. Education.

648 Stone, Lawrence, ed. Oxford and Cambridge from the 14th to
the Early 19th Century. Vol. I. of his The University in
Society. Princeton, N.J.: Princeton Univ. Press, 1975.
Oxford University. Cambridge University.

•648a Stone, Lawrence, and Jeanne C. Fawtier Stone. An Open
Elite? England, 1540-1880. New York: Oxford Univ.
Press, 1984. Social structure [challenges standard opinion
that wealthy middle class had easy entry into ranks of landed
elite]. The aristocracy. The middle class. Gentry.

649 Streatfield, David C. "Art and Nature in the English Landscape Garden: Design Theory and Practice, 1700-1818." In
David C. Streatfield and Alistair M. Duckworth's Landscape
in the Gardens and the Literature of Eighteenth-Century
England. Los Angeles: Clark Memorial Library, U.C.L.A.,
1981, pp. 3-87. Landscape gardening.

650 Stromberg, Roland N. Religious Liberalism in Eighteenth-Century England. London: Cumberlege, 1954. Christianity.

651 Summerson, John. English Architecture, 1530-1830. Pelican
History of Art. Baltimore: Penguin, 1953. Architecture.

652 Summerson, John. Georgian London. 1945. Rev. ed. London: Pleiades, 1948. London. Architecture.

653 Sutherland, Lucy. "The City of London in Eighteenth-Century
Politics." In Essays Presented to Sir Lewis Namier. Ed.

Richard Pares and A. J. P. Taylor. 1956; rpt. Freeport,
N.Y.: Books for Libraries Press, 1971. Rpt. in Aristo-
cratic Government and Society in Eighteenth-Century Eng-
land: The Foundations of Stability. Ed. Daniel A. Baugh.
New York: New Viewpoints, 1975, pp. 158-82. London.
Politics.

654 Sutherland, Lucy. The University of Oxford in the Eighteenth
     Century: A Reconsideration. Oxford: Blackwell, 1973.
     [1972 lecture]. Oxford University.

•655 Sykes, Norman. Church and State in Eighteenth-Century Eng-
     land. 1934; rpt. Hamden, Conn.: Archon, 1962. The
     Church. Latitudinarianism. The clergy.

656 Tate, William E. The English Village Community and the En-
     closure Movements. London: Gollancz, 1967. Villages.
     Country life. Enclosures.

657 Taylor, Arthur J., ed. The Standard of Living in Britain in
     the Industrial Revolution. London: Methuen, 1975. Stand-
     ard of living. Wages. Working classes.

658 Taylor, Douglas. Fielding's England. Living in England
     Series. London: Dobson, 1966. Social background.

659 Thomas, David. "The Social Origins of Marriage Partners of
     the British Peerage in the Eighteenth and Nineteenth Cen-
     turies." Population Studies, 26 (1972), 99-111. Marriage.
     The aristocracy.

660 Thomas, P. D. G. The House of Commons in the Eighteenth
     Century. Oxford: Clarendon Press, 1971. House of Com-
     mons.

661 Thompson, Edward Palmer. The Making of the English Work-
     ing Class. London: Gollancz, 1963. Working classes.

662 Tinker, Chauncey Brewster. Nature's Simple Plan: A Phase
     of Radical Thought in the Mid-Eighteenth Century. 1922;
     rpt. New York: Gordian Press, 1964. Intellectual back-
     ground. Nature. Liberty. Primitivism.

663 Tinker, Chauncey Brewster. Painter and Poet: Studies in
     the Literary Relations of English Painting. The Charles
     Eliot Norton Lectures for 1937-1938. Cambridge, Mass.:
     Harvard Univ. Press, 1938. Aesthetic theory and back-
     ground. Literature and the other arts. Hogarth.

664 Tinker, Chauncey Brewster. The Salon and English Letters:
     Chapters on the Interrelations of Literature and Society in

the Age of Johnson. New York: Macmillan, 1915. The
salon. The writer in society. Intellectual background.

665 Tobias, J. T. Crime and Police in England, 1700-1900. New
York: St. Martin's, 1979. Crime and punishment.

666 Tomasson, Katherine, and Francis Buist. Battles of the '45.
New York: Macmillan, 1962. Jacobitism. Rebellion of 1745.

667 Tompson, Richard S. Classics or Charity? The Dilemma of
the Eighteenth-Century Grammar School. Manchester: Manchester Univ. Press, 1971. Education. Grammar schools.

668 Trease, Geoffrey. The Grand Tour. New York: Holt, Rinehart, Winston, 1967. Grand tour.

669 Trevelyan, George M. England Under Queen Anne. 3 vols.
London: Longman, 1930-34. History. Politics.

670 Trevelyan, George M. Illustrated English Social History. Vol.
3: The Eighteenth Century. 1942; rpt. London: Longman, 1954. Social background. Politics.

671 Trickett, Rachel. "The Growth of Literary Taste in the Eighteenth Century." In Silver Renaissance: Essays in Eighteenth-Century English History. Ed. Alex Natan. London:
Macmillan, 1961, pp. 142-64. Popular culture.

672 Trumbach, Randolph. The Rise of the Egalitarian Family:
Aristocratic Kinship and Domestic Relations in Eighteenth-
Century England. New York: Academic Press, 1978. The
family. The aristocracy. Pregnancy and childbirth. Children.

673 Tucker, Susie I. Enthusiasm: A Study in Semantic Change.
Cambridge: Cambridge Univ. Press, 1972. Enthusiasm.
Semantics.

674 Tucker, Susie I. Protean Shape: A Study in Eighteenth-
Century Vocabulary and Usage. London: Athlone Press,
1967. Semantics.

675 Turberville, A. S. The House of Lords in the XVIIIth Century. 1913; rpt. Westport, Conn.: Greenwood Press, 1970.
House of Lords.

•676 Turberville, A. S., ed. Johnson's England: An Account of
the Life and Manners of His Age. 2 vols. 1933. Rev. ed.
Oxford: Clarendon Press, 1952. [Collection of essays].
Social background. The Church. The navy. The army.
Exploration. Travel. Communications. London. Towns.

Industry and trade. Agriculture. Country life. The poor.
Crime and punishment. Philanthropy. Manners. Meals.
Domestic life. Sport and recreation. Dress and fashion.
Taste. Art. Architecture. Landscape gardening. Interior
design. The theater. Music. Education. Science. Medi-
cine. Law. Booksellers. Newspapers.

677 Turner, Michael. "Parliamentary Enclosure and Population
Change in England, 1750-1830." Explorations in Economic
History, 13 (1976), 463-68. For a reply see Gordon Philpot,
"Reply to 'Parliamentary Enclosure and Population Change
in England, 1750-1830,'" ibid., 469-71. Enclosures. Popu-
lation.

678 Tuveson, Ernest. "The Importance of Shaftesbury." ELH: A
Journal of English Literary History, 20 (1953), 267-99.
Shaftesbury.

679 Tuveson, Ernest. "Shaftesbury and the Age of Sensibility."
In Studies in Criticism and Aesthetics, 1660-1800: Essays in
Honor of Samuel Holt Monk. Ed. Howard Anderson and John
S. Shea. Minneapolis: Univ. of Minnesota Press, 1967, pp.
73-93. Shaftesbury. Sensibility.

680 Uphaus, Robert W. "Mandeville and the Force of Prejudice."
In his The Impossible Observer: Reason and the Reader in
18th-Century Prose. Lexington: Univ. Press of Kentucky,
1979, pp. 28-45. Mandeville.

681 Vaid, Sudesh. "The Eighteenth-Century Woman: Education,
Economics, and Law." In The Divided Mind: Studies in
Defoe and Richardson. New Delhi: Associated Publishing
House, 1980, pp. 13-47. Women. Education. Economics.
Law.

682 Vale, Edmund. The Mail-Coach Men of the Late Eighteenth
Century. London: Cassell, 1960. Post office. The mail-
coachman. Coaching.

683 Vann, Richard T. The Social Development of English Quakerism, 1655-1755. Cambridge, Mass.: Harvard Univ. Press,
1969. Quakerism.

684 Varma, Devendra P. The Evergreen Tree of Diabolical Knowledge. Washington, D.C.: Consortium Press, 1972. Book
trade. Reading public. Circulating libraries.

685 Vereker, Charles. Eighteenth-Century Optimism: A Study of
the Interrelations of Moral and Social Theory in English and
French Thought Between 1689 and 1789. Liverpool: Liverpool Univ. Press, 1967. Optimism. Intellectual background.

686 Vichert, Gordon. "The Theory of Conspicuous Consumption in the 18th Century." In The Varied Pattern: Studies in the 18th Century. Ed. Peter Hughes and David Williams. Toronto: Hakkert, 1971, pp. 253-67. "Conspicuous consumption." Luxury. Economics.

687 Vincent, W. A. L. The Grammar Schools: Their Continuing Tradition, 1660-1714. London: Murray, 1969. Education. Grammar schools.

688 Viner, Jacob. "Satire and Economics in the Augustan Age of Satire." In The Augustan Milieu: Essays Presented to Louis A. Landa. Ed. Henry Knight Miller, Eric Rothstein, and George S. Rousseau. Oxford: Clarendon Press, 1970, pp. 77-101. Satire. Economics.

689 Walker, Robert G. "Public Death in the Eighteenth Century." Research Studies, 48 (1980), 11-24. Crime and punishment.

690 Wall, Cecil. The History of the Surgeon's Company, 1745-1800. London: Hutchinson, 1937. Medicine.

691 Wall, Cecil; H. Charles Cameron; and E. Ashworth Underwood. A History of the Worshipful Society of Apothecaries of London. Vol. I: 1617-1815. London: Oxford Univ. Press, 1963--. Medicine.

692 Walters, John. Splendour and Scandal: The Reign of Beau Nash. London: Murray, 1968. "Beau" Richard Nash. Bath.

693 Walvin, James. The Black Presence: A Documentary History of the Negro in England, 1555-1860. 1971; rpt. New York: Schocken, 1972. Blacks.

694 Walvin, James. "The Rise of British Popular Sentiment for Abolition, 1787-1832." In Anti-Slavery, Religion, and Reform: Essays in Memory of Roger Anstey. Ed. Christine Bolt and Seymour Drescher. Hamden, Conn.: Archon, 1980, pp. 149-62. Slavery.

695 Walvin, James. Slavery and British Society, 1776-1846. Baton Rouge: Louisiana State Univ. Press, 1982. Slavery.

696 Ward, W. R. The English Land Tax in the Eighteenth Century. London: Oxford Univ. Press, 1953. Taxation.

697 Ward, W. R. Georgian Oxford: University Politics in the 18th Century. Oxford: Clarendon Press, 1958. Oxford University. Politics.

698   Wark, Robert R.   "Hogarth's Narrative Method in Practice and
      Theory."   In England in the Restoration and Early Eight-
      eenth Century: Essays on Culture and Society.   Ed. H. T.
      Swedenberg, Jr.   Berkeley: Univ. of California Press,
      1970, pp. 161-72.   Hogarth.   Narrative technique.

699   Warner, James H.   "'Education of the Heart':   Observations on
      the Eighteenth-Century English Sentimental Movement."   Pa-
      pers of the Michigan Academy of Science, Arts and Letters,
      29 (1943), 553-60.   Sentimentalism.

699a Warren, Leland E.   "Turning Reality Round Together: Guides
      to Conversation in Eighteenth-Century England."   Eighteenth-
      Century Life, 8, N.S. 3, No. 1 (1983), pp. 65-87.   Conver-
      sation.

700   Waterhouse, Ellis.   Painting in Britain, 1530-1790.   Pelican
      History of Art.   Baltimore: Penguin, 1953.   Art.

701   Watson, J. Steven.   "Dissent and Toleration."   In Silver Ren-
      aissance: Essays in Eighteenth-Century English History.
      Ed. Alex Natan.   London: Macmillan, 1961, pp. 1-19.
      Toleration.   Dissenters.

•702 Watson, J. Steven.   The Reign of George III, 1760-1815.   Ox-
      ford: Clarendon Press, 1960.   History.   Politics.   Eco-
      nomics.   Social structure.

703   Wearmouth, R. I.   Methodism and the Common People of the
      Eighteenth Century.   London: Epworth Press, 1945.
      Methodism.

704   Webb, Robert Kiefer.   The British Working Class Reader,
      1790-1848:   Literacy and Social Tension.   London: Allen &
      Unwin, 1955.   Reading public.   Literacy.   Working classes.

705   Webb, Sidney, and Beatrice Webb.   English Local Government
      from the Revolution to the Municipal Corporations Act.   Lon-
      don: Longman, 1908.   Poor law.   Law.   The "trading jus-
      tice."

706   Webb, Sidney, and Beatrice Webb.   English Local Government:
      The Story of the King's Highway.   London: Longman, 1913.
      Transportation.   Turnpikes and roads.   Bridges.

707   Webb, Sidney, and Beatrice Webb.   English Prisons Under
      Local Government.   London: Longman, 1922.   Prisons.
      John Howard.

708   Weitzman, Arthur J.   "Eighteenth-Century London: Urban
      Paradise or Fallen City?"   Journal of the History of Ideas,
      36 (1975), 469-80.   London.

709 Welch, Barbara A. "Curiosities and Reflections: British Trav-
     elers on the Continent in the Eighteenth Century." Modern
     Language Studies, 10, No. 2 (1980), 10-25. Travel.

710 Westerfield, Ray B. Middlemen in English Business, Particu-
     larly Between 1660-1760. 1915; rpt. New York: Kelly,
     1981. Economics. Industry and trade. The tradesman.

711 Western, J. R. The English Militia in the Eighteenth Century:
     The Story of a Political Issue, 1660-1802. Toronto: Univ.
     of Toronto Press, 1965. The militia. Politics.

712 Whinney, Margaret. Sculpture in Britain, 1530-1830. Pelican
     History of Art. Harmondsworth: Penguin, 1964. Sculpture.

713 White, R. J. "The Grand Tour." In Silver Renaissance: Es-
     says in Eighteenth-Century English History. Ed. Alex Natan.
     London: Macmillan, 1961, pp. 122-41. Grand tour.

714 Wiles, Richard C. "Mercantilism and the Idea of Progress."
     Eighteenth-Century Studies, 8 (1974), 56-74. Mercantilism.
     Progress.

715 Wiles, Roy M. "Crowd-Pleasing Spectacles in Eighteenth-Cen-
     tury England." Journal of Popular Culture, 1 (1967), 90-
     105. Sport and recreation [e.g., hangings, play-going,
     balloon flights]. The mob.

716 Wiles, Roy M. "Felix que ...: Standards of Happiness in
     Eighteenth-Century England." In Studies on Voltaire and
     the Eighteenth Century. Ed. Theodore Besterman. Geneva:
     Droz, 1967, pp. 1857-67. [Johnson, Pope, Goldsmith].
     Happiness.

717 Wiles, Roy M. Freshest Advices: Early Provincial Newspapers
     in England. Columbus: Ohio State Univ. Press, 1965.
     Newspapers [includes chapter on "Literary Features and
     Fillers"].

718 Wiles, Roy M. "Middle-Class Literacy in Eighteenth-Century
     England: Fresh Evidence." Studies in the Eighteenth Cen-
     tury. Ed. R. F. Brissenden. Canberra: Australia National
     Univ. Press, 1968, pp. 49-65. Literacy. Reading public.
     The middle class.

719 Wiles, Roy M. "Provincial Culture in Early Georgian England."
     In The Triumph of Culture: 18th-Century Perspectives.
     Eds. Paul Fritz and David Williams. Toronto: Hakkert,
     1972, pp. 49-68. Country life. Newspapers. Popular cul-
     ture.

720 Wiles, Roy M. "The Relish for Reading in Provincial England

Two Centuries Ago." In The Widening Circle: Essays on
the Circulation of Literature in Eighteenth-Century Europe.
Ed. Paul J. Korshin. Philadelphia: Univ. of Pennsylvania
Press, 1976, pp. 87-115. Reading public.

721 Wiles, Roy M. Serial Publication in England Before 1750.
Cambridge: Cambridge Univ. Press, 1957. Journalism.

722 Willcox, William B. The Age of Aristocracy, 1688-1830. 2nd
ed. Lexington, Mass.: Heath, 1971. The aristocracy.
Social structure.

723 Willey, Basil. The Eighteenth-Century Background: Studies
on the Idea of Nature. 1940; rpt. New York: Columbia
Univ. Press, 1962. Intellectual background. "Cosmic Toryism." Nature.

•724 Williams, Basil. The Whig Supremacy, 1714-1760. 1939. 2nd
ed., rev. by Charles H. Stuart. Oxford: Clarendon Press,
1952. History. Politics. Social background. Whigs.

725 Williams, E. Neville. The Eighteenth-Century Constitution,
1688-1815, Documents and Commentary. Cambridge: Cambridge Univ. Press, 1960. Constitution of Great Britain.

726 Williams, E. Neville. Life in Georgian England. London:
Batsford, 1962. Social background.

727 Williams, E. Neville. "'Our Merchants Are Princes': The English Middle Classes in the Eighteenth Century." History To-
day, 12 (1962), 548-57. The merchant. Social structure.
The middle class.

•728 Williams, Raymond. The Country and the City. New York:
Oxford, 1973. Country vs. city.

729 Willis, Peter. "The Visual Arts." In The Eighteenth Century.
Ed. Pat Rogers. New York: Holmes & Meier, 1978, pp.
208-39. Architecture. Art. Landscape gardening. Interior
design.

730 Wilson, Bruce L. "'Sex and the Single Girl' in the Eighteenth
Century: An Essay on Marriage and the Puritan Myth."
Journal of Women's Studies in Literature, 1 (1979), 195-219.
Women. Sex. Marriage. Puritanism.

731 Wilson, Charles. England's Apprenticeship, 1603-1763. London: Longman, 1965. Economics. Social background.

732 Wilson, Charles, and Geoffrey Parker. An Introduction to the
Sources of European Economic History, 1500-1800. Ithaca,

N.Y.: Cornell Univ. Press, 1977. Economics. Social background. Statistics.

733 Winstanley, D. A. The University of Cambridge in the Eighteenth Century. Cambridge: Cambridge Univ. Press, 1922. Cambridge University.

734 Winstanley, D. A. Unreformed Cambridge: A Study of Certain Aspects of the University in the Eighteenth Century. Cambridge: Cambridge Univ. Press, 1935. Cambridge University.

735 Wood, Theodore E. B. The Word "Sublime" and Its Context, 1650-1760. The Hague: Mouton, 1972. The sublime and the beautiful. Semantics.

736 Woodforde, John. Georgian Houses for All. London: Routledge & Kegan Paul, 1978. Domestic life. Architecture.

737 Wrigley, E. A. "A Simple Model of London's Importance in Changing English Society and Economy, 1650-1750." In Aristocratic Government and Society in Eighteenth-Century England: The Foundations of Stability. Ed. Daniel A. Baugh. New York: New Viewpoints, 1975, pp. 62-95. Originally published in Past and Present, No. 37 (1967), pp. 44-70. London. Economics.

738 Yolton, John W. Materialism in Eighteenth-Century Britain. Minneapolis: Univ. of Minnesota Press, 1984. [Not seen]. Intellectual background. Materialism.

739 Young, Percy M. A History of British Music. London: Benn, 1967. Music.

740 Zaller, Robert. "The Continuity of British Radicalism in the Seventeenth and Eighteenth Centuries." Eighteenth-Century Life, 6, Nos. 2-3 (1981), 17-38. Radicalism.

741 Zucker, Paul. "Ruins--An Aesthetic Hybrid." Journal of Aesthetics and Art Criticism, 20 (1961), 119-30. Ruins. Aesthetic theory and background. Art. Landscape gardening.

PART IV: GENERAL CRITICISM OF THE
EIGHTEENTH-CENTURY BRITISH NOVEL
AND RELATED STUDIES

742 Adams, M. Ray. Studies in the Literary Backgrounds of English Radicalism. 1947; rpt. New York: Greenwood Press,
1968. [Hays, Robinson]. Radicalism.

▫743 Adams, Percy G. "The Anti-Hero in Eighteenth-Century Fiction." Studies in the Literary Imagination, 9 (1976), 29-51.
Anti-hero [picaresque anti-hero, villain-hero, rake, menda-
cious narrator].

•744 Adams, Percy G. Travel Literature and the Evolution of the
Novel. Lexington: Univ. Press of Kentucky, 1983. Travel
literature. Hero/heroine. Realism. Romanticism. Plot,
structure, and design. Point of view and narrator. Characterization. Coaching. Inns. Style and language.

745 Adams, Percy G. Travelers and Travel-Liars, 1660-1800.
Berkeley: Univ. of California Press, 1962. Travel literature.

746 Allen, Walter. "The Virtues of the Epistolary Novel." Times
Literary Supplement, January 26, 1973, pp. 97-98. Epistolary novel. Characterization.

•747 Alter, Robert. Rogue's Progress: Studies in the Picaresque
Novel. Cambridge, Mass.: Harvard Univ. Press, 1964.
[Moll Flanders, Roderick Random, Tom Jones]. Picaresque
novel. Rogue hero.

747a Altman, Janet Gorkin. Epistolarity: Approaches to a Form.
Columbus: Ohio State Univ. Press, 1982. Epistolary novel.

748 Andersen, Jorgen. "Giant Dreams: Piranesi's Influence in
England." English Miscellany, 3 (1952), 49-59. [Beckford,
Walpole]. Gothic novel. Sources, analogues, and influ-
ences. Piranesi.

749 Anderson, George K. The Legend of the Wandering Jew.
Providence, R.I.: Brown Univ. Press, 1965. Wandering
Jew.

750 Anderson, Howard. "Gothic Heroes." In The English Hero,
     1660-1800. Ed. Robert Folkenflik. Newark: Univ. of Dela-
     ware Press, 1982, pp. 205-21. [Walpole, Radcliffe, Lewis].
     Gothic hero [differences in characterization]. Characteriza-
     tion.

751 Auty, Susan. The Comic Spirit of Eighteenth-Century Novels.
     Port Washington, N.Y.: Kennikat Press, 1975. [Fielding,
     Coventry, Lennox, Goldsmith, Graves, Smollett, Sterne].
     Comedy. Benevolence.

752 Backscheider, Paula R. "Woman's Influence." Studies in the
     Novel, 11 (1979), 3-22. [Barker, Haywood, Lennox, F.
     Brooke, Burney, S. Scott, Richardson, Inchbald]. Women
     [women's need to influence men]. Man vs. Woman. Marriage
     [women's methods of avoiding an unwanted marriage].

•753 Baker, Ernest A. Intellectual Realism: From Richardson to
     Sterne. Vol. 4 of The History of the English Novel. 10
     vols. 1936; rpt. New York: Barnes & Noble, 1966. His-
     tory of the novel. "Intellectual realism."

•754 Baker, Ernest A. The Later Romances and the Establishment
     of Realism. Vol. 3 of The History of the English Novel. 10
     vols. 1936; rpt. New York: Barnes & Noble, 1966. His-
     tory of the novel. Realism.

•755 Baker, Ernest A. The Novel of Sentiment and the Gothic Ro-
     mance. Vol. 5 of The History of the English Novel. 10 vols.
     1936; rpt. New York: Barnes & Noble, 1966. History of
     the novel. Oriental novel. Sentimental novel. Gothic novel.
     Novel of sensibility. Novel of doctrine.

■756 Baker, Sheridan. "The Idea of Romance in Eighteenth-Century
     Fiction." Publications of the Michigan Academy of Arts,
     Sciences and Letters, 49 (1964), 507-22. Romance.

757 Barnett, George, ed. Eighteenth-Century British Novelists on
     the Novel. New York: Appleton-Century-Crofts, 1968.
     [Anthology of criticism]. Novelists on the novel. Theory
     and practice of the novel.

758 Bator, Robert. "Eighteenth-Century England Versus the Fairy
     Tale." Research Studies, 39 (1971), 1-10. Fairy tale.
     Children's literature.

759 Bator, Robert. "Out of the Ordinary Road: John Locke and
     English Juvenile Fiction in the Eighteenth Century." In The
     Great Excluded: Critical Essays on Children's Literature.
     Ed. Francelia Butler. Storrs: Univ. of Connecticut Press,
     1972, pp. 46-53. Children's literature. Locke.

760 Batten, Charles L., Jr. Pleasurable Instruction: Form and
     Convention in Eighteenth-Century Travel Literature. Berke-
     ley: Univ. of California Press, 1978. Travel literature.

•761 Battestin, Martin C. The Providence of Wit: Aspects of Form
     in Augustan Literature and the Arts. Oxford: Clarendon
     Press, 1974. [Fielding, Goldsmith, Swift, Sterne]. Chris-
     tianity. Plot, structure, and design. Style and language.
     Order.

762 Bayer-Berenbaum, Linda. The Gothic Imagination: Expansion
     in Gothic Literature and Art. East Brunswick, N.J.: As-
     sociated Univ. Presses, 1982. [Not seen]. Imagination.
     Gothic novel. Art.

•763 Beasley, Jerry C. Novels of the 1740s. Athens: Univ. of
     Georgia Press, 1982. Incorporates his "English Fiction in
     the 1740's: Some Glances at the Major and Minor Novels,"
     Studies in the Novel, 5 (1973), 155-75; and "Romance and
     the 'New' Novels of Richardson, Fielding, and Smollett,"
     Studies in English Literature, 16 (1976), 437-50. [Esp.
     Richardson, Fielding, Smollett]. Romance. Realism. Inno-
     vation. Popular novel. Criminal biography. Spiritual biog-
     raphy. Comparison of novelists.

764 Beasley, Jerry C. "Politics and Character in the Eighteenth
     Century: Glances at Some Rhetorical Types." In Studies
     in Eighteenth-Century Culture. Ed. O M Brack, Jr. Vol.
     13. Madison: Univ. of Wisconsin Press, 1984, pp. 3-18.
     Politics. Allegory. Characterization [of political figures,
     types, ideologies].

765 Beasley, Jerry C. "Portraits of a Monster: Robert Walpole
     and Early English Prose Fiction." Eighteenth-Century
     Studies, 14 (1981), 406-31. Sir Robert Walpole. Satire.

766 Behrendt, Stephen C. "Art as Deceptive Intruder: Audience
     Entrapment in Eighteenth-Century Verbal and Visual Art."
     Papers on Language and Literature, 19 (1983), 37-52.
     Author-reader relationship. Art. Narrative technique.

767 Bentley, G. E., ed. Editing Eighteenth-Century Novels
     [1973]. Toronto: Hakkert, 1975. [Fielding, Richardson,
     Sterne, Smollett]. Textual editing.

768 Berger, Morroe. Real and Imagined Worlds: The Novel and
     Social Science. Cambridge, Mass.: Harvard Univ. Press,
     1977. [Fielding, Defoe]. Social criticism in the novel.
     Realism. Mandeville.

769 Birkhead, Edith. "Sentiment and Sensibility in the Eighteenth-

Century Novel." Essays and Studies by Members of the
English Association, 11 (1925), 92-116. Sentimentalism.
Sensibility.

770 Birkhead, Edith. The Tale of Terror: A Study of the Gothic
Romance. 1921; rpt. New York: Russell & Russell, 1963.
Gothic novel.

771 Bissell, Benjamin. The American Indian in English Literature
of the Eighteenth Century. 1925; rpt. [Hamden, Conn.]:
Archon, 1968, pp. 78-117. The Indian.

772 Black, Frank Gees. "The Technique of Letter Fiction from
1740 to 1800." Harvard Studies and Notes in Philology and
Literature, 15 (1933), 291-312. Epistolary novel.

773 Black, Sidney J. "Eighteenth-Century 'Histories' as a Fictional
Mode." Boston University Studies in English, 1 (1955), 38-
44. Historical façade.

774 Blackburn, Alexander. The Myth of the Picaro: Continuity
and Transformation of the Picaresque Novel, 1554-1954.
Chapel Hill: Univ. of North Carolina Press, 1979. [Defoe,
Fielding, Smollett]. Picaresque novel. Rogue hero. Prog-
ress [in Colonel Jack]. Satire [on picaresque in Jonathan
Wild]. Satanic hero [in Ferdinand, Count Fathom].

775 Bland, D. S. "Endangering the Reader's Neck: Background
Description in the Novel." Criticism, 3 (1961), 121-39.
Setting.

776 Blondel, Jacques. "On 'Metaphysical Prisons.'" Durham University Journal, N.S. 32 (1971), 133-38. Gothic novel.
Imprisonment.

777 Bloom, Edward A., and Lillian D. Bloom. Satire's Persuasive
Voice. Ithaca, N.Y.: Cornell Univ. Press, 1979. Satire.
Point of view and narrator. Morality.

●778 Booth, Wayne C. The Rhetoric of Fiction. 1961. 2nd ed.
Chicago: Univ. of Chicago Press, 1983, pp. 211-40.
[Fielding, Sterne]. Point of view and narrator [intrusive
narrator]. Author-reader relationship. Digressions and interpolated stories. Critical revaluation [reestablishment of
"telling" over "showing" in fiction].

779 Booth, Wayne C. A Rhetoric of Irony. Chicago: Univ. of
Chicago Press, 1974. Irony.

■780 Booth, Wayne C. "The Self-Conscious Narrator in Comic Fiction Before Tristram Shandy." PMLA, 67 (1952), 163-85.
Point of view and narrator.

781 Boyce, Benjamin. "The Effect of the Restoration on Prose
     Fiction." Tennessee Studies in Literature, 6 (1961), 77-83.
     History of the novel.

781a Boyce, Benjamin. "English Short Fiction in the Eighteenth
     Century: A Preliminary View." Studies in Short Fiction,
     5 (1968), 95-112. Short fiction [its conventions and matter
     influence the early novel]. Conventions of the Georgian
     novel.

782 Bradbrook, Frank W. Jane Austen and Her Predecessors.
     Cambridge: Cambridge Univ. Press, 1966. Influence and
     imitation. Morality. The picaresque. Women novelists.

783 Brady, Frank. "Prose Style and the 'Whig' Tradition." Bul-
     letin of the New York Public Library, 66 (1962), 455-63.
     Cf. Donald J. Greene, "Is There a 'Tory' Prose Style?"
     ibid., 449-54. Style and language. Whigs. Tories.

784 Braudy, Leo. "The Form of the Sentimental Novel." Novel,
     7 (1973), 5-13. [Mackenzie, Sterne]. Sentimental novel.
     Plot, structure, and design.

785 Braudy, Leo. Narrative Form in History and Fiction: Hume,
     Fielding, and Gibbon. Princeton, N.J.: Princeton Univ.
     Press, 1970. Plot, structure, and design. Style and lan-
     guage. Historiography.

•786 Brissenden, R. F. Virtue in Distress: Studies in the Novel
     of Sentiment From Richardson to Sade. New York: Macmil-
     lan, 1974. [Richardson, Sterne, Goldsmith, Mackenzie].
     Sentimental novel. Sentimentalism.

787 Brooks, Douglas. Number and Pattern in the Eighteenth-Cen-
     tury Novel: Defoe, Fielding, Smollett and Sterne. London:
     Routledge & Kegan Paul, 1973. Numerology. Plot, struc-
     ture, and design. Symbolism.

787a Brooks-Davies, Douglas. "The Mythology of Love: Venerian
     (and Related) Iconography in Pope, Fielding, Cleland and
     Sterne." In Sexuality in Eighteenth-Century Britain. Ed.
     Paul-Gabriel Boucé. Totowa, N.J.: Barnes & Noble, 1982,
     pp. 176-97. Love. Myth [Venus, Narcissis, Adonis].

788 Brown, Huntington. "The Age of the Novel." In his Rabelais
     in English Literature. 1933; rpt. New York: Octagon,
     1967, pp. 178-206. [Fielding, Amory, Goldsmith, Johnson,
     Smollett, Sterne]. Rabelais. Comedy. Sources, analogues,
     and influences.

789 Brown, Laura S. "Drama and Novel in Eighteenth-Century

England." <u>Genre</u>, 13 (1980), 287-304. Dramatic conventions in the novel.

790 Brown, Wallace Cable. "Prose Fiction and English Interest in the Near East, 1775-1825," <u>PMLA</u>, 53 (1938), 827-36. Orientalism.

791 Butt, John. <u>The Mid-Eighteenth Century</u>. Ed. and completed by Geoffrey Carnall. Vol. 8 of the <u>Oxford History of English Literature</u>. Oxford: Clarendon Press, 1979. History of the novel.

792 Byrd, Max. <u>London Transformed: Images of the City in the Eighteenth Century</u>. New Haven, Conn.: Yale Univ. Press, 1978. [Defoe, Fielding, Johnson, Smollett]. London. Humanism. Imagery [the body, theaters, rivers, language].

793 Byrd, Max. "The Madhouse, the Whorehouse, and the Convent." <u>Partisan Review</u>, 44 (1977), 268-78. [Defoe, Richardson, Lewis]. Sex. Imprisonment. Insanity. Symbolism [the locking away of unreason in an age of reason].

794 Byrd, Max. <u>Visits to Bedlam: Madness and Literature in the Eighteenth Century</u>. Columbia: Univ. of South Carolina Press, 1974. [Swift, Johnson]. Reason. Insanity. Melancholy.

795 Bystrom, Valerie Ann. "The Abyss of Sympathy: The Conventions of Pathos in Eighteenth- and Nineteenth-Century British Novels." <u>Criticism</u>, 23 (1981), 211-31. Sympathy. Conventions of the Georgian novel.

796 Canepa, Andrew M. "From Degenerate Scoundrel to Noble Savage: The Italian Stereotype in Eighteenth-Century British Travel Literature." <u>English Miscellany</u>, 22 (1971), 107-46. National stereotypes. The Italian. The Englishman. Travel literature.

797 Carnochan, W. B. <u>Confinement and Flight: An Essay on English Literature of the Eighteenth Century</u>. Berkeley: Univ. of California Press, 1977. [Defoe, Swift, Sterne, Godwin, Johnson]. Flight. Imprisonment. Loneliness. Psychology of characters.

798 Chandler, Frank W. <u>The Literature of Roguery</u>. 2 vols. 1907; rpt. New York: Burt Franklin, 1958. Picaresque novel.

799 Clements, Frances M. "The Rights of Women in the Eighteenth-Century Novel." <u>Enlightenment Essays</u>, 4 (1973), 63-70. Women.

800 Cockshut, A. O. J. Man and Woman: A Study of Love and
     the Novel, 1740-1940. 1977; rpt. New York: Oxford Univ.
     Press, 1978. [Richardson, Fielding, Sterne]. Love. Sex.
     Comparison of novelists.

801 Cockshut, A. O. J. "Sentimentality in Fiction." Twentieth
     Century, 161 (1957), 354-64. Sentimentalism.

802 Cohen, Murray. "Eighteenth-Century English Literature and
     Modern Critical Methodologies." The Eighteenth Century:
     Theory and Interpretation, 20 (1979), 5-23. Critical revalu-
     ation. Pedagogical approach.

803 Conant, Martha Pike. The Oriental Tale in English in the
     Eighteenth Century. Columbia University Studies in Com-
     parative Literature. New York: Columbia Univ. Press,
     1908. Oriental tale. Rasselas-Candide comparison.

804 Cooke, Arthur L. "Some Side Lights on the Theory of the
     Gothic Romance." Modern Language Quarterly, 12 (1951),
     429-36. Gothic novel.

805 Copeland, Edward. "What's a Competence? Jane Austen, Her
     Sister Novelists, and the 5%'s." Modern Language Studies,
     9, No. 3 (1979), 161-68. Money. Women novelists.

806 Coveney, Peter. "The 'Cult of Sensibility' and the 'Romantic
     Child.'" In his The Image of Childhood. Rev. ed. Balti-
     more: Penguin, 1967, pp. 37-51. The child. Sensibility.

807 Cox, Stephen D. "The Stranger Within Thee": Concepts of
     the Self in Late-Eighteenth-Century Literature. Pittsburgh:
     Univ. of Pittsburgh Press, 1980. [Clarissa]. The self.
     Sensibility. Intellectual background.

808 Dalnekoff, Donna Isaacs. "A Familiar Stranger: The Out-
     sider of Eighteenth-Century Satire." Neophilologus, 57
     (1973), 121-34. [Goldsmith]. The wanderer. Satire.

809 Daniel, Stephen H. "Political and Philosophical Uses of Fables
     in Eighteenth-Century England." The Eighteenth Century:
     Theory and Interpretation, 23 (1982), 151-71. The fable.
     Politics. Philosophy of novelist.

810 Danziger, Marlies K. "The Eighteenth-Century Novel: A
     Comparative Approach." College English, 23 (1962), 646-48.
     Pedagogical approach.

811 Davies, Hugh Sykes. "Irony and the Engish Tongue." In
     The World of Jonathan Swift. Ed. Brian Vickers. Cam-
     bridge, Mass.: Harvard Univ. Press, 1968, pp. 129-53.
     Irony.

812 Davies, Paul C. "Augustan Smells." Essays in Criticism, 25
     (1975), 395–406. Smells. Imagery.

813 Davis, Lennard J. "A Social History of Fact and Fiction: Au-
     thorial Disavowal in the Early English Novel." In Factual
     Fictions: Studies in the Origin of the English Novel. Ed.
     Edward W. Said. Baltimore: The Johns Hopkins Univ.
     Press, 1980, pp. 120–48. Historical façade. Point of view
     and narrator.

814 Davis, Lennard J. "Wicked Actions and Feigned Words: Crim-
     inals, Criminality, and the Early English Novel." Yale
     French Studies, 59 (1980), 106–18. Novel as subversive
     form. The criminal. Style and language.

815 Davis, Robert Gorham. "The Sense of the Real in English Fic-
     tion." Comparative Literature, 3 (1951), 200–17. Realism.

816 Day, Robert Adams. "Speech Acts, Orality, and the Epistolary
     Novel." The Eighteenth Century: Theory and Interpreta-
     tion, 21 (1980), 187–97. [Moll Flanders, Clarissa, Tom
     Jones]. Speech and dialogue. Point of view and narrator.
     Epistolary novel.

817 Day, Robert Adams. Told in Letters: Epistolary Fiction Be-
     fore Richardson. Ann Arbor: Univ. of Michigan Press,
     1966. Epistolary novel. Bibliography of primary sources
     [many minor novelists listed].

818 Dircks, Richard J. "Cumberland, Richardson, and Fielding:
     Changing Patterns in the Eighteenth-Century Novel." Re-
     search Studies, 38 (1970), 291–99. Comparison of novelists
     [Cumberland's novels reflect changing social patterns].

819 Dobrée, Bonamy. English Literature in the Early Eighteenth
     Century, 1700–1740. Vol. 7 of the Oxford History of Eng-
     lish Literature. Oxford: Clarendon Press, 1959. History
     of the novel.

820 Donaldson, Ian. "The Clockwork Novel: Three Notes on an
     Eighteenth-Century Analogy." Review of English Studies,
     N.S. 21 (1970), 14–22. [Fielding, Richardson, S. Fielding,
     Sterne]. "Clockwork" analogy. Symbolism. Comparison of
     novelists.

821 Donovan, Robert Alan. The Shaping Vision: Imagination in
     the English Novel from Defoe to Dickens. Ithaca, N.Y.:
     Cornell Univ. Press, 1966. [Defoe, Richardson, Fielding,
     Sterne, Smollett]. Imagination. Plot, structure, and design.

822 Doody, Margaret Anne. "Deserts, Ruins and Troubled Waters:

Female Dreams in Fiction and the Development of the Gothic Novel." Genre, 10 (1977), 529-72. [Lennox, Barker, Haywood, Richardson, Mackenzie, Burney, Reeve, Lee, Smith, Radcliffe]. Dreams. Gothic novel. Women. Imagery. Ruins.

823   Dooley, D. J. "Some Uses and Mutations of the Picaresque." Dalhousie Review, 37 (1958), 363-77. Picaresque novel. Influence and imitation.

824   Duckworth, Alistair M. "Fiction and Some Uses of the Country House Setting from Richardson to Scott." In David C. Streatfield and Alistair M. Duckworth's Landscape in the Gardens and the Literature of Eighteenth-Century England. Los Angeles: Clark Memorial Library, U.C.L.A., 1981, pp. 91-128. [Sir Charles Grandison, Humphry Clinker, Mysteries of Udolpho]. Setting. Country house. Country life.

■825   Duncan, Jeffrey L. "The Rural Ideal in Eighteenth-Century Fiction." Studies in English Literature, 8 (1968), 517-35. [Fielding, Smollett, Sterne, Goldsmith]. Rural ideal [as symbol of values]. Pastoral tradition. Retirement.

●826   Dussinger, John A. The Discourse of the Mind in Eighteenth-Century Fiction. The Hague: Mouton, 1974. [Richardson, Goldsmith, Sterne]. Epistemology. The self.

827   Eastman, Richard M. A Guide to the Novel. New York: Chandler, 1965. Introductory guide [elements of literary analysis].

828   Echeruo, Michael J. C. "The Exo-cultural Hero of the Enlightenment." In his The Conditioned Imagination from Shakespeare to Conrad: Studies in the Exo-cultural Stereotype. London: Macmillan, 1978, pp. 71-92. Noble savage. Blacks. The Jew. Hero/heroine.

829   Ehrenpreis, Irvin. Literary Meaning and Augustan Values. Charlottesville: Univ. Press of Virginia, 1974. Critical revaluation.

830   Elkin, P. K. The Augustan Defence of Satire. Oxford: Clarendon Press, 1973. Satire.

831   Erskine-Hill, Howard. The Augustan Idea in English Literature. Baltimore: Edward Arnold, 1983. Augustanism.

832   Fabian, Bernhard. "English Books and Their Eighteenth-Century German Readers." In The Widening Circle: Essays on the Circulation of Literature in Eighteenth-Century Europe. Ed. Paul J. Korshin. Philadelphia: Univ. of Penn-

sylvania Press, 1976, pp. 117-96. Influence and reputation
abroad. Germany.

833 Flanders, W. Austin. Structures of Experience: History, Society, and Personal Life in the Eighteenth-Century British
Novel. Columbia: Univ. of South Carolina Press, 1984.
[Richardson, Fielding]. Liberalism. The self. Style and
language. Family. Bastardy. Orphans. Crime and punishment. City life.

834 Folkenflik, Robert. "'Homo Alludens' in the Eighteenth Century." Criticism, 24 (1982), 218-32. [Sterne, Fielding,
Swift]. Allusion.

835 Foster, James R. "The Abbé Prévost and the English Novel."
PMLA, 42 (1927), 443-64. [Lee, Reeve, Radcliffe, Smith].
Prévost. Novel of sensibility.

836 Foster, James R. History of the Pre-Romantic Novel in Eng-
land. 1949; rpt. New York: Kraus Reprint, 1966. Pre-
Romantic novel. Sentimentalism. Sensibility. Deism.
Prévost.

837 Foxon, David. Libertine Literature in England, 1660-1745.
New Hyde Park, N.Y.: University Books, 1965. [Esp.
Cleland]. Pornographic novel. Libertinism. Book trade.

838 Friedman, Arthur. "Aspects of Sentimentalism in Eighteenth-
century Literature." In The Augustan Milieu: Essays Presented to Louis A. Landa. Ed. Henry Knight Miller, Eric
Rothstein, and George S. Rousseau. Oxford: Clarendon
Press, 1970, pp. 247-61. Sentimentalism.

■839 Frye, Northrop. "Towards Defining an Age of Sensibility."
ELH: A Journal of English Literary History, 23 (1956), 144-
52. Rpt. in Eighteenth-Century English Literature: Modern
Essays in Criticism. Ed. James L. Clifford. New York:
Oxford Univ. Press, 1959, pp. 311-18. Sensibility.

840 Fussell, Paul. The Rhetorical World of Augustan Humanism:
Ethics and Imagery from Swift to Burke. Oxford: Oxford
Univ. Press, 1965. Imagery [fortification and warfare,
architecture, clothing, travel, open road]. Humanism.
Ethics.

841 Galbraith, Lois Hall. The Established Clergy as Depicted in
English Prose Fiction from 1740 to 1800. Philadelphia:
[Privately printed dissertation, University of Pennsylvania],
1950. The clergy.

842 Gallaway, W. F., Jr. "The Conservative Attitude Toward Fic-

tion, 1770-1830." PMLA, 55 (1940), 1041-59. Eighteenth-
century criticism and reviews of the novel. Conservatism.

843 Garber, Frederick. "Meaning and Mode in Gothic Fiction." In
     Studies in Eighteenth-Century Culture: Racism in the Eight-
     eenth Century. Vol. 2. Ed. Harold E. Pagliaro. Cleveland:
     The Press of Case Western Reserve Univ., 1973, pp. 155-70.
     Gothic novel [an amalgam of genres].

844 Garver, Joseph. "Context of the 'Interesting' Heroine." Eng-
     lish Studies, 63 (1982), 318-34. [Richardson, Sterne, Rad-
     cliffe]. Style and language. Sensibility. Characterizaiton.
     Hero/heroine.

845 Goad, Caroline. Horace in the English Literature of the Eight-
     eenth Century. Yale Studies in English, 58. New Haven,
     Conn.: Yale Univ. Press, 1918. Horace. Classical allu-
     sions.

846 Goldgar, Bertrand A. Walpole and the Wits: The Relation of
     Politics to Literature, 1722-1742. Lincoln: Univ. of Nebraska
     Press, 1976. Sir Robert Walpole. Politics.

■847 Goldknopf, David. "How the Novel Began" and "The Confes-
     sional Increment: A New Look at the I-Narrator." In his
     The Life of the Novel. Chicago: Univ. of Chicago Press,
     1972, pp. 1-41. History of the novel. Innovation. Point
     of view and narrator.

■848 Göller, Karl Heinz. "The Emancipation of Women in Eighteenth-
     Century English Literature." Anglia, 101 (1983), 78-98.
     Women novelists. Feminism [replacement of feminism by
     sentimentalism in women's novels]. Sentimentalism.

849 Gordon, Ian A. "The Century of Prose, 1660-1760." In his
     The Movement of English Prose. Bloomington: Indiana Univ.
     Press, 1966. Style and language [speech-based prose style].

850 Graham, John. "Character Description and Meaning in the
     Romantic Novel." Studies in Romanticism, 5 (1966), 208-18.
     [Fielding, Godwin, Smith, Lewis]. Characterization [shift
     from emphasis on character's action to internal development].
     Physiognomy. Romantic novel.

851 Greene, Donald. "The Study of Eighteenth-Century Literature:
     Past, Present, and Future." In New Approaches to Eight-
     eenth-Century Literature. Ed. Phillip Harth. New York:
     Columbia Univ. Press, 1974, pp. 1-32. Critical revaluation.
     Pedagogical approach.

852 Gregory, Allene. The French Revolution and the English Novel.

1915; rpt. New York: Haskell House, 1966. [Bage, Inchbald, Smith, Wollstonecraft, Holcroft, Godwin]. Jacobin
novel. French Revolution. Radicalism.

853 Greiner, Walter F., ed. English Theories of the Novel. Vol.
II: Eighteenth Century. Tübingen: Max Niemeyer Verlag,
1970. [Anthology of criticism]. Theory and practice of the
novel. Eighteenth-century criticism and reviews of the
novel. Novelists on the novel.

854 Guilhamet, Leon. "The Novel of Sincerity." In his The Sin-
cere Ideal: Studies on Sincerity in Eighteenth-Century English Literature. Montreal: McGill-Queen's Univ. Press,
1974, pp. 287-99. [Richardson]. Sincerity. Novel of
sincerity.

855 Hagstrum, Jean H. "'Such, Such Were the Joys': The Boy-
hood of the Man of Feeling." In Changing Taste in Eighteenth-Century Art and Literature: Papers Read at a Clark
Library Seminar April 17, 1971. Ed. Robert E. Moore and
Jean H. Hagstrum. Los Angeles: Clark Memorial Library,
U.C.L.A., 1972, pp. 43-62. "Man of Feeling." The adolescent.

856 Halsband, Robert. "Ladies of Letters in the Eighteenth Cen-
tury." In Irvin Ehrenpreis and Robert Halsband's The
Lady of Letters in the Eighteenth Century. Los Angeles:
Clark Memorial Library, U.C.L.A., 1969, pp. 30-51. Women.
The bluestocking.

857 Halsband, Robert. "Lady Mary Wortley Montagu and Eighteenth-Century Fiction." Philological Quarterly, 45 (1966),
145-56. Eighteenth-century criticism and reviews of the
novel. Lady Mary Wortley Montagu.

858 Halsband, Robert. "Women and Literature in 18th-Century
England." In Woman in the 18th Century and Other Essays.
Ed. Paul Fritz and Richard Morton. Toronto: Hakkert,
1976, pp. 55-71. Women. Women novelists.

859 Hart, Francis Russell. "The Experience of Character in the
English Gothic Novel." In Experience in the Novel: Selected
Papers from the English Institute. Ed. Roy Harvey Pearce.
New York: Columbia Univ. Press, 1968, pp. 83-105. Char-
acterization. Gothic novel ["a naturalizing of myth and
romance"].

860 Hart, Francis Russell. "Limits of the Gothic: The Scottish
Example." In Studies in Eighteenth-Century Culture. Vol.
3. Ed. Harold E. Pagliaro. Cleveland: Press of Case
Western Reserve Univ., 1973, pp. 137-54. [Smollett]. Gothic
novel. Scottish novel. The grotesque. Horror and terror.

861 Hart, Francis Russell. The Scottish Novel: From Smollett to
    Spark. Cambridge, Mass.: Harvard Univ. Press, 1978.
    Scottish novel.

862 Hayden, Lucy K. "The Black Presence in Eighteenth-Century
    British Novels." College Language Association Journal, 24
    (1981), 400-15. Blacks.

863 Hayman, John G. "On Reading an Eighteenth-Century Page."
    Essays in Criticism, 12 (1962), 388-401. [Thrale, Fielding,
    Johnson]. Style and language.

864 Heffernan, William. "The Slave Trade and Abolition in Travel
    Literature." Journal of the History of Ideas, 34 (1973),
    185-208. Travel literature. Slavery.

865 Heilman, Robert Bechtold. America in English Fiction, 1760-
    1800: The Influence of the American Revolution. 1937; rpt.
    New York: Octagon, 1968. American Revolution. The
    American. Radicalism. Satire. Politics. Economics.

866 Hemmings, F. W. J. "Realism and the Novel: The Eighteenth-
    Century Beginnings." In The Age of Realism. Ed. F. W. J.
    Hemmings. Harmondsworth: Penguin, 1974, pp. 9-35.
    Realism.

867 Hilliard, Raymond F. "Desire and the Structure of Eighteenth-
    Century Fiction." In Studies in Eighteenth-Century Culture.
    Vol. 9. Ed. Roseann Runte. Madison: Univ. of Wisconsin
    Press, 1979, pp. 357-70. Plot, structure, and design. De-
    sire.

868 Hogle, Jerrold E. "The Restless Labyrinth: Cryptonymy in
    the Gothic Novel." Arizona Quarterly, 36 (1980), 330-58.
    [Walpole, Radcliffe, Lewis, Beckford]. Cryptonymy. Gothic
    novel.

869 Holland, Norman N., and Leona F. Sherman. "Gothic Possibil-
    ities." New Literary History, 8 (1977), 279-94. Gothic
    novel. Symbolism. Psychology. Epistemology.

870 Horn, András. Byron's "Don Juan" and the Eighteenth-Century
    English Novel. Swiss Studies in English, 51. Bern:
    Francke Verlag, 1962. [Fielding, Smollett, Sterne]. Moral-
    ity. Picaresque novel. Subjectivity. Byron.

871 Horner, Joyce M. "The English Women Novelists and Their
    Connection with the Feminist Movement (1688-1797)." Smith
    College Studies in Modern Languages, 11, Nos. 1, 2, 3
    (1929-1930), 1-152. [Manley, Haywood, S. Fielding, Lennox,
    Radcliffe, Barker, Burney]. Feminism. Women novelists.

•872 Howells, Coral Ann. Love, Mystery and Misery: Feeling in
      Gothic Fiction. London: Athlone Press, 1978. [Radcliffe,
      Lewis]. Gothic novel. Love. Mystery. Misery. Minerva
      Press.

873   Hughes, Helen Sard. "English Epistolary Fiction Before Pam-
      ela." In The Manly Anniversary Studies in Language and
      Literature. 1923; rpt. Freeport, N.Y.: Books for Li-
      braries Press, 1968, pp. 156-69. Epistolary novel.

874   Hughes, Helen Sard. "The Middle-Class Reader and the Eng-
      lish Novel." Journal of English and Germanic Philology,
      25 (1926), 362-78. Reading public. The middle class.

875   Hughes, Peter. "Allusion and Expression in Eighteenth-Cen-
      tury Literature." In The Author in His Works: Essays on
      a Problem in Criticism. Eds. Louis L. Martz and Aubrey
      Williams. New Haven, Conn.: Yale Univ. Press, 1978, pp.
      297-317. Allusion.

876   Hughes, Peter. "Language, History & Vision: An Approach
      to 18th-Century Literature." In The Varied Pattern:
      Studies in the 18th Century. Ed. Peter Hughes and David
      Williams. Toronto: Hakkert, 1971, pp. 77-96. Style and
      language.

877   Hume, Martin. "The Picaresque and Peripatetic Novels in
      England." In his Spanish Influence on English Literature.
      1904; rpt. New York: Haskell House, 1964, pp. 156-83.
      Picaresque novel. Sources, analogues, and influences.
      Spain.

■878 Hume, Robert D. "Gothic Versus Romance: A Revaluation of
      the Gothic Novel." PMLA, 84 (1969), 282-90. See also
      Robert L. Platzner and Robert D. Hume, "'Gothic Versus
      Romantic': A Rejoinder [an exchange]," PMLA, 86 (1971),
      266-74. Gothic novel. Romanticism. Horror and terror.
      Critical revaluation.

879   Hunter, J. Paul. "Biography and the Novel." Modern Lan-
      guage Studies, 9 (1979), 68-84. Historical façade. Biog-
      raphy.

880   Hunter, J. Paul. "The Insistent I." Novel, 13 (1979), 19-37.
      The self. Subjectivity. Point of view and narrator.

881   Hunter, J. Paul. "'Peace' and the Augustans: Some Implica-
      tions of Didactic Method and Literary Form." In Studies in
      Change and Revolution: Aspects of English Intellectual His-
      tory, 1640-1800. Ed. Paul J. Korshin. Menston, Yorkshire:
      Scolar Press, 1972, pp. 161-89. Didacticism. Philosophy of
      novelist. Social criticism in the novel.

882 Hunter, Kathryn. "The Informing Word: Verbal Strategies
     in Visual Satire." In Studies in Eighteenth-Century Culture.
     Vol. 4. Ed. Harold E. Pagliaro. Madison: Univ. of Wis-
     consin Press, 1975, pp. 271-96. Style and language.

883 Jefferson, D. W. "Speculations on Three Eighteenth-Century
     Prose Writers." In Of Books and Humankind: Essays and
     Poems Presented to Bonamy Dobrée. Ed. John Butt. Lon-
     don: Routledge & Kegan Paul, 1964, pp. 81-91. [Gold-
     smith, Johnson, Smollett]. Style and language.

884 Johnson, Clifford R. Plots and Characters in the Fiction of
     Eighteenth-Century English Authors: Volume I: Jonathan
     Swift, Daniel Defoe, and Samuel Richardson. Hamden,
     Conn.: Shoe String Press, 1977. Volume II: Henry Field-
     ing, Tobias Smollett, Laurence Sterne, Samuel Johnson, and
     Oliver Goldsmith. Hamden, Conn.: Shoe String Press,
     1978. Synopses.

885 Kahane, Claire. "Gothic Mirrors and Feminine Identity."
     Centennial Review, 24 (1980), 43-64. Women. Gothic novel.

•886 Karl, Frederick R. A Reader's Guide to the Eighteenth-Cen-
     tury English Novel. New York: Noonday, 1974. See esp.
     "Introduction: The Novel as Subversion," pp. 3-54, and
     "The Development of Technique in the Eighteenth-Century
     Novel," pp. 290-336. [Includes discussion of many minor
     novelists]. Conventions of the Georgian novel. Innovation.
     Narrative technique. Novel as subversive form. Realism
     [useful list of fifteen recurring elements of eighteenth-
     century literary realism, pp. 13-14].

887 Kaufman, Pamela. "Burke, Freud, and the Gothic." Studies
     in Burke and His Time, 13 (1972), 2179-92. Gothic novel.
     Burke. Freud. Horror and terror.

888 Kay, Donald. Short Fiction in "The Spectator." University:
     Univ. of Alabama Press, 1975. Short fiction [varied types
     of]. The Spectator. Addison and Steele.

889 Kearful, Frank J. "Spanish Rogues and English Foundlings:
     On the Disintegration of Picaresque." Genre, 4 (1971), 376-
     91. Picaresque novel.

890 Keech, James M. "The Survival of the Gothic Response."
     Studies in the Novel, 6 (1974), 130-44. Gothic novel.

891 Kelly, Gary D. The English Jacobin Novel, 1780-1805. Ox-
     ford: Clarendon Press, 1976. [Bage, Inchbald, Holcroft,
     Godwin]. Jacobin novel. Social criticism in the novel.
     Politics.

892   Kelly, Gary D. "'Intellectual Physicks': Necessity and the
      English Jacobin Novel." Etudes Anglaises, 31 (1978), 161-
      75. Jacobin novel. Necessity.

892a Kenny, Virginia C. The Country-House Ethos in English Lit-
      erature, 1688-1750: Themes of Personal Retreat and National
      Expansion. New York: St. Martin's, 1984. [Defoe]. Coun-
      try house. Retirement. British Empire.

893   Kern, Jean B. "The Fallen Woman, from the Perspective of
      Five Early Eighteenth-Century Women Novelists." In Studies
      in Eighteenth-Century Culture. Vol. 10. Ed. Harry C.
      Payne. Madison: Univ. of Wisconsin Press, 1981, pp. 457-
      68. [Aubin, Hearn, Haywood, Manley, "Ma A"]. The "fallen
      woman." Women novelists. Sex. Realism. Novel of man-
      ners.

894   Kettle, Arnold. "The Eighteenth Century." In his An Intro-
      duction to the English Novel. 1951; rpt. New York:
      Harper, 1960, I, 41-86. History of the novel.

895   Kettle, Arnold. "The Precursors of Defoe: Puritanism and
      the Rise of the Novel." In On the Novel: A Present for
      Walter Allen on His 60th Birthday from His Friends and Col-
      leagues. Ed. B. S. Benedikz. London: Dent, 1971, pp.
      206-17. Puritanism. Realism.

896   Kiely, Robert. The Romantic Novel in England. Cambridge,
      Mass.: Harvard Univ. Press, 1972. [Walpole, Beckford,
      Radcliffe, Godwin, Lewis]. Romantic novel. Gothic novel.

897   Klein, Michael, and Gillian Parker, eds. The English Novel
      and the Movies. New York: Ungar, 1981. [Robinson
      Crusoe, Joseph Andrews, Tom Jones]. Film and the novel.

898   Knowles, A. S., Jr. "Defoe, Swift, and Fielding: Notes on
      the Retirement Theme." In Quick Springs of Sense: Studies
      in the Eighteenth Century. Ed. Larry S. Champion. Athens:
      Univ. of Georgia Press, 1974, pp. 121-36. Retirement.
      Comparison of novelists. Rural ideal.

899   Knox, Norman. The Word "Irony" and Its Context, 1500-1755.
      Durham, N.C.: Duke Univ. Press, 1961. Irony. Semantics.

900   Kooiman-Van Middendorp, Gerarda Maria. The Hero in the
      Feminine Novel. 1931; rpt. New York: Haskell House,
      1966. Characterization. Women novelists. Hero/heroine.

901   Korshin, Paul J. "The Development of Abstracted Typology in
      England, 1650-1820." In Literary Uses of Typology from the
      Late Middle Ages to the Present. Ed. Earl Miner. Prince-

ton, N.J.: Princeton Univ. Press, 1976, pp. 147-203.
Typology.

902 Korshin, Paul J. "Probability and Character in the Eighteenth
Century." In Probability, Time, and Space in Eighteenth-
Century Literature. Ed. Paula Backscheider. New York:
AMS Press, 1979, pp. 63-77. Characterization. Probability.

903 Korshin, Paul J. "Typology and the Novel." In his Typol-
ogies in England, 1650-1820. Princeton, N.J.: Princeton
Univ. Press, 1982, pp. 186-268. Typology. Narrative techniques.

904 Kovačević, Ivanka. "Part I: Introduction." In her Fact into
Fiction: English Literature and the Industrial Scene, 1750-
1850. Leicester: Leicester Univ. Press, 1975, pp. 11-128.
Industrial Revolution [survey of literary responses to indus-
trialism].

905 Kramnick, Isaac. "Children's Literature and Bourgeois Ideology: Observations on Culture and Industrial Capitalism in
the Later Eighteenth Century." In Culture and Politics from
Puritanism to the Enlightenment. Ed. Perez Zagorin. Berkeley: Univ. of California Press, 1980, pp. 203-40. Children's
literature. Capitalism. Bourgeois ideology.

906 Krieger, Murray. "Fiction and Historical Reality: The Hour-
glass and the Sands of Time." In Literature and History.
Papers Read at a Clark Library Seminar, March 3, 1973.
Los Angeles: Clark Memorial Library, U.C.L.A., 1974.
Time. Historical façade. Realism.

907 Kropf, Carl R. "Libel and Satire in the Eighteenth Century."
Eighteenth-Century Studies, 8 (1974-1975), 153-68. Libel.
Satire. Law.

■908 Kropf, Carl R. "Unity and the Study of Eighteenth-Century
Literature." The Eighteenth Century: Theory and Interpretation, 21 (1980), 25-40. Unity [not a desideratum in
eighteenth-century literary theory and practice]. Critical
revaluation.

909 Lerenbaum, Miriam. "'Mistresses of Orthodoxy': Education in
the Lives and Writings of Late Eighteenth-Century English
Women Writers." Proceedings of the American Philosophical
Society, 121 (1977), 281-301. Education. Women novelists.

910 Le Tellier, Robert Ignatius. An Intensifying Vision of Evil:
The Gothic Novel (1764-1820) as a Self-Contained Literary
Cycle. Salzburg: Inst. für Anglistik und Amerikanistik,
Univ. of Salzburg, 1980. [Esp. Radcliffe, Walpole, Lewis,

Beckford]. Gothic novel. Evil. Gothic hero [types of].
Setting. Plot, structure, and design.

911 Levin, Harry. "The Wages of Satire." In Literature and So-
ciety: Selected Papers from the English Institute, 1978.
Ed. Edward W. Said. Baltimore: The Johns Hopkins Univ.
Press, 1980, pp. 1-14. Satire.

912 Lewis, Paul. "Beyond Mystery: Emergence from Delusion as
a Pattern in Gothic Fiction." Gothic, 2 (1980), 7-13. Plot,
structure, and design. Gothic novel. Delusion. Mystery.

913 Lewis, Paul. "Fearful Lessons: The Didacticism of the Early
Gothic Novel." College Language Association Journal, 23
(1980), 470-84. [Radcliffe, Lewis]. Gothic novel. Didacticism.

914 Lewis, Paul. "Mysterious Laughter: Humor and Fear in Gothic
Fiction." Genre, 14 (1981), 309-27. Comedy. Fear. Gothic
novel.

915 Lovecraft, H. P. "Supernatural Horror in Fiction." 1927;
rpt. in his Dagon and Other Macabre Tales. Ed. August
Derleth. Sauk City, Wis.: Arkham, 1965. Gothic novel.
Horror and terror.

916 Lutwack, Leonard. "Mixed and Uniform Prose Styles in the
Novel." Journal of Aesthetics and Art Criticism, 18 (1959-
1960), 350-57. Style and language.

917 Lyndenberg, Robin. "Gothic Architecture and Fiction: A
Survey of Critical Responses." Centennial Review, 22
(1978), 95-109. Gothic novel. Architecture. Survey of
criticism.

918 Lyons, John O. The Invention of the Self: The Hinge of
Consciousness in the Eighteenth Century. Carbondale:
Southern Illinois Univ. Press, 1978. [Fielding, Cleland,
Sterne]. The self. Travel. Pornographic novel.

919 MacAndrew, Elizabeth. The Gothic Tradition in Fiction. New
York: Columbia Univ. Press, 1979. Gothic novel. Characterization.

920 MacCarthy, B. G. The Later Women Novelists, 1744-1818.
Oxford: Blackwell, 1947. [Aubin, Reeve, Haywood, Sheridan, Lennox, F. Brooke, Robinson, Burney, Smith, Radcliffe, Wollstonecraft, Hays, Inchbald]. Women novelists.

921 MacCarthy, B. G. Women Writers: Their Contribution to the
English Novel, 1621-1744. Oxford: Blackwell, 1944. [Man-

ley, Haywood, Rowe, Barker, Aubin, Davys, S. Fielding].
Women novelists.

922 MacDonald, Ruth K. Literature for Children in England:
     1659-1774. Troy, N.Y.: Whitston, 1982. Children's liter-
     ature.

923 Macey, Samuel L. "Clocks and Chronology in the Novels from
     Defoe to Austen." Eighteenth-Century Life, 7 (1982), 96-
     104. Time. Symbolism [clocks, watches]. "Clockwork"
     analogy.

924 MacLean, Kenneth. John Locke and English Literature of the
     Eighteenth Century. New Haven, Conn.: Yale Univ.
     Press, 1936. Locke. Sources, analogues, and influences.
     Intellectual background.

925 Madoff, Mark. "The Useful Myth of Gothic Ancestry." Studies
     in Eighteenth-Century Culture. Vol. 8. Ed. Roseann
     Runte. Madison: Univ. of Wisconsin Press, 1979, pp. 337-
     50. [Reeve, Lewis]. Gothic background. Gothic novel.

926 Major, John Campbell. The Role of Personal Memoirs in Eng-
     lish Biography and Novel. Philadelphia: Univ. of Pennsyl-
     vania Press, 1935. Memoirs. Biography.

927 Malins, Edward. English Landscaping and Literature, 1660-
     1840. London: Oxford Univ. Press, 1966. Literature and
     the other arts. Aesthetic theory and background. Land-
     scape gardening.

928 Maresca, Thomas E. Epic to Novel. Columbus: Ohio State
     Univ. Press, 1974. [Swift, Fielding]. Epic. Plot, struc-
     ture, and design. Contrast as technique [structural paral-
     lels in Fielding's novels].

929 Marshall, Roderick. Italy in English Literature, 1755-1815:
     Origins of the Romantic Interest in Italy. Columbia Univer-
     sity Studies in English and Comparative Literature. New
     York: Columbia Univ. Press, 1934. [Beckford, Radcliffe].
     Italy. Setting.

930 Martin, Robert Bernard. "Notes Toward a Comic Fiction." In
     The Theory of the Novel: New Essays. Ed. John Halperin.
     New York: Oxford Univ. Press, 1974, pp. 71-90. Comedy.

930a Matthews, William. "Some Eighteenth-Century Vulgarisms."
     Review of English Studies, O.S. 13 (1937), 307-25. Style
     and language [vulgarisms and misspellings, esp. by servants,
     are means in the literature of burlesquing lack of education].
     Parody.

931 May, Georges. "The Influence of English Fiction on the
     French Mid-Eighteenth Century Novel." In Aspects of the
     Eighteenth Century. Ed. Earl R. Wasserman. Baltimore:
     The Johns Hopkins Univ. Press, 1965, pp. 265-80. Influ-
     ence and reputation abroad. France.

932 May, Keith M. "The Eighteenth Century." In his Characters
     of Women in Narrative Literature. New York: St. Martin's,
     1981, pp. 33-57. [Defoe, Richardson, Fielding]. Women.
     Characterization. Comparison of novelists.

933 Mayo, Robert D. The English Novel in the Magazines, 1740-
     1815. With a Catalogue of 1375 Magazine Novels and Novel-
     ettes. Evanston, Ill.: Northwestern Univ. Press, 1962.
     Novel in magazines. Bibliography of primary sources.

934 Mayo, Robert D. "How Long Was Gothic Fiction in Vogue?"
     Modern Language Notes, 58 (1943), 58-64. Gothic back-
     ground. Reading public. Best sellers.

935 McCullen, J. T., Jr. "Tobacco: A Recurrent Theme in Eight-
     eenth-Century Literature." Bulletin of the Rocky Mountain
     Modern Language Association, 22 (1968), 30-39. Tobacco.

936 McCullough, N. Verrle. The Negro in English Literature: A
     Critical Introduction. Ilfracombe, Devon: Arthur H. Stock-
     well, 1962. Blacks.

937 McGlinchee, Claire. "'The Smile of Reason': Its Metamorphosis
     in Late 18th-Century Architecture and Literature." Studies
     on Voltaire and the Eighteenth Century, 89 (1972), 993-1001.
     Architecture. Reason.

938 McGlynn, Paul D. "Microcosm and the Aesthetics of Eight-
     eenth-Century British Literature." Studies in English Liter-
     ature, 19 (1979), 363-85. Microcosm. Theory and practice
     of the novel.

939 McGuirk, Carol. "Sentimental Encounter in Sterne, Mackenzie,
     and Burns." Studies in English Literature, 20 (1980), 505-
     15. Sentimentalism. Sympathy.

940 McIntosh, Carey. "Quantities of Qualities: Nominal Style and
     the Novel." In Studies in Eighteenth-Century Culture. Vol.
     4. Ed. Harold E. Pagliaro. Madison: Univ. of Wisconsin
     Press, 1975, pp. 139-53. For a response see Elizabeth Mac-
     Andrew, ibid., pp. 155-59. Style and language.

941 McIntyre, Clara F. "The Later Career of the Elizabethan Vil-
     lain-Hero." PMLA, 40 (1925), 874-80. Characterization.
     Villain. Hero/heroine.

942 McKee, John B. Literary Irony and the Literary Audience:
     Studies in the Victimization of the Reader in Augustan Fic-
     tion. Amsterdam: Rodopi, 1974. [Tom Jones, Gulliver's
     Travels, Tristram Shandy]. Irony. Point of view and nar-
     rator. Author-reader relationship.

943 McKenzie, Alan T. "The Countenance You Showed Me: Read-
     ing the Passions in the Eighteenth Century." Georgia Re-
     view, 32 (1978), 758-73. The passions. Physiognomy.

•944 McKillop, Alan Dugald. The Early Masters of English Fiction.
     Lawrence: Univ. of Kansas Press, 1956. [Defoe, Richard-
     son, Fielding, Smollett, Sterne]. Introductory guide [excel-
     lent account of main issues].

945 McKillop, Alan Dugald. English Literature from Dryden to
     Burns. New York: Appleton-Century-Crofts, 1948. Intro-
     ductory guide.

946 McVeagh, John. Tradefull Merchants: The Portrayal of the
     Capitalist in Literature. London: Routledge & Kegan Paul,
     1981, esp. pp. 53-127. [Defoe, Fielding, Smollett]. The
     merchant. Capitalism. Economics.

947 Mews, Hazel. Frail Vessels: Women's Roles in Women's Novels
     from Fanny Burney to George Eliot. London: Athlone
     Press, 1969. Women. Women novelists.

948 Miles, Josephine. "A Change in the Language in Literature."
     Eighteenth-Century Studies, 2 (1968), 35-44. Style and
     language.

949 Milic, Louis T. "Observations on Conversational Style." In
     English Writers of the Eighteenth Century. Ed. John H.
     Middendorf. New York: Columbia Univ. Press, 1971, pp.
     273-87. Style and language.

950 Miller, Henry Knight. "Augustan Prose Fiction and the Ro-
     mance Tradition." Studies in the Eighteenth Century III.
     Ed. R. F. Brissenden and J. C. Eade. Toronto: Univ. of
     Toronto Press, 1976, pp. 241-55. Romance. Sources, ana-
     logues, and influences.

951 Miller, Nancy K. The Heroine's Text: Readings in the French
     and English Novel, 1722-1782. New York: Columbia Univ.
     Press, 1980. [Moll Flanders, Pamela, Fanny Hill, Clarissa].
     Women. Plot, structure, and design. Hero/heroine.

952 Miller, Stuart. The Picaresque Novel. Cleveland: The Press
     of Case Western Reserve Univ., 1967. Picaresque novel.
     Plot, structure, and design. Rogue hero [traits of]. Point
     of view and narrator. Style and language. Closure.

953 Mish, Charles C. "Early Eighteenth-Century Best Sellers in
     English Prose Fiction." Papers of the Bibliographical Society
     of America, 75 (1981), 413-18. [Before Richardson]. Best
     sellers. Book trade.

954 Mish, Charles C. "A Note on the Fiction Reprint Market in
     the Early Eighteenth Century." Newberry Library Bulletin,
     3 (1954), 201-05. Book trade. Best sellers.

955 Modder, Montagu Frank. The Jew in the Literature of Eng-
     land to the End of the 19th Century. Philadelphia: Jewish
     Publication Society of America, 1939. The Jew.

956 Monk, Samuel H. The Sublime: A Study of the Critical The-
     ories in XVIII-Century England. 1935; rpt. Ann Arbor:
     Univ. of Michigan Press, 1962. Aesthetic theory and back-
     ground. The sublime and the beautiful.

957 Monteser, Frederick. "The Picaro in British Literature." In
     his The Picaresque Element in Western Literature. Studies
     in the Humanities, No. 5. University: Univ. of Alabama
     Press, 1975, pp. 41-70. Picaresque novel. Rogue hero.

958 Moore, C. A. "The English Malady." In his Backgrounds of
     English Literature, 1700-60. Minneapolis: Univ. of Minnesota
     Press, 1953, pp. 179-235. Melancholy.

959 Moore, Robert Etheridge. Hogarth's Literary Relationships.
     1948; rpt. New York: Octagon, 1969. [Fielding, Smollett].
     Hogarth.

960 Morgan, Charlotte E. The Rise of the Novel of Manners: A
     Study of English Prose Fiction Between 1600 and 1740. 1911;
     rpt. New York: Russell & Russell, 1963. Novel of manners.
     Popular novel.

961 Muecke, D. C. The Compass of Irony. London: Methuen,
     1969. Irony.

962 Mylne, Vivienne. "The Punctuation of Dialogue in Eighteenth-
     Century French and English Fiction." Library, 1 (1979),
     43-61. Speech and dialogue. Punctuation.

963 Nelson, Lowry, Jr. "Night Thoughts on the Gothic Novel."
     Yale Review, 52 (1962), 236-57. Gothic background. The
     wanderer.

■964 New, Melvyn. "'The Grease of God': The Form of 18th-Cen-
     tury English Fiction." PMLA, 91 (1976), 235-44. Provi-
     dence. Christianity. Plot, structure, and design.

965   Newell, A. G. "Early Evangelical Fiction." Evangelical Quar-
      terly, 38 (1967), 3-21, 81-98. [More, R. Hill, L. Richmond,
      Mrs. Sherwood]. Evangelical fiction.

966   Newlin, Claude M. "The English Periodicals and the Novel,
      1709-1740." Papers of the Michigan Academy of Sciences,
      Arts and Letters, 16 (1932), 467-76. Novel in magazines.

967   Noel, Thomas. Theories of the Fable in the Eighteenth Cen-
      tury. New York: Columbia Univ. Press, 1975. Fable.

968   Norton, Rictor. "Aesthetic Gothic Horror." Yearbook of Com-
      parative and General Literature, 21 (1972), 31-40. Gothic
      novel. Horror and terror.

969   Novak, Maximillian E. "The Extended Moment: Time, Dream,
      History, and Perspective in Eighteenth-Century Fiction."
      In Probability, Time, and Space in Eighteenth-Century Lit-
      erature. Ed. Paula Backscheider. New York: AMS Press,
      1979, pp. 141-66. Time. Dreams. Historiography.

■970 Novak, Maximillian E. "Fiction and Society in the Early Eight-
      eenth Century." In England in the Restoration and Early
      Eighteenth Century: Essays on Culture and Society. Ed.
      H. T. Swedenberg, Jr. Berkeley: Univ. of California
      Press, 1972, pp. 51-70. Reading public [preferences in fic-
      tion]. Social background [how fiction influenced and was
      influenced by social change].

971   Novak, Maximillian E. "Freedom, Libertinism, and the Picar-
      esque." In Studies in Eighteenth-Century Culture. Vol. 3.
      Ed. Harold E. Pagliaro. Cleveland: Press of Case Western
      Reserve Univ., 1973, pp. 35-48. Picaresque novel. Liber-
      tinism.

972   Novak, Maximillian E. "Gothic Fiction and the Grotesque."
      Novel, 13 (1979), 50-67. [Esp. Radcliffe]. Gothic novel.
      The grotesque. Supernatural [demons represent a sudden
      revelation of the uncontrolled forces of the mind]. Land-
      scape.

973   Novak, Maximillian E. "The Wild Man Comes to Tea." In The
      Wild Man Within: An Image in Western Thought from the
      Renaissance to Romanticism. Ed. Edward Dudley and Maxi-
      millian E. Novak. Pittsburgh: Univ. of Pittsburgh Press,
      1972, pp. 183-221. [Defoe, Swift]. Noble Savage.

974   Noyes, Robert Gale. "Congreve and His Comedies in the
      Eighteenth-Century Novel." Philological Quarterly, 39 (1960),
      464-80. Congreve. Comedy.

•975 Noyes, Robert Gale. The Neglected Muse: Restoration and
      Eighteenth-Century Tragedy in the Novel (1740-1780).
      Providence, R.I.: Brown Univ. Press, 1958. Tragedy.
      Dramatic conventions in the novel.

•976 Noyes, Robert Gale. The Thespian Mirror: Shakespeare in
      the Eighteenth-Century Novel. Providence, R.I.: Brown
      Univ. Press, 1953. Shakespearean influence.

977   Olshin, Toby. "Form and Theme in Novels About Non-Human
      Characters, a Neglected Sub-Genre." Genre, 2 (1969), 43-
      54. [Fielding, Coventry, Johnstone, Smollett]. Novel about
      non-human characters.

978   Ousby, Ian. Bloodhounds of Heaven: The Detective in Eng-
      lish Fiction from Godwin to Doyle. Cambridge, Mass.: Har-
      vard Univ. Press, 1976. [Defoe, Fielding, Godwin]. The
      detective. Crime and punishment. Jonathan Wild.

■979 Park, William. "What Was New About the 'New Species of Writ-
      ing'?" Studies in the Novel, 2 (1970), 112-30. Conventions
      of the Georgian novel. Innovation.

980   Parke, Catherine. "Vision and Revision: A Model for Reading
      the Eighteenth-Century Novel of Education." Eighteenth-
      Century Studies, 16 (1982-83), 162-74. [A Sentimental
      Journey, Evelina]. Novel of education. Plot, structure, and
      design.

981   Parker, Alexander A. "The Picaresque Tradition in England
      and France." In his Literature and the Delinquent: The
      Picaresque Novel in Spain and Europe, 1599-1753. Edin-
      burgh: The University Press, 1967, pp. 99-137. Picaresque
      novel. Rogue hero.

982   Parkinson, C. Northcote. Portsmouth Point: The British Navy
      in Fiction, 1793-1815. 1948. Rpt. West Orange, N.J.:
      Saifer, n.d. The navy. Naval novel.

983   Parks, George B. "The Turn of the Romantic in the Travel
      Literature of the Eighteenth Century." Modern Language
      Quarterly, 25 (1964), 22-33. Nature. Travel literature.

984   Parnell, Paul E. "The Sentimental Mask." PMLA, 78 (1963),
      529-35. Sentimentalism.

985   Patterson, Sylvia. "Eighteenth-Century Children's Literature
      in England: A Mirror of Its Culture." Journal of Popular
      Culture, 13 (1979), 38-43. Children's literature.

986   Pattison, Robert. "The Preromantic English Tradition." In his

The Child Figure in English Literature. Athens: Univ. of
Georgia Press, 1978, pp. 21-75. [Tom Jones, Tristram
Shandy]. Children.

987 Paulson, Ronald. The Fictions of Satire. Baltimore: The
Johns Hopkins Univ. Press, 1967. [Esp. Swift]. Satire.

988 Paulson, Ronald. "Gothic Fiction and the French Revolution."
ELH: A Journal of English Literary History, 48 (1981),
532-54. [The Monk]. Gothic novel [connects horror in
novels of 1790s with the horror of events in France]. French
Revolution. Rebellion. Sex.

989 Paulson, Ronald. "Life as Journey and as Theater: Two
Eighteenth-Century Narrative Structures." New Literary
History, 8 (1976), 43-58. Journey. Theater motif. Plot,
structure, and design. Hogarth.

•990 Paulson, Ronald. Satire and the Novel in Eighteenth-Century
England. New Haven, Conn.: Yale Univ. Press, 1967.
[Esp. Fielding, Smollett, Sterne]. Satire. Realism. Ro-
mance. Sentimentalism. Novel of manners.

991 Perry, Ruth. Women, Letters, and the Novel. AMS Studies
in the Eighteenth Century, No. 4. New York: AMS Press,
1980. Women.

992 Pickering, Samuel F., Jr. "The Evolution of a Genre: Fictional Biographies for Children in the Eighteenth Century."
Journal of Narrative Technique, 7 (1977), 1-23. Children's
literature. Biography.

993 Pickering, Samuel F., Jr. John Locke and Children's Literature in Eighteenth-Century England. Knoxville: Univ. of
Tennessee Press, 1981. Children's literature. Locke.

994 Pickering, Samuel F., Jr. The Moral Tradition in English
Fiction, 1785-1850. Hanover, N.H.: The University Press
of New England, 1976. Morality.

995 Pierce, Robert B. "Moral Education in the Novel of the 1750's."
Philological Quarterly, 44 (1965), 73-87. [Fielding, Lennox,
Haywood, Cleland]. Morality. Didacticism.

996 Piper, William Bowman. "Common Sense as a Basis of Literary
Style." Texas Studies in Literature and Language, 18
(1977), 624-41. Common sense. Style and language.

997 Pitcher, Edward W. "Changes in Short Fiction in Britain,
1785-1810: Philosophic Tales, Gothic Tales, and Fragments
and Visions." Studies in Short Fiction, 13 (1976), 331-54.
Short fiction.

998   Pitcher, Edward W. "On the Conventions of Eighteenth-Cen-
      tury British Short Fiction: Part I: 1700-1760; Part II:
      1760-1785." Studies in Short Fiction, 12 (1975), 199-212,
      327-41. Short fiction. Conventions of the Georgian novel.

999   Politi, Jina. The Novel and Its Presuppositions: Changes in
      the Conceptual Structure of Novels in the 18th and 19th
      Centuries. Amsterdam: Hakkert, 1976. Philosophy of
      novelist. Epistemology. Theory and practice of the novel.

1000 Porte, Joel. "In the Hands of an Angry God: Religious Ter-
      ror in Gothic Fiction." In The Gothic Imagination: Essays
      in Dark Romanticism. Ed. G. R. Thompson. N.p.: Wash-
      ington State Univ. Press, 1974, pp. 42-64. Horror and
      terror. Christianity.

1001 Praz, Mario. The Romantic Agony. Trans. Angus Davidson.
      1933. 2nd ed. London: Oxford Univ. Press, 1951. [Rad-
      cliffe, Lewis, Richardson]. Gothic hero. Women. Sade.
      Romantic novel.

•1002 Preston, John. The Created Self: The Reader's Role in
      Eighteenth-Century Fiction. New York: Barnes & Noble,
      1970. [Defoe, Richardson, Fielding, Sterne]. Author-
      reader relationship.

1003 Preston, Thomas R. "From Typology to Literature: Hermen-
      eutics and Historical Narrative in Eighteenth-Century Eng-
      land." The Eighteenth-Century: Theory and Interpreta-
      tion, 23 (1982), 181-96. Historiography. Typology. Her-
      meneutics.

•1004 Preston, Thomas R. Not in Timon's Manner: Feeling, Mis-
      anthropy, and Satire in Eighteenth-Century England. Uni-
      versity: Univ. of Alabama Press, 1975. [Smollett, John-
      son, Fielding, S. Fielding, Burney, Bage, Goldsmith, Mac-
      kenzie]. Misanthropy ["Benevolent misanthropy"]. Satire.
      "Man of Feeling."

■1004a Price, John Valdimir. "Patterns of Sexual Behaviour in Some
      Eighteenth-Century Novels." In Sexuality in Eighteenth-
      Century Britain. Ed. Paul-Gabriel Boucé. Totowa, N.J.:
      Barnes & Noble, 1982, pp. 159-75. [Defoe, Fielding, Rich-
      ardson, Smollett]. Sex.

1005 Price, Lawrence Marsden. The Reception of English Litera-
      ture in Germany. 1932; rpt. New York: Blom, 1968,
      pp. 190-256. [Richardson, Fielding, Sterne, Goldsmith].
      Influence and reputation abroad. Germany.

•1006 Price, Martin. To the Palace of Wisdom: Studies in Order

and Energy from Dryden to Blake. Garden City, N.Y.:
Doubleday, 1964. [Swift, Defoe, Richardson, Fielding,
Sterne]. Intellectual background [interaction of ideas and
literary form]. Order. Shaftesbury. Mandeville. Aesthetic theory and background. Rasselas-Candide comparison.

1007 Proctor, Mortimer R. "Decline of the Universities." In his
The English University Novel. University of California
Publications, English Studies, 15. Berkeley: Univ. of
California Press, 1957, pp. 33-50. University novel. Ox-
ford University. Cambridge University.

1008 Proper, Coenraad. Social Elements in English Prose Fiction
Between 1700 and 1832. Amsterdam: H. J. Paris, 1929.
Social criticism in the novel.

■1009 Punter, David. "Fictional Representation of the Law in the
Eighteenth Century." Eighteenth-Century Studies, 16
(1982), 47-74. Law.

1010 Punter, David. The Literature of Terror: A History of
Gothic Fictions from 1765 to the Present Day. New York:
Longman, 1980. [Smollett, Walpole, Reeve, Lee, Radcliffe,
Lewis, Godwin]. Gothic novel. Horror and terror. Ro-
manticism. Sentimentalism.

1011 Quennell, Peter. Romantic England: Writing and Painting,
1717-1851. New York: Macmillan, 1970. Romanticism.
Gothic background. Art.

1012 Rader, Ralph W. "Defoe, Richardson, Joyce, and the Concept of Form in the Novel." In Autobiography, Biography,
and the Novel. Papers read at a Clark Library Seminar,
May 13, 1982. Ed. William Matthews and Ralph W. Rader.
Los Angeles: Clark Memorial Library, U.C.L.A., 1973, pp.
29-72. Plot, structure, and design. Comparison of novelists. Point of view and narrator.

1013 Radner, John B. "The Youthful Harlot's Curse: The Prostitute as Symbol of the City in 18th-Century English Literature." Eighteenth-Century Life, 2 (1976), 59-64. The
prostitute [symbol of vice and decay of the city]. Symbolism. London [its corruption causes prostitution].

●1014 Reed, Walter L. An Exemplary History of the Novel: The
Quixotic Versus the Picaresque. Chicago: Univ. of Chicago Press, 1981. [Moll Flanders, Joseph Andrews, Tristram Shandy]. Quixotic novel. Picaresque novel.

●1015 Richetti, John J. Popular Fiction Before Richardson: Narra-

tive Patterns, 1700-1739. Oxford: Clarendon Press, 1969.
[Defoe, Manley, Haywood, Aubin, Barker, Rowe]. Morality.
Plot, structure, and design. Popular novel. Criminal biog-
raphy. Didacticism. Scandal chronicles. Travel literature.
The pirate. Rogue hero. The prostitute.

1016 Richetti, John J. "The Portrayal of Women in Restoration and
Eighteenth-Century Literature." In What Manner of Woman:
Essays on English and American Life and Literature. Ed.
Marlene Springer. New York: New York Univ. Press,
1977, pp. 65-97. [Defoe, Swift, Richardson, Fielding].
Women.

1017 Richmond, H. W. "The Naval Officer in Fiction." Essays and
Studies, 30 (1945), 7-25. The sailor.

1018 Riggan, William. Picaros, Madmen, Naïfs, and Clowns: The
Unreliable First-Person Narrator. Norman: Univ. of Okla-
homa Press, 1981. [Moll Flanders, Tristram Shandy].
Point of view and narrator. Picaresque novel.

1019 Rivers, Isabel. "'Strangers and Pilgrims': Sources and Patterns of Methodist Narrative." In Augustan Worlds: New
Essays in Eighteenth-Century Literature. Eds. J. C. Hil-
son, M. M. B. Jones, and J. R. Watson. New York:
Barnes & Noble, 1978, pp. 189-203. Methodism. Methodist
fiction.

1020 Robert, Marthe. "Crusoism and Quixotery." In her Origins
of the Novel [1972]. Trans. Sacha Rabinovitch. Bloomington: Univ. of Indiana Press, 1980, pp. 81-148. Crusoism.
Quixotic novel. History of the novel.

1021 Robinson, Charles N. The British Tar in Fact and Fiction.
London: Harper, 1909. [Defoe, Smollett]. The sailor.
Naval novel.

1022 Rogal, Samuel J. "Enlightened Enthusiasm: Anti-Methodism
in the Literature of the Mid- and Late-Eighteenth Century."
Enlightenment Essays, 5, No. 1 (1974), 3-13. Methodism.

1023 Rogers, Katharine M. "Reason vs. Folly and Romantic Illusion: The Restoration and the Eighteenth Century." In
her The Troublesome Helpmate: A History of Misogyny in
Literature. Seattle: Univ. of Washington Press, 1966, pp.
160-88. Man vs. woman. Misogyny.

1023a Rogers, Pat. Eighteenth-Century Encounters: Essays on
Literature and Society in the Age of Walpole. New York:
Barnes & Noble, [forthcoming]. Social background [inter-
action of literature and society].

■1024 Rogers, Winfield H. "The Reaction Against Melodramatic
       Sentimentality in the English Novel, 1796-1830." PMLA, 49
       (1934), 98-122. Parody. Sentimentalism. Eighteenth-
       century criticism and reviews of the novel. Novelists on
       the novel.

1025   Romberg, Bertil. Studies in the Narrative Technique of the
       First-Person Novel. Trans. Michael Taylor and Harold B.
       Borland. Stockholm: Almqvist & Wiksell, 1962. Point of
       view and narrator.

1026   Rosenberg, Edgar. From Shylock to Svengali: Jewish
       Stereotypes in English Fiction. Stanford, Cal.: Stanford
       Univ. Press, 1960. The Jew.

●1027 Rothstein, Eric. Systems of Order and Inquiry in Later
       Eighteenth-Century Fiction. Berkeley: Univ. of California
       Press, 1975. [Rasselas, Tristram Shandy, Humphry Clink-
       er, Amelia, Caleb Williams]. Point of view and narrator.
       Epistemology. Plot, structure, and design. Order.

■1028 Rousseau, George S. "Threshold and Explanation: The So-
       cial Anthropologist and the Critic of Eighteenth-Century
       Literature." The Eighteenth Century: Theory and Inter-
       pretation, 22 (1981), 127-52. [Sterne, Richardson, Smol-
       lett]. Critical revaluation. Pedagogical approach.

1029   Runte, Roseann. "Dying Words: The Vocabulary of Death
       in Three Eighteenth-Century English and French Novels."
       Canadian Review of Comparative Literature, 6 (1979), 360-
       68. [Clarrissa]. Style and language. Death. Imagery
       [angel, poison, veil, hunt, flower].

1030   Russell, H. K. "Unity in Eighteenth-Century Episodic Nov-
       els." In Quick Springs of Sense: Studies in the Eight-
       eenth Century. Ed. Larry S. Champion. Athens: Univ.
       of Georgia Press, 1974, pp. 183-96. Conventions of the
       Georgian novel. Plot, structure, and design. Picaresque
       novel. Unity.

1031   Saagpakk, Paul F. "A Survey of Psychopathology in British
       Literature from Shakespeare to Hardy." Literature and
       Psychology, 18 (1968), 135-65. Psychology of characters.
       Insanity.

1032   Sacks, Sheldon. Fiction and the Shape of Belief: A Study
       of Henry Fielding with Glances at Swift, Johnson, and
       Richardson. Berkeley: Univ. of California Press, 1964.
       Theory and practice of the novel. Rhetorical novel. Di-
       dacticism. Author-reader relationship. Digressions and
       interpolated stories.

1033   Schulz, Dieter. "The Coquette's Progress from Satire to
       Sentimental Novel." Literatur in Wissenschaft und Unter-
       richt, 6 (1973), 77-89. The coquette.

■1034 Schulz, Dieter. "'Novel,' 'Romance,' and Popular Fiction in
       the First Half of the Eighteenth Century." Studies in
       Philology, 70 (1973), 77-91. History of the novel. Ro-
       mance. Popular novel. Critical revaluation [early novel a
       reaction to popular fiction, not to romance].

1035   Sedgwick, Eve Kosofsky. "The Character in the Veil: Imag-
       ery of the Surface in the Gothic Novel." PMLA, 96 (1981),
       255-70. [Radcliffe, Lewis]. Imagery [veils]. Gothic nov-
       el. Characterization.

1036   Shepherd, T. B. Methodism and the Literature of the Eight-
       eenth Century. London: Epworth Press, 1940. Methodism.

1037   Shepperson, Archibald Bolling. The Novel in Motley: A His-
       tory of the Burlesque Novel in English. Cambridge, Mass.:
       Harvard Univ. Press, 1936. Burlesque novel. Parody.

■1038 Sherbo, Arthur. "Character Description in the Novel." In
       his Studies in the Eighteenth-Century English Novel. Ann
       Arbor: Michigan State Univ. Press, 1969, pp. 177-207.
       Physiognomy. Physiology. Characterization. Conventions
       of the Georgian novel.

■1039 Sherwood, Irma Z. "The Novelists as Commentators." In
       The Age of Johnson: Essays Presented to Chauncey Brew-
       ster Tinker. Ed. Frederick W. Hilles and Wilmarth S.
       Lewis. New Haven, Conn.: Yale Univ. Press, 1949, pp.
       113-25. Point of view and narrator.

1040   Shroff, Homai J. The Eighteenth-Century Novel: The Idea
       of the Gentleman. New Delhi: Arnold-Heinemann, 1978.
       [Richardson, Fielding, Smollett, Goldsmith, Mackenzie,
       Sterne, Burney]. The gentleman.

1041   Shugrue, Michael F. "The Sincerest Form of Flattery: Imi-
       tation in the Early Eighteenth-Century Novel." South At-
       lantic Quarterly, 70 (1971), 248-55. Influence and imita-
       tion. Popular novel [popular works influenced fictional
       techniques and audience expectations].

1042   Sieber, Harry. The Picaresque. The Critical Idiom Series.
       London: Methuen, 1977. Picaresque novel [introductory
       guide].

1043   Simmons, Ernest J. "The English Novel in Eighteenth-Century
       Russia" and "English Sentimentalism in Russian Literature."

In his English Literature and Culture in Russia (1553-1840).
1935; rpt. New York: Octagon, 1964, pp. 134-203. Influence and reputation abroad. Russia.

1044   Singer, Godfrey Frank. The Epistolary Novel: Its Origin,
Development, Decline, and Residuary Influence. 1933; rpt.
New York: Russell & Russell, 1963. Epistolary novel.

•1045 Sitter, John. Literary Loneliness in Mid-Eighteenth-Century
England. Ithaca, N.Y.: Cornell Univ. Press, 1982.
[Fielding, Richardson]. Loneliness.

1046   Skilton, David. "Quoxitic and Picaresque Fiction." In his
The English Novel: Defoe to the Victorians. Newton Abbot, Devon.: David & Charles, 1977, pp. 32-44. Introductory guide. Quixotic novel. Picaresque novel.

1047   Slagle, Kenneth Chester. The English Country Squire As
Depicted in English Prose Fiction from 1740 to 1800. 1938;
rpt. New York: Octagon, 1971. The squire. Country
life. Manners. Sport and recreation.

1048   Sloman, Judith. "The Female Quixote as an Eighteenth-Cen-
tury Character Type." In Transactions of the Samuel
Johnson Society of the Northwest. Vol. 4. Ed. Robert H.
Carnie. Calgary, Alberta: Samuel Johnson Society of the
Northwest, 1972, pp. 86-101. [Steele, Lennox, Smollett].
"Female Quixote."

1049   Smith, Warren Hunting. Architecture in English Fiction.
1934; rpt. Hamden, Conn.: Archon, 1970. Architecture.

1050   Sokolyansky, Mark G. "The Diary and Its Role in the Genesis of the English Novel." Zeitschrift für Anglistik und
Amerikanistik, 28 (1980), 341-49. Diary. History of the
novel.

1051   Solomon, Stanley J. "Subverting Propriety as a Pattern of
Irony in Three Eighteenth-Century Novels: The Castle of
Otranto, Vathek, and Fanny Hill." Erasmus Review, 1
(1971), 107-16. [Walpole, Beckford, Cleland]. Propriety.
Irony. Comparison of novelists.

1052   Spacks, Patricia Meyer. The Adolescent Idea: Myths of
Youth and the Adult Imagination. New York: Basic Books,
1981. Incorporates "The Dangerous Age," Eighteenth-
Century Studies, 11 (1978), 417-38. [Richardson, Fielding,
Smollett, Goldsmith, Burney, Radcliffe]. The adolescent.

■1053 Spacks, Patricia Meyer. "Early Fiction and the Frightened
Male." Novel, 8 (1974), 5-15. Rpt. in Towards a Poetics

of Fiction. Ed. Mark Spilka. Bloomington: Indiana Univ.
Press, 1977, pp. 255-65. Women [fear of]. Man vs. woman. Impotence.

■1054 Spacks, Patricia Meyer. "'Ev'ry Woman Is at Heart a Rake.'"
Eighteenth-Century Studies, 8 (1974), 27-46. Women.
Sex.

1055   Spacks, Patricia Meyer. "Female Identities." In her Imagining a Self: Autobiography and Novel in Eighteenth-Century
England. Cambridge, Mass.: Harvard Univ. Press, 1976,
pp. 57-91. The self. Autobiographical elements in the
novel. Women.

1056   Spearman, Diana. The Novel and Society. New York:
Barnes & Noble, 1966. [Defoe, Richardson, Fielding].
Social criticism in the novel.

1056a Speck, W. A. Society and Literature in England, 1700-60.
Atlantic Highlands, N.J.: Humanities Press, 1983. [Field-
ing, Smollett]. Politics. Social structure. Fortune.
Country vs. city. History. Reading public. The writer
in society.

1057   Squires, Michael. "The Development of the Pastoral Novel."
In his The Pastoral Novel: Studies in George Eliot, Thomas
Hardy, and D. H. Lawrence. Charlottesville: Univ.
Press of Virginia, 1974, pp. 22-52. Pastoral novel.

1058   Stamm, James R. "The Use and Types of Humor in the Picaresque Novel." Hispania, 42 (1959), 482-87. Comedy.
Picaresque novel.

1059   Starkie, Walter F. "Miguel de Cervantes and the English
Novel." Essays by Divers Hands, Being the Transactions
of the Royal Society of Literature, 34 (1966), 159-79.
Cervantes. Sources, analogues, and influences. Quixotic
hero.

1060   Starr, George A. "'Only a Boy': Notes on Sentimental Nov-
els." Genre, 10 (1977), 501-27. [Esp. Defoe's Colonel
Jack, Mackenzie's The Man of Feeling]. Sentimental novel.
Sentimental hero. The adolescent. Speech and dialogue.

●1060a Stauffer, Donald A. "Biography and the Novel." In his
The Art of Biography in Eighteenth-Century England.
Princeton, N.J.: Princeton Univ. Press, 1941, pp. 65-131.
[Manley, Defoe, Richardson, Smollett, Fielding, Sterne,
Robinson, Burney]. Biography [reciprocal influences of
biography and novel].

1061   Staves, Susan. "British Seduced Maidens." Eighteenth-
       Century Studies, 14 (1980), 109-34. Women. Seduction.
       The seduced maiden.

1062   Staves, Susan. "Don Quixote in Eighteenth-Century Eng-
       land." Comparative Literature, 24 (1972), 193-215.
       [Fielding, Lennox, Sterne]. Quixotic hero. Satire.

1063   Steele, F. M. "Catholicism and English Literature in the
       Eighteenth Century." American Catholic Quarterly Review,
       36 (1911), 634-59. Catholicism.

1064   Steeves, Edna L. "Pre-Feminism in Some Eighteenth-Century
       Novels." Texas Quarterly, 16, No. 3 (1973), 48-57.
       Feminism.

1065   Steeves, Harrison R. Before Jane Austen: The Shaping of
       the English Novel in the Eighteenth Century. New York:
       Holt, Rinehart, Winston, 1965. [Useful for Goldsmith, Mac-
       kenzie, Burney, Johnson, Beckford, Walpole, Radcliffe,
       Lewis, Bage, Holcroft, Godwin, Wollstonecraft]. Introduc-
       tory guide.

1066   Stevenson, Lionel. The English Novel: A Panorama. Bos-
       ton: Houghton Mifflin, 1960. History of the novel.

1067   Stevick, Philip. "The Augustan Nose." University of Toronto
       Quarterly, 34 (1965), 110-17. Smells. Imagery [smelling,
       noses].

1068   Stevick, Philip. "Miniaturization in Eighteenth-Century Eng-
       lish Literature." University of Toronto Quarterly, 38
       (1969), 159-73. [Fielding, Sterne, Swift]. Miniaturization.
       Imagery [size]. Epistemology.

1069   Stewart, Keith. "History, Poetry, and the Terms of Fiction
       in the Eighteenth Century." Modern Philology, 66 (1968),
       110-20. Theory and practice of the novel. Historical fa-
       çade.

1070   Stock, R. D. "Spiritual Horror in the Novel: Richardson,
       Radcliffe, Beckford, Lewis." In his The Holy and the
       Daemonic from Sir Thomas Browne to William Blake. Prince-
       ton, N.J.: Princeton Univ. Press, 1982, pp. 259-313.
       [Clarissa, St. Leon, The Italian, Vathek, The Monk].
       Horror and terror. Supernatural. Gothic novel.

1071   Streeter, Harold Wade. The Eighteenth-Century English Nov-
       el in French Translation: A Bibliographical Study. 1936;
       rpt. New York: Blom, 1970. Influence and reputation
       abroad. France. Bibliography of primary sources.

1072   Summers, Montague. "Architecture and the Gothic Novel."
       Architectural Design, 2 (1931), 78-81. [Walpole, Reeve,
       Radcliffe]. Architecture. Strawberry Hill.

1073   Summers, Montague. The Gothic Quest: A History of the
       Gothic Novel. 1938; rpt. New York: Russell & Russell,
       1964. Gothic novel. Romanticism. Book trade. Circulat-
       ing libraries. Sources, analogues, and influences.

1074   Sutherland, James R. "Some Aspects of Eighteenth-Century
       Prose." In Essays on the Eighteenth Century Presented to
       David Nichol Smith. 1945; rpt. New York: Russell &
       Russell, 1963, pp. 94-110. Style and language.

1075   Sypher, Wylie. "Anti-Slavery Fiction." In his Guinea's Cap-
       tive Kings: British Anti-Slavery Literature of the XVIIIth
       Century. 1942; rpt. New York: Octagon, 1969, pp. 257-
       316. [Defoe, Smith, Bage, Day]. Slavery. Anti-slavery
       fiction.

1076   Tarr, Sister Mary Muriel. Catholicism in Gothic Fiction: A
       Study of the Nature and Function of Catholic Materials in
       Gothic Fiction in England (1762-1820). Washington, D.C.:
       Catholic Univ. of America Press, 1946. Gothic novel.
       Catholicism.

•1077 Tave, Stuart M. The Amiable Humorist: A Study in the
       Comic Theory and Criticism of the Eighteenth and Early
       Nineteenth Centuries. Chicago: Univ. of Chicago Press,
       1960. [Swift, Fielding, Sterne]. Characterization. Come-
       dy. "Amiable Humorist." "Good-natured Man."

1078   Taylor, John Tinnon. Early Opposition to the English Novel:
       The Popular Reaction from 1760 to 1830. New York:
       King's Crown Press, 1943. Reading public. Eighteenth-
       century criticism and reviews of the novel [opposition to
       the novel]. Women. Circulating libraries.

1079   Taylor, S. Ortiz. "Episodic Structure and the Picaresque
       Novel." Journal of Narrative Technique, 7 (1977), 218-25.
       Picaresque novel. Plot, structure, and design.

1080   Thacker, Christopher. "'Wish'd, Wint'ry, Horrors': The
       Storm in the Eighteenth Century." Comparative Literature,
       19 (1967), 36-57. Nature. Setting. Storms.

1081   Thorslev, Peter L., Jr. The Byronic Hero: Types and
       Prototypes. Minneapolis: Univ. of Minnesota Press, 1962.
       Gothic hero. "Man of Feeling." Child of nature. Byron.

1082   Tieje, Arthur J. "The Expressed Aim of the Long Prose Fic-

tion from 1579 to 1740." Journal of English and Germanic
Philology, 11 (1912), 402-32. Theory and practice of the
novel. Conventions of the Georgian novel.

1083   Tieje, Arthur J. "A Peculiar Phase of the Theory of Realism
in Pre-Richardsonian Fiction." PMLA, 28 (1913), 213-52.
Realism.

1084   Tieje, Arthur J. The Theory of Characterization in Prose
Fiction Prior to 1740. Minneapolis: Univ. of Minnesota
Press, 1916. Characterization. Theory and practice of the
novel.

1085   Tillyard, E. M. W. The Epic Strain in the English Novel.
London: Chatto & Windus, 1958. [Defoe, Fielding]. Epic.
Sources, analogues, and influences.

1086   Tillyard, E. M. W. "Retirement." In his Myth and the English Mind: From Piers Plowman to Edward Gibbon. 1961;
rpt. New York: Collier, 1962, pp. 65-95. Retirement.
Myth. Country vs. city. Rural ideal.

1087   Todd, Janet. Women's Friendship in Literature. New York:
Columbia Univ. Press, 1980. [Richardson, Cleland, Woll-
stonecraft, Haywood, Lennox, Burney, Fielding, Manley,
S. Scott, Defoe]. Women's friendship.

1088   Tompkins, J. M. S. The Popular Novel in England, 1770-
1800. 1932; rpt. Lincoln: Univ. of Nebraska Press, 1961.
Popular novel. Women novelists. Novel of doctrine. Didacticism. Sensibility. Gothic novel. Book trade.

1089   Tracy, Ann B. The Gothic Novel, 1790-1830: Plot Summaries
and Index to Motifs. Lexington: Univ. Press of Kentucky,
1981. Synopses. Gothic novel. Motif index.

1090   Tripathi, P. D. The Doctrinal English Novel (Later Eighteenth Century). Calcutta: K. P. Bagchi, 1977. Social
criticism in the novel. Politics. Novel of doctrine.

1091   Turner, Paul. "Novels, Ancient and Modern." Novel, 2
(1968), 15-24. Sources, analogues, and influences [ancient
Greek novels]. Classical allusions.

•1092   Uphaus, Robert W. The Impossible Observer: Reason and
the Reader in 18th-Century Prose. Lexington: Univ. Press
of Kentucky, 1979. [Swift, Defoe, Richardson, Fielding,
Johnson, Sterne, Godwin]. Reason. Author-reader relationship. Epistemology. Mandeville.

1093   Utter, Robert P., and Gwendolyn B. Needham. Pamela's

Daughters. New York: Macmillan, 1936. Influence and imitation. Sentimental heroine.

1094 Van der Veen, H. R. S. Jewish Characters in Eighteenth-Century English Fiction and Drama. Groningen-Batavia: J. B. Wolters' Uitgerers-Maatschappij, 1935. The Jew.

1095 Varma, Devendra P. The Gothic Flame. Being a History of the Gothic Novel in England: Its Origins, Efflorescence, Disintegration, and Residuary Influences. 1957; rpt. New York: Russell & Russell, 1966. [Beckford, Godwin, Lewis, Radcliffe, Reeve, Walpole]. Gothic novel.

1096 Wardroper, John. Kings, Lords and Wicked Libellers: Satire and Protest, 1760-1837. London: Murray, 1973. Satire [political]. Politics. Social background.

1097 Watson, Harold Francis. The Sailor in English Fiction and Drama, 1550-1800. 1931; rpt. New York: AMS Press, 1966. The sailor. Naval novel.

■1098 Watt, Ian. "The Ironic Voice." 1967; rpt. in his The Augustan Age: Approaches to Its Literature, Life and Thought. Greenwich, Conn.: Fawcett, 1968, pp. 101-14. Irony. Style and language.

●1099 Watt, Ian. The Rise of the Novel: Studies in Defoe, Richardson and Fielding. 1957; rpt. Berkeley: Univ. of California Press, 1962. History of the novel. Realism. "Formal realism." Plot, structure, and design. Space. Time. Critical revaluation [the most influential study of the eighteenth-century British novel].

1100 Watt, Ian. "Serious Thoughts on The Rise of the Novel." Novel, 1 (1968), 206-18. Critical revaluation.

1101 Weinstein, Arnold. Fictions of the Self: 1550-1800. Princeton, N.J.: Princeton Univ. Press, 1981. [Defoe, Richardson, Fielding, Sterne]. The self. Characterization.

1102 Weitzman, Arthur J. "The Oriental Tale in the Eighteenth Century: A Reconsideration." Studies on Voltaire and the Eighteenth Century, 58 (1967), 1839-55. [Johnson, Beckford]. Oriental novel.

1103 Welsh, Alexander. Reflections on the Hero as Quixote. Princeton, N.J.: Princeton Univ. Press, 1981. Quixotic hero.

1104 Whitbourn, Christine J., ed. Knaves and Swindlers: Essays on the Picaresque Novel in Europe. London: Oxford Univ.

Press, 1974. [Anthology of criticism]. Picaresque novel. Rogue hero.

1105 Whitney, Lois. Primitivism and the Idea of Progress in English Popular Literature of the Eighteenth Century. 1934; rpt. New York: Octagon, 1965. Primitivism. Progress. Popular novel.

1106 Whittuck, C. A. The "Good Man" of the XVIIIth Century: A Monograph on XVIIIth-Century Didactic Literature. London: George Allen, 1901. "Good Man." Rasselas-Candide comparison.

1107 Wicks, Ulrich. "The Nature of Picaresque Narrative: A Modal Approach." PMLA, 89 (1975), 240-49. Picaresque novel.

1108 Wicks, Ulrich. "Picaro, Picaresque: The Picaresque in Literary Scolarship." Genre, 5 (1972), 153-92. Picaresque novel. Survey of criticism.

1109 Wicks, Ulrich. "The Romance of the Picaresque." Genre, 11 (1978), 29-44. Romance. Picaresque novel.

1110 Williams, Ioan. The Idea of the Novel in Europe, 1600-1800. New York: New York Univ. Press, 1979. [Defoe, Richardson, Fielding, Sterne]. Theory and practice of the novel.

1111 Williams, Ioan, ed. Novel and Romance, 1700-1800: A Documentary Record. New York: Barnes & Noble, 1970. Eighteenth-century criticism and reviews of the novel.

1112 Williamson, George. "The Rhetorical Pattern of Neo-Classical Wit." Modern Philology, 33 (1935), 55-81. Rhetoric. Comedy.

1113 Wilson, W. Daniel. "Science, Natural Law, and Unwitting Sibling Incest in Eighteenth-Century Literature." In Studies in Eighteenth-Century Culture. Ed. O M Brack, Jr. Vol. 13. Madison: Univ. of Wisconsin Press, 1984, pp. 249-70. [Moll Flanders]. Incest.

1114 Wolf, Edward C. J. Rowlandson and His Illustrations of Eighteenth-Century English Literature. Copenhagen: Einar Munksgaard, 1945. Rowlandson. Illustration.

1115 Wolff, Cynthia Griffin. "The Problem of Eighteenth-Century Secular Heroinism." Modern Language Studies, 4, No. 2 (1974), 35-42. Women. Sentimentalism. Style and language.

1116   Wright, Terence. "'Metaphors for Reality': Mind and Object
       and the Problem of Form in the Early Novel." Durham Uni-
       versity Journal, 38 (1977), 239-48. [Defoe, Richardson,
       Sterne]. Realism. Epistemology. Time.

1117   Wright, Walter Francis. Sensibility in English Prose Fiction,
       1760-1814: A Reinterpretation. Urbana: Univ. of Illinois
       Press, 1937. Sensibility.

PART V: MAJOR NOVELISTS

DANIEL DEFOE
(1660-1731)

PRINCIPAL FICTION

Robinson Crusoe, 1719

Memoirs of a Cavalier, 1720

Captain Singleton, 1720

A Journal of the Plague Year, 1722

Moll Flanders, 1722

Colonel Jacque, 1722

The Fortunate Mistress (Roxana), 1724

BIBLIOGRAPHIES AND SURVEYS OF CRITICISM

1118 Burch, Charles E. "British Criticism of Defoe as a Novelist, 1719-1860." Englische Studien, 67 (1933), 178-98. Survey of criticism.

1119 Higdon, David L. "The Critical Fortunes and Misfortunes of Defoe's Roxana." Bucknell Review, 20, No. 1 (1972), 67-82. Survey of criticism.

1120 Moore, John Robert. A Checklist of the Writings of Daniel Defoe. Bloomington: Univ. of Indiana Press, 1960. See also Pat Rogers, "Addenda and Corrigenda: Moore's Checklist of Defoe." Papers of the Bibliographical Society of America, 75 (1981), 60-64. Bibliography of primary sources.

1121 Novak, Maximillian E. "Defoe." In The English Novel: Select Bibliographical Guides. Ed. A. E. Dyson. London: Oxford Univ. Press, 1974, pp. 16-35. Bibliography of criticism. Survey of criticism.

1122   O'Brien, C. J. H. Moll Among the Critics. Armidale, N.S.W.,
       Australia: Univ. of New England Publishing Unit, 1979.
       Survey of criticism. Critical revaluation. Irony. Psychol-
       ogy of characters.

1123   Payne, William L. "An Annotated Bibliography of Works About
       Daniel Defoe, 1719-1974: Part I." Bulletin of Bibliography,
       32, No. 1 (1975), 3-14. "Part II." Ibid., No. 2, 63-75,
       87. "Part III." Ibid., No. 3, 89-100, 132. Bibliography
       of criticism [annotated].

1124   Stoler, John A. Daniel Defoe: An Annotated Bibliography of
       Modern Criticism. New York: Garland, [forthcoming].
       Bibliography of criticism [annotated].

1125   Watt, Ian. "The Recent Critical Fortunes of Moll Flanders."
       Eighteenth-Century Studies, 1 (1967), 109-26. Survey of
       criticism.

CRITICAL AND BIOGRAPHICAL STUDIES

1126   Aldrich, Pearl G. "Daniel Defoe: The Father of Soap Opera."
       Journal of Popular Culture, 8 (1975), 767-74. "Soap opera."
       Popular culture. Influence and imitation.

1127   Alkon, Paul K. Defoe and Fictional Time. Athens: Univ.
       of Georgia Press, 1979. Time. Setting.

1128   Alkon, Paul K. "The Odds Against Friday: Defoe, Bayes,
       and Inverse Probability." In Probability, Time, and Space
       in Eighteenth-Century Literature. Ed. Paula Backscheider.
       New York: AMS Press, 1979, pp. 29-61. Probability.

■1129 Alter, Robert. "A Bourgeois Picaroon." In his Rogue's Prog-
       ress: Studies in the Picaresque Novel. Cambridge, Mass.:
       Harvard Univ. Press, 1964, pp. 35-57. Rpt. in Twentieth
       Century Interpretations of "Moll Flanders." Ed. Robert C.
       Elliott. Englewood Cliffs, N.J.: Prentice-Hall, 1970, pp.
       63-77. [Moll Flanders]. Picaresque novel. Rogue hero.

■1130 Anderson, Hans H. "The Paradox of Trade and Morality in
       Defoe." Modern Philology, 39 (1941), 23-46. Morality
       [tension between financial and ethical imperatives]. Philos-
       ophy of novelist. Industry and trade. Mercantilism.

1131   Ayers, Robert W. "Robinson Crusoe: 'Allusive Allegorick
       History.'" PMLA, 82 (1967), 399-407. Puritanism.
       Sources, analogues, and influences. Allegory.

1132   Backscheider, Paula. "Defoe's Prodigal Sons." Studies in the Literary Imagination, 15, No. 2 (1982), 3-18. Prodigal son motif. Typology. Influence and imitation [Defoe's use of the prodigal son motif influences structure and resolution of the Georgian novel].

1133 Backscheider, Paula. "Defoe's Women: Snares and Prey." In Studies in Eighteenth-Century Culture. Vol. 5. Ed. Ronald C. Rosbottom. Madison: Univ. of Wisconsin Press, 1976, pp. 103-20. Women.

1134 Baer, Joel H. "'The Complicated Plot of Piracy': Aspects of English Criminal Law and the Image of the Pirate in Defoe." The Eighteenth Century: Theory and Interpretation, 23 (1982), 3-26. [General History of the Pyrates, Captain Singleton]. Law. Crime and punishment. The pirate.

1135 Baine, Rodney M. Daniel Defoe and the Supernatural. Athens: Univ. of Georgia Press, 1968. Angelology. Supernatural.

1136 Baine, Rodney M. "Roxana's Georgian Setting." Studies in English Literature, 15 (1975), 459-71. Setting. Time [chronology of Roxana's life].

1137 Bastian, Frank. Defoe's Early Life. London: Macmillan, 1981. Biography.

1138 Bastian, Frank. "Defoe's Journal of the Plague Year Reconsidered." Review of English Studies, N.S. 16 (1965), 151-73. Point of view and narrator.

1139 Beberfall, Lester. "The 'Picaro' in Context." Hispania, 37 (1954), 288-92. Rogue hero.

1140 Bell, Robert H. "Moll's Grace Abounding." Genre, 8 (1975), 267-82. Point of view and narrator. Rogue biography. Spiritual biography and autobiography.

1141 Benjamin, Edwin B. "Symbolic Elements in Robinson Crusoe." Philological Quarterly, 30 (1951), 206-11. Symbolism. Allegory. Christianity.

1142 Berne, Eric. "The Psychological Structure of Space with Some Remarks on Robinson Crusoe." Psychoanalytic Quarterly, 25 (1956), 549-67. Space. Psychology of characters. Personality of novelist.

1143 Bishop, Jonathan. "Knowledge, Action, and Interpretation in Defoe's Novels." Journal of the History of Ideas, 13 (1952), 3-16. Epistemology [influence of Locke]. Characterization [the mind reacting to its environment].

1144   Bjornson, Richard. "The Ambiguous Success of the Picaresque
       Hero in Defoe's Moll Flanders." In his The Picaresque Hero
       in European Fiction. Madison: Univ. of Wisconsin Press,
       1977, pp. 188-206. Rogue hero. Ambiguity [of middle-
       class view of success].

1145   Blackburn, Timothy C. "The Coherence of Defoe's Captain
       Singleton." Huntington Library Quarterly, 41 (1978), 119-
       36. Plot, structure, and design.

1146   Blair, Joel. "Defoe's Art in A Journal of the Plague Year."
       South Atlantic Quarterly, 72 (1973), 243-54. Plot, struc-
       ture, and design. Point of view and narrator. Philosophy
       of novelist.

1147   Blewett, David. "Changing Attitudes Toward Marriage in the
       Time of Defoe: The Case of Moll Flanders." Huntington
       Library Quarterly, 44 (1981), 77-88. Marriage.

•1148 Blewett, David. Defoe's Art of Fiction: "Robinson Crusoe,"
       "Moll Flanders," "Colonel Jack" and "Roxana." Toronto:
       Univ. of Toronto Press, 1979. Incorporates his "Jacobite
       and Gentleman: Defoe's Use of Jacobitism in Colonel Jack,"
       English Studies in Canada, 4 (1978), 15-24; and "'Roxana'
       and the Masquerades," Modern Language Review, 65 (1970),
       499-502. Unity. Narrative technique. Plot, structure,
       and design. Setting. Morality. Style and language.
       Jacobitism. The gentleman. Masquerade.

1149   Blewett, David. "The Double Time-Scheme of Roxana: Furth-
       er Evidence." In Studies in Eighteenth-Century Culture.
       Ed. O M Brack, Jr. Vol. 13. Madison: Univ. of Wiscon-
       sin Press, 1984, pp. 19-28. Time. Setting [in both Res-
       toration and early Georgian periods]. Morality [dissolute-
       ness of both periods].

1150   Blewett, David. "The Retirement Myth in Robinson Crusoe:
       A Reconsideration." Studies in the Literary Imagination,
       15, No. 2 (1982), 37-50. Retirement. Myth.

1151   Boardman, Michael M. Defoe and the Uses of Narrative.
       New Brunswick, N.J.: Rutgers Univ. Press, 1983. Point
       of view and narrator. Conventions of the Georgian novel.
       Characterization.

1152   Boardman, Michael M. "Defoe's Political Rhetoric and the
       Problem of Irony." Tulane Studies in English, 22 (1977),
       87-102. Politics. Irony. Rhetoric.

1153   Borck, Jim Springer. "One Woman's Prospects: Defoe's Moll
       Flanders and the Ironies in Restoration Self-Image." Forum

[Houston, Texas], 17, No. 1 (1979), 10-16. Characterization. Philosophy of novelist [Hobbesian basis].

1154 Bordner, Marsha. "Defoe's Androgynous Vision: In Moll Flanders and Roxana." Gypsy Scholar, 2 (1975), 76-93. Androgyny.

1155 Boreham, Frank W. The Gospel of Robinson Crusoe. London: Epworth Press, 1955. Christianity.

∎1156 Boyce, Benjamin. "The Question of Emotion in Defoe." Studies in Philology, 1 (1953), 45-58. Characterization. Sensibility.

1157 Boyce, Benjamin. "The Shortest Way: Characteristic Defoe Fiction." In Quick Springs of Sense: Studies in the Eighteenth Century. Ed. Larry S. Champion. Athens: Univ. of Georgia Press, 1974, pp. 1-13. Characterization. Point of view and narrator. Journalism.

1158 Braudy, Leo. "Daniel Defoe and the Anxieties of Autobiography." Genre, 7 (1973), 76-97. Autobiography. Point of view and narrator. The self.

1159 Brooks, Douglas. "Defoe: Robinson Crusoe, Captain Singleton, Colonel Jack" and "Defoe: Moll Flanders and Roxana." In his Number and Pattern in the Eighteenth-Century Novel. London: Routledge & Kegan Paul, 1973, pp. 18-64. Incorporates his "Moll Flanders: An Interpretation," Essays in Criticism, 19 (1969), 46-59. Numerology. Plot, structure, and design. Symbolism.

1160 Brown, Homer Obed. "The Displaced Self in the Novels of Daniel Defoe." ELH: A Journal of English Literary History, 38 (1971), 562-90. Rpt. in Studies in Eighteenth-Century Culture. Vol. 4. Ed. Harold E. Pagliaro. Madison: Univ. of Wisconsin Press, 1975, pp. 69-94.

1161 Brown, Lloyd W. "Defoe and the Feminine Mystique." In Transactions of the Samuel Johnson Society of the Northwest. Vol. 4. Ed. Robert H. Carnie. Calgary, Alberta: Samuel Johnson Society of the Northwest, 1972, pp. 4-18. [Moll Flanders, Roxana]. Women [Defoe's ambivalent view of women's liberation].

1162 Burch, Charles E. "Daniel Defoe's Views on Education." London Quarterly Review, 151 (1930), 202-29. Education.

1163 Burch, Charles E. "The Moral Elements in Defoe's Fiction." London Quarterly and Holburn Review, 162 (1937), 207-13. Morality.

1164 Burke, John J., Jr. "Observing the Observer in Historical
      Fictions by Defoe." Philological Quarterly, 61 (1982), 13-
      32. [Memoirs of a Cavalier, A Journal of the Plague Year].
      Historical novel. Point of view and narrator [autobiograph-
      ical form].

1165 Butler, Mary E. "The Effect of the Narrator's Rhetorical
      Uncertainty on the Fiction of Robinson Crusoe." Studies
      in the Novel, 15 (1983), 77-90. Style and language. Point
      of view and narrator. Rhetoric.

1166 Castle, Terry. "'Amy, Who Knew My Disease': A Psycho-
      sexual Pattern in Defoe's Roxana." ELH: A Journal of
      English Literary History, 46 (1979), 81-96. Psychology of
      characters. Sex.

1167 Chaber, Lois A. "Matriarchal Mirror: Women and Capital in
      Moll Flanders." PMLA, 97 (1982), 212-26. Social criticism
      in the novel. Women. Money. Capitalism. The mother.

1168 Cohan, Steven M. "Other Bodies: Roxana's Confession of
      Guilt." Studies in the Novel, 8 (1976), 406-17. Charac-
      terization. Point of view and narrator.

1169 Columbus, Robert T. "Conscious Artistry in Moll Flanders."
      Studies in English Literature, 3 (1963), 415-32. Charac-
      terization. Plot, structure, and design.

1170 Cottom, Daniel. "Robinson Crusoe: The Emperor's New
      Clothes." The Eighteenth Century: Theory and Inter-
      pretation, 22 (1981), 271-86. State of nature. Insanity.
      Characterization.

1171 Curtis, Laura. The Elusive Daniel Defoe. New York:
      Barnes & Noble, [forthcoming]. Personality of novelist.
      Ambivalence.

1172 Damrosch, Leopold. "Defoe as Ambiguous Impersonator."
      Modern Philology, 71 (1973), 153-59. Point of view and
      narrator.

1173 Dennis, Nigel. "Swift and Defoe." In his Jonathan Swift:
      A Short Character. New York: Macmillan, 1964, pp. 122-
      33. Comparison of novelists.

1174 Dollerup, Cay. "Does the Chronology of Moll Flanders Tell
      Us Something About Defoe's Method of Writing?" English
      Studies, 53 (1973), 234-35. Time. Composition of the nov-
      el.

1175 Donoghue, Denis. "The Values of Moll Flanders." Sewanee
      Review, 71 (1963), 287-303. Morality. Industry and trade.

1176 Donovan, Robert Alan. "The Two Heroines of Moll Flanders."
      In his The Shaping Vision: Imagination in the English Nov-
      el from Defoe to Dickens. Ithaca, N.Y.: Cornell Univ.
      Press, 1966, pp. 21-46. Characterization. Point of view
      and narrator. Plot, structure, and design.

1177 Doody, Terrence. "Three Confessional Novels: Moll Fland-
      ers, Notes from the Underground, Moby Dick." In his
      Confession and Community in the Novel. Baton Rouge:
      Louisiana State Univ. Press, 1980, pp. 39-90. Confessional
      novel.

1178 Earle, Peter. The World of Defoe. New York: Atheneum,
      1977. Biography. Economics. Philosophy of novelist.
      Social structure.

1179 Edwards, Lee. "Between the Real and the Moral: Problems
      in the Structure of Moll Flanders." In Twentieth Century
      Interpretations of "Moll Flanders." Ed. Robert C. Elliott.
      Englewood Cliffs, N.J.: Prentice-Hall, 1970, pp. 95-107.
      Plot, structure, and design. Realism. Morality. Didacti-
      cism.

1180 Egan, James. "Crusoe's Monarchy and the Puritan Concept
      of the Self." Studies in English Literature, 13 (1973), 451-
      60. Puritanism. Imagery [monarch]. The self.

1181 Erickson, Robert A. "Moll's Fate: 'Mother Midnight' and
      Moll Flanders." Studies in Philology, 76 (1979), 75-100.
      Characterization.

1182 Erickson, Robert A. "Starting Over with Robinson Crusoe."
      Studies in the Literary Imagination, 15, No. 2 (1982), 51-
      73. Rebirth. Characterization. Typology. Symbolism.

1183 Ermarth, Elizabeth Deeds. "Time and Eternity: The Cases
      of Robinson Crusoe and Pamela." In her Realism and Con-
      sensus in the English Novel. Princeton, N.J.: Princeton
      Univ. Press, 1983, pp. 95-143. Time. Realism. Compari-
      son of novelists.

1184 Flanders, W. Austin. "Defoe's Journal of the Plague Year
      and the Modern Urban Experience." Centennial Review, 16
      (1972), 328-48. Psychology of characters. Dread. Anxi-
      ety. City life.

1185 Ganzel, Dewey. "Chronology in Robinson Crusoe." Philologi-
      cal Quarterly, 40 (1961), 495-512. Time.

1186 Gaskin, Bob. "Moll Flanders: Consistency in a Psychopath."
      Lamar Journal of the Humanities, 6, No. 1 (1980), 5-18.
      Psychology of characters. Insanity.

1187 Gerber, Richard. "The English Island Myth: Remarks on the Englishness of Utopian Fiction." Critical Quarterly, 1 (1959), 36-43. [Defoe, Swift]. Myth. Utopian Fiction.

1188 Gifford, George E., Jr. "Daniel Defoe and Maryland." Maryland Historical Magazine, 52 (1957), 307-15. Maryland [Defoe's knowledge of].

1189 Girdler, Lew. "Defoe's Education at Newington Green Academy." Studies in Philology, 50 (1953), 573-91. Education. Dissenting academies.

1190 Goldberg, M. A. "Moll Flanders: Christian Allegory in a Hobbesian Mode." University Review, 33 (1967), 267-78. Allegory. Christianity. Hobbes. Materialism.

■1191 Goldknopf, David. "The I-Narrator in the Pseudomemoir: Daniel Defoe." In his The Life of the Novel. Chicago: Univ. of Chicago Press, 1972, pp. 42-58. Point of view and narrator. Autobiographical façade.

1192 Goldstein, Laurence. "Roxana and Empire." In his Ruins and Empire: The Evolution of a Theme in Augustan and Romantic Literature. Pittsburgh: Univ. of Pittsburgh Press, 1977, pp. 59-72. Allegory [of national spiritual decay]. Imperialism.

1193 Gray, Christopher W. "Defoe's Literalizing Imagination." Philological Quarterly, 57 (1978), 66-81. Style and language. Characterization. Loneliness.

1194 Green, Martin. "Defoe." In his Dreams of Adventure, Deeds of Empire. New York: Basic Books, 1979, pp. 66-96. [Robinson Crusoe, Captain Singleton]. Mercantilism. Imperialism.

1195 Greif, Martin J. "The Conversion of Robinson Crusoe." Studies in English Literature, 6 (1966), 551-74. Conversion and repentance. Allegory. Symbolism. Christianity.

1196 Hahn, H. George. "An Approach to Character Development in Defoe's Narrative Prose." Philological Quarterly, 51 (1972), 845-58. Characterization [three patterns of character development]. Plot, structure, and design [formula of Defoe's plots].

1197 Halewood, William. "Religion and Invention in Robinson Crusoe." Essays in Criticism, 14 (1964), 339-51. Puritanism. Sources, analogues, and influences.

1198 Hammond, Brean S. "Repentance: Solution to the Clash of

Moralities in Moll Flanders." English Studies, 61 (1980), 329-37. Characterization. Morality. Conversion and repentance.

1199 Harlan, Virginia. "Defoe's Narrative Style." Journal of English and Germanic Philology, 30 (1931), 55-73. Style and language.

1200 Harris, R. W. "Defoe and Economic Individualism." In his Reason and Nature in the Eighteenth Century. New York: Barnes & Noble, 1969, pp. 112-31. Individualism. Capitalism. Colonialism.

1201 Hartog, Curt. "Aggression, Femininity, and Irony in Moll Flanders." Literature and Psychology, 22 (1972), 121-38. Aggression [in male and female characters compared]. Femininity. Irony. Psychology of characters.

1202 Hartog, Curt. "Authority and Autonomy in Robinson Crusoe." Enlightenment Essays, 5, No. 2 (1974), 33-43. Philosophy of novelist. Psychology of characters.

1203 Hartveit, Lars. "A Chequer-Work of Formulae: A Reading of Defoe's Colonel Jack." English Studies, 63 (1982), 122-33. Picaresque novel. Social structure. Social criticism in the novel.

1204 Hastings, William T. "Errors and Inconsistencies in Defoe's Robinson Crusoe." Modern Language Notes, 27 (1912), 161-66. Defects in the novel [esp. errors in chronology]. Time. Narrative technique. Autobiographical elements in the novel [disproved].

1205 Häusermann, Hans W. "Aspects of Life and Thought in Robinson Crusoe." Review of English Studies, O.S. 11 (1935), 299-312, 439-56. Characterization. The tradesman.

1206 Hearne, John. "The Naked Footprint: An Inquiry into Crusoe's Island." Review of English Literature, 8 (1967), 97-107. Introductory guide.

1207 Higdon, David Leon. "Daniel Defoe's Moll Flanders and Roxana." In his Time and English Fiction. Totowa, N.J.: Rowman & Littlefield, 1977, pp. 56-73. Incorporates his "The Chronology of Moll Flanders." English Studies, 56 (1975), 316-19. Time. Plot, structure, and design.

1208 Howard, William J. "Truth Preserves Her Shape: An Unexplored Influence on Defoe's Prose Style." Philological Quarterly, 47 (1968), 193-205. Style and language. Sources, analogues, and influences.

1209 Hume, Robert D. "The Conclusion of Defoe's Roxana: Fiasco
      or Tour de Force?" Eighteenth-Century Studies, 3 (1970),
      475-90. Plot, structure, and design. Morality. Closure.

•1210 Hunter, J. Paul. The Reluctant Pilgrim: Defoe's Emblematic
      Method and Quest for Form in "Robinson Crusoe." Balti-
      more: The Johns Hopkins Univ. Press, 1966. Plot, struc-
      ture, and design. Puritanism. Providence. Conversion
      and repentance. Spiritual biography and autobiography.
      "Guide" tradition. Pilgrim allegory. Sources, analogues,
      and influences.

1211 Jackson, Wallace. "Roxana and the Development of Defoe's
      Fiction." Studies in the Novel, 7 (1975), 181-94. Psychol-
      ogy of characters. Artistic development.

1212 James, E. Anthony. Daniel Defoe's Many Voices: A Rhetori-
      cal Study of Prose Style and Literary Method. Amsterdam:
      Editions Rodopi, 1972. Point of view and narrator. Style
      and language.

1213 James, E. Anthony. "Defoe's Narrative Artistry: Naming
      and Describing in Robinson Crusoe." Costerus, 5 (1972),
      51-73. Names of characters.

1214 Jenkins, Ralph E. "The Structure of Roxana." Studies in
      the Novel, 2 (1970), 145-58. Plot, structure, and design.

1215 Johnson, Abby A. "Old Bones Uncovered: A Reconsidera-
      tion of Robinson Crusoe." College Language Association
      Journal, 17 (1973), 271-78. Racism.

1216 Johnson, Clifford. "Defoe's Reaction to Enlightened Secular-
      ism: A Journal of the Plague Year." Enlightenment Essays,
      3 (1972), 169-77. Christianity. Science.

1217 Karl, Frederick R. "Daniel Defoe: The Politics of Necessity."
      In his A Reader's Guide to the Eighteenth-Century English
      Novel. New York: Noonday, 1974, pp. 68-98. [Robinson
      Crusoe, Moll Flanders]. Necessity. Myth.

1218 Karl, Frederick R. "Moll's Many-Colored Coat: Veil and
      Disguise in the Fiction of Defoe." Studies in the Novel, 5
      (1973), 86-97. Disguise. Characterization.

1219 Kavanagh, Thomas M. "Unraveling Robinson: The Divided
      Self in Defoe's Robinson Crusoe." Texas Studies in Liter-
      ature and Language, 20 (1978), 416-32. The self. Char-
      acterization.

1220 Kettle, Arnold. "In Defense of Moll Flanders." In Of Books

and Humankind: Essays and Poems Presented to Bonamy
Dobrée. London: Routledge & Kegan Paul, 1964, pp. 55-
67. Critical revaluation. Defects in the novel.

1221 Kettle, Arnold. "The Precursors of Defoe: Puritanism and
the Rise of the Novel." In On the Novel: A Present for
Walter Allen On His 60th Birthday from His Friends and
Colleagues. Ed. B. S. Benedikz. London: Dent, 1971,
pp. 206-17. Puritanism. History of the novel.

∎1222 Koonce, Howard L. "Moll's Muddle: Defoe's Use of Irony in
Moll Flanders." ELH: A Journal of English Literary His-
tory, 30 (1963), 377-94. Rpt. in Twentieth Century Inter-
pretations of "Moll Flanders." Ed. Robert C. Elliott.
Englewood Cliffs, N.J.: Prentice-Hall, 1970, pp. 49-59.
Irony.

1223 Kraft, Quentin G. "Robinson Crusoe and the Story of the
Novel." College English, 41 (1980), 535-48. Narrative
technique. History of the novel.

1224 Krier, William J. "A Courtesy Which Grants Integrity: A
Literal Reading of Moll Flanders." ELH: A Journal of English Literary History, 38 (1971), 397-410. Characterization.

1225 Kropf, Carl R. "Theme and Structure in Defoe's Roxana."
Studies in English Literature, 12 (1972), 467-80. Plot,
structure, and design. Unity [plot unified by the destruction of Roxana's soul].

1226 Laird, John. "Robinson Crusoe's Philosophy." In his Philosophical Incursions into English Literature. 1946; rpt.
New York: Russell & Russell, 1962, pp. 21-33. Philosophy
of novelist.

1227 Leinster-Mackay, D. P. The Educational World of Daniel Defoe. Victoria: Univ. of Victoria, 1981. [Little on the nov-
els]. Education. Intellectual background.

1228 Lerenbaum, Miriam. "Moll Flanders: 'A Woman on her own
Account.'" In The Authority of Experience: Essays in
Feminist Criticism. Ed. Arlyn Diamond and Lee R. Edwards. Amherst: Univ. of Massachusetts Press, 1977, pp.
101-17. Feminism. Characterization.

1229 Levett, Ada E. "Daniel Defoe." In Social & Political Ideas
of Some Thinkers of the Augustan Age, A. D. 1650-1750.
Ed. F. J. C. Hearnshaw. 1923; rpt. New York: Barnes
& Noble, 1950, pp. 157-88. Politics. Social criticism in
the novel. Philosophy of novelist.

1230 Macaree, David. Daniel Defoe and the Jacobite Movement.
      Salzburg: Institut für Anglistik und Amerikanistik, 1980.
      Politics. Jacobitism.

1231 Macaree, David. "Daniel Defoe, the Church of Scotland, and
      the Union of 1707." Eighteenth-Century Studies, 7 (1973),
      62-77. Scotland. Presbyterianism. Politics.

1232 MacDonald, Robert H. "The Creation of an Ordered World in
      Robinson Crusoe." Dalhousie Review, 56 (1976), 23-34.
      Order vs. disorder. The self. Characterization. Myth.

1233 MacLaine, Allan H. "Robinson Crusoe and the Cyclops."
      Studies in Philology, 52 (1955), 599-604. Classical allusions.

1233a Maddox, James H., Jr. "Interpreter Crusoe." ELH: A
      Journal of English Literary History, 51 (1984), 33-52.
      Psychology of characters [Crusoe's skeptical search for a
      myth to interpret his life].

1234 Manlove, C. N. "Defoe." In his Literature and Reality,
      1600-1800. New York: St. Martin's, 1978, pp. 99-113.
      Survival. Realism.

■1235 Martin, Terence. "The Unity of Moll Flanders." Modern Lan-
      guage Quarterly, 22 (1961), 115-24. Unity. Plot, struc-
      ture, and design.

1236 Mason, Shirlene. Daniel Defoe and the Status of Women. St.
      Alban's, Vt.: Eden Press, 1978. Women.

1237 Maxfield, Ezra Kempton. "Daniel Defoe and the Quakers."
      PMLA, 47 (1932), 179-90. Quakerism [Defoe no friend to
      the Quakers, esp. in Captain Singleton].

■1238 McBurney, William H. "Colonel Jacque: Defoe's Definition of
      the Complete Gentleman." Studies in English Literature, 2
      (1962), 321-26. The gentleman.

1239 McCoy, Kathleen. "The Femininity of Moll Flanders." In
      Studies in Eighteenth-Century Culture. Vol. 7. Ed. Rose-
      ann Runte. Madison: Univ. of Wisconsin Press, 1978, pp.
      413-22. Femininity. Characterization.

■1240 McKillop, Alan Dugald. "Daniel Defoe." In his The Early
      Masters of English Fiction. Lawrence: Univ. Press of
      Kansas, 1956, pp. 1-46. Introductory guide [excellent ac-
      count of main issues].

1241 McMaster, Juliet. "The Equation of Love and Money in Moll
      Flanders." Studies in the Novel, 2 (1970), 131-44. Love.
      Money. Morality.

1242 McVeagh, John. "'The Blasted Race of Old Cham': Daniel Defoe and the African." Ibadan Studies in English, 1 (1969), 85-109. [Not seen]. Blacks. Africa.

1243 McVeagh, John. "Defoe and the Romance of Trade." Durham University Journal, 70 (1978), 141-47. Industry and trade.

1244 Megroz, R. L. The Real Robinson Crusoe. London: Cresset Press, [1939]. [Biography of Alexander Selkirk]. Sources, analogues, and influences. Alexander Selkirk.

1245 Merrett, Robert J. Daniel Defoe's Moral and Rhetorical Ideas. Victoria: Univ. of Victoria, 1980. Philosophy of novelist. Morality. Rhetoric. Didacticism. Style and language.

1246 Merrett, Robert J. "Defoe's Presentation of Crime and Criminals: An Examination of His Social Philosophy." Transactions of the Samuel Johnson Society of the Northwest. Vol. IV. Ed. Robert H. Carnie. Calgary: Samuel Johnson Soc. of the Northwest, 1972, pp. 68-85. The criminal. Philosophy of novelist [human nature as criminal].

1247 Michie, J. A. "The Unity of Moll Flanders." In Knaves and Swindlers. Ed. C. J. Whitbourn. New York: Oxford Univ. Press, 1974, pp. 75-92. Unity.

1248 Moore, Catherine E. "Robinson and Xury and Inkle and Yarico." English Language Notes, 19 (1981), 24-29. Christianity. Sources, analogues, and influences.

1249 Moore, Catherine E. "Robinson Crusoe's Two Servants: The Measure of His Conversion." In A Fair Day in the Affections: Literary Essays in Honor of Robert B. White, Jr. Ed. Jack D. Durant and M. Thomas Hester. Raleigh, N.C.: Winston, 1980, pp. 111-18. Conversion and repentance. Characterization. Noble savage.

•1250 Moore, John Robert. Daniel Defoe: Citizen of the Modern World. Chicago: Univ. of Chicago Press, 1958. Biography.

1251 Moore, John Robert. "Daniel Defoe: Precursor of Samuel Richardson." In Restoration and Eighteenth-Century Literature: Essays in Honor of Alan Dugald McKillop. Ed. Carroll Camden. Chicago: Univ. of Chicago Press, 1963, pp. 351-69. Comparison of novelists.

1252 Moore, John Robert. "Defoe and Shakespeare." Shakespeare Quarterly, 19 (1968), 71-80. [Robinson Crusoe]. Shakespearean influence.

1253 Moore, John Robert. "Mandeville and Defoe." In Mandeville

Studies: New Explorations in the Art and Thought of Dr.
Bernard Mandeville, 1670-1733. Ed. Irwin Primer. The
Hague: Nijhoff, 1975, pp. 119-25. Mandeville. Philosophy
of novelist.

1254   Napier, Elizabeth R. "Objects and Order in Robinson Crusoe."
South Atlantic Quarterly, 80 (1981), 84-94. Characterization.

1255   Needham, J. D. "Moll's 'Honest Gentleman.'" Southern Review: An Australian Journal of Literary Studies, 3 (1969),
366-74. Characterization.

1256   Nicholson, Watson. The Historical Sources of Defoe's "Journal of the Plague Year." 1919; rpt. Port Washington,
N.Y.: Kennikat Press, 1966. Sources, analogues, and influences.

1257   Novak, Maximillian E. "Colonel Jack's Thieving Roguing Trade
to Mexico and Defoe's Attack on Economic Individualism."
Huntington Library Quarterly, 24 (1961), 349-53. "Economic individualism." Social criticism in the novel.

■1258   Novak, Maximillian E. "Conscious Irony in Moll Flanders:
Facts and Problems." College English, 26 (1964), 198-204.
Irony.

1259   Novak, Maximillian E. "Crime and Punishment in Defoe's
Roxana." Journal of English and Germanic Philology, 65
(1966), 445-65. Morality. Crime and punishment.

1260   Novak, Maximillian E. "Crusoe the King and the Political
Evolution of his Island." Studies in English Literature, 2
(1962), 337-50. Authority. Politics.

1261   Novak, Maximillian E. "Defoe and the Disordered City."
PMLA, 92 (1977), 241-52. [A Journal of the Plague Year].
Realism. London. The poor. Disease. Sympathy. Point
of view and narrator.

●1262   Novak, Maximillian E. Defoe and the Nature of Man. Oxford:
Oxford Univ. Press, 1963. Natural law. Intellectual back-
ground. Necessity. Courage. Philosophy of novelist.
Love. Marriage. Loneliness. "State of nature."

1263   Novak, Maximillian E. "Defoe's 'Indifferent Monitor': The
Complexity of Moll Flanders." Eighteenth-Century Studies,
3 (1970), 351-65. Style and language.

■1264   Novak, Maximillian E. "Defoe's Theory of Fiction." Studies
in Philology, 61 (1964), 650-58. Theory and practice of the

novel. Eighteenth-century criticism and reviews of the
novel.

1265   Novak, Maximillian E. "Defoe's Use of Irony." In Stuart
and Georgian Moments. Ed. Earl Miner. Berkeley: Univ.
of California Press, 1972, pp. 189-220. Point of view and
narrator. Irony.

•1266   Novak, Maximillian E. Economics and Fiction of Daniel Defoe.
Berkeley: Univ. of California Press, 1962. Economics.
The poor. Prostitution. Marriage. The pirate. Colonial-
ism. Luxury.

1267   Novak, Maximillian E. "Imaginary Islands and Real Beasts:
The Imaginative Genesis of Robinson Crusoe." Tennessee
Studies in Literature, 19 (1974), 57-78. Sources, ana-
logues, and influences. Composition of the novel.

1268   Novak, Maximillian E. "Moll Flanders' First Love." Papers
of the Michigan Academy of Science, Arts and Letters, 46
(1961), 635-43. Satire. Point of view and narrator.

1269   Novak, Maximillian E. "The Problem of Necessity in Defoe's
Fiction." Philological Quarterly, 40 (1961), 513-24. Necessity. Philosophy of novelist.

1270   Novak, Maximillian E. Realism, Myth, and History in Defoe's
Fiction. Lincoln: Univ. of Nebraska Press, 1983. Narrative technique. Realism. Myth. Historiography. Criminal
biography. Crime and punishment.

1271   Novak, Maximillian E. "Robinson Crusoe and Economic Utopia."
Kenyon Review, 25 (1963), 474-90. Economics. Utopia.

1272   Novak, Maximillian E. "Robinson Crusoe's Fear and the
Search for Natural Man." Modern Philology, 58 (1961),
238-45. State of nature. Intellectual background. Psychology of characters.

1273   Novak, Maximillian E. "The Unmentionable and the Ineffable
in Defoe's Fiction." Studies in the Literary Imagination,
15, No. 2 (1982), 85-102. Style and language. Psychology
of characters. Sex. Horror and terror.

1274   Novak, Maximillian E. "A Whiff of Scandal in the Life of
Daniel Defoe." Huntington Library Quarterly, 34 (1970),
35-42. Biography [sexual misconduct, 1707-08].

1275   Olshin, Toby. "'Thoughtful of the Main Chance': Defoe and
the Cycle of Anxiety." Hartford Studies in Literature, 6
(1974), 117-28. Anxiety. Psychology of characters. Biography [psychological].

1276 Parker, George. "The Allegory of Robinson Crusoe." His-
      tory, 10 (1925), 11-25. Autobiographical elements in the
      novel. Allegory [Crusoe's life as allegory of Defoe's].

1277 Pearlman, E. "Robinson Crusoe and the Cannibals." Mosaic,
      10, No. 1 (1976), 39-55. Cannibals. Sex. Violence.
      Psychology of characters.

1278 Peck, H. Daniel. "Robinson Crusoe: The Moral Geography
      of Limitation." Journal of Narrative Technique, 3 (1973),
      20-31. Setting. Morality.

■1279 Peterson, Spiro. "The Matrimonial Theme of Defoe's Roxana."
      PMLA, 70 (1955), 166-91. Marriage. Marriage law.

1280 Piper, William Bowman. "Moll Flanders as a Structure of
      Topics." Studies in English Literature, 9 (1969), 489-502.
      Plot, structure, and design.

1281 Preston, John. "Moll Flanders: 'The Satire of the Age.'"
      In his The Created Self: The Reader's Role in Eighteenth-
      Century Fiction. New York: Barnes & Noble, 1970, pp.
      8-37. Author-reader relationship. Plot, structure, and de-
      sign.

■1282 Price, Martin. "Defoe's Novels." In his To the Palace of
      Wisdom: Studies in Order and Energy from Dryden to
      Blake. Garden City, N.Y.: Doubleday, 1964, pp. 262-75.
      Order vs. disorder [energy]. Characterization [the "ener-
      gy of impulse" of Defoe's characters].

1283 Pugh, Charles W. "Defoe's Repentance Theme." Southern
      University Bulletin, 46 (1959), 57-64. Conversion and
      repentance.

1284 Rader, Ralph W. "Defoe, Richardson, Joyce, and the Con-
      cept of Form in the Novel." In Autobiography, Biography,
      and the Novel: Papers Read at a Clark Library Seminar,
      May 13, 1972. Ed. William Matthews and Ralph W. Rader.
      Los Angeles: Clark Memorial Library, U.C.L.A., 1973, pp.
      31-72. Plot, structure, and design.

1285 Raleigh, John Henry. "Style and Structure and Their Import
      in Defoe's Roxana." University of Kansas City Review, 20
      (1953), 128-35. Style and language. Plot, structure, and
      design.

1286 Ray, J. Karen. "The Feminist Role in Robinson Crusoe, Rox-
      ana, and Clarissa." Emporia State Research Studies, 24
      (1976), 28-33. Feminism.

1287   Reed, Walter L. "Moll Flanders and the Picaresque: The
       Transvaluation of Virtue." In his An Exemplary History
       of the Novel: The Quixotic versus the Picaresque. Chi-
       cago: Univ. of Chicago Press, 1981, pp. 93-116. Picar-
       esque novel. Plot, structure, and design.

•1288 Richetti, John J. Defoe's Narratives: Situations and Struc-
       tures. Oxford: Clarendon Press, 1975. Plot, structure,
       and design. Point of view and narrator. The self. Char-
       acterization.

1289   Richetti, John J. "The Family, Sex, and Marriage in Defoe's
       Moll Flanders and Roxana." Studies in the Literary Imagina-
       tion, 15, No. 2 (1982), 19-35. Family. Sex. Marriage.

1290   Robins, Harry F. "How Smart Was Robinson Crusoe?"
       PMLA, 67 (1952), 782-89. Characterization [Crusoe's mis-
       takes and errors of judgment].

1291   Rodway, A. E. "Moll Flanders and Manon Lescaut." Essays
       in Criticism, 3 (1953), 303-20. Comparison of novelists
       [Defoe, Prévost]. Love.

1292   Rogal, Samuel J. "The Profit and Loss of Moll Flanders."
       Studies in the Novel, 5 (1973), 98-103. Money [sixty-five
       financial transactions]. Characterization.

1293   Rogers, Henry N., III. "The Two Faces of Moll." Journal
       of Narrative Technique, 9 (1979), 117-25. Characterization.
       Male novelist assuming female identity.

1294   Rogers, Katharine M. "The Feminism of Daniel Defoe." In
       Woman in The 18th Century and Other Essays. Ed. Paul
       Fritz and Richard Morton. Toronto: Hakkert, 1976, pp.
       3-24. Feminism.

1295   Rogers, Pat. "Crusoe's Home." Essays in Criticism. 24
       (1974), 375-90. Domestic life. Setting.

1296   Rogers, Pat, ed. Defoe: The Critical Heritage. Critical
       Heritage Series. London: Routledge & Kegan Paul, 1972.
       Eighteenth-century criticism and reviews of the novel.

1297   Rogers, Pat. "Moll's Memory." English, 24 (1975), 67-72.
       Characterization. Point of view and narrator. Time.

•1298 Rogers, Pat. Robinson Crusoe. London: Allen & Unwin,
       1979. Travel. Allegory. Christianity. Philosophy of nov-
       elist. Plot, structure, and design. Survey of criticism.

1299   Rogers, Pat. "Speaking Within Compass: The Ground Cov-

ered in Two Works by Defoe." <u>Studies in the Literary
Imagination</u>, 15, No. 2 (1982), 103-13. [<u>Tour Thro' Great
Britain</u>, <u>Captain Singleton</u>]. Journey. Narrative tech-
nique.

1300 Ross, John F. <u>Swift and Defoe: A Study in Relationship</u>.
Berkeley: Univ. of California Press, 1941. Comparison of
novelists. Point of view and narrator.

1301 Sagarin, Edward. "Moll Flanders: Happy Are the Days of
the Penitent." In his <u>Raskolnikov and Others: Literary
Images of Crime, Punishment, Redemption, and Atonement</u>.
New York: St. Martin's, 1981, pp. 40-59. Characterization. Crime and punishment. Morality. Conversion and
repentance.

1302 Sankey, Margaret. "Meaning Through Intertextuality: Iso-
morphism of Defoe's <u>Robinson Crusoe</u> and Tournier's <u>Ven-
dredi ou les limbes du Pacifique</u>." <u>Australian Journal of
French Studies</u>, 18 (1981), 77-88. Influence and imitation.
Intertextuality.

1303 Schonhorn, Manuel. "Defoe, the Language of Politics, and
the Past." <u>Studies in the Literary Imagination</u>, 15, No. 2
(1982), 75-83. Style and language. Allusions.

■1304 Schonhorn, Manuel. "Defoe: The Literature of Politics and
the Politics of Some Fictions." In <u>English Literature in the
Age of Disguise</u>. Ed. Maximillian E. Novak. Berkeley:
Univ. of California Press, 1977, pp. 15-56. Politics.

■1305 Schonhorn, Manuel. "Defoe's <u>Captain Singleton</u>: A Reassessment with Observations." <u>Papers on Language and Litera-
ture</u>, 7 (1971), 38-51. Realism. The pirate. Sources,
analogues, and influences.

1306 Schonhorn, Manuel. "Defoe's <u>Journal of the Plague Year</u>:
Topography and Intention." <u>Review of English Studies</u>,
N.S. 19 (1968), 387-402. Setting. London.

■1306a Schorer, Mark. "A Study in Defoe: Moral Vision and Structural Form." <u>Thought</u>, 25 (1950), 275-87. Morality.
Plot, structure, and design.

■1306b Schrock, Thomas S. "Considering Crusoe." <u>Interpretation:
A Journal of Political Philosophy</u>, 1 (1970), 76-106; 2 (1971),
169-232. Critical revaluation [refutes religious interpreta-
tion]. Politics [secular political philosophy of the novel].
Christianity [anti-religious drift to Crusoe's story].

1307 Scrimgeour, Gary J. "The Problem of Realism in Defoe's

Captain Singleton." Huntington Library Quarterly, 27
(1963), 21-37. Realism.

1308   Secord, Arthur W. Robert Drury's Journal and Other Studies.
       Urbana: Univ. of Illinois Press, 1961. Sources, analogues,
       and influences.

1309   Secord, Arthur W. Studies in the Narrative Method of Defoe.
       1924; rpt. New York: Russell & Russell, 1963. Sources,
       analogues, and influences. Narrative technique.

1310   Seidel, Michael. "Crusoe in Exile." PMLA, 96 (1981), 363-
       74. Estrangement. The exile. Allegory. Plot, structure,
       and design.

1311   Sherbo, Arthur. "Moll Flanders: Defoe as Transvestite?"
       and "Moll's Friends." In his Studies in the Eighteenth-
       Century English Novel. East Lansing: Michigan State
       Univ. Press, 1969, pp. 136-76. Characterization. Male
       novelist assuming female identity. Style and language.
       Women's friendship.

•1312- Shinagel, Michael. Daniel Defoe and Middle-Class Gentility.
   13   Cambridge, Mass.: Harvard Univ. Press, 1968. Social
        structure. The middle class. The gentleman. The trades-
        man. Gentility [and other middle-class themes related to
        it].

1314   Sill, Geoffrey M. Defoe and the Idea of Fiction, 1713-1719.
       Newark: Univ. of Delaware Press, 1983. [Robinson Cru-
       soe]. Theory and practice of the novel [Defoe's political
       experiences condition his fiction]. Politics [Defoe's ideol-
       ogy]. Whigs. Allegory [Crusoe as allegory of moral and
       self restraint].

1315   Sill, Geoffrey M. "Defoe's Two Versions of the Outlaw."
       English Studies, 64 (1983), 122-28. The criminal [Defoe's
       earlier heroic view becomes a critical view].

1316   Sill, Geoffrey M. "Rogues, Strumpets, and Vagabonds: De-
       foe on Crime in the City." Eighteenth-Century Life, 2
       (1976), 74-78. Crime and punishment. City life. Social
       criticism in the novel.

1317   Skydsgaard, Niels Jørgen. "Defoe on the Art of Fiction."
       In Essays Presented to Knud Schibsbye on His 75th Birth-
       day, 29 November 1979. Ed. Michael Chesnutt et al.
       Copenhagen: Akademisk, 1979, pp. 164-71. Theory and
       practice of the novel.

1318   Sloman, Judith. "The Time Scheme of Defoe's Roxana."

English Studies in Canada, 5 (1979), 406-19. Time. Plot,
structure, and design.

1319   Smith, Leroy W. "Daniel Defoe: Incipient Pornographer."
       Literature and Psychology, 22 (1972), 165-78. [Moll Fland-
       ers, Roxana]. Pornography.

1320   Snow, Malinda. "Diabolic Intervention in Defoe's Roxana."
       Essays in Literature, 3 (1976), 52-60. Characterization.
       Puritanism. Supernatural.

1321   Snow, Malinda. "The Origins of Defoe's First-Person Narra-
       tive Technique: An Overlooked Aspect of the Rise of the
       Novel." Journal of Narrative Technique, 6 (1976), 175-87.
       Point of view and narrator. Narrative technique. Sources,
       analogues, and influences.

1322   Spacks, Patricia Meyer. "The Soul's Imaginings: Daniel De-
       foe, William Cowper." PMLA, 91 (1976), 420-35. Rev. and
       rpt. in Imagining a Self: Autobiography and Novel in
       Eighteenth-Century England. Cambridge, Mass.: Harvard
       Univ. Press, 1976, pp. 28-56. The self. Autobiographical
       elements in the novel. Characterization. Narrative tech-
       nique.

1323   Spadaccini, Nicholas. "Daniel Defoe and the Spanish Picar-
       esque Tradition: The Case of Moll Flanders." Ideologies
       and Literature: A Journal of Hispanic and Luso-Brazilian
       Studies, 2, No. 6 (1978), 10-26. Picaresque novel.
       Sources, analogues, and influences.

■1324 Stamm, Rudolf G. "Daniel Defoe: An Artist in the Puritan
       Tradition." Philological Quarterly, 15 (1936), 225-46.
       Puritanism. Philosophy of novelist.

1325   Starr, George A. Defoe and Casuistry. Princeton, N.J.:
       Princeton Univ. Press, 1971. Casuistry. Morality. Intel-
       lectual background. Christianity. Philosophy of novelist.

•1326 Starr, George A. Defoe and Spiritual Autobiography.
       Princeton, N.J.: Princeton Univ. Press, 1965. Spiritual
       biography and autobiography. Puritanism. Sources, ana-
       logues, and influences.

1327   Starr, George A. "Defoe's Prose Style: 1. The Language
       of Interpretation." Modern Philology, 71 (1974), 277-94.
       Style and language.

1328   Starr, George A. "Sympathy v. Judgment in Roxana's First
       Liaison." In The Augustan Milieu: Essays Presented to
       Louis A. Landa. Eds. Henry Knight Miller, Eric Rothstein,

and George S. Rousseau. Oxford: Clarendon Press, 1970, pp. 59-76. Sympathy vs. judgment. Characterization.

1329 Stein, William Bysshe. "Robinson Crusoe: The Trickster Tricked." Centennial Review, 9 (1965), 271-88. Point of view and narrator. Narrative technique. Morality. Imagery [religious, clothing].

1330 Stephanson, Raymond. "Defoe's 'Malade Imaginaire': The Historical Foundation of Mental Illness in Roxana." Huntington Library Quarterly, 45 (1982), 99-118. Insanity [novel reflects eighteenth-century medical opinion]. Melancholy.

1331 Stephanson, Raymond. "Defoe's Roxana: The Unresolved Experiment in Characterization." Studies in the Novel, 12 (1980), 279-88. Characterization.

1332 Strange, Sallie Minter. "Moll Flanders: A Good Calvinist." South Central Bulletin, 36 (1976), 152-54. Characterization. Calvinism.

•1333 Sutherland, James R. Daniel Defoe: A Critical Study. Cambridge, Mass.: Harvard Univ. Press, 1971. Introductory guide [excellent account of main issues].

•1334 Sutherland, James R. Defoe. 1937. Rev. ed. London: Methuen, 1950. Biography.

1335 Sutherland, James R. "The Relation of Defoe's Fiction to His Non-fictional Writings." In Imagined Worlds: Essays on Some English Novels and Novelists in Honour of John Butt. Ed. Maynard Mack and Ian Gregor. London: Methuen, 1968, pp. 37-50. Introductory guide.

1336 Swados, Harvey. "Robinson Crusoe, the Man Alone." In Twelve Original Essays on Great English Novels. Ed. Charles Shapiro. Detroit: Wayne State Univ. Press, 1960, pp. 1-21. Loneliness. Sources, analogues, and influences [Selkirk's shipwreck]. Alexander Selkirk.

1337 Swann, George Rogers. "Defoe and Individualistic Realism." In his Philosophical Parallelisms in Six English Novelists: The Conception of Good, Evil, and Human Nature. Philadelphia: Univ. of Pennsylvania, 1929, pp. 8-26. Philosophy of novelist. Aristotle. Realism.

1338 Taube, Myron. "Moll Flanders and Fanny Hill: A Comparison." Ball State University Forum, 9 (1968), 76-80. Comparison of novelists [Defoe, Cleland].

1339   Taylor, Anne Robinson. "This Beautiful Lady Whose Words
       He Speaks: Defoe and His Female Masquerades." In her
       Male Novelists and Their Female Voices: Literary Masquer-
       ades. Troy, N.Y.: Whitston, 1981, pp. 29-55. [Moll
       Flanders, Roxana]. Male novelist assuming female identity.
       Women. Autobiographical elements in the novel. Masquer-
       ade.

1340   Tillyard, E. M. W. "Defoe." In his The Epic Strain in the
       English Novel. Fair Lawn, N.J.: Essential Books, 1958,
       pp. 25-50. Epic [Robinson Crusoe as an English epic].
       Allegory.

1341   Uphaus, Robert W. "Defoe, Deliverance, and Dissimulation."
       In his The Impossible Observer: Reason and the Reader
       in 18th-Century Prose. Lexington: Univ. Press of Ken-
       tucky, 1979, pp. 46-70. Author-reader relationship.
       Point of view and narrator.

1342   Vaid, Sudesh. "Defoe and Richardson and the Eighteenth-
       Century Woman's Debate" and "Moll Flanders and Roxana."
       In The Divided Mind: Studies in Defoe and Richardson.
       New Delhi: Associated Publishing House, 1980, pp. 48-150.
       Women. Social criticism in the novel. Comparison of novel-
       ists.

■1343 Van Ghent, Dorothy. "On Moll Flanders." In her The Eng-
       lish Novel: Form and Function. New York: Holt, Rine-
       hart, Winston, 1953, pp. 33-44. Rpt. in Twentieth Century
       Interpretations of "Moll Flanders." Ed. Robert C. Elliott.
       Englewood Cliffs, N.J.: Prentice-Hall, 1970, pp. 30-39.
       Irony. Materialism.

1344   Walton, James. "The Romance of Gentility: Defoe's Heroes
       and Heroines." In Literary Monographs. Vol. 4. Ed.
       Eric Rothstein. Madison: Univ. of Wisconsin Press, 1971,
       pp. 91-135. Gentility. Characterization. Hero/heroine.

1345   Watson, Tommy G. "Defoe's Attitude Toward Marriage and
       the Position of Women as Revealed in Moll Flanders."
       Southern Quarterly, 3 (1964), 1-8. Marriage. Women.

1346   Watt, Ian. "Defoe and Richardson on Homer: A Study of
       the Relation of Novel and Epic in the Early Eighteenth Cen-
       tury." Review of English Studies, N.S. 4 (1953), 325-40.
       Homer. Epic.

1347   Watt, Ian. "The Naming of Characters in Defoe, Richardson,
       and Fielding." Review of English Studies, O.S. 25 (1949),
       322-38. Names of characters.

1348 Watt, Ian. "Robinson Crusoe as a Myth." Essays in Criti-
      cism, 1 (1951), 95-119. Myth [of modern economic and so-
      cial order].

■1349 Watt, Ian. "Robinson Crusoe, Individualism and the Novel"
      and "Defoe as Novelist: Moll Flanders." In his The Rise
      of the Novel: Studies in Defoe, Richardson and Fielding.
      1957; rpt. Berkeley: Univ. of California Press, 1962, pp.
      60-134. Individualism. Realism.

1350 Weinstein, Arnold. "The Self-Made Woman, I: Moll Flanders."
      In his Fictions of the Self: 1550-1800. Princeton, N.J.:
      Princeton Univ. Press, 1981, pp. 85-100. The self. Indi-
      vidualism [power of the individual]. Characterization.

1351 Woodcock, George. "Colonel Jack and Tom Jones: Aspects
      of a Changing Century." Wascana Review, 5 (1970), 67-73.
      Comparison of novelists [Defoe, Fielding].

1352 Zimmerman, Everett. "Defoe and Crusoe." ELH: A Journal
      of English Literary History, 38 (1971), 377-96. Character-
      ization.

1353 Zimmerman, Everett. Defoe and the Novel. Berkeley: Univ.
      of California Press, 1975. Artistic development. Point of
      view and narrator. Plot, structure, and design. Epistem-
      ology. The self.

1354 Zimmerman, Everett. "H. F.'s Meditations: A Journal of the
      Plague Year." PMLA, 87 (1972), 417-23. Allegory. Plot,
      structure, and design. Providence.

1355 Zimmerman, Everett. "Language and Character in Defoe's
      Roxana." Essays in Criticism, 21 (1971), 227-35. Style
      and language. Characterization.

      SEE ALSO ITEMS 334, 768, 774, 792, 793, 797, 816,
      884, 892a, 897, 898, 932, 946, 951, 973, 978, 1004a,
      1012, 1015, 1016, 1018, 1021, 1056, 1060, 1060a, 1075,
      1087, 1110, 1113, 1116.

                        HENRY FIELDING
                         (1707-1754)

PRINCIPAL FICTION

An Apology for the Life of Mrs. Shamela Andrews, 1741

Joseph Andrews, 1742

Jonathan Wild the Great, 1743

Tom Jones, 1749

Amelia, 1751

BIBLIOGRAPHIES AND SURVEYS OF CRITICISM

1356 Battestin, Martin C. "Fielding." In The English Novel: Se-
      lect Bibliographical Guides. Ed. A. E. Dyson. Oxford:
      Oxford Univ. Press, 1974, pp. 71-89. Bibliography of
      criticism. Survey of criticism.

1357 Blanchard, Frederic T. Fielding the Novelist: A Study in
      Historical Criticism. New Haven, Conn.: Yale Univ.
      Press, 1926. Eighteenth-century criticism and reviews of
      the novel. Survey of criticism.

1358 Hahn, H. George. Henry Fielding: An Annotated Bibliogra-
      phy. Metuchen, N.J.: Scarecrow Press, 1979. Bibliogra-
      phy of criticism [annotated, evaluative].

1359 Hahn, H. George. "Main Lines of Criticism of Fielding's
      Joseph Andrews, 1925-1978." British Studies Monitor, 10,
      No. 3 (1981), 4-17. Survey of criticism.

1360 Hahn, H. George. "Main Lines of Criticism of Fielding's Tom
      Jones, 1900-1978." British Studies Monitor, 10, No. 1
      (1980), 8-35. Survey of criticism.

1361 McKillop, Alan Dugald. "Some Recent Views of Tom Jones."
      College English, 21 (1959), 17-22. Survey of criticism.

1362 Morrissey, L. J. Henry Fielding: A Reference Guide. Bos-
      ton: G. K. Hall, 1980. Bibliography of criticism [anno-
      tated]. Bibliography of primary sources.

1363 Stoler, John A., and Richard D. Fulton. Henry Fielding:
      An Annotated Bibliography of Twentieth-Century Criticism,
      1900-1977. New York: Garland, 1980. Bibliography of
      criticism [annotated].

BIOGRAPHICAL AND CRITICAL STUDIES

1364 Allott, Miriam. "A Note on Fielding's Mr. Square." Modern
      Language Review, 56 (1961), 69-72. Characterization.
      Christianity.

•1365 Alter, Robert. Fielding and the Nature of the Novel. Cam-
       bridge, Mass.: Harvard Univ. Press, 1968. Plot, struc-
       ture, and design. Style and language. Irony. Charac-
       terization. Critical revaluation [attacks criticism of Fielding
       based on puritanical and tragic standards].

1366 Alter, Robert. "The Picaroon Domesticated." In his Rogue's
       Progress: Studies in the Picaresque Novel. Cambridge,
       Mass.: Harvard Univ. Press, 1964, pp. 80-105. [Tom
       Jones]. Rogue hero. Picaresque novel.

1367 Amory, Hugh, ed. "Henry Fielding." In his Poets and Men
       of Letters. Vol. VII of Sale Catalogues of Libraries of
       Eminent Persons. London: Mansell, with Sotheby Publica-
       tions, 1973, pp. 123-58. Library of novelist.

1368 Amory, Hugh. "Henry Fielding and the Criminal Legislation
       of 1751-2." Philological Quarterly, 50 (1970), 175-92. Law.
       Crime and punishment. Philosophy of novelist.

1369 Amory, Hugh. "Magistrate or Censor? The Problem of Au-
       thority in Fielding's Later Writings." Studies in English
       Literature, 12 (1972), 503-18. [Amelia]. Authority.
       Characterization.

1370 Amory, Hugh. "Shamela as Aesopic Satire." ELH: A Jour-
       nal of English Literary History, 38 (1971), 239-53. Satire.
       Parody.

1371 Anderson, Howard. "Answers to the Author of Clarissa:
       Theme and Narrative Technique in Tom Jones and Tristram
       Shandy." Philological Quarterly, 51 (1972), 859-73. Nar-
       rative technique.

1372 Baker, John Ross. "From Imitation to Rhetoric: The Chicago
       Critics, Wayne C. Booth, and Tom Jones." Novel, 6
       (1973), 197-217. Plot, structure, and design. Point of
       view and narrator.

1373 Baker, Sheridan. "Bridget Allworthy: The Creative Pres-
       sures of Fielding's Plot." Papers of the Michigan Academy
       of Science, Arts and Letters, 52 (1967), 345-56. Charac-
       terization. Plot, structure, and design [plot generates
       character].

1374 Baker, Sheridan. "Fielding and the Irony of Form." Eight-
       eenth-Century Studies, 2 (1968), 138-54. [Joseph Andrews,
       Tom Jones]. Irony. Aesthetic distance.

1375 Baker, Sheridan. "Fielding's Amelia and the Materials of Ro-
       mance." Philological Quarterly, 41 (1962), 437-49. Romance.

1376   Baker, Sheridan. "Fielding's Comic Epic-in-Prose Romances
        Again." Philological Quarterly, 58 (1979), 63-81. Romance.

1377   Baker, Sheridan. "Henry Fielding and the Cliché." Criti-
        cism, 1 (1959), 354-61. Style and language. Imagery.

■1378   Baker, Sheridan. "Henry Fielding's Comic Romances." Pa-
        pers of the Michigan Academy of Science, Arts and Letters,
        45 (1960), 411-19. [Joseph Andrews, Tom Jones]. Ro-
        mance [acceptance of romantic love, mockery of heroic ad-
        venture].

1379   Battestin, Martin C. "Fielding's Changing Politics and Joseph
        Andrews." Philological Quarterly, 39 (1960), 39-55. Auto-
        biographical elements in the novel. Politics.

■1380   Battestin, Martin C. "Fielding's Definition of Wisdom: Some
        Functions of Ambiguity and Emblem in Tom Jones." ELH:
        A Journal of English Literary History, 35 (1968), 188-217.
        Rpt. in his The Providence of Wit: Aspects of Form in
        Augustan Literature and the Arts. Oxford: Clarendon
        Press, 1974, pp. 164-92. Wisdom [as chief theme]. Am-
        biguity. Emblem.

1381   Battestin, Martin C. "Henry Fielding, Sarah Fielding, and
        'the Dreadful Sin of Incest.'" Novel, 13 (1979), 6-18.
        [Amelia]. Incest. Biography.

●1382   Battestin, Martin C. The Moral Basis of Fielding's Art: A
        Study of "Joseph Andrews." Middletown, Conn.: Wesleyan
        Univ. Press, 1959. Philosophy of novelist. Christianity.
        Latitudinarianism. Morality. The clergy. Rural ideal.
        Plot, structure, and design.

1383   Battestin, Martin C. "Osborne's Tom Jones: Adopting a
        Classic." Virginia Quarterly Review, 42 (1966), 378-93.
        Film and the novel.

1384   Battestin, Martin C. "The Problem of Amelia: Hume, Bar-
        row, and the Conversion of Captain Booth." ELH: A
        Journal of English Literary History, 41 (1974), 613-48.
        Philosophy of novelist. Artistic development. Intellectual
        background.

■1385   Battestin, Martin C. "Tom Jones: The Argument of Design."
        In The Augustan Milieu: Essays Presented to Louis A.
        Landa. Ed. Henry Knight Miller, Eric Rothstein, and
        George S. Rousseau. Oxford: Clarendon Press, 1970, pp.
        289-319. Rpt. in his The Providence of Wit: Aspects of
        Form in Augustan Literature and the Arts. Oxford: Clar-
        endon Press, 1974, pp. 141-63. Plot, structure, and design

[symbolizes Fielding's Christian view of life]. Providence.
Philosophy of novelist.

1386   Battestin, Martin C. "Tom Jones and 'His Egyptian Majesty':
       Fielding's Parable of Government." PMLA, 82 (1967), 68-
       77. Politics. Digressions and interpolated stories.

1387   Battestin, Martin C., with R. R. Battestin. "Fielding, Bed-
       ford, and the Westminster Election of 1749." Eighteenth-
       Century Studies, 11 (1977-78), 143-85. Politics. Biogra-
       phy.

1388   Beasley, Jerry C. "Fiction as Artifice: The Achievement of
       Henry Fielding." In his Novels of the 1740s. Athens:
       Univ. of Georgia Press, 1982, pp. 184-210. Innovation.
       Achievement and reputation.

1389   Beatty, Richmond Croom. "Criticism in Fielding's Narratives
       and His Estimate of Critics." PMLA, 49 (1934), 1087-1100.
       Theory and practice of the novel. Novelists on the novel.

1390   Behrens, Laurence. "The Argument of Tom Jones." Liter-
       ature/Film Quarterly, 8 (1980), 22-34. Film and the novel.

1391   Bell, Michael. "A Note on Drama and the Novel: Fielding's
       Contribution." Novel, 3 (1970), 119-28. [Tom Jones].
       Dramatic conventions in the novel. Speech and dialogue.
       Style and language. Marriage proposal.

1392   Berland, K. J. H. "Satire and the Via Media: Anglican Dia-
       logue in Joseph Andrews." In Satire in the Eighteenth
       Century. Ed. J. D. Browning. New York: Garland,
       1983, pp. 83-99. Satire. Anglicanism. Via media. Ethics.

1393   Bevan, C. H. K. "The Unity of Fielding's Amelia." Renais-
       sance and Modern Studies, 14 (1970), 90-110. Plot, struc-
       ture, and design. Unity.

1394   Bissell, Frederick Olds, Jr. Fielding's Theory of the Novel.
       1933; rpt. New York: Cooper Square, 1969. Theory and
       practice of the novel. Novelists on the novel.

1395   Bliss, Michael. "Fielding's Bill of Fare in Tom Jones." ELH:
       A Journal of English Literary History, 30 (1963), 236-43.
       Author-reader relationship. Point of view and narrator.

1396   Bloch, Tuvia. "Amelia and Booth's Doctrine of the Passions."
       Studies in English Literature, 13 (1973), 461-73. Philos-
       ophy of novelist [Fielding abandons his doctrine of "good
       nature"]. Characterization. The passions.

1397   Bloch, Tuvia. "The Prosecution of the Maidservant in Ame-
       lia." English Language Notes, 6 (1969), 269–71. Charac-
       terization. Law.

1398   Bort, Barry D. "Incest Theme in Tom Jones." American
       Notes and Queries, 3 (1965), 83–84. Incest.

1399   Bradbury, Malcolm. "The Comic Novel in Sterne and Field-
       ing." In The Winged Skull: Papers from the Laurence
       Sterne Bicentenary Conference. Ed. Arthur H. Cash and
       John M. Stedmond. Kent, Ohio: Kent State Univ. Press,
       1971, pp. 124–31. Comparison of novelists. Comedy.

1400   Braudy, Leo. "Fielding: Public History and Individual Per-
       ception." In his Narrative Form in History and Fiction:
       Hume, Fielding, and Gibbon. Princeton, N.J.: Princeton
       Univ. Press, 1970, pp. 91–212. Plot, structure, and design.
       Point of view and narrator. Artistic development. Histori-
       ography. Epistemology.

1401   Brogan, Howard O. "Fiction and Philosophy in the Education
       of Tom Jones, Tristram Shandy, and Richard Feverel."
       College English, 14 (1952), 144–49. Education. Comparison
       of novelists.

1402   Brooks, Douglas. "Abraham Adams and Parson Trulliber:
       The Meaning of Joseph Andrews, Book II, Chapter 14."
       Modern Language Review, 63 (1968), 794–801. Biblical al-
       lusions. Classical allusions.

1403   Brooks, Douglas. "Fielding: Joseph Andrews" and "Fielding:
       Tom Jones and Amelia." In his Number and Pattern in the
       Eighteenth-Century Novel. London: Routledge & Kegan
       Paul, 1973, pp. 65–122. Numerology. Plot, structure, and
       design. Symbolism.

1404   Brooks, Douglas. "The Interpolated Tales in Joseph Andrews
       Again." Modern Philology, 65 (1968), 208–13. Digressions
       and interpolated stories. Marriage.

1405   Brooks, Douglas. "Richardson's Pamela and Fielding's Joseph
       Andrews." Essays in Criticism, 18 (1967), 158–68. See al-
       so A. M. Kearney, "Pamela and Joseph Andrews," ibid.,
       105–07. Comparison of novelists.

1406   Brown, Homer Obed. "Tom Jones: The 'Bastard' of History."
       Boundary, 7, No. 2 (1979), 201–33. Allegory. Politics.

1407   Burke, John J., Jr. "History Without History: Fielding's
       Theory of Fiction." In A Provision of Human Nature: Es-
       says on Fielding and Others in Honor of Miriam Austin

Locke. Ed. Donald Kay. University: Univ. of Alabama
Press, 1977, pp. 45-63. Theory and practice of the novel.
Historiography.

■1408 Cauthen, I. B., Jr. "Fielding's Digressions in Joseph Andrews." College English, 17 (1956), 379-82. Digressions
and interpolated stories [digressions are exempla of themes
in the novel proper]. Plot, structure, and design.

1409 Cleary, Thomas R. "Fielding: Style for an Age of Sensibility." In Transactions of the Samuel Johnson Society of the
Northwest. Vol. VI. Calgary: Samuel Johnson Society of
the Northwest, 1973, pp. 91-96. Novel of sensibility.
Style and language.

1410 Cleary, Thomas R. "Henry Fielding and the Great Jacobite
Paper War of 1747-49." Eighteenth-Century Life, 5 (1978),
1-11. Jacobitism. Politics.

1411 Cleary, Thomas R. "Jacobitism in Tom Jones: The Basis for
an Hypothesis." Philological Quarterly, 52 (1973), 239-51.
Jacobitism. Rebellion of 1745. Politics. Digressions and
interpolated stories.

1412 Cockshut, A. O. J. "Richardson and Fielding." In his Man
and Woman: A Study of Love and the Novel, 1740-1940.
1977; rpt. New York: Oxford Univ. Press, 1978, pp. 32-
45. Love. Sex. Comparison of novelists.

1413 Coley, W. B. "The Background of Fielding's Laughter."
ELH: A Journal of English Literary History, 26 (1959),
229-52. Sources, analogues, and influences. Satires.

1414 Coley, W. B. "Henry Fielding and the Two Walpoles." Philological Quarterly, 45 (1966), 157-78. Sir Robert Walpole.
Horace Walpole. Politics.

1415 Coley, W. B. "Notes Toward a 'Class Theory' of Augustan
Literature: The Example of Fielding." In Literary Theory
and Structure: Essays in Honor of William K. Wimsatt.
Ed. Frank Brady, et al. New Haven, Conn.: Yale Univ.
Press, 1973, pp. 131-50. Social structure. Patronage.

1416 Combs, William W. "The Return to Paradise Hall: An Essay
on Tom Jones." South Atlantic Quarterly, 67 (1968), 419-
36. Evil. Philosophy of novelist. Plot, structure, and
design. The "fortunate fall."

1417 Cooke, Arthur L. "Fielding and the Writers of Heroic Romance." PMLA, 62 (1947), 984-94. Romance.

■1418 Coolidge, John S. "Fielding and the 'Conservation of Char-
       acter.'" Modern Philology, 57 (1960), 245-59. [Tom
       Jones, Amelia]. Characterization. Artistic development.

■1419 Crane, R. S. "The Plot of Tom Jones." Journal of General
       Education, 4 (1950), 112-30. Plot, structure, and design
       [intricate scheme of probabilities, moral choices, mistaken
       judgments, accidents of fortune]. Unity. Author-reader
       relationship.

●1420 Cross, Wilbur L. The History of Henry Fielding. 3 vols.
       New Haven, Conn.: Yale Univ. Press, 1918. Biography.

 1421 DeBlois, Peter B. "Ulysses at Upton: A Consideration of
       the Comic Effect of Fielding's Mock-Heroic Style in Tom
       Jones." Thoth, 11, No. 3 (1971), 3-8. Comedy. Style
       and language. Parody.

 1422 De Voogd, Peter Jan. Henry Fielding and William Hogarth:
       The Correspondences of the Arts. Amsterdam: Rodopi,
       1981. [Esp. Amelia]. Hogarth. Literature and the other
       arts.

 1423 Digeon, Aurélien. The Novels of Fielding. 1923; rpt. Lon-
       don: Routledge & Kegan Paul, 1925. Plot, structure, and
       design. Realism. Artistic development.

 1424 Dircks, Richard J. "The Perils of Heartfree: A Sociological
       Review of Fielding's Adaptation of Dramatic Convention."
       Texas Studies in Literature and Language, 8 (1966), 5-13.
       Dramatic conventions in the novel. Sentimentalism. Plot,
       structure, and design.

 1425 Donaldson, Ian. "Fielding, Richardson, and the Ends of the
       Novel." Essays in Criticism, 32 (1982), 26-47. Closure.
       Characterization.

 1426 Donaldson, Ian. "High and Low Life: Fielding and the Uses
       of Inversion." In his The World Upside-Down: Comedy
       from Jonson to Fielding. Oxford: Clarendon Press, 1970,
       pp. 183-206. Comedy. Social structure.

 1427 Donovan, Robert Alan. "Joseph Andrews as Parody." In his
       The Shaping Vision: Imagination in the English Novel from
       Defoe to Dickens. Ithaca, N.Y.: Cornell Univ. Press,
       1966, pp. 68-88. Parody.

 1428 Driskell, Leon V. "Interpolated Tales in Joseph Andrews
       and Don Quixote: The Dramatic Method as Instruction."
       South Atlantic Bulletin, 33, No. 3 (1968), 5-8. Digressions
       and interpolated stories. Don Quixote.

1429   Dudden, F. Homes. Henry Fielding: His Life, Works, and
        Times. 2 vols. Oxford: Clarendon Press, 1952. Biogra-
        phy.

■1430   Dyson, A. E. "Satiric and Comic Theory in Relation to Field-
        ing." Modern Language Quarterly, 18 (1957), 225-37. Rpt.
        in Crazy Fabric: Essays in Irony. London: Macmillan,
        1965, pp. 14-32. Satire. Comedy [humor undermines sat-
        ire]. Irony. Artistic development [shift from satiric ideal
        to comic norm].

1431   Eaves, T. C. Duncan. "Amelia and Clarissa." In A Provi-
        sion of Human Nature: Essays on Fielding and Others in
        Honor of Miriam Austin Locke. Ed. Donald Kay. Univer-
        sity: Univ. of Alabama Press, 1977, pp. 95-110. Compari-
        son of novelists.

1432   Ehrenpreis, Irvin. Fielding: "Tom Jones." London: Ed-
        ward Arnold, 1964. Introductory guide.

1433   Ehrenpreis, Irvin. "Fielding's Use of Fiction: The Autonomy
        of Joseph Andrews." In Twelve Original Essays on Great
        English Novels. Ed. Charles Shapiro. Detroit: Wayne
        State Univ. Press, 1960, pp. 23-41. Plot, structure, and
        design. Unity.

1434   Ek, Grete. "Glory, Jest, and Riddle: The Masque of Tom
        Jones in London." English Studies, 60 (1979), 148-58.
        Characterization [Tom analyzed by Fielding in a theatrical
        framework]. Gestures and mannerisms. Dramatic conven-
        tions in the novel. Masquerade.

1435   Empson, William "Tom Jones." Kenyon Review, 20 (1958),
        217-49. For a response see C. J. Rawson, "Professor Emp-
        son's Tom Jones," Notes and Queries, 204 (1959), 400-04.
        Irony. Author-reader relationship. Morality. Philosophy
        of novelist.

1436   Evans, David L. "The Theme of Liberty in Jonathan Wild."
        Papers on Language and Literature, 3 (1967), 302-13.
        Liberty. Philosophy of novelist.

1437   Evans, James E. "Fielding, The Whole Duty of Man, Shamela,
        and Joseph Andrews." Philological Quarterly, 61 (1982),
        212-19. Sources, analogues, and influences. Morality.

1438   Evans, James E. "The Social Design of Fielding's Novels."
        College Literature, 7 (1980), 91-103. Charity. Social
        criticism in the novel. Plot, structure, and design. Set-
        ting [communities focus the theme of social obligation].

1439   Farrell, William J. "Fielding's Familiar Style." ELH: A
       Journal of English Literary History, 34 (1967), 65-77.
       Style and language. Speech and dialogue. Point of view
       and narrator.

1440   Farrell, William J. "The Mock-Heroic Form of Jonathan Wild."
       Modern Philology, 63 (1966), 216-26. Plot, structure, and
       design. Parody.

1441   Farringdon, Michael G. A Concordance and Word-Lists to
       Henry Fielding's "Shamela." West Cross, Swansea: Ariel
       House, 1982. Concordance.

1442   Farringdon, Michael G. A Concordance and Word-Lists to
       Henry Fielding's "Joseph Andrews." West Cross, Swansea:
       Ariel House, 1984. Concordance.

1443   Felsenstein, Frank. "'Newgate with the Mask On': A View
       of Jonathan Wild." Zeitschrift für Anglistik und Ameri-
       kanistik, 28 (1980), 211-18. Satire.

1444   Folkenflik, Robert. "Purpose and Narration in Fielding's
       Amelia." Novel, 6 (1973), 168-74. Point of view and nar-
       rator. Tragedy. Shakespearean influence.

1445   Folkenflik, Robert. "Tom Jones, the Gypsies, and the Mas-
       querade." University of Toronto Quarterly, 44 (1975),
       224-37. Contrast as technique. Digressions and interpo-
       lated stories. Masquerade.

1446   Freedman, William. "Joseph Andrews: Clothing and the Con-
       cretization of Character." Discourse, 4 (1961), 304-10.
       Characterization. Imagery. Clothing.

1447   Freedman, William. "Joseph Andrews: Fielding's Garden of
       the Perverse." Tennessee Studies in Literature, 16 (1971),
       35-46. Characterization. Imagery [animal].

1448   Giddings, Robert. "Fielding, Smollett, and Eighteenth-Century
       Criticism of the Novel." In his The Tradition of Smollett.
       London: Methuen, 1967, pp. 46-70. Comparison of novel-
       ists. Theory and practice of the novel. Eighteenth-century
       criticism and reviews of the novel.

1449   Goldberg, Homer. The Art of "Joseph Andrews." Chicago:
       Univ. of Chicago Press, 1969. Incorporates a revision of
       "The Interpolated Stories in Joseph Andrews or 'The His-
       tory of the World in General' Satirically Revised," Modern
       Philology, 63 (1966), 295-310. Digressions and interpolated
       stories. Sources, analogues, and influences. Don Quixote.

1450 Goldberg, Homer. "Comic Prose Epic or Comic Romance:
      The Argument of the Preface to Joseph Andrews." Philo-
      logical Quarterly, 43 (1964), 193-215. Theory and practice
      of the novel. Epic. Romance.

1451 Golden, Morris. Fielding's Moral Psychology. Amherst:
      Univ. of Massachusetts Press, 1966. Psychology of char-
      acters. Philosophy of novelist. Morality. The self.

1451a Golden, Morris. "Public Context and Imagining a Self in Tom
      Jones." Papers on Language and Literature, 20 (1984), 273-
      92. Autobiographical elements in the novel. Politics.

■1452 Goldknopf, David. "The Failure of Plot in Tom Jones."
      Criticism, 11 (1969), 262-74. Rpt. and rev. in his The
      Life of the Novel. Chicago: Univ. of Chicago Press, 1972,
      pp. 125-42. Plot, structure, and design. Point of view
      and narrator. Defects in the novel [plot lacks tension and
      energy].

1453 Gottfried, Leon. "The Odysseyan Form." In Essays in Euro-
      pean Literature: In Honor of Liselotte Dieckmann. Ed.
      P. U. Hofendahl, H. Lindenberger, and E. Schwarz. St.
      Louis: Washington Univ. Press, 1972, pp. 19-43. Plot,
      structure, and design. Classical allusions.

1454 Greene, J. Lee. "Fielding's Gypsy Episode and Sancho Pan-
      za's Governorship." South Atlantic Bulletin, 39 (1974),
      117-21. Politics. Digressions and interpolated stories.
      Sources, analogues, and influences. Don Quixote.

1455 Guthrie, William B. "The Comic Celebrant of Life in Tom
      Jones." Tennessee Studies in Literature, 19 (1974), 91-
      105. Comedy. Point of view and narrator [narrator's
      festive spirit].

1456 Hagstrum, Jean H. "Henry Fielding and Amelia." In his
      Sex and Sensibility: Ideal and Erotic Love from Milton to
      Mozart. Chicago: Univ. of Chicago Press, 1980, pp. 178-
      90. Love. Sensibility. Sex.

1457 Hall, Michael L. "Incest and Morality in Tom Jones." South
      Central Bulletin, 41 (1981), 101-04. Incest. Morality.

1458 Harris, R. W. "Richardson, Fielding, and the New Morality."
      In his Reason and Nature in the Eighteenth Century. New
      York: Barnes & Noble, 1969, pp. 251-79. Morality. Bene-
      volence. Comparison of novelists.

•1459 Harrison, Bernard. Henry Fielding's "Tom Jones": The Nov-
      elist as Moral Philosopher. Sussex: Sussex Univ. Press,

1975. [Includes a chapter on Jonathan Wild, pp. 127-38].
Morality. Philosophy of novelist. "Good-natured Man."
Characterization. Irony. Intellectual background.

1460   Hartwig, Robert J. "Pharsamon and Joseph Andrews." Texas
Studies in Literature and Language, 14 (1972), 45-52.
Sources, analogues, and influences. Narrative technique.
Author-reader relationship.

1461   Hassall, Anthony J. "Fielding's Amelia: Dramatic and Authorial Narration." Novel, 5 (1972), 225-33. Point of view
and narrator.

1462   Hassall, Anthony J. "Fielding and the Novel as Parody."
Southern Review: Literary and Interdisciplinary Essays,
13 (1980), 30-40. Parody. Sources, analogues, and influences.

1463   Hassall, Anthony J. "Fielding's Puppet Image." Philological
Quarterly, 53 (1974), 71-83. Imagery.

1464   Hassall, Anthony J. Henry Fielding's "Tom Jones." Sydney:
Sydney Univ. Press, 1979. Style and language [texture].
Theory and practice of the novel [relationship between life
and art].

•1465   Hatfield, Glenn W. Henry Fielding and the Language of
Irony. Chicago: Univ. of Chicago Press, 1968. Incorporates "Puffs and Pollitricks: Jonathan Wild and the Political Corruption of Language," Philological Quarterly, 46
(1967), 248-67; "Quacks, Pettifoggers, and Parsons: Fielding's Case Against the Learned Professions," Texas Studies
in Literature and Language, 9 (1967), 69-83; and "'The
Serpent and the Dove': 'Prudence' in Tom Jones," Modern
Philology, 65 (1967), 17-32. Irony. Style and language.
Satire. Politics. The professions. Prudence [as theme].
Quackery.

1466   Herman, George. "Fielding Defends Allworthy." Iowa English Yearbook, 10 (1965), 64-70. Characterization.

1467   Hill, Rowland M. "Setting in the Novels of Henry Fielding."
Bulletin of the Citadel, 7 (1943), 26-52. Setting.

■1468   Hilles, Frederick W. "Art and Artifice in Tom Jones." In
Imagined Worlds: Essays on Some English Novels and Nov-
elists in Honour of John Butt. Ed. Maynard Mack and Ian
Gregor. London: Methuen, 1968, pp. 91-110. Plot,
structure, and design [includes a diagram of the plot].
Critical revaluation [shows "contrivance" as a merit].

1469 Hopkins, Robert H. "Language and Comic Play in Fielding's
      Jonathan Wild." Criticism, 8 (1966), 213-28. Speech and
      dialogue. Style and language. Satire.

1470 Hughes, Leo. "The Influence of Fielding's Milieu upon His
      Humor." Studies in English (1944), pp. 269-97. Comedy.
      Autobiographical elements in the novel.

■1471 Humphreys, A. R. "Fielding's Irony: Its Methods and Ef-
      fects." Review of English Studies, O. S. 18 (1942), 183-
      96. Irony. Comparison of novelists [Fielding, Swift].

1472 Hunt, Russell A. "Johnson on Fielding and Richardson: A
      Problem in Literary Moralism." Humanities Association Re-
      view, 27 (1976), 412-20. Eighteenth-century criticism and
      reviews of the novel. Comparison of novelists. Morality.
      Dr. Johnson.

1473 Hunter, J. Paul. "Fielding and the Disappearance of Heroes."
      In The English Hero, 1660-1800. Ed. Robert Folkenflik.
      Newark: Univ. of Delaware Press, 1982, pp. 116-42.
      Hero/heroine [Tom Jones as modern hero maturing in a
      world bereft of old values].

1474 Hunter, J. Paul. "The Lesson of Amelia." In Quick Springs
      of Sense: Studies in the Eighteenth Century. Ed. Larry
      S. Champion. Athens: Univ. of Georgia Press, 1974, pp.
      157-82. Defects in the novel. Critical revaluation.

●1475 Hunter, J. Paul. Occasional Form: Henry Fielding and the
      Chains of Circumstance. Baltimore: The Johns Hopkins
      Univ. Press, 1975. Incorporates "Fielding's Reflexive Plays
      and the Rhetoric of Discovery," Studies in the Literary
      Imagination, 5 (1972), 65-100. Politics. Social background.
      Artistic development [Fielding's literary adjustment to cul-
      tural changes]. Plot, structure, and design. Journey.
      Country vs. city.

●1476 Hutchens, Eleanor Newman. Irony in "Tom Jones." Univer-
      sity: Univ. of Alabama Press, 1965. Irony.

1477 Hutchens, Eleanor Newman. "O Attic Shape! The Cornering
      of Square." In A Provision of Human Nature: Essays on
      Fielding and Others in Honor of Miriam Austin Locke. Ed.
      Donald Kay. University: Univ. of Alabama Press, 1977,
      pp. 37-44. Symbolism [geometric]. Setting.

●1478 Irwin, Michael. Henry Fielding: The Tentative Realist. Ox-
      ford: Clarendon Press, 1967. Realism. Plot, structure,
      and design. Morality. Dichotomy of intention [Fielding's

split intentions between moralizing and entertaining make
his realism tentative].

•1479 Irwin, W. R. The Making of "Jonathan Wild": A Study in
the Literary Method of Henry Fielding. 1941; rpt. Hamden, Conn.: Archon, 1966. Satire. Parody [of criminal
biography and rogue story]. Morality. Goodness vs.
greatness.

1480 Irwin, W. R. "Satire and Comedy in the Works of Henry
Fielding." ELH: A Journal of English Literary History,
13 (1946), 168-88. Satire. Comedy. Artistic development
[from early satire on affectation he progressed to narrative
comedy with ethical and technical refinements].

1481 Iser, Wolfgang. "The Role of the Reader in Fielding's Joseph
Andrews and Tom Jones." In his Implied Reader: Patterns
of Communications in Prose Fiction from Bunyan to Beckett.
Baltimore: The Johns Hopkins Univ. Press, 1974, pp. 29-
56. [Originally published in German in 1972]. Author-
reader relationship.

1482 Jarvis, Rupert C. "Fielding and the Forty-Five." Notes and
Queries, N.S. 3 (1956), 391-94, 479-82; N.S. 4 (1957), 19-
34. Politics. Rebellion of 1745.

1483 Jenkins, Owen. "Richardson's Pamela and Fielding's 'Vile
Forgeries.'" Philological Quarterly, 44 (1965), 200-10.
Comparison of novelists.

1484 Jensen, Gerard E. "Fashionable Society in Fielding's Time."
PMLA, 31 (1916), 79-89. Social background. Social structure.

•1485 Johnson, Maurice. Fielding's Art of Fiction: Eleven Essays
on "Shamela," "Joseph Andrews," "Tom Jones," and "Amelia." Philadelphia: Univ. of Pennsylvania Press, 1961.
Theory and practice of the novel. Point of view and narrator. Plot, structure, and design. Satire. Style and
language. Characterization. Imagery [muff]. Parody.
Romance [Joseph Andrews develops from a burlesque to a
romance]. Biblical allusions. Names of characters. Digressions and interpolated stories. "Life as art." Narrative technique.

1486 Jones, B. M. Henry Fielding: Novelist and Magistrate.
London: Allen & Unwin, 1933. Law. Biography.

1487 Jones, Claude E. "Satire and Certain English Satirists of the
Enlightenment." Studies on Voltaire and the Eighteenth
Century, 25 (1963), 885-97. Satire [on fashion, lack of

taste, law, politics, quackery, the Dutch, the French, the Scots]. Hogarth.

1488 Jordan, Robert M. "The Limits of Illusion: Faulkner, Fielding, and Chaucer." Criticism, 2 (1960), 278-305. Point of view and narrator. Epistemology. Plot, structure, and design.

1489 Kalpakgian, Mitchell. The Marvellous in Fielding's Novels. Washington, D.C.: University Press of America, 1981. [Joseph Andrews, Tom Jones, Amelia]. The marvellous. Providence. Fortune. The sublime and the beautiful.

1490 Kaplan, Fred. "Fielding's Novel About Novels: The 'Prefaces' and the 'Plot' of Tom Jones." Studies in English Literature, 13 (1973), 535-49. Theory and practice of the novel. Digressions and interpolated stories. Plot, structure, and design [prefaces maintain their own plot].

1491 Karl, Frederick R. "Henry Fielding: The Novel, the Epic, and the Comic Sense of Life." In his A Reader's Guide to the Eighteenth-Century English Novel. New York: Noonday, 1974, pp. 146-82. Style and language. Comedy. Epic. Plot, structure, and design.

1492 Kaul, A. N. "The Adjudication of Fielding's Comedy." In his The Action of English Comedy: Studies in the Encounter of Abstraction and Experience from Shakespeare to Shaw. New Haven, Conn.: Yale Univ. Press, 1970, pp. 151-92. Love [sentimental vs. sensual love]. Contrast as technique. Comedy.

1493 Kearney, Anthony. "Tom Jones and the Forty-Five." Ariel: A Review of International English Literature, 4, No. 2 (1973), 68-78. Rebellion of 1745. Order vs. disorder.

1494 Kermode, Frank. "Richardson and Fielding." Cambridge Journal, 4 (1950), 106-14. Comparison of novelists. Style and language. Plot, structure, and design.

1495 Kishler, Thomas C. "Fielding's Experiments with Fiction in The Champion." Journal of Narrative Technique, 1 (1971), 95-107. Narrative technique. Artistic development. Newspapers.

1496 Kishler, Thomas C. "Heartfree's Function in Jonathan Wild." Satire Newsletter, 1 (1964), 32-34. "Good Man." Contrast as technique. Goodness vs. greatness. Characterization.

1497 Knight, Charles A. "Multiple Structures and the Unity of Tom Jones." Criticism, 14 (1972), 227-42. Unity. Plot, structure, and design [four main structures].

1498 Knight, Charles A. "The Narrative Structure of Fielding's
      Amelia." Ariel: A Review of International English Litera-
      ture, 11, No. 1 (1980), 31-46. Plot, structure, and design.

1499 Knight, Charles A. "Tom Jones: The Meaning of the 'Main
      Design.'" Genre, 12 (1979), 379-99. Plot, structure, and
      design.

1500 Koppel, Gene S. "Sexual Education and Sexual Values in
      Tom Jones: Confusion at the Core?" Studies in the Novel,
      12 (1980), 1-11. Sex. Defects in the novel.

1501 Kropf, Carl R. "Educational Theory and Human Nature in
      Fielding's Works." PMLA, 89 (1974), 113-20. Education.
      Philosophy of novelist.

1502 LaFrance, Marston. "Fielding's Use of the 'Humor' Tradition."
      Bucknell Review, 17 (1969), 53-63. Characterization. The
      humors.

1503 Lavin, Henry St. C. "Rhetoric and Realism in Tom Jones."
      University Review (UKCR), 32 (1965), 19-25. Speech and
      dialogue.

1504 Lenta, M. "From Pamela to Joseph Andrews: An Investiga-
      tion of the Relationship Between Two Originals." English
      Studies in Africa, 23 (1980), 63-74. Comparison of novel-
      ists.

1505 Lentin, A. "Fielding, Lord Chancellor Hardwicke and the
      'Court of Conscience' in Tom Jones." Notes and Queries,
      N.S. 27 (1980), 400-04. Law.

1506 LePage, Peter. "The Prison and the Dark Beauty of Amelia."
      Criticism, 9 (1967), 337-54. Plot, structure, and design.
      Symbolism. Imprisonment.

1507 Levine, George R. Henry Fielding and the Dry Mock: A
      Study of the Techniques of Irony in His Early Works. The
      Hague: Mouton, 1967. Irony.

1508 Lindboe, Berit R. "'O, Shakespear, Had I Thy Pen!':
      Fielding's Use of Shakespeare in Tom Jones." Studies in
      the Novel, 14 (1982), 303-15. Allusions. Shakespearean
      influence.

■1509 Lockwood, Thomas. "Matter and Reflection in Tom Jones."
      ELH: A Journal of English Literary History, 45 (1978),
      226-35. Point of view and narrator.

1510 Loftis, John E. "Imitation in the Novel: Fielding's Amelia."

Rocky Mountain Review of Language and Literature, 31
(1977), 214-29. Epic. Plot, structure, and design. Setting. Adultery.

1511 Longmire, Samuel E. "Allworthy and Barrow: The Standards
of Good Judgment." Texas Studies in Literature and Language, 13 (1972), 630-39. Characterization. Good judgment.

1512 Longmire, Samuel E. "Amelia as a Comic Action." Tennessee
Studies in Literature, 17 (1972), 67-80. Plot, structure,
and design. Comedy.

1513 Longmire, Samuel E. "Booth's Conversion in Amelia." South
Atlantic Bulletin, 40, No. 4 (1975), 12-17. Christianity.
Characterization.

1514 Longmire, Samuel E. "Partridge's Ghost Story." Studies in
Short Fiction, 11 (1974), 423-26. Digressions and interpolated stories. Contrast as technique.

1515 Lynch, James J. "Structural Techniques in Tom Jones."
Zeitschrift für Anglistik und Amerikanistik, 7 (1959), 5-16.
Plot, structure, and design.

1516 Macallister, Hamilton. Fielding. 1967; rpt. New York: Arco, 1971. Introductory guide.

1517 MacAndrew, Elizabeth. "Fielding's Use of Names in Joseph
Andrews." Names, 16 (1968), 362-70. Characterization.
Names of characters.

1518 Mack, Edward C. "Pamela's Stepdaughters: The Heroines
of Smollett and Fielding." College English, 8 (1947), 293-
301. Comparison of novelists. Women. Hero/heroine.

1519 Mack, Maynard. "Introduction." In his edition, Joseph
Andrews. Rinehart Edition. New York: Holt, 1948, pp.
ii-xxiv. Rpt. in Fielding: A Collection of Critical Essays.
Ed. Ronald Paulson. Twentieth Century Views Series.
Englewood Cliffs, N.J.: Prentice-Hall, 1962, pp. 52-58.
Introductory guide.

1520 Mandel, Jerome. "The Man of the Hill and Mrs. Fitzpatrick:
Character and Narrative Technique in Tom Jones." Papers
on Language and Literature, 5 (1969), 26-38. Digressions
and interpolated stories. Contrast as technique.

1521 Manlove, C. N. "Fielding." In his Literature and Reality,
1600-1800. New York: St. Martin's, 1978, pp. 136-48.
Morality. Realism.

1522   Maresca, Thomas E. "Fielding." In his Epic to Novel. Co-
        lumbus: Ohio State Univ. Press, 1974, pp. 181-234. Epic.
        Plot, structure, and design. Sources, analogues, and in-
        fluences.

1523   McCrea, Brian. Henry Fielding and the Politics of Mid-Eight-
        eenth-Century England. Athens: Univ. of Georgia Press,
        1981. Politics. Rebellion of 1745.

1524   McCrea, Brian. "Romances, Newspapers, and the Style of
        Fielding's True History." Studies in English Literature, 21
        (1981), 471-80. Style and language. Satire. Romance.
        Newspapers.

1525   McDowell, Alfred. "Fielding's Rendering of Speech in Joseph
        Andrews and Tom Jones." Language and Style, 6 (1973),
        83-96. Speech and dialogue.

1526   McKenzie, Alan T. "The Physiology of Deceit in Fielding's
        Works." Dalhousie Review, 62 (1982), 140-52. The pas-
        sions. Physiology. Psychology of characters. Deceit.

1527   McKenzie, Alan T. "The Processes of Discovery in Tom
        Jones." Dalhousie Review, 54 (1974-75), 720-40. Discov-
        ery. Characterization.

■1528 McKillop, Alan Dugald. "Henry Fielding." In his The Early
        Masters of English Fiction. Lawrence: Univ. Press of
        Kansas, 1956, pp. 98-146. Introductory guide [excellent
        account of main issues].

1529   McKillop, Alan Dugald. "The Personal Relations Between
        Fielding and Richardson." Modern Philology, 28 (1931),
        423-33. Personal relations between authors.

1530   McNamara, Susan P. "Mirrors of Fiction Within Tom Jones:
        The Paradox of Self-Reference." Eighteenth-Century
        Studies, 12 (1979), 372-90. Realism. Author-reader rela-
        tionship. Point of view and narrator.

1531   Merrett, Robert. "The Principles of Fielding's Legal Satire
        and Social Reform." Dalhousie Review, 62 (1982), 238-53.
        Law. Satire. Social criticism in the novel.

1532   Merrett, Robert. "Empiricism and Judgment in Fielding's Tom
        Jones." Ariel: A Review of International English Litera-
        ture, 11, No. 3 (1980), 3-21. Epistemology. Good judg-
        ment. Author-reader relationship.

1533   Miller, Henry Knight. "The 'Digressive' Tales in Fielding's
        Tom Jones and the Perspective of Romance." Philological

Quarterly, 54 (1975), 258-74. Digressions and interpolated stories. Romance.

•1534 Miller, Henry Knight. Henry Fielding's "Tom Jones" and the Romance Tradition. English Literary Studies Monograph Series, No. 6. Victoria: Univ. of Victoria Press, 1976. Romance [the novel is understood by romance conventions, not by concepts of realism]. Plot, structure, and design [exile, initiation, return motif]. Myth. Style and language. Characterization. Setting. Time. Philosophy of novelist [belief in a Providential universe].

1535 Miller, Henry Knight. "Some Functions of Rhetoric in Tom Jones." Philological Quarterly, 45 (1966), 209-35. Style and language. Point of view and narrator. Speech and dialogue.

1536 Miller, Henry Knight. "The Voices of Henry Fielding: Style in Tom Jones." In The Augustan Milieu: Essays Presented to Louis A. Landa. Ed. Henry Knight Miller, Eric Rothstein, and George S. Rousseau. Oxford: Clarendon Press, 1970, pp. 262-88. Point of view and narrator. Style and language.

1537 Miller, Susan. "Eighteenth-Century Play and the Game of Tom Jones." In A Provision of Human Nature: Essays on Fielding and Others in Honor of Miriam Austin Locke. Ed. Donald Kay. University: Univ. of Alabama Press, 1977, pp. 83-93. Characterization [games define Tom's development]. Sport and recreation. Author-reader relationship.

1538 Moore, Robert Etheridge. "Dr. Johnson on Fielding and Richardson." PMLA, 66 (1951), 162-81. Eighteenth-century criticism and reviews of the novel. Dr. Johnson. Comparison of novelists.

1539 Moore, Robert Etheridge. "Hogarth's Role in Fielding's Novels." In his Hogarth's Literary Relationships. 1948; rpt. New York: Octagon, 1969, pp. 107-62. Hogarth. Sources, analogues, and influences. Characterization. Caricature. Setting.

1539a Mulford, Carla. "Booth's Progress and the Resolution of Amelia." Studies in the Novel, 16 (1984), 20-31. Plot, structure, and design. Closure. Characterization.

1540 Nassar, Eugene Paul. "Complex Irony in Tom Jones." In his Rape of Cinderella: Essays in Literary Continuity. Bloomington: Indiana Univ. Press, 1970, pp. 71-84. Irony [tonal irresolution between sentiment and skepticism].

1541 Nathan, Sabine. "The Anticipation of Nineteenth-Century
      Ideological Trends in Fielding's Amelia." Zeitschrift für
      Anglistik und Amerikanistik, 6 (1958), 382-409. Bourgeois
      ideology [missionary sense, sentimentalism, sincerity, sin-
      gleness of purpose, morality, simple way of life].

1542 Oakman, Robert L. "The Character of the Hero: A Key to
      Fielding's Amelia." Studies in English Literature, 16 (1976),
      473-90. Plot, structure, and design. Closure. Charac-
      terization. Philosophy of novelist. Social criticism in the
      novel.

1543 Olsen, Flemming. "Notes on the Structure of Joseph Andrews."
      English Studies, 50 (1969), 340-51. Plot, structure, and
      design.

1544 Osland, Dianne. "Fielding's Amelia: Problem Child or Prob-
      lem Reader?" Journal of Narrative Technique, 10 (1980),
      56-67. Author-reader relationship.

1545 Palmer, E. Taiwo. "Fielding's Joseph Andrews: A Comic
      Epic in Prose." English Studies, 52 (1971), 331-39.
      Morality. Comedy. Epic.

1546 Palmer, E. Taiwo. "Irony in Tom Jones." Modern Language
      Review, 66 (1971), 497-510. Irony.

1547 Palmer, Eustace. "Amelia--The Decline of Fielding's Art."
      Essays in Criticism, 21 (1971), 135-51. Defects in the nov-
      el.

■1548 Park, William. "Fielding and Richardson." PMLA, 81 (1966),
      381-88. Comparison of novelists [their important similari-
      ties]. Theory and practice of the novel. Philosophy of
      novelist [common assumptions about man, society, and the
      world].

1549 Park, William. "Ironist and Moralist: The Two Readers of
      Tom Jones." Studies in Eighteenth-Century Culture. Vol.
      8. Ed. Roseann Runte. Madison: Univ. of Wisconsin
      Press, 1979, pp. 233-42. Irony. Morality. Author-reader
      relationship.

1550 Park, William. "Tom and Oedipus." Hartford Studies in Lit-
      erature, 7 (1975), 207-15. Incest. Comedy. Classical
      allusions.

1551 Parker, Alexander A. "Fielding and the Structure of Don
      Quixote." Bulletin of Hispanic Studies, 33 (1956), 1-16.
      Plot, structure, and design. Don Quixote.

1552 Paulson, Ronald. "Fielding in Tom Jones: The Historian,
      the Poet, and the Mythologist." In Augustan Worlds: Es-
      says in Honour of A. R. Humphreys. Ed. J. C. Hilson et
      al. Leicester: Leicester Univ. Press, 1977, pp. 175-87.
      Rebellion of 1745. Historiography.

■1553 Paulson, Ronald. "Fielding the Satirist," "Fielding the Anti-
      Romanticist," "Fielding the Novelist." In his Satire and
      the Novel in Eighteenth-Century England. New Haven,
      Conn.: Yale Univ. Press, 1967, pp. 52-164. Satire.
      Satiric techniques. Romance.

1554 Paulson, Ronald. "Models and Paradigms: Joseph Andrews,
      Hogarth's Good Samaritan, and Fénelon's Télémaque."
      Modern Language Notes, 91 (1976), 1186-1207. Sources,
      analogues, and influences. Hogarth.

1555 Paulson, Ronald. "The Pilgrimage and the Family: Struc-
      tures in the Novels of Fielding and Smollett." Tobias Smol-
      lett: Bicentennial Essays Presented to Lewis M. Knapp.
      Ed. George S. Rousseau and Paul-Gabriel Boucé. New
      York: Oxford Univ. Press, 1971, pp. 57-78. Plot, struc-
      ture, and design. Journey. Family.

1556 Paulson, Ronald, and Thomas Lockwood, eds. Henry Field-
      ing: The Critical Heritage. Critical Heritage Series.
      London: Routledge & Kegan Paul, 1969. Eighteenth-cen-
      tury criticism and reviews of the novel.

1557 Penner, Allen R. "Fielding's Adaptation of Cervantes' Knight
      and Squire: The Character of Joseph." Revue de Littéra-
      ture Comparée, 41 (1967), 508-14. Quixotic hero. Sources,
      analogues, and influences. Don Quixote.

1558 Perl, Jeffrey M. "Anagogic Surfaces: How to Read Joseph
      Andrews." The Eighteenth Century: Theory and Inter-
      pretation, 22 (1981), 249-70. Allegory [anagogy]. Biblical
      allusions. Classical allusions.

1559 Poovey, Mary. "Journeys from This World to the Next: The
      Providential Promise in Clarissa and Tom Jones." ELH: A
      Journal of English Literary History, 43 (1976), 300-15.
      Providence. Comparison of novelists. Philosophy of novel-
      ist.

1560 Poston, Charles D. "The Novel as 'Exemplum': A Study of
      Fielding's Amelia." West Virginia University Philological
      Papers, 18 (1971), 23-29. Artistic development. Exemplum.

1561 Powers, Lyall H. "The Influence of the Aeneid on Fielding's

Amelia." <u>Modern Language Notes</u>, 71 (1956), 330-36. Epic.
Classical allusions. Sources, analogues, and influences.
Virgil.

1562 Preston, John. "The Ironic Mode: A Comparison of <u>Jonathan</u>
<u>Wild</u> and <u>The Beggar's Opera</u>." <u>Essays in Criticism</u>, 16
(1966), 268-80. Irony.

1563 Preston, John. "<u>Tom Jones</u> (i): Plot as Irony" and "<u>Tom</u>
<u>Jones</u> (ii): The 'Pursuit of True Judgment.'" In his <u>The</u>
<u>Created Self: The Reader's Role in Eighteenth-Century</u>
<u>Fiction</u>. New York: Barnes & Noble, 1970, pp. 94-132.
Author-reader relationship. Plot, structure, and design.
Irony.

1564 Price, John Valdimir. "Sex and the Foundling Boy: The
Problem in <u>Tom Jones</u>." <u>Review of English Literature</u>, 8
(1967), 45-52. Sex [Tom's adventures are guiltless, and
Fielding's irony defends them].

1565 Price, Martin. "Fielding: The Comedy of Forms." In his
<u>To the Palace of Wisdom: Studies in Order and Energy</u>
<u>from Dryden to Blake</u>. Garden City, N.Y.: Doubleday,
1964, pp. 285-311. Philosophy of novelist. Plot, structure, and design. Characterization.

1566 Pringle, Patrick. <u>Hue and Cry: The Story of Henry and</u>
<u>John Fielding and Their Bow Street Runners</u>. London:
Morrow, 1955. Biography. Law. Crime and punishment.
Sir John Fielding.

1567 Radzinowicz, Leon. "The Trend of the Proposed Reforms:
Henry Fielding and the Committee of 1750." In his <u>History</u>
<u>of English Criminal Law</u>. New York: Macmillan, 1948, I,
399-424. Law. Reform.

1568 Rawson, C. J. "Cannibalism and Fiction: Part II: Love
and Eating in Fielding, Mailer, Genet, and Wittig." <u>Genre</u>,
11 (1978), 227-313, esp. 227-34. Sex. Imagery [food,
eating].

1569 Rawson, C. J. "Circles, Catalogues and Conversations:
Swift, with Reflections on Fielding, Flaubert, Ionesco."
In his <u>Gulliver and the Gentle Reader: Studies in Swift</u>
<u>and Our Time</u>. London: Routledge & Kegan Paul, 1973,
pp. 84-99. Comparison of novelists. Style and language.

1570 Rawson, C. J. "Fielding's 'Good' Merchant: The Problem of
Heartfree in <u>Jonathan Wild</u> (with Comments on Other 'Good'
Characters in Fielding)." <u>Modern Philology</u>, 69 (1972),
292-313. Characterization. Goodness vs. greatness. Ambiguity [sentiment vs. sarcasm].

1571 Rawson, C. J. <u>Henry Fielding</u>. Profiles in Literature Series.
London: Routledge & Kegan Paul, 1968. Introductory
guide.

1572 Rawson, C. J. <u>Henry Fielding and the Augustan Ideal under</u>
<u>Stress: "Nature's Dance of Death" and Other Studies</u>.
London: Routledge & Kegan Paul, 1972. Philosophy of
novelist. Order vs. disorder. Good breeding. Providence.
Goodness vs. greatness. Style and language. Point of
view and narrator. Artistic development.

1573 Rawson, C. J. "Language, Dialogue, and Point of View in
Fielding: Some Considerations." In <u>Quick Springs of</u>
<u>Sense: Studies in the Eighteenth Century</u>. Ed. Larry S.
Champion. Athens: Univ. of Georgia Press, 1974, pp.
137-54. Style and language. Speech and dialogue. Point
of view and narrator.

1574 Rawson, C. J. "Some Considerations on Authorial Intrusion
in Fielding's Novels and Plays." <u>Durham University Jour-</u>
<u>nal</u>, 33 (1971), 32-44. Point of view and narrator. Speech
and dialogue. Style and language.

1575 Reed, Walter L. "<u>Joseph Andrews</u> and the Quixotic: The
Politics of the Classic." In his <u>An Exemplary History of</u>
<u>the Novel: The Quixotic versus the Picaresque</u>. Chicago:
Univ. of Chicago Press, 1981, pp. 117-36. Quixotic novel.
Theory and practice of the novel.

1576 Reid, B. L. "Utmost Merriment, Strictest Decency: <u>Joseph</u>
<u>Andrews</u>." <u>Sewanee Review</u>, 18 (1956), 559-84. Rpt. in
his <u>The Long Boy and Others: Eighteenth-Century</u>
<u>Studies</u>. Athens: Univ. of Georgia Press, 1969, pp. 52-
77. Journey. Good will.

1577 Ribble, Frederick G. "Aristotle and the 'Prudence' Theme of
<u>Tom Jones</u>." <u>Eighteenth-Century Studies</u>, 15 (1981), 26-47.
Prudence. Aristotle.

1578 Ribble, Frederick G. "The Constitution of the Mind and the
Concept of Emotion in Fielding's <u>Amelia</u>." <u>Philological Quar-</u>
<u>terly</u>, 56 (1977), 104-22. Characterization. Sensibility.

1579 Rinehart, Hollis. "Fielding's Chapter 'Of Proverbs' (<u>Jonathan</u>
<u>Wild</u> [1743], Book 2, Chapter 12): Sources, Allusions, and
Interpretation." <u>Modern Philology</u>, 77 (1980), 291-96. Biblical allusions. Sources, analogues, and influences.

1580 Rinehart, Hollis. "<u>Jonathan Wild</u> and the Cant Dictionary."
<u>Philological Quarterly</u>, 48 (1969), 220-25. Style and lan-
guage.

1581   Rinehart, Hollis. "The Role of Walpole in Fielding's Jonathan
       Wild." Eighteenth-Century Studies, 5 (1979), 420-31. Sir
       Robert Walpole.

1582   Robinson, Roger. "Henry Fielding and the English Rococo."
       In Studies in the Eighteenth Century II. Ed. R. F. Bris-
       senden. Toronto: Univ. of Toronto Press, 1973, pp. 93-
       112. Narrative technique. Rococo. Digressions and inter-
       polated stories.

1583   Rogers, Katharine M. "Sensitive Feminism vs. Conventional
       Sympathy: Richardson and Fielding on Women." Novel, 9
       (1976), 256-70. Rpt. as "Richardson's Empathy with Wom-
       en" in The Authority of Experience: Essays in Feminist
       Criticism. Ed. Arlyn Diamond and Lee R. Edwards. Am-
       herst: Univ. of Massachusetts Press, 1977. For a response,
       see Anthony J. Hassall, "Critical Exchange: Women in
       Richardson and Fielding," Novel, 14 (1981), 168-74. Wom-
       en. Comparison of novelists.

1584   Rogers, Pat. Henry Fielding. New York: Scribner, 1979.
       Biography.

1585   Røstvig, Maren-Sofie. "New Perspectives on Fielding's Nar-
       rative Art." In Papers from the First Nordic Conference
       for English Studies, Oslo. Oslo: Institute of English
       Studies, Univ. of Oslo, 1981, pp. 183-97. Narrative tech-
       nique.

1586   Røstvig, Maren-Sofie. "Tom Jones and the Choice of Her-
       cules." In Fair Forms: Essays in English Literature from
       Spenser to Jane Austen. Cambridge: D. S. Brewer, 1975,
       pp. 147-77. Classical allusions. Plot, structure, and de-
       sign. Philosophy of novelist.

■1587 Rothstein, Eric. "Amelia." In his Systems of Order and In-
       quiry in Later Eighteenth-Century Fiction. Berkeley:
       Univ. of California Press, 1975, pp. 154-207. Point of
       view and narrator. Plot, structure, and design. Epistem-
       ology.

1588   Rothstein, Eric. "The Framework of Shamela." ELH: A
       Journal of English Literary History, 35 (1968), 381-402.
       Plot, structure, and design. Satire.

1589   Ruthven, K. K. "Fielding, Square, and the Fitness of
       Things." Eighteenth-Century Studies, 5 (1971), 243-55.
       Characterization. Christianity.

1590   Sacks, Sheldon. Fiction and the Shape of Belief: A Study
       of Henry Fielding with Glances at Swift, Johnson, and

Richardson. Berkeley: Univ. of California Press, 1964.
Author-reader relationship. Philosophy of novelist. Theory and practice of the novel.

1591 Schilling, Bernard N. "Fielding's 'Preface' and Joseph Andrews" and "Slipslop, Lady Booby, and the Ladder of De-
pendence." In his Comic Spirit: Boccaccio to Thomas
Mann. Detroit: Wayne State Univ. Press, 1965, pp. 43-
97. Comedy. Contrast as technique [Adams vs. vain and
hypocritical characters]. Characterization [vanity and
hypocrisy].

1592 Schonhorn, Manuel. "Fielding's Digressive-Parodic Artistry:
Tom Jones and the Man of the Hill." Texas Studies in Literature and Language, 10 (1968), 207-14. Digressions and
interpolated stories. Parody.

1593 Schonhorn, Manuel. "Fielding's Ecphrastic Moment: Tom
Jones and His Egyptian Majesty." Studies in Philology, 78
(1981), 305-23. Classical allusions. Digressions and interpolated stories.

1594 Schonhorn, Manuel. "Heroic Allusion in Tom Jones: Hamlet
and the Temptations of Christ." Studies in the Novel, 6
(1974), 218-27. Characterization. Allegory. Biblical allusions. Shakespearean influence.

1595 Seamon, R. G. "The Rhetorical Pattern of Mock-Heroic Satire." Humanities Association Bulletin, 17 (1966), 37-41.
[Jonathan Wild]. Parody. Plot, structure, and design.

1596 Sheehan, David. "Pope and Palladio, Hogarth and Fielding:
Kinds of Discipline in Interdisciplinary Studies." Eighteenth-Century Life, 5, No. 3 (1979), 76-82. Pedagogical
approach. Art. Hogarth.

1597 Shepperson, Archibald B. "Fielding on Liberty and Democracy." University of Virginia Studies, 5 (1951), 265-75.
Politics. Liberty. Democracy.

■1598 Sherbo, Arthur. "The Narrator in Fielding's Novels," "'In-
side' and 'Outside' Readers in Fielding's Novels," "Some
Aspects of Fielding's Style," "Fielding's Amelia: A Reinterpretation," "The 'Moral Basis' of Joseph Andrews," and
"'Naked Innocence' in Joseph Andrews." In his Studies in
the Eighteenth-Century English Novel. East Lansing:
Michigan State Univ. Press, 1969, pp. 1-127. Critical revaluation [corrects excesses of some major critics]. Point
of view and narrator. Author-reader relationship. Style
and language. Philosophy of novelist.

1599   Sherbo, Arthur. "The Time Scheme in Amelia." Boston Uni-
       versity Studies in English, 4 (1960), 223-28. Time. De-
       fects in the novel.

■1600 Sherburn, George. "Fielding's Amelia: An Interpretation."
       ELH: A Journal of English Literary History, 3 (1936), 1-
       14. Rpt. in Studies in the Literature of the Augustan Age:
       Essays Collected in Honor of Arthur Ellicott Case. Ed.
       Richard C. Boys. Augustan Reprint Society. Ann Arbor,
       Mich.: George Wahr, 1953, pp. 266-80. Artistic develop-
       ment. Classical allusions. Epic. Social criticism in the
       novel. Philosophy of novelist.

■1601 Sherburn, George. "Fielding's Social Outlook." Philological
       Quarterly, 35 (1956), 1-23. Rpt. in Eighteenth-Century
       English Literature. Ed. James L. Clifford. New York:
       Oxford Univ. Press, 1959, pp. 251-73. Philosophy of nov-
       elist [Fielding's belief in a divine plan, stratified society,
       human moral responsibility, individual's sense of duty].
       Social criticism in the novel. Morality.

1602   Shesgreen, Sean. Literary Portraits in the Novels of Henry
       Fielding. DeKalb: Northern Illinois Univ. Press, 1972.
       Characterization [four types of literary portraits]. Morality
       [characters as ethical emblems].

1603   Shesgreen, Sean. "The Moral Function of Thwackum, Square,
       and Allworthy." Studies in the Novel, 2 (1970), 159-67.
       Allegory. Morality. Characterization.

1604   Simon, Irene. "Early Theories of Prose Fiction: Congreve
       and Fielding." In Imagined Worlds: Essays on Some Eng-
       lish Novels and Novelists in Honour of John Butt. Ed.
       Maynard Mack and Ian Gregor. London: Methuen, 1968,
       pp. 19-36. Theory and practice of the novel.

1605   Smith, J. Oates. "Masquerade and Marriage: Fielding's
       Comedies of Identity." Ball State University Forum, 6
       (1965), 10-21. Symbolism. Marriage. Masquerade.

1606   Smith, Leroy W. "Fielding and Mandeville: The 'War Against
       Virtue.'" Criticism, 3 (1961), 7-15. Philosophy of novel-
       ist. Charity. Self-interest. Mandeville.

1607   Smith, Raymond. "The Ironic Structure of Fielding's Jonathan
       Wild." Ball State University Forum, 6 (1965), 3-9. Irony.
       Self-interest. Benevolence.

1608   Smith, Robert A. "The 'Great Man' Motif in Jonathan Wild
       and The Beggar's Opera." College Language Association
       Journal, 2 (1959), 183-84. The "Great Man." Symbolism
       [evil, mismanagement, tyrannical rule, ambition, cruelty].

1609 Snow, Malinda. "The Judgment of Evidence in Tom Jones."
South Atlantic Review, 48, No. 2 (1983), 37-51. Plot,
structure, and design [despite similarities, the plot of the
novel essentially different from that of detective fiction].
Judgment。

1610 Sokolyansky, Mark G. "Poetics of Fielding's Comic Epics."
Zeitschrift für Anglistik und Amerikanistik, 22 (1974), 251-
65. Theory and practice of the novel. Characterization.
Time.

1611 Spacks, Patricia Meyer. "Young Men's Fancies: James Bos-
well, Henry Fielding" and "Laws of Time: Fielding and
Boswell." In her Imagining a Self: Autobiography and
Novel in Eighteenth-Century England. Cambridge, Mass.:
Harvard Univ. Press, 1976, pp. 227-99. The self. Time.
Autobiographical elements in the novel. Boswell.

1612 Spearman, Diana. "Fielding." In her Novel and Society.
New York: Barnes & Noble, 1966, pp. 199-224. Social
criticism in the novel. Realism.

1613 Speer, Blanche C., and Robert W. Lovett. "Dialects and the
Dialect in Fielding's Novels." The SECOL Bulletin: South-
eastern Conference on Linguistics, 3 (1979), 57-62. Speech
and dialogue.

■1614 Spilka, Mark. "Comic Resolution in Fielding's Joseph Andrews." College English, 15 (1953), 11-19. Comedy. Allegory [Adams, Joseph, Fanny as touchstones of virtue].

1615 Spilka, Mark. "Fielding and the Epic Impulse." Criticism,
11 (1969), 68-77. Epic. Innovation.

1616 Stanzel, Franz. "The Authorial Novel: Tom Jones." In his
Narrative Situations in the Novel: "Tom Jones," "Moby
Dick," "The Ambassadors," "Ulysses." Trans. from the
German by James P. Pusack. Bloomington: Indiana Univ.
Press, 1971, pp. 38-58. Point of view and narrator.
Epistemology. Narrative technique.

1617 Stephanson, Raymond. "The Education of the Reader in
Fielding's Joseph Andrews." Philological Quarterly, 61
(1982), 243-58. Author-reader relationship. Satire [on
reader].

1618 Stephens, John C., Jr. "The Verge of the Court and Arrest
for Debt in Fielding's Amelia." Modern Language Notes,
63 (1948), 104-09. Law.

1619 Stevick, Philip. "Fielding and the Meaning of History."
PMLA, 79 (1964), 561-68. Philosophy of novelist. History.

1620   Stevick, Philip. "On Fielding Talking." College Literature,
       1 (1974), 19-33. Point of view and narrator. Author-
       reader relationship. Epistemology. Style and language.

1621   Stewart, Keith. "History, Poetry, and the Terms of Fiction
       in the Eighteenth Century." Modern Philology, 66 (1968),
       110-20. Historiography. Realism.

1622   Stitzel, Judith G. "Blifil and Henry Fielding's Conception of
       Evil." West Virginia University Philological Papers, 17 (1970),
       16-24. Evil. Characterization. Philosophy of novelist.

1623   Stumpf, Thomas A. "Tom Jones from the Outside." In The
       Classic British Novel. Ed. Howard M. Harper, Jr., and
       Charles Edge. Athens: Univ. of Georgia Press, 1972, pp.
       3-20. Characterization.

1624   Swann, George Rogers. "Fielding and Empirical Realism."
       In his Philosophical Parallelisms in Six English Novelists:
       The Conception of Good, Evil and Human Nature. Philadel-
       phia: Univ. of Pennsylvania, 1929, pp. 46-64. Philosophy
       of novelist. Realism. Hume.

1625   Swingewood, Alan. "Fielding, Tom Jones, and the Rise of
       the Novel." In Diana T. Laurenson and Alan Swingewood's
       Sociology of Literature. New York: Schocken, 1972, pp.
       175-206. Social structure. Social criticism in the novel.
       Gentry. Symbolism [Tom as symbol of the declining gentry
       in a vanishing rural England].

1626   Tannenbaum, Earl. "A Note on Tom Jones and the Man of
       the Hill." College Language Association Journal, 4 (1961),
       215-17. Digressions and interpolated stories. Contrast as
       technique.

1627   Taylor, Dick, Jr. "Joseph as Hero in Joseph Andrews."
       Tulane Studies in English, 7 (1957), 91-109. Characteri-
       zation. Critical revaluation.

1628   Taylor, Houghton W. "Fielding upon Cibber." Modern Phi-
       lology, 29 (1931), 73-90. Colley Cibber [in Joseph An-
       drews, inter alia].

1629   Thomas, D. S. "Fortune and the Passions in Fielding's
       Amelia." Modern Language Review, 60 (1965), 176-87.
       The passions. Fortune. Philosophy of novelist.

1630   Thornbury, E. Margaret. Henry Fielding's Theory of the
       Comic Prose Epic. 1931; rpt., New York: Russell & Rus-
       sell, 1966. Epic. Theory and practice of the novel.
       Sources, analogues, and influences. Realism. The mar-
       vellous.

1631	Tillyard, E. M. W. "Tom Jones." In his The Epic Strain in the English Novel. Fair Lawn, N.J.: Essential Books, 1958, pp. 51-58. Epic [Tom Jones not an epic].

1632	Torrance, Robert M. "Moral Rake and Masterful Lackey." In his The Comic Hero. Cambridge, Mass.: Harvard Univ. Press, 1978, pp. 177-205. [Tom Jones, Jacques the Fatalist]. Morality. Comedy. The rake.

1633	Towers, A. R. "Amelia and the State of Matrimony." Review of English Studies, N.S. 5 (1954), 145-57. Marriage. Contrast as technique.

1634	Tucker, Edward F. J. "Fielding and Rolle's Abridgement." Modern Philology, 79 (1981), 173-76. Law [in The Champion]. Satire [of legal jargon].

1635	Ulanov, Barry. "Sterne and Fielding: The Allegory of Irony." In his Sources and Resources: The Literary Traditions of Christian Humanism. Westminster, Md.: Newman Press, 1960, pp. 206-77. Comparison of novelists. Morality. Irony.

1636	Uphaus, Robert W. "Clarissa, Amelia, and the State of Probation." In his The Impossible Observer: Reason and the Reader in Eighteenth-Century Prose. Lexington: Univ. Press of Kentucky, 1979, pp. 71-88. Author-reader relationship. Philosophy of novelist.

1637	Van der Voorde, Frans P. Henry Fielding: Critic and Satirist. 1931; rpt. New York: Haskell House, 1966. Satire.

■1638	Van Ghent, Dorothy. "On Tom Jones." In her English Novel: Form and Function. 1953; rpt. New York: Harper, 1961, pp. 65-81. Plot, structure, and design ["comic curve"]. Contrast as technique ["form vs. feeling"].

1639	Vopat, James B. "Narrative Technique in Tom Jones: The Balance of Art and Nature." Journal of Narrative Technique, 4 (1974), 144-54. Plot, structure, and design. Point of view and narrator. Narrative technique. Nature vs. art.

1640	Warner, John M. "The Interpolated Narratives in the Fiction of Fielding and Smollett: An Epistemological View." Studies in the Novel, 5 (1973), 271-83. Digressions and interpolated stories. Epistemology. Comparison of novelists. Unity.

1641	Warren, Leland E. "Fielding's Problem and Ours: Allworthy and Authority in Tom Jones." Essays in Literature, 5 (1978), 15-25. Authority. Characterization.

1642 Warren, Leland E. "History-as-Literature and the Narrative
      Stance of Henry Fielding." Clio, 9 (1979), 89–109. His-
      torical façade. Point of view and narrator.

1643 Warren, Leland E. "'This Intrepid and Gallant Spirit': Henry
      Fielding's Sentimental Satiric Voyage." Essays in Literature,
      9 (1982), 43–54. [Journal of a Voyage to Lisbon]. Auto-
      biographical elements in the novel. Travel literature.

■1644 Watt, Ian. "Fielding and the Epic Theory of the Novel" and
      "Fielding as Novelist: Tom Jones." In his The Rise of the
      Novel: Studies in Defoe, Richardson, and Fielding. 1957;
      rpt. Berkeley: Univ. of California Press, 1962, pp. 239–
      89. Epic. Theory and practice of the novel.

1645 Watt, Ian. "The Naming of Characters in Defoe, Richardson,
      and Fielding." Review of English Studies, O.S. 25 (1949),
      322–38. Characterization. Names of characters.

1646 Watt, Ian. "Shamela." Introduction to his edition of An
      Apology for the Life of Mrs. Shamela Andrews. Augustan
      Reprint Society, No. 57. Los Angeles: Clark Memorial Li-
      brary, U.C.L.A., 1956, pp. 1–11. Rpt. in Fielding: A
      Collection of Critical Essays. Ed. Ronald Paulson. Twenti-
      eth Century Views Series. Englewood Cliffs, N.J.: Pren-
      tice-Hall, 1962, pp. 45–51. Satire. Parody.

1647 Weinbrot, Howard. "Chastity and Interpolation: Two Aspects
      of Joseph Andrews." Journal of English and Germanic
      Philology, 69 (1970), 14–31. Chastity. Digressions and
      interpolated stories.

1648 Weinstein, Arnold. "The Body Beautiful: Joseph Andrews."
      In his Fictions of the Self: 1550–1800. Princeton, N.J.:
      Princeton Univ. Press, 1981, pp. 114–28. The self. Indi-
      vidualism [power of the individual]. Symbolism [the human
      body as Nature].

1649 Weissman, Judith. "The Man of the Hill and the Gypsies in
      Tom Jones: Satire, Utopia, and the Novel." Ball State
      University Forum, 22 (1981), 60–68. Narrative technique.
      Comparison of novelists [Swift, Johnson]. Digressions and
      interpolated stories.

1650 Wells, John Edwin. "Fielding's Political Purpose in Jonathan
      Wild." PMLA, 28 (1913), 1–55. Politics. Sir Robert Wal-
      pole [as satiric emblem of political corruption]. Satire [on
      Walpole].

■1651 Wendt, Allan. "The Moral Allegory of Jonathan Wild." ELH:
      A Journal of English Literary History, 24 (1957), 306–20.

Morality. Allegory. Charity. Self-interest. Philosophy
of novelist [derives from Hoadly and Shaftesbury].

■1652 Wendt, Allan. "The Naked Virtue of Amelia." ELH: A
Journal of English Literary History, 27 (1960), 131-48.
Benevolence. Characterization. Philosophy of novelist.
Providence.

■1653 Wess, Robert V. "The Probable and the Marvelous in Tom
Jones." Modern Philology, 68 (1970), 32-45. The marvellous [many coincidences are plausible].

1654 Wiesenfarth, Joseph. "'High' People and 'Low' in Joseph
Andrews: A Study of Structure and Style." College Language Association Journal, 16 (1973), 357-65. Social structure. Social criticism in the novel.

1655 Williams, Aubrey. "Interpositions of Providence and the Design of Fielding's Novels." South Atlantic Quarterly, 70
(1971), 265-86. Plot, structure, and design. Providence
[informs the grand design of his novels]. The marvellous.

1656 Williams, Murial Brittain. Marriage: Fielding's Mirror of
Morality. University: Univ. of Alabama Press, 1973.
Marriage. Marriage law.

1657 Williamson, Eugene. "Guiding Principles in Fielding's Criti-
cism of the Critics." In A Provision of Human Nature:
Essays on Fielding and Others in Honor of Miriam Austin
Locke. Ed. Donald Kay. University: Univ. of Alabama
Press, 1977, pp. 1-24. Eighteenth-century criticism and
reviews of the novel.

1658 Wolff, Cynthia Griffin. "Fielding's Amelia: Private Virtue
and Public Good." Texas Studies in Literature and Language, 10 (1968), 37-55. Autobiographical elements in the
novel. Philosophy of novelist. Morality. Law. Defects
in the novel. "Good Man."

1659 Wood, Carl. "Shamela's Subtle Satire: Fielding's Characterization of Mrs. Jewkes and Mrs. Jervis." English Language Notes, 13 (1976), 266-70. Satire. Characterization.

1660 Woodcock, George. "Colonel Jack and Tom Jones: Aspects
of a Changing Century." Wascana Review, 5 (1970), 67-73.
Comparison of novelists [Defoe, Fielding].

■1661 Woods, Charles B. "Fielding and the Authorship of Shamela."
Philological Quarterly, 25 (1946), 248-72. Satire [on des-
picable priests, inter alia]. The clergy. Pamela-Shamela.

■1662 Work, James A. "Henry Fielding, Christian Censor." In
       The Age of Johnson: Essays Presented to Chauncey Brew-
       ster Tinker. Ed. Frederick W. Hilles and Wilmarth S.
       Lewis. New Haven, Conn.: Yale Univ. Press, 1949, pp.
       139-48. Philosophy of novelist. Morality [Fielding as most
       important moralist of his time]. Christianity [orthodox, low
       Church, conservative]. Social criticism in the novel [Field-
       ing traces England's evils to its neglect of religion].

●1663 Wright, Andrew. Henry Fielding: Mask and Feast. Berke-
       ley: Univ. of California Press, 1965. Comedy [stresses
       comic over moral intention]. Characterization. Point of
       view and narrator [festive stance]. Plot, structure, and
       design. Style and language.

1664   Wynne, Edith J. "Latitudinarian Philosophy in Fielding's
       Amelia." Publications of the Missouri Philological Associa-
       tion, 4 (1979), 33-38. Latitudinarianism.

1665   Zirker, Malvin R. "Fielding and Reform in the 1750s."
       Studies in English Literature, 7 (1967), 433-65. Law. Re-
       form.

1666   Zirker, Malvin R. Fielding's Social Pamphlets: A Study of
       "An Enquiry into the Causes of the Late Increase of Rob-
       bers" and "A Proposal for Making an Effectual Provision for
       the Poor." Berkeley: Univ. of California Press, 1966.
       [Little on novels]. Social background. Social criticism in
       the novel. The poor. Crime and punishment. Critical
       revaluation [questions the romantically liberal picture of
       Fielding]. Conservatism.

       SEE ALSO ITEMS 240, 334, 537, 641, 751, 761, 763,
       767, 768, 774, 778, 787a, 788, 792, 816, 820, 825, 833,
       834, 850, 863, 870, 884, 897, 898, 918, 932, 942, 946,
       977, 978, 986, 995, 1004, 1004a, 1005, 1016, 1040,
       1045, 1052, 1056, 1056a, 1060a, 1062, 1068, 1077, 1087,
       1110, 1728, 1942, 2542.

                         SAMUEL RICHARDSON
                           (1689-1761)

PRINCIPAL FICTION

       Pamela, 1740-41

       Clarissa, 1747-48

       Sir Charles Grandison, 1753-54

BIBLIOGRAPHIES AND SURVEYS OF CRITICISM

1667 Carroll, John. "Richardson (1689–1761)." In The English
      Novel: Select Bibliographical Guides. Ed. A. E. Dyson.
      London: Oxford Univ. Press, 1974, pp. 56–70. Bibliog-
      raphy of criticism. Survey of criticism.

1668 Doederlein, Sue Warrick. "Clarissa in the Hands of the
      Critics." Eighteenth-Century Studies, 16 (1983), 401–14.
      Survey of criticism [of the rape of Clarissa]. Rape.

1669 Hannaford, Richard Gordon. Samuel Richardson: An Anno-
      tated Bibliography of Critical Studies. New York: Gar-
      land, 1980. Bibliography of criticism [annotated, evalua-
      tive].

1670 Sale, William M., Jr. Samuel Richardson: A Bibliographical
      Record of His Literary Career with Historical Notes. New
      Haven, Conn.: Yale Univ. Press, 1936. Bibliography of
      primary sources.

BIOGRAPHICAL AND CRITICAL STUDIES

1671 Allentuck, Marcia Epstein. "Narration and Illustration: The
      Problem of Richardson's Pamela." Philological Quarterly,
      51 (1972), 874–86. Illustration.

1672 Anderson, Howard. "Answers to the Author of Clarissa:
      Theme and Narrative Technique in Tom Jones and Tristram
      Shandy." Philological Quarterly, 51 (1972), 859–73. Com-
      parison of novelists. Narrative technique. Point of view
      and narrator.

1673 Babb, Howard S. "Richardson's Narrative Mode in Clarissa."
      Studies in English Literature, 16 (1976), 451–60. Style
      and language. Narrative technique. Contrast as technique.

1674 Ball, Donald L. "Pamela II: A Primary Link in Richardson's
      Development as a Novelist." Modern Philology, 65 (1968),
      334–42. Artistic development.

1675 Ball, Donald L. "Richardson's Resourceful Wordmaking."
      South Atlantic Bulletin, 41, No. 4 (1976), 56–65. Style and
      language.

•1676 Ball, Donald L. Samuel Richardson's Theory of Fiction. The
      Hague: Mouton, 1971. Theory and practice of the novel.
      Characterization. Morality. Epistolary novel. Plot, struc-
      ture, and design. Didacticism. Narrative technique.

1677 Barker, Gerard A. "Clarissa's 'Command of her Passions':

Self-Censorship in the Third Edition." Studies in English
Literature, 10 (1970), 525-39. Characterization [Richardson
lessened the degree of Clarissa's affection for Lovelace].
Composition of the novel.

■1678 Barker, Gerard A. "The Complacent Paragon: Exemplary
Characterization in Richardson." Studies in English Literature, 9 (1969), 503-19. Philosophy of novelist [belief in
self-judgment]. Morality. Characterization [self-approval
inseparable from virtue].

1679 Beer, Gillian. "Richardson, Milton, and the Status of Evil."
Review of English Studies, N.S. 19 (1968), 261-70. Milton.
Morality. Evil. Characterization.

1680 Bell, Michael Davitt. "Pamela's Wedding and the Marriage of
the Lamb." Philological Quarterly, 49 (1970), 100-12.
Love. Christianity. Style and language [religious conno-
tations of words].

1681 Biggs, Penelope. "Hunt, Conquest, Trial: Lovelace and the
Metaphors of the Rake." In Studies in Eighteenth-Century
Culture. Vol. 11. Ed. Harry C. Payne. Madison: Univ.
of Wisconsin Press, 1982, pp. 51-64. The rake. Imagery.

1682 Binkley, Harold C. "A Novelist in Letters." Papers of the
Michigan Academy of Science, Arts and Letters, 8 (1927),
333-40. Introductory guide. Epistolary novel.

1683 Braudy, Leo. "Penetration and Impenetrability in Clarissa."
In New Approaches to Eighteenth-Century Literature. Ed.
Phillip Harth. New York: Columbia Univ. Press, 1974,
pp. 177-206. The self. Sex. Characterization.

1684 Bredsdorff, Thomas. "Whatever Happened to Women's Lust?"
In Essays Presented to Knud Schibsbye on His 75th Birthday, 29 November 1979. Ed. Michael Chestnutt et al.
Copenhagen: Akademisk Forlag, 1979, pp. 175-80. [Pam-
ela]. Women. Sex. Social criticism in the novel.

1685 Brissenden, R. F. "Clarissa: The Sentimental Tragedy."
In Virtue in Distress: Studies in the Novel of Sentiment
from Richardson to Sade. New York: Macmillan, 1974, pp.
159-86. Sentimentalism. Sentimental novel.

1686 Brissenden, R. F. "Le Philosophie dans le boudoir; or, A
Young Lady's Entrance into the World." In Studies in
Eighteenth-Century Culture: Irrationalism in the Eighteenth
Century. Ed. Harold E. Pagliaro. Vol. 2. Cleveland:
The Press of Case Western Reserve Univ., 1972, pp. 113-
41. Rpt. in his Virtue in Distress: Studies in the Novel

of Sentiment from Richardson to Sade. New York: Macmillan, 1974, pp. 268-93. Sade. Sentimentalism. Initiation.

1687   Brooks, Douglas. "Richardson's Pamela and Fielding's Joseph
       Andrews." Essays in Criticism, 17 (1967), 158-68. Com-
       parison of novelists.

•1688 Brophy, Elizabeth Bergen. Samuel Richardson: The Tri-
       umph of Craft. Knoxville: Univ. of Tennessee Press,
       1974. Theory and practice of the novel. Realism. Moral-
       ity. Didacticism. Epistolary novel. Narrative technique.

1689   Brown, Herbert Ross. "Richardson and Seduction." In his
       The Sentimental Novel in America. New York: Pageant
       Books, 1940, pp. 28-51. Seduction. Sentimental novel.
       Influence and reputation abroad. America.

1690   Brownstein, Rachel M. "'An Exemplar to Her Sex':   Richard-
       son's Clarissa." Yale Review, 67 (1977), 30-47. Rpt. in
       her Becoming a Heroine: Reading About Women in Novels.
       New York: Viking, 1982, pp. 32-77. Imagery [house,
       clothing, entrapment, coffin]. Characterization. Didacti-
       cism [Clarissa as exemplar]. Man vs. woman.

1691   Brückmann, Patricia. "The Settings in Pamela." Transac-
       tions of the Samuel Johnson Society of the Northwest. Vol.
       6. Calgary: Samuel Johnson Society of the Northwest,
       1973, pp. 1-10. Setting [related to Pamela's growth].

1692   Bullen, John Samuel. Time and Space in the Novels of Samuel
       Richardson. Logan: Utah State Univ. Press, 1965. Time.
       Space. Setting.

1692a Butler, Janet. "The Garden: Early Symbol of Clarissa's
       Complicity." Studies in English Literature, 24 (1984), 527-
       44. Symbolism.

1693   Carroll, John. "Lovelace as Tragic Hero." University of
       Toronto Quarterly, 42 (1972), 14-25. Characterization.
       Tragic hero.

1694   Carroll, John. "Richardson at Work: Revisions, Allusions,
       and Quotations in Clarissa." In Studies in the Eighteenth
       Century II. Ed. R. F. Brissenden. Toronto: Univ. of
       Toronto Press, 1973, pp. 53-71. Composition of the novel.
       Biblical allusions. Classical allusions. Characterization.

1695   Carroll, John. "Richardson on Pope and Swift." University
       of Toronto Quarterly, 33 (1963), 19-29. Pope. Swift.

1696   Castle, Terry. Clarissa's Ciphers: Meaning and Disruption

in Richardson's "Clarissa." Ithaca, N.Y.: Cornell Univ.
Press, 1982. Letter-writing. Author-reader relationship.
Symbolism.

1697 Castle, Terry. "Lovelace's Dream." In Studies in Eighteenth-Century Culture. Ed. O M Brack, Jr. Vol. 13.
Madison: Univ. of Wisconsin Press, 1984, pp. 29-42.
[Clarissa]. Plot, structure, and design [the dream as
emblem of the novel's structure].

1698 Castle, Terry. "P/B: Pamela as Sexual Fiction." Studies
in English Literature, 22 (1982), 469-90. Sex.

1699 Chalker, John. "Virtue Rewarded: The Sexual Theme in
Richardson's Pamela." Literary Half-Yearly [Bangalore
Central College, India], 2 (1961), 58-64. Sex. Morality.

1700 Cockshut, A. O. J. "Richardson and Fielding." In his Man
and Woman: A Study of Love and the Novel. New York:
Oxford Univ. Press, 1977, pp. 32-45. Love. Sex. Morality. Comparison of novelists.

1701 Cohan, Steven M. "Clarissa and the Individuation of Character." ELH: A Journal of English Literary History, 43
(1976), 163-83. Characterization. The self.

1702 Cohen, Richard. Literary References and Their Effect upon
Characterization in the Novels of Samuel Richardson.
Bangor, Me.: Husson College Press, 1970. Characteriza-
tion. Allusions.

1703 Cohen, Richard. "The Social-Christian and Christian-Social
Doctrines of Samuel Richardson." Hartford Studies in Lit-
erature, 4 (1972), 136-46. Christianity. Characterization.
Philosophy of novelist.

∎1704 Copeland, Edward. "Allegory and Analogy in Clarissa: The
'Plan' and the 'No-Plan.'" ELH: A Journal of English Literary History, 39 (1972), 254-65. Dichotomy of intention
[tension between the allegorical and universal and the social
and personal].

1705 Copeland, Edward. "Clarissa and Fanny Hill: Sisters in
Distress." Studies in the Novel, 4 (1972), 343-52. Comparison of novelists. Conventions of the Georgian novel.

1706 Copeland, Edward. "Samuel Richardson and Naive Allegory:
Some Beauties of the Mixed Metaphor." Novel, 4 (1971),
231-39. Theory and practice of the novel. Allegory.
Style and language.

1707   Costa, Richard Hauer. "The Epistolary Monitor in Pamela."
       Modern Language Quarterly, 31 (1970), 38-47. Epistolary
       novel [letters as a plot device]. Characterization [Pamela
       writes to change Mr. B, knowing he will intercept and read
       her letters].

1708   Cox, Stephen D. "Defining the Self: Samuel Richardson's
       Clarissa." In his "The Stranger Within Thee": Concepts
       of the Self in Late-Eighteenth-Century Literature. Pitts-
       burgh: Univ. of Pittsburgh Press, 1980, pp. 59-81. The
       self. Sensibility. Characterization.

1709   Crabtree, Paul R. "Propriety, Grandison, and the Novel of
       Manners." Modern Language Quarterly, 41 (1980), 151-61.
       Novel of manners. Propriety.

1710   Daiches, David. "Samuel Richardson." In his Literary Es-
       says. 1956; rpt. Edinburgh: Oliver & Boyd, 1966, pp.
       26-49. Introductory guide.

1711   Dalziel, Margaret. "Richardson and Romance." Journal of
       the Australasian Universities Language and Literature As-
       sociation, 33 (1970), 5-24. Romance [use of romance con-
       ventions].

1712   Denton, Ramona. "Anna Howe and Richardson's Ambivalent
       Artistry in Clarissa." Philological Quarterly, 58 (1979),
       53-62. Characterization. Plot, structure, and design.
       Marriage. Women. Sex.

1713   Donaldson, Ian. "Fielding, Richardson, and the Ends of the
       Novel." Essays in Criticism, 32 (1982), 26-47. Closure.
       Characterization.

1714   Donovan, Robert Alan. "The Problem of Pamela." In his
       The Shaping Vision: Imagination in the English Novel from
       Defoe to Dickens. Ithaca, N.Y.: Cornell Univ. Press,
       1966, pp. 47-67. Originally published as "The Problem of
       Pamela, or Virtue Unrewarded," Studies in English Litera-
       ture, 3 (1963), 377-95. Social structure. Man vs. woman.
       Plot, structure, and design.

•1715 Doody, Margaret Anne. A Natural Passion: A Study of the
       Novels of Samuel Richardson. Oxford: Clarendon Press,
       1974. Pastoral tradition [Pamela]. Sources, analogues, and
       influences. Narrative technique. Imagery. Artistic de-
       velopment. Tragedy [Clarissa]. The gentleman [Sir
       Charles Grandison]. Love. Seduction. The passions.
       Comedy [Sir Charles Grandison]. Characterization.
       Philosophy of novelist. Death [Clarissa].

1716 Downs, Brian W. Richardson. 1928; rpt. London: Cass,
      1969. Biography. Introductory guide.

■1717 Dussinger, John A. "Clarissa: The Curse of Intellect." In
      his The Discourse of the Mind in Eighteenth-Century Fic-
      tion. The Hague: Mouton, 1974, pp. 77-126. Epistemol-
      ogy. The self. Psychology of characters. Authority.
      Death.

■1718 Dussinger, John A. "Conscience and the Pattern of Christian
      Perfection in Clarissa." PMLA, 81 (1966), 236-45. Chris-
      tianity. Perfectionism.

1718a Dussinger, John A. "Love and Consanguinity in Richardson's
      Novels." Studies in English Literature, 24 (1984), 513-26.
      Love [erotic love as motive toward social good]. Sex.
      Family. Philanthropy.

1719 Dussinger, John A. "Pamela: Towards the Governance of
      Time." In his The Discourse of the Mind in Eighteenth-
      Century Fiction. The Hague: Mouton, 1974, pp. 53-76.
      Incorporates, with revisions, his "What Pamela Knew: An
      Interpretation," Journal of English and Germanic Philology,
      69 (1970), 377-93. Epistemology. The self. Psychology
      of characters. Initiation. Point of view and narrator.

1720 Dussinger, John A. "Richardson's 'Christian Vocation.'"
      Papers on Language and Literature, 3 (1967), 3-19.
      Christianity. Philosophy of novelist.

1721 Dussinger, John A. "Richardson's Tragic Muse." Philologi-
      cal Quarterly, 46 (1967), 18-33. Tragedy. Shakespearean
      influence. Dramatic conventions in the novel [the distressed
      heroine of seventeenth-century tragedy].

1722 Eagleton, Terry. The Rape of Clarissa: Writing, Sexuality,
      and Class Struggle in Samuel Richardson. Minneapolis:
      Univ. of Minnesota Press, 1982. Bourgeois ideology. Writ-
      ing [psychological examination of the act of writing of both
      Richardson and his characters]. Psychology of characters.
      Rape.

1723 Eaves, T. C. Duncan. "Amelia and Clarissa." In A Provi-
      sion of Human Nature: Essays on Fielding and Others in
      Honor of Miriam Austin Locke. Ed. Donald Kay. University:
      Univ. of Alabama Press, 1977, pp. 95-110. Influence and
      imitation.

1724 Eaves, T. C. Duncan. "Graphic Illustrations of the Novels
      of Samuel Richardson, 1740-1810." Huntington Library
      Quarterly, 14 (1951), 349-83. Illustration.

1725 Eaves, T. C. Duncan, and Ben D. Kimpel. "The Composition
      of Clarissa and Its Revision Before Publication." PMLA,
      83 (1968), 416-28. Composition of the novel.

1726 Eaves, T. C. Duncan, and Ben D. Kimpel. "Richardson's
      Connection with Sir William Harrington." Papers on Lan-
      guage and Literature, 4 (1968), 276-87. Novelists on the
      novel. Personal relations between novelists [Richardson,
      Anna Meades].

1727 Eaves, T. C. Duncan, and Ben D. Kimpel. "Richardson's
      Revisions of Pamela." Studies in Bibliography, 20 (1967),
      61-88. Composition of the novel.

•1728 Eaves, T. C. Duncan, and Ben D. Kimpel. Samuel Richard-
      son: A Biography. Oxford: Clarendon Press, 1971.
      Biography. Eighteenth-century criticism and reviews of
      the novel. Comparison of novelists [Richardson, Fielding].
      Influence and imitation. Artistic development. Philosophy
      of novelist. Achievement and reputation.

1729 Erickson, Robert A. "Mother Jewkes, Pamela, and the Mid-
      wives." ELH: A Journal of English Literary History, 43
      (1976), 500-16. The midwife.

1730 Ermarth, Elizabeth Deeds. "Time and Eternity: The Cases
      of Robinson Crusoe and Pamela." In her Realism and Con-
      sensus in the English Novel. Princeton, N.J.: Princeton
      Univ. Press, 1983, pp. 95-143. Time. Realism. Compari-
      son of novelists.

1731 Farrell, William J. "The Style and the Action in Clarissa."
      Studies in English Literature, 3 (1963), 365-75. Rpt. in
      Samuel Richardson: A Collection of Critical Essays. Ed.
      John Carroll. Englewood Cliffs, N.J.: Prentice-Hall, 1969,
      pp. 92-101. Style and language [Richardson adapts con-
      ventions of literary prose]. Sources, analogues, and in-
      fluences [courtly love letter, "she-tragedy"].

1732 Fiedler, Leslie A. "The Novel's Audience and the Sentimental
      Love Religion," "Richardson and the Tragedy of Seduction,"
      "The Bourgeois Sentimental Novel and the Female Audience,"
      "Clarissa in America: Toward Marjorie Morningstar," and
      "Good Good Girls and Good Bad Boys: Clarissa as a Juve-
      nile." In his Love and Death in the American Novel. Rev.
      ed. New York: Stein and Day, 1966, pp. 39-104 and 217-
      90. Influence and reputation abroad. America. Love.
      Seduction. Sentimentalism. Women.

1733 Flynn, Carol Houlihan. Samuel Richardson: A Man of Let-
      ters. Princeton, N.J.: Princeton Univ. Press, 1982.

Perfectionism. Morality. Women. Sex. Prostitution.
Fairy tale. The rake. Characterization. Letter-writing.

■1734 Folkenflik, Robert. "A Room of Pamela's Own." ELH: A
Journal of English Literary History, 39 (1972), 585-96.
Women. Setting. The self.

1735 Fortuna, James Louis, Jr. "The Unsearchable Wisdom of
God": A Study of Providence in Richardson's "Pamela."
Gainesville: Univ. Presses of Florida, 1980. Providence.
Christianity.

1736 Frank, Frederick S. "From Boudoir to Castle Crypt: Richardson and the Gothic Novel." Revue des Langues Vivantes,
41 (1975), 49-59. Influence and imitation. Gothic novel
[Gothic elements in Richardson's fiction].

1737 Garber, Frederick. The Autonomy of the Self from Richardson to Huysmans. Princeton, N.J.: Princeton Univ. Press,
1982. [Clarissa, passim]. The self. Imagery [of desire].

1738 Garber, Frederick. "Richardson, Rousseau, and the Autonomy
of the Elect." Canadian Review of Comparative Literature,
5 (1978), 154-68. Imprisonment. Rousseau.

1739 Gillis, Christine Marsden. "Private Room and Public Space:
The Paradox of Form in Clarissa." Studies on Voltaire and
the Eighteenth Century, 176 (1979), 153-68. The self.
Privacy. Setting. Space.

●1740 Golden, Morris. Richardson's Characters. Ann Arbor:
Univ. of Michigan Press, 1963. Characterization. Psychology of characters. Dominance. "Bourgeois aristocracy."

1741 Golden, Morris. "Richardson's Repetitions." PMLA, 82
(1967), 64-67. Characterization. Plot, structure, and design.

1742 Goldknopf, David. "The Meaning of the Epistolary Format in
Clarissa." In his The Life of the Novel. Chicago: Univ.
of Chicago Press, 1972, pp. 59-78. Point of view and narrator. Epistolary novel.

1743 Gopnik, Irwin. A Theory of Style and Richardson's "Clarissa." The Hague: Mouton, 1970. Style and language.

1744 Greenstein, Susan. "Dear Reader, Dear Friend: Richardson's Readers and the Social Response to Character." College English, 41 (1980), 524-34. Author-reader relationship.

1745   Griffith, Philip Mahone. "Fire-Scenes in Richardson's Clarissa
        and Smollett's Humphry Clinker: A Study of a Literary
        Relationship in the Structure of the Novel." Tulane Studies
        in English, 11 (1961), 39-51. Setting. Fire scenes. Par-
        ody.

1746   Guilhamet, Leon M. "From Pamela to Grandison: Richard-
        son's Moral Revolution in the Novel." In Studies in Change
        and Revolution: Aspects of English Intellectual History,
        1640-1800. Ed. Paul J. Korshin. Menston, Yorkshire:
        Scolar Press, 1972, pp. 191-210. Characterization. Ex-
        emplum. Didacticism. Morality.

1747   Hagstrum, Jean H. "Richardson." In his Sex and Sensibil-
        ity: Ideal and Erotic Love from Milton to Mozart. Chicago:
        Univ. of Chicago Press, 1980, pp. 186-218. Love. Sen-
        sibility. Sex.

1748   Hardwick, Elizabeth. "Seduction and Betrayal." In Seduction
        and Betrayal: Women and Literature. New York: Random
        House, 1974, esp. pp. 196-202. Seduction. Women.

■1749   Harris, Jocelyn. "'As if they had been living friends': Sir
        Charles Grandison into Mansfield Park." Bulletin of Re-
        search in the Humanities, 83 (1980), 360-405. Influence
        and imitation. Marriage. Characterization. Education.
        Friendship. Propriety. Setting. Morality.

1750   Harris, Jocelyn. "The Reviser Observed: The Last Volume
        of Sir Charles Grandison." Studies in Bibliography, 29
        (1976), 1-31. Composition of the novel.

1751   Harris, R. W. "Richardson, Fielding, and the New Morality."
        In his Reason and Nature in the Eighteenth Century. New
        York: Barnes & Noble, 1969, pp. 251-79. Morality.
        Benevolence. Comparison of novelists.

1752   Hartveit, Lars. "Samuel Richardson, Pamela I. The Impact
        of Moral Exemplum: The Dilemma of the Didactic Writer."
        In his The Art of Persuasion: A Study of Six Novels.
        Bergen: Universitetsforlaget, 1977, pp. 14-32. Didacticism.
        Morality. Characterization.

1753   Harvey, A. D. "Clarissa and the Puritan Tradition." Essays
        in Criticism, 28 (1978), 38-51. Puritanism [morality in
        Clarissa not Puritanism]. Women. Morality [new obsession
        with virginity].

■1754   Hill, Christopher. "Clarissa Harlowe and Her Times." In his
        Puritanism and Revolution: Studies in Interpretation of the
        English Revolution of the 17th Century. 1958; rpt. New

York: Shocken Books, 1964, pp. 367-94. Rpt. in Samuel
Richardson: A Collection of Critical Essays. Ed. John
Carroll. Englewood Cliffs, N.J.: Prentice-Hall, 1969, pp.
102-23. Originally printed in Essays in Criticism, 5
(1955), 315-40. Marriage [the economics of marriage].
Social structure. Family. The middle class. Morality.
Puritanism.

■1755 Hilles, Frederick W. "The Plan of Clarissa." Philological
Quarterly, 45 (1966), 236-48. Rpt. in Samuel Richardson:
A Collection of Critical Essays. Ed. John Carroll. Englewood Cliffs, N.J.: Prentice-Hall, 1969, pp. 80-91. Plot,
structure, and design [highly symmetrical plot]. Composition of the novel.

1756 Hopkinson, H. T. "Robert Lovelace, the Romantic Cad."
Horizon, 10 (1944), 80-104. Characterization. The cad.
Man vs. woman.

1757 Hornbeak, Katherine G. "Richardson's 'Familiar Letters' and
the Domestic Conduct Books." Smith College Studies in
Modern Languages, 19 (1938), 1-29. Letter-writing. Conduct books.

1758 Hughes, Helen Sard. "Characterization in Clarissa Harlowe."
Journal of English and Germanic Philology, 13 (1914), 110-
23. Characterization.

1759 Hughes, Leo. "Theatrical Convention in Richardson: Some
Observations on a Novelist's Technique." In Restoration
and Eighteenth-Century Literature: Essays in Honor of
Alan Dugald McKillop. Ed. Carroll Camden. Chicago:
Univ. of Chicago Press, 1963, pp. 239-50. Dramatic con-
ventions in the novel.

1760 Humphreys, A. R. "Richardson's Novels: Words and the
'Movements Within.'" Essays and Studies, N.S. 23 (1970),
34-50. Style and language. Narrative technique. Innovation.

1761 Hunt, Russell A. "Johnson on Fielding and Richardson: A
Problem in Literary Moralism." Humanities Association Review, 27 (1976), 412-20. Eighteenth-century criticism and
reviews of the novel. Dr. Johnson. Comparison of novelists. Morality.

1762 Itzoe, Linda V. "The Chapel-Church Motif in Pamela: An
Analysis." Essays in Literature, 8 (1981), 91-96. Setting
[four church scenes punctuate Pamela's development from
serving girl to lady].

1763 Jeffrey, David K. "The Epistolary Format of Pamela and
      Humphry Clinker." In A Provision of Human Nature: Es-
      says on Fielding and Others in Honor of Miriam Austin
      Locke. Ed. Donald Kay. University: Univ. of Alabama
      Press, 1977, pp. 145-54. Epistolary novel. Comparison
      of novelists.

1764 Jenkins, Owen. "Richardson's Pamela and Fielding's 'Vile
      Forgeries.'" Philological Quarterly, 44 (1965), 200-10.
      Parody. Pamela-Shamela.

1765 Johnson, Glen M. "Richardson's 'Editor' in Clarissa." Jour-
      nal of Narrative Technique, 10 (1980), 99-114. Point of
      view and narrator.

1766 Kaplan, Fred. "'Our Short Story': The Narrative Devices
      of Clarissa." Studies in English Literature, 11 (1971),
      549-62. Plot, structure, and design. Narrative technique
      [use of flashback, foreshortening, time, reported dialogue,
      multiple points of view].

1767 Karl, Frederick. "Samuel Richardson and Clarissa." In A
      Reader's Guide to the Eighteenth-Century English Novel.
      New York: Noonday, 1974, pp. 99-145. Innovation. Nar-
      rative technique. Characterization. Plot, structure, and
      design.

1768 Kay, Donald. "Pamela and the Poultry." Satire Newsletter,
      10, No. 1 (1973), 25-27. Imagery [fowl].

■1769 Kearney, Anthony M. "Clarissa and the Epistolary Form."
      Essays in Criticism, 16 (1966), 44-56. Epistolary novel.
      Narrative technique.

1770 Kearney, Anthony M. "A Recurrent Motif in Richardson's
      Novels." Neophilologus, 55 (1971), 447-50. Symbolism
      [fowler, bird].

■1771 Kearney, Anthony M. "Richardson's Pamela: The Aesthetic
      Case." Review of English Literature, 7 (1966), 78-90.
      Rpt. in Samuel Richardson: A Collection of Critical Essays.
      Ed. John Carroll. Englewood Cliffs, N.J.: Prentice-Hall,
      1969, pp. 28-38. Critical revaluation [turns from the ques-
      tion of Pamela's motivations to consider the novel as an
      artistic whole]. Point of view and narrator [Pamela both
      "character" and "author"]. Narrative technique.

1772 Kearney, Anthony M. Samuel Richardson. Profiles in Liter-
      ature Series. London: Routledge & Kegan Paul, 1968.
      Introductory guide.

1773 Kearney, Anthony M. Samuel Richardson: "Clarissa."
      London: Edward Arnold, 1975. Introductory guide.

1774 Kermode, Frank. "Richardson and Fielding." Cambridge
      Journal, 4 (1950), 106-14. Comparison of novelists.

1775 Kinkead-Weekes, Mark. "Clarissa Restored?" Review of
      English Studies, N.S. 10 (1959), 156-71. Composition of
      the novel. Textual editing.

1776 Kinkead-Weekes, Mark. "Defoe and Richardson--Novelists of
      the City." In Dryden to Johnson. Ed. Roger Lonsdale.
      Vol. 4 of the History of Literature in the English Language.
      London: Barrie & Jenkins, 1971. Comparison of novelists.
      City life.

•1777 Kinkead-Weekes, Mark. Samuel Richardson: Dramatic Novel-
      ist. Ithaca, N.Y.: Cornell Univ. Press, 1973. Charac-
      terization. Dramatic conventions in the novel. Artistic de-
      velopment. "Writing to the moment." "Social realism."
      Social criticism in the novel.

1778 Klotman, Phyllis R. "Sin and Sublimation in the Novels of
      Samuel Richardson." College Language Association Journal,
      20 (1977), 365-73. Puritanism. Sex. Psychology of char-
      acters. Morality.

1779 Knight, Charles A. "The Function of Wills in Richardson's
      Clarissa." Texas Studies in Literature and Language, 11
      (1969), 1183-90. Wills [last wills and testaments]. Plot,
      structure, and design.

1780 Konigsberg, Ira. Samuel Richardson & the Dramatic Novel.
      Lexington: Univ. Press of Kentucky, 1968. Incorporates
      his "The Dramatic Background of Richardson's Plots and
      Characters," PMLA, 83 (1968), 42-53; and his "The Tragedy
      of Clarissa," Modern Language Quarterly, 27, No. 3 (1966),
      285-98. Innovation. Narrative technique. Dramatic con-
      ventions in the novel. Sources, analogues and influences.
      Characterization. Tragedy.

1781 Kovacs, Anna-Maria. "Pamela's Poverty." Revues des
      Langues Vivantes, 44 (1978), 3-14. Social structure.
      Servants. The poor.

•1782 Kreissman, Bernard. "Pamela"-"Shamela": A Study of the
      Criticisms, Burlesques, Parodies, and Adaptations of Rich-
      ardson's "Pamela." Lincoln: Univ. of Nebraska Press,
      1960. Parody. Influences and imitation. Pamela-Shamela.

1782a Lansbury, Coral. "The Triumph of Clarissa: Richardson's

Divine Comedy." Thalia: Studies in Literary Humor, 1,
No. 1 (1978), 9-17. Death [Clarissa's death a Christian
triumph]. Marriage [virtue prepares Clarissa for marriage
to Christ]. Christianity [Richardson's certainty of immor-
tality].

1783 Larson, Kerry C. "'Naming the Writer': Exposure, Author-
ity, and Desire in Pamela." Criticism, 23 (1981), 126-40.
Point of view and narrator. Author-reader relationship.
Psychology of characters.

1784 Lauren, Barbara. "Clarissa and The Newgate Calendar
(1768): A Perspective on the Novel Twenty Years Later."
Modern Language Studies, 8, No. 3 (1978), 5-11. Newgate
Calendar [historical analogue to Clarissa's rape]. Rape.

1785 Laurence-Anderson, Judith. "Changing Affective Life in
Eighteenth-Century England and Samuel Richardson's Pam-
ela." In Studies in Eighteenth-Century Culture. Vol. 10.
Ed. Harry C. Payne. Madison: Univ. of Wisconsin Press,
1981, pp. 445-56. Servants. Psychology of characters.
Sex.

1786 Leed, Jacob. "Richardson's Pamela and Sidney's." Journal
of the Australian Universities Language and Literature Association, 40 (1973), 240-45. Sources, analogues, and influences.

1787 Lefever, Charlotte. "Richardson's Paradoxical Success."
PMLA, 48 (1933), 856-60. Realism.

1788 Lesser, Simon O. "A Note on Pamela." In The Whispered
Meanings: Selected Essays. Ed. Robert Sprich and Richard W. Noland. Boston: Univ. of Massachusetts Press,
1977, pp. 14-19. Originally published in College English,
14 (1952), 13-17. Defects in the novel. Fairy tale.
Cinderella.

•1789 Levin, Gerald. Richardson the Novelist: The Psychological
Patterns. Atlantic Highlands, N.J.: Humanities Press,
1978. Incorporates his "Lovelace's Dream," Literature and
Psychology, 29 (1970), 121-27; "Richardson's Pamela:
'Conflicting Trends,'" American Imago, 28 (1971), 319-29;
and "Character and Fantasy in Richardson's Sir Charles
Grandison," Connecticut Review, 7, No. 1 (1973), 93-99.
Psychology of characters. Masochism ["moral masochism"
and "feminine masochism"]. Sex.

1790 Lindley, Arthur. "Richardson's Lovelace and the Self-drama-
tizing Hero of the Restoration." In The English Hero, 1660-
1800. Newark: Univ. of Delaware Press, 1982, pp. 195-204.
Hero/heroine [Lovelace's theatrical concept of himself].

1791 Loesberg, Jonathan. "Allegory and Narrative in Clarissa."
      Novel, 15 (1981), 39-59. Narrative technique. Allegory.

1792 Lyles, Albert M. "Pamela's Trials." College Language As-
      sociation Journal, 8 (1965), 290-92. Imagery [trial].
      Characterization [Mr. B., appropriately a justice of the
      peace, is Pamela's "judge"].

1793 Maddox, James H., Jr. "Lovelace and the World of Ressenti-
      ment in Clarissa." Texas Studies in Literature and Lan-
      guage, 24 (1982), 271-92. Characterization. Psychology
      of characters. Ressentiment.

1794 Manheim, Leonard H. "The Absurd Miss Pamela and the
      Tragic Miss Clarissa: A Brief Study of Samuel Richardson
      as a Developing Artist." Nassau Review, 2 (1970), 1-10.
      Artistic development.

1795 McIntosh, Carey. "Pamela's Clothes." ELH: A Journal of
      English Literary History, 35 (1968), 75-83. Rpt. in Twen-
      tieth Century Interpretations of "Pamela": A Collection of
      Critical Essays. Ed. Rosemary Cowler. Englewood Cliffs,
      N.J.: Prentice-Hall, 1969, pp. 89-96. Clothing. Symbol-
      ism [social, sexual significance of clothes].

1796 McKillop, Alan Dugald. "Epistolary Technique in Richard-
      son's Novels." Rice Institute Pamphlet, 38, No. 1 (1951),
      36-54. Rpt. in Studies in the Literature of the Augustan
      Age: Essays Collected in Honor of Arthur Ellicott Case.
      Ed. Richard C. Boys. Augustan Reprint Society. Ann
      Arbor, Mich.: George Wahr, 1952, pp. 198-217. Epistolary
      novel.

1797 McKillop, Alan Dugald. "The Mock Marriage Device in Pam-
      ela." Philological Quarterly, 26 (1947), 285-88. Marriage.
      Sources, analogues, and influences.

1798 McKillop, Alan Dugald. "The Personal Relations Between
      Fielding and Richardson." Modern Philology, 28 (1931),
      423-33. Personal relations between authors.

■1799 McKillop, Alan Dugald. "Samuel Richardson." In his The
      Early Masters of English Fiction. Lawrence: Univ. of
      Kansas Press, 1956, pp. 47-97. Introductory guide [excel-
      lent account of main issues].

•1800 McKillop, Alan Dugald. Samuel Richardson, Printer and Nov-
      elist. 1936; rpt. Hamden, Conn.: Shoe String Press,
      1960. Biography. Theory and practice of the novel.
      Sources, analogues, and influences. Composition of the nov-
      el. Achievement and reputation.

1801   McKillop, Alan Dugald. "Wedding Bells for Pamela." Philo-
       logical Quarterly, 28 (1949), 323-25. Reading public
       [popularity of Pamela].

1802   Miller, Nancy K. "Novels of Innocence: Fiction of Loss."
       Eighteenth-Century Studies, 11 (1978), 325-39. Women.
       Innocence. Initiation.

1803   Moore, John Robert. "Daniel Defoe: Precursor of Samuel
       Richardson." In Restoration and Eighteenth-Century Lit-
       erature: Essays in Honor of Alan Dugald McKillop. Ed.
       Carroll Camden. Chicago: Univ. of Chicago Press, 1963,
       pp. 351-69. Comparison of novelists.

1804   Moore, Robert Etheridge. "Dr. Johnson on Fielding and
       Richardson." PMLA, 66 (1951), 162-81. Eighteenth-century
       criticism and reviews of the novel. Dr. Johnson. Compari-
       son of novelists.

1805   Morton, Donald E. "Theme and Structure in Pamela." Studies
       in the Novel, 3 (1971), 242-57. Plot, structure, and design.
       Conversion and repentance [of Mr. B shapes the plot].

1806   Moynihan, Robert D. "Clarissa and the Enlightened Woman as
       Literary Heroine." Journal of the History of Ideas, 36
       (1975), 159-66. Women. Characterization. Marriage.
       Family.

1807   Muecke, D. C. "Beauty and Mr. B." Studies in English Lit-
       erature, 7 (1967), 467-74. Fairy tale.

1808   Munro, James S. "Richardson, Marivaux and the French
       Romance Tradition." Modern Language Review, 70 (1975),
       752-59. Marivaux. Romance. Sources, analogues, and
       influences.

■1809 Napier, Elizabeth R. "'Tremble and Reform': The Inversion
       of Power in Richardson's Clarissa." ELH: A Journal of
       English Literary History, 42 (1975), 214-23. Power. Plot,
       structure, and design. Imagery [hunting, government,
       serpents, sovereignty].

1810   Needham, Gwendolyn B. "Richardson's Characterization of
       Mr. B. and Double Purpose in Pamela." Eighteenth-Century
       Studies, 3 (1970), 433-74. Characterization [sound under-
       standing of Mr. B's character and psychological motivation].

1811   Noble, Yvonne. "Clarissa: Paradise Irredeemably Lost." In
       Transactions of the Fourth International Congress on the
       Enlightenment. Oxford: Voltaire Foundation, 1976, pp.
       1529-45. Milton [comparison of Paradise Lost with Clarissa].
       Christianity. Philosophy of novelist. Initiation.

1812 Olivier, Theo. "Pamela and Shamela: A Reassessment."
      English Studies in Africa, 17 (1974), 59-70. Parody.
      Pamela-Shamela.

■1813 Palmer, William J. "Two Dramatists: Lovelace and Richard-
      son in Clarissa." Studies in the Novel, 5 (1973), 7-21.
      Autobiographical elements in the novel [Lovelace expresses
      Richardson's unconscious desires]. Characterization.
      Dramatic conventions in the novel [Lovelace as author of a
      play-within-a-novel].

1814 Park, William. "Clarissa as Tragedy." Studies in English
      Literature, 16 (1976), 461-71. Tragedy.

■1815 Park, William. "Fielding and Richardson." PMLA, 81 (1966),
      381-88. Comparison of novelists [their important similari-
      ties]. Theory and practice of the novel. Philosophy of
      novelist [common assumptions about man, society, and the
      world].

1816 Parker, Dorothy. "The Time Scheme of Pamela and the Char-
      acter of B." Texas Studies in Literature and Language, 11
      (1969), 695-704. Time [letters written over 17 months].
      Characterization [only as Pamela matures do we see the real
      Mr. B].

1817 Peters, Dolores. "The Pregnant Pamela: Characterization
      and Popular Medical Attitudes in the Eighteenth Century."
      Eighteenth-Century Studies, 14 (1981), 432-51. Character-
      ization [owes much to medical attitudes]. Women. Medicine.
      Pregnancy and childbirth.

1818 Pierson, Robert C. "The Revisions of Richardson's Sir
      Charles Grandison." Studies in Bibliography, 21 (1968),
      163-89. Composition of the novel. Textual editing.

1819 Poovey, Mary. "Journeys from This World to the Next: The
      Providential Promise in Clarissa and Tom Jones." ELH: A
      Journal of English Literary History, 43 (1976), 300-15.
      Comparison of novelists. Providence. Philosophy of novel-
      ist.

1820 Preston, John. "Clarissa (i): A Process of Estrangement"
      and "Clarissa (ii): A Form of Freedom." In his The Cre-
      ated Self: The Reader's Role in Eighteenth-Century Fic-
      tion. New York: Barnes & Noble, 1970, pp. 38-93.
      Author-reader relationship. Estrangement.

1821 Price, Martin. "Clarissa and Lovelace." In his To the Palace
      of Wisdom: Studies in Order and Energy from Dryden to
      Blake. Garden City: Doubleday, 1964, pp. 276-84. Char-
      acterization.

1822 Rabkin, Norman. "Clarissa: A Study in the Nature of Con-
      vention." ELH: A Journal of English Literary History, 23
      (1956), 204-17. Characterization. Propriety. The pas-
      sions.

1823 Ray, J. Karen. "The Feminist Role in Robinson Crusoe,
      Roxana, and Clarissa." Emporia State Research Studies,
      24 (1976), 28-33. Feminism.

1824 Reid, B. L. "Justice to Pamela." Hudson Review, 9 (1956-
      57), 516-33. Rpt. in his The Long Boy and Others. Ath-
      ens: Univ. of Georgia Press, 1969, pp. 31-51. Realism.

1825 Rogers, Katharine M. "Sensitive Feminism vs. Conventional
      Sympathy: Richardson and Fielding on Women." Novel, 9
      (1976), 256-70. Rpt. as "Richardson's Empathy with Wom-
      en." In The Authority of Experience: Essays in Feminist
      Criticism. Ed. Arlyn Diamond and Lee R. Edwards. Am-
      herst: Univ. of Massachusetts Press, 1977, pp. 118-36.
      For a response, see Anthony J. Hassall, "Critical Exchange:
      Women in Richardson and Fielding," Novel, 14 (1981), 168-
      74. Women. Comparison of novelists.

1826 Romberg, Bertil. "Clarissa." In his Studies in the Narrative
      Technique of the First-Person Novel. Trans. Michael Tay-
      lor and Harold B. Borland. Stockholm: Almqvist & Wik-
      sell, 1962, pp. 117-235. Point of view and narrator.

1827 Rousseau, George S. "III. Whores: Pamela." In his
      "Threshold and Explanation: The Social Anthropologist
      and the Critic of Eighteenth-Century Literature." The
      Eighteenth Century: Theory and Interpretation, 22 (1981),
      137-40. Servants. Sex. Marriage.

1828 Roussel, Roy. "Reflections on the Letter: The Reconciliation
      of Distance and Presence in Pamela." ELH: A Journal of
      English Literary History, 41 (1974), 375-99. Letter-writing.
      Love. The self. Characterization. Privacy.

1829 Sabor, Peter. "Richardson and His Readers." Humanities
      Association Bulletin, 30 (1979), 161-73. Composition of the
      novel [Richardson's soliciting critical opinion as he wrote].
      Eighteenth-century criticism and reviews of the novel.

1830 Sacks, Sheldon. "Clarissa and the Tragic Traditions." In
      Studies in Eighteenth-Century Culture: Irrationalism in the
      Eighteenth Century. Ed. Harold E. Pagliaro. Vol. 2
      Cleveland: The Press of Case Western Reserve Univ.,
      1972, pp. 195-221. Tragedy. Dramatic conventions in the
      novel. Sentimental novel.

1831 Sale, William M., Jr. "From Pamela to Clarissa." In The

Age of Johnson: Essays Presented to Chauncey Brewster
Tinker. Ed. Frederick W. Hilles and Wilmarth S. Lewis.
New Haven, Conn.: Yale Univ. Press, 1949, pp. 127-38.
Rpt. in Samuel Richardson: A Collection of Critical Essays.
Ed. John Carroll. Englewood Cliffs, N.J.: Prentice-Hall,
1969, pp. 39-48. Social structure. Artistic development.

•1832   Sale, William M., Jr. Samuel Richardson: Master Printer.
        Ithaca, N.Y.: Cornell Univ. Press, 1950. Biography.

1833   Schmitz, Robert M. "Death and Colonel Morden in Clarissa."
        South Atlantic Quarterly, 69 (1970), 346-53. Death.
        Characterization.

1834   Scrutton, Mary. "Bourgeois Cinderellas." Twentieth Century,
        155 (1954), 351-63, esp. 351-55. Myth. Marriage. Bour-
        geois ideology [middle-class virtue rewarded by prosperous
        marriage].

1835   Sharrock, Roger. "Richardson's Pamela: The Gospel and
        the Novel." Durham University Journal, N.S. 27 (1966),
        67-74. Christianity. Characterization.

1836   Shepperson, Archibald Bolling. "Richardson and Fielding:
        Shamela and Shamelia." In his The Novel in Motley: A
        History of the Burlesque Novel in English. 1936; rpt.
        New York: Octagon, 1967, pp. 9-38. Parody. Pamela-
        Shamela. Burlesque novel.

1837   Sherbo, Arthur. "Time and Place in Richardson's Clarissa."
        Boston University Studies in English, 3 (1957), 139-46.
        Setting [place, time].

1838   Sherburn, George. "Samuel Richardson's Novels and the
        Theatre: A Theory Sketched." Philological Quarterly, 41
        (1962), 325-29. Dramatic conventions in the novel.
        Sources, analogues, and influences.

1839   Sherburn, George. "Writing to the Moment: One Aspect."
        In Restoration and Eighteenth-Century Literature: Essays
        in Honor of Alan Dugald McKillop. Ed. Carroll Camden.
        Chicago: Univ. of Chicago Press for William Marsh Rice
        Univ., 1963, pp. 201-09. Rpt. in Samuel Richardson: A
        Collection of Critical Essays. Ed. John Carroll. Englewood
        Cliffs, N.J.: Prentice-Hall, 1969, pp. 152-60. "Writing to
        the moment." Characterizaiton [visual details]. Gestures
        and mannerisms.

1840   Shroff, Homai J. "The Woman's Gentleman, or the Anatomy
        of the Rake--Samuel Richardson." In her The Eighteenth-
        Century Novel: The Idea of the Gentleman. New Delhi:

Arnold-Heinemann, 1978, pp. 96-122. The gentleman. The rake.

1841 Shuman, R. Baird. "Censorship as a Controlling Theme in Pamela and Clarissa." Notes and Queries, N.S. 3 (1956), 30-32. Censorship. Social criticism in the novel. Symbolism.

1842 Siegel, June Sigler. "Lovelace and Rameau's Nephew: Roots of Poetic Amoralism." Diderot Studies, 19 (1978), 163-74. Comparison of novelists [Richardson, Diderot]. Characterization [new type of character marked by intensity, dichotomy].

1843 Smidt, Kristian. "Character and Plot in the Novels of Samuel Richardson." Critical Quarterly, 17 (1975), 155-66. Characterization. Plot, structure, and design.

1844 Spacks, Patricia Meyer. "The Sense of Audience: Samuel Richardson, Colley Cibber." In her Imagining a Self: Autobiography and Novel in Eighteenth-Century England. Cambridge, Mass.: Harvard Univ. Press, 1976, pp. 193-226. The self.

1845 Spearman, Diana. "Richardson." In her The Novel and Society. London: Routledge & Kegan Paul, 1966, pp. 173-98. Social background.

1846 Stein, William B. "Pamela: The Narrator as Unself-Conscious Hack." Bucknell Review, 20, No. 1 (1972), 39-66. Conventions of the Georgian novel. Point of view and narrator [Pamela as novice author using literary stereotypes then in vogue].

◼1847 Stevenson, John Allen. "The Courtship of the Family: Clarissa and the Harlowes Once More." ELH: A Journal of English Literary History, 48 (1981), 757-77. Family. Marriage. Psychology of characters [endogamous urge in the Harlowes leaves Clarissa trapped between incest and rape].

1848 Swann, George Rogers. "Richardson and the Idealism of the Moral Will." In his Philosophical Parallelisms in Six English Novelists. 1929; rpt. Folcroft, Pa.: Folcroft Press, 1969, pp. 27-45. Philosophy of novelist. Kant.

1849 Taylor, Anne Robinson. "An Odd and Grotesque Figure: Samuel Richardson and Clarissa." In her Male Novelists and Their Female Voices: Literary Masquerades. Troy, N.Y.: Whitston, 1981, pp. 57-90. Male novelist assuming female identity. Masquerade [Richardson's art based on assuming other identities]. Personality of novelist. Domi-

nance [struggle for dominance over Clarissa]. Characterization [characters seen as evocations of the author].

1850 Ten Harmsel, Henrietta. "The Villain-Hero in Pamela and
Pride and Prejudice." College English, 23 (1961), 104-08.
Characterization. Social structure.

■1851 Todd, Janet. "Sentimental Friendship: Samuel Richardson's
Clarissa." In her Women's Friendship in Literature. New
York: Columbia Univ. Press, 1980, pp. 9-68. Women's
friendship. Sentimentalism.

1852 Traugott, John. "Clarissa's Richardson: An Essay to Find
the Reader." In English Literature in the Age of Disguise.
Ed. Maximillan E. Novak. Los Angeles: Univ. of California
Press, 1977, pp. 157-208. Author-reader relationship.
Personality of novelist. The rake. Comedy [juxtaposed
with sentimental realism]. Contrast as technique. Characterization.

1853 Uhrström, Wilhelm. Studies on the Language of Samuel Richardson. 1907; rpt. Folcroft, Pa.: Folcroft Press, 1969.
Style and language.

1854 Ulmer, Gregory L. "Clarissa and La Nouvelle Héloïse." Comparative Literature, 24 (1972), 289-308. Rousseau. Comparison of novelists [Rousseau inverts the plot of Clarissa].

1855 Uphaus, Robert W. "Clarissa, Amelia, and the State of Pro-
bation." In his The Impossible Observer: Reason and the
Reader in 18th-Century Prose. Lexington: Univ. Press
of Kentucky, 1979, pp. 71-88. Author-reader relationship.
Reason.

1856 Utter, Robert P., and Gwendolyn B. Needham. Pamela's
Daughters. New York: Macmillan, 1936. Influence and
imitation.

1857 Vaid, Sudesh. "Defoe and Richardson and the Eighteenth-
Century Woman's Debate" and "Pamela and Clarissa." In
The Divided Mind: Studies in Defoe and Richardson.
New Delhi: Associated Publishing House, 1980, pp. 48-91,
151-224. Women. Social criticism in the novel. Comparison
of novelists.

1858 Van Ghent, Dorothy. "Clarissa and Emma as Phèdre." Par-
tisan Review, 17 (1950), 820-33. Love.

■1859 Van Ghent, Dorothy. "On Clarissa Harlowe." In her The
English Novel: Form and Function. 1953; rpt. New York:
Holt, Rinehart, Winston, 1964, pp. 45-63. Rpt. in Samuel

Richardson: A Collection of Critical Essays. Ed. John
Carroll. Englewood Cliffs, N.J.: Prentice-Hall, 1969, pp.
49-66. Myth [Puritan myth, myth of social class, sexual
myth]. Symbolism ["Clarissa-symbol"]. Plot, structure,
and design. Characterization. Women. Sex. Family.

1860 Van Marter, Shirley. "Hidden Virtue: An Unsolved Problem
      in Clarissa." Yearbook of English Studies, 4 (1974), 140-
      48. Composition of the novel. Characterization.

1861 Van Marter, Shirley. "Richardson's Debt to Hestor Mulso
      Concerning the Curse in Clarissa." Papers on Language
      and Literature, 14 (1978), 22-31. Hester Mulso. Composi-
      tion of the novel.

1862 Ward, H. G. "Samuel Richardson and the English Philosoph-
      ers." Notes and Queries, 11th series, 3 (1911), 5-6.
      Berkeley. Mandeville. Shaftesbury.

1863 Warner, William Beatty. Reading "Clarissa": The Struggles
      of Interpretation. New Haven, Conn.: Yale Univ. Press,
      1980. Critical revaluation. Survey of criticism. Author-
      reader relationship.

1864 Watt, Ian. "Defoe and Richardson on Homer: A Study of the
      Relation of Novel and Epic in the Early Eighteenth Century."
      Review of English Studies, N.S. 4 (1953), 325-40. Epic.
      Homer.

■1865 Watt, Ian. "Love and The Novel: Pamela," "Private Experi-
      ence and the Novel," and "Richardson as Novelist: Claris-
      sa." In his The Rise of the Novel: Studies in Defoe,
      Richardson and Fielding. 1957; rpt. Berkeley: Univ. of
      California Press, 1971, pp. 135-238. Theory and practice
      of the novel. Love. Marriage. Women. Sex. Author-
      reader relationship.

1866 Watt, Ian. "The Naming of Characters in Defoe, Richardson,
      and Fielding." Review of English Studies, O.S. 25 (1949),
      322-38. Names of characters.

1867 Weinstein, Arnold. "Huis Clos: Clarissa." In his Fictions
      of the Self: 1550-1800. Princeton, N.J.: Princeton Univ.
      Press, 1981, pp. 165-81. The self. Symbolism.

1868 Wendt, Allan. "Clarissa's Coffin." Philological Quarterly, 39
      (1960), 481-95. Morality. Symbolism [coffin].

1869 Wills, Antony. "The World of Clarissa." Rendezvous, 9,
      Nos. 1-2 (1974), 1-14. Critical revaluation [emphasizes
      mythic and allegorical structure as corrective to Watt's em-

phasis on realism]. Allegory [Clarissa a female Job; Lovelace, the epitome of evil].

1870 Wilson, Angus. "Evil in the English Novel." Kenyon Review,
      29 (1967), 167-94. Evil [sees Clarissa as first novel to de-
      velop the sense of evil].

1871 Wilson, Stuart. "Richardson's Pamela: An Interpretation."
      PMLA, 88 (1973), 79-91. Characterization. Unity. Plot,
      structure, and design. Imagery. Symbolism.

1872 Wilt, Judith. "He Could Go No Farther: A Modest Proposal
      About Lovelace and Clarissa." PMLA, 92 (1977), 19-32.
      For a response and an additional comment, see Robert M.
      Schmitz and Judith Wilt, "Lovelace and Impotence," ibid.,
      1005-6. Characterization. Impotence. Women [Richardson's
      ambivalent attitude towards].

1873 Winner, Anthony. "Richardson's Lovelace: Character and
      Prediction." Texas Studies in Literature and Language, 14
      (1972), 53-75. Characterization.

•1874 Wolff, Cynthia Griffin. Samuel Richardson and the Eighteenth-
       Century Puritan Character. Hamden, Conn.: Archon,
       1972. Characterization. Puritanism. Sources, analogues,
       and influences [Puritan devotional literature].

1875 Wolff, Renate C. "Pamela as Myth and Dream." Costerus,
      7 (1973), 223-35. Fairy tale. Dreams [novel a projection
      of Pamela's (and the author's) unconscious, culminating in
      wish-fulfillment]. Myth.

1875a Yates, Mary V. "The Christian Rake in Sir Charles Grandi-
       son." Studies in English Literature, 24 (1984), 545-61.
       The rake. Didacticism.

1876 Zach, Wolfgang. "Mrs. Aubin and Richardson's Earliest Lit-
      erary Manifesto." English Studies, 62 (1981), 271-81.
      Comparison of novelists. Theory and practice of the novel
      [suggests that Richardson wrote the Preface to a 1739
      posthumous collection of Aubin's novels].

      SEE ALSO ITEMS 334, 442, 752, 763, 767, 793, 816,
      820, 822, 824, 833, 844, 854, 884, 932, 951, 1001, 1004a,
      1005, 1012, 1016, 1029, 1032, 1045, 1052, 1056, 1060a,
      1070, 1110, 1116.

TOBIAS SMOLLETT
(1721-1777)

PRINCIPAL FICTION

Roderick Random, 1748

Peregrine Pickle, 1751

Ferdinand, Count Fathom, 1753

Sir Launcelot Greaves, 1760-61, 1762

The Expedition of Humphry Clinker, 1771

BIBLIOGRAPHIES AND SURVEYS OF CRITICISM

1877   Boege, Fred W. Smollett's Reputation as a Novelist. 1947;
       rpt. New York: Octagon, 1969. Survey of criticism.
       Eighteenth-century criticism and reviews of the novel.
       Achievement and reputation.

1878   Boucé, Paul-Gabriel. "Eighteenth- and Nineteenth-Century
       Biographies of Smollett." In Tobias Smollett: Bicentennial
       Essays Presented to Lewis M. Knapp. Ed. George S.
       Rousseau and Paul-Gabriel Boucé. New York: Oxford
       Univ. Press, 1971, pp. 201-30. Biography [survey of].

1879   Boucé, Paul-Gabriel. "Smollett: Roderick Random (1748):
       A Selective and Critical Bibliography." Bulletin de la So-
       ciété d'Etudes Anglo-Américaines des XVIIe et XVIIIe Si-
       ècles, 13 (1981), 43-51. Bibliography of criticism [1971-
       1981].

1880   Cordasco, Francesco. Tobias George Smollett: A Biblio-
       graphical Guide. New York: AMS Press, 1978. Bibliog-
       raphy of primary sources. Bibliography of criticism.

1881   Knapp, Lewis M. "Smollett." In The English Novel: Select
       Bibliographical Guides. Ed. A. E. Dyson. London: Ox-
       ford Univ. Press, 1974, pp. 112-27. Bibliography of criti-
       cism. Survey of criticism.

1882   Rousseau, George S. "Beef and Bouillon: A Voice for
       Tobias Smollett, with Comments on His Life, Works, and
       Modern Critics." British Studies Monitor, 7, No. 1 (1977),
       4-56. Survey of criticism. Critical revaluation.

1883   Spector, Robert D. Tobias Smollett: A Reference Guide.

Boston: G. K. Hall, 1980. Bibliography of criticism [annotated, evaluative].

1884   Thorson, Connie Capers. "Smollett and Humphry Clinker: A Bibliographical Essay." In Tobias Smollett: "Humphry Clinker": An Authoritative Text, Contemporary Responses, Criticism. Ed. James L. Thorson. Norton Critical Editions. New York: Norton, 1983, pp. 427-33. Survey of criticism.

1884a Wagoner, Mary. Tobias Smollett: A Checklist of Editions of His Works and an Annotated Secondary Bibliography. New York: Garland [forthcoming]. Bibliography of primary sources. Bibliography of criticism [annotated].

BIOGRAPHICAL AND CRITICAL STUDIES

■1885 Alter, Robert. "The Picaroon as Fortune's Plaything." In his The Rogue's Progress: Studies in the Picaresque Novel. Cambridge, Mass.: Harvard Univ. Press, 1964, pp. 58-79. [Roderick Random]. Picaresque novel. Rogue hero.

1886   Anderson, Earl R. "Footnotes More Pedestrian Than Sublime: A Historical Background for the Foot-Races in Evelina and Humphry Clinker." Eighteenth-Century Studies, 14 (1980), 56-68. Sources, analogues, and influences.

1887   Andres, Sophia. "Tobias Smollett's Satiric Spokesman in Humphry Clinker." Studies in Scottish Literature. Vol. 13. Ed. G. Ross Roy. Columbia: Univ. of South Carolina Press, 1978, pp. 100-10. Satire. Characterization. Point of view and narrator.

■1888 Baker, Sheridan. "Humphry Clinker as Comic Romance." Papers of the Michigan Academy of Science, Arts and Letters, 46 (1961), 645-54. Rpt. in Essays on the Eighteenth-Century Novel. Ed. Robert D. Spector. Bloomington: Indiana Univ. Press, 1965. Burlesque novel [burlesque of traditional romance]. Satire. Romance.

1889   Barlow, Sheryl. "The Deception of Bath: Malapropisms in Smollett's Humphry Clinker." Michigan Academician, 2 (1970), 13-24. Speech and dialogue.

1890   Bates, Robin. "Smollett's Struggle for a New Mode of Expression." Thalia, 1, No. 3 (1978-79), 25-31. Innovation.

1891   Batten, Charles L., Jr. "Humphry Clinker and Eighteenth-Century Travel Literature." Genre, 7 (1974), 392-408. Travel literature.

1892 Beasley, Jerry C. "Roderick Random: The Picaresque
      Transformed." College Literature, 6 (1979), 211-20.
      Picaresque novel.

1892a Beasley, Jerry C. "Smollett's Novels: Ferdinand, Count
      Fathom for the Defense." Papers on Language and Litera-
      ture, 20 (1984), 165-84. Critical revaluation.

1893 Bertelsen, Lance. "The Smollettian View of Life." Novel, 11
      (1978), 115-27. Plot, structure, and design [stress on
      dynamics of action]. Unity. Artistic development. Philos-
      ophy of novelist [life as a web in which people and activity
      are inextricably linked].

1894 Bjornson, Richard. "The Picaresque Hero as Young Noble-
      man: Victimization and Vindication in Smollett's Roderick
      Random." In his The Picaresque Hero in European Fiction.
      Madison: Univ. of Wisconsin Press, 1977, pp. 228-48.
      Rogue hero. Social criticism in the novel [of the middle-
      class ethic].

1895 Bloch, Tuvia. "Smollett's Quest for Form." Modern Philology,
      65 (1967), 103-13. Artistic development. Plot, structure,
      and design.

1896 Boggs, W. Arthur. "Dialectical Ingenuity in Humphry Clink-
      er." Papers on Language and Literature, 1 (1965), 327-37.
      Speech and dialogue.

1897 Boggs, W. Arthur. "A Win Jenkins' Lexicon." Bulletin of
      the New York Public Library, 68 (1964), 323-30. Speech
      and dialogue.

1898 Boggs, W. Arthur. "Win Jenkins' Malapropisms." Jammie and
      Kashmir University Review, 4 (1961), 130-40. Speech and
      dialogue.

1899 Boucé, Paul-Gabriel. "The Duke of Newcastle's Levee in
      Smollett's Humphry Clinker." Yearbook of English Studies,
      5 (1975), 136-41. Realism. Setting.

•1900 Boucé, Paul-Gabriel. The Novels of Tobias Smollett. Trans.
      Antonia White in collaboration with the author. London:
      Longman, 1976. Autobiographical elements in the novel.
      Plot, structure, and design. Morality. Realism. Comedy.

1901 Brooks, Douglas. "Smollett: Roderick Random, Peregrine
      Pickle, Ferdinand, Count Fathom" and "Smollett: Humphry
      Clinker." In his Number and Pattern in the Eighteenth-
      Century Novel. London: Routledge & Kegan Paul, 1975,
      pp. 123-43. Numerology. Plot, structure, and design.
      Symbolism.

1902 Bruce, Donald. <u>Radical Doctor Smollett</u>. 1964; rpt. Boston:
      Houghton Mifflin, 1965. Biography.

1903 Bruce, Donald. "Smollett and the Sordid Knaves." <u>Contem-
      porary Review</u>, 220 (1972), 133-38. Whigs [criticism of
      their corruption]. Satire.

1904 Buck, Howard Swazey. <u>A Study in Smollett, Chiefly "Pere-
      grine Pickle," with a Complete Collation of the First and
      Second Editions</u>. 1925; rpt. Mamaroneck, N.Y.: Paul R.
      Appel, 1973. Composition of the novel. Plot, structure,
      and design.

1905 Bunn, James H. "Signs of Randomness in <u>Roderick Random</u>."
      <u>Eighteenth-Century Studies</u>, 14 (1981), 452-69. Plot,
      structure, and design. Narrative technique. Chance.

1906 Butt, John. "Smollett's Achievement as Novelist." In <u>Tobias
      Smollett: Bicentennial Essays Presented to Lewis M. Knapp</u>.
      Ed. George S. Rousseau and Paul-Gabriel Boucé. New
      York: Oxford Univ. Press, 1971, pp. 9-23. Introductory
      guide. Achievement and reputation.

1907 Chandler, Frank W. "Tobias Smollett." In his <u>The Literature
      of Roguery</u>. Boston: Houghton Mifflin, 1907, II, 309-20.
      Picaresque novel.

1908 Collins, R. G. "The Hidden Bastard: A Question of Illegiti-
      macy in Smollett's <u>Peregrine Pickle</u>." <u>PMLA</u>, 94 (1979),
      91-105. Bastardy. Plot, structure, and design.

1909 Copeland, Edward. "<u>Humphry Clinker</u>: A Comic Pastoral
      Poem in Prose?" <u>Texas Studies in Literature and Language</u>,
      16 (1974), 493-501. Pastoral tradition.

1910 Daiches, David. "Smollett Reconsidered." In <u>From Smollett
      to James: Studies in the Novel and Other Essays Presented
      to Edgar Johnson</u>. Ed. Samuel I. Mintz et al. Charlottes-
      ville: Univ. Press of Virginia, 1981, pp. 11-47. Critical
      revaluation [stresses moral over comic tone]. Morality.

1910a Day, Robert Adams. "Sex, Scatology, Smollett." In <u>Sexual-
      ity in Eighteenth-Century Britain</u>. Ed. Paul-Gabriel
      Boucé. Totowa, N.J.: Barnes & Noble, 1982, pp. 225-43.
      Sex [homosexual-excremental myth]. Scatology.

1911 Day, Robert Adams. "Ut Pictura Poesis? Smollett, Satire, and
      the Graphic Arts." In <u>Studies in Eighteenth-Century Cul-
      ture</u>. Vol. 10. Ed. Harry C. Payne. Madison: Univ. of
      Wisconsin Press, 1981, pp. 297-312. Satire. Caricature.
      Scatology.

1912 Dempsey, I. Lindsay. "The Metamorphosis of Humphry
      Clinker." New Laurel Review, 4, Nos. 1-2 (1975), 19-26.
      Contrast as technique [Matt vs. Tabitha]. Symbolism.
      Journey. Characterization.

1913 Donovan, Robert Alan. "Humphry Clinker and the Novelist's
      Imagination." In his The Shaping Vision: Imagination in
      the English Novel. Ithaca, N.Y.: Cornell Univ. Press,
      1966, pp. 118-39. Point of view and narrator. Plot, struc-
      ture, and design. Family. Imagination.

1914 Drinker, Cecil K. "Doctor Smollett." Annals of Medical His-
      tory, 7 (1925), 31-47. Medicine.

1915 Driskell, Leon V. "Looking for Dustwich." Texas Studies in
      Lit. and Lang., 9 (1967), 85-90. Appearance vs. reality.

1916 Dunn, Richard J. "Humphry Clinker's Humane Humor." Texas
      Studies in Lit. and Lang., 18 (1976), 229-39. Comedy.

1917 Ellison, Lee Monroe. "Elizabethan Drama and the Works of
      Smollett." PMLA, 44 (1929), 842-62. Shakespearean influ-
      ence. Sources, analogues, and influences.

1918 Evans, David L. "Humphry Clinker: Smollett's Tempered Au-
      gustanism." Criticism, 9 (1967), 257-74. Gentry. Rural
      ideal.

1919 Evans, David L. "Peregrine Pickle: The Complete Satirist."
      Studies in the Novel, 3 (1971), 258-74. Satire. Character-
      ization.

1920 Evans, James E. "Smollett's Verbal Performances in Peregrine
      Pickle." Notre Dame English Journal, 8 (1973), 87-97.
      Style and language.

1921 Fabel, Robin. "The Patriotic Briton: Tobias Smollett and Eng-
      lish Politics, 1756-1771." Eighteenth-Century Studies, 8
      (1974), 100-14. Politics [opposed to partisan government].

1922 Flanders, W. Austin. "The Significance of Smollett's Memoirs
      of A Lady of Quality." Genre, 8 (1975), 146-64. Defects
      in the novel [conventional endings]. Closure.

■1923 Folkenflik, Robert. "Self and Society: Comic Union in
      Humphry Clinker." Philological Quarterly, 53 (1974), 195-
      204. Self vs. society [reconciliation of self-interest and
      social union]. Unity.

1924 Franke, Wolfgang. "Smollett's Humphry Clinker as a 'Party
      Novel.'" Studies in Scottish Literature, 9 (1971-72), 97-
      106. Politics. Scotland.

1925 Fredman, Alice G. "The Picaresque in Decline: Smollett's
      First Novel." In English Writers of the Eighteenth Century.
      Ed. John H. Middendorf. New York: Columbia Univ.
      Press, 1971, pp. 189-207. [Roderick Random]. Picaresque
      novel.

1926 Garrow, Scott. "A Study of the Organization of Smollett's
      The Expedition of Humphry Clinker." Southern Quarterly,
      4 (1966), 349-63. Cont'd, ibid., 5 (1966), 22-46. Plot,
      structure, and design. Travel literature.

1927 Gassman, Byron. "The Briton and Humphry Clinker."
      Studies in English Literature, 3 (1963), 397-414. Politics.

■1928 Gassman, Byron. "The Economy of Humphry Clinker." In
      Tobias Smollett: Bicentennial Essays Presented to Lewis
      M. Knapp. Ed. George S. Rousseau and Paul-Gabriel
      Boucé. New York: Oxford Univ. Press, 1971, pp. 155-
      68. Plot, structure, and design. Unity.

1929 Gassman, Byron. "Humphry Clinker and the Two Kingdoms
      of George III." Criticism, 16 (1974), 95-108. Social criti-
      cism in the novel. Rural ideal.

1930 Gassman, Byron. "Religious Attitudes in the World of
      Humphry Clinker." Brigham Young University Studies, 6
      (1965), 65-72. Satire. Methodism.

1931 Giddings, Robert. "Matthew Bramble's Bath: Smollett and
      the West Indian Connection." In Smollett: Author of the
      First Distinction. Ed. Alan Bold. London: Vision Press,
      1982, pp. 47-63. [Humphry Clinker]. Bath. Industry
      and trade. West Indies. Social criticism in the novel.
      Luxury.

1932 Giddings, Robert. The Tradition of Smollett. London:
      Methuen, 1967. Picaresque novel. Social criticism in the
      novel. Satire.

1933 Goldberg, M. A. Smollett and the Scottish School: Studies
      in Eighteenth-Century Thought. Albuquerque: Univ. of
      New Mexico Press, 1959. Intellectual background.
      Sources, analogues, and influences. Plot, structure, and
      design. Scottish "Common Sense School." Philosophy of
      novelist.

1934 Grant, Damian. "Roderick Random: Language as Projectile."
      In Smollett: Author of the First Distinction. Ed. Alan
      Bold. London: Vision Press, 1982, pp. 129-47. Speech
      and dialogue [verbal aggression of the characters]. Vio-
      lence.

•1935 Grant, Damian. *Tobias Smollett: A Study in Style*. Man-
       chester: Manchester Univ. Press, 1977. Style and lan-
       guage.

1936   Griffith, Philip Mahone. "Fire-Scenes in Richardson's *Clarissa*
       and Smollett's *Humphry Clinker*: A Study of a Literary Re-
       lationship in the Structure of the Novel." *Tulane Studies*
       in English, 11 (1961), 39-51. Parody. Setting. Fire
       scenes.

1937   Hambridge, Roger A. "Smollett's Legalese: Giles Jacob's
       New Law Dictionary and *Sir Launcelot Greaves*." *Revue*
       des Langues Vivantes, 44, No. 1 (1978), 37-44. Law.
       Style and language.

1938   Hames, Louise. "The Pronunciation of Tabitha Bramble."
       Journal of English Linguistics, 14 (1980), 6-19. Speech
       and dialogue.

1939   Helmick, E. T. "Voltaire and *Humphry Clinker*." *Studies*
       on Voltaire and the Eighteenth Century, 67 (1969), 59-64.
       Sources, analogues, and influences. Artistic development.
       Voltaire.

1940   Highsmith, James M. "Smollett's Nancy Williams: A Mirror
       for Maggie." *English Miscellany*, 23 (1972), 113-23.
       Sources, analogues, and influences [mirror literature].

1941   Hopkins, Robert H. "The Function of Grotesque in *Humphry*
       Clinker." *Huntington Library Quarterly*, 32 (1969), 163-
       77. The grotesque.

1942   Humphreys, A. R. "Fielding and Smollett." In *From Dryden*
       to Johnson. Ed. Boris Ford. Vol. 4 of the *Pelican History*
       of English Literature. Harmondsworth: Penguin, 1957, pp.
       313-32. Comparison of novelists.

1943   Iser, Wolfgang. "The Generic Control of the Aesthetic Dis-
       tance: An Examination of Smollett's *Humphry Clinker*."
       Southern Humanities Review, 3 (1969), 243-57. Aesthetic
       distance. Plot, structure, and design. Realism.

1944   Jack, R. D. S. "Appearance and Reality in *Humphry Clinker*."
       In *Smollett: Author of the First Distinction*. Ed. Alan
       Bold. London: Vision Press, 1982, pp. 209-27. Appear-
       ance vs. reality.

1945   Jackson, Holbrook. "Tobias Smollett." In his *Great English*
       Novelists. London: Grant Richards, 1908, pp. 87-107.
       Picaresque novel. Morality.

1946 Jeffrey, David K. "'Ductility and Dissimulation': The Unity
      of Ferdinand, Count Fathom." Tennessee Studies in Liter-
      ature, 23 (1978), 47-60. Imagery [sickness, health, Satan,
      angels]. Plot, structure, and design. Appearance vs.
      reality. Unity.

1947 Jeffrey, David K. "The Epistolary Format of Pamela and
      Humphry Clinker." In A Provision of Human Nature: Es-
      says on Fielding and Others in Honor of Miriam Austin
      Locke. Ed. Donald Kay. University: Univ. of Alabama
      Press, 1977, pp. 145-54. Epistolary novel. Characteriza-
      tion. Comparison of novelists.

1948 Jeffrey, David K. "Religious Metaphors in Humphry Clinker."
      New Rambler, Serial C, No. 16 (1975), pp. 26-28. Imagery.

1949 Jeffrey, David K. "Roderick Random: The Form and Struc-
      ture of a Romance." Revue Belge de Philologie et d'His-
      toire, 58 (1980), 604-14. Romance. Plot, structure, and
      design.

1950 Jeffrey, David K. "Smollett's Irony in Peregrine Pickle."
      Journal of Narrative Technique, 6 (1976), 137-46. Irony.

1951 Jones, Claude E. "Smollett and the Navy." In his Smollett
      Studies. 1942; rpt. New York: Phaeton, 1970. The
      navy.

1952 Jones, Claude E. "Tobias Smollett (1721-1771)--the Doctor
      as Man of Letters." Journal of the History of Medicine and
      Allied Sciences, 12 (1957), 337-48. Medicine. Characteri-
      zation. Setting.

1953 Kahrl, George. "The Influence of Shakespeare on Smollett."
      In Essays in Dramatic Literature: The Parrott Presentation
      Volume. Ed. Hardin Craig. Princeton, N.J.: Princeton
      Univ. Press, 1935, pp. 399-420. Shakespearean influence.

1954 Kahrl, George. "Smollett as Caricaturist." In Tobias Smol-
      lett: Bicentennial Essays Presented to Lewis M. Knapp.
      Ed. George S. Rousseau and Paul-Gabriel Boucé. New
      York: Oxford Univ. Press, 1971, pp. 169-200. Caricature.

1955 Kahrl, George. Tobias Smollett: Traveler-Novelist. 1945;
      rpt. New York: Octagon, 1968. Travel. Style and lan-
      guage. Plot, structure, and design. Characterization.

1956 Karl, Frederick R. "Smollett's Humphry Clinker: The Chol-
      eric Temper." In his A Reader's Guide to the Eighteenth-
      Century English Novel. New York: Noonday, 1974, pp.
      183-204. Social criticism in the novel. Defects in the novel.

1957 Kline, Judd. "Three Doctors and Smollett's Lady of Qual-
      ity." Philological Quarterly, 27 (1948), 219-28. Charac-
      terization.

1958 Klukoff, Philip J. "Smollett and the Critical Review: Criti-
      cism of the Novel, 1756-1763." Studies in Scottish Litera-
      ture, 4 (1966), 89-100. Theory and practice of the novel.
      Eighteenth-century criticism and reviews of the novel.

1959 Knapp, Lewis M. "Early Scottish Attitudes Toward Tobias
      Smollett." Philological Quarterly, 45 (1966), 262-69.
      Biography.

1960 Knapp, Lewis M. "The Naval Scenes in Roderick Random."
      PMLA, 49 (1934), 593-98. Sources, analogues, and influ-
      ences. The navy. Setting.

1961 Knapp, Lewis M. "Smollett's Self-Portrait in The Expedition
      of Humphry Clinker." In The Age of Johnson: Essays
      Presented to Chauncey Brewster Tinker. Ed. Frederick
      W. Hilles and Wilmarth S. Lewis. New Haven, Conn.:
      Yale Univ. Press, 1949, pp. 149-58. Autobiographical ele-
      ments in the novel.

•1962 Knapp, Lewis M. Tobias Smollett: Doctor of Men and Man-
      ners. Princeton, N.J.: Princeton Univ. Press, 1949.
      Biography.

1963 Korte, Donald M. "Verse Satire and Smollett's Humphry
      Clinker." Studies in Scottish Literature, 7 (1970), 188-92.
      Satire. Sources, analogues, and influences.

1964 Mack, Edward C. "Pamela's Stepdaughters: The Heroines of
      Smollett and Fielding." College English, 8 (1947), 293-301.
      Women. Comparison of novelists. Hero/heroine.

•1965 Martz, Louis L. The Later Career of Tobias Smollett. 1942;
      rpt. Hamden, Conn.: Archon, 1968. Biography. Style
      and language.

1966 Martz, Louis L. "Smollett and the Expedition to Carthagena."
      PMLA, 56 (1941), 428-46. [Roderick Random]. Autobio-
      graphical elements in the novel. The navy. Satire [on
      the military].

■1967 McKillop, Alan Dugald. "Tobias Smollett." In his The Early
      Masters of English Fiction. Lawrence: Univ. Press of
      Kansas, 1956, pp. 147-81. Introductory guide [excellent
      account of main issues].

1968 McVeagh, John. "Smollett and the Sceptical Reader." Notes

and Queries, N.S. 27 (1980), 34-40. Author-reader relationship.

1969 Miles, Peter. "Platonic Topography and the Locations of
      Humphry Clinker." Trivium, 16 (1981), 81-98. Epistemol-
      ogy. Imagery [water, hollows, mists, heights, depths].

1970 Moore, Robert Etheridge. "Hogarth and Smollett." In his
      Hogarth's Literary Relationships. 1948; rpt. New York:
      Octagon, 1969, pp. 162-95. Hogarth. Caricature.
      Sources, analogues, and influences.

1971 Moss, Harold Gene. "The Surgeon's Mate: Tobias Smollett
      and The Adventures of Roderick Random." In Medicine and
      Literature. Ed. Enid Rhodes Peschel. New York: Watson,
      1980, pp. 35-38. Medicine.

1972 Musher, Daniel M. "The Medical Views of Dr. Tobias Smollett
      (1721-1771)." Bulletin of the History of Medicine, 41
      (1967), 455-62. Medicine.

1973 Nemoianu, Virgil. "The Semantics of Bramble's Hypochondria:
      A Connection Between Illness and Style in the Eighteenth
      Century." Clio, 9 (1979), 39-50. Hypochondria. Style
      and language. Characterization.

1974 Niehus, Edward L. "Quixote Figures in the Novels of Smol-
      lett." Durham University Journal, 71 (1979), 233-43.
      Quixotic hero. Characterization.

1975 Orowitz, Milton. "Smollett and the Art of Caricature."
      Spectrum, 2 (1958), 155-67. Caricature. Characterization.

1976 Pannill, Linda. "Some Patterns of Imagery in Humphry Clink-
      er." Thoth, 13, No. 3 (1974), 37-43. Imagery [animal,
      hell, monsters, disharmony]. Journey.

1977 Park, William. "Fathers and Sons--Humphry Clinker." Lit-
      erature and Psychology, 16 (1966), 166-74. Psychology of
      characters. Fatherhood.

1978 Parker, Alice. "Tobias Smollett and the Law." Studies in
      Philology, 39 (1942), 545-58. Autobiographical elements in
      the novel. Law.

1979 Parreaux, André. Smollett's London: A Course of Lectures
      Delivered at the University of Paris, 1963-64. Paris:
      A. G. Nizet, 1965. London [as depicted in Smollett's nov-
      els].

1980 Paulson, Ronald. "The Pilgrimage and the Family: Structures

in the Novels of Fielding and Smollett." In <u>Tobias Smollett:</u>
<u>Bicentennial Essays Presented to Lewis M. Knapp</u>. Ed.
George S. Rousseau and Paul-Gabriel Boucé. New York:
Oxford Univ. Press, 1971, pp. 57-78. Journey. Family.
Plot, structure, and design.

1981 Paulson, Ronald. "Satire in the Early Novels of Smollett."
      <u>Journal of English and Germanic Philology</u>, 59 (1960), 381-
      402. Substantially rev. and rpt. in his <u>Satire and the</u>
      <u>Novel in Eighteenth-Century England</u>. New Haven, Conn.:
      Yale Univ. Press, 1967, pp. 165-218. Satire. Point of
      view and narrator. Comparison of novelists [Smollett,
      Sterne].

1982 Paulson, Ronald. "Smollett and Hogarth: The Identity of
      Pallet." <u>Studies in English Literature</u>, 4 (1964), 351-59.
      Characterization.

■1983 Paulson, Ronald. "Smollett: The Satirist as a Character
      Type." In his <u>Satire and the Novel in Eighteenth-Century</u>
      <u>England</u>. New Haven, Conn.: Yale Univ. Press, 1967,
      pp. 165-218. Characterization. Point of view and narrator.
      Satire.

■1984 Piper, William Bowman. "The Large Diffused Picture of Life
      in Smollett's Early Novels." <u>Studies in Philology</u>, 60
      (1963), 45-56. Characterization. Setting.

1985 Pratt, T. K. "Linguistics, Criticism, and Smollett's <u>Roderick</u>
      <u>Random</u>." <u>University of Toronto Quarterly</u>, 42 (1972), 26-
      39. Style and language.

1986 Preston, Thomas R. "Disenchanting the Man of Feeling:
      Smollett's <u>Ferdinand, Count Fathom</u>." In <u>Quick Springs of</u>
      <u>Sense: Studies in the Eighteenth Century</u>. Ed. Larry S.
      Champion. Athens: Univ. of Georgia Press, 1974, pp.
      223-39. "Man of Feeling." Sentimentalism.

1987 Preston, Thomas R. "Smollett Among the Indians." <u>Philo-</u>
      <u>logical Quarterly</u>, 61 (1982), 231-41. [<u>Humphry Clinker</u>].
      The Indian.

1988 Preston, Thomas R. "Smollett and the Benevolent Misanthrope
      Type." <u>PMLA</u>, 79 (1964), 51-57. Characterization. Mis-
      anthropy.

1989 Preston, Thomas R. "The 'Stage Passions' and Smollett's
      Characterization." <u>Studies in Philology</u>, 71 (1974), 105-25.
      Characterization. Dramatic conventions in the novel.

■1990 Preston, Thomas R. "Tobias Smollett--A Risible Misanthrope."

In his Not in Timon's Manner: Feeling, Misanthropy, and Satire in Eighteenth-Century England. University: Univ. of Alabama Press, 1975, pp. 69-120. Misanthropy. "Man of Feeling." Comedy. Satire [blends social satire with comedy].

1991 Price, John Valdimir. "Smollett and the Reader in Sir Launcelot Greaves." In Smollett: Author of the First Distinction. Ed. Alan Bold. London: Vision Press, 1982, pp. 193-208. Author-reader relationship. Point of view and narrator.

1992 Price, John Valdimir. Tobias Smollett: "The Expedition of Humphry Clinker." London: Edward Arnold, 1973. Plot, structure, and design. Point of view and narrator. Characterization.

1993 Punter, David. "Smollett and the Logic of Domination." Literature and History, No. 2 (1975), pp. 60-83. Social criticism in the novel. Capitalism.

1994 Putney, Rufus. "The Plan of Peregrine Pickle." PMLA, 60 (1945), 1051-65. Plot, structure, and design. Satire. Social criticism in the novel.

1995 Puzon, Bridget. "The Hidden Meaning in Humphry Clinker." Harvard Library Bulletin, 24 (1976), 40-54. Bildungsroman [of middle age].

1996 Read, Herbert. "Tobias Smollett." In his Reason and Romanticism: Essays in Literary Criticism. 1926; rpt. London: Faber & Faber, 1938, pp. 234-46. Critical revaluation. Style and language [obscenity]. Philosophy of novelist [rationalism vs. sensibility].

1997 Reid, B. L. "Smollett's Healing Journey." Virginia Quarterly Review, 41 (1965), 549-70. Rpt. in his The Long Boy and Others: Eighteenth-Century Studies. Athens: Univ. of Georgia Press, 1969, pp. 78-99. Characterization. Health. Journey.

1998 Rogers, Deborah C. "Further Shakespearean Echoes in Humphry Clinker." American Notes and Queries, 14 (1976), 98-102. Shakespearean influence.

■1999 Rosenblum, Michael. "Smollett and the Old Conventions." Philological Quarterly, 55 (1976), 389-402. Conventions of the Georgian novel. Romance [sequence of romance motifs of disinheritance, exile, and restoration in his novels].

■2000 Rosenblum, Michael. "Smollett as Conservative Satirist."

ELH: A Journal of English Literary History, 42 (1975),
556-79. Satire. Social criticism in the novel. Conservatism.

2001 Ross, Angus. "The 'Show of Violence' in Smollett's Novels."
Yearbook of English Studies, 2 (1972), 118-29. Violence.

2002 Ross, Ian Campbell. "Language, Structure and Vision in
Smollett's Roderick Random." Etudes Anglaises, 31 (1978),
52-63. Style and language. Plot, structure, and design.
Philosophy of novelist.

2003 Ross, Ian Campbell. "'With Dignity and Importance': Peregrine Pickle as Country Gentleman." In Smollett: Author
of the First Distinction. Ed. Alan Bold. London: Vision
Press, 1982, pp. 148-69. The gentleman. Social criticism
in the novel. Country vs. city. Politics. Characterization.

■2004 Rothstein, Eric. "Humphry Clinker." In his Systems of Order and Inquiry in Later Eighteenth-Century Fiction.
Berkeley: Univ. of California Press, 1975, pp. 109-53.
Point of view and narrator [multiple perspective]. Plot,
structure, and design. Epistemology.

2005 Rothstein, Eric. "Scotophilia and Humphry Clinker: The
Politics of Beggary, Bugs, and Buttocks." University of
Toronto Quarterly, 52 (1982), 63-78. National stereotypes.
Scotland.

2006 Rousseau, George S. "Matt Bramble and the Sulphur Controversy in the XVIIIth Century: Medical Background of
Humphry Clinker." Journal of the History of Ideas, 28
(1967), 577-89. Medicine.

2007 Rousseau, George S. "'No Boasted Academy of Christendom':
Smollett and the Society of Arts." Journal of the Royal
Society of Arts, 121 (1973), 468-75, 532-35, 623-28. Social
criticism in the novel.

2008 Rousseau, George S. "Pineapples, Pregnancy, Pica, and
Peregrine Pickle." In Tobias Smollett: Bicentennial Essays
Presented to Lewis M. Knapp. Ed. George S. Rousseau
and Paul-Gabriel Boucé. New York: Oxford Univ. Press,
1971, pp. 79-110. Medicine. Pregnancy and Childbirth.

2009 Rousseau, George S. "Smollett and Sterne: A Revaluation."
Archiv für das Studium der Neueren Sprachen und Litera-
turen, 208 (1972), 286-97. Comparison of novelists.

2010 Rousseau, George S. "Smollett and the Picaresque: Some
Questions about a Label." Studies in Burke and His Time,

12 (1971), 1886-1904. Reply by Paul-Gabriel Boucé, "Smollett's Pseudo-Picaresque: A Response to Rousseau's 'Smollett and the Picaresque,'" Studies in Burke and His Time,
13 (1972), 73-79. Picaresque novel.

2011 Runte, Roseann. "Gil Blas and Roderick Random: Food for
Thought." French Review, 50 (1977), 698-705. Imagery
[food, meals].

2012 Scott, Tom. "The Note of Protest in Smollett's Novels." In
Smollett: Author of the First Distinction. Ed. Alan Bold.
London: Vision Press, 1982, pp. 106-25. Social criticism
in the novel. Morality [Smollett's ethical compassion].

■2013 Sekora, John. "Smollett and Luxury" and "The Attack upon
Luxury and the Forms of Humphry Clinker." In his Luxury:
The Concept in Western Thought. Baltimore: The Johns
Hopkins Univ. Press, 1977, pp. 135-211, 215-95. Luxury
[as chief human vice]. Philosophy of novelist. Social
criticism in the novel. Politics. Characterization. Plot,
structure, and design.

2014 Sekora, John. "Some Political Figures in Humphry Clinker."
Notes and Queries, N.S. 24 (1977), 270-73. Politics.
Characterization.

2015 Sena, John F. "Ancient Designs and Modern Folly: Architecture in The Expedition of Humphry Clinker." Harvard
Library Bulletin, 27 (1979), 86-113. Architecture [sym-
bolizes Smollett's criticism of England's moral decline].
Setting. Symbolism.

2016 Sena, John F. "Smollett's Matthew Bramble and the Tradition
of the Physician-Satirist." Papers on Language and Literature, 11 (1975), 380-96. Health. Point of view and narrator. Characterization.

2017 Sena, John F. "Smollett's Portrait of Narcissa's Aunt: The
Genesis of an 'Original.'" English Language Notes, 14
(1977), 270-75. Characterization. Medicine. Hysteria.

2018 Sherbo, Arthur. "Win Jenkins' Language." Papers on Language and Literature, 5 (1969), 199-204. Speech and dialogue.

2019 Shroff, Homai J. "Angry Young Gentleman and 'A Most
Risible Misanthrope'--Tobias Smollett." In her The Eighteenth-Century Novel: The Idea of the Gentleman. New
Delhi: Arnold-Heinemann, 1978, pp. 161-91. The gentleman.

2020 Siebert, Donald T. "The Role of the Senses in Humphry
      Clinker." Studies in the Novel, 6 (1974), 17-26. Imagery
      [comfort, discomfort]. Locke.

2021 Simpson, K. G. "Roderick Random and the Tory Dilemma."
      Scottish Literary Journal, 2, No. 2 (1975), 5-17. Politics.
      Tories.

2022 Simpson, K. G. "Tobias Smollett: The Scot as English Nov-
      elist." In Smollett: Author of the First Distinction. Ed.
      Alan Bold. London: Vision Press, 1982, pp. 64-105. In-
      novation. Scotland [its literary tradition prominent in
      Smollett's novels].

2023 Spector, Robert D. Tobias George Smollett. Twayne's Eng-
      lish Authors Series. New York: Twayne, 1968. Intro-
      ductory guide.

2024 Starr, Nathan Comfort. "Smollett's Sailors." American Nep-
      tune, 32 (1972), 81-99. The sailor. Comedy.

2025 Stevick, Philip. "Smollett's Picaresque Games." In Tobias
      Smollett: Bicentennial Essays Presented to Lewis M. Knapp.
      Ed. George S. Rousseau and Paul-Gabriel Boucé. New
      York: Oxford Univ. Press, pp. 111-30. Picaresque novel.
      Comedy. Rogue hero.

■2026 Stevick, Philip. "Stylistic Energy in Early Smollett." Studies
      in Philology, 64 (1967), 712-19. Style and language [hyper-
      bolic style].

2027 Strauss, Albrecht B. "On Smollett's Language: A Paragraph
      in Ferdinand, Count Fathom." In Style in Prose Fiction:
      English Institute Essays, 1958. Ed. Harold C. Martin.
      New York: Columbia Univ. Press, 1959, pp. 25-54. Style
      and language. Imagery. Speech and dialogue [dialect].

2028 Thomas, Joel J. "Smollett and Ethical Sensibility: Ferdinand,
      Count Fathom." Studies in Scottish Literature, 14 (1979),
      145-64. Morality. Sensibility.

2029 Thorson, James L. "Reflections of Oxford in The Expedition
      of Humphry Clinker." Oxford, 34 (1982), 34-44. [Not
      seen]. Oxford University.

2030 Treadwell, T. O. "The Two Worlds of Ferdinand, Count
      Fathom." In Tobias Smollett: Bicentennial Essays Pre-
      sented to Lewis M. Knapp. Ed. George S. Rousseau and
      Paul-Gabriel Boucé. New York: Oxford Univ. Press, 1971,
      pp. 131-53. Realism. Romance. Plot, structure, and de-
      sign.

2031 Underwood, E. Ashworth. "Medicine and Science in the Writings of Smollett." Proceedings of the Royal Society of Medicine, 30 (1938), 961-74. Medicine.

2032 Underwood, Gary N. "Linguistic Realism in Roderick Random." Journal of English and Germanic Philology, 69 (1970), 32-40. Speech and dialogue [use of dialect]. Realism.

2033 Uphaus, Robert W. "Sentiment and Spleen: Travels with Sterne and Smollett." Centennial Review, 15 (1971), 406-21. Comparison of novelists. Personal relations between authors.

2034 Wagenknecht, Edward. "Smollett and the Novel of Humors." In his Cavalcade of the English Novel. New York: Holt, Rinehart, Winston, 1954, pp. 69-77. Novel of humors. The humors.

2035 Wagoner, Mary. "On the Satire in Humphry Clinker." Papers on Language and Literature, 2 (1966), 109-16. Satire. Sources, analogues, and influences [its satire derives from Swift and Pope].

2036 Warner, John M. "The Interpolated Narratives in the Fiction of Fielding and Smollett: An Epistemological View." Studies in the Novel, 5 (1973), 271-83. Digressions and interpolated stories. Comparison of novelists. Epistemology. Unity.

2037 Warner, John M. "Smollett's Development as a Novelist." Novel, 5 (1972), 148-61. Artistic development.

2038 Webster, Grant T. "Smollett's Microcosms: A Satiric Device in the Novel." Satire Newsletter, 5 (1967), 34-37. Microcosm. Satiric techniques.

2039 Weinsheimer, Joel. "Defects and Difficulties in Smollett's Peregrine Pickle." Ariel: A Review of International English Literature, 9, No. 3 (1978), 49-62. Defects in the novel.

2040 Weinsheimer, Joel. "Impedance as Value: Roderick Random and Pride and Prejudice." PTL: A Journal For Descriptive Poetics and Theory, 3 (1978), 139-66. Impedance. Defects in the novel.

2041 West, William A. "Matt Bramble's Journey to Health." Texas Studies in Literature and Language, 11 (1969), 1197-1208. Characterization. Journey. Medicine.

SEE ALSO ITEMS 240, 641, 751, 763, 767, 774, 788, 792, 824, 825, 860, 870, 883, 884, 946, 977, 1004a, 1010, 1021, 1028, 1048, 1052, 1056a, 1060a, 2067.

LAURENCE STERNE
(1713-1768)

PRINCIPAL FICTION

Tristram Shandy, 1760-67

A Sentimental Journey Through France and Italy, 1768

BIBLIOGRAPHIES AND SURVEYS OF CRITICISM

2042 Hartley, Lodwick. Laurence Sterne: An Annotated Bibliog-
      raphy, 1965-77, with an Introductory Essay-Review of the
      Scholarship. Boston: G. K. Hall, 1978. Bibliography of
      criticism [annotated, evaluative]. Survey of criticism.

2043 Hartley, Lodwick. Laurence Sterne in the Twentieth Century:
      An Essay and a Bibliography of Sternean Studies, 1900-
      1968. Rev. ed. Chapel Hill: Univ. of North Carolina
      Press, 1968. Survey of criticism. Bibliography of criticism
      [annotated, evaluative].

2044 Hartley, Lodwick. "Yorick Redivivus: A Bicentenary Review
      of Studies on Laurence Sterne." Studies in the Novel, 1
      (1969), 81-87. Survey of criticism.

2045 Hicks, John H. "The Critical History of Tristram Shandy."
      Boston University Studies in English, 2 (1956), 65-84.
      Survey of criticism.

2046 Howes, Alan B. Yorick and the Critics: Sterne's Reputation
      in England, 1760-1868. New Haven, Conn.: Yale Univ.
      Press, 1958. Survey of criticism. Eighteenth-century
      criticism and reviews of the novel.

2047 Isles, Duncan. "Sterne." In The English Novel: Select
      Bibliographical Guides. Ed. A. E. Dyson. London: Ox-
      ford Univ. Press, 1974, pp. 90-111. Bibliography of criti-
      cism. Survey of criticism.

2048 McKillop, Alan Dugald. "The Reinterpretation of Laurence
      Sterne." Etudes Anglaises, 7 (1954), 36-47. Survey of
      criticism.

BIOGRAPHICAL AND CRITICAL STUDIES

2049   Aldridge, A. Owen. "From Sterne to Machado de Assis." In
       The Winged Skull: Papers from the Laurence Sterne Bicen-
       tenary Conference. Ed. Arthur H. Cash and John M. Sted-
       mond. Kent, Ohio: Kent State Univ. Press, 1971, pp.
       170-85。 Influence and reputation abroad. Brazil.

2050   Allentuck, Marcia Epstein. "In Defense of an Unfinished
       Tristram Shandy." In The Winged Skull: Papers from the
       Laurence Sterne Bicentenary Conference. Ed. Arthur H.
       Cash and John M. Stedmond. Kent, Ohio: Kent State
       Univ. Press, 1971, pp. 145-55. Closure. Composition of
       the novel. Plot, structure, and design.

2051   Alter, Robert. "Sterne and the Nostalgia For Reality." In
       his Partial Magic: The Novel as a Self-Conscious Genre.
       Berkeley: Univ. of California Press, 1975, pp. 30-56.
       Realism. Point of view and narrator.

■2052 Alter, Robert. "Tristram Shandy and the Game of Love."
       American Scholar, 37 (1968), 316-23. Love. Sex. Style
       and language.

2053   Anderson, Howard. "Answers to the Author of Clarissa:
       Theme and Narrative Technique in Tom Jones and Tristram
       Shandy." Philological Quarterly, 51 (1972), 859-73. Point
       of view and narrator. Author-reader relationship. Narra-
       tive technique.

■2054 Anderson, Howard. "Associationism and Wit in Tristram
       Shandy." Philological Quarterly, 48 (1969), 27-41. As-
       sociationism. Comedy. Locke. Sources, analogues, and
       influences.

2055   Anderson, Howard. "Tristram Shandy and the Reader's
       Imagination." PMLA, 86 (1971), 966-73. Author-reader
       relationship。

2056   Anderson, Howard. "A Version of the Pastoral: Class and
       Society in Tristram Shandy." Studies in English Literature,
       7 (1967), 509-29. Social structure. Characterization.
       Rural ideal. Pastoral tradition.

2057   Baird, Theodore. "The Time-Scheme of Tristram Shandy and
       a Source." PMLA, 51 (1936), 803-20. Time. Plot, struc-
       ture, and design. Locke. Sources, analogues, and influ-
       ences.

2058   Baker, Van R. "Whatever Happened to Lydia Sterne?" Eight-
       eenth-Century Life, 2 (1975), 6-11. Lydia Sterne. Biog-
       raphy.

2059 Banerjee, Chinmoy. "John Locke and the Comedy of Com-
      munication in Tristram Shandy." Visvabharati Quarterly,
      38, No. 1-2 (1972-73), 119-33. Locke. Comedy.

2060 Banerjee, Chinmoy. "Tristram Shandy and the Association
      of Ideas." Texas Studies in Literature and Language, 15
      (1974), 693-706. Psychology of characters. Association-
      ism.

2061 Battestin, Martin C. "A Sentimental Journey and the Syntax
      of Things." In Augustan Worlds: New Essays in Eight-
      eenth-Century Literature. Ed. J. C. Hilson, M. M. B.
      Jones, and J. R. Watson. New York: Harper & Row,
      1978, pp. 223-40. Journey. Estrangement. Communion.

2062 Battestin, Martin C. "Swift and Sterne: The Disturbance
      of Form." In his The Providence of Wit: Aspects of Form
      in Augustan Literature and the Arts. Oxford: Clarendon
      Press, 1974, pp. 215-69. Comparison of novelists. Order.
      Plot, structure, and design. Sensibility. The hobby-
      horse.

2063 Bethune, John. "A Sentimental Journey: A Fragment."
      Massachusetts Studies in English, 8 (1982), 9-16. Plot,
      structure, and design.

2064 Booth, Wayne C. "Did Sterne Complete Tristram Shandy?"
      Modern Philology, 48 (1951), 172-83. Composition of the
      novel. Closure.

•2065 Booth, Wayne C. The Rhetoric of Fiction. Chicago: Univ.
      of Chicago Press, 1961, pp. 221-40, 430-32. Point of view
      and narrator. Unity. Author-reader relationship.

2066 Bowman, Joel P. "Structural Values in Tristram Shandy."
      Re: Arts and Letters, 6, No. 1 (1972), 16-26. Plot,
      structure, and design. Time. Musical novel.

2067 Boys, Richard C. "Tristram Shandy and the Conventional
      Novel." Papers of the Michigan Academy of Science, Arts
      and Letters, 37 (1951), 423-36. [Smollett, Sterne]. In-
      novation. Conventions of the Georgian novel. Comparison
      of novelists.

2068 Bradbury, Malcolm. "The Comic Novel in Sterne and Field-
      ing." In The Winged Skull: Papers from the Laurence
      Sterne Bicentenary Conference. Ed. Arthur H. Cash and
      John M. Stedmond. Kent, Ohio: Kent State Univ. Press,
      1971, pp. 124-31. Comedy. Comparison of novelists.

2069 Brady, Frank. "Tristram Shandy: Sexuality, Morality, and

Sensibility." Eighteenth-Century Studies, 4 (1970), 41-56.
Sex. Morality. Sensibility. Plot, structure, and design.

2070 Brienza, Susan D. "Volume VII of Tristram Shandy--A Dance
      of Life." University of Dayton Review, 10, No. 3 (1974),
      59-62. Sex.

2071 Brissenden, R. F. "The Sentimental Comedy: Tristram
      Shandy" and "The Sentimental Comedy: A Sentimental
      Journey." In his Virtue in Distress: Studies in the Novel
      of Sentiment from Richardson to Sade. New York: Barnes
      & Noble, 1974, pp. 187-217, 220-42. Sentimental novel.
      Comedy.

2072 Brissenden, R. F. "Sterne and Painting." In Of Books and
      Humankind: Essays and Poems Presented to Bonamy Do-
      brée. Ed. John Butt. London: Routledge & Kegan Paul,
      1964, pp. 93-108. Art. Hogarth.

2073 Brissenden, R. F. "'Trusting to Almighty God': Another
      Look at the Composition of Tristram Shandy." In The
      Winged Skull: Papers from the Laurence Sterne Bicentenary
      Conference. Ed. Arthur H. Cash and John M. Stedmond.
      Kent, Ohio: Kent State Univ. Press, 1971, pp. 258-69.
      Composition of the novel.

2074 Brogan, Howard O. "Fiction and Philosophy in the Education
      of Tom Jones, Tristram Shandy, and Richard Feverel."
      College English, 14 (1952), 144-49. Education. Comparison
      of novelists [Fielding, Sterne, Meredith].

2075 Brooks, Douglas. "Sterne: Tristram Shandy." In his Num-
      ber and Pattern in the Eighteenth-Century Novel. London:
      Routledge & Kegan Paul, 1973, pp. 160-82. Numerology.
      Symbolism. Plot, structure, and design.

2076 Brown, Herbert Ross. "Sterne and Sensibility." In his The
      Sentimental Novel in America. 1940; rpt. New York:
      Pageant Books, 1959, pp. 74-99. Influence and reputation
      abroad. Sentimental novel. America.

2077 Burckhardt, Sigurd. "Tristram Shandy's Law of Gravity."
      ELH: A Journal of English Literary History, 28 (1961), 70-
      88. Locke. Irony.

2078 Cash, Arthur H. "The Birth of Tristram Shandy: Sterne
      and Dr. Burton." In Studies in the Eighteenth Century.
      Ed. R. F. Brissenden. Canberra: Australian National
      Univ. Press, 1968, pp. 133-54. Pregnancy and childbirth.

•2079 Cash, Arthur H. Laurence Sterne: The Early and Middle
      Years. London: Methuen, 1975. Biography.

■2080 Cash, Arthur H. "The Lockean Psychology of Tristram
       Shandy." ELH: A Journal of English Literary History, 22
       (1955), 125-35. Locke. Associationism [not the organizing
       principle of the novel]. Plot, structure, and design.

2081   Cash, Arthur H. "The Sermon in Tristram Shandy." ELH:
       A Journal of English Literary History, 31 (1964), 395-417.
       The sermon. Composition of the novel.

●2082 Cash, Arthur H. Sterne's Comedy of Moral Sentiments: The
       Ethical Dimensions of "The Journey." Pittsburgh: Duquesne
       Univ. Press, 1966. [A Sentimental Journey]. Comedy.
       Morality. Sentimentalism.

2083   Chadwick, Joseph. "Infinite Jest: Interpretation in Sterne's
       A Sentimental Journey." Eighteenth-Century Studies, 12
       (1978-79), 190-205. Epistemology.

2084   Chatterjee, Ambarnath. "Dramatic Technique in Tristram
       Shandy." Indian Journal of English Studies, 6 (1965), 33-
       43. Dramatic conventions in the novel.

2085   Cockshut, A. O. J. "Sterne." In his Man and Woman: A
       Study of Love and the Novel, 1740-1940. 1977; rpt. New
       York: Oxford Univ. Press, 1978, pp. 46-53. Sex. Moral-
       ity.

2086   Connely, Willard. Laurence Sterne as Yorick. London:
       Bodley Head, 1958. Biography [later years].

2087   Connolly, Cyril. "Sterne and Swift." Atlantic Monthly,
       June 1945, 94-96. Comparison of novelists.

2088   Conrad, Peter. Shandyism: The Character of Romantic
       Irony. New York: Harper & Row, 1978. Shandyism.
       Characterization. Irony.

2089   Cook, Albert Spaulding. "Reflexive Attitudes: Sterne, Go-
       gol, Gide." Criticism, 2 (1960), 164-74. Rpt. in his The
       Meaning of Fiction. Detroit: Wayne State Univ. Press,
       1960, pp. 24-37. Reflexivity. Point of view and narrator.

●2090 Cross, Wilbur L. The Life and Times of Laurence Sterne.
       2 vols. 3rd ed. New Haven, Conn.: Yale Univ. Press,
       1929. Biography.

2091   Curtis, Lewis Perry. The Politicks of Laurence Sterne.
       Oxford: Oxford Univ. Press, 1929. Politics. Biography.

2092   Davidson, Arnold E., and Cathy N. Davidson. "Yorick con-
       tra Hobbes: Comic Synthesis in Sterne's A Sentimental

Journey." Centennial Review, 21 (1977), 282-93. Hobbes.
Comedy. Contrast as technique.

2093 Davies, Richard A. "Tristram Shandy: Eccentric Public
      Orator." English Studies in Canada, 5 (1979), 154-66.
      Speech and dialogue. Characterization. Sources, ana-
      logues, and influences [public oratory].

2094 Davis, Robert Gorham. "Sterne and the Delineation of the
      Modern Novel." In The Winged Skull: Papers from the
      Laurence Sterne Bicentenary Conference. Ed. Arthur H.
      Cash and John M. Stedmond. Kent, Ohio: Kent State
      Univ. Press, 1971, pp. 21-41. Sources, analogues, and
      influences. Ambiguity. Psychology of characters. Mod-
      ernity.

2095 Day, W. G. "Sterne's Books." Library, 31 (1976), 245-48.
      Library of novelist.

2096 Dilworth, Ernest Nevin. "Sterne: Some Devices." Notes
      and Queries, 197 (1952), 165-66. Style and language.
      Rhythm.

2097 Dilworth, Ernest Nevin. The Unsentimental Journey of Laur-
      ence Sterne. New York: King's Crown Press, 1948.
      [Tristram Shandy, A Sentimental Journey]. Sentimentalism.
      Comedy. Satire. Biography.

2098 Donoghue, Denis. "Sterne, Our Contemporary." In The
      Winged Skull: Papers from the Laurence Sterne Bicentenary
      Conference. Ed. Arthur H. Cash and John M. Stedmond.
      Kent, Ohio: Kent State Univ. Press, 1971, pp. 42-58.
      Influence and imitation.

2099 Donovan, Robert Alan. "Sterne and the Logos." In his The
      Shaping Vision: Imagination in the English Novel from De-
      foe to Dickens. Ithaca, N.Y.: Cornell Univ. Press, 1966,
      pp. 89-117. Style and language. Speech and dialogue.

2100 Dowling, William C. "Tristram Shandy's Phantom Audience."
      Novel, 13 (1980), 284-95. Author-reader relationship.

2101 Dussinger, John A. "A Sentimental Journey: 'A Sort of
      Knowingness.'" In his The Discourse of the Mind in Eight-
      eenth-Century Fiction. The Hague: Mouton, 1974, pp.
      173-200. Epistemology. Psychology of characters.

2102 Dyson, A. E. "Sterne: The Novelist as Jester." Critical
      Quarterly, 4 (1962), 309-20. Rpt. in his The Crazy Fabric:
      Essays in Irony. London: Macmillan, 1965, pp. 33-48.
      Comedy.

2103 Eaves, T. C. Duncan. "George Romney: His 'Tristram
      Shandy' Paintings and Trip to Lancaster." Huntington
      Library Quarterly, 7 (1944), 321-26. George Romney.
      Illustration.

2104 Ehlers, Leigh A. "Mrs. Shandy's 'Lint and Basilicon': The
      Importance of Women in Tristram Shandy." South Atlantic
      Bulletin, 46, No. 1 (1981), 61-75. Women.

2105 Eskin, Stanley G. "Tristram Shandy and Oedipus Rex: Re-
      flections on Comedy and Tragedy." College English, 24
      (1963), 271-77. Tragedy.

2106 Evans, James E. "Tristram as Critic: Momus's Glass vs.
      Hobby-Horse." Philological Quarterly, 50 (1971), 669-71.
      Characterization.

2107 Evans, Walter. "Teaching Tristram Shandy." English Record,
      29 (1978), 8-11. Pedagogical approach.

2108 Fabian, Bernhard. "Tristram Shandy and Parson Yorick
      Among Some German Greats." In The Winged Skull: Pa-
      pers from the Laurence Sterne Bicentenary Conference.
      Ed. Arthur H. Cash and John M. Stedmond. Kent, Ohio:
      Kent State Univ. Press, 1971, pp. 194-209. Influence and
      reputation abroad. Germany.

2109 Fabricant, Carole. "Tristram Shandy and Moby-Dick: A
      Cock and Bull Story and a Tale of a Tub." Journal of
      Narrative Technique, 7 (1977), 57-69. Epistemology.
      Imagery [sex, architecture, incompletion]. Narrative tech-
      nique. Sources, analogues, and influences.

■2110 Farrell, William J. "Nature versus Art as a Comic Pattern in
      Tristram Shandy." ELH: A Journal of English Literary
      History, 30 (1963), 16-35. Nature vs. art. Comedy.
      Plot, structure, and design. Parody. Style and language.

2111 Faurot, Ruth M. "Mrs. Shandy Observed." Studies in Eng-
      lish Literature, 10 (1970), 579-89. Characterization.

2112 Fluchère, Henri. Laurence Sterne: From Tristram to Yorick.
      1961. Trans. and abridged by Barbara Bray. Oxford:
      Oxford Univ. Press, 1965. Plot, structure, and design.
      Style and language. Time.

2113 Francis, C. J. "Sterne: The Personal and the Real." In
      A Festschrift for Edgar Ronald Seary: Essays in English
      Language and Literature Presented by Colleagues and Former
      Students. Ed. A. A. Macdonald et al. St. Johns: Mem-
      orial University of Newfoundland, 1975, pp. 90-115. Point

of view and narrator. Epistemology. Autobiographical elements in the novel.

2114   Fredman, Alice G. Diderot and Sterne. New York: King's Crown Press, 1955. Diderot. Romanticism. Comparison of novelists.

2115   Freedman, William. Laurence Sterne and the Origins of the Musical Novel. Athens: Univ. of Georgia Press, 1978. Musical novel. Plot, structure, and design. Narrative technique. Characterization. Time. Rhythm. Unity.

2116   Freedman, William. "Tristram Shandy: The Art of Literary Counterpoint." Modern Language Quarterly, 32 (1971), 268-80. Contrast as technique. Digressions and interpolated stories.

2117   Froe, Arie de. Laurence Sterne and His Novels Studied in the Light of Modern Psychology. 1925; rpt. Philadelphia: West, 1977. Biography [psychological]. Autobiographical elements in the novel.

2118   Furst, Lilian R. "The Dual Face of the Grotesque in Sterne's Tristram Shandy and Lenz's Der Waldruder." Comparative Literature Studies, 13 (1976), 15-21. The grotesque.

2119   Garvey, James W. "Translation, Equivocation, and Reconciliation in Sterne's Sentimental Journey." Southern Humanities Review, 12, (1978), 339-49. Style and language. Point of view and narrator.

2120   Golden, Morris. "Sterne's Journeys and Sallies." Studies in Burke and His Time, 16 (1974), 47-62. Journey. Psychology of characters.

2121   Goodin, George. "The Comic as a Critique of Reason: Tristram Shandy." College English, 29 (1967), 206-23. Comedy. Reason.

2122   Graves, Lila. "Locke's Essay and Sterne's Work Itself." Journal of Narrative Technique, 12 (1982), 36-47. Epistemology. Locke.

2123   Griffin, Robert J. "Tristram Shandy and Language." College English, 23 (1961), 108-12. Style and language.

2124   Grossvogel, David I. "Sterne: Tristram Shandy." In his Limits of the Novel: Evolution of a Form from Chaucer to Robbe-Grillet. Ithaca, N.Y.: Cornell Univ. Press, 1968, pp. 136-59. Plot, structure, and design. Characterization.

2125   Hafter, Ronald. "Garrick and Tristram Shandy." Studies in
       English Literature, 7 (1967), 475-89. David Garrick.
       Dramatic conventions in the novel.

2126   Hagen, June Steffenson. "The Salon, the Queen of the
       Blues, and Laurence Sterne." Susquehanna University
       Studies, 10 (1975), 5-15. The salon. The bluestocking.
       Mrs. Edward Montagu. Biography.

2127   Hagstrum, Jean H. "Sterne." In his Sex and Sensibility:
       Ideal and Erotic Love from Milton to Mozart. Chicago:
       Univ. of Chicago Press, 1980, pp. 247-59. Love. Sensi-
       bility. Sex.

2128   Hall, Joan Joffe. "The Hobbyhorsical World of Tristram
       Shandy." Modern Language Quarterly, 24 (1963), 131-43.
       Hobbyhorse. Characterization. Plot, structure, and design.
       Point of view and narrator.

2129   Hammond, Lansing Van der Heyden. Laurence Sterne's "Ser-
       mons of Mr. Yorick." New Haven, Conn.: Yale Univ.
       Press, 1948. The sermon. Christianity. Sources, ana-
       logues, and influences.

2130   Harries, Elizabeth W. "Sterne's Novels: Gathering up the
       Fragments." ELH: A Journal of English Literary History,
       49 (1982), 35-49. Narrative technique. Closure.

2131   Hartley, Lodwick. "The Dying Soldier and the Love-Lorn
       Virgin: Notes on Sterne's Early Reception in America."
       Southern Humanities Review, 4 (1970), 69-80. Influence
       and reputation abroad. America.

•2132 Hartley, Lodwick. Laurence Sterne: A Biographical Essay.
       Chapel Hill: Univ. of North Carolina Press, 1968. Biog-
       raphy.

2133   Hartley, Lodwick. "Laurence Sterne and the Eighteenth-Cen-
       tury Stage." Papers on Language and Literature, 4 (1968),
       144-57. Dramatic conventions in the novel.

•2134 Hartley, Lodwick. This Is Lorence: A Narrative of the
       Reverend Laurence Sterne. Chapel Hill: Univ. of North
       Carolina Press, 1943. Biography.

2135   Hartley, Lodwick. "'Tis a picture of Myself': The Author in
       Tristram Shandy." Southern Humanities Review, 4 (1970),
       301-13. Autobiographical elements in the novel. Point of
       view and narrator.

2136   Hay, John A. "Rhetoric and Historiography: Tristram Shan-

dy's First Nine Kalendar Months." In Studies in the Eighteenth Century II. Ed. R. F. Brissenden. Toronto: Univ.
of Toronto Press, 1973, pp. 73-91. Rhetoric. Historiography. Style and language.

2137   Hnatko, Eugene. "Sterne's Conversational Style." In The
       Winged Skull: Papers from the Laurence Sterne Bicentenary
       Conference. Ed. Arthur H. Cash and John M. Stedmond.
       Kent, Ohio: Kent State Univ. Press, 1971, pp. 229-36.
       Speech and dialogue. Style and language. Point of view
       and narrator.

2138   Hnatko, Eugene. "Sterne's Whimsical Syntax: The Pseudo-
       Archaic Style." Style, 3 (1969), 168-81. Syntax. Style
       and language.

2139   Hnatko, Eugene. "Tristram Shandy's Wit." Journal of Eng-
       lish and Germanic Philology, 65 (1966), 47-64. Comedy.

2140   Holland, Norman N. "The Laughter of Laurence Sterne."
       Hudson Review, 9 (1956), 422-30. Comedy.

2141   Holtz, William V. Image and Immortality: A Study of "Tris-
       tram Shandy." Providence, R.I.: Brown Univ. Press,
       1970. Incorporates his "The Journey and the Picture: The
       Art of Sterne and Hogarth," Bulletin of the New York Pub-
       lic Library, 71 (1967), 25-38; "Pictures for Parson Yorick:
       Laurence Sterne's London Visit of 1760," Eighteenth-Cen-
       tury Studies, 1 (1967), 169-84; "The Faces of Yorick,"
       Queen's Quarterly, 76 (1969), 379-91. Imagery. Immortal-
       ity. Style and language. Characterization. Point of view
       and narrator. Time. Art. Hogarth.

2142   Holtz, William V. "Typography, Tristram Shandy, the Aposi-
       opesis, etc." In The Winged Skull: Papers from the
       Laurence Sterne Bicentenary Conference. Ed. Arthur H.
       Cash and John M. Stedmond. Kent, Ohio: Kent State
       Univ. Press, 1971, pp. 247-57. Typography. Style and
       language.

2143   Howes, Alan B., ed. Sterne: The Critical Heritage. The
       Critical Heritage Series. London: Routledge & Kegan Paul,
       1974. Eighteenth-century criticism and reviews of the nov-
       el.

2144   Hughes, Helen Sard. "A Precursor of Tristram Shandy."
       Journal of English and Germanic Philology, 17 (1918), 227-
       51. Sources, analogues, and influences.

2145   Hunter, J. Paul. "Response as Reformation: Tristram Shandy
       and the Art of Interruption." Novel, 4 (1971), 132-46.

Narrative technique. Author-reader relationship. The sermon.

2146 Jackson, H. J. "Sterne, Burton, and Ferriar: Allusions to
the Anatomy of Melancholy in Volumes Five to Nine of Tristram Shandy." Philological Quarterly, 54 (1975), 457-70.
Robert Burton. Sources, analogues, and influences.

2147 James, Overton Philip. The Relation of "Tristram Shandy" to
the Life of Sterne. The Hague: Mouton, 1966. Autobiographical elements in the novel.

■2148 Jefferson, D. W. "Tristram Shandy and the Tradition of
Learned Wit." Essays in Criticism, 1 (1951), 225-48.
Sources, analogues, and influences. Plot, structure, and
design. Comedy.

■2149 Karl, Frederick R. "Tristram Shandy, the Sentimental Novel
and Sentimentalists." In his A Reader's Guide to the
Eighteenth-Century English Novel. New York: Noonday,
1974, pp. 205-34, esp. 205-20. Sentimental novel. Innovation. Conventions of the Georgian novel.

2150 Khazoum, Violet. "The Inverted Comedy of Tristram Shandy."
Hebrew University Studies in English, 7 (1979), 139-60.
Comedy. Characterization.

2151 Kirby, Paul F. "Sterne in Italy." In The Winged Skull:
Papers from the Laurence Sterne Bicentenary Conference.
Ed. Arthur H. Cash and John M. Stedmond. Kent, Ohio:
Kent State Univ. Press, 1971, pp. 210-26. Influence and
reputation abroad. Italy.

2152 Klotman, Phyllis R. "'Reconciliation of Contrasts' in Tristram
Shandy." College Language Association Journal, 20 (1976),
48-56. Contrast as technique.

2153 Koppel, Gene S. "Fulfillment Through Frustration: Some
Aspects of Sterne's Art of the Incomplete in A Sentimental
Journey." Studies in the Novel, 2 (1970), 168-72. Sex.
Psychology of characters.

2154 Korkowski, Eugene. "The Second Tale of a Tub: A Link
from Swift to Sterne?" Studies in the Novel, 16 (1974),
470-74. Sources, analogues, and influences.

2155 Kroeger, Frederick P. "Uncle Toby's Pipe and Whistle."
Papers of the Michigan Academy of Science, Arts and Letters, 47 (1962), 669-85. Characterization.

2156 Laird, John. "Shandean Philosophy." In his Philosophical

Incursions into English Literature. Cambridge: Cambridge
Univ. Press, 1946, pp. 74-91. Locke. Philosophy of novelist.

2157 Lamb, Jonathan. "The Comic Sublime and Sterne's Fiction."
      ELH: A Journal of English Literary History, 48 (1981),
      110-43. Comedy. Parody [mock-heroic].

2158 Lamb, Jonathan. "Language and Hartleian Associationism in
      A Sentimental Journey." Eighteenth-Century Studies, 13
      (1980), 285-312. Style and language. David Hartley. As-
      sociationism.

2159 Lamb, Jonathan. "'Uniting and Reconciling Everything':
      Book-Wit in Tristram Shandy." Southern Review: An Aus-
      tralian Journal of Literary Studies, 7 (1974), 236-45.
      Comedy.

2160 Landa, Louis A. "The Shandean Homunculus: The Back-
      ground of Sterne's 'Little Gentleman.'" Restoration and
      Eighteenth-Century Literature: Essays in Honor of Alan
      Dugald McKillop. Ed. Carroll Camden. Chicago: Univ.
      of Chicago Press, 1963, pp. 49-68. The homunculus.

2161 Landor, Mikhail. "Sterne in Russia." Soviet Literature, 4
      (1968), 170-76. Influence and reputation abroad. Russia.

2162 Landow, George P. "Tristram Shandy and the Comedy of
      Context." Brigham Young University Studies, 7 (1966),
      208-24. Comedy. Style and language.

2163 Lanham, Richard A. "Tristram Shandy": The Games of
      Pleasure. Berkeley: Univ. of California Press, 1973.
      Sensibility. Sympathy. Sport and recreation. Comedy.
      Point of view and narrator. Shakespearean influence
      [Yorick].

■2164 Lehman, B. H. "Of Time, Personality, and the Author: A
      Study of Tristram Shandy: Comedy." In Studies in the
      Comic. Berkeley: Univ. of California Press, 1941, pp.
      233-50. Rpt. in Essays on the Eighteenth-Century Novel.
      Ed. Robert Donald Spector. Bloomington: Univ. of Indiana
      Press, 1965, pp. 165-84. Comedy. Characterization.
      Point of view and narrator.

2165 Lockridge, Ernest H. "A Vision of the Sentimental Absurd:
      Sterne and Camus." Sewanee Review, 72 (1964), 652-67.
      The absurd. Sentimentalism.

2166 Lounsberry, Barbara. "Sermons and Satire: Anti-Catholicism
      in Sterne." Philological Quarterly, 55 (1976), 403-17. The

sermon. Satire. Catholicism [Sterne's anti-Catholicism not merely comic, but also a reflection of his view of Catholicism as a threat].

2167 Loveridge, Mark. Laurence Sterne and the Argument About Design. Totowa, N.J.: Barnes & Noble, 1982. Plot, structure, and design. Characterization. Sentimentalism. Locke.

2168 Macaffee, C. H. G. "The Obstetrical Aspects of Tristram Shandy." Ulster Medical Journal, 19 (1950), 12-22. Pregnancy and childbirth.

2169 MacLean, Kenneth. "Imagination and Sympathy: Sterne and Adam Smith." Journal of the History of Ideas, 10 (1949), 399-410. Characterization. Imagination. Sympathy. Adam Smith.

2170 Maskell, Duke. "Locke and Sterne, or Can Philosophy Influence Literature?" Essays in Criticism, 23 (1973), 22-40. Locke. Sources, analogues, and influences.

2171 Mayoux, Jean-Jacques. "Variations on the Time-Sense in Tristram Shandy." In The Winged Skull: Papers from the Laurence Sterne Bicentenary Conference. Ed. Arthur H. Cash and John M. Stedmond. Kent, Ohio: Kent State Univ. Press, 1971, pp. 3-18. Time.

■2172 McGlynn, Paul D. "Orthodoxy versus Anarchy in Sterne's Sentimental Journey." Papers on Language and Literature, 7 (1971), 242-51. Philosophy of novelist. Morality. Sensibility.

2173 McGlynn, Paul D. "Sterne's Maria: Madness and Sentimentality." Eighteenth-Century Life, 3 (1976), 39-43. Insanity. Sentimentalism. Characterization.

■2174 McKillop, Alan Dugald. "Laurence Sterne." In his The Early Masters of English Fiction. Lawrence: Univ. of Kansas Press, 1956, pp. 182-219. Introductory guide [excellent account of main issues].

2175 McMaster, Juliet. "Experience to Expression: Thematic Character Contrasts in Tristram Shandy." Modern Language Quarterly, 32 (1971), 42-57. Rpt. and rev. in Juliet McMaster and Rowland McMaster's The Novel from Sterne to James: Essays on the Relation of Literature to Life. Totowa, N.J.: Barnes & Noble, 1981, pp. 1-18. Characterization. Contrast as technique.

2176 Mellown, Elgin W. "Narrative Technique in Tristram Shandy."

Papers on Language and Literature, 9 (1973), 263-70. Narrative technique. Plot, structure, and design. Digressions
and interpolated stories.

■2177 Mendilow, A. A. "Time, Structure, and Tristram Shandy."
In his Time and the Novel. 1952; rpt. New York: Humanities Press, 1972, pp. 158-99. Time. Plot, structure,
and design.

2178 Milic, Louis T. "Information Theory and the Style of Tris-
tram Shandy." In The Winged Skull: Papers from the
Laurence Sterne Bicentenary Conference. Ed. Arthur H.
Cash and John M. Stedmond. Kent, Ohio: Kent State
Univ. Press, 1971, pp. 237-46. Information theory. Style
and language.

2179 Moglen, Helene. "Laurence Sterne and the Contemporary Vision." In The Winged Skull: Papers from the Laurence
Sterne Bicentenary Conference. Ed. Arthur H. Cash and
John M. Stedmond. Kent, Ohio: Kent State Univ. Press,
1971, pp. 59-75. Epistemology. Locke.

■2180 Moglen, Helene. The Philosophical Irony of Laurence Sterne.
Gainesville: Univ. of Florida Press, 1975. Irony. Philosophy of novelist. Intellectual background.

2181 Monkman, Kenneth. "Sterne, Hamlet, and Yorick: Some New
Material." In The Winged Skull: Papers from the Laurence
Sterne Bicentenary Conference. Ed. Arthur H. Cash and
John M. Stedmond. Kent, Ohio: Kent State Univ. Press,
1971, pp. 112-23. Shakespearean influence.

2182 Moss, Roger B. "Sterne's Punctuation." Eighteenth-Century
Studies, 15 (1981), 179-200. Punctuation.

2183 Muir, Edwin. "Laurence Sterne." In his Essays on Literature
and Society. London: Hogarth Press, 1949, pp. 49-56.
Style and language.

2184 Myers, Walter. "O, the Hobby-Horse." Virginia Quarterly
Review, 19 (1943), 268-77. Characterization.

2185 Nänny, Max. "Similarity and Contiguity in Tristram Shandy."
English Studies, 60 (1979), 422-35. Style and language.
Symbolism. Characterization [the total Shandy man a com-
bination of Walter and Toby, symbols of similarity and con-
tiguity].

2186 New, Melvyn. "The Dunce Revisited: Colley Cibber and
Tristram Shandy." South Atlantic Quarterly, 72 (1973),
547-59. Colley Cibber. Point of view and narrator.

2187 New, Melvyn. "Laurence Sterne and Henry Baker's The
      Microscope Made Easy." Studies in English Literature, 10
      (1970), 591-604. Time. Science. Philosophy of novelist.
      Sources, analogues, and influences.

•2188 New, Melvyn. Laurence Sterne as Satirist: A Reading of
      "Tristram Shandy." Gainesville: Univ. of Florida Press,
      1969. Satire. Philosophy of novelist. Critical revaluation
      [Sterne's ties to Augustan satire].

2189 New, Melvyn. "Sterne and Swift: Sermons and Satire."
      Modern Language Quarterly, 30 (1969), 198-211. Compari-
      son of novelists. The sermon. Satire. Christianity.
      Latitudinarianism.

2190 New, Melvyn. "Sterne as Editor: The 'Abuses of Conscience'
      Sermon." In Studies in Eighteenth-Century Culture. Vol.
      8. Ed. Roseann Runte. Madison: Univ. of Wisconsin
      Press, 1979, 243-51. Composition of the novel. The sermon.

2191 New, Melvyn. "Sterne, Warburton, and the Burden of Exu-
      berant Wit." Eighteenth-Century Studies, 15 (1982), 245-
      74. Biography. William Warburton. Sources, analogues,
      and influences.

2192 Oates, J. C. T. Shandyism and Sentiment, 1760-1800. Cam-
      bridge: Cambridge Bibliographical Society, 1968. Influence
      and imitation. Sentimentalism. Shandyism.

2193 Olshin, Toby A. "Genre and Tristram Shandy: The Novel
      of Quickness." Genre, 4 (1971), 360-75. Innovation.
      Sympathy. Satire [on Tristram]. Time. Author-reader
      relationship.

2194 Parish, Charles. "The Nature of Mr. Tristram Shandy, Au-
      thor." Boston University Studies in English, 5 (1961), 74-
      90. Characterization. Point of view and narrator.

2195 Parish, Charles. "The Shandy Bull Vindicated." Modern
      Language Quarterly, 31 (1970), 48-52. Sex. Digressions
      and interpolated stories. Imagery [animal].

2196 Parish, Charles. "A Table of Contents for Tristram Shandy."
      College English, 22 (1960), 143-50. Introductory guide.
      Synopsis.

■2197 Park, William. "Tristram Shandy and the New Novel of Sen-
      sibility." Studies in the Novel, 6 (1974), 268-79. Novel
      of sensibility. Conventions of the Georgian novel. Influ-
      ence and imitation.

2198 Parks, A. Franklin. "Yorick's Sympathy for the 'little': A

Measure of his Sentimentality in Sterne's Sentimental Journey." Literature and Psychology, 28 (1978), 119–24. Psychology of characters.

■2199 Paulson, Ronald. "Satire and Sentimentality." In his Satire and the Novel in Eighteenth-Century England. New Haven, Conn.: Yale Univ. Press, 1967, pp. 219–65. Sentimentalism. Satire.

2200 Petrakis, Byron. "Jester in the Pulpit: Sterne and Pulpit Eloquence." Philological Quarterly, 51 (1972), 430–37. The sermon. Speech and dialogue.

■2201 Petrie, Graham. "Rhetoric as Fictional Technique in Tristram Shandy." Philological Quarterly, 48 (1969), 479–94. Narrative technique. Rhetoric. Author–reader relationship.

2202 Petrie, Graham. "A Rhetorical Topic in Tristram Shandy." Modern Language Review, 65 (1970), 261–66. Rhetoric. Speech and dialogue.

2203 Piper, William Bowman. Laurence Sterne. Twayne's English Authors Series. New York: Twayne, 1965. Introductory guide.

■2204 Piper, William Bowman. "Tristram Shandy's Digressive Artistry." Studies in English Literature, 1 (1961), 65–76. Digressions and interpolated stories. Plot, structure, and design.

2205 Piper, William Bowman. "Tristram Shandy's Tragi-comical Testimony." Criticism, 3 (1961), 171–85. Author–reader relationship. Point of view and narrator. Characterization.

2206 Porter, Dennis. "Fictions of Art and Life: Tristram Shandy and Henry Brulard." Modern Language Notes, 91 (1976), 1257–66. [Sterne, Stendhal]. Composition of the novel. Point of view and narrator.

2207 Posner, Roland. "Semiotic Paradoxes in Language Use, with Particular Reference to Tristram Shandy." The Eighteenth Century: Theory and Interpretation, 20 (1979), 148–63. Style and language.

2208 Preston, John. "Tristram Shandy (i): The Reader as Author" and "Tristram Shandy (ii): The Author as Reader." In his The Created Self: The Reader's Role in Eighteenth-Century Fiction. New York: Barnes & Noble, 1970, pp. 133–95. Author–reader relationship. Plot, structure, and design.

2209 Price, Lawrence Marsden. "Sterne and the Sentimental Nov-
      el." In his English Literature in Germany. Berkeley:
      Univ. of California Press, 1953, pp. 193-206. Influence
      and reputation abroad. Sentimental novel.

2210 Price, Martin. "Sterne: Art and Nature." In his To the
      Palace of Wisdom: Studies in Order and Energy from Dry-
      den to Blake. New York: Doubleday, 1964, pp. 312-41.
      Philosophy of novelist. Nature vs. art.

2211 Putney, Rufus. "The Evolution of A Sentimental Journey."
      Philological Quarterly, 19 (1940), 349-69. Composition of
      the novel. Plot, structure, and design. Sentimentalism.
      Satire.

2212 Putney, Rufus. "Laurence Sterne: Apostle of Laughter."
      In The Age of Johnson: Essays Presented to Chauncey
      Brewster Tinker. Ed. Frederick W. Hilles and Wilmarth S.
      Lewis. New Haven, Conn.: Yale Univ. Press, 1949, pp.
      274-84. Comedy. Irony. Sentimentalism.

2213 Quennell, Peter. "Laurence Sterne." Horizon, 8 (1943), 337-
      49; ibid., 10 (1945), 36-57. Rpt. in his Four Portraits:
      Boswell, Gibbon, Sterne, Wilkes. New York: Viking,
      1945, pp. 139-94. Biography.

2214 Read, Herbert. "Sterne." In his The Sense of Glory. New
      York: Harcourt, Brace, 1930, pp. 123-51. Introductory
      guide.

2215 Reed, Walter L. "Tristram Shandy: Displacement as Signifi-
      cation." In his An Exemplary History of the Novel: The
      Quixotic Versus the Picaresque. Chicago: Univ. of Chicago
      Press, 1981, pp. 137-61. Characterization. Quixotic novel.

2216 Reid, B. L. "The Sad Hilarity of Sterne." Virginia Quarter-
      ly Review, 32 (1956), 107-30. Comedy.

2217 Richter, David H. "The Reader as Ironic Victim." Novel, 14
      (1981), 135-51, esp. 138-43. [A Sentimental Journey].
      Irony. Satire [on reader].

2218 Rodgers, James S. "'Life' in the Novel: Tristram Shandy
      and Some Aspects of Eighteenth-Century Physiology."
      Eighteenth-Century Life, 6, (1980), 1-20. Characterization.
      Physiology.

2219 Rogers, Pat. "Sterne and Journalism." In The Winged Skull:
      Papers from the Laurence Sterne Bicentenary Conference.
      Ed. Arthur H. Cash and John M. Stedmond. Kent, Ohio:

Kent State Univ. Press, 1971, pp. 132-44. Autobiographical elements in the novel. Journalism.

2220 Rogers, Pat. "Tristram Shandy's Polite Conversation." Essays in Criticism, 32 (1982), 305-20. Style and language. Speech and dialogue.

2221 Rohrberger, Mary, and Samuel H. Woods, Jr. "Alchemy of the Word: Surrealism in Tristram Shandy." Interpretations, 11 (1979), 24-34. Surrealism.

2222 Rosenblum, Michael. "The Sermon, the King of Bohemia, and the Art of Interpolation in Tristram Shandy." Studies in Philology, 75 (1978), 472-91. The sermon. Digressions and interpolated stories. Narrative technique.

2223 Rosenblum, Michael. "Shandean Geometry and the Challenge of Contingency." Novel, 10 (1977), 237-47. Probability. Plot, structure, and design. Narrative technique.

2224 Roth, Martin. "Laurence Sterne in America." Bulletin of the New York Public Library, 74 (1970), 428-36. Influence and reputation abroad. America.

■2225 Rothstein, Eric. "Tristram Shandy." In his Systems of Order and Inquiry in Later Eighteenth-Century Fiction. Berkeley: Univ. of California Press, 1975, pp. 62-108. Point of view and narrator. Plot, structure, and design. Epistemology.

2226 Rousseau, George S. "Smollett and Sterne: A Revaluation." Archiv, 208, Nos. 4-6 (1972), 289-97. Comparison of novelists. Critical revaluation.

2227 Rousseau, George S. "Widows: Tristram Shandy." In his "Threshold and Explanation: The Social Anthropologist and the Critic of Eighteenth-Century Literature." The Eighteenth Century: Theory and Interpretation, 22 (1981), 133-37. The widow. Characterization.

2228 Russell, H. K. "Tristram Shandy and the Technique of the Novel." Studies in Philology, 42 (1945), 581-93. Characterization.

2229 Ryan, Marjorie. "Tristram Shandy and the Limits of Satire." Kansas Quarterly, 1, No. 3 (1969), 58-63. Satire.

2230 Sallé, Jean-Claude. "A State of Warfare: Some Aspects of Time and Chance in Tristram Shandy." In Quick Springs of Sense: Studies in the Eighteenth Century. Ed. Larry S. Champion. Athens: Univ. of Georgia Press, 1974, pp. 211-21. Time. Chance.

2231 Schackford, John B. "Sterne's Use of Catachresis in Tristram Shandy." Iowa English Yearbook, No. 6 (1961), pp.
74-79. Style and language. Rhetoric。

2232 Scher, Steven Paul. "Hoffman and Sterne: Unmediated Par-
allels in Narrative Method." Comparative Literature, 28
(1976), 309-25. Narrative technique.

2233 Seidel, Michael. "Gravity's Inheritable Line: Sterne's Tristram Shandy." In his Satiric Inheritance: Rabelais to
Sterne. Princeton, N.J.: Princeton Univ. Press, 1979,
pp. 250-62. Narrative technique. Satire.

2234 Seltzer, Alvin J. "A Thousand Splinters: The Deliberately
Distorted Narrative of Tristram Shandy." In his Chaos in
the Novel, The Novel in Chaos. New York: Schocken,
1974, pp. 29-51. Narrative technique. Plot, structure,
and design.

2235 Shaw, Margaret R. B. Laurence Sterne: The Making of a
Humorist, 1713-1762. London: Richards Press, 1957.
Biography.

2236 Sherbo, Arthur. "Some Not-So-Hidden Allusions in Tristram
Shandy." In his Studies in the Eighteenth-Century English
Novel. East Lansing: Michigan State Univ. Press, 1969,
pp. 128-35. Biblical allusions.

2237 Shroff, Homai J. "'The Heart Rather Than the Head'--Oliver
Goldsmith, Henry Mackenzie, Laurence Sterne." In her
The Eighteenth Century Novel: The Idea of the Gentleman.
New Delhi: Arnold-Heinemann, 1978, pp. 192-235. The
gentleman.

2238 Shumuta, Natsuo. "Laurence Sterne and Japan." In The
Winged Skull: Papers from the Laurence Sterne Bicentenary Conference. Ed. Arthur H. Cash and John M. Stedmond. Kent, Ohio: Kent State Univ. Press, 1971, pp.
186-93. Influence and reputation abroad. Japan.

2239 Sinfield, Mark. "Uncle Toby's Potency: Some Critical and
Authorial Confusions in Tristram Shandy." Notes and
Queries, N.S. 25 (1978), 54-55。 Characterization.

2240 Singleton, Marvin K. "Deduced Knowledge as Shandean Nub:
Paracelsian Hermetic as Metaphoric Bridge in Tristram
Shandy." Zeitschrift für Anglistik und Amerikanistik, 16
(1968), 274-84. Style and language. Imagery [diabolic,
learned].

2241 Singleton, Marvin K. "Trismegistic Tenor and Vehicle in

Sterne's Tristram Shandy." Papers on Language and Literature, 4 (1968), 158-69. Style and language. Names of characters.

2242 Smitten, Jeffrey R. "Gesture and Expression in Eighteenth-Century Fiction: A Sentimental Journey." Modern Language Studies, 9 (1979), 85-97. Gestures and mannerisms. Characterization.

2243 Smitten, Jeffrey R. "Spatial Form as Narrative Technique in A Sentimental Journey." Journal of Narrative Technique, 5 (1975), 208-18. Space. Narrative technique. Plot, structure, and design.

2244 Smitten, Jeffrey R. "Tristram Shandy and Spatial Form." Ariel: A Review of International English Literature, 8, No. 4 (1977), 43-59. [Vol. III of Tristram Shandy]. Space. Plot, structure, and design. Imagery [physical destruction, circumstances, sexuality, imprisonment of sentiment].

2245 Snow, Kathleen R. "Homunculus in Paracelsus, Tristram Shandy, and Faust." Journal of English and Germanic Philology, 79 (1980), 67-74. The homunculus.

2246 Sokolyansky, Mark G. "The Rhythmical Pattern of Tristram Shandy." Durham University Journal, 73 (1980), 23-26. Rhythm. Plot, structure, and design. Style and language.

2247 Spacks, Patricia Meyer. "The Beautiful Oblique: Tristram Shandy." In her Imagining a Self: Autobiography and Novel in Eighteenth-Century England. Cambridge, Mass.: Harvard Univ. Press, 1976, pp. 127-57. The self. Autobiographical elements in the novel.

2248 Speck, Paul Surgi. "Frustration, Curiosity and Rumor: Sterne's Use of Women to Define Impotence in Tristram Shandy." Publications of the Arkansas Philological Association, 5, No. 2-3 (1979), 30-35. Impotence. Man vs. woman. Symbolism [widows, nuns, keyholes, clocks, handles, ends, breeches].

•2249 Stedmond, John M. The Comic Art of Laurence Sterne: Convention and Innovation in "Tristram Shandy" and "A Sentimental Journey." Toronto: Univ. of Toronto Press, 1967. Incorporates his "Genre and Tristram Shandy," Philological Quarterly, 38 (1959), 37-51; "Satire and Tristram Shandy," Studies in English Literature, 1 (1961), 53-63; "Sterne as a Plagiarist," English Studies, 41 (1960), 308-12; and "Style and Tristram Shandy," Modern Language Quarterly, 20 (1959), 243-51. Comedy. Satire. Style and language. Characterization. Conventions of the Georgian novel. Innovation.

2250 Stewart, Jack F. "Romantic Theories of Humor Relating to
      Sterne." The Personalist, 50 (1968), 459-73. Comedy
      [Sterne's romantic irony as central example in Romantic
      theory].

2251 Stewart, Jack F. "Some Critical Metaphors for Shandean
      Style." College Language Association Journal, 13 (1969),
      183-87. Rhythm. Style and language [described by critics
      metaphorically as flow, whirl, mosaic, logopoeia].

2252 Stewart, Jack F. "Sterne's Absurd Comedy." University of
      Windsor Review, 5, No. 2 (1970), 81-95. Comedy. The
      absurd [absurd elements in Tristram Shandy].

2253 Stobie, Margaret. "Walter Shandy: Generative Grammarian."
      Humanities Association Bulletin, 17, No. 1 (1966), 13-19.
      Modernity [Sterne anticipates transformational grammar].
      Grammar.

2254 Stout, Gardner D. "Some Borrowings in Sterne from Rabelais
      and Cervantes." English Language Notes, 3 (1965-66), 111-
      18. Sources, analogues, and influences. Cervantes.
      Rabelais.

2255 Stout, Gardner D. "Yorick's Sentimental Journey: A Comic
      'Pilgrim's Progress' for the Man of Feeling." ELH: A
      Journal of English Literary History, 30 (1963), 395-412.
      Comedy. Sentimentalism. "Man of Feeling."

2256 Swearingen, James E. Reflexivity in "Tristram Shandy":
      An Essay in Phenomenological Criticism. New Haven, Conn.:
      Yale Univ. Press, 1977. Reflexivity. Hobbyhorse. The
      self. Subjectivity. Time. Style and language. Psychol-
      ogy of characters.

2257 Tave, Stuart M. The Amiable Humorist: A Study in the
      Comic Theory and Criticism of the Eighteenth and Early
      Nineteenth Century. Chicago: Univ. of Chicago Press,
      1960, pp. 148-51, 171-77, 222-27, 233-35. "Amiable Hu-
      morist." Comedy. Eighteenth-century criticism and re-
      views of the novel. Theory and practice of the novel.

2258 Thomson, David. Wild Excursions: The Life and Fiction of
      Laurence Sterne. New York: McGraw-Hill, 1972. Biogra-
      phy.

2259 Thomson, J. E. P. "Contrasting Scenes and Their Part in
      the Structure of A Sentimental Journey." Journal of the
      Australasian Universities Language and Literature Associa-
      tion, 32 (1969), 206-13. Contrast as technique. Setting.
      Plot, structure, and design.

2260 Thomson, J. E. P. "The Morality of Sterne's Yorick." Jour-
      nal of the Australasian Universities Language and Literature
      Association, 27 (1967), 71-78. Morality. Characterization.

2261 Towers, A. R. "Sterne's Cock and Bull Story." ELH: A
      Journal of English Literary History, 24 (1957), 12-29.
      Characterization. Comedy. Sex.

2262 Tracy, Clarence. "As Many Chapters as Steps." In The
      Winged Skull: Papers from the Laurence Sterne Bicentenary
      Conference. Ed. Arthur H. Cash and John M. Stedmond.
      Kent, Ohio: Kent State Univ. Press, 1971, pp. 97-111.
      Plot, structure, and design. Conventions of the Georgian
      novel [biographical form].

•2263 Traugott, John L. Tristram Shandy's World: Sterne's Philo-
      sophical Rhetoric. Berkeley: Univ. of California Press,
      1954. Locke. Point of view and narrator [novel controlled
      by Tristram as "facetious rhetor"]. Characterization.
      Comedy. Sentimentalism. Rhetoric. Philosophy of novelist.

2264 Tuveson, Ernest. "Locke and Sterne." In Reason and the
      Imagination: Studies in the History of Ideas, 1660-1800.
      Ed. J. A. Mazzeo. New York: Columbia Univ. Press,
      1962, pp. 255-77. Rpt. in English Literature and British
      Philosophy. Ed. S. P. Rosenbaum. Chicago: Univ. of
      Chicago Press, 1971, pp. 86-108. Locke. Psychology of
      characters. Epistemology.

2265 Tyson, Gerald P. "The Rococo Style of Tristram Shandy."
      Bucknell Review, 24, No. 2 (1978), 38-55. Rococo. Style
      and language.

2266 Ulanov, Barry. "Sterne and Fielding: The Allegory of
      Irony." In his Sources and Resources: The Literary
      Traditions of Christian Humanism. Westminster, Md.:
      Newman Press, 1960, pp. 206-27. Irony. Comparison of
      novelists.

2267 Uphaus, Robert W. "Sentiment and Spleen: Travels with
      Sterne and Smollett." Centennial Review, 15 (1971), 406-
      21. Comparison of novelists. Personal relations between
      authors.

2268 Uphaus, Robert W. "Sterne's Sixth Sense." In his The Im-
      possible Observer: Reason and the Reader in 18th-Century
      Prose. Lexington: Univ. Press of Kentucky, 1979, pp.
      108-22. Author-reader relationship.

2269 Van Ghent, Dorothy. "On Tristram Shandy." In her The
      English Novel, Form and Function. New York: Rinehart,

1953, pp. 83-98. Plot, structure, and design [the "opera-
tive character of consciousness"]. Characterization.

2270 Wagoner, Mary. "Satire of the Reader in Tristram Shandy."
      Texas Studies in Literature and Language, 7 (1966), 337-
      44. Author-reader relationship. Satire.

2271 Walker, Robert G. "A Sign of the Satirist's Wit: The Nose
      in Tristram Shandy." Ball State University Forum, 19, No.
      2 (1978), 52-54. Satire [on Tristram]. Symbolism [nose].

2272 Warren, Leland E. "The Constant Speaker: Aspects of Con-
      versation in Tristram Shandy." University of Toronto
      Quarterly, 46 (1976), 51-67. Speech and dialogue.

2273 Watkins, Walter B. C. "Yorick Revisited." In his Perilous
      Balance: The Tragic Genius of Swift, Johnson, and Sterne.
      Princeton, N.J.: Princeton Univ. Press, 1939, pp. 99-156.
      Personality of novelist.

2274 Watt, Ian. "The Comic Syntax of Tristram Shandy." In
      Studies in Criticism and Aesthetics, 1660-1800. Ed. Howard
      Anderson and John S. Shea. Minneapolis: Univ. of Min-
      nesota Press, 1967, pp. 315-31. Plot, structure, and design.
      Style and language. Comedy.

2275 Watt, Ian. "Realism and the Later Tradition: A Note." In
      his The Rise of the Novel: Studies in Defoe, Richardson,
      and Fielding. Berkeley: Univ. of California Press, 1957,
      pp. 290-301, esp. 290-96. Realism. Time.

2276 Weales, Gerald. "Tristram Shandy's Anti-book." In Twelve
      Original Essays on Great English Novels. Ed. Charles
      Shapiro. Detroit, Mich.: Wayne State Univ. Press, 1960,
      pp. 43-47. Digressions and interpolated stories. Unity
      [of attitude].

2277 Weinstein, Arnold. "New Worlds and Old Worlds: Tristram
      Shandy." In his Fictions of the Self: 1550-1800. Prince-
      ton, N.J.: Princeton Univ. Press, 1981, pp. 214-32. The
      self. Style and language [language and imagination vs.
      matter and experience].

2278 White, F. Eugene. "Sterne's Quiet Journey of the Heart:
      Unphilosophic Projection of Enlightened Benevolence." En-
      lightenment Essays, 2 (1971), 103-10. Benevolence. Phi-
      losophy of novelist.

■2279 Work, James A. "Introduction." In his edition of Tristram
      Shandy. New York: Odyssey, 1940, pp. ix-lxxii. Intro-
      ductory guide [excellent account of main issues].

2280   Wright, Andrew. "The Artifice of Failure in Tristram Shan-
       dy." Novel, 2 (1969), 212-20. Narrative technique.

2281   Wright, Arnold, and William Lutley Sclater. Sterne's Eliza,
       Some Account of Her Life in India: With Her Letters Writ-
       ten Between 1757 and 1774. London: Heinemann, 1922.
       Elizabeth Draper. Biography.

2282   Yoseloff, Thomas. A Fellow of Infinite Jest. New York:
       Prentice-Hall, 1945. Biography [popular].

       SEE ALSO ITEMS 242, 751, 761, 767, 778, 784, 787a,
       788, 797, 820, 825, 834, 844, 870, 884, 918, 939, 942,
       980, 986, 1005, 1018, 1060a, 1062, 1068, 1110, 1116.

PENELOPE AUBIN
(1685-1731)

PRINCIPAL FICTION

Madam de Beaumont, 1721

The Count de Vinevil, 1721

Lucinda, 1722

The Noble Slaves, 1722

The Lady Lucy, 1726

The Young Count Albertus, 1728

BIBLIOGRAPHIES AND SURVEYS OF CRITICISM

2283 Backscheider, Paula, et al. "Penelope Aubin." In their An Annotated Bibliography of Twentieth-Century Critical Studies of Women and Literature, 1660-1800. New York: Garland, 1977, p. 92. Bibliography of criticism [annotated].

BIOGRAPHICAL AND CRITICAL STUDIES

2284 Dooley, Roger B. "Penelope Aubin: Forgotten Catholic Novelist." Renascence, 11 (1959), 65-71. Catholicism. Characterization [admirable Catholic characters].

2285 McBurney, William H. "Mrs. Penelope Aubin and the Early Eighteenth-Century English Novel." Huntington Library Quarterly, 20 (1957), 245-67. Introductory guide. Theory and practice of the novel.

SEE ALSO ITEMS 893, 920, 921, 1015.

ROBERT BAGE
(1728-1801)

PRINCIPAL FICTION

Mount Henneth, 1781

Barham Downs, 1784

The Fair Syrian, 1787

James Wallace, 1788

Man as He Is, 1792

Hermsprong, 1796

BIBLIOGRAPHIES AND SURVEYS OF CRITICISM

2286 Beasley, Jerry C. "Robert Bage (1728-1801)." In his English Fiction, 1660-1800: A Guide to Information Sources. Detroit: Gale, 1978, pp. 53-55. Bibliography of criticism [annotated].

2287 Moran, Michael G. "Robert Bage (1728-1801): A Bibliography." Bulletin of Bibliography, 38 (1981), 173-78. Bibliography of criticism. Bibliography of primary sources.

BIOGRAPHICAL AND CRITICAL STUDIES

2288 Faulkner, Peter. "Man as He Is Not." Durham University Journal, 26 (1965), 137-47. Social criticism in the novel.

2289 Faulkner, Peter. Robert Bage. Twayne's English Authors Series. Boston: Twayne, 1979. Introductory guide.

2290 Grabo, C. H. "Robert Bage, a Forgotten Novelist." Midwest Quarterly, 5 (1917), 201-26. Introductory guide.

2291 Gregory, Allene. "The Novels of Robert Bage." In her The French Revolution and the English Novel. 1915; rpt. New York: Haskell House, 1966, pp. 161-80. Jacobin novel. French Revolution.

2292 Kelly, Gary D. "Robert Bage." In his The English Jacobin Novel: 1780-1805. Oxford: Oxford Univ. Press, 1976, pp. 20-63. Jacobin novel. Politics.

■2293 Sutherland, John H. "Robert Bage: Novelist of Ideas."

Philological Quarterly, 36 (1957), 211-20. Philosophical
novel. Point of view and narrator [multiple points of view
essential to novel of ideas]. Critical revaluation [counters
usual association of Bage with the novelists of doctrine].

SEE ALSO ITEMS 1004, 1065, 1075.

JANE BARKER
(1675-1743)

PRINCIPAL FICTION

Love Intrigues, or The History of the Amours of Bosvil and
    Galesia, 1713

Exilius, 1715

A Patchwork Screen for the Ladies, 1723

The Lining of the Patchwork Screen, 1726

BIBLIOGRAPHIES AND SURVEYS OF CRITICISM

2294 Backsheider, Paula, et al. "Jane Barker." In their An An-
      notated Bibliography of Twentieth-Century Critical Studies
      of Women and Literature, 1660-1800. New York: Garland,
      1977, p. 95. Bibliography of criticism [annotated].

BIOGRAPHICAL AND CRITICAL STUDIES

2295 McBurney, William H. "Edmund Curll, Mrs. Jane Barker, and
      the English Novel." Philological Quarterly, 37 (1958), 385-
      99. Edmund Curll. Sources, analogues, and influences.
      Influence and imitation. Innovation. Morality.

SEE ALSO ITEMS 752, 822, 871, 921, 1015.

WILLIAM BECKFORD
(1760-1844)

PRINCIPAL FICTION

Vathek, 1786

Modern Novel Writing, or the Elegant Enthusiast, 1796

Azemia, 1797-98

BIBLIOGRAPHIES AND SURVEYS OF CRITICISM

2296 Chapman, Guy, and John Hodgkin. A Bibliography of William
      Beckford of Fonthill. London: Constable, 1930. Bibliog-
      raphy of primary sources.

2297 Gemmett, Robert J. "An Annotated Checklist of the Works of
      William Beckford." Papers of the Bibliographical Society of
      America, 61 (1967), 243-58. Bibliography of primary
      sources.

2298 McNutt, Dan J. "William Beckford (1760-1844)." In his The
      Eighteenth-Century Gothic Novel: An Annotated Bibliogra-
      phy of Criticism and Selected Texts. New York: Garland,
      1975, pp. 265-310. Bibliography of criticism [annotated].
      Bibliography of primary sources.

SEE ALSO ITEM 67.

BIOGRAPHICAL AND CRITICAL STUDIES

2299 Alexander, Boyd. "The Decay of Beckford's Genius." In
      William Beckford of Fonthill, 1760-1844. Bicentenary Es-
      says. Ed. Fatma Moussa Mahmoud. Port Washington, N.Y.:
      Kennikat, 1972. Artistic decline.

2300 Alexander, Boyd. England's Wealthiest Son: A Study of Wil-
      liam Beckford. London: Centaur, 1962. Biography. Per-
      sonality of novelist.

2301 Alexander, Boyd. "William Beckford, Man of Taste." History
      Today, 10 (1960), 686-94. Taste. Fonthill.

2302 Brockman, H. A. N. The Caliph of Fonthill. London: Wern-
      er Laurie, 1956. Architecture. Fonthill. Biography.

2303 Bullough, Geoffrey. "Beckford's Early Travels and His
      'Dream of Delusion.'" In William Beckford of Fonthill, 1760-
      1844. Bicentenary Essays. Ed. Fatma Moussa Mahmoud.
      Port Washington, N.Y.: Kennikat, 1972. Travel. Biogra-
      phy.

•2304 Chapman, Guy. Beckford. 2nd ed. London: Rupert Hart-
      Davis, 1952. Biography.

2305 Folsom, James K. "Beckford's Vathek and the Tradition of Oriental Satire." Criticism, 6 (1964), 53-69. Oriental novel. Satire.

2306 Gemmett, Robert J. "Beckford's Fonthill: The Landscape as Art." Gazette des Beaux-Arts, 80 (1972), 335-56. Fonthill. Landscape gardening. The picturesque.

2307 Gemmett, Robert J. "The Critical Reception of William Beckford's Fonthill." English Miscellany, 19 (1968), 133-51. Fonthill. Architecture. Landscape gardening. The picturesque.

•2308 Gemmett, Robert J. William Beckford. Twayne's English Authors Series. Boston: Twayne, 1977. Introductory guide. Orientalism.

2309 Giddey, Ernest. "Byron and Beckford." The Byron Journal, 6 (1978), 38-47. Influence and imitation. Byron.

2310 Graham, Kenneth W. "Beckford's Adaptation of the Oriental Tale in Vathek." Enlightenment Essays 5, No. 1 (1974), 24-33. Oriental novel. Sources, analogues, and influences.

2311 Graham, Kenneth W. "Beckford's Design for The Episodes: A Review and a History." Papers of the Bibliographical Society of America, 71 (1977), 336-43. Composition of the novel.

2312 Graham, Kenneth W. "Beckford's Vathek: A Study in Ironic Dissonance." Criticism, 14 (1972), 243-52. Philosophy of novelist. Irony. Skepticism.

■2313 Graham, Kenneth W. "Implications of the Grotesque: Beckford's Vathek and the Boundaries of Fictional Reality." Tennessee Studies in Literature, 23 (1978), 61-74. The grotesque. Realism. Innovation.

2314 Graham, Kenneth W. "Vathek in English and French." Studies in Bibliography, 28 (1975), 153-66. Composition of the novel.

2315 Hume, Robert D. "Exuberant Gloom, Existential Agony, and Heroic Despair: Three Varieties of Negative Romanticism." In The Gothic Imagination: Essays in Dark Romanticism. Ed. G. R. Thompson. Pullman: Washington State Univ. Press, 1974, pp. 109-127, esp. pp. 113-17. Romanticism.

2316 Hussain, Imdad. "Beckford, Wainewright, De Quincey, and Oriental Exoticism." Venture, 1 (1960), 234-48. Orientalism. The exotic.

2317 Kiely, Robert. "Vathek." In his The Romantic Novel in
      England. Cambridge, Mass.: Harvard Univ. Press, 1972,
      pp. 43-64. Romantic novel. Autobiographical elements in
      the novel.

2318 Lees-Milne, James. William Beckford. Tisbury, Wiltshire:
      Compton Russell, 1976. Biography.

2318a Liu, Alan. "Toward a Theory of Common Sense: Beckford's
      Vathek and Johnson's Rasselas." Texas Studies in Litera-
      ture and Language, 26 (1984), 183-217. Common sense.
      Comparison of novelists.

2319 Mahmoud, Fatma Moussa. "Beckford, Vathek and the Oriental
      Tale." In William Beckford of Fonthill, 1760-1844. Bicen-
      tenary Essays. Ed. Fatma Moussa Mahmoud. Port Washing-
      ton, N.Y.: Kennikat, 1972. Oriental novel.

2320 Mahmoud, Fatma Moussa. "Rasselas and Vathek." In Bicen-
      tenary Essays on "Rasselas." Ed. Magdi Wahba. Cairo:
      Société orientale de publicité, 1959, pp. 51-57. Comparison
      of novelists [Johnson, Beckford]. Orientalism.

2321 Manzalaoui, Mahmoud. "Pseudo-Orientalism in Transition:
      The Age of Vathek." In William Beckford of Fonthill, 1760-
      1844. Bicentenary Essays. Ed. Fatma Moussa Mahmoud.
      Port Washington, N.Y.: Kennikat, 1972. Oriental novel.

2322 Maynard, Temple. "Depictions of Persepolis and William Beck-
      ford's Istakar." Eighteenth-Century Life, 3 (1977), 119-22.
      Setting. Sources, analogues, and influences.

2323 Maynard, Temple. "The Landscape of Vathek." Transactions
      of the Samuel Johnson Society of the Northwest, 7 (1974),
      79-98. See also a reply by David McCracken, ibid., pp.
      99-103. Imagery. Setting.

2324 More, Paul Elmer. "William Beckford." In his The Drift of
      Romanticism. Boston: Houghton Mifflin, 1913, pp. 3-36.
      Romanticism.

2325 Oliver, J. W. The Life of William Beckford. London: Ox-
      ford Univ. Press, 1932. Biography.

■2326 Parreaux, André. "The Caliph and the Swinish Multitude."
      In William Beckford of Fonthill, 1760-1844. Bicentenary
      Essays. Ed. Fatma Moussa Mahmoud. Port Washington,
      N.Y.: Kennikat, 1972. [Modern Novel Writing, Azemia].
      Politics. Satire.

■2327 Rieger, James Henry. "Au Pied de la Lettre: Stylistic Un-

certainty in Vathek." Criticism, 4 (1962), 302-12. Style
and language. Defects in the novel. Composition of the
novel.

2328 Scott, John. "The Rise and Fall of Fonthill Abbey." British
      History Illustrated, August 1975, pp. 2-11. Fonthill.
      Architecture.

2329 Sena, John F. "Drawing from Blots: The Landscapes of
      Vathek and the Paintings of Alexander Cozens." Etudes
      Anglaises, 26 (1973), 210-15. Setting. Landscape. Par-
      ticular vs. general. Alexander Cozens [influence on Beck-
      ford].

2330 Wahba, Magdi. "Beckford, Portugal and 'Childish Error.'"
      in William Beckford of Fonthill, 1760-1844. Bicentenary
      Essays. Ed. Fatma Moussa Mahmoud. Port Washington,
      N.Y.: Kennikat, 1972. Personality of novelist [childish-
      ness, pederasty]. Portugal.

2331 Wiener, Harold S. L. "Byron and the East: Literary Sources
      of the Turkish Tales." Nineteenth-Century Studies. Ed.
      Herbert Davis et al. 1940; rpt. New York: Greenwood
      Press, 1968, esp. pp. 95-103. Influence and imitation.
      Byron.

      SEE ALSO ITEMS 748, 868, 910, 929, 1051, 1065, 1070,
      1095, 1102.

                        ARTHUR BLACKAMORE
                           (c.1679-?)

PRINCIPAL FICTION

    The Perfidious Brethren, 1720

    Luck at Last, or The Happy Unfortunate, 1723

BIBLIOGRAPHIES AND SURVEYS OF CRITICISM

None.

BIOGRAPHICAL AND CRITICAL STUDIES

2332 Davis, Richard Beale. "Arthur Blackamore: The Virginia
      Colony and the Early English Novel." Virginia Magazine of

History and Biography, 75 (1967), 22-34. Introductory
guide. Virginia.

FRANCES MOORE BROOKE
(1724-1789?)

PRINCIPAL FICTION

The History of Lady Julia Mandeville, 1763

The History of Emily Montague, 1769

All's Right at Last, or The History of Frances West, 1774

The Excursion, 1777

BIBLIOGRAPHIES AND SURVEYS OF CRITICISM

None.

BIOGRAPHICAL AND CRITICAL STUDIES

2333 Edwards, Mary Jane. "The Brookes and Protestantism in
      Quebec in the 1760s." Huguenot Trails, 11, No. 4 (1978),
      4-5. Biography. Anglicanism. Canada.

2334 Edwards, Mary Jane. "Frances Brooke's Politics and The
      History of Emily Montague." In Beginnings: A Critical
      Anthology. Ed. John Moss. Toronto: N C Press, 1980,
      pp. 19-27. Politics. Canada.

2335 McMullen, Lorraine. "All's Right at Last: An Eighteenth-
      Century Canadian Novel." Journal of Canadian Fiction, 21
      (1977-78), 95-104. Canada. Introductory guide.

2336 McMullen, Lorraine. "The Divided Self." Atlantis: A Wom-
      en's Studies Journal, 5, No. 2 (1980), 53-67, esp. 53-58.
      [The History of Emily Montague]. Women novelists. Women.
      Contrast as technique [unconventional woman juxtaposed
      with a conventional woman].

2337 McMullen, Lorraine. "Frances Brooke's Early Fiction." Cana-
      dian Literature, 86 (1980), 31-40. Sources, analogues, and
      influences. Novel of sensibility. Narrative technique.
      Feminism.

2338   Pacey, Desmond. "The First Canadian Novel." <u>Dalhousie</u>
       <u>Review</u>, 26, No. 2 (1946), 143-50. Canada.

2339   Rogers, Katharine M. "Sensibility and Feminism: The Nov-
       els of Frances Brooke." <u>Genre</u>, 11 (1980), 159-71. Senti-
       mentalism [her "novels are in no way especially sentimen-
       tal"]. Women.

2340   Shohet, Linda. "An Essay on <u>The History of Emily Montague</u>."
       In <u>Beginnings: A Critical Anthology</u>. Ed. John Moss.
       Toronto: N C Press, 1980, pp. 28-34. Introductory
       guide. Canada.

       SEE ALSO ITEMS 752, 920.

                          <u>HENRY BROOKE</u>
                           (1703-1783)

PRINCIPAL FICTION

       <u>The Fool of Quality</u>, 1764-70

       <u>Juliet Grenville, or The History of the Human Heart</u>, 1774

BIBLIOGRAPHIES AND SURVEYS OF CRITICISM

2341   Beasley, Jerry C. "Henry Brooke (1703-83)." In his <u>Eng-</u>
       <u>lish Fiction, 1660-1800: A Guide to Information Sources</u>.
       Detroit: Gale, 1978, pp. 69-71. Bibliography of criticism
       [annotated].

BIOGRAPHICAL AND CRITICAL STUDIES

2342   Foster, James R. <u>History of the Pre-Romantic Novel in Eng-</u>
       <u>land</u>. 1949; rpt. New York: Modern Language Associa-
       tion, 1966, pp. 164-69. Introductory guide.

2343   Scheuermann, Mona. "More Than 'A Few Passages': Henry
       Brooke's <u>The Fool of Quality</u> as the Source for Thomas
       Day's <u>The History of Sandford and Merton</u>." <u>Durham Uni-</u>
       <u>versity Journal</u>, N.S. 44, No. 2 (1983), 55-59. Comparison
       of novelists. Influence and imitation.

2344   Scurr, Helen Margaret. <u>Henry Brooke</u>. Minneapolis: Univ.
       of Minnesota Press, 1927. Biography.

2345 Tompkins, J. M. S. The Popular Novel in England, 1770–
      1800. 1932; rpt. Lincoln: Univ. of Nebraska Press, 1961,
      pp. 30-33. Introductory guide.

                    FANNY BURNEY, MME. D'ARBLAY
                              (1752-1840)

PRINCIPAL FICTION

      Evelina, 1778

      Cecilia, 1782

      Camilla, 1796

      The Wanderer, 1814

BIBLIOGRAPHIES AND SURVEYS OF CRITICISM

2346 Backscheider, Paula, et al. "Fanny Burney." In their An
      Annotated Bibliography of Twentieth-Century Critical Studies
      of Women and Literature, 1660-1800. New York: Garland,
      1977, pp. 111-20. Bibliography of criticism [annotated].

2347 Grau, Joseph A. Fanny Burney: An Annotated Bibliography.
      New York: Garland, 1981. Bibliography of primary sources.
      Bibliography of criticism [annotated].

BIOGRAPHICAL AND CRITICAL STUDIES

2348 Adelstein, Michael E. Fanny Burney. Twayne's English Au-
      thors Series. New York: Twayne, 1968. Introductory
      guide.

2349 Anderson, Earl R. "Footnotes More Pedestrian Than Sublime:
      A Historical Background for the Foot-Races in Evelina and
      Humphry Clinker." Eighteenth-Century Studies, 14 (1980),
      56-68. See also Arthur Sherbo, "Addenda to 'Footnotes
      More Pedestrian Than Sublime,'" ibid., 14 (1981), 313-16.
      Sport and recreation. Social background.

2350 Barker, Gerard A. "The Two Mrs. Selwyns: Evelina and
      The Man of the World." Papers on Language and Litera-
      ture, 13 (1977), 80-84. Comparison of novelists [Burney,
      Mackenzie]. Characterization.

2351 Beasley, Jerry C. "Fanny Burney and Jane Austen's Pride
      and Prejudice." English Miscellany, 24 (1973-74), 153-66.
      Influence and imitation.

2352 Bloom, Lillian D. "Fanny Burney's Camilla: The Author as
      Editor." Bulletin of Research in the Humanities, 82 (1979),
      367-93. Composition of the novel.

■2353 Bloom, Lillian D., and Edward A. Bloom. "Fanny Burney's
      Novels: The Retreat from Wonder." Novel, 12 (1979),
      215-35. Artistic decline. Biography. Autobiographical
      elements in the novel. Fairy tale.

2354 Bradford, Gamaliel. "Madame d'Arblay." 1914; rpt. in his
      Portraits of Women. Boston: Houghton Mifflin, 1916, pp.
      67-87. Personality of novelist.

■2355 Cecil, David. "Fanny Burney's Novels." In Essays on the
      Eighteenth Century Presented to David Nichol Smith. 1945;
      rpt. New York: Russell & Russell, 1963, pp. 212-24.
      Introductory guide.

2356 Copeland, Edward. "Money in the Novels of Fanny Burney."
      Studies in the Novel, 8 (1976), 24-37. Money. Artistic
      development. Plot, structure, and design. Women.

2357 Cruse, Amy. "The Subscribers to Camilla." In her The
      Englishman and His Books in the Early Nineteenth Century.
      1930; rpt. New York: Blom, 1968, pp. 21-36. Reading
      public.

2358 Cutting, Rose Marie. "Defiant Women: The Growth of Femin-
      ism in Fanny Burney's Novels." Studies in English Litera-
      ture, 17 (1977), 519-30. Feminism. Women.

2359 Cutting, Rose Marie. "A Wreath for Fanny Burney's Last
      Novel: The Wanderer's Contribution to Women's Studies."
      College Language Association Journal, 20 (1976), 57-67.
      Women. Feminism.

2360 Deitz, Jonathan, and Sidonie Smith. "From Precept to Proper
      Social Action: Empirical Maturation in Fanny Burney's
      Evelina." Eighteenth-Century Life, 3 (1977), 85-88. Char-
      acterization. Maturation.

2361 Eaves, T. C. Duncan. "Edward Burney's Illustrations to
      Evelina." PMLA, 62 (1947), 995-99. Illustration.

2362 Edwards, Averyl. Fanny Burney: A Biography. London:
      Staples Press, 1948. Biography [popular].

2363 Erickson, James P. "Evelina and Betsy Thoughtless." Texas
     Studies in Literature and Language, 6 (1964), 96-103. Com-
     parison of novelists [Burney, Haywood]. Innovation.

■2364 Glock, Waldo S. "Appearance and Reality: The Education of
     Evelina." Essays in Literature, 2 (1975), 32-41. Appear-
     ance vs. reality. Propriety. Characterization.

2365 Hahn, Emily. A Degree of Prudery: A Biography of Fanny
     Burney. Garden City, N.Y.: Doubleday, 1950. Biography
     [hostile].

2366 Hale, Will Taliaferro. "Madame D'Arblay's Place in the De-
     velopment of the English Novel." Indiana University
     Studies, 3 (1916), 5-35. Artistic decline [deterioration of
     style, speech, humor, plot, and characterization after suc-
     cess of Evelina].

■2367 Hemlow, Joyce. "Fanny Burney and the Courtesy Books."
     PMLA, 65 (1950), 732-61. Courtesy books. Propriety.
     Morality. Women. Sources, analogues, and influences.

●2368 Hemlow, Joyce. The History of Fanny Burney. Oxford:
     Clarendon Press, 1958. Biography.

2369 Jeffrey, David K. "Manners, Morals, Magic and Evelina."
     Enlightenment Essays, 9 (1978), 35-47. Epistolary novel.
     Women. Comparison of novelists [Richardson, Smollett,
     Burney].

2370 Kilpatrick, Sarah. Fanny Burney. New York: Stein & Day,
     1981. Biography.

2371 Malone, Kemp. "Evelina Revisited." Papers on Language
     and Literature, 1 (1965), 3-19. Introductory guide.

2372 Montague, Edwine, and Louis L. Martz. "Fanny Burney's
     Evelina." In The Age of Johnson: Essays Presented to
     Chauncey Brewster Tinker. Ed. Frederick W. Hilles and
     Wilmarth S. Lewis. New Haven, Conn.: Yale Univ.
     Press, 1949, pp. 171-81. [A dialogue]. Narrative tech-
     nique.

2373 More, Paul Elmer. "Fanny Burney." In his Shelburne Es-
     says, Fourth Series. New York: Putnam, 1907, pp. 35-61.
     Introductory guide.

2374 Newton, Judith Lowder. "Evelina." In her Women, Power,
     and Subversion: Social Strategies in British Fiction, 1778-
     1860. Athens: Univ. of Georgia Press, 1981, pp. 23-54.
     Feminism. Social criticism in the novel. Man vs. woman.

2375 Newton, Judith Lowder. "Evelina: Or, the History of a
      Young Lady's Entrance into the Marriage Market." Modern
      Language Studies, 6, No. 1 (1976), 48-56. Marriage.
      Women.

■2376 Olshin, Toby. "'To Whom I Most Belong': The Role of the
      Family in Evelina." Eighteenth-Century Life, 6 (1980), 29-
      42. Family.

2377 Overman, Antoinette A. An Investigation into the Character
      of Fanny Burney. Amsterdam: H. J. Paris, 1933. Biog-
      raphy [psychoanalytic approach].

2378 Patterson, Emily H. "Family and Pilgrimage Themes in Bur-
      ney's Evelina." New Rambler, 18 (1977), 41-48. Family.
      Journey.

2379 Patterson, Emily H. "Unearned Irony in Fanny Burney's
      Evelina." Durham University Journal, 36 (1975), 200-04.
      Irony [unintentional].

2380 Rubenstein, Jill. "The Crisis of Identity in Fanny Burney's
      Evelina." New Rambler, 112 (1972), 45-50. The self.
      Characterization.

2381 Scrutton, Mary. "Bourgeois Cinderellas." Twentieth Cen-
      tury, 155 (1954), 351-63 [esp. 355-60]. Myth. Marriage.
      Bourgeois ideology [middle-class virtue rewarded by pros-
      perous marriage].

■2382 Spacks, Patricia Meyer. "Dynamics of Fear: Fanny Burney."
      In her Imagining a Self: Autobiography and Novel in Eight-
      eenth-Century England. Cambridge, Mass.: Harvard Univ.
      Press, 1976, pp. 158-92. For a response, see Peter Glass-
      man, "Acts of Enclosure," Hudson Review, 30 (1977), 138-
      46. The self. Autobiographical elements in the novel [nov-
      els may reveal more of Burney's private self than do her
      diaries]. Women [virtue requires self-concealment]. Anxi-
      ety [women's fears]. Writing.

■2383 Staves, Susan. "Evelina; or, Female Difficulties." Modern
      Philology, 73 (1976), 368-81. Women.

2384 Stowell, Helen Elizabeth. "Fanny Burney." In her Quill
      Pens and Petticoats: A Portrait of Women and Letters.
      London: Wayland, 1970. Introductory guide.

2385 Vopat, James B. "Evelina: Life as Art--Notes Toward Be-
      coming a Performer on the Stage of Life." Essays in Liter-
      ature, 2 (1975), 42-52. Characterization. Initiation.
      "Life as art."

2386 Voss-Clesly, Patricia. Tendencies of Character Depiction in
      the Domestic Novels of Burney, Edgeworth, and Austen:
      A Consideration of "Subjective" and "Objective" World. 3
      vols. Salzburg: Institut für Anglistik und Amerikanistik,
      1978. Characterization.

2387 White, Eugene. "Fanny Burney." In Minor British Novelists.
      Ed. Charles A. Hoyt. Carbondale: Southern Illinois Univ.
      Press, 1967, pp. 3-12. Introductory guide.

2388 White, Eugene. Fanny Burney, Novelist: A Study in Tech-
      nique. Hamden, Conn.: Shoe String Press, 1960. Plot,
      structure, and design. Characterization. Narrative tech-
      nique. Style and language.

      SEE ALSO ITEMS 126, 620, 752, 822, 871, 920, 980,
      1004, 1040, 1052, 1060a, 1065, 1087.

                          JOHN CLELAND
                          (1709-1789)

PRINCIPAL FICTION

      Fanny Hill, 1748-49

      Memoirs of a Coxcomb, 1751

BIBLIOGRAPHIES AND SURVEYS OF CRITICISM

2389 Beasley, Jerry C. "John Cleland (1709-89)." In his English
      Fiction, 1660-1800: A Guide to Information Sources. De-
      troit: Gale, 1978, pp. 87-90. Bibliography of criticism
      [annotated].

2390 Lonsdale, Roger. "New Attributions to John Cleland." Re-
      view of English Studies, N.S. 30 (1979), 268-90. Bibliog-
      raphy of primary sources. Theory and practice of the nov-
      el.

BIOGRAPHICAL AND CRITICAL STUDIES

2391 Bradbury, Malcolm. "Fanny Hill and the Comic Novel."
      Critical Quarterly, 13 (1971), 263-75. Comedy. Conven-
      tions of the Georgian novel.

■2392 Braudy, Leo. "Fanny Hill and Materialism." Eighteenth-

Century Studies, 4 (1970), 21-40. Materialism. Social criticism in the novel.

2393   Charney, Maurice. "Two Sexual Lives, Entrepreneurial and Compulsive: Fanny Hill and My Secret Life." In his Sexual Fiction. London: Methuen, 1981, pp. 71-92. Sex. Style and language [sexual rhetoric]. Capitalism [Fanny as entrepreneur].

2394   Copeland, Edward. "Clarissa and Fanny Hill: Sisters in Distress." Studies in the Novel, 4 (1972), 343-52. Comparison of novelists. Conventions of the Georgian novel.

•2395   Epstein, William H. John Cleland: Images of a Life. New York: Columbia Univ. Press, 1974. Biography.

2396   Foxon, David. "John Cleland and the Publication of the Memoirs of a Woman of Pleasure." Book Collector, 12 (1963), 476-87. Rpt. in his Libertine Literature in England, 1660-1745. New Hyde Park, N.Y.: University Books, 1965, pp. 52-63. Book trade.

2397   Hollander, John. "The Old Last Act: Some Observations on Fanny Hill." Encounter, 21, No. 4 (1963), 69-77. Characterization. Style and language.

2398   Illo, John. "The Idyll of Unreproved Pleasures Free." Carolina Quarterly, 17, No. 2 (1965), 19-26. Style and language. Sex.

2399   Ivker, Barry. "John Cleland and the Marquis d'Argens: Eroticism and Natural Morality in Mid-Eighteenth Century English and French Fiction." Mosaic, 8, No. 2 (1975), 141-48. Eroticism. Morality.

■2400   Miller, Nancy K. "'I's' in Drag: The Sex of Recollection." Eighteenth Century: Theory and Interpretation, 22 (1981), 47-57. [Fanny Hill]. Male novelist assuming female identity.

2401   Rembar, Charles. The End of Obscenity: The Trials of "Lady Chatterly," "Tropic of Cancer," and "Fanny Hill." New York: Random House, 1968. Pornography. Censorship.

2402   Shinagel, Michael. "Memoirs of a Woman of Pleasure: Pornography and the Mid-Eighteenth Century Novel." In Studies in Change and Revolution: Aspects of English Intellectual History, 1640-1800. Ed. Paul J. Korshin. Menston, Yorkshire: Scolar Press, 1972, pp. 211-36. Pornography.

2403 Slepian, B., and L. J. Morrissey. "What Is Fanny Hill?"
      Essays in Criticism, 14 (1964), 65-75. [Review article].
      Pornography. Narrative technique. Style and language.

2404 Sossaman, Stephen. "Sex, Love, and Reason in the Novels
      of John Cleland." Massachusetts Studies in English, 6
      (1978), 93-106. Sex. Love. Reason.

2405 Stewart, Douglas J. "Pornography, Obscenity and Capital-
      ism." Antioch Review, 35 (1977), 389-98. [Fanny Hill].
      Pornography. Capitalism. Imagery [sexual relations, sex-
      ual organs].

2406 Taube, Myron. "Moll Flanders and Fanny Hill: A Compari-
      son." Ball State University Forum, 9 (1968), 76-80. Com-
      parison of novelists. Characterization.

2407 Todd, Janet. "Erotic Friendship: John Cleland's Fanny
      Hill." In her Women's Friendship in Literature. New York:
      Columbia Univ. Press, 1980, pp. 69-100. Women's friend-
      ship.

2408 Whitley, Raymond K. "The Libertine Hero and Heroine in the
      Novels of John Cleland." In Studies in Eighteenth-Century
      Culture. Vol. 9. Ed. Roseann Runte. Madison: Univ.
      of Wisconsin Press, 1979, 387-404. Libertinism. Charac-
      terization.

      SEE ALSO ITEMS 787a, 918, 951, 995, 1051.

                        FRANCIS COVENTRY
                         (1728-1759?)

PRINCIPAL FICTION

      The History of Pompey the Little, 1751

BIBLIOGRAPHIES AND SURVEYS OF CRITICISM

None.

BIOGRAPHICAL AND CRITICAL STUDIES

2409 Olshin, Toby. "Pompey the Little: A Study in Fielding's In-
      fluence." Revue des Langues Vivantes, 36 (1970), 117-24.
      Sources, analogues, and influences.

2410 Scott, William. "Francis Coventry's Pompey the Little, 1751
      and 1752." Notes and Queries, N.S. 15 (1968), 215-19.
      Eighteenth-century criticism and reviews of the novel.
      Composition of the novel.

      SEE ALSO ITEMS 751, 977.

                      RICHARD CUMBERLAND
                         (1732-1811)

PRINCIPAL FICTION

      Arundel, 1789

      Henry, 1795

      John de Lancaster, 1809

BIBLIOGRAPHIES AND SURVEYS OF CRITICISM

      See Dircks, Richard Cumberland, below, pp. 157-61.

BIOGRAPHICAL AND CRITICAL STUDIES

2411 Dircks, Richard J. Richard Cumberland. Twayne's English
      Authors Series. Boston: Twayne, 1976. Introductory
      guide. Comparison of novelists [Cumberland, Richardson,
      Fielding].

                        MARY DAVYS
                       (1674-1732)

PRINCIPAL FICTION

      The Reformed Coquet, 1724

      The Accomplished Rake, or The Modern Fine Gentleman,
      1727

BIBLIOGRAPHIES AND SURVEYS OF CRITICISM

2412 Backscheider, Paula, et al. "Mary Davys." In their An An-

notated Bibliography of Twentieth-Century Critical Studies
of Women and Literature, 1660-1800. New York: Garland,
1977, p. 138. Bibliography of criticism [annotated].

BIOGRAPHICAL AND CRITICAL STUDIES

2413 McBurney, William H. "Mrs. Mary Davys: Forerunner of
      Fielding." PMLA, 74 (1959), 348-55. Introductory guide.
      Theory and practice of the novel.

      SEE ALSO ITEM 921.

THOMAS DAY
(1748-1789)

PRINCIPAL FICTION

The History of Sandford and Merton, 1783-89

The Story of Little Jack, 1788

BIBLIOGRAPHIES AND SURVEYS OF CRITICISM

2414 Beasley, Jerry C. "Thomas Day (1748-89)." In his English
      Fiction, 1660-1800: A Guide to Information Sources. De-
      troit: Gale, 1978, pp. 91-93. Bibliography of criticism
      [annotated].

BIOGRAPHICAL AND CRITICAL STUDIES

2415 Gignilliat, George Warren, Jr. The Author of Sandford and
      Merton: A Life of Thomas Day, Esq. New York: Columbia
      Univ. Press, 1932. Biography. Children's literature.

2416 Sadleir, Michael. Thomas Day: An English Disciple of Rous-
      seau. Cambridge: Cambridge Univ. Press, 1928. Compar-
      ison of novelists [Day, Rousseau]. Sources, analogues,
      and influences. Rousseau.

2417 Scheuermann, Mona. "More Than 'A Few Passages': Henry
      Brooke's The Fool of Quality as the Source for Thomas
      Day's The History of Sandford and Merton." Durham Uni-
      versity Journal, N.S. 44, No. 2 (1983), 55-59. Comparison
      of novelists. Sources, analogues, and influences.

2418 Scott, H. W. The Exemplary Mr. Day, 1748-1789. London:
      Faber & Faber, 1935. Biography [critical].

      SEE ALSO ITEM 1075.

                        SARAH FIELDING
                         (1710-1768)

PRINCIPAL FICTION

      David Simple, 1744-53

      The Lives of Cleopatra and Octavia, 1757

      The Countess of Dellwyn, 1759

      The History of Ophelia, 1760

BIBLIOGRAPHIES AND SURVEYS OF CRITICISM

2419 Backscheider, Paula, et al. "Sarah Fielding." In their An
      Annotated Bibliography of Twentieth-Century Critical
      Studies of Women and Literature, 1660-1800. New York:
      Garland, 1977, pp. 150-51. Bibliography of criticism [anno-
      tated].

2420 Beasley, Jerry C. "Sarah Fielding (1710-68)." In his Eng-
      lish Fiction, 1660-1800: A Guide to Information Sources.
      Detroit: Gale, 1978, pp. 135-38. Bibliography of criticism
      [annotated].

BIOGRAPHICAL AND CRITICAL STUDIES

2421 Battestin, Martin C. "Henry Fielding, Sarah Fielding, and
      'the dreadful Sin of Incest.'" Novel, 13 (1979), 6-18. In-
      cest. Biography.

2422 Donaldson, Ian. "The Clockwork Novel: Three Notes on an
      Eighteenth-Century Analogy." Review of English Studies,
      N.S. 21 (1970), 14-22. [Fielding, Richardson, S. Fielding].
      "Clockwork" analogy. Symbolism. Comparison of novelists.

2423 Hunting, Robert. "Fielding's Revisions of David Simple."
      Boston University Studies in English, 3 (1957), 117-21.
      Style and language. Personal relations between authors
      [Fielding, Sarah Fielding].

SEE ALSO ITEMS 871, 921, 1004.

WILLIAM GODWIN
(1756-1836)

PRINCIPAL FICTION

   Imogen, A Pastoral Romance, 1784

   Caleb Williams, 1794

   St. Leon, 1799

   Fleetwood, 1805

   Mandeville, 1817

   Cloudesley, 1830

   Deloraine, 1833

BIBLIOGRAPHIES AND SURVEYS OF CRITICISM

2424   Marken, Jack W. "The Canon and Chronology of William God-
       win's Early Works." Modern Language Notes, 69 (1954),
       176-80. Bibliography of primary sources.

2425   Pollin, Burton R. Godwin Criticism: A Synoptic Bibliography.
       Toronto: Univ. of Toronto Press, 1967. Bibliography of
       criticism [annotated].

       SEE ALSO ITEM 67.

BIOGRAPHICAL AND CRITICAL STUDIES

2426   Allen, B. Sprague. "William Godwin as a Sentimentalist."
       PMLA, 33 (1918), 1-29. Sentimentalism.

2427   Barker, Gerard A. "Ferdinando Falkland's Fall: Grandison
       in Disarray." Papers on Language and Literature, 16
       (1980), 376-86. Comparison of novelists [Richardson, God-
       win]. Characterization.

2428   Barker, Gerard A. "Justice to Caleb Williams." Studies in
       the Novel, 6 (1974), 377-88. Characterization [novel cen-
       ters on Caleb's moral growth and maturation]. Closure
       [published ending superior].

2429 Blunden, Edmund. "G's Library Catalogue." Keats-Shelley
      Memorial Bulletin, 9 (1958), 27-29. Library of novelist.

■2430 Boulton, J. T. "William Godwin, Philosopher and Novelist."
      In his The Language of Politics in the Age of Wilkes and
      Burke. London: Routledge & Kegan Paul, 1963, pp. 207-
      49. Style and language. Burke.

2431 Brown, Ford K. The Life of William Godwin. London: Dent,
      1926. Biography.

2432 Butler, Marilyn. "Godwin, Burke and Caleb Williams." Es-
      says in Criticism, 32 (1982), 237-57. Social criticism in the
      novel. Radicalism. Politics. Burke. Hierarchy.

2433 Clifford, Gay. "Caleb Williams and Frankenstein: First-Per-
      son Narrative and 'Things as They Are.'" Genre, 10 (1977),
      601-17. Point of view and narrator.

2434 Cobb, Joann P. "Godwin's Novels and Political Justice." En-
      lightenment Essays, 4 (1973), 15-28. Philosophy of novel-
      ist. Social criticism in the novel.

2435 Cruttwell, Patrick. "On Caleb Williams." Hudson Review, 11
      (1958), 87-95. Psychology of characters.

2435a De Porte, Michael. "The Consolations of Fiction: Mystery
      in Caleb Williams." Papers on Language and Literature, 20
      (1984), 154-64. Mystery.

2436 Detre, Jean. A Most Extraordinary Pair: Mary Wollstone-
      craft and William Godwin. New York: Doubleday, 1975.
      Biography.

2437 Dumas, D. Gilbert. "Things as They Were: The Original
      Ending of Caleb Williams." Studies in English Literature, 6
      (1966), 575-97. Composition of the novel. Closure [new
      ending altered the political theme].

2438 England, Martha Winburn. "Further Discussion of Godwin's
      Imogen: Felix Culpa." Bulletin of the New York Public
      Library, 67 (1963), 115-18. Defects in the novel [failure
      of Imogen contrasted with success of Caleb Williams]. Art-
      istic development.

2439 Farouk, Marion O. "Mandeville, a Tale of the Seventeenth
      Century: Historical Novel or Psychological Study?" In
      Life and Literature of the Working Class: Essays in Honour
      of William Gallacher. Berlin: Humboldt-Universität zu Ber-
      lin, 1966, pp. 111-17. Historical novel.

2440 Flanders, Wallace A. "Godwin and Gothicism: St. Leon."

Texas Studies in Literature and Language, 8 (1967), 533–45. Gothic novel.

2441 Fleisher, David. William Godwin: A Study in Liberalism. London: Allen & Unwin, 1951. Biography. Politics. Liberalism. Philosophy of novelist.

2442 Furbank, P. N. "Godwin's Novels." Essays in Criticism, 5 (1955), 214–28. Introductory guide. Confessional novel. Politics.

■2443 Gold, Alex, Jr. "It's Only Love: The Politics of Passion in Godwin's Caleb Williams." Texas Studies in Literature and Language, 19 (1977), 135–60. Love. Characterization. Psychology of characters. Philosophy of novelist.

2443a Graham, Kenneth W. "The Gothic Unity of Godwin's Caleb Williams." Papers on Language and Literature, 20 (1984), 47–59. Unity. Psychology of characters [solipsism distorts reality].

2444 Gregory, Allene. "Revolutionary Philosophers. Section 1. William Godwin." In her The French Revolution and the English Novel. 1915; rpt. New York: Haskell House, 1966, pp. 86–119. Introductory guide.

■2445 Gross, Harvey. "The Pursuer and the Pursued: A Study of Caleb Williams." Texas Studies in Literature and Language, 1 (1959), 401–11. Self vs. society. Pursuit. Social structure. Social criticism in the novel.

2446 Grylls, Rosalie Glynn. William Godwin and His World. London: Oldhams Press, 1952. Biography. Social background.

■2447 Harvey, A. D. "The Nightmare of Caleb Williams." Essays in Criticism, 26 (1976), 236–49. Myth [of the isolated individual trapped by society]. Realism [novel not realistic]. Social criticism in the novel [generalized, not based on plausible detail]. Philosophy of novelist. Dreams.

2448 Hogle, Jerrold E. "The Texture of the Self in Godwin's Things as They Are." Boundary, 7, No. 2 (1979), 261–81. The self. Style and language. Characterization.

2449 Kelly, Gary D. "Godwin, Wollstonecraft, and Rousseau." Women & Literature, 3, No. 2 (1975), 21–26. Rousseau.

2450 Kelly, Gary D. "History and Fiction: Bethlem Gabor in Godwin's St. Leon." English Language Notes, 14 (1976), 117–20. Theory and practice of the novel. Defects in the novel [flawed attempt to meld historical figure and fictional character].

2451 Kelly, Gary D. "'Intellectual Physicks': Necessity and the
      English Jacobin Novel." Etudes Anglaises, 31 (1978), 161-
      75. [Godwin, Holcroft]. Necessity. Jacobin novel.

2452 Kelly, Gary D. "William Godwin." In his The English Jacobin
      Novel: 1780-1805. Oxford: Oxford Univ. Press, 1976,
      pp. 179-260. Jacobin novel.

2453 Kiely, Robert. "Caleb Williams: William Godwin." In his
      The Romantic Novel in England. Cambridge, Mass.: Har-
      vard Univ. Press, 1972, pp. 81-97. Romantic novel.

■2454 Kropf, Carl R. "Caleb Williams and the Attack on Romance."
      Studies in the Novel, 8 (1976), 81-87. Theory and practice
      of the novel. Romance [falsifies reality]. Education.

2455 Kuczynski, Ingrid. "Pastoral Romance and Political Justice."
      In Life and Literature of the Working Class: Essays in
      Honour of William Gallacher. Berlin: Humboldt-Universität
      zu Berlin, 1966, pp. 101-10o [Imogen]. Social criticism in
      the novel.

2456 Lessenich, Rolf P. "Godwin and Shelley: Rhetoric Versus
      Revolution." Studia Neophilologica, 47 (1975), 40-52.
      Radicalism. Social criticism in the novel.

●2457 Locke, Don. A Fantasy of Reason: The Life and Thought of
      William Godwin. London: Routledge & Kegan Paul, 1980.
      Biography. Philosophy of novelist.

2458 McCracken, David. "Godwin's Caleb Williams: A Fictional
      Rebuttal of Burke." Studies in Burke and His Time, 11
      (1970), 1442-52. Politics. Burke [as source of Falkland].

■2459 McCracken, David. "Godwin's Literary Theory: The Alliance
      Between Fiction and Political Philosophy." Philological Quar-
      terly, 49 (1970), 113-33. Theory and practice of the novel
      [novel serves to instruct, as fiction and philosophy are in-
      separable]. Novel of doctrine.

2460 McCracken, David. "Godwin's Reading in Burke." English
      Language Notes, 7 (1970), 264-70. Sources, analogues, and
      influences. Burke.

2461 Miller, Jacqueline T. "The Imperfect Tale: Articulation,
      Rhetoric, and Self in Caleb Williams." Criticism, 20 (1978),
      366-82. Style and language [Godwin's theory of language
      informs the novel]. Characterization. The self.

2462 Monro, David Hector. Godwin's Moral Philosophy: An Inter-
      pretation of William Godwin. Oxford: Oxford Univ. Press,
      1953. Philosophy of novelist. Morality.

■2463 Myers, Mitzi. "Godwin's Changing Conception of Caleb Wil-
       liams." Studies in English Literature, 12 (1972), 591-628.
       Theory and practice of the novel. Dichotomy of intention
       [vision of novel evolved during its writing]. Characteri-
       zation [Godwin's interest in characters as complex moral be-
       ings]. Morality [shapes the novel, not politics]. Closure.

2464   Ousby, Ian. "'My Servant Caleb': Godwin's Caleb Williams
       and the Political Trials of the 1790's." University of Tor-
       onto Quarterly, 44 (1974), 47-55. Rev. and incorporated
       in "Caleb Williams." In his Bloodhounds of Heaven: The
       Detective in English Fiction from Godwin to Doyle. Cam-
       bridge, Mass.: Harvard Univ. Press, 1976, pp. 12-42.
       Characterization. The spy [Godwin's dislike for detectives
       aligns him with Falkland]. The detective.

2465   Pesta, John. "Caleb Williams: A Tragedy of Wasted Love."
       Tennessee Studies in Literature, 16 (1971), 67-76. Tragedy.
       Characterization [spiritual father-son relationsip].

2466   Plamenatz, John. "The Radical Utilitarians. 2. Godwin."
       In his The English Utilitarians. Oxford: Blackwell, 1966,
       pp. 88-96. Utilitarianism. Philosophy of novelist.

●2467 Pollin, Burton R. Education and Enlightenment in the Works
       of William Godwin. New York: Las Americas Publishing
       Company, 1962. Intellectual elite. Education. Reason.
       Progress. Philosophy of novelist.

2468   Pollin, Burton R. "Primitivism in Imogen." Bulletin of the
       New York Public Library, 67 (1963), 186-90. Primitivism.

2469   Pollin, Burton R. "The Significance of Names in the Fiction
       of William Godwin." Revue des Langues Vivantes, 37
       (1971), 388-99. Names of characters.

2470   Preu, James A. "Anti-Monarchism in Swift and Godwin."
       Studies in English and American Literature, 19 (1955), 11-
       28. Politics. Comparison of novelists.

2471   Preu, James A. The Dean and the Anarchist. Tallahassee:
       Florida State Univ. Press, 1959. Incorporates his "Swift's
       Influence on Godwin's Doctrine of Anarchism," Journal of
       the History of Ideas, 15 (1954), 371-83. [Little on novels].
       Sources, analogues, and influences [Swift's influence on
       Godwin]. Comparison of novelists [Godwin, Swift]. Poli-
       tics.

2472   Primer, Irwin. "Further Discussion of Godwin's Imogen:
       Some Implications of Irony." Bulletin of the New York Pub-
       lic Library, 67 (1963), 257-60. Irony. Parody. Pastoral
       tradition.

2473 Rodway, A. E., ed. "Introduction" to his Godwin and the
      Age of Transition. London: Harrap, 1952, pp. 13-50.
      [Anthology of writings by Godwin and his contemporaries].
      Social background. Philosophy of novelist. Influence and
      imitation.

2474 Roemer, Donald. "The Achievement of Godwin's Caleb Wil-
      liams: The Proto-Byronic Squire Falkland." Criticism, 18
      (1976), 43-56. Characterization [anticipates Byronic hero].
      Innovation.

2475 Rosen, Frederick. "Godwin and Holcroft." English Language
      Notes, 5 (1968), 183-86. Personal relations between authors
      [breaking off of long friendship].

2476 Rothstein, Eric. "Allusion and Analogy in the Romance of
      Caleb Williams." University of Toronto Quaterly, 37 (1967),
      18-30. Bildungsroman. Spiritual biography and autobiogra-
      phy. Morality. Biblical allusions. Imprisonment [and al-
      lusions to the criminal Jack Sheppard].

2477 Rothstein, Eric. "Caleb Williams." In his Systems of Order
      and Inquiry in Later Eighteenth-Century Fiction. Los Ange-
      les: Univ. of California Press, 1975, pp. 208-42. Epis-
      temology. Order.

2478 Scheuermann, Mona. "From Mind to Society: Caleb Williams
      as a Psychological Novel." Dutch Quaterly Review of Anglo-
      American Letters, 7 (1977), 115-27. Psychology of charac-
      ters.

2479 Scrivener, Michael H. "Godwin's Philosophy: A Revaluation."
      Journal of the History of Ideas, 39 (1978), 615-26. Philos-
      ophy of novelist. Progress.

2480 Sherburn, George. "Godwin's Later Novels." Studies in Ro-
      manticism, 1 (1962), 65-82. Artistic development. Charac-
      terization. Plot, structure, and design. Misanthropy.

2481 Smith, Elton Edward, and Esther Greenwell Smith. William
      Godwin. Twayne's English Authors Series. New York:
      Twayne, 1965. Introductory guide.

2482 Stallbaumer, Virgil R. "Holcroft's Influence on Political Jus-
      tice." Modern Language Quarterly, 14 (1953), 21-30.
      Sources, analogues, and influences. Holcroft.

2483 Stamper, Rexford. "Caleb Williams: The Bondage of Truth."
      Southern Quarterly, 12 (1973), 39-50. Characterization.
      Initiation. Morality. Law.

■2484 Storch, Rudolf F. "Metaphors of Private Guilt and Social Re-

bellion in Godwin's Caleb Williams." ELH: A Journal of
English Literary History, 34 (1967), 188-207. Psychology
of characters. Guilt. Rebellion.

•2485 Tysdahl, B. J. William Godwin as Novelist. London: Ath-
       lone Press, 1981. Theory and practice of the novel [ex-
       plores "his relationsip to his most important literary mod-
       els"].

■2486 Uphaus, Robert W. "Caleb Williams: Godwin's Epoch of
       Mind." Studies in the Novel, 9 (1977), 279-96. Rev. and
       rpt. as "Moral and Tendency in Caleb Williams." In his
       The Impossible Observer: Reason and the Reader in 18th-
       Century Prose. Lexington: Univ. Press of Kentucky,
       1979, pp. 123-36. Author-reader relationship [Falkland's
       trunk as a "reading paradigm of the novel's psychological
       appeal"]. Psychology of characters.

2487   Walton, James. "'Mad Feary Father': Caleb Williams and the
       Novel Form." Salzburg Studies in English Literature.
       Salzburg: Institut für Englische Sprache und Literatur,
       Universität Salzburg, 1975, pp. 1-61. Characterization.
       Social structure.

2488   Woodcock, George. "Things as They Might Be: Things as
       They Are: Notes on the Novels of William Godwin." Dal-
       housie Review, 54 (1974-75), 685-97. Introductory guide.
       Self vs. society.

2489   Woodcock, George. William Godwin: A Biographical Study.
       London: Porcupine Press, 1946. Biography. Education.
       Philosophy of novelist.

       SEE ALSO ITEMS 538, 797, 850, 1010, 1065, 1070, 1095.

                         OLIVER GOLDSMITH
                          (1730?-1774)

PRINCIPAL FICTION

       The Vicar of Wakefield, 1766

BIBLIOGRAPHIES AND SURVEYS OF CRITICISM

2490   Quintana, Ricardo. "The Vicar of Wakefield: The Problem of
       Critical Approach." Modern Philology, 71 (1973-74), 59-65.
       Survey of criticism.

2491 Scott, Temple. Oliver Goldsmith Bibliographically and Bio-
      graphically Considered. London: Maggs, 1928. Bibliogra-
      phy of primary sources.

2492 Williams, Iolo A. "Oliver Goldsmith." In Seven Eighteenth-
      Century Bibliographies. 1924; rpt. New York: Burt
      Franklin, 1968. Bibliography of primary sources.

2493 Woods, Samuel H., Jr. "The Goldsmith 'Problem.'" Studies
      in Burke and His Time, 19 (1978), 47-60. Survey of criti-
      cism.

2494 Woods, Samuel H., Jr. "The Vicar of Wakefield and Recent
      Goldsmith Scholarship." Eighteenth-Century Studies, 9
      (1976-77), 429-43. Survey of criticism.

BIOGRAPHICAL AND CRITICAL STUDIES

■2495 Adelstein, Michael E. "Duality of Theme in The Vicar of
       Wakefield." College English, 22 (1961), 315-21. Prudence
       [lack of in Primrose family]. Fortitude. Plot, structure,
       and design [prudence as key theme early in the novel
       yields to fortitude as dominant theme later].

2496 Amory, Hugh. "Oliver Goldsmith." In his Poets and Men of
      Letters. Vol. VII of Sales Catalogues of Libraries of Emi-
      nent Persons. London: Mansell, with Sotheby Publica-
      tions, 1973, pp. 227-46. Library of novelist.

2497 Bäckman, Sven. This Singular Tale: A Study of "The Vicar
      of Wakefield" and Its Literary Background. Lund Studies
      in English, 40. Ed. Claes Schaar and Jan Svartvik. Lund:
      C. W. K. Gleerup, 1971. Plot, structure, and design.
      Setting. Characterization. Narrative technique. Dramatic
      conventions in the novel. Sources, analogues, and influ-
      ences.

2498 Bataille, Robert A. "City and Country in The Vicar of Wake-
      field." Eighteenth-Century Life, 3 (1977), 112-14. Coun-
      try vs. city [not an oversimple juxtaposition of the innocent
      and the wicked].

■2499 Battestin, Martin C. "Goldsmith: The Comedy of Job." In
       his The Providence of Wit: Aspects of Form in Augustan
       Literature and the Arts. Oxford: Clarendon Press, 1974,
       pp. 193-214. Biblical allusions. Christianity. Providence.

■2500 Bell, Howard J. "The Deserted Village and Goldsmith's Social
       Doctrines." PMLA, 59 (1944), 747-72. Social criticism in
       the novel [of luxury, plutocracy, and commerce]. Luxury.

2501 Bligh, John. "Neglected Aspects of The Vicar of Wakefield."
      Dalhousie Review, 56 (1976), 103-11. Social criticism in the
      novel. Politics. Morality.

2502 Brissenden, R. F. "The Vicar of Wakefield, The Man of Feel-
      ing and Werther: Comic, Pathetic and Tragic Versions of
      the Distressed and Virtuous Hero." In his Virtue in Dis-
      tress: Studies in the Novel of Sentiment from Richardson
      to Sade. New York: Barnes & Noble, 1974, pp. 243-67,
      esp. 243-50. Sentimental novel [its conventions]. "Man
      of Feeling." Comparison of novelists [Goldsmith, Mac-
      kenzie].

2503 Cole, Richard C. "Oliver Goldsmith's Reputation in Ireland,
      1762-74." Modern Philology, 68 (1970), 65-70. Influence
      and reputation abroad. Eighteenth-century criticism and
      reviews of the novel. Ireland.

■2504 Dahl, Curtis. "Patterns of Disguise in The Vicar of Wake-
      field." ELH: A Journal of English Literary History, 25
      (1958), 90-104. Disguise. Appearance vs. reality. Plot,
      structure, and design. Unity.

■2505 Durant, David. "The Vicar of Wakefield and the Sentimental
      Novel." Studies in English Literature, 17 (1977), 477-91.
      Sentimental novel [through Primrose's sentimentalism, Gold-
      smith criticizes the sentimental novel]. Characterization.
      Philosophy of novelist [impracticality of a life of principle
      in a fallen world].

2506 Dussinger, John A. "Oliver Goldsmith: Citizen of the
      World." Studies on Voltaire and the Eighteenth Century,
      55 (1967), 445-61. Intellectual background. Philosophy of
      novelist.

2507 Dussinger, John A. "The Vicar of Wakefield: A 'Sickly Sen-
      sibility' and the Rewards of Fortune." In his The Dis-
      course of the Mind in Eighteenth-Century Fiction. The
      Hague: Mouton, 1974, pp. 148-72. Point of view and nar-
      rator. Epistemology. Psychology of characters. Sensibil-
      ity. Defects in the novel.

■2508 Emslie, Macdonald. Goldsmith: "The Vicar of Wakefield."
      Great Neck, N.Y.: Barron's Educational Series, 1963.
      Introductory guide [excellent account of main issues].
      Characterization. Sentimental novel. Philosophy of novel-
      ist. Charity. Wealth. Plot, structure, and design.
      Style and language.

■2509 Ferguson, Oliver W. "Dr. Primrose and Goldsmith's Clerical

Ideal." Philological Quarterly, 54 (1975), 323-32. The
clergy. The church. Characterization.

2510 Ferguson, Oliver W. "Goldsmith." South Atlantic Quarterly,
66 (1967), 465-72. Introductory guide.

2511 Friedman, Arthur. "The Time of Composition of Goldsmith's
Edwin and Angelina." In Restoration and Eighteenth-
Century Literature. Ed. Carroll Camden. Chicago: Univ.
of Chicago Press, 1963, pp. 155-59. Composition of the
novel [before 1762]. Poems in the novel.

2512 Gallaway, W. F., Jr. "The Sentimentalism of Goldsmith."
PMLA, 48 (1933), 1167-81. Sentimentalism. Satire [on
sentimentalism].

2513 Golden, Morris. "The Family-Wanderer Theme in Goldsmith."
ELH: A Journal of English Literary History, 25 (1958),
181-93. The family. The wanderer. Autobiographical elements in the novel [yearning for family, despair at its dis-
appearance].

2514 Golden, Morris. "Goldsmith, The Vicar of Wakefield, and the
Periodicals." Journal of English and Germanic Philology,
76 (1977), 525-36. The writer in society. Sources, analogues, and influences.

2515 Golden, Morris. "Goldsmith's Reputation in His Day." Papers
on Language and Literature, 16 (1980), 213-38. Eighteenth-
century criticism and reviews of the novel. Survey of
criticism. Achievement and reputation.

2516 Golden, Morris. "Image Frequency and the Split in The Vicar
of Wakefield." Bulletin of the New York Public Library, 63
(1959), 473-77. Composition of the novel. Imagery [96
similes and metaphors].

2517 Golden, Morris. "Sidney Bidulph and The Vicar of Wakefield." Modern Language Studies, 9, No. 2 (1979), 33-35.
Sources, analogues, and influences.

2518 Golden, Morris. "The Time of Writing of The Vicar of Wakefield." Bulletin of the New York Public Library, 65 (1961),
442-50. Composition of the novel [1759-63]. Sources,
analogues, and influences.

2519 Green, Mary Elizabeth. "Oliver Goldsmith and the Wisdom of
the World." Studies in Philology, 77 (1980), 202-12.
Philosophy of novelist. Morality.

2520 Grudis, Paul J. "The Narrator and the Vicar of Wakefield."
       Essays in Literature (Univ. of Denver), 1, No. 1 (1973),
       51-66. Point of view and narrator [Primrose as foolish
       character but wise narrator].

2521 Harp, Richard L. "New Perspectives for Goldsmith's Biogra-
       phy." The Eighteenth Century: Theory and Interpreta-
       tion, 21 (1980), 162-75. Biography.

2522 Helgerson, Richard. "The Two Worlds of Oliver Goldsmith."
       Studies in English Literature, 13 (1973), 516-34. Country
       vs. city. Philosophy of novelist.

2523 Hilliard, Raymond F. "The Redemption of Fatherhood in The
       Vicar of Wakefield." Studies in English Literature, 23
       (1983), 465-80. Characterization [Primrose as delinquent
       husband and father]. Fatherhood. Biblical allusions.

■2524 Hopkins, Robert H. "Fortune and the Heavenly Bank: The
       Vicar of Wakefield as Sustained Satire." In his The True
       Genius of Oliver Goldsmith. Baltimore: The Johns Hopkins
       Univ. Press, 1969, pp. 166-230. Satire. Characterization.

2525 Hopkins, Robert H. "Matrimony in The Vicar of Wakefield
       and the Marriage Act of 1753." Studies in Philology, 74
       (1977), 322-39. Marriage. Marriage law.

2526 Hopkins, Robert H. "Social Stratification and the Obsequious
       Curve: Goldsmith and Rowlandson." In Studies in the
       Eighteenth Century III. Ed. R. F. Brissenden and J. C.
       Eade. Toronto: Univ. of Toronto Press, 1976, pp. 55-71.
       Social structure. Rowlandson. Satire. Obsequiousness.
       Illustration.

2527 Hunting, Robert. "The Poems in The Vicar of Wakefield."
       Criticism, 15 (1973), 234-41. Satire [on Primrose]. Poems
       in the novel. Digressions and interpolated stories.

2528 Jaarsma, Richard J. "Satiric Intent in The Vicar of Wake-
       field." Studies in Short Fiction, 5 (1968), 331-41. Satire
       [on ideal of rural innocence, the sentimental novel, belief
       in innate goodness of man].

2529 Jeffares, A. Norman. "Goldsmith: The Good Natured Man."
       Hermathena, 119 (1975), 5-19. Personality of novelist.

2530 Jefferson, D. W. "Observations on The Vicar of Wakefield."
       Cambridge Journal, 3 (1950), 621-28. Satire. Narrative
       technique. Style and language.

2531 Kent, Elizabeth Eaton. Goldsmith and His Booksellers. Cor-

nell Studies in English, 20.   Ithaca, N.Y.:   Cornell Univ.
Press, 1933.   Book trade.

2532   Kirk, Clara.   Oliver Goldsmith.   Twayne's English Authors
Series.   New York: Twayne, 1967.   Introductory guide.

2533   Lehmann, James H.   "The Vicar of Wakefield: Goldsmith's
Sublime, Oriental Job."   ELH: A Journal of English Literary History, 46 (1979), 97-121.   Biblical allusions.   Humanism.   Orientalism.

2534   MacLennan, Munro.   The Secret of Oliver Goldsmith.   New
York: Vantage Press, 1975.   Biography [color-blindness].
Imagery [colors].

2535   May, James E.   "Goldsmith's Theory of Composition: 'my
heart dictates the whole.'"   Papers on Language and Literature, 15 (1979), 418-21.   Composition of the novel.

2536   McAdam, E. L., Jr.   "Goldsmith, The Good-Natured Man."
In The Age of Johnson: Essays Presented to Chauncey
Brewster Tinker.   Ed. Frederick W. Hilles and Wilmarth S.
Lewis.   New Haven, Conn.:   Yale Univ. Press, 1949, pp.
41-47.   [Little on The Vicar of Wakefield].   Biography.
Benevolence.

2537   McCracken, David.   "Goldsmith and the 'Natural Revolution of
Things.'"   Journal of English and Germanic Philology, 78
(1979), 33-48.   Historiography.   Philosophy of novelist.

2538   McDonald, Daniel.   "The Vicar of Wakefield: A Paradox."
College Language Association Journal, 10 (1966), 23-33.
Defects in the novel [Primrose's poor judgment undermines
his status as moral spokesman].   Ambiguity.

2539   Murray, Christopher.   "The Operation of Generosity and Justice in the Writings of Oliver Goldsmith."   Canadian Journal
of Irish Studies, 6, No. 1 (1980), 23-35.   Generosity.
Justice.   Plot, structure, and design.

2540   Nathan, Sabine.   "The Place of The Vicar of Wakefield Within
the Realistic Tradition of the Eighteenth Century."   Wissen-
schaftliche Zeitschrift der Universität Rostock, 23 (1974),
413-20.   Social criticism in the novel.   Pastoral novel [not
a pastoral novel].   Realism.

2541   Paulson, Ronald.   "Dr. Primrose: The Ironic Hero."   In his
Satire and the Novel in Eighteenth-Century England.   New
Haven, Conn.:   Yale Univ. Press, 1967, pp. 269-75.   Novel
of manners.   Irony.

2542 Privateer, Paul C. "Goldsmith's Vicar of Wakefield: The Re-
      union of the Alienated Artist." Enlightenment Essays, 6
      (1975), 27-36. Characterization. Symbolism [art-society
      relationship figured in Thornhill]. The wanderer. Com-
      parison of novelists [Goldsmith, Fielding].

■2543 Quintana, Ricardo. "Comedy, Idyllic and Romantic: The
      Vicar of Wakefield." In his Oliver Goldsmith: A Georgian
      Study. New York: Macmillan, 1967, pp. 99-115. Comedy.
      Plot, structure, and design.

2544 Quintana, Ricardo. "Oliver Goldsmith, Ironist to the Geor-
      gians." Eighteenth-Century Studies in Honor of Donald F.
      Hyde. Ed. W. F. Bond. New York: Grolier, 1970, pp.
      297-310. Irony.

2545 Reynolds, W. Vaughan. "Goldsmith's Critical Outlook." Re-
      view of English Studies, O.S. 14 (1938), 155-72. Theory
      and practice of the novel. Didacticism.

2546 Rothstein, Eric, and Howard Weinbrot. "The Vicar of Wake-
      field, Mr. Wilmot, and the 'Whistonean Controversy.'"
      Philological Quarterly, 55 (1976), 225-40. The clergy.
      Marriage. Composition of the novel.

2547 Rousseau, George S., ed. Goldsmith: The Critical Heritage.
      Critical Heritage Series. London: Routledge & Kegan Paul,
      1974. Eighteenth-century criticism and reviews of the nov-
      el.

2548 Seitz, Robert W. "The Irish Background of Goldsmith's Social
      and Political Thought." PMLA, 52 (1937), 405-11. Ireland.
      Politics. Social criticism in the novel.

2549 Sells, Arthur L. Oliver Goldsmith: His Life and Works. New
      York: Barnes & Noble, 1974, esp. pp. 251-82. Biography.
      Introductory guide.

2550 Sherwin, Oscar. Goldy: The Life and Times of Oliver Gold-
      smith. New York: Twayne, 1961. Biography.

2551 Sutherland, W. O. S., Jr. "Satiric Ambiguity: The Vicar
      of Wakefield and the Kindly Satirist." In his The Art of
      the Satirist: Essays on the Satire of Augustan England.
      Austin: Univ. of Texas Press, 1965, pp. 83-91. Satire.
      Ambiguity.

2552 Wardle, Ralph M. Oliver Goldsmith. 1957; rpt. Hamden,
      Conn.: Archon, 1969. Biography.

■2553 Winchcombe, George. Oliver Goldsmith and the Moonrakers.
      London: Thab, 1972. Sources, analogues, and influences.

SEE ALSO ITEMS 716, 751, 761, 788, 808, 825, 883, 884, 1004, 1005, 1040, 1052, 1065.

RICHARD GRAVES
(1715-1804)

PRINCIPAL FICTION

The Spiritual Quoxite, 1773

Columella, 1779

BIBLIOGRAPHIES AND SURVEYS OF CRITICISM

2554 Beasley, Jerry C. "Richard Graves (1715-1804)." In his
      English Fiction, 1660-1800: A Guide to Information Sources.
      Detroit: Gale, 1978, pp. 153-55. Bibliography of criticism
      [annotated].

BIOGRAPHICAL AND CRITICAL STUDIES

2555 Ellis, Havelock. "Richard Graves and The Spiritual Quixote."
      Nineteenth Century, 77 (1915), 848-60. Methodism. Come-
      dy. Quixotic novel.

2556 Hill, Charles Jarvis. "The Literary Career of Richard
      Graves." Smith College Studies in Modern Languages, 16,
      Nos. 1-3 (1934-35), 1-148. Biography. Artistic develop-
      ment. Methodism. Quixotic novel. Journey.

2557 Hill, Charles Jarvis. "Shenstone and Richard Graves's Colu-
      mella." PMLA, 49 (1934), 566-76. Sources, analogues,
      and influences [originals of characters]. William Shenstone
      [the original of Columella].

2558 Lyons, N. J. "The Spiritual Quixote: A New Key to the
      Characters in Graves's Novel." Notes and Queries, N.S.
      18 (1971), 63-67. Sources, analogues, and influences
      [originals of characters].

2559 Rymer, Michael. "Satiric Technique in The Spiritual Quixote."
      Durham University Journal, 34 (1972), 54-64. For a re-
      sponse, see N. J. Lyons, "Satiric Technique in The Spirit-
      ual Quixote: Some Comments," ibid., 35 (1975), 266-77.
      Methodism [Graves's attitude towards debated]. Satire.

SEE ALSO ITEM 751.

JOHN HAWKESWORTH
(1715-1773)

PRINCIPAL FICTION

Almoran and Hamet, 1761

BIBLIOGRAPHIES AND SURVEYS OF CRITICISM

None.

BIOGRAPHICAL AND CRITICAL STUDIES

2559a Abbott, John Lawrence. John Hawkesworth: Eighteenth-
        Century Man of Letters. Madison: Univ. of Wisconsin
        Press, 1982. Biography. Oriental novel.

MARY HAYS
(1760-1843)

PRINCIPAL FICTION

Memoirs of Emma Courtney, 1796

The Victim of Prejudice, 1799

BIBLIOGRAPHIES AND SURVEYS OF CRITICISM

2560 Backscheider, Paula, et al. "Mary Hays." In their An An-
        notated Bibliography of Twentieth-Century Critical Studies
        of Women and Literature, 1660-1800. New York: Garland,
        1977, p. 158. Bibliography of criticism [annotated].

BIOGRAPHICAL AND CRITICAL STUDIES

2561 Adams, M. Ray. "Mary Hays, Disciple of William Godwin."
        In his Studies in the Literary Backgrounds of English Radi-
        calism. 1947; rpt. New York: Greenwood Press, 1968,
        pp. 83-103. Introductory guide. Radicalism.

2562 Wedd, Annie F. The Love-Letters of Mary Hays. London:
        Methuen, 1925. Biography. Letter-writing.

SEE ALSO ITEMS 742, 920.

<u>ELIZA HAYWOOD</u>
(1693-1756)

PRINCIPAL FICTION

<u>Love in Excess</u>, 1719

<u>Lasselia</u>, 1723

<u>Idalia</u>, 1723

<u>Memoirs of a Certain Island Adjacent to Utopia</u>, 1725

<u>The Mercenary Lover</u>, 1726

<u>The Court of Caramania</u>, 1727

<u>Philidore and Placentia</u>, 1727

<u>Anti-Pamela</u>, 1741

<u>The Fortunate Foundlings</u>, 1744

<u>The History of Miss Betsy Thoughtless</u>, 1751

<u>The History of Jenny and Jemmy Jessamy</u>, 1753

BIBLIOGRAPHIES AND SURVEYS OF CRITICISM

2563 Backscheider, Paula, et al. "Eliza Haywood." In their <u>An
      Annotated Bibliography of Twentieth-Century Critical
      Studies of Women and Literature, 1660-1800</u>. New York:
      Garland, 1977, pp. 159-61. Bibliography of criticism [an-
      notated].

2564 Beasley, Jerry C. "Eliza Haywood (1693-1756)." In his <u>Eng-
      lish Fiction, 1660-1800: A Guide to Information Sources</u>.
      Detroit: Gale, 1978, pp. 157-60. Bibliography of criticism
      [annotated].

BIOGRAPHICAL AND CRITICAL STUDIES

2565 Erickson, James P. "<u>Evelina</u> and <u>Betsy Thoughtless</u>." <u>Texas
      Studies in Literature and Language</u>, 6 (1964), 96-103.
      Comparison of novelists [Burney, Haywood].

2566 Schofield, Mary Anne. "The Awakening of the Eighteenth-
      Century Heroine: Eliza Haywood's New Women." <u>CEA
      Critic</u>, 43 (1981), 9-13. Women.

2567 Schofield, Mary Anne. Quiet Rebellion: The Fictional Hero-
      ines of Eliza Fowler Haywood. Washington, D.C.: Univ.
      Press of America, 1982. Characterization. Women.

2568 Whicher, George Frisbie. The Life and Romances of Mrs.
      Eliza Haywood. New York: Columbia Univ. Press, 1915.
      Biography. Introductory guide.

      SEE ALSO ITEMS 752, 822, 871, 893, 920, 921, 995,
      1087.

                        THOMAS HOLCROFT
                          (1745-1809)

PRINCIPAL FICTION

      Alwyn, 1780

      Anna St. Ives, 1792

      Hugh Trevor, 1794-97

      Bryan Perdue, 1805

BIBLIOGRAPHIES AND SURVEYS OF CRITICISM

2569 Beasley, Jerry C. "Thomas Holcroft (1745-1809)." In his
      English Fiction, 1660-1800: A Guide to Information Sources.
      Detroit: Gale, 1978, pp. 161-64. Bibliography of criticism
      [annotated].

2570 Colby, Elbridge. A Bibliography of Thomas Holcroft. New
      York: New York Public Library, 1922. Bibliography of
      primary sources.

BIOGRAPHICAL AND CRITICAL STUDIES

•2571 Baine, Rodney M. Thomas Holcroft and the Revolutionary
      Novel. Athens: Univ. of Georgia Press, 1965. Jacobin
      novel. Philosophy of novelist. Social criticism in the nov-
      el.

2572 Gregory, Allene. "A Representative Revolutionist: Thomas
      Holcroft." In The French Revolution and the English Novel.
      1915; rpt. New York: Haskell House, 1966, pp. 49-85.
      Jacobin novel. French Revolution.

2573 Kelly, Gary D. "'Intellectual Physicks': Necessity and the
      English Jacobin Novel." Etudes Anglaises, 31 (1978), 161-
      75. [Godwin, Holcroft]. Necessity. Jacobin novel.

2574 Kelly, Gary D. "Thomas Holcroft." In his The English
      Jacobin Novel: 1780-1805. Oxford: Oxford Univ. Press,
      1976, pp. 114-78. Jacobin novel. Politics.

2575 Rosen, Frederick. "Godwin and Holcroft." English Language
      Notes, 5 (1968), 183-86. Personal relations between au-
      thors [breaking off of long friendship].

2576 Stallbaumer, Virgil R. "Holcroft's Influence on Political Jus-
      tice." Modern Language Quarterly, 14 (1953), 21-30.
      Politics. Philosophy of novelist. Godwin. Biography.

2577 Stallbaumer, Virgil R. "Thomas Holcroft as a Novelist."
      ELH: A Journal of English Literary History, 15 (1948),
      194-218. Theory and practice of the novel. Innovation.
      Artistic development.

2578 Teissedou, Janie. "Thomas Holcroft: A Radical Novelist."
      In Politics in Literature in the Nineteenth Century. Lille,
      France: Univ. de Lille, 1974, pp. 11-30. Politics. Jacobin
      novel. Radicalism [condemnation of government, religious
      intolerance, corrupt aristocracy, private property]. Social
      criticism in the novel.

2579 Ter-Abramova, V. G. "Thomas Holcroft and the English
      Democratic Novel at the End of the 18th Century." Zeit-
      schrift für Anglistik und Amerikanistik, 26 (1978), 293-304.
      Democracy. Godwin [influence of his ideas]. Social criti-
      cism in the novel.

      SEE ALSO ITEM 1065.

                        ELIZABETH INCHBALD
                          (1753-1821)

PRINCIPAL FICTION

      A Simple Story, 1791

      Nature and Art, 1796

BIBLIOGRAPHIES AND SURVEYS OF CRITICISM

2580 Backscheider, Paula, et al. "Elizabeth Inchbald." In their
      An Annotated Bibliography of Twentieth-Century Critical
      Studies of Women and Literature, 1660-1800. New York:
      Garland, 1977, pp. 165-66. Bibliography of criticism [an-
      notated].

2581 Joughin, G. Louis. "An Inchbald Bibliography." University
      of Texas Studies in English, 14 (1934), 59-74. Bibliogra-
      phy of primary sources.

BIOGRAPHICAL AND CRITICAL STUDIES

2582 Gregory, Allene. "Some Typical Lady Novelists of the Revo-
      lution: Mrs. Elizabeth Inchbald." In her The French
      Revolution and the English Novel. 1915; rpt. New York:
      Haskell House, 1966, pp. 191-202. Jacobin novel. French
      Revolution. Women novelists.

2583 Kelly, Gary D. "Elizabeth Inchbald." In his The English
      Jacobin Novel: 1780-1805. Oxford: Oxford Univ. Press,
      1976, pp. 64-113. Jacobin novel. Politics.

2584 Littlewood, S. R. Elizabeth Inchbald and Her Circle. Lon-
      don: Daniel O'Connor, 1921. Biography.

2585 Mckee, William. Elizabeth Inchbald, Novelist. Washington,
      D.C.: Catholic University, 1935. Plot, structure, and de-
      sign. Characterization.

2586 Patterson, Emily H. "Elizabeth Inchbald's Treatment of the
      Family and the Pilgrimage in A Simple Story." Etudes Ang-
      laises, 29 (1976), 196-98. Plot, structure, and design.
      Family. Journey.

2587 Rogers, Katharine M. "Inhibitions on Eighteenth-Century
      Women Novelists: Elizabeth Inchbald and Charlotte Smith."
      Eighteenth-Century Studies, 11 (1977), 63-78. Women nov-
      elists. The writer in society. Characterization [of women
      limited by notions of propriety]. Propriety.

2588 Stebbins, Lucy Poate. "My Lady Restless: Elizabeth Simp-
      son Inchbald, 1753-1821." In her London Ladies: True
      Tales of the Eighteenth Century. New York: Columbia
      Univ. Press, 1952, pp. 29-58. Biography.

SEE ALSO ITEMS 752, 920.

CHARLES JOHNSTONE
(1719-1800?)

PRINCIPAL FICTION

Chrysal, 1760-65

BIBLIOGRAPHIES AND SURVEYS OF CRITICISM

None.

BIOGRAPHICAL AND CRITICAL STUDIES

2589 Bartz, F. K. "A New Edition and New Identifications: Johnstone's Chrysal." Notes and Queries, N.S. 27 (1980), 46-
47. Characterization [sources of characters].

SEE ALSO ITEM 977.

SOPHIA LEE
(1750-1824)

PRINCIPAL FICTION

The Recess, or A Tale of Other Times, 1785

BIBLIOGRAPHIES AND SURVEYS OF CRITICISM

None.

BIOGRAPHICAL AND CRITICAL STUDIES

2590 Roberts, Bette B. "Sophia Lee's The Recess (1785): The
Ambivalence of Female Gothicism." Massachusetts Studies
in English, 6 (1978), 68-82. Psychology of characters.
Gothic novel. Women.

SEE ALSO ITEMS 822, 835, 1010.

CHARLOTTE RAMSAY LENNOX
(1720?-1804)

PRINCIPAL FICTION

The Life of Harriot Stuart, 1750

The Female Quixote, 1752

Henrietta, 1758

Sophia, 1760-61

Euphemia, 1790

BIBLIOGRAPHIES AND SURVEYS OF CRITICISM

2591 Backscheider, Paula, et al. "Charlotte Lennox." In their
      An Annotated Bibliography of Twentieth-Century Critical
      Studies of Women and Literature, 1660-1800. New York:
      Garland, 1977, pp. 173-75. Bibliography of criticism [an-
      notated].

2592 Beasley, Jerry C. "Charlotte Ramsay Lennox (1720-1804)."
      In his English Fiction, 1660-1800: A Guide to Information
      Sources. Detroit: Gale, 1978, pp. 177-80. Bibliography
      of criticism [annotated]. Bibliography of primary sources.

BIOGRAPHICAL AND CRITICAL STUDIES

2593 Isles, Duncan. "Johnson and Charlotte Lennox." New Ram-
      bler, Series C, 3 (1967), 34-48. Personal relations between
      authors.

2594 Isles, Duncan. "Johnson, Richardson, and The Female Qui-
      xote." An appendix to The Female Quixote, or the Adven-
      tures of Arabella. Ed. Margaret Dalziel. Oxford English
      Novels. London: Oxford Univ. Press, 1970, pp. 418-27.
      Composition of the novel. Personal relations between novel-
      ists.

2595 Kauvar, Elaine M. "Jane Austen and The Female Quixote."
      Studies in the Novel, 2 (1970), 211-21. Comparison of
      novelists. Initiation.

2596 Maynadier, Gustavus Howard. The First American Novelist?
      Cambridge, Mass.: Harvard Univ. Press, 1940. Biography.

2597   Séjourné, Philippe. The Mystery of Charlotte Lennox: First
       Novelist of Colonial America (1727?-1804). Aix-en-Provence:
       Publications des Annales de la Faculté des Lettres, 1967.
       Biography.

2598   Small, Miriam Rossiter. Charlotte Ramsay Lennox: An Eight-
       eenth-Century Lady of Letters. 1935; rpt. Hamden,
       Conn.: Archon, 1969. Biography. Quixotic novel.

■2599 Warren, Leland E. "Of the Conversation of Women: The
       Female Quixote and the Dream of Perfection." In Studies
       in Eighteenth-Century Culture. Vol. 11. Ed. Harry C.
       Payne. Madison: Univ. of Wisconsin Press, 1982, pp.
       367-80. Characterization. Speech and dialogue. Propri-
       ety. Women.

       SEE ALSO ITEMS 751, 752, 822, 871, 920, 995, 1048,
       1062, 1087.

MATTHEW GREGORY LEWIS
(1775-1818)

PRINCIPAL FICTION

The Monk, 1796

BIBLIOGRAPHIES AND SURVEYS OF CRITICISM

2600   Beasley, Jerry C. "Matthew Gregory Lewis (1775-1818)." In
       his English Fiction, 1660-1800: A Guide to Information
       Sources. Detroit: Gale, 1978, pp. 181-84. Bibliography
       of criticism [annotated].

2601   McNutt, Dan J. "Matthew Gregory Lewis (1775-1818)." In
       his The Eighteenth-Century Gothic Novel: An Annotated
       Bibliography of Criticism and Selected Texts. New York:
       Garland, 1975, pp. 226-64. Bibliography of criticism [an-
       notated]. Bibliography of primary sources .

       SEE ALSO ITEM 67.

BIOGRAPHICAL AND CRITICAL STUDIES

2602   Anderson, Howard. "The Manuscript of M. G. Lewis's The
       Monk: Some Preliminary Notes." Papers of the Bibliograph-

ical Society of America, 62 (1968), 427-34. Composition of
the novel.

■2603 Brooks, Peter. "Virtue and Terror: The Monk." ELH: A
Journal of English Literary History, 40 (1973), 249-63.
Philosophy of novelist. Gothic novel. Horror and terror.

2604 Conger, Syndy McMillen. "An Analysis of The Monk and Its
German Sources." In her Matthew G. Lewis, Charles Robert
Maturin and the Germans: An Interpretative Study of the
Influence of German Literature on Two Gothic Novels.
Salzburg: Institut für Englische Sprache und Literatur,
1977, pp. 12-159. Sources, analogues, and influences.
Germany.

2605 Fogle, Richard H. "The Passions of Ambrosio." In The
Classic British Novel. Ed. Howard M. Harper, Jr., and
Charles Edge. Athens: Univ. of Georgia Press, 1972, pp.
36-50. Plot, structure, and design.

2606 Gose, Elliott B., Jr. "The Monk." In his Imagination In-
dulged: The Irrational in the Nineteenth-Century Novel.
Montreal: McGill-Queen's Univ. Press, 1972, pp. 27-40.
Irrationality. The romance.

2607 Grudin, Peter. "The Monk: Matilda and the Rhetoric of Deceit." Journal of Narrative Technique, 5 (1975), 136-46.
Characterization. Evil.

■2608 Howells, Coral Ann. "M. G. Lewis, The Monk." In her
Love, Mystery, and Misery: Feeling in Gothic Fiction.
London: Athlone Press, 1978, pp. 62-79. Innovation.
Sensationalism. Sex. Irrationality. Gothic novel.

2609 Irwin, Joseph James. M. G. "Monk" Lewis. Twayne's English Authors Series. Boston: Twayne, 1976. Introductory
guide.

2610 Kiely, Robert. "The Monk." In his The Romantic Novel in
England. Cambridge, Mass.: Harvard Univ. Press, 1972,
pp. 98-117. Characterization. Romantic novel.

2611 Lyndenberg, Robin. "Ghostly Rhetoric: Ambivalence in
M. G. Lewis's The Monk." Ariel: A Review of International
English Literature, 10, No. 2 (1979), 65-79. Ambivalence.
Author-reader relationship. Dichotomy of intention.

●2612 Parreaux, André. The Publication of "The Monk": A Literary Event, 1796-1798. Paris: Didier, 1960. Eighteenth-
century criticism and reviews of the novel. The writer in
society. Social background. Influence and imitation.

•2613 Peck, Louis F. A Life of Matthew G. Lewis. Cambridge,
       Mass.: Harvard Univ. Press, 1961. Biography.

2614   Praz, Mario. "Matthew Gregory Lewis's 'Gothic Novel': The
       Monk." In Le romantisme anglo-américain: Mélanges offerts
       à Louis Bonnerot. Paris: Didier, 1971. Achievement and
       reputation.

2615   Romero, Christiane Zehl. "M. G. Lewis's The Monk and E. T.
       A. Hoffmann's Die Elixiere des Teufels: Two Versions of
       the Gothic." Neophilologus, 63 (1979), 574-82. Gothic
       novel.

2616   Taylor, Archer. "The Three Sins of the Hermit." Modern
       Philology, 20 (1922), 61-94. Sources, analogues, and in-
       fluences.

2617   Varma, Devendra P. In his The Gothic Flame. 1957; rpt.
       New York: Russell & Russell, 1966, pp. 139-54 and passim.
       Gothic novel. Horror and terror.

       SEE ALSO ITEMS 538, 750, 793, 850, 868, 910, 913, 925,
       988, 1001, 1010, 1035, 1065, 1070.

                        HENRY MACKENZIE
                         (1745-1831)

PRINCIPAL FICTION

       The Man of Feeling, 1771

       The Man of the World, 1773

       Julia de Roubigné, 1777

BIBLIOGRAPHIES AND SURVEYS OF CRITICISM

2618   Beasley, Jerry C. "Henry Mackenzie (1745-1831)." In his
       English Fiction, 1660-1800: A Guide to Information Sources.
       Detroit: Gale, 1978, pp. 185-88. Bibliography of criticism
       [annotated].

BIOGRAPHICAL AND CRITICAL STUDIES

2619   Barker, Gerard A. Henry Mackenzie. Twayne's English Au-
       thors Series. Boston: Twayne, 1975. Introductory guide.
       Sentimentalism. "Man of Feeling." Sensibility.

2620 Barker, Gerard A. "The Two Mrs. Selwyns: Evelina and
      The Man of the World." Papers on Language and Litera-
      ture, 13 (1977), 80-84. Influence and imitation.

■2621 Brissenden, R. F. "The Vicar of Wakefield, The Man of Feel-
      ing and Werther: Comic, Pathetic and Tragic Versions of
      the Distressed and Virtuous Hero." In his Virtue in Dis-
      tress: Studies in the Novel of Sentiment from Richardson
      to Sade. New York: Barnes & Noble, 1974, pp. 243-67,
      esp. 250-58. Sentimental novel [its conventions]. "Man of
      Feeling." Comparison of novelists [Goldsmith, Mackenzie].

2622 Gilman, Sander L. "Seeing the Insane: Mackenzie, Kleist,
      William James." Modern Language Notes, 93 (1978), 871-87,
      esp. 872-74. Insanity. Bedlam. Hogarth.

2623 Jenkins, Ralph E. "The Art of the Theorist: Rhetorical
      Structure in The Man of Feeling." Studies in Scottish Lit-
      erature, 9 (1971), 3-15. Plot, structure, and design.
      Contrast as technique. Didacticism.

2624 Kramer, Dale. "The Structural Unity of The Man of Feeling."
      Studies in Short Fiction, 1 (1964), 191-99. Unity. Plot,
      structure, and design.

2625 Platzner, Robert L. "Mackenzie's Martyr: The Man of Feel-
      ing as Saintly Fool." Novel, 10 (1976), 59-64. "Man of
      Feeling." Sympathy [for the wretched that makes Harley
      more than merely benevolent]. Love. Social criticism in
      the novel. Contemptus mundi [to find himself Harley must
      lose the world].

2626 Ramsey, Roger. "The Man of Feeling's Best Friend." Studies
      in Scottish Literature, 14 (1979), 252-56. Imagery [dogs].

■2627 Rymer, Michael. "Henry Mackenzie's The Man of Feeling."
      Durham University Journal, 37 (1976), 62-69. Sentimental-
      ism [Mackenzie's presentation and criticism]. Satire [on
      Harley and his values]. Critical revaluation.

2628 Spencer, David G. "Henry Mackenzie, A Practical Sentimental-
      ist." Papers on Language and Literature, 3 (1967), 314-26.
      Philosophy of novelist. Intellectual background. Sentimen-
      talism.

2629 Thompson, Harold William. A Scottish Man of Feeling: Henry
      Mackenzie. London: Oxford Univ. Press, 1931, esp. pp.
      92-128. Sentimental novel. "Man of Feeling." Biography.

      SEE ALSO ITEMS 784, 822, 939, 1004, 1040, 1060, 1065.

<u>DELARIVIERE MANLEY</u>
(1672-1724)

PRINCIPAL FICTION

Letters Written by Mrs. Manley, 1696; (reissued as <u>A</u>
<u>Stage Coach Journey to Exeter</u>, 1725)

The Secret History of Queen Zarah, 1705

The New Atalantis, 1709

Memoirs of Europe towards the Close of the Eighth Century,
1710

The Adventures of Rivella, 1714

BIBLIOGRAPHIES AND SURVEYS OF CRITICISM

2630 Backscheider, Paula, et al. "Mary Delarivière Manley." In
      their An Annotated Bibliography of Twentieth-Century
      Critical Studies of Women and Literature, 1660-1800. New
      York: Garland, 1977, pp. 177-79. Bibliography of criti-
      cism [annotated].

2631 Beasley, Jerry C. "Mary Delarivière Manley (1672-1724)."
      In his English Fiction, 1660-1800: A Guide to Information
      Sources. Detroit: Gale, 1978, pp. 189-91. Bibliography
      of criticism [annotated].

2632 Palomo, Dolores. "A Woman Writer and the Scholars: A Re-
      view of Mary Manley's Reputation." Women and Literature,
      6, No. 1 (1978), 36-46. Survey of criticism.

BIOGRAPHICAL AND CRITICAL STUDIES

2633 Anderson, Paul B. "Delarivière Manley's Prose Fiction."
      Philological Quarterly, 13 (1934), 168-88. Introductory
      guide.

2634 Anderson, Paul B. "Mistress Delarivière Manley's Biography."
      Modern Philology, 33 (1936), 261-78. Biography.

2635 Köster, Patricia. "Delarivière Manley and the DNB: A Cau-
      tionary Tale About Following Black Sheep, with a Challenge
      to Cataloguers." Eighteenth-Century Life, 3 (1977), 106-
      11. Misattribution ["Mary" as her Christian name an incor-
      rect interpolation].

2636 Köster, Patricia. "Humanism, Feminism, Sensationalism: Mrs.
      Manley vs. Society." In Transactions of the Samuel John-
      son Society of the Northwest. Vol. IV. Ed. Robert H.
      Carnie. Calgary, Alberta: Samuel Johnson Soc. of the
      Northwest, 1972, pp. 42-53. Education [misguided reading
      a possible forerunner of seduction]. Women. Social criti-
      cism in the novel [attacks moral and educational double
      standards].

2637 Needham, Gwendolyn B. "Mary de la Rivière Manley, Tory
      Defender." Huntington Library Quarterly, 12 (1949), 253-
      88. Satire. Politics. Tories.

2638 Needham, Gwendolyn B. "Mrs. Manley: An Eighteenth-Cen-
      tury Wife of Bath." Huntington Library Quarterly, 14
      (1951), 259-84. Biography.

      SEE ALSO ITEMS 871, 893, 921, 1015, 1060a, 1087.

                        JOHN MOORE
                        (1729-1802)

PRINCIPAL FICTION

      Zeluco, 1786

      Edward, 1796

      Mordaunt, 1800

BIBLIOGRAPHIES AND SURVEYS OF CRITICISM

      None.

BIOGRAPHICAL AND CRITICAL STUDIES

2639 Fulton, Henry L. "An Eighteenth-Century Best Seller."
      Papers of the Bibliographical Society of America, 66 (1972),
      428-33. Best sellers [A View of Society and Manners in
      France, Switzerland, Germany, 1779]. Grand Tour.

ANN RADCLIFFE
(1764-1823)

PRINCIPAL FICTION

The Castles of Athlin and Dunbayne, 1789

A Sicilian Romance, 1790

The Romance of the Forest, 1791

The Mysteries of Udolpho, 1794

The Italian, 1797

BIBLIOGRAPHIES AND SURVEYS OF CRITICISM

2640 Backscheider, Paula, et al. "Ann Radcliffe." In their An
      Annotated Bibliography of Twentieth-Century Critical
      Studies of Women and Literature, 1660-1800. New York:
      Garland, 1977, pp. 204-09. Bibliography of criticism [an-
      notated].

2641 Frank, Frederick S. "A Bibliography of Writings about Ann
      Radcliffe." Extrapolation, 17 (1975), 54-62. Bibliography
      of criticism.

2642 McNutt, Dan J. "Ann (Ward) Radcliffe (1764-1823)." In his
      The Eighteenth-Century Gothic Novel: An Annotated Bib-
      liography of Criticism and Selected Texts. New York:
      Garland, 1975, pp. 186-225. Bibliography of criticism [an-
      notated]. Bibliography of primary sources.

      SEE ALSO ITEM 67.

BIOGRAPHICAL AND CRITICAL STUDIES

2643 Allen, M. L. "The Black Veil: Three Versions of a Symbol."
      English Studies, 47 (1966), 286-89. Symbolism. Imagery
      [veil].

2644 Broadwell, Elizabeth P. "The Veil Image in Ann Radcliffe's
      The Italian." South Atlantic Bulletin, 40, No. 4 (1975),
      76-87. Symbolism. Imagery [veil].

2645 Butler, Marilyn. "The Woman at the Window: Ann Radcliffe
      in the Novels of Mary Wollstonecraft and Jane Austen."
      Women & Literature, N.S. 1 (1980), 128-48. Influence and
      imitation.

■2646 Durant, David. "Aesthetic Heroism in The Mysteries of
       Udolpho." The Eighteenth Century: Theory and Inter-
       pretation, 22 (1981), 175–88. Theory and practice of the
       novel. Realism [novel cannot be mimetic if it is to be real-
       istic]. Imagination. Gothic novel [Udolpho as critique of
       Gothic novel].

■2647 Durant, David. "Ann Radcliffe and the Conservative Gothic."
       Studies in English Literature, 22 (1982), 519–30. Conser-
       vatism. Philosophy of novelist.

2648   Epstein, Lynne. "Mrs. Radcliffe's Landscapes: The Influ-
       ence of Three Landscape Painters on Her Nature Descrip-
       tions." Hartford Studies in Literature, 1 (1969), 107–20.
       Setting. Sources, analogues, and influences. Landscape.
       Nature.

2649   Fawcett, Mary Laughlin. "Udolpho's Primal Mystery."
       Studies in English Literature, 23 (1983), 481–94. Gothic
       novel [psychoanalytic approach]. Sex. Psychology of
       characters.

2650   Garrett, John. "The Eternal Appeal of the Gothic." Sphinx:
       A Magazine of Literature and Society, 8 (1977), 1–7. [Pri-
       marily on Radcliffe's novels]. Characterization. Conserva-
       tism [social and psychological]. Ambivalence.

2651   Grant, Aline. Ann Radcliffe: A Biography. Denver: Alan
       Swallow, 1951. Biography [not scholarly; unsympathetic].

2652   Havens, Raymond D. "Ann Radcliffe's Nature Descriptions."
       Modern Language Notes, 66 (1951), 251–55. Setting. Na-
       ture. Narrative technique.

■2653 Howells, Coral Ann. "Ann Radcliffe, The Mysteries of Udol-
       pho." In her Love, Mystery, and Misery: Feeling in
       Gothic Fiction. London: Athlone Press, 1978, pp. 28–61.
       Innovation. Sensationalism. Narrative technique [interplay
       between visual and emotional perspectives]. Gothic novel.

2654   Kelly, Gary D. "'A Constant Vicissitude of Interesting Pas-
       sions': Ann Radcliffe's Perplexed Narratives." Ariel: A
       Review of International English Literature, 10, No. 2
       (1979), 45–64. Innovation [expands Walpole's techniques].
       Comparison of novelists [Radcliffe, Walpole]. Narrative
       technique.

2655   Kiely, Robert. "The Mysteries of Udolpho." In his The
       Romantic Novel in England. Cambridge, Mass.: Harvard
       Univ. Press, 1972, pp. 65–80. Romantic novel.

2656 Mayo, Robert D. "Ann Radcliffe and Ducray-Duminil." Mod-
      ern Language Review, 36 (1941), 501-05. [The Romance
      of the Forest]. Sources, analogues, and influences.

2657 McIntyre, Clara F. Ann Radcliffe in Relation to Her Time.
      1920; rpt. Hamden, Conn.: Archon, 1970. Eighteenth-
      century criticism and reviews of the novel. Social back-
      ground. Innovation.

2658 McIntyre, Clara F. "Were the 'Gothic Novels' Gothic?" PMLA,
      36 (1921), 644-67. Gothic novel. Sources, analogues, and
      influences.

2659 McKillop, Alan Dugald. "Mrs. Radcliffe on the Supernatural
      in Poetry." Journal of English and Germanic Philology, 31
      (1932), 352-59. Supernatural. Horror and terror.

2660 Murray, E. B. Ann Radcliffe. Twayne's English Authors
      Series. New York: Twayne, 1972. Introductory guide.

■2661 Poovey, Mary. "Ideology and The Mysteries of Udolpho."
      Criticism, 21 (1979), 307-30. Philosophy of novelist.
      Sentimentalism. Women.

2662 Ruff, William. "Ann Radcliffe, or, the Hand of Taste." In
      The Age of Johnson: Essays Presented to Chauncey Brew-
      ster Tinker. Ed. Frederick W. Hilles and Wilmarth S.
      Lewis. New Haven, Conn.: Yale Univ. Press, 1949, pp.
      183-93. Taste. Novel of taste. Defects in the novel.

■2663 Smith, Nelson C. "Sense, Sensibility and Ann Radcliffe."
      Studies in English Literature, 13 (1973), 577-90. Sensibil-
      ity. Sense vs. sensibility.

2664 Swigart, Ford H., Jr. "Ann Radcliffe's Veil Imagery."
      Studies in the Humanities, 1, No. 1 (1969), 55-59. Sym-
      bolism. Imagery [veil].

■2665 Sypher, Wylie. "Social Ambiguity in a Gothic Novel." Parti-
      san Review, 12 (1945), 50-60. [Udolpho]. Dichotomy of
      intention [incomplete rebellion against middle-class values].
      Ambiguity [bourgeois morality at odds with romantic aes-
      thetics]. Romanticism. Morality. Gothic novel.

2666 Thomas, Donald. "The First Poetess of Romantic Fiction:
      Ann Radcliffe, 1764-1823." English, 15 (1964), 91-95.
      Introductory guide.

2667 Thomson, John. "Seasonal and Lighting Effects in Ann Rad-
      cliffe's Fiction." Journal of the Australasian Universities
      Language and Literature Association, 56 (1981), 191-200.

Setting.   Innovation [seasonal and atmospheric effects].
Imagery.

2668   Varma, Devendra P.   "Mrs. Ann Radcliffe: The Craft of
       Terror."   In his The Gothic Flame.   1957; rpt.   New York:
       Russell & Russell, 1966, pp. 85-128.   Gothic novel.   Horror
       and terror.

2669   Ware, Malcolm.   "Mrs. Radcliffe's 'Picturesque Embellishment.'"
       Tennessee Studies in Literature, 5 (1960), 67-71.   Horror
       and terror.

2670   Ware, Malcolm.   Sublimity in the Novels of Ann Radcliffe:
       A Study of the Influence upon her Craft of Edmund
       Burke's Enquiry into the Origin of our Ideas of the Sub-
       lime and Beautiful.   Essays and Studies on English Lan-
       guage and Literature, XXV.   English Institute, Uppsala
       University.   Uppsala: Lundeqvistska, 1963.   The sublime
       and the beautiful.   Burke.   Sources, analogues, and influ-
       ences.   Setting.

2671   Ware, Malcolm.   "The Telescope Reversed: Ann Radcliffe and
       Natural Scenery."   In A Provision of Human Nature: Essays
       on Fielding and Others in Honor of Miriam Austin Locke.
       Ed. Donald Kay.   University: Univ. of Alabama Press,
       1977, pp. 169-89.   Setting.   Nature.   Narrative technique.
       The picturesque.

2672   Wieten, Alida Alberdina Sibbellina.   Mrs. Radcliffe; Her Re-
       lation Towards Romanticism.   Amsterdam: H. J. Paris,
       1926.   Romanticism.

2673   Wolff, Cynthia Griffin.   "The Radcliffean Gothic Model: A
       Form for Feminine Sexuality."   Modern Language Studies,
       9, No. 3 (1979), 98-113.   Women.   Sex.

       SEE ALSO ITEMS 750, 822, 824, 835, 844, 868, 871,
       910, 913, 920, 929, 972, 1001, 1010, 1035, 1052, 1065,
       1070, 1072, 2697.

                          CLARA REEVE
                          (1729-1807)

PRINCIPAL FICTION

       The Champion of Virtue, 1777; (reissued as The Old Eng-
       lish Baron, 1778)

The Two Mentors, 1783

The Exiles, 1788

The School for Widows, 1791

Sir Roger de Clarendon, 1793

Destination, 1799

BIBLIOGRAPHIES AND SURVEYS OF CRITICISM

2674 Beasley, Jerry C. "Clara Reeve (1729-1807)." In his Eng-
      lish Fiction, 1660-1800: A Guide to Information Sources.
      Detroit: Gale, 1978, pp. 199-201. Bibliography of criticism
      [annotated].

2675 McNutt, Dan J. "Clara Reeve (1729-1807)." In his The
      Eighteenth-Century Gothic Novel: An Annotated Bibliogra-
      phy of Criticism and Selected Texts. New York: Garland,
      1975, pp. 166-72. Bibliography of criticism [annotated].
      Bibliography of primary sources.

      SEE ALSO ITEM 67.

BIOGRAPHICAL AND CRITICAL STUDIES

2676 Ehlers, Leigh A. "A Striking Lesson to Posterity: Provi-
      dence and Character in Clara Reeve's The Old English
      Baron." Enlightenment Essays, 9 (1978), 62-76. Provi-
      dence. Characterization. Didacticism.

2677 Kievitt, Frank David. "Clara Reeve's The School for Widows."
      Mid-Hudson Language Studies, 3 (1980), 73-84. The widow.

      SEE ALSO ITEMS 822, 835, 920, 925, 1010, 1072, 1095.

MARY DARBY ROBINSON
(1758-1800)

PRINCIPAL FICTION

Vancenza, 1792

Walsingham, or The Pupil of Nature, 1797

BIBLIOGRAPHIES AND SURVEYS OF CRITICISM

2678 Backscheider, Paula, et al. "Mary Robinson." In their An
      Annotated Bibliography of Twentieth-Century Critical
      Studies of Women and Literature, 1660-1800. New York:
      Garland, 1977, p. 210. Bibliography of criticism [anno-
      tated].

BIOGRAPHICAL AND CRITICAL STUDIES

2679 Adams, M. Ray. "Mrs. Mary Robinson: A Study of Her
      Later Career." In his Studies in the Literary Backgrounds
      of English Radicalism. 1947; rpt. New York: Greenwood
      Press, 1968, pp. 104-29. Introductory guide. Radicalism.

2680 Steen, M. The Lost One: A Biography of Mary--Perdita--
      Robinson. London: Methuen, 1937. Biography.

      SEE ALSO ITEMS 742, 920, 1060a.

                    ELIZABETH SINGER ROWE
                         (1674-1737)

PRINCIPAL FICTION

      Letters Moral and Entertaining, 1729-33

BIBLIOGRAPHIES AND SURVEYS OF CRITICISM

2681 Backscheider, Paula, et al. "Elizabeth Singer Rowe." In
      their An Annotated Bibliography of Twentieth-Century
      Critical Studies of Women and Literature, 1660-1800. New
      York: Garland, 1977, p. 211. Bibliography of criticism
      [annotated].

BIOGRAPHICAL AND CRITICAL STUDIES

2682 Hughes, Helen Sard. "Elizabeth Rowe and the Countess of
      Hertford." PMLA, 59 (1944), 726-46. Biography.

■2683 Richetti, John J. "Mrs. Elizabeth Rowe: The Novel as
      Polemic." PMLA, 82 (1967), 522-29. Didacticism. Love.
      Death. Christianity.

2684 Stecher, Henry F. Elizabeth Singer Rowe, the Poetess of

Frome: A Study in Eighteenth-Century English Pietism.
Bern: Lang, 1973. Biography. Pietism.

2685   Wright, H. Bunker.   "Matthew Prior and Elizabeth Singer."
       Philological Quarterly, 24 (1945), 71-82.   Letter-writing
       [account of correspondence with Prior].

       SEE ALSO ITEMS 921, 1015.

SARAH SCOTT
(1723-1795)

PRINCIPAL FICTION

The History of Cornelia, 1750

Millenium Hall, 1762

Sir George Ellison, 1766

BIBLIOGRAPHIES AND SURVEYS OF CRITICISM

2686   Backscheider, Paula, et al.   "Sarah Scott."   In their An An-
       notated Bibliography of Twentieth-Century Critical Studies
       of Women and Literature, 1660-1800.   New York: Garland,
       1977, p. 212.   Bibliography of criticism [annotated].

BIOGRAPHICAL AND CRITICAL STUDIES

2687   Grow, L. M.   "Sarah Scott: A Reconsideration."   Coranto,
       9, No. 1 (1973), 9-15.   Defects in the novel [moral instruc-
       tion impedes creativity].

2688   Onderwyzer, Gaby E.   "Sarah Scott's Agreeable Ugliness, a
       Translation."   Modern Language Notes, 70 (1955), 578-80.
       Misattribution [not her novel, but her translation of La
       Place's].

       SEE ALSO ITEM 752.

<u>FRANCES SHERIDAN</u>
(1724-1766)

PRINCIPAL FICTION

<u>Sidney Bidulph</u>, 1761

<u>Nourjahad</u>, 1766

BIBLIOGRAPHIES AND SURVEYS OF CRITICISM

2689 Backscheider, Paula, et al. "Frances Sheridan." In their
      <u>An Annotated Bibliography of Twentieth-Century Critical
      Studies of Women and Literature, 1660-1800</u>. New York:
      Garland, 1977, p. 216. Bibliography of criticism [anno-
      tated].

BIOGRAPHICAL AND CRITICAL STUDIES

2690 Golden, Morris. "<u>Sidney Bidulph</u> and <u>The Vicar of Wake-
      field</u>." <u>Modern Language Studies</u>, 9, No. 2 (1979), 33-35.
      Influence and imitation.

2691 Russell, Norma. "Some Uncollected Authors XXXVIII: Fran-
      ces Sheridan, 1724-1766." <u>Book Collector</u>, 13 (1964), 196-
      205. Introductory guide.

2692 Wilson, Mona. "The Mother of Richard Brinsley Sheridan."
      In her <u>These Were the Muses</u>. London: Sidgwick & Jackson,
      1924, pp. 27-49. Biography.

SEE ALSO ITEM 920.

<u>CHARLOTTE TURNER SMITH</u>
(1749-1806)

PRINCIPAL FICTION

<u>Emmeline</u>, 1788

<u>Ethelinde</u>, 1789

<u>Celestina</u>, 1791

<u>Desmond</u>, 1792

The Old Manor House, 1793

The Banished Man, 1794

Montalbert, 1795

Marchmont, 1796

The Young Philosopher, 1798

BIBLIOGRAPHIES AND SURVEYS OF CRITICISM

2693 Backscheider, Paula, et al. "Charlotte Smith." In their An
      Annotated Bibliography of Twentieth-Century Critical
      Studies of Women and Literature, 1660-1800. New York:
      Garland, 1977, pp. 219-20. Bibliography of criticism [an-
      notated].

2694 Beasley, Jerry C. "Charlotte Smith (1749-1806)." In his
      English Fiction, 1660-1800: A Guide to Information Sources.
      Detroit: Gale, 1978, pp. 219-22. Bibliography of criticism
      [annotated].

2695 McNutt, Dan J. "Charlotte (Turner) Smith (1749-1806)." In
      his The Eighteenth-Century Gothic Novel: An Annotated
      Bibliography of Criticism and Selected Texts. New York:
      Garland, 1975, pp. 173-85. Bibliography of criticism [anno-
      tated]. Bibliography of primary sources.

      SEE ALSO ITEM 67.

BIOGRAPHICAL AND CRITICAL STUDIES

2696 Ellis, Katherine. "Charlotte Smith's Subversive Gothic."
      Feminist Studies, 3, No. 3/4 (1976), 51-53. [Desmond].
      Rebellion. Social criticism in the novel [of the bourgeois
      family]. Gothic novel.

■2697 Foster, James R. "Charlotte Smith, Pre-Romantic Novelist."
      PMLA, 43 (1928), 463-75. Sentimental novel. Romanticism.
      Influence and imitation [Radcliffe].

2698 Foster, James R. "Liberal Opinions." In his History of the
      Pre-Romantic Novel in England. New York: Kraus, 1949,
      pp. 239-50 and passim. Autobiographical elements in the
      novel. Politics. Sentimental novel. Setting.

2699 Gregory, Allene. "Some Typical Lady Novelists of the Revo-
      lution: Mrs. Charlotte Smith." In her The French Revo-

lution and the English Novel. 1914; rpt. New York:
Haskell House, 1966, pp. 213-22. Jacobin novel. French
Revolution. Women novelists.

2700   Hilbish, Florence. Charlotte Smith, Poet and Novelist (1749-
       1806). Philadelphia: Univ. of Pennsylvania Press, 1941.
       Biography. Theory and practice of the novel. Innovation.

2701   Rogers, Katharine M. "Inhibitions on Eighteenth-Century
       Women Novelists: Elizabeth Inchbald and Charlotte Smith."
       Eighteenth-Century Studies, 11 (1977), 63-78. Women
       novelists. The writer in society. Characterization [of
       women limited by notions of propriety]. Propriety.

   SEE ALSO ITEMS 822, 835, 850, 920, 1075.

                        GEORGE WALKER
                         (1772-1847)

PRINCIPAL FICTION

   The Vagabond, 1799

BIBLIOGRAPHIES AND SURVEYS OF CRITICISM

   None.

BIOGRAPHICAL AND CRITICAL STUDIES

2702   Harvey, A. D. "George Walker and the Anti-Revolutionary
       Novel." Review of English Studies, N.S. 28 (1977), 290-
       300. Anti-Revolutionary novel. Satire [on Godwin]. Con-
       servatism. Godwin.

                        HORACE WALPOLE
                         (1717-1797)

PRINCIPAL FICTION

   The Castle of Otranto, 1764

BIBLIOGRAPHIES AND SURVEYS OF CRITICISM

2703 Beasley, Jerry C. "Horace Walpole (1717-1797)." In his
      English Fiction, 1660-1800: A Guide to Information Sources.
      Detroit: Gale, 1978, pp. 269-73. Bibliography of criticism
      [annotated].

2704 Hazen, Allen T. A Bibliography of Horace Walpole. 1948;
      rpt. New York: Barnes & Noble, 1973. Bibliography of
      primary sources.

2705 McNutt, Dan J. "Horace Walpole, 4th Earl of Orford (1717-
      1797)." In his The Eighteenth-Century Gothic Novel: An
      Annotated Bibliography of Criticism and Selected Texts.
      New York: Garland, 1975, pp. 136-66. Bibliography of
      criticism [annotated]. Bibliography of primary sources.

      SEE ALSO ITEM 67.

BIOGRAPHICAL AND CRITICAL STUDIES

2706 Ames, Dianne S. "Strawberry Hill: Architecture of the 'As
      If.'" In Studies in Eighteenth-Century Culture. Vol. 8.
      Ed. Roseann Runte. Madison: Univ. of Wisconsin Press,
      1979, pp. 351-63. Strawberry Hill. Architecture.

2707 Brooke, John. "Horace Walpole and the Politics of the Early
      Years of the Reign of George III." In Horace Walpole:
      Writer, Politician, and Connoisseur. Essays on the 250th
      Anniversary of Walpole's Birth. New Haven, Conn.: Yale
      Univ. Press, 1967, pp. 3-23. Politics.

2708 Burney, E. L. "Shakespeare in Otranto." Manchester Re-
      view, 12 (1972), 61-64. Shakespearean influence.

2709 Chase, Isabel Wakelin Urban. Horace Walpole: Gardenist.
      An Edition of Walpole's "The History of the Modern Taste
      in Gardening" with an "Estimate of Walpole's Contribution
      to Landscape Architecture." Princeton, N.J.: Princeton
      Univ. Press, 1943. Landscape gardening.

2710 Coley, W. B. "Henry Fielding and the Two Walpoles."
      Philological Quarterly, 45 (1966), 157-78. Personal rela-
      tions between authors.

■2711 Conger, Syndy McMillen. "Faith and Doubt in The Castle
      of Otranto." Gothic, 1 (1979), 51-59. Christianity [Wal-
      pole's skepticism]. Irrationality. Supernatural [providence,
      miracles].

2712 DeKoven, Anna. Horace Walpole and Madame Du Deffand: An
      Eighteenth-Century Friendship. New York: Appleton,
      1928. Biography.

2713 Dobrée, Bonamy. "Horace Walpole." In Restoration and
      Eighteenth Century Literature: Essays in Honor of Alan
      Dugald McKillop. Ed. Carroll Camden. Chicago: Univ.
      of Chicago Press, 1963, pp. 301-10. Introductory guide.

■2714 Ehlers, Leigh A. "The Gothic World as Stage: Providence
      and Character in The Castle of Otranto." Wascana Review,
      14, No. 2 (1979), 17-30. Providence. Characterization.
      Dramatic conventions in the novel. Shakespearean influ-
      ence.

2715 Foord, Archibald S. "'The Only Unadulterated Whig.'" In
      Horace Walpole: Writer, Politician, and Connoisseur. Es-
      says on the 250th Anniversary of Walpole's Birth. New
      Haven, Conn.: Yale Univ. Press, 1967, pp. 25-43. Poli-
      tics.

2716 Harfst, Betsy Perteit. Horace Walpole and the Unconscious:
      An Experiment in Freudian Analysis. New York: Arno
      Press, 1980. [Not seen]. Personality of novelist [psycho-
      analytic approach]. Autobiographical elements in the novel
      [examines relationship of the novel to Walpole's unconscious].

2717 Havens, Munson Aldrich. Horace Walpole and the Strawberry
      Hill Press, 1757-1789. 1901; rpt. Folcroft, Pa.: Folcroft
      Press, 1969. Strawberry Hill Press.

2718 Hazen, Allen T. A Catalogue of Horace Walpole's Library.
      With "Horace Walpole's Library" by Wilmarth S. Lewis. 3
      vols. New Haven, Conn.: Yale Univ. Press, 1969. Li-
      brary of novelist.

2719 Kallich, Martin. Horace Walpole. Twayne's English Authors
      Series. New York: Twayne, 1971. Introductory guide.

2720 Kallich, Martin. "Horace Walpole Against Edmund Burke: A
      Study in Antagonism." Studies in Burke and His Time, 9,
      Nos. 2-3 (1968), 834-63, 927-45. Politics. Burke.

●2721 Ketton-Cremer, R. W. Horace Walpole: A Biography. 1940.
      3rd ed. London: Methuen, 1964. Biography.

2722 Kiely, Robert. "The Castle of Otranto." In his The Roman-
      tic Novel in England. Cambridge, Mass.: Harvard Univ.
      Press, 1972, pp. 27-42. Romantic novel.

2723 Lam, George L. "Walpole and The Duke of Newcastle." In
      Horace Walpole: Writer, Politician, and Connoisseur. Es-
      says on the 250th Anniversary of Walpole's Birth. New
      Haven, Conn.: Yale Univ. Press, 1967, pp. 57-84. Biog-
      raphy.

2724 Lewis, Wilmarth S. "The Genesis of Strawberry Hill." Metro-
      politan Museum Studies, 5, Pt. 1 (1934), 57-92. Strawberry
      Hill. Architecture.

2725 Lewis, Wilmarth S. Horace Walpole. The A. W. Mellon Lec-
      tures in the Fine Arts, 1960. New York: Pantheon, 1960.
      Biography. Politics. Strawberry Hill.

2726 Lewis, Wilmarth S. Horace Walpole's Library. Cambridge:
      Cambridge Univ. Press, 1958. Library of novelist.

2727 Mehrota, K. K. Horace Walpole and the English Novel: A
      Study of the Influence of "The Castle of Otranto," 1764-
      1820. 1934; rpt. New York: Russell & Russell, 1970.
      Gothic novel. Influence and imitation.

2728 Quaintance, Richard E. "Walpole's Whig Interpretation of
      Landscaping History." In Studies in Eighteenth-Century
      Culture. Vol. 9. Ed. Roseann Runte. Madison: Univ.
      of Wisconsin Press, 1979, 285-300. Landscape gardening.
      Whigs.

2729 Riely, John C. "Horace Walpole and 'the Second Hogarth.'"
      Eighteenth-Century Studies, 9 (1975), 28-44. Caricature.
      Henry William Bunbury.

2730 Rogal, Samuel J. "Horace Walpole and the Methodists." Uni-
      versity of Dayton Review, 12, No. 3 (1976), 107-19.
      Methodism.

2731 Sedgwick, Romney. "Horace Walpole's Political Articles, 1747-
      49." In Horace Walpole: Writer, Politician, and Connois-
      seur. Essays on the 250th Anniversary of Walpole's Birth.
      New Haven, Conn.: Yale Univ. Press, 1967, pp. 45-55.
      Politics.

2732 Smith, Horatio E. "Horace Walpole Anticipates Victor Hugo."
      Modern Language Notes, 41 (1926), 458-61. The grotesque.

2733 Smith, Robert A. "Walpole's Reflections on the Revolution in
      France." In Horace Walpole: Writer, Politician, and Con-
      noisseur. Essays on the 250th Anniversary of Walpole's
      Birth. New Haven, Conn.: Yale Univ. Press, 1967, pp.
      91-114. French Revolution. Politics.

2734 Stein, Jess M. "Horace Walpole and Shakespeare." Studies
      in Philology, 31 (1934), 51-68. Shakespearean influence.

2735 Summers, Montague. "Architecture and the Gothic Novel."
      Architectural Design, 2 (1931), 78-81. Gothic novel. Set-
      ting. Architecture.

2736 Tatar, Maria M. "The Houses of Fiction: Toward a Defini-
      tion of the Uncanny." Comparative Literature, 33 (1981),
      167-82. The supernatural.

2737 Varma, Devendra P. "The First Gothic Tale: Its Potential-
      ities." In his The Gothic Flame. 1957; rpt. New York:
      Russell & Russell, 1966, pp. 42-73. [The Castle of Otran-
      to]. Gothic novel.

      SEE ALSO ITEMS 748, 750, 868, 910, 1010, 1051, 1065,
      1072.

                    MARY WOLLSTONECRAFT
                        (1759-1797)

PRINCIPAL FICTION

      Mary, A Fiction, 1788

      Maria; or The Wrongs of Woman, 1798

BIBLIOGRAPHIES AND SURVEYS OF CRITICISM

2738 Backscheider, Paula, et al. "Mary Wollstonecraft." In their
      An Annotated Bibliography of Twentieth-Century Critical
      Studies of Women and Literature, 1660-1800. New York:
      Garland, 1977, pp. 228-32. Bibliography of criticism [an-
      notated].

2739 Todd, Janet. Mary Wollstonecraft: An Annotated Bibliogra-
      phy. New York: Garland, 1976. Bibliography of criticism
      [annotated].

BIOGRAPHICAL AND CRITICAL STUDIES

2740 Butler, Marilyn. "The Woman at the Window: Ann Radcliffe
      in the Novels of Mary Wollstonecraft and Jane Austen."
      Women & Literature, N.S. 1 (1980), 128-48. Sources, ana-
      logues, and influences.

2741 Detre, Jean. A Most Extraordinary Pair: Mary Wollstone-
      craft and William Godwin. New York: Doubleday, 1975.
      Biography.

2742 Flexner, Eleanor. Mary Wollstonecraft. New York: Coward,
      1972. Biography. Philosophy of novelist.

2743   George, Margaret. One Woman's "Situation": A Study of
       Mary Wollstonecraft. Urbana: Univ. of Illinois Press,
       1970. Biography. Women. Feminism.

2744   Gregory, Allene. "The French Revolution and the Rights of
       Woman. Section 2. Mary Wollstonecraft." In her The
       French Revolution and the English Novel. 1915; rpt.
       New York: Haskell House, 1966, pp. 239-58. Introductory
       guide.

2745   Kelly, Gary D. "Godwin, Wollstonecraft, and Rousseau."
       Women & Literature, 3, No. 2 (1975), 21-26. Rousseau.

■2746 Myers, Mitzi. "Unfinished Business: Wollstonecraft's Maria."
       Wordsworth Circle, 11 (1980), 107-14. Dichotomy of in-
       tention ["coalition of 'female Werter' and rational reformer"].
       Philosophy of novelist. Reason. Sensibility. Women.
       Narrative technique.

2747   Nixon, Edna. Mary Wollstonecraft: Her Life and Times.
       London: Dent, 1971. Biography [popular].

■2748 Poovey, Mary. "Mary Wollstonecraft: The Gender of Genres
       in Late Eighteenth-Century England." Novel, 15 (1982),
       111-26. Point of view and narrator [problems peculiar to
       the eighteenth-century woman novelist]. Women novelists.
       Women. Sentimental novel. Sentimentalism.

2749   Sunstein, Emily W. A Different Face: The Life of Mary
       Wollstonecraft. New York: Harper & Row, 1975. Biogra-
       phy [psychology, feminism].

■2750 Todd, Janet. "Political Friendship: Mary Wollstonecraft's
       Mary, A Fiction; Mary Wollstonecraft's The Wrongs of Wom-
       an." In her Women's Friendship in Literature. New York:
       Columbia Univ. Press, 1980, pp. 191-226. Women's friend-
       ship.

2751   Todd, Janet. "Reason and Sensibility in Mary Wollstonecraft's
       The Wrongs of Woman." Frontiers, 5, No. 3 (1980), 17-20.
       Didacticism.

2752   Tomalin, Claire. The Life and Death of Mary Wollstonecraft.
       New York: Harcourt, Brace, 1974. Biography. Philosophy
       of novelist.

2753   Wardle, Ralph M. Mary Wollstonecraft: A Critical Biography.
       Lincoln: Univ. of Nebraska Press, 1951. Biography.

       SEE ALSO ITEMS 920, 1065.

SAMUEL JOHNSON
(1709-1784)

PRINCIPAL FICTION

Rasselas, 1759

BIBLIOGRAPHIES AND SURVEYS OF CRITICISM

2754 Clifford, James L., and Donald Greene. Samuel Johnson: A Survey and Bibliography of Critical Studies. Minneapolis: Univ. of Minnesota Press, 1970. Bibliography of criticism. Survey of criticism.

2755 Courtney, W. P., and D. Nichol Smith. A Bibliography of Samuel Johnson. 1915; rpt. Oxford: Clarendon Press, 1968. See also R. W. Chapman and Allen T. Hazen. "Johnsonian Bibliography: A Supplement to Courtney." Proceedings of the Oxford Bibliographical Society, 5 (1939), 119-66. Bibliography of primary sources.

2756 Fleeman, J. D. "Samuel Johnson in the British Press, 1749-1784: A Chronological Checklist." Analytical and Enumerative Bibliography, 1 (1977), 209-14. Eighteenth-century criticism and reviews of the novel.

2757 Greene, Donald. "The Development of the Johnson Canon." In Restoration and Eighteenth-Century Literature: Essays in Honor of Alan Dugald McKillop. Ed. Carroll Camden. Chicago: Univ. of Chicago Press, 1963, pp. 407-27. Bibliography of primary sources.

2758 Kenney, William. "Johnson's Rasselas After Two Centuries." Boston University Studies in English, 3 (1957), 88-96. Survey of criticism.

2759 Lascelles, Mary. "Rasselas: A Rejoinder." Review of English Studies, N.S. 21 (1970), 49-56. Survey of criticism.

2760 McGuffie, Helen Louise. Samuel Johnson in the British Press, 1749-1784: A Chronological Checklist. New York: Garland, 1976. Eighteenth-century criticism and reviews of the novel.

BIOGRAPHICAL AND CRITICAL STUDIES

2761 Abdul Hamid Al Aoun, Dina. "Some Remarks on a Second Reading of Rasselas." In Bicentenary Essays on "Rasselas." Ed. Magdi Wahba. Cairo: Société orientale de publicité, 1959, pp. 15-20. Education.

2762 Aden, John M. "Rasselas and The Vanity of Human Wishes." Criticism, 3 (1961), 295-303. Satire [on states of the mind]. Melancholy. Pessimism.

•2763 Alkon, Paul K. Samuel Johnson and Moral Discipline. Evanston, Ill.: Northwestern Univ. Press, 1967. Morality. Philosophy of novelist. The passions. Intelligence. Locke. Delusion. Liberty.

2764 Babbitt, Irving. "Dr. Johnson and Imagination." Southwest Review, 13 (1927), 25-35. Imagination.

■2765 Baker, Sheridan. "Rasselas: Psychological Irony and Romance." Philological Quarterly, 45 (1966), 249-61. Imagination. Reality. Irony. Romance.

2766 Balderston, Katharine C. "Johnson's Vile Melancholy." In The Age of Johnson: Essays Presented to Chauncey Brewster Tinker. Ed. Frederick W. Hilles and Wilmarth S. Lewis. New Haven, Conn.: Yale Univ. Press, 1949, pp. 3-14. Melancholy. Personality of novelist [masochism].

2767 Barnouw, Jeffrey. "Readings of Rasselas: 'Its Most Obvious Moral' and the Moral Role of Literature." Enlightenment Essays, 7 (1976), 17-39. Morality. Philosophy of novelist.

•2768 Bate, W. Jackson. The Achievement of Samuel Johnson. New York: Oxford Univ. Press, 1955. Morality. Imagination. Reason vs. imagination. Achievement and reputation.

■2769 Bate, W. Jackson. "Johnson and Satire Manqué." In Eighteenth-Century Studies in Honor of Donald F. Hyde. Ed. W. H. Bond. New York: Grolier, 1971, pp. 145-60. Satire [his satiric intentions blunted by his compassion]. Comedy.

•2770 Bate, W. Jackson. Samuel Johnson. New York: Harcourt, Brace, 1977. Biography.

2771   Bernard, F. V.   "The Hermit of Paris and the Astronomer in
       Rasselas."   Journal of English and Germanic Philology, 67
       (1968), 272-78.   Sources, analogues, and influences.

2772   Bloom, Edward A.   Samuel Johnson in Grub Street.   Provi-
       dence, R.I.:   Brown Univ. Press, 1957.   Grub Street.
       Biography.

2773   Boas, Guy.   "Dr. Johnson on Schools and Schoolmasters."
       English, 1 (1937), 537-49.   Education.

2774   Bogle, Frederic V.   "Fables of Knowing: Melodrama and Re-
       lated Forms."   Genre, 11 (1978), 83-108.   Fable.   Epistem-
       ology.

2775   Boulton, J. T., ed.   Johnson: The Critical Heritage.   Criti-
       cal Heritage Series.   London: Routledge & Kegan Paul,
       1971.   Eighteenth-century criticism and reviews of the nov-
       el.

2776   Brinton, George.   "Rasselas and the Problem of Evil."   Pa-
       pers on Literature and Language, 8 (1972), 92-96.   Evil.
       Philosophy of novelist.

2777   Broadhead, Glenn J.   "The Journey and the Stream: Space
       and Time Imagery in Johnson's Rasselas."   Exploration, 8
       (1980), 15-24.   Imagery.   Space.   Time.   Journey.

•2778 Bronson, Bertrand H.   Johnson Agonistes and Other Essays.
       Berkeley: Univ. of California Press, 1965.   Incorporates
       his "Johnson Agonistes," in his Johnson and Boswell:
       Three Essays, Berkeley: Univ. of California, 1944, pp.
       363-98; and his "The Double Tradition of Dr. Johnson,"
       ELH: A Journal of English Literary History, 18 (1951), 90-
       106.   Personality of novelist [ebullient temperament].   Con-
       servatism.

2779   Brown, Stuart Gerry.   "Dr. Johnson and the Religious Prob-
       lem."   English Studies, 20 (1938), 1-17, 67.   Christianity.

2780   Butterick, George F.   "The Comedy of Johnson's Rasselas."
       Studies in the Humanities, 2 (1970-71), 25-31.   Comedy.
       Tragicomedy.

2781   Byrd, Max.   "Johnson's Spiritual Anxiety."   Modern Philology,
       78 (1981), 368-78.   Personality of novelist.

2782   Cairns, William T.   "The Religion of Dr. Johnson."   In The
       Religion of Dr. Johnson and Other Essays.   1946; rpt.
       Freeport, N.Y.:   Books for Libraries Press, 1969, pp. 1-23.
       Christianity.   Death.   Biography [Johnson's last days].

2783 Cameron, Kenneth Neill. "Rasselas and Alastor: A Study in
      Transmutation." Studies in Philology, 40 (1943), 58-78.
      Influence and imitation.

●2784 Chapin, Chester F. The Religious Thought of Samuel John-
       son. Ann Arbor: Univ. of Michigan Press, 1968. Chris-
       tianity. Anglicanism.

●2785 Clifford, James L. Dictionary Johnson: The Middle Years of
       Samuel Johnson. New York: McGraw-Hill, 1979. Biogra-
       phy.

2786 Clifford, James L. "Some Remarks on Candide and Rasselas."
      In Bicentenary Essays on "Rasselas." Ed. Magdi Wahba.
      Cairo: Société orientale de publicité, 1959, pp. 7-14.
      Rasselas-Candide comparison.

●2787 Clifford, James L. Young Sam Johnson. New York: Mc-
       Graw-Hill, 1955. Biography.

2788 Conrad, Lawrence H., Jr. "Samuel Johnson on Education."
      Ball State University Forum, 8, No. 2 (1967), 20-26.
      Education [his liberal views].

2789 Curley, Thomas M. "Mythic and Historic Travel in the Crea-
      tion of Rasselas." In his Samuel Johnson and the Age of
      Travel. Athens: Univ. of Georgia Press, 1976, pp. 147-
      82. Journey. Travel literature. Biblical allusions. Clas-
      sical allusions.

■2790 Curley, Thomas M. "The Spiritual Journey Moralized in Ras-
       selas." Anglia, 91 (1973), 35-55. Journey. Allegory.
       Bunyan's The Pilgrim's Progress. Morality.

2791 Eberwein, Robert. "The Astronomer in Johnson's Rasselas."
      Michigan Academician, 5 (1972), 9-15. Humanism. Insan-
      ity.

2792 Ehrenpreis, Irvin. "Rasselas and Some Meanings of 'Struc-
      ture' in Literary Criticism." Novel, 14 (1981), 101-17.
      Autobiographical elements in the novel. Plot, structure,
      and design. Oriental novel.

2793 Einbond, Bernard L. "Rasselas: The Happy Valley as Alle-
      gorical Metaphor." In his Samuel Johnson's Allegory. The
      Hague: Mouton, 1971, pp. 83-96. Allegory. Critical re-
      valuation [only Happy Valley, not all of Rasselas, is allegor-
      ical].

2794 Emden, Cecil S. "Rhythmical Features in Dr. Johnson's
      Prose." Review of English Studies, O.S. 25 (1949), 38-54.
      Style and language. Rhythm.

2795 Eversole, Richard. "Imlac and the Poets of Persia and Arabia." Philological Quarterly, 58 (1979), 155-70. Orientalism.

2796 Fisher, Marvin. "The Pattern of Conservatism in Johnson's Rasselas and Hawthorne's Tales." Journal of the History of Ideas, 19 (1958), 173-96. Philosophy of novelist. Conservatism.

2797 Folkenflik, Robert. "The Tulip and Its Streaks: Contexts of Rasselas X." Ariel: A Review of International English Literature, 9, No. 2 (1978), 57-71. Imagery [Johnson's vs. Imlac's view of poetry]. Particular vs. general.

2798 Fulton, Henry L. "Theme and Structure in Rasselas." Michigan Academician, 1, Nos. 3-4 (1969), 75-80. Plot, structure, and design. Education [as theme].

2799 Fussell, Paul. "The Choice of Life." In his Samuel Johnson and the Life of Writing. New York: Harcourt, Brace, 1971, pp. 216-45. The writer in society. Composition of the novel.

2800 Gaba, Phyllis. "'A Succession of Amusements': The Moralization in Rasselas of Locke's Account of Time." Eighteenth-Century Studies, 10 (1977), 451-63. Time. Locke.

2801 Gold, Joel J. "Johnson's Translation of Lobo." PMLA, 80 (1965), 51-61. Sources, analogues, and influences.

2802 Goodyear, Louis E. "Rasselas' Journey From Amhara to Cairo Viewed from Arabia." In Bicentenary Essays on "Rasselas." Ed. Magdi Wahba. Cairo: Société orientale de publicité, 1959, pp. 21-29. Geography. Setting. Journey. Places in the novel.

2803 Grange, Kathleen M. "Dr. Samuel Johnson's Account of a Schizophrenic Illness in Rasselas." Medical History, 6 (1962), 162-69, 291. Insanity.

2804 Greene, Donald. "Johnson, Stoicism, and the Good Life." In The Unknown Samuel Johnson. Ed. John J. Burke, Jr., and Donald Kay. Madison: Univ. of Wisconsin Press, 1983, pp. 17-38. Philosophy of novelist. Stoicism [Johnson not a stoic]. Christianity.

2805 Greene, Donald. "'Pictures to the Mind': Johnson and Imagery." In Johnson, Boswell, and Their Circle: Essays Presented to Lawrence Fitzroy Powell in Honour of His Eighty-Fourth Birthday. Oxford: Clarendon Press, 1965, pp. 137-58. Imagery. Particular vs. general.

•2806   Greene, Donald. The Politics of Samuel Johnson. New Hav-
        en, Conn.: Yale Univ. Press, 1960. Politics. Critical
        revaluation.

2807   Greene, Donald. Samuel Johnson. Twayne's English Authors
        Series. New York: Twayne, 1970. Introductory guide.

2808   Greene, Donald. Samuel Johnson's Library: An Annotated
        Guide. Victoria: Univ. of Victoria, 1975₀ Library of
        novelist.

2809   Gross, Gloria Sybil. "Sanity, Madness and the Family in
        Samuel Johnson's Rasselas." Psychocultural Review, 1
        (1977), 152-59. Psychology of characters [psychoanalytic
        issues]. Insanity. Marriage. Family.

2810   Hagstrum, Jean H. "On Dr. Johnson's Fear of Death." ELH:
        A Journal of English Literary History, 14 (1947), 308-19.
        Christianity. Death.

2811   Hagstrum, Jean H. Samuel Johnson's Literary Criticism.
        Chicago: Univ. of Chicago Press, 1952. Theory and prac-
        tice of the novel. Reason. Nature. The sublime and the
        beautiful. Style and language. Particular vs. general.

2812   Hansen, Marlene R. "Rasselas, Milton, and Humanism."
        English Studies, 60 (1979), 14-22. Humanism. Milton.
        Sources, analogues, and influences.

■2813   Hardy, J. P. "Rasselas." In his Samuel Johnson: A Criti-
        cal Study. London: Routledge & Kegan Paul, 1979, pp.
        127-48. Optimism. Imagination. Symbolism [the Nile].

2814   Hart, Francis Russell. "Johnson as Philosophic Traveler:
        The Perfecting of an Idea." ELH: A Journal of English
        Literary History, 36 (1969), 679-95. Allegory. The wan-
        derer. Journey.

2815   Hartley, Lodwick. "Johnson, Reynolds, and the Notorious
        Streaks of the Tulip Again." Eighteenth-Century Studies,
        8 (1975), 329-36. Particular vs. general. Parody [of the
        grand style].

2816   Havens, Raymond D. "Johnson's Distrust of the Imagination."
        ELH: A Journal of English Literary History, 10 (1943),
        243-55. Reason vs. imagination. Imagination.

2817   Hilles, Frederick W. "Rasselas, An 'Uninstructive Tale₀'" In
        Johnson, Boswell and Their Circle: Essays Presented to
        Lawrence Fitzroy Powell in Honour of His Eighty-Fourth
        Birthday. Oxford: Clarendon Press, 1965, pp. 111-21.
        Didacticism.

2818 Hovey, Richard B. "Dr. Samuel Johnson, Psychiatrist."
      Modern Language Quarterly, 15 (1954), 321-25. Autobio-
      graphical elements in the novel. Melancholy. Psychology
      of characters.

2819 Hunt, Russell A. "Johnson on Fielding and Richardson: A
      Problem in Literary Moralism." Humanities Association Bul-
      letin, 27 (1976), 412-20. Morality. Comparison of novel-
      ists.

2820 Irwin, George. Samuel Johnson: A Personality in Conflict.
      Auckland, N.Z.: Auckland Univ. Press, 1971. Incorpor-
      ates his "Doctor Johnson's Troubled Mind," Literature and
      Psychology, 13 (1963), 6-11. Biography [psychological].
      Personality of novelist.

2821 Isles, Duncan. "Johnson and Charlotte Lennox." New Ram-
      bler, Ser. C, 3 (1967), 34-48. Personal relations between
      authors.

2822 Jack, Ian. "'The Choice of Life' in Johnson and Matthew
      Prior." Journal of English and Germanic Philology, 49
      (1950), 523-30. Sources, analogues, and influences.

2823 Jemielity, Thomas. "Dr. Johnson and the Uses of Travel."
      Philological Quarterly, 51 (1972), 448-59. Travel [as a
      means to improve judgment].

2824 Jenkins, Harold D. "Some Aspects of the Background of Ras-
      selas." In Studies in English in Honor of Raphael Dorman
      O'Leary and Selden Lincoln Whitcomb. Univ. of Kansas
      Publications, Humanistic Studies. Lawrence: Univ. of
      Kansas, 1940, pp. 8-14. Sources, analogues, and influences.
      Places in the novel.

2825 Jones, Emrys. "The Artistic Form of Rasselas." Review of
      English Studies, N.S., 18 (1967), 387-401. Plot, structure,
      and design.

2826 Joost, Nicholas. "Whispers of Fancy; or, The Meaning of
      Rasselas." Modern Age, 1 (1957), 166-73. Allegory.
      Christianity [fideistic tendency, denial of rationalism].

2827 Kallich, Martin. "Samuel Johnson's Principles of Criticism and
      Imlac's 'Dissertation upon Poetry.'" Journal of Aesthetics
      and Art Criticism, 25 (1966), 71-82. Theory and practice
      of the novel. Autobiographical elements in the novel. Par-
      ticular vs. general.

2828 Kaul, R. K. "The Philosopher of Nature in 'Rasselas.'" In-
      dian Journal of English Studies, 3 (1962), 116-20. Nature.

2829 Kearney, Anthony. "Johnson's Rasselas and the Poets."
      English Studies, 53 (1972), 514-18. Milton. Shakespeare.

2830 Keener, Frederick M. "Conflict, Declamation, and Self-As-
      sessment in Rasselas." In his The Chain of Becoming:
      The Philosophical Tale, the Novel, and a Neglected Realism
      of the Enlightenment. New York: Columbia Univ. Press,
      1983, pp. 217-40. Philosophical tale. Didacticism. Psy-
      chology of characters.

2831 Kenney, William. "Rasselas and the Theme of Diversification."
      Philological Quarterly, 38 (1959), 84-89. Response by
      George Sherburn in "Rasselas Returns--To What?" ibid.,
      383-84. Diversification. Happiness. Journey [return to
      Abyssinia, not to Happy Valley].

2832 Kolb, Gwin J. "The Intellectual Background of the Discourse
      on the Soul in Rasselas." Philological Quarterly, 54 (1975),
      357-69. Intellectual background. Immortality.

2833 Kolb, Gwin J. "Johnson's 'Dissertation on Flying.'" In New
      Light on Dr. Johnson: Essays on the Occasion of His
      250th Birthday. Ed. Frederick W. Hilles. 1959; rpt. New
      York: Archon, 1967, pp. 91-106. Rev. of his "Johnson's
      'Dissertation on Flying' and John Wilkins' Mathematical Ma-
      gick," Modern Philology, 47 (1949), 24-31. Composition of
      the novel. Sources, analogues, and influences. Science.

2834 Kolb, Gwin J. "The 'Paradise' in Abyssinia and the 'Happy
      Valley' in Rasselas." Modern Philology, 56 (1958), 10-16.
      Sources, analogues, and influences.

2835 Kolb, Gwin J. "Rousseau and the Background of the 'Life
      Led According to Nature' in Chapter 22 of Rasselas."
      Modern Philology, 73, No. 4, Part 2 (1976), S66-73.
      Nature. Rousseau. Sources, analogues, and influences.

■2836 Kolb, Gwin J. "The Structure of Rasselas." PMLA, 66 (1951),
      698-717. Plot, structure, and design. Apologue. Happi-
      ness.

2837 Kolb, Gwin J. "Textual Cruxes in Rasselas." In Johnsonian
      Studies. Ed. Magdi Wahba. Cairo: n.p., 1962, pp. 257-
      62. Closure. Characterization.

2838 Kolb, Gwin J. "The Use of Stoical Doctrines in Rasselas,
      Chapter XVIII." Modern Language Notes, 68 (1953), 439-
      47. Stoicism. Intellectual background.

2839 Korshin, Paul J. "Johnson and Swift: A Study in the Gene-
      sis of Literary Opinion." Philological Quarterly, 48 (1969),

464-78. Eighteenth-century criticism and reviews of the
novel. Philosophy of novelist.

2840 Krutch, Joseph Wood. "Rasselas." In his Samuel Johnson.
      1944; rpt. New York: Harcourt, Brace, 1963, pp. 161-84.
      Biography. Composition of the novel.

2841 Landa, Louis A. "Johnson's Feathered Man: 'A Dissertation
      on the Art of Flying' Considered." In Eighteenth-Century
      Studies in Honor of Donald F. Hyde. Ed. W. H. Bond.
      New York: Grolier, 1970, pp. 161-78. Science. Philos-
      ophy of novelist.

2842 Lascelles, Mary. "Rasselas Reconsidered." In Essays and
      Studies, 4 (1951), 37-52. Critical revaluation.

2843 Leyburn, Ellen Douglass. "No Romantick Absurdities or In-
      credible Fictions: The Relations of Johnson's Rasselas to
      Lobo's Voyage to Abyssinia." PMLA, 70 (1955), 1059-67.
      Orientalism. Sources, analogues, and influences.

2844 Leyburn, Ellen Douglass. "Two Allegorical Treatments of
      Man: Rasselas and La Peste." Criticism, 4 (1962), 197-
      209. Allegory. Humanism. Existentialism.

2845 Link, Frederick M. "Rasselas and the Quest for Happiness."
      Boston University Studies in English, 3 (1957), 121-23.
      Happiness. Morality.

2845a Liu, Alan. "Toward a Theory of Common Sense: Beckford's
      Vathek and Johnson's Rasselas." Texas Studies in Litera-
      ture and Language, 26 (1984), 183-217. Common sense.
      Comparison of novelists.

2846 Lockhart, Donald M. "'The Fourth Son of the Mighty Emper-
      or': The Ethiopian Background of Johnson's Rasselas."
      PMLA, 78 (1963), 516-28. Composition of the novel.
      Sources, analogues, and influences.

2847 Lombardo, Agostino. "The Importance of Imlac." In Bicen-
      tenary Essays on "Rasselas." Ed. Magdi Wahba. Cairo:
      Société orientale de publicité, 1959, pp. 31-49. Character-
      ization. Autobiographical façade.

2848 Mahmoud, Fatma Moussa. "Rasselas and Vathek." In Bicen-
      tenary Essays on "Rasselas." Ed. Magdi Wahba. Cairo:
      Société orientale de publicité, 1959, pp. 51-57. Oriental-
      ism. Composition of the novel. Comparison of novelists
      [Johnson, Beckford].

2849 Manzalaoui, Mahmoud. "Rasselas and Some Mediaeval Ancil-

laries." In Bicentenary Essays on "Rasselas." Ed. Magdi
Wahba. Cairo: Société orientale de publicité, 1959, pp.
59-73. Sources, analogues, and influences. Christianity.
Education [Fürstenspiegel tradition]. Setting.

2850 Margolis, John D. "Pekuah and the Theme of Imprisonment
in Johnson's Rasselas." English Studies, 53 (1972), 339-
43. Imprisonment.

2851 McAdam, E. L., Jr. Dr. Johnson and the English Law. Syracuse, N.Y.: Syracuse Univ. Press, 1951. Law.

2852 McCrea, Brian. "Style or Styles: The Problem of Johnson's
Prose." Style, 14 (1980), 201-15. Style and language.

2853 McIntosh, Carey. "Johnson's Debate with Stoicism." ELH:
A Journal of English Literary History, 33 (1966), 327-36.
Stoicism. Philosophy of novelist.

■2854 McIntosh, Carey. "Rasselas." In his The Choice of Life:
Samuel Johnson and the World of Fiction. New Haven,
Conn.: Yale Univ. Press, 1973, pp. 163-212. Pessimism.
Happiness. Plot, structure, and design. Ambiguity.
Philosophy of novelist. Theory and practice of the novel.
Rasselas-Candide comparison.

2855 Misenheimer, James B., Jr. "Dr. Johnson on Prose Fiction."
New Rambler, Ser. C, 4 (1968), 12-18. Theory and practice of the novel [insistence on realism and morality].
Eighteenth-century criticism and reviews of the novel
[praise of novel over romance].

2856 Misenheimer, James B., Jr. "Dr. Johnson's Concept of Literary Fiction." Modern Language Review, 62 (1967), 598-
605. Theory and practice of the novel.

2857 Monie, Willis J. "Samuel Johnson's Contribution to the Novel." New Rambler, Ser. C, 17 (1976), 39-44. [Rasselas].
Theory and practice of the novel [realism and interest in
plot, characters, background].

2858 Moore, John Robert. "Rasselas and the Early Travelers to
Abyssinia." Modern Language Quarterly, 15 (1954), 36-41.
Sources, analogues, and influences.

2859 Moore, Robert Etheridge. "Dr. Johnson on Fielding and
Richardson." PMLA, 66 (1951), 162-81. Comparison of
novelists. Theory and practice of the novel.

2860 O'Flaherty, Patrick. "Dr. Johnson as Equivocator: The
Meaning of Rasselas." Modern Language Quarterly, 31
(1970), 195-208. Ambiguity. Christianity. Existentialism.

2861 Orr, Leonard. "The Structural and Thematic Importance of
      the Astronomer in Rasselas." Recovering Literature: A
      Journal of Contextualist Criticism, 9 (1981), 15-21. Plot,
      structure, and design [pyramidal plot].

2862 Pagliaro, Harold E. "Structural Patterns of Control in Ras-
      selas." In English Writers of the Eighteenth Century.
      Ed. John H. Middendorf. New York: Columbia Univ. Press,
      1971, pp. 208-29. Plot, structure, and design. Contrast
      as technique.

2863 Parke, Catherine. "Imlac and Autobiography." In Studies
      in Eighteenth-Century Culture. Vol. 6. Ed. Ronald C.
      Rosbottom. Madison: Univ. of Wisconsin Press, 1977, pp.
      183-98. Autobiographical façade. Point of view and nar-
      rator.

2864 Pierce, Charles E. "The Conflict of Faith and Fear in John-
      son's Moral Writing." Eighteenth-Century Studies, 15
      (1982), 317-38. Philosophy of novelist. Christianity.
      Existentialism.

■2865 Preston, Thomas R. "The Biblical Context of Johnson's Ras-
      selas." PMLA, 84 (1969), 274-81. Response by D. M.
      Korte in "Johnson's Rasselas," ibid., 87 (1972), 100-01.
      Biblical allusions. Happiness [futility of seeking perfect
      happiness].

2866 Probyn, Clive T. "Johnson, James Harris, and the Logic of
      Happiness." Modern Language Review, 73 (1978), 256-66.
      Happiness. Sources, analogues, and influences. Philos-
      ophy of novelist.

2867 Pyles, Thomas. "The Romantic Side of Dr. Johnson." ELH:
      A Journal of English Literary History, 11 (1944), 192-212.
      Reason. Romanticism.

2868 Quinlan, Maurice J. Samuel Johnson: A Layman's Religion.
      Madison: Univ. of Wisconsin Press, 1964. Christianity.
      Anglicanism. Charity. Conversion and repentance. Intel-
      lectual background.

2869 Reade, Aleyn Lyell. Johnsonian Gleanings. 11 vols. 1909-
      46; rpt. New York: Octagon, 1968. Biography.

2870 Reed, Kenneth T. "'This Tasteless Tranquility': A Freudian
      Note on Johnson's Rasselas." Literature and Psychology,
      19 (1969), 61-62. Imagery [pre-natal symbolism].

2871 Reichard, Hugo M. "The Pessimist's Helpers in Rasselas."
      Texas Studies in Literature and Language, 10 (1968), 57-64.
      Pessimism. Narrative technique.

2872 Reynolds, W. Vaughan. "Johnson's Opinions on Prose Style."
      Review of English Studies, O.S. 9 (1933), 433-46. Style
      and language.

2873 Richter, David H. "Aspects of the Eighteenth-Century Rhe-
      torical Novel: Johnson's Rasselas and Voltaire's Candide."
      In his Fable's End: Completeness and Closure in Rhetorical
      Fiction. Chicago: Univ. of Chicago Press, 1974, pp. 22-
      60. Apologue. Rhetorical novel. Plot, structure, and de-
      sign. Rasselas-Candide comparison.

2874 Rogers, Donald O. "Samuel Johnson's Concept of the Imagi-
      nation." South Central Bulletin, 33 (1973), 213-18. Imagi-
      nation.

2875 Rothstein, Eric. "Rasselas." In his Systems of Order and
      Inquiry in Later Eighteenth-Century Fiction. Los Angeles:
      Univ. of California Press, 1975, pp. 23-61. Plot, struc-
      ture, and design. Epistemology.

2876 Sachs, Arieh. "The Folly of Utopia." In his Passionate In-
      telligence: Imagination and Reason in the Work of Samuel
      Johnson. Baltimore: The Johns Hopkins Univ. Press,
      1967, pp. 91-108. [Rasselas]. Satire. Utopia. Christian-
      ity. Comparison of novelists [Johnson, Swift].

2877 Sachs, Arieh. "Generality and Particularity in Johnson's
      Thought." Studies in English Literature, 5 (1965), 491-511.
      Particular vs. general.

2878 Sacks, Sheldon. "The Special Demands of Apologue: Ras-
      selas." In his Fiction and the Shape of Belief: A Study
      of Henry Fielding with Glances at Swift, Johnson and Rich-
      ardson. Berkeley: Univ. of California Press, 1964, pp.
      49-60. Apologue. Narrative technique.

2879 Schwartz, Richard. "Johnson's Day, and Boswell's." In
      The Unknown Samuel Johnson. Ed. John J. Burke, Jr.,
      and Donald Kay. Madison: Univ. of Wisconsin Press,
      1983, pp. 76-90. The writer in society. Social back-
      ground.

2880 Schwartz, Richard. "Johnson's Philosopher of Nature: Ras-
      selas, Chapter 22." Modern Philology, 74 (1976), 196-200.
      Nature. Philosophy of novelist.

2881 Schwartz, Richard. Samuel Johnson and the New Science.
      Madison: Univ. of Wisconsin Press, 1971. Science.

•2882 Schwartz, Richard. Samuel Johnson and the Problem of Evil.
      Madison: Univ. of Wisconsin Press, 1975. Evil [psycho-

logical form of evil in Rasselas].   Philosophy of novelist.
Intellectual background.

2883   Scouten, Arthur H.   "Dr. Johnson and Imlac."   Eighteenth-
Century Studies, 6 (1973), 506-08.   Plot, structure, and
design.   Style and language.

2884   Sewall, Richard B.   "Dr. Johnson, Rousseau, and Reform."
In The Age of Johnson: Essays Presented to Chauncey
Brewster Tinker.   Ed. Frederick W. Hilles and Wilmarth S.
Lewis.   New Haven, Conn.:   Yale Univ. Press, 1949, pp.
307-17.   Rousseau.   Philosophy of novelist.

2885   Sewall, Richard B.   "Rousseau's Second Discourse in England
from 1755 to 1762."   Philological Quarterly, 17 (1938), 96-
111.   Rousseau.   Satire [on Rousseau's state of nature].
State of nature.

2886   Sklenicka, Carol J.   "Samuel Johnson and the Fiction of Activ-
ity."   South Atlantic Quarterly, 78 (1979), 214-23.   [Ras-
selas].   Happiness.

2887   Smitten, Jeffrey R.   "Johnson and the Sin of Sloth."   Renascence, 30 (1977), 3-18.   Sloth.   Christianity.

2888   Sternbach, Robert.   "Pascal and Dr. Johnson on Immortality."
Journal of the History of Ideas, 39 (1978), 483-89.   Pascal.
Immortality.

2889   Suderman, Elmer F.   "Candide, Rasselas and Optimism."   Iowa
English Yearbook, No. 11 (1966), pp. 37-43.   Rasselas-
Candide comparison.   Optimism [as futile].   Philosophy of
novelist.

2890   Sutherland, W. O. S., Jr.   "Satiric Ambiguity: The Plot of
Rasselas."   In his The Art of the Satirist: Essays on the
Satire of Augustan England.   Austin: Univ. of Texas
Press, 1965, pp. 83, 92-104.   Satire.   Ambiguity.   Plot,
structure, and design.

2891   Tillotson, Geoffrey.   "Imlac and the Business of a Poet."   In
Studies in Criticism and Aesthetics, 1660-1800:   Essays in
Honor of Samuel Holt Monk.   Ed. Howard Anderson and
John S. Shea.   Minneapolis: Univ. of Minnesota Press,
1967, pp. 296-314.   Characterization.

2892   Tillotson, Geoffrey.   "Rasselas."   In his Augustan Studies.
London: Athlone Press, 1961, pp. 229-48.   Introductory
guide.

2893   Tillotson, Geoffrey.   "Rasselas and the Persian Tales."   In his Essays in Criticism and Research. Cambridge: Cambridge Univ. Press, 1942, pp. 111-16. Sources, analogues, and influences. Orientalism.

2894   Tillotson, Geoffrey. "Time in Rasselas." In Bicentenary Essays on "Rasselas." Ed. Magdi Wahba. Cairo: Société orientale de publicité, 1959, pp. 97-103. Rpt. in his Augustan Studies. London: Athlone Press, 1961, pp. 249-55. Time [its use as a measure of life's worth].

2895   Tomarken, Edward. "Travels into the Unknown: Rasselas and A Journey to the Western Islands of Scotland." In The Unknown Samuel Johnson. Ed. John J. Burke, Jr., and Donald Kay. Madison: Univ. of Wisconsin Press, 1983, pp. 150-67. Journey. Closure.

2896   Tracy, Clarence. "'Democritus, Arise!' A Study of Dr. Johnson's Humor." Yale Review, 39 (1949), 294-310, esp. 305-10. Comedy.

2897   Tracy, Clarence. "Johnson and the Common Reader: The Roy M. Wiles Memorial Lecture for 1976." Dalhousie Review, 57 (1977), 405-23. Author-reader relationship. Point of view and narrator.

2898   Uphaus, Robert W. "Johnson's Equipoise and the State of Man." In his The Impossible Observer: Reason and the Reader in 18th-Century Prose. Lexington: Univ. Press of Kentucky, 1979, pp. 89-107. Equipoise. Author-reader relationship.

2899   Verbeek, E. The Measure and the Choice: A Pathographic Essay on Samuel Johnson. Ghent: E. Story-Scientia, 1971. Personality of novelist.

2900   Vesterman, William. "Johnson and Rasselas." In his The Stylistic Life of Samuel Johnson. New Brunswick, N.J.: Rutgers Univ. Press, 1977, pp. 69-104. Narrative technique. Style and language.

2901   Voitle, Robert. Samuel Johnson the Moralist. Cambridge, Mass.: Harvard Univ. Press, 1961. Morality. Reason. Empiricism. Charity. Liberty.

2902   Voitle, Robert. "Stoicism and Samuel Johnson." In Essays in English Literature of the Classical Period. Ed. Daniel W. Patterson and Albrecht B. Strauss. (Studies in Philology, Extra Series, No. 4.) Chapel Hill: Univ. of North Carolina Press, 1967, pp. 107-27. Stoicism.

2903   Wahba, Magdi. "A Note on the Manner of Concluding in Ras-

selas." In his Bicentenary Essays on "Rasselas." Société
orientale de publicité, 1959, pp. 105-10. Closure.

2904 Wain, John. Samuel Johnson: A Biography. New York:
Viking, 1974. Biography.

2905 Walker, Robert G. Eighteenth-Century Arguments for Immortality and Johnson's "Rasselas." Victoria: Univ. of Victoria, 1977. Immortality. Intellectual background.

■2906 Wasserman, Earl R. "Johnson's Rasselas: Implicit Contexts."
Journal of English and Germanic Philology, 74 (1975), 1-25.
Morality. Irony. Happiness. Plot, structure, and design.

2907 Weinbrot, Howard. "The Reader, the General, and the Particular: Johnson and Imlac in Chapter Ten of Rasselas."
Eighteenth-Century Studies, 5 (1971), 80-96. Point of view
and narrator. Author-reader relationship. Particular vs.
general.

2908 Weitzman, Arthur J. "More Light on Rasselas: The Background of the Egyptian Episodes." Philological Quarterly,
48 (1969), 42-58. Composition of the novel. Sources, analogues, and influences.

2909 West, Paul. "Rasselas: The Humanist as Stoic." English, 13
(1961), 181-85. Stoicism. Humanism.

2910 Whibley, Leonard. "Dr. Johnson and the Universities."
Blackwood's Magazine, 226 (1929), 369-83. Education.
Oxford University. Cambridge University.

2911 White, Ian. "On Rasselas." Cambridge Quarterly, 6 (1973),
6-31. Philosophy of novelist. Characterization. Happiness.

■2912 Whitley, Alvin. "The Comedy of Rasselas." ELH: A Journal
of English Literary History, 23 (1956), 48-70. Comedy.
Satire [on philosophic errors]. Plot, structure, and design.

2913 Wiles, Roy M. "Felix qui ...: Standards of Happiness in
Eighteenth-Century England." Studies on Voltaire and the
Eighteenth Century, 58 (1967), 1857-67. [Rasselas]. Hap-
piness. Philosophy of novelist.

2914 Willard, Nedd. "Zadig and Rasselas Considered." In Bicentenary Essays on "Rasselas." Ed. Magdi Wahba. Cairo:
Société orientale de publicité, 1959, pp. 111-23. Sources,
analogues, and influences.

2915 Wimsatt, W. K. "In Praise of Rasselas: Four Notes (Con-
verging)." In Imagined Worlds: Essays on Some English

Novels and Novelists in Honour of John Butt. Ed. Maynard
Mack and Ian Gregor. London: Methuen, 1968, pp. 111-
36. Composition of the novel. Plot, structure, and design.
Realism. Comedy.

•2916 Wimsatt, W. K. The Prose Style of Samuel Johnson. 1941;
rpt. New Haven, Conn.: Yale Univ. Press, 1963. Style
and language. Composition of the novel. Theory and practice of the novel.

2917 Winnett, A. R. "Johnson and Hume." New Rambler, Ser.
C., 1 (1966), pp. 2-14. Hume. Philosophy of novelist.

SEE ALSO ITEMS 334, 478, 716, 788, 792, 794, 797,
803, 863, 883, 884, 1004, 1006, 1065, 1102, 1106.

JONATHAN SWIFT
(1667-1745)

PRINCIPAL FICTION

Gulliver's Travels, 1726

BIBLIOGRAPHIES AND SURVEYS OF CRITICISM

2918 Bond, Donald. "Jonathan Swift (1667-1745)." In his The
Eighteenth Century. Goldentree Bibliographies. Northbrook, Ill.: AHM Press, 1975, pp. 133-42. Bibliography
of criticism.

2919 Clifford, James L. "The Eighteenth Century." Modern Language Quarterly, 26 (1965), 111-34, esp. 126-130. Fourth
voyage issues. Survey of criticism.

2920 Clifford, James L. "Gulliver's Fourth Voyage: 'Hard' and
'Soft' Schools of Interpretation." In Quick Springs of
Sense: Studies in the Eighteenth Century. Ed. Larry S.
Champion. Athens: Univ. of Georgia Press, 1974, pp. 33-
50. Survey of criticism [important delineation of main is-
sues]. Fourth voyage issues.

2921 Clubb, Merrel D. "The Criticism of Gulliver's 'Voyage to the
Houyhnhnms,' 1726-1914." Stanford Studies in Language
and Literature, 1941. Stanford, Cal.: Stanford Univ.
Press, 1941. Survey of criticism. Fourth voyage issues.

2922 Davis, Herbert. "Recent Studies of Swift: A Survey." Uni-

versity of Toronto Quarterly, 7 (1938), 273-88. Survey of
criticism.

2923 Falle, George. "Swift's Writings and a Variety of Commentators." University of Toronto Quarterly, 34 (1965), 294-312.
[Review article]. Survey of criticism.

2924 Keesey, Donald. "The Distorted Image: Swift's Yahoos and
the Critics." Papers on Language and Literature, 15
(1979), 320-32. Survey of criticism. Fourth voyage issues.
The Yahoos.

2925 Landa, Louis A. "Swift, 1667-1745." In The English Novel:
Select Bibliographical Guides. Ed. A. E. Dyson. Oxford:
Oxford Univ. Press, 1974, pp. 36-55. Bibliography of
criticism. Survey of criticism.

2926 Landa, Louis A., and James E. Tobin. Jonathan Swift: A
List of Critical Studies Published from 1895 to 1945. New
York: Cosmopolitan Science & Art Service Co., 1945.
Bibliography of criticism.

2927 Mayhew, George P. "Recent Swift Scholarship." In Jonathan
Swift, 1667-1967: A Dublin Tercentenary Tribute. Ed.
Roger McHugh and Philip Edwards. Chester Springs, Pa.:
Dufour Editions, 1968, pp. 187-97. Survey of criticism.

2928 Quintana, Ricardo. "A Modest Appraisal: Swift Scholarship
and Criticism, 1945-65." In Fair Liberty Was All His Cry:
A Tercentenary Tribute to Jonathan Swift, 1667-1745. Ed.
A. Norman Jeffares. London: Macmillan, 1967, pp. 342-
55. Survey of criticism.

2928a Rodino, Richard H. Swift Studies, 1965-1980: An Annotated
Bibliography. New York: Garland, [forthcoming]. Bibliography of criticism [annotated].

2929 Rosenheim, Edward, Jr. "The Fifth Voyage of Lemuel Gulliver: A Footnote." Modern Philology, 60 (1962), 103-19.
Survey of criticism.

2930 Sherburn, George. "Methods in Books About Swift." Studies
in Philology, 35 (1938), 635-56. Survey of criticism.

2931 Stathis, James J. A Bibliography of Swift Studies, 1945-1965.
Nashville, Tenn.: Vanderbilt Univ. Press, 1967. Bibliography of criticism [annotated].

2932 Teerink, Herman. A Bibliography of the Writings of Jonathan
Swift. 1937. 2nd ed., rev. by A. H. Scouten. Philadelphia: Univ. of Pennsylvania Press, 1963. Bibliography of
primary sources. Bibliography of criticism [through 1895].

2933 Voigt, Milton. "Gulliver's Travels." In his Swift and the
      Twentieth Century. Detroit: Wayne State Univ. Press,
      1964, pp. 65-123. Incorporates a revision of his "Swift and
      Psychoanalytic Criticism." Western Humanities Review, 16
      (1962), 361-67. Survey of criticism. Psychoanalytic issues.

BIOGRAPHICAL AND CRITICAL STUDIES

2934 Allison, Alexander W. "Concerning Houyhnhnm Reason."
      Sewanee Review, 76 (1968), 480-92. The Houyhnhnms.
      Reason.

2935 Barker, Rosalind Allen. "A Case for Religious Interpretation
      in Part III of Gulliver's Travels." In A Festschrift for
      Professor Marguerite Roberts, on the Occasion of Her Re-
      tirement from Westhampton College, University of Richmond,
      Virginia. Ed. Frieda Elaine Penniger. Richmond: Univ.
      of Richmond, 1976, pp. 101-13. Christianity.

■2936 Barroll, J. Leeds, III. "Gulliver and the Struldbruggs."
      PMLA, 73 (1958), 43-50. The Struldbruggs. Free think-
      ing. Immortality.

2937 Battestin, Martin C. "Swift: Order from Confusion." In his
      The Providence of Wit: Aspects of Form in Augustan Lit-
      erature and the Arts. Oxford: Clarendon Press, 1974,
      pp. 216-41. Plot, structure, and design. Order.

2938 Beauchamp, Gordon. "Gulliver's Return to the Cave: Plato's
      Republic and Book IV of Gulliver's Travels." Michigan
      Academician, 7 (1974), 201-09. Fourth voyage issues.
      The Houyhnhnms. Plato.

2939 Beaumont, Charles Allen. "Gulliver's Travels." In his
      Swift's Use of the Bible: A Documentation and a Study in
      Allusion. Athens: Univ. of Georgia Press, 1965, pp. 53-
      63. Biblical allusions.

2940 Beaumont, Charles Allen. Swift's Classical Rhetoric. Athens:
      Univ. of Georgia Press, 1961. Rhetoric [excludes Gulliver's
      Travels].

2941 Bentman, Raymond. "Satiric Structure and Tone in the Con-
      clusion of Gulliver's Travels." Studies in English Litera-
      ture, 11 (1971), 535-48. Plot, structure, and design.
      Satiric techniques. Characterization.

2942 Bloom, Allan. "An Outline of Gulliver's Travels." In An-
      cients and Moderns: Essays on the Tradition of Political
      Philosophy in Honor of Leo Strauss. Ed. Joseph Cropsey.

New York: Basic Books, 1964, pp. 238-58. Ancients vs. Moderns. Politics. Intellectual background.

2943 Borkat, Roberta Sarfatt. "Pride, Progress, and Swift's Struldbruggs." Durham University Journal, N.S. 37 (1976), 126-34. The Struldbruggs. Pride. Progress. Satire [on optimistic Moderns].

2944 Bracher, Frederick. "The Maps in Gulliver's Travels." Huntington Library Quarterly, 8 (1944), 59-74. Maps.

2945 Bracher, Frederick. "The Name 'Lemuel Gulliver.'" Huntington Library Quarterly, 12 (1949), 409-13. Names of characters.

2946 Brady, Frank. "Vexations and Diversions: Three Problems in Gulliver's Travels." Modern Philology, 75 (1978), 346-67. Critical revaluation. Comedy [jokes]. Degeneration. Fourth voyage issues.

■2947 Bredvold, Louis I. "The Gloom of the Tory Satirists." In Pope and His Contemporaries: Essays Presented to George Sherburn. Ed. James L. Clifford and Louis A. Landa. Oxford: Clarendon Press, 1949, pp. 1-19. Rpt. in Eighteenth-Century English Literature: Modern Essays in Criticism. Ed. James A. Clifford. New York: Oxford Univ. Press, 1959, pp. 3-20. [Swift, Pope]. Pessimism. Satire. Philosophy of novelist. Tories.

2948 Brown, James. "Swift as Moralist." Philological Quarterly, 33 (1954), 368-87. Morality. Philosophy of novelist.

■2949 Brown, Norman O. "The Excremental Vision." In his Life Against Death: The Psychoanalytical Meaning of History. Middletown, Conn.: Wesleyan Univ. Press, 1959, pp. 179-201. Rpt. in Swift: A Collection of Critical Essays. Ed. Ernest Tuveson. Twentieth Century Views Series. Englewood Cliffs, N.J.: Prentice Hall, 1964, pp. 31-54. Scatology. Psychoanalytic issues.

2950 Brückmann, Patricia. "Gulliver, Cum Grano Salis." Satire Newsletter, 1 (1963), 5-11. Imagery [salt].

2951 Bryan, Margaret B. "Swift's Use of the Looking-Glass in Gulliver's Travels." Connecticut Review, 8, No. 1 (1974), 90-94. Imagery [mirror].

●2952 Bullitt, John M. Jonathan Swift and the Anatomy of Satire: A Study of Satiric Technique. Cambridge, Mass.: Harvard Univ. Press, 1953. Satiric techniques.

2953 Byrd, Max. "Gulliver's Clothes: An Enlightenment Motif."
      Enlightenment Essays, 3, No. 1 (1972), 41-46. Clothing.
      Symbolism。

2954 Carnochan, W. B. "The Consolations of Satire." In The
      Art of Jonathan Swift. Ed. Clive T. Probyn. New York:
      Barnes & Noble, 1978, pp。 19-42. Satire [Swift's personal
      motives].

•2955 Carnochan, W. B. Lemuel Gulliver's Mirror for Man. Berke-
      ley: Univ. of California Press, 1968. Incorporates his
      "The Complexity of Swift: Gulliver's Fourth Voyage,"
      Studies in Philology, 60 (1963), 23-44; and "Gulliver's
      Travels: An Essay on the Human Understanding," Modern
      Language Quarterly, 25 (1964), 5-21. Satire. Point of
      view and narrator. Characterization.

2956 Carnochan, W. B. "Some Roles of Lemuel Gulliver." Texas
      Studies in Literature and Language, 5 (1964), 520-29.
      Characterization.

■2957 Case, Arthur E. "Personal and Political Satire in Gulliver's
      Travels." In his Four Essays on "Gulliver's Travels."
      1945; rpt. Gloucester, Mass.: Peter Smith, 1958, pp. 69-
      96. Rpt. in Discussions of Jonathan Swift. Ed. John
      Traugott. Boston: Heath, 1962, pp. 105-20. Satire.
      Politics.

2958 Castle, Terry. "Why the Houyhnhnms Don't Write: Swift,
      Satire and the Fear of the Text." Essays in Literature, 7
      (1980), 31-44. Satire. Grammaphobia. Autobiographical
      elements in the novel.

2959 Champion, Larry S. "Gulliver's Voyages: The Framing
      Events as a Guide to Interpretation." Texas Studies in
      Literature and Language, 10 (1969), 529-36. Plot, struc-
      ture, and design.

2960 Clark, J。 Kent. "Swift and the Dutch." Huntington Library
      Quarterly, 17 (1954), 345-56. The Dutch [Swift's hatred
      of].

2960a Clark, John R. "Lures, Limetwigs, and the Swiftean Swindle."
      Studies in the Literary Imagination, 17 (1984), 27-34. Au-
      thor-reader relationship ["reader entrapment"]. Point of
      view and narrator。

2961 Clark, Paul O. "A Gulliver Dictionary." Studies in Philology,
      50 (1953), 592-624. "Little language."

2962 Clark, Paul O., and Roland M. Smith. "Swift's Little Language

and Nonsense Names." Journal of English and Germanic
Philology, 56 (1957), 154-62. [An exchange]. "Little language." Style and language.

2963 Clayborough, Arthur. "Swift: The Fantasy of Extreme Logic." In his The Grotesque in English Literature. Oxford:
Clarendon Press, 1965, pp. 112-57. The grotesque.

2964 Cohan, Steven M. "Gulliver's Fiction." Studies in the Novel,
6 (1974), 7-16. Psychology of characters. Plot, structure,
and design.

2965 Cook, Richard I. Jonathan Swift as a Tory Pamphleteer.
Seattle: Univ. of Washington Press, 1967. Tories. Politics. Biography [pre-Gulliver].

2966 Cook, Terry. "'Dividing the Swift Mind': A Reading of Gulliver's Travels." Critical Quarterly, 22, No. 3 (1980), 35-
47. Plot, structure, and design.

2967 Corder, Jim. "Gulliver in England." College English, 23
(1961), 98-103. Setting. Point of view and narrator.
The Houyhnhnms [as the English].

2968 Crane, R. S. "The Houyhnhnms, the Yahoos, and the History of Ideas." In Reason and the Imagination: Studies in
the History of Ideas, 1660-1800. Ed. J. A. Mazzeo. New
York: Columbia Univ. Press, 1962, pp. 231-53. Intellectual
background. The Houyhnhnms. The Yahoos. Fourth voyage issues.

■2969 Crane, R. S. "The Rationale of the Fourth Voyage" [1955
lecture]. In Jonathan Swift: "Gulliver's Travels." Ed.
Robert A. Greenberg. 1961. Rev. ed. Norton Critical
Editions. New York: Norton, 1970, pp. 331-38. Fable
[Fourth voyage as moral and psychological fable]. Fourth
voyage issues.

2970 Darnall, F. M. "Old Wine in New Bottles." South Atlantic
Quarterly, 41 (1942), 53-63. Social criticism in the novel.

2971 Davis, Herbert. "The Conciseness of Swift." In Essays on
the Eighteenth Century Presented to David Nichol Smith.
1945; rpt. New York: Russell & Russell, 1963, pp. 15-32.
Style and language.

■2972 Davis, Herbert. "Moral Satire--Lemuel Gulliver." In his
The Satire of Jonathan Swift. New York: Macmillan, 1947,
pp. 77-109. Rpt. in his Jonathan Swift: Essays on his
Satire and Other Studies. New York: Oxford Univ. Press,
1964, pp. 143-60. Morality. Satire.

2973 Davis, Herbert. Stella: A Gentlewoman of the Eighteenth
      Century. New York: Macmillan, 1942. "Stella" [biography
      of Esther Johnson].

2974 Davis, Herbert. "Swift's Use of Irony." In The World of
      Jonathan Swift. Ed. Brian Vickers. Cambridge, Mass.:
      Harvard Univ. Press, 1968, pp. 154-70. Rpt. in Stuart
      and Georgian Moments. Ed. Earl Miner. Berkeley: Univ.
      of California Press, 1972, pp. 221-43. Irony. Satiric tech-
      niques.

2975 Dennis, Nigel. Jonathan Swift: A Short Character. London:
      Macmillan, 1964. Introductory guide. Biography. Com-
      parison of novelists [Swift, Defoe].

2976 Dennis, Nigel. "On Swift and Satire." Encounter, 22, No.
      3 (1964), 14-28. Introductory guide.

2977 Dircks, Richard J. "Gulliver's Tragic Rationalism." Criti-
      cism, 2 (1960), 134-49. Fourth voyage issues. Reason.
      Insanity.

2978 Donoghue, Denis. "The Lame Beggar." In his Jonathan
      Swift: A Critical Introduction. Cambridge: Cambridge
      Univ. Press, 1969, pp. 160-87. Introductory guide [Gul-
      liver's Travels].

2979 Dooley, D. J. "Image and Point of View in Swift." Papers
      on Language and Literature, 6 (1970), 125-35. Gulliver-
      Swift relationship. Point of view and narrator.

2980 Downie, J. A. "Political Characterization in Gulliver's Tra-
      vels." Yearbook of English Studies, 7 (1977), 108-20.
      Politics. Characterization.

2981 Duthie, Elizabeth. "Gulliver Art." Scriblerian, 10 (1978),
      127-31. Illustration.

2982 Dyson, A. E. "Swift: The Metamorphosis of Irony." Eng-
      lish Studies, 11 (1958), 53-67. Rpt. in his The Crazy
      Fabric: Essays in Irony. London: Macmillan, 1965, pp.
      1-13. Irony.

2983 Eddy, William A. "Gulliver's Travels": A Critical Study.
      1923; rpt. Gloucester, Mass.: Peter Smith, 1963. Imag-
      inary voyage. Philosophic voyage. Sources, analogues,
      and influences. Influence and imitation. Fourth voyage
      issues.

2984 Ehrenpreis, Irvin. "The Meaning of Gulliver's Last Voyage."
      Review of English Literature, 3, No. 3, (1962), 18-38.

Philosophy of novelist. Author-reader relationship. Fourth
voyage issues.

•2985 Ehrenpreis, Irvin. The Personality of Jonathan Swift. 1958;
rpt. New York: Barnes & Noble, 1969. Incorporates his
"The Origins of Gulliver's Travels." PMLA, 72 (1957),
880-99. Personality of novelist. Autobiographical elements
in the novel. Fourth voyage issues. Composition of the
novel. Allegory. Politics.

2986 Ehrenpreis, Irvin. "Swift and the Comedy of Evil." In The
World of Jonathan Swift. Ed. Brian Vickers. Cambridge,
Mass.: Harvard Univ. Press, 1968, pp. 213-19. Comedy.
Evil.

2987 Ehrenpreis, Irvin. "Swift and Satire." College English, 13
(1952), 309-12. Satiric techniques.

•2988 Ehrenpreis, Irvin. Swift: The Man, His Works, and the
Age. 3 vols. Cambridge, Mass.: Harvard Univ. Press,
1962-83. Biography.

2989 Ehrenpreis, Irvin. "Swiftian Dilemmas." In Satire in the
Eighteenth Century. Ed. J. D. Browning. New York:
Garland, 1983, pp. 214-31. [Gulliver's Travels]. Comedy
[comic form rests on the opposition between mind and
body].

2990 Elder, Lucius W. "The Pride of the Yahoo." Modern Language Notes, 35 (1920), 206-11. Pride. Irrationality.
Intellectual background. Fourth voyage issues.

2991 Elliott, Robert C. "Gulliver as Literary Aritst." ELH: A
Journal of English Literary History, 19 (1952), 49-63.
Point of view and narrator.

■2992 Elliott, Robert C. "Gulliver's Travels." In his The Power
of Satire: Magic, Ritual, Art. Princeton, N.J.: Princeton
Univ. Press, 1960, pp. 184-222. Satire. Point of view and
narrator. Satiric techniques. Gulliver-Swift relationship.
Fourth voyage issues.

2993 Elliott, Robert C. "Jonathan Swift." In his The Literary
Persona. Chicago: Univ. of Chicago Press, 1982, pp. 107-
64. Point of view and narrator. Satire.

2994 Elliott, Robert C. "Swift's 'I.'" Yale Review, 62 (1973), 372-
91. Point of view and narrator.

2995 Elliott, Robert C. "Swift's Satire: Rules of the Game." ELH:
A Journal of English Literary History, 41 (1974), 413-28.
Satire. Satiric techniques.

2996   Ewald, William Bragg, Jr.   "The Character of Lemuel Gulliver"
       and "Gulliver and His Hosts."   In his The Masks of Jona-
       than Swift.   Cambridge, Mass.:   Harvard Univ. Press,
       1954, pp. 124-62.   Point of view and narrator.   Satiric
       techniques.   Fourth voyage issues.   Masquerade.

2997   Fabricant, Carole.   Swift's Landscape.   Baltimore: The Johns
       Hopkins Univ. Press, 1982.   Landscape.   Setting.   Epistem-
       ology.   Politics.   Social criticism in the novel.   Scatology.
       Rural ideal [country house ideal, pastoral vision rejected].

2998   Ferenczi, Sandor.   "Gulliver Phantasies."   International Jour-
       nal of Psychoanalysis, 9 (1928), 283-300.   Psychoanalytic
       issues.   Psychology of characters.

2999   Ferguson, Oliver W.   Jonathan Swift and Ireland.   Urbana:
       Univ. of Illinois Press, 1962.   Ireland.   Politics.

3000   Fink, Zera S.   "Political Theory in Gulliver's Travels."   ELH:
       A Journal of English Literary History, 14 (1947), 151-61.
       Politics.

3001   Firth, Charles H.   "The Political Significance of Gulliver's
       Travels."   Proceedings of the British Academy, 9 (1919-20),
       237-59.   Rpt. in Essays, Historical and Literary.   Oxford:
       Oxford Univ. Press, 1938, pp. 210-41.   Politics.   Allegory.

3002   Fitzgerald, Robert P.   "The Allegory of Luggnagg and the
       Struldbruggs in Gulliver's Travels."   Studies in Philology.
       65 (1968), 657-76.   Allegory.   The Luggnaggians.   The
       Struldbruggs.

■3003 Fitzgerald, Robert P.   "The Structure of Gulliver's Travels."
       Studies in Philology, 71 (1974), 247-63.   Plot, structure,
       and design.   Social criticism in the novel.

3003a Fitzgerald, Robert P.   "Swift's Immortals: The Satiric Point."
       Studies in English Literature, 24 (1984), 483-95.   The
       Struldbruggs.   Satire [on the pursuit of fame].

3004   French, David P.   "Swift and Hobbes--A Neglected Parallel."
       Boston University Studies in English, 3 (1957), 243-55.
       Hobbes.   Philosophy of novelist.

3005   Frese, Jerry.   "Swift's Houyhnhnms and Utopian Law."   Hart-
       ford Studies in Literature, 9 (1977), 187-95.   The Houy-
       hnhnms.   Utopia.   Law.   Morality.

■3006 Frye, Roland Mushat.   "Swift's Yahoo and the Christian Sym-
       bols for Sin."   Journal of the History of Ideas, 15 (1954),
       201-17.   Rpt. in part in Twentieth Century Interpretations

of "Gulliver's Travels": A Collection of Critical Essays.
Ed. Frank Brady. Englewood Cliffs, N.J.: Prentice-Hall,
1968, pp. 104-06. For a response, see W. A. Murray,
"Mr. Roland M. Frye's Article on Swift's Yahoo," Journal
of the History of Ideas, 15 (1954), 599-601. The Yahoos
[symbols of sin and depravity]. Symbolism. Christianity.
Biblical allusions. Fourth voyage issues.

3007 Fussell, Paul. "The Frailty of Lemuel Gulliver." In Essays
      in Literary History Presented to J. Milton French. Eds.
      Rudolph Kirk and C. F. Main. New Brunswick, N.J.:
      Rutgers Univ. Press, 1960, pp. 113-25. Characterization.

3008 Geering, R. G. "Swift's Struldbruggs: The Critics Consid-
      ered." Journal of the Australasian Universities Modern
      Language Association, 7 (1957), 5-15. The Struldbruggs.
      Pride [satire on]. Critical revaluation.

3009 Gilbert, Jack G. Jonathan Swift: Romantic and Cynic Moral-
      ist. Austin: Univ. of Texas Press, 1966. Philosophy
      of novelist. Morality [of Gulliver's Travels].

3010 Gill, James E. "Beast over Man: Theriophilic Paradox in
      Gulliver's 'Voyage to the Country of the Houyhnhnms.'"
      Studies in Philology, 67 (1970), 532-49. Theriophily. Para-
      dox.

3011 Gill, James E. "Discovery and Alienation, Nature and Reason
      in Gulliver's Travels, Parts I-III." Tennessee Studies in
      Literature, 22 (1977), 85-104. Discovery. Loneliness.
      Characterization.

3012 Gill, James E. "Man and Yahoo: Dialectic and Symbolism in
      Gulliver's 'Voyage to the Country of the Houyhnhnms.'" In
      The Dress of Words: Essays on Restoration and Eighteenth-
      Century Literature in Honor of Richmond P. Bond. Ed.
      Robert B. White, Jr. Lawrence: Univ. of Kansas Libraries,
      1978, pp. 67-90. Symbolism. The Yahoos. Plot, structure,
      and design. Fourth voyage issues.

3013 Gold, Maxwell B. Swift's Marriage to Stella. Cambridge,
      Mass.: Harvard Univ. Press, 1937. "Stella" [Esther John-
      son]. Biography.

3014 Golden, Morris. "Swift." In his The Self Observed: Swift,
      Johnson, Wordsworth. Baltimore: The Johns Hopkins
      Univ. Press, 1972, pp. 33-66. The self. Philosophy of
      novelist.

3015 Goldgar, Bertrand A. The Curse of Party: Swift's Relations
      with Addison and Steele. Lincoln: Univ. of Nebraska

Press, 1961. Politics [1707-29]. Biography. Addison and
Steele. Tories. Whigs.

3016 Goldgar, Bertrand A. "Gulliver's Travels and the Opposition
to Walpole." In The Augustan Milieu: Essays Presented to
Louis A. Landa. Eds. Henry Knight Miller, Eric Rothstein,
and George S. Rousseau. Oxford: Clarendon Press, 1970,
pp. 155-73. Politics. Sir Robert Walpole.

3017 Goldgar, Bertrand A. "Satires on Man and 'The Dignity of
Human Nature.'" PMLA, 80 (1965), 535-41. Eighteenth-
century criticism and reviews of the novel.

3018 Greenacre, Phyllis. Swift and Carroll: A Psychoanalytic
Study of Two Lives. New York: International Univ.
Press, 1955. Psychology of characters. Psychoanalytic
issues. Autobiographical elements in the novel.

3019 Greene, Donald. "The Education of Lemuel Gulliver." In
The Varied Pattern: Studies in the 18th Century. Ed.
Peter Hughes and David Williams. Toronto: Hakkert, 1971,
pp. 3-20. Characterization.

3020 Greene, Donald. "Swift: Some Caveats." In Studies in the
Eighteenth Century II. Ed. R. F. Brissenden. Toronto:
Univ. of Toronto Press, 1973, pp. 341-58. Philosophy of
novelist.

3021 Grennan, Margaret R. "Lilliput and Leprecan: Gulliver and
the Irish Tradition." ELH: A Journal of English Literary
History, 12 (1945), 188-202. The Lilliputians. Ireland.

3022 Guskin, Phyllis J. "'A Very Remarkable Book': Abel Boyer's
View of Gulliver's Travels." Studies in Philology, 72 (1975),
439-53. Eighteenth-century criticism and reviews of the
novel.

3023 Halewood, William H. "Gulliver's Travels I, vi." ELH: A
Journal of English History, 33 (1966), 422-33. Utopia.
Plutarch. Sources, analogues, and influences. Plot, struc-
ture, and design. Satiric techniques.

3024 Halewood, William H. "Plutarch in Houyhnhnmland: A Neglected Source of Gulliver's Fourth Voyage." Philological
Quarterly, 44 (1965), 185-94, esp. 192-94. Fourth voyage
issues. Plutarch. Classical allusions. Sources, analogues,
and influences.

3025 Halewood, William H., and Marvin Levich. "Houyhnhnm Est
Animal Rationale." Journal of the History of Ideas, 26
(1965), 273-81. The Houyhnhnms [as ideal]. Reason.
Fourth voyage issues.

3026 Hall, Basil. "'An Inverted Hypocrite': Swift the Church-
      man." In The World of Jonathan Swift. Ed. Brian Vick-
      ers. Cambridge, Mass.: Harvard Univ. Press, 1968, pp.
      38-68. Christianity.

3027 Hammond, Eugene R. "Nature-Reason-Justice in Utopia and
      Gulliver's Travels." Studies in English Literature, 22
      (1982), 445-68. Fourth voyage issues. Utopia. Sir Thomas
      More.

3028 Hardy, Evelyn. The Conjured Spirit: A Study in the Rela-
      tionship of Swift, Stella, and Vanessa. London: Hogarth
      Press, 1949. Biography. Psychoanalytic issues. "Stella"
      [Esther Johnson]. "Vanessa" [Esther Vanhomrigh].

3029 Hart, Jeffrey. "The Ideologue as Artist. Some Notes on
      Gulliver's Travels." Criticism, 2 (1960), 125-33. Order.
      Politics.

3030 Harth, Phillip. "The Problem of Political Allegory in Gulliver's
      Travels." Modern Philology, 73, No. 4 (1976), Part 2, S
      40-47. [First voyage]. Politics. Allegory. Critical re-
      valuation.

3031 Hassall, Anthony J. "Discontinuities in Gulliver's Travels."
      Sydney Studies in English, 5 (1979-80), 3-14. Defects in
      the novel. Author-reader relationship.

3032 Higgins, Ian. "Swift and Sparta: The Nostalgia of Gulliver's
      Travels." Modern Language Review, 78 (1983), 513-31.
      Classical allusions [influence of Spartan politics and ethics
      on Swift]. Politics. Morality.

3033 Holly, Grant. "Travel and Translation: Textuality in Gul-
      liver's Travels." Criticism, 21 (1979), 134-52. "Textual-
      ity." Ambiguity. Author-reader relationship.

3034 Horrell, Joseph. "What Gulliver Knew." Sewanee Review, 51
      (1943), 476-504. Narrative technique. Fourth voyage is-
      sues.

3035 Horsley, Lee Sonsteng. "'Of All Fictions the Most Simple':
      Swift's Shared Imagery." Yearbook of English Studies, 5
      (1975), 98-114. Imagery.

3036 Hunting, Robert. Jonathan Swift. Twayne's English Authors
      Series. New York: Twayne, 1967. Introductory guide.

3037 Jarrett, James L. "A Yahoo Versus Jonathan Swift." Western
      Humanities Review, 8 (1954), 195-200. Defects in the novel.

3038   Johnson, James W. "Swift's Historical Outlook." Journal of
       British Studies, 4, No. 2 (1965), 52-77. Historiography.

3039   Johnston, Denis. In Search of Swift. New York: Barnes &
       Noble, 1959. Biography.

3040   Kallich, Martin. The Other End of the Egg: Religious Satire
       in "Gulliver's Travels." Bridgeport, Conn.: Conference
       on British Studies at the University of Bridgeport, 1970.
       Satire. Christianity. Satiric techniques. Fourth voyage
       issues.

3041   Kallich, Martin. "Three Ways of Looking at a Horse: Jona-
       than Swift's 'Voyage to the Houyhnhnms' Again." Criticism,
       2 (1960), 107-24. The Houyhnhnms. Christianity. Fourth
       voyage issues. Satire [on Deism]. Deism.

3042   Karpman, Benjamin. "A Modern Gulliver: A Study in Copro-
       philia." Psychoanalytic Review, 26 (1949), 162-85, 260-82.
       Psychoanalytic issues. Scatology.

3043   Karpman, Benjamin. "Neurotic Traits of Jonathan Swift, as
       Revealed in Gulliver's Travels." Psychoanalytic Review, 29
       (1942), 26-45, 165-84. Autobiographical elements in the
       novel. Psychoanalytic issues.

3044   Keener, Frederick M. "Gulliver's Habits and Prejudices." In
       his The Chain of Becoming: The Philosophical Tale, the
       Novel, and a Neglected Realism of the Enlightenment. New
       York: Columbia Univ. Press, 1983, pp. 89-126. Philo-
       sophical tale. Didacticism. Psychology of characters.

3045   Kelling, H. D. "Gulliver's Travels: A Comedy of Humours."
       University of Toronto Quarterly, 21 (1952), 362-75. Come-
       dy. The humors. Gulliver-Swift relationship. Fourth
       voyage issues. Characterization.

3046   Kelling, H. D. "Gulliver's Travels IV, Once More." Scholia
       Satyrica, 2, No. 2 (1976), 3-12. Fourth voyage issues.
       Author-reader relationship.

3047   Kelling, H. D. "Some Significant Names in Gulliver's Travels."
       Studies in Philology, 48 (1951), 761-78. Names of charac-
       ters.

3048   Kelly, Ann Cline. "After Eden: Gulliver's (Linguistic) Trav-
       els." ELH: A Journal of English Literary History, 45
       (1978), 33-54. Style and language. Speech and dialogue.

3049   Kelly, Ann Cline. "Swift's Explorations of Slavery in Houy-
       hnhnmland and Ireland." PMLA, 91 (1976), 846-55. Slav-
       ery. Ireland. Politics.

3050 Kelsall, M. M. "Iterum Houyhnhnm: Swift's Sextumvirate
and the Horses." Essays in Criticism, 19 (1969), 35-45.
The Houyhnhnms. Fourth voyage issues. Classical allusions.

■3051 Kliger, Samuel. "The Unity of Gulliver's Travels." Modern
Language Quarterly, 6 (1945), 401-15. Unity. Contrast as
technique. Characterization. Imagery [return, animal,
clothing]. Fourth voyage issues.

3052 Korshin, Paul J. "The Intellectual Context of Swift's Flying
Island." Philological Quarterly, 50 (1971), 630-46. Satire.
Sources, analogues, and influences. Intellectual background.
Science.

3053 LaCasce, Steward. "The Fall of Gulliver's Master." Essays
in Criticism, 20 (1970), 327-33. Characterization. The
Houyhnhnms.

3054 LaCasce, Steward. "Gulliver's Fourth Voyage: A New Look
at the Critical Debate." Satire Newsletter, 8, No. 1 (1970),
5-7. Fourth voyage issues.

3055 LaCasce, Steward. "Swift on Medical Extremism." Journal of
the History of Ideas, 31 (1970), 599-606. [Fourth voyage].
Medicine. Satire.

3056 Landa, Louis A. "The Dismal Science in Houyhnhnmland."
Novel, 13 (1979), 38-49. Mercantilism. Luxury. Economics.

3057 Landa, Louis A. "Jonathan Swift and Charity." Journal of
English and Germanic Philology, 44 (1945), 337-50. Charity. Biography.

■3058 Landa, Louis A. "Jonathan Swift: The Critical Significance
of Biographical Evidence." In English Institute Essays,
1946. New York: Columbia Univ. Press, 1947, pp. 20-40.
Rpt. in Studies in the Literature of the Augustan Age:
Essays Collected in Honor of Arthur Ellicott Case. Ed.
Richard C. Boys. Ann Arbor, Mich.: George Wahr, 1952,
176-97. Christianity [Fourth voyage as Christian apolo-
getics]. Allegory. Biography.

3059 Landa, Louis A. Swift and the Church of Ireland. Oxford:
Clarendon Press, 1954. Biography [religious life]. The
Church.

3060 Landa, Louis A. "Swift's Economic Views and Mercantilism."
ELH: A Journal of English Literary History, 10 (1943),
310-35. Economics. Mercantilism.

3061 Lawlis, Merritt. "Swift's Use of Narrative: The Third Chapter of The Voyage to Lilliput." Journal of English and Germanic Philology, 72 (1973), 1-16. Narrative technique. Point of view and narrator.

3062 Lawry, Jon S. "Dr. Lemuel Gulliver and 'The Thing Which Was Not.'" Journal of English and Germanic Philology, 67 (1968), 212-34. Point of view and narrator. Characterization.

3063 Leavis, F. R. "The Irony of Swift." Scrutiny, 2 (1934), 364-78. Rpt. in Discussions of Jonathan Swift. Ed. John Traugott. Boston: Heath, 1962, pp. 35-43. Irony.

3064 LeBrocquy, Sybil. Cadenus: A Reassessment in the Light of New Evidence of the Relationships Between Swift, Stella and Vanessa. Dublin: Dolmen Press, 1962. Biography [romantic life]. "Stella" [Esther Johnson]. "Vanessa" [Esther Vanhomrigh].

3065 Lee, Jae Num. "Scatology in Gulliver's Travels." In his Swift and Scatological Satire. Albuquerque: Univ. of New Mexico Press, 1971, pp. 98-120. Scatology. Satiric techniques.

3066 Leyburn, Ellen Douglass. "Gulliver's Clothes." Satire Newsletter, 1 (1964), 35-40. Imagery. Clothing.

3067 Leyburn, Ellen Douglass. "Satiric Journeys I: Gulliver's Travels." In her Satiric Allegory: Mirror of Man. New Haven, Conn.: Yale Univ. Press, 1956, pp. 71-91. Allegory. Satire. Journey.

3068 Leyburn, Ellen Douglass. "Swift's Language Trifles." Huntington Library Quarterly, 15 (1952), 195-200. Style and language [little on Gulliver's Travels].

3069 Leyburn, Ellen Douglass. "Swift's View of the Dutch." PMLA, 66 (1951), 734-45. The Dutch.

•3070 Lock, F. P. The Politics of "Gulliver's Travels." Oxford: Clarendon Press, 1980. Politics.

3071 Louis, Frances Deutsch. "Travelling On: Gulliver's Travels." In her Swift's Anatomy of Misunderstanding: A Study of Swift's Epistemological Imagination in "A Tale of a Tub" and "Gulliver's Travels." Totowa, N.J.: Barnes & Noble, 1981, pp. 126-67. Epistemology. The Laputans. The Brobdingnagians. The Lilliputians. The Houyhnhnms. The Yahoos.

3072 Maresca, Thomas E. "Swift." In his Epic to Novel. Columbus: Ohio State Univ. Press, 1974, pp. 135-80. Epic.

3073 McCracken, George. "Homerica in Gulliver's Travels." Classical Journal, 29 (1934), 535-38. Homer. Classical allusions.

3074 McDowell, R. B. "Swift as a Political Thinker." In Jonathan Swift, 1667-1967: A Dublin Tercentenary Tribute. Ed. Roger McHugh and Philip Edwards. Chester Springs, Pa.: Dufour Editions, 1968, pp. 176-86. Politics.

3075 McKenzie, Gordon. "Swift: Reason and Some of Its Consequences." In Five Studies in Literature. Univ. of California Publications in English, Vol. 8, No. 1. Berkeley: Univ. of California Press, 1940, pp. 101-29. Reason [as ideal]. Philosophy of novelist.

3076 McManmon, John J. "The Problem of a Religious Interpretation of Gulliver's Fourth Voyage." Journal of the History of Ideas, 27 (1966), 59-72. Christianity. Fourth voyage issues. Survey of criticism.

3077 Mercier, Vivian. "Swift and Irish Satire in the English Language." In The Irish Comic Tradition. Oxford: Clarendon Press, 1962, pp. 182-209. Satiric techniques. Ireland.

3078 Metscher, Thomas. "The Radicalism of Swift: Gulliver's Travels and the Irish Point of View." Zeitschrift für Anglistik und Amerikanistik, No. 4 (1982), pp. 293-310. Radicalism. Ireland. Social criticism in the novel.

3079 Mezciems, Jenny. "Gulliver and Other Heroes." In The Art of Jonathan Swift. Ed. Clive Probyn. New York: Barnes & Noble, 1978, pp. 189-208. Characterization. Comparison of novelists [Swift, Defoe].

■3080 Mezciems, Jenny. "The Unity of Swift's 'Voyage to Laputa': Structure as Meaning in Utopian Fiction." Modern Language Review, 72 (1977), 1-21. Unity. Plot, structure, and design. The Laputans. Utopian fiction.

3081 Mezciems, Jenny. "Utopia and 'The Thing Which Is Not': More, Swift, and Other Lying Idealists." University of Toronto Quarterly, 52 (1982), 40-62. Style and language. Utopia. Idealism. Point of view and narrator. Sir Thomas More.

3082 Milic, Louis T. A Quantitative Approach to the Style of Jonathan Swift. The Hague: Mouton, 1967. Style and language.

■3083 Monk, Samuel H. "The Pride of Lemuel Gulliver." Sewanee Review, 63 (1955), 48-71. Rpt. in Eighteenth-Century English Literature: Modern Essays in Criticism. Ed. James L.

Clifford. New York: Oxford Univ. Press, 1959, pp. 112-
29. Pride. Christianity. Satire [on Gulliver]. Gulliver-
Swift relationship. Misanthropy [Swift not a misanthrope].
Fourth voyage issues.

3084   Moore, John Brooks. "The Role of Gulliver." Modern Philology, 25 (1928), 469-80. Gulliver-Swift relationship. Misanthropy.

3085   Moore, John Robert. "The Geography of Gulliver's Travels."
Journal of English and Germanic Philology, 40 (1941), 214-
28. Setting. Geography.

3086   Moore, John Robert. "Was Jonathan Swift a Moderate?"
South Atlantic Quarterly, 53 (1954), 260-67. Politics.
Christianity.

3087   Morris, John N. "Wishes for Horses: A Word for the Houyhnhnms." Yale Review, 62 (1973), 355-71. Author-reader
relationship. The Houyhnhnms.

3088   Morrissey, L. J. Gulliver's Progress. Hamden, Conn.:
Archon, 1978. Characterization. Christianity. Biblical
allusions. Plot, structure, and design. Time [dates as
Christian allegory].

3089   Munro, John M. "Book III of Gulliver's Travels Once More."
English Studies, 49 (1968), 429-36. Composition of the novel. Plot, structure, and design.

3090   Murry, John Middleton. Jonathan Swift: A Critical Biography. 1954; rpt. New York: Noonday, 1955. Biography.

3091   Nicolson, Marjorie. "The Microscope and English Imagination."
Smith College Studies in Modern Languages, 16, No. 4
(1935), 1-92, esp. 50-56. Rpt. in Science and Imagination.
Ithaca, N.Y.: Great Seal Books, 1956, pp. 155-234. [First
and second voyages]. Microscope. Science.

3092   Nicolson, Marjorie, with Nora M. Mohler. "The Scientific
Background of Swift's Voyage to Laputa." Annals of Science, 2 (1937), 299-334. Rpt. in Science and Imagination.
Ithaca, N.Y.: Great Seal Books, 1956, pp. 110-54. Science. Intellectual background.

3093   Orwell, George. "Politics vs. Literature: An Examination of
Gulliver's Travels." In his Shooting an Elephant and Other
Essays. New York: Harcourt, Brace, 1945, pp. 53-76.
Rpt. in Discussions of Jonathan Swift. Ed. John Traugott.
Boston: Heath, 1962, pp. 80-91. Politics.

3094   Palomo, Dolores. "The Dutch Connection: The University of
       Leiden and Swift's Academy of Lagado." Transactions of
       the Samuel Johnson Society of the Northwest, 7 (1974),
       119-34. Satire. Science. "Little language." Names of
       characters.

3095   Paulson, Ronald. "Swiftean Picaresque: Gulliver's Travels."
       In his The Fictions of Satire. Baltimore: The Johns Hop-
       kins Univ. Press, 1967, pp. 162-85. Picaresque novel.
       Satiric techniques.

■3096 Peake, Charles. "Swift and the Passions." Modern Language
       Review, 55 (1960), 169-80. Rpt. in A Casebook on Gulliver
       Among the Houyhnhnms. Ed. Milton P. Foster. New York:
       Crowell, 1961, pp. 282-98. Fourth voyage issues. The
       passions [not reprehensible to Swift]. The Houyhnhnms.
       The Yahoos.

3097   Philmus, Robert M. "Swift, Gulliver, and 'The Thing Which
       Was Not.'" ELH: A Journal of English Literary History,
       38 (1971), 62-79. Point of view and narrator. Irony.

3098   Pierre, Gerald J. "Gulliver's Voyage to China and Moor Park:
       The Influence of Sir William Temple upon Gulliver's Travels."
       Texas Studies in Literature and Language, 17 (1975), 427-
       37. Sources, analogues, and influences. Fourth voyage
       issues.

3099   Pinkus, Philip. Swift's Vision of Evil: A Comparative Study
       of "A Tale of a Tub" and "Gulliver's Travels." 2 vols.
       English Literary Studies Monograph Series, 3-4. Victoria:
       Department of English, Univ. of Victoria, 1975. Evil.
       Imagery [bestial]. Irrationality. Fourth voyage issues.
       Existentialism.

3100   Piper, William Bowman. "The Sense of Gulliver's Travels."
       Rice University Studies, 61, No. 1 (1975), 75-106. Plot,
       structure, and design. Style and language. The Yahoos.
       The Houyhnhnms. Author-reader relationship.

3101   Poll, Max. The Sources of "Gulliver's Travels." Univ. of Cin-
       cinnati, Bulletin No. 24. Cincinnati: Univ. of Cincinnati
       Press, 1904. Sources, analogues, and influences.

3102   Potter, George Reuben. "Swift and Natural Science." Philo-
       logical Quarterly, 20 (1941), 97-118. Science. Satire.

3103   Preu, James A. The Dean and the Anarchist. Tallahassee:
       Florida State Univ. Press, 1959. Politics. Influence and
       imitation. Comparison of novelists [Swift, Godwin].

3104 Price, Martin. "Swift: Order and Obligation." In his To
the Palace of Wisdom: Studies in Order and Energy from
Dryden to Blake. 1964; rpt. New York: Doubleday, 1965,
pp. 180-204, esp. pp. 197-204. Order vs. disorder. Contrast as technique.

▪3105 Price, Martin. "The Symbolic Works." In his Swift's Rhetor-
ical Art: A Study in Structure and Meaning. 1953; rpt.
Hamden, Conn.: Archon, 1963, pp. 75-102. Symbolism.
Plot, structure, and design. Rhetoric. Satiric techniques.
Author-reader relationship. Fourth voyage issues.

3106 Probyn, Clive T. "Gulliver and the Relativity of Things: A
Commentary on Method and Mode, with a Note on Smollett."
Renaissance and Modern Studies, 18 (1974), 63-76. Rela-
tivity. Morality. Satiric techniques.

3107 Probyn, Clive T. "Swift and Linguistics: The Context Be-
hind Lagado and Around the Fourth Voyage." Neophilo-
logus, 58 (1974), 425-39. Style and language. Satire [on
language].

3108 Pullen, Charles H. "Gulliver: Student of Nature." Dalhousie
Review, 51 (1971), 77-89. Characterization.

3109 Quinlan, Maurice J. "Swift's Use of Literalization as a Rhetorical Device." PMLA, 82 (1967), 516-21. Style and language.
Satiric techniques.

3110 Quinlan, Maurice J. "Treason in Lilliput and in England."
Texas Studies in Literature and Language, 11 (1970), 1317-
32. Politics. Allegory. Satire.

▪3111 Quintana, Ricardo. "Gulliver's Travels." In his The Mind
and Art of Jonathan Swift. 1936; rpt. London: Oxford
Univ. Press, 1953, pp. 289-328. Philosophy of novelist.
Intellectual background. Satiric techniques. Fourth voyage
issues.

3112 Quintana, Ricardo. "Gulliver's Travels: The Satiric Intent
and Execution." In Jonathan Swift, 1667-1967: A Dublin
Tercentenary Tribute. Ed. Roger McHugh and Philip Edwards. Chester Springs, Pa.: Dufour Editions, 1968, pp.
78-93. Introductory guide. Satire.

3113 Quintana, Ricardo. "Situational Satire: A Commentary on the
Method of Swift." University of Toronto Quarterly, 17
(1948), 130-36. Rpt. in Studies in the Literature of the
Augustan Age: Essays Collected in Honor of Arthur Ellicott
Case. Ed. Richard C. Boys. Ann Arbor, Mich.: George
Wahr, 1952, pp. 258-65. Satiric techniques. Gulliver-Swift
relationship.

•3114 Quintana, Ricardo. Swift: An Introduction. London: Ox-
       ford Univ. Press, 1955. Introductory guide [excellent ac-
       count of main issues]. Fourth voyage issues.

3115   Quintana, Ricardo. Two Augustans: John Locke, Jonathan
       Swift. Madison: Univ. of Wisconsin Press, 1978. Intel-
       lectual background. Locke.

3116   Radner, John B. "The Struldbruggs, the Houyhnhnms, and
       the Good Life." Studies in English Literature, 17 (1977),
       419-33. Christianity. Immortality. The Struldbruggs.
       The Houyhnhnms.

3117   Rawson, C. J. "Gulliver and the Gentle Reader." In his
       Gulliver and the Gentle Reader: Studies in Swift and Our
       Time. London: Routledge & Kegan Paul, 1973, pp. 1-32.
       Author-reader relationship. Satiric techniques.

3118   Reichard, Hugo M. "Gulliver the Pretender." Papers on
       Language and Literature, 1 (1965), 316-26. Characteriza-
       tion.

3119   Reichard, Hugo M. "Satiric Snobbery: The Houyhnhnms'
       Man." Satire Newsletter, 4 (1967), 51-57. Characteriza-
       tion. Satire. Snobbery.

3120   Reichert, John F. "Plato, Swift, and the Houyhnhnms."
       Philological Quarterly, 47 (1968), 179-92. [Fourth voyage].
       The Houyhnhnms. Plato.

3121   Reilly, Patrick. "Curiosity and Contamination: Forbidden
       Knowledge in Gulliver's Travels" and "The Displaced Per-
       son." In his Jonathan Swift: The Brave Desponder. Car-
       bondale: Southern Illinois Univ. Press, 1982, pp. 152-209.
       Modernity. Forbidden knowledge. Estrangement. Chris-
       tianity. Philosophy of novelist [influence of Hobbes].
       Pessimism.

3122   Reiss, Edmund. "The Importance of Swift's Glubbdubrib Epi-
       sode." Journal of English and Germanic Philology, 59
       (1960), 223-28. Plot, structure, and design. Characteri-
       zation.

3123   Roberts, Donald R. "A Freudian View of Jonathan Swift."
       Literature and Psychology, 6 (1956), 8-17. Psychoanalytic
       issues. Autobiographical elements in the novel.

3124   Rogers, Pat. "Swift, Walpole, and the Rope-Dancers." Pa-
       pers on Language and Literature, 8 (1972), 159-71. Poli-
       tics. Allegory. Sir Robert Walpole.

3125   Rogers, Pat. "Gulliver and the Engineers." Modern Lan-

guage Review, 70 (1975), 260-70. [Lagado episode]. Industry and trade. Satire. Social background.

3126   Rogers, Pat. "Gulliver's Glasses." In The Art of Jonathan
       Swift. Ed. Clive T. Probyn. New York: Barnes & Noble,
       1978, pp. 179-88. Symbolism [glasses]. Characterization.

3127   Rogers, Pat. "Swift and the Idea of Authority." In The
       World of Jonathan Swift. Ed. Brian Vickers. Cambridge,
       Mass.: Harvard Univ. Press, 1968, pp. 25-37. Authority.
       Philosophy of novelist.

•3128   Rosenheim, Edward W., Jr. Swift and the Satirist's Art.
       Chicago: Univ. of Chicago Press, 1963, 90-102, 154-67,
       207-36. Satiric techniques. Fourth voyage issues.

3129   Ross, Angus. "The Social Circumstances of Certain Remote
       Nations." In The World of Jonathan Swift. Ed. Brian
       Vickers. Cambridge, Mass.: Harvard Univ. Press, 1968,
       pp. 220-32. Social structure.

■3130   Ross, John F. "The Final Comedy of Lemuel Gulliver." In
       Studies in the Comic. Univ. of California Publications in
       English, Vol. 8, No. 2. Berkeley: Univ. of California
       Press, 1941, pp. 175-96. Rpt. in Swift: A Collection of
       Critical Essays. Ed. Ernest Tuveson. Twentieth Century
       Views Series. Englewood Cliffs, N.J.: Prentice-Hall, 1964,
       pp. 71-90. Comedy. Fourth voyage issues. Gulliver-Swift
       relationship [their separate identities]. Satiric techniques.
       Misanthropy [Gulliver, not Swift, a misanthrope].

3131   Ross, John F. Swift and Defoe: A Study in Relationship.
       Berkeley: Univ. of California Press, 1941. Comparison of
       novelists.

3132   Ryley, Robert M. "Gulliver, Flimnap's Wife, and the Critics."
       Studies in the Literary Imagination, 5, No. 2 (1972), 53-63.
       [First voyage]. Comedy. Characterization.

3133   Sams, Henry W. "Swift's Satire of the Second Person." ELH:
       A Journal of English Literary History, 26 (1959), 36-44.
       Satire [on reader]. Author-reader relationship. Satiric
       techniques.

3134   Samuel, Irene. "Swift's Reading of Plato." Studies in Philol-
       ogy, 73 (1976), 440-62. Plato. Socrates.

3135   Seelye, John D. "Hobbes' Leviathan and the Giantism Com-
       plex in the First Book of Gulliver's Travels." Journal of
       English and Germanic Philology, 60 (1961), 228-39. Hobbes.
       Satire [on Hobbes]. Politics.

3136 Seidel, Michael. "Strange Dispositions: Swift's Gulliver's Travels." In his Satiric Inheritance: Rabelais to Sterne. Princeton, N.J.: Princeton Univ. Press, 1979, pp. 201-25. Narrative technique. Satire.

3137 Selby, Hopewell R. "The Cell and the Garret: Fictions of Confinement in Swift's Satires and Personal Writings." In Studies in Eighteenth-Century Culture. Vol. 6. Ed. Ronald C. Rosbottom. Madison: Univ. of Wisconsin Press, 1977, pp. 133-56. Imprisonment.

3138 Sena, John F. "The Language of Gestures in Gulliver's Travels." Papers on Language and Literature, 19 (1983), 145-66. Gestures and mannerisms. Speech and dialogue.

3139 Sena, John F. "Swift, the Yahoos, and 'The English Malady.'" Papers on Language and Literature, 7 (1971), 300-03. The Yahoos. Medicine. Satire.

3140 Sherbo, Arthur. "Swift and Travel Literature." Modern Language Studies, 9, No. 3 (1979), 114-27. Travel literature. Parody.

■3141 Sherburn, George. "Errors Concerning the Houyhnhnms." Modern Philology, 61 (1958), 92-97. The Houyhnhnms [not objects of satire]. Fourth voyage issues.

3142 Siebert, Donald T., Jr. "Masks and Masquerades: The Animus of Swift's Satire." South Atlantic Quarterly, 74 (1975), 535-45. Satire. Point of view and narrator. Autobiographical elements in the novel. Masquerade.

3142a Smith, Frederik N. "The Danger of Reading Swift: The Double Binds of Gulliver's Travels." Studies in the Literary Imagination, 17 (1984), 35-47. Author-reader relationship ["reader entrapment"].

3143 Smith, Raymond J., Jr. "The 'Character' of Lemuel Gulliver." Tennessee Studies in Literature, 10 (1965), 133-40. Characterization.

3144 Smith, Roland M. "Swift's Little Language and Nonsense Names." Journal of English and Germanic Philology, 53 (1954), 178-96. Names of characters [Irish sources]. "Little language." Style and language.

3145 Speck, W. A. "From Principles to Practice: Swift and Party Politics." In The World of Jonathan Swift. Ed. Brian Vickers. Cambridge, Mass.: Harvard Univ. Press, 1968, pp. 69-86. Politics.

3146 Speck, W. A. Swift. 1969; rpt. New York: Arco, 1970.
      Introductory guide.

3147 Starkman, Miriam. "Swift's Rhetoric: The 'Overfraught Pin-
      nace'?" South Atlantic Quarterly, 68 (1967), 188-97. Sat-
      iric techniques.

3148 Steele, Peter. Jonathan Swift: Preacher and Jester. Ox-
      ford: Clarendon Press, 1978. Satire [on fools]. Point of
      view and narrator. Narrative technique. The grotesque.

■3149 Stone, Edward. "Swift and the Horses: Misanthropy or
      Comedy?" Modern Language Quarterly, 10 (1949), 367-76.
      The Houyhnhnms. Misanthropy. Comedy [fourth voyage
      comic, not misanthropic]. Fable. Fourth voyage issues.
      Gulliver-Swift relationship.

3150 Suits, Conrad. "The Role of the Horses in 'A Voyage to the
      Houyhnhnms.'" University of Toronto Quarterly, 34 (1965),
      118-32. Characterization. Insanity. The Houyhnhnms.

3150a Sullivan, E. E. "Houyhnhnms and Yahoos: From Technique
      to Meaning." Studies in English Literature, 24 (1984), 497-
      511. Fourth voyage issues. Satiric techniques.

3151 Sutherland, John H. "A Reconsideration of Gulliver's Third
      Voyage." Studies in Philology, 54 (1957), 45-52. Unity.
      Plot, structure, and design.

3152 Sutherland, W. O. S., Jr. "Satire and the Use of History:
      Gulliver's Third Voyage." In his The Art of the Satirist:
      Essays on the Satire of Augustan England. Austin: Univ.
      of Texas Press, 1965, pp. 107-28. Plot, structure, and de-
      sign. History.

3153 Tallman, Warren. "Swift's Fool: A Comment upon Satire in
      Gulliver's Travels." Dalhousie Review, 40 (1961), 470-78.
      Characterization. The fool. Christianity.

3154 Taylor, Dick, Jr. "Gulliver's Pleasing Visions: Self-Decep-
      tion as a Major Theme in Gulliver's Travels." Tulane
      Studies in English, 12 (1962), 7-61. Characterization.
      Self-deception.

3155 Thornburg, Thomas R. Swift and the Ciceronian Tradition.
      Ball State Monograph Series. Muncie, Ind.: Ball State
      Univ. Press, 1980. [Little on Gulliver's Travels]. Cicero.
      Style and language.

3156 Thorpe, Annette P. "Jonathan Swift's Prescriptions Concern-
      ing the English Language." College Language Association

Journal, 3 (1960), 173-80. [Not on Gulliver's Travels].
Style and language.

3157 Tilton, John W. "Gulliver's Travels as a Work of Art."
      Bucknell Review, 8 (1959), 246-59. Plot, structure, and
      design. Characterization. Point of view and narrator.

3158 Timpe, Eugene F. "Swift as Railleur." Journal of English
      and Germanic Philology, 69 (1970), 41-49. Satiric tech-
      niques.

3159 Todd, Dennis. "Laputa, the Whore of Babylon, and the Idols
      of Science." Studies in Philology, 75 (1978), 93-120. Sat-
      ire. Biblical allusions. Science.

3160 Torchiana, Donald T. "Jonathan Swift, the Irish, and the
      Yahoos: The Case Reconsidered." Philological Quarterly,
      54 (1975), 195-212. The Irish. Irish stereotype. The
      Yahoos.

3161 Tracy, Clarence. "The Unity of Gulliver's Travels."
      Queen's Quarterly, 68 (1962), 597-609. Unity. Plot, struc-
      ture, and design.

3162 Traldi, Ila Dawson. "Gulliver the 'Educated Fool': Unity in
      the Voyage to Laputa." Papers on Language and Literature,
      4 (1968), 35-50. Unity. Characterization. The fool.

3163 Traugott, John. "Swift's Allegory: The Yahoo and the Man-
      of-Mode." University of Toronto Quarterly, 33 (1963), 1-
      18. Social criticism in the novel.

3164 Traugott, John. "A Voyage to Nowhere with Thomas More
      and Jonathan Swift." Sewanee Review, 69 (1961), 534-65.
      Utopia. Sir Thomas More.

3165 Treadwell, J. M. "Jonathan Swift: The Satirist as Project-
      or." Texas Studies in Literature and Language, 17 (1975),
      439-60. [Third and Fourth voyages]. Satire [on Swift].
      Autobiographical elements in the novel. Satiric techniques.

3166 Treadwell, Michael. "Swift, Richard Coleire, and the Origins
      of Gulliver's Travels." Review of English Studies, N.S. 34
      (1983), 304-11. Sources, analogues, and influences.

■3167 Tuveson, Ernest. "Swift: The Dean as Satirist." University
      of Toronto Quarterly, 22 (1953), 368-75. [Fourth voyage].
      Satire. Allegory. Christianity. The Houyhnhnms [not
      ideal]. Fourth voyage issues.

3168 Tuveson, Ernest. "Swift: The View from Within the Satire."

In The Satirist's Art. Ed. H. James Jensen and Malvin R.
Zirker, Jr. Bloomington: Indiana Univ. Press, 1972, pp.
55-85. Satiric techniques. Author-reader relationship.

3169 Uphaus, Robert W. "Gulliver's Travels, A Modest Proposal,
and the Problematical Nature of Meaning." Papers on Language and Literature, 10 (1974), 268-78. Rpt. in his The
Impossible Observer: Reason and the Reader in 18th-
Century Prose. Lexington: Univ. Press of Kentucky,
1979, pp. 9-27. Author-reader relationship.

3170 Vance, John A. "The 'Odious Vermin': Gulliver's Progres-
sion Towards Misanthropy." Enlightenment Essays, 10
(1979), 65-73. Misanthropy.

3171 Vickers, Brian. "The Satiric Structure of Gulliver's Travels
and More's Utopia." In The World of Jonathan Swift. Ed.
Brian Vickers. Cambridge, Mass.: Harvard Univ. Press,
1968, pp. 233-57. Satiric techniques. Sources, analogues,
and influences. Sir Thomas More.

3172 Walton, J. K. "The Unity of the Travels." Hermathena, 104
(1967), 5-50. Unity. Politics.

3173 Wasiolek, Edward. "Relativity in Gulliver's Travels." Philological Quarterly, 37 (1958), 110-16. Relativity [as means
of satire]. Contrast as technique.

■3174 Wedel, T. O. "On the Philosophical Background of Gulliver's
Travels." Studies in Philology, 23 (1926), 434-50. Rpt. in
Twentieth Century Interpretations of "Gulliver's Travels":
A Collection of Critical Essays. Ed. Frank Brady. Twen-
tieth Century Interpretations Series. Englewood Cliffs,
N.J.: Prentice-Hall, 1968, pp. 23-34. Intellectual back-
ground. Christianity. Fourth voyage issues.

3175 White, Douglas H. "Swift and the Definition of Man." Modern Philology, 73 (1976), S 48-55. Intellectual background.
Satire [on natural religion]. Fourth voyage issues.

3176 Wilding, Michael. "The Politics of Gulliver's Travels." In
Studies in the Eighteenth Century II. Ed. R. F. Brissen-
den. Toronto: Univ. of Toronto Press, 1973, pp. 303-22.
Politics.

3177 Williams, Harold. Dean Swift's Library. Cambridge: Cambridge Univ. Press, 1932. Library of novelist.

3178 Williams, J. David. Questions That Count: British Literature
to 1750. Lanham, Md.: University Press of America, [forth-
coming]. Fourth voyage issues. Pedagogical approach
[questions establishing reading goals].

3179   Williams, Kathleen. "'Animal Rationis Capax': A Study of
       Certain Aspects of Swift's Imagery." ELH: A Journal of
       English Literary History, 21 (1954), 193-207. Rpt. in her
       Jonathan Swift and the Age of Compromise. Lawrence:
       Univ. of Kansas Press, 1965, pp. 154-209. Compromise.
       Satire. Philosophy of novelist. Imagery [physicality].
       Reason.

■3180 Williams, Kathleen. "Gulliver's Voyage to the Houyhnhnms."
       ELH: A Journal of English Literary History, 18 (1951),
       275-86. The Houyhnhnms [Swift's criticism of]. Fourth
       voyage issues.

3181   Williams, Kathleen. "Restoration Themes in the Major Satires
       of Swift." Review of English Studies, N.S. 16 (1965), 258-
       71. Intellectual background.

3182   Williams, Kathleen, ed. Swift: The Critical Heritage. Criti-
       cal Heritage Series. New York: Barnes & Noble, 1970.
       Eighteenth-century criticism and reviews of the novel.

3183   Wilson, James R. "Swift, the Psalmist, and the Horse."
       Tennessee Studies in Literature, 3 (1958), 17-23. The
       Houyhnhnms. Biblical allusions. Imagery [horse].

■3184 Winton, Calhoun. "Conversion on the Road to Houyhnhnm-
       land." Sewanee Review, 68 (1960), 20-33. Christianity.
       Deism. Satire [on Deism]. Fourth voyage issues. Conver-
       sion and repentance.

3185   Wood, James O. "Gulliver and the Monkey of Tralee."
       Studies in English Literature, 9 (1969), 415-26. Allegory.
       Sources, analogues, and influences.

3186   Yeomans, W. E. "The Houyhnhnm as Menippean Horse."
       College English, 26 (1966), 449-54. Rpt. in Swift: Modern
       Judgments. Ed. A. Norman Jeffares. London: Macmillan,
       1968, pp. 258-66. Fourth voyage issues. Satire.

3187   Zimansky, Curt A. "Gulliver, Yahoos, and Critics." College
       English, 27 (1965), 45-49. Pedagogical approach [history
       of ideas]. The Yahoos.

3188   Zimmerman, Everett. "Gulliver the Preacher." PMLA, 89
       (1974), 1024-32. Christianity. Morality. Characterization.
       Imposture.

       SEE ALSO ITEMS 334, 761, 794, 797, 834, 884, 898,
       942, 973, 987, 1016, 1032, 1068, 1077, 1471, 2876.

INDEX OF CRITICS AND SCHOLARS

Abbott, John Lawrence 2559a
Abdul Hamid Al Aoun, Dina 2761
Abernethy, Peter L. 1
Adams, M. Ray 742, 2561, 2679
Adams, Percy G. 3, 743, 744,
745
Adamson, John William 78
Adelstein, Michael E. 2348,
2495
Aden, John M. 2762
Albert, William 79
Aldrich, Pearl G. 1126
Aldridge, A. Owen 2049
Alexander, Boyd 2299, 2300, 2301
Alkon, Paul K. 1127, 1128, 2763
Allen, B. Sprague 80, 2426
Allen, M. L. 2643
Allen, Robert J. 81
Allen, Walter 746, 747
Allentuck, Marcia Epstein 1671,
2050
Allibone, S. Austin 4
Allison, Alexander W. 2934
Allott, Miriam 1364
Alter, Robert 747, 1129, 1365,
1366, 1885, 2051, 2052
Altick, Richard D. 82, 83
Altman, Janet Gurkin 747a
Ames, Dianne S. 2706
Amory, Hugh 84, 1369, 1370,
2496
Andersen, Jorgen 748
Anderson, Earl R. 1886, 2349
Anderson, George K. 749
Anderson, Hans H. 1130
Anderson, Howard 85, 750,
1371, 1672, 2053, 2054, 2055,
2056, 2602
Anderson, Paul B. 2633, 2634
Andres, Sophia 1887
Antal, Frederick 86, 87
Appleton, William W. 88
Archer, John 89
Armstrong, Anthony 90
Armstrong, Robert L. 91
Armytage, W. H. G. 92, 93
Ashton, Thomas S. 94, 95, 96

Asquith, Herbert Henry 97
Atherton, Herbert M. 98, 99, 100
Aubin, Robert A. 101
Auty, Susan 751
Ayers, Robert W. 1131

Babb, Howard S. 1673
Babbitt, Irving 2764
Bäckman, Sven 2497
Backscheider, Paula 6, 752, 1132,
1133, 2283, 2294, 2346, 2412,
2419, 2560, 2563, 2580, 2591,
2630, 2640, 2678, 2681, 2686,
2689, 2693, 2738
Baer, Joel H. 1134
Baine, Rodney M. 1135, 1136, 2571
Baird, Donald 10
Baird, Theodore 2057
Baker, Ernest A. 753, 754, 755
Baker, Frank 102
Baker, John Ross 1372
Baker, Norman 103
Baker, Sheridan 756, 1373, 1374,
1375, 1376, 1377, 1378, 1888,
2765
Baker, Van R. 2058
Balderston, Katharine C. 2766
Ball, Donald L. 1674, 1675, 1676
Banerjee, Chinmoy 2059, 2060
Barasch, Frances K. 104
Barker, Gerard A. 1677, 1678,
2350, 2427, 2428, 2619, 2620
Barker, Rosalind Allen 2935
Barlow, Richard B. 105
Barlow, Sheryl 1889
Barnes, Warner 7
Barnett, George 757
Barnouw, Jeffrey 2767
Barrell, John 106
Barroll, J. Leeds, III 2936
Barrow, Andrew 107
Bartel, Roland 108
Bartz, F. K. 2589
Bassin, Joan 109
Bastian, Frank 1137, 1138
Bataille, Robert A. 2498

Bate, W. Jackson 110, 2768, 2769, 2770
Bates, Robin 1890
Bateson, F. W. 18
Bator, Robert 758, 759
Batten, Charles L., Jr. 760, 1891
Battestin, Martin C. 761, 1356, 1379, 1380, 1381, 1382, 1383, 1384, 1385, 1386, 1387, 2061, 2062, 2421, 2499, 2937
Battestin, R. R. 1387
Baugh, Daniel A. 111, 112
Bayer-Berenbaum, Linda 762
Bayne-Powell, Rosamond 113, 114, 115, 116, 117
Beasley, Jerry C. 8, 9, 763, 764, 765, 1388, 1892, 1892a, 2286, 2341, 2351, 2389, 2414, 2420, 2554, 2564, 2569, 2592, 2600, 2618, 2631, 2674, 2694, 2703
Beattie, J. M. 118, 119, 120, 121
Beatty, Richard Croom 1389
Beauchamp, Gordon 2938
Beaumont, Charles Allen 2939, 2940
Bebb, Evelyn D. 122
Beberfall, Lester 1139
Becker, Carl A. 123
Beer, Gillian 1679
Beers, Henry A. 124
Behrendt, Stephen C. 766
Behrens, Laurence 1390
Belanger, Terry 125
Bell, Howard J. 2500
Bell, Inglis F. 10
Bell, Michael 1391
Bell, Michael Davitt 1680
Bell, Robert H. 1140
Benjamin, Edwin B. 1141
Benkovitz, Miriam J. 126
Bentley, G. E. 767
Bentman, Raymond 2941
Berger, Morroe 768
Berland, K. J. H. 1392
Bernard, F. V. 2771
Berne, Eric 1142
Bertelsen, Lance 1893
Bethune, John 2063
Bevan, C. H. K. 1393
Biggs, Penelope 1681
Binkley, Harold C. 1682
Birkhead, Edith 769, 770
Bishop, Jonathan 1143
Bissell, Benjamin 771

Bissell, Frederick Olds, Jr. 1394
Bjornson, Richard 1144, 1894
Black, Frank Gees 11, 772
Black, Sidney 773
Blackburn, Alexander 774
Blackburn, Timothy C. 1145
Blair, Joel 1146
Blakey, Dorothy 127
Blanchard, Frederic T. 1357
Blanco, Richard L. 128
Bland, D. S. 129, 775
Blewett, David 1147, 1148, 1149, 1150
Bligh, John 2501
Bliss, Michael 1395
Bloch, Tuvia 1396, 1397, 1895
Block, Andrew 12
Blondel, Jacques 776
Bloom, Allan 2942
Bloom, Edward A. 777, 2353, 2772
Bloom, Lillian D. 777, 2352, 2353
Blunden, Edmund 2429
Boardman, Michael M. 1151, 1152
Boas, Guy 2773
Boase, T. S. R. 327
Bodek, Evelyn Gordon 130
Boege, Fred W. 1877
Boersch, A. 131
Boggs, W. Arthur 1896, 1897, 1898
Bogle, Frederic V. 2774
Bond, Donald F. 13, 2918
Bond, Richmond P. 132
Bonheim, Helmut W. 14
Booth, Alan 133
Booth, Wayne C. 778, 779, 780, 2064, 2065
Borck, Jim Springer 1153
Bordner, Marsha 1154
Boreham, Frank W. 1155
Borkat, Roberta Sarfatt 2943
Bort, Barry D. 1398
Bossy, John 134
Boucé, Paul-Gabriel 1004a, 1878, 1879, 1899, 1900, 1910a, 2010
Boulton, J. T. 2430, 2775
Bovill, E. W. 135
Bowden, Witt 136
Bowman, Joel P. 2066
Boyce, Benjamin 781, 1156, 1157
Boys, Richard C. 2067
Bracher, Frederick 2944, 2945
Brack, O M, Jr. 16
Bradbrook, Frank W. 782
Bradbury, Malcolm 1399, 2068, 2391
Bradford, Gamaliel 2354
Bradley, James E. 137
Bradley, Rose M. 138

Brady, Frank 783, 2069, 2946
Brander, Michael 139
Braudy, Leo 784, 785, 1158,
1400, 1683, 2392
Brauer, George C. 140
Bredsdorff, Thomas 1684
Bredvold, Louis I. 141, 142, 143,
2947
Brewer, John 144, 145, 487
Brienza, Susan D. 2070
Briggs, Asa 146
Brinton, Crane 147
Brinton, George 2776
Brissenden, R. F. 786, 1685,
1686, 2071, 2072, 2073, 2502,
2621
Broadhead, Glenn J. 2777
Broadwell, Elizabeth P. 2644
Brockman, H. A. N. 2302
Brogan, Howard O. 1401, 2074
Bronson, Bertrand H. 148, 149,
2778
Brooke, John 150, 509, 2707
Brooks, Douglas 787, 1159, 1402,
1403, 1404, 1405, 1687, 1901,
2075
Brooks, Peter 2603
Brooks-Davies, Douglas 787a
Brophy, Elizabeth Bergen 1688
Brown, Ford K. 2431
Brown, Herbert Ross 1689, 2076
Brown, Homer Obed 1160, 1406
Brown, Huntington 788
Brown, James 2948
Brown, Laura S. 789
Brown, Lloyd W. 1161
Brown, Norman O. 2949
Brown, Philip Anthony 151
Brown, R. G. 489
Brown, Stuart Gerry 2779
Brown, Wallace Cable 790
Brownstein, Rachel M. 1690
Bruce, Donald 1902, 1903
Brückmann, Patricia 1691,
2950
Bryan, Margaret B. 2951
Bryson, Gladys 153
Buck, Anne 154
Buck, Howard Swazey 1904
Buer, M. C. 155
Buist, Francis 666
Bullen, John Samuel 1692
Bullitt, John M. 2952
Bullough, Bonnie 156
Bullough, Geoffrey 2303
Bullough, Vern 156
Bunn, James H. 157, 1905

Burch, Charles E. 1118, 1162, 1163
Burckhardt, Sigurd 2077
Burke, John J., Jr. 1164, 1407
Burke, Joseph 158
Burney, E. L. 2708
Burton, Elizabeth 159
Butler, Janet 1692a
Butler, Marilyn 160, 2432, 2645,
2740
Butler, Mary 1165
Butt, John 791, 1906
Buttman, William A. 17
Butterfield, Herbert 161
Butterick, George F. 2780
Byrd, Max 792, 793, 794, 2781,
2953
Bystrom, Valerie Ann 795

Cairnes, William T. 2782
Cameron, H. Charles 691, 2783
Camp, John 162
Canepa, Andrew M. 796
Carnochan, W. B. 797, 2954, 2955,
2956
Carpenter, Spencer Cecil 163
Carr, Raymond 164
Carroll, John 1667, 1693, 1694,
1695
Carse, Adam 165
Case, Arthur E. 2957
Cash, Arthur H. 2078, 2079, 2080,
2081, 2082
Cassirer, Ernst 166
Castle, Terry 166a, 1166, 1696,
1697, 1698, 2958
Cauthen, I. B., Jr. 1408
Cecil, David 2355
Chaber, Lois A. 1167
Chadwick, Joseph 2083
Chalker, John 1699
Chalklin, C. W. 167, 168
Chambers, J. D. 169, 170, 171
Champion, Larry S. 2959
Chandler, Frank W. 798, 1907
Chapin, Chester F. 2784
Chapman, Guy 2296, 2304
Charney, Maurice 2393
Chase, Isabel Wakelin Urban 2709
Chatterjee, Ambarnath 2084
Cherry, S. 172
Christie, Ian R. 173, 174
Clark, George 175, 176
Clark, H. F. 177
Clark, J. Kent 2960
Clark, John R. 2960a
Clark, Kenneth 178, 179

Clark, Paul O. 2961, 2962
Clark, Peter 180
Clarke, M. L. 181
Clarkson, L. A. 181, 182
Clayborough, Arthur 2963
Cleary, Thomas R. 1409, 1410,
  1411
Clements, Frances M. 799
Clifford, Gay 2433
Clifford, James L. 19, 184, 185,
  186, 2754, 2785, 2786, 2787,
  2919, 2920
Clubb, Merrel D. 2921
Coats, A. W. 187, 188
Cobb, Joann P. 2434
Cobban, Alfred 189
Cockburn, J. S. 190
Cockshut, A. O. J. 800, 801,
  1412, 1700, 2085
Cohan, Steven M. 1168, 1701,
  2964
Cohen, Murray 191, 802
Cohen, Richard 1702, 1703
Colby, Elbridge 2570
Cole, G. D. H. 192
Cole, Richard C. 2503
Cole, W. A. 229
Coleman, Donald Cuthbert 193
Coleman, Patrick 194
Coley, W. B. 1413, 1414, 1415,
  2710
Colley, Linda 195
Collins, Arthur S. 196, 197, 198
Collins, R. G. 1908
Columbus, Robert T. 1169
Combs, William W. 1416
Conant, Martha Pike 803
Cone, Carl B. 199
Conger, Syndy McMillen 2604,
  2711
Connely, Willard 200, 2086
Connolly, Cyril 2087
Conrad, James L. 2787
Conrad, Lawrence H., Jr. 2788
Conrad, Peter 2088
Constantine, J. Robert 201
Cook, Albert Spaulding 2089
Cook, Richard I. 2965
Cook, Terry 2966
Cooke, Arthur L. 804, 1417
Coolidge, John S. 1418
Cooper, Robert Alan 202
Copeland, Edward 805, 1704,
  1705, 1706, 1909, 2356, 2394
Copeman, W. S. C. 203
Cordasco, Francesco 1880
Corder, Jim 2967

Costa, Richard Hauer 1707
Cottom, Daniel 1170
Courtney, W. P. 2755
Coveney, Peter 806
Cowie, Leonard W. 204
Cowles, Virginia 205
Cox, Edward Godfrey 21
Cox, Stephen D. 807, 1708
Crabtree, Paul R. 1709
Cragg, Gerald R. 206, 207
Crane, R. S. 208, 209, 210, 1419,
  2968, 2969
Cranfield, Geoffrey Alan 211
Cressey, David 212
Creswell, John 213
Crocker, Lester G. 214
Crook, J. Mordaunt 215
Cross, Wilbur L. 1420, 2090
Cruse, Amy 2357
Cruttwell, Patrick 2435
Cummings, Dorothea 216
Cummings, Frederick J. 217
Cunnington, Cecil W. 218
Cunnington, Phillis 218
Curley, Thomas M. 2789, 2790
Curtis, Laura 1171
Curtis, Lewis P. 219
Curtis, Lewis Perry 2091
Cutting, Rose Marie 2358, 2359

Daghlian, Philip B. 85
Dahl, Curtis 2504
Daiches, David 1710, 1910
Dainton, Courtney 220
Dalnekoff, Donna Isaacs 808
Dalziel, Margaret 1711
Damrosch, Leopold 1172
Daniel, Stephen H. 809
Danziger, Marlies K. 810
Darby, H. C. 221
Darnall, F. M. 2970
Davidson, Arnold E. 2092
Davidson, Cathy N. 2092
Davies, E. 222
Davies, Hugh Sykes 811
Davies, Paul C. 812
Davies, Richard A. 2093
Davis, Herbert 2922, 2972, 2973,
  2974
Davis, Lennard J. 813, 814
Davis, Ralph 225, 226
Davis, Richard Beale 2332
Davis, Robert Gorham 815, 2094
Davis, Terence 227
Day, Robert Adams 23, 816, 817,
  1910a, 1911

Day, W. G. 2095
Deane, Phyllis 228, 229, 498
Debb, E. D. 230
De Beer, E. S. 231
De Blois, Peter B. 1421
Deitz, Jonathan 2360
De Koven, Anna 2712
Dempsey, I. Lindsay 1912
Dennis, Nigel 1173, 2975, 2976
Denton, Ramona 1712
De Porte, Michael 2435a
Detre, Jean 2436, 2741
Devine, T. M. 232
De Voogd, Peter Jan 1422
Dickinson, H. T. 233
Dickson, G. M. 234
Digeon, Aurélien 1423
Dilworth, Ernest Nevin 2096,
    2097
Dircks, Richard J. 818, 1424,
    2411, 2977
Ditchfield, G. M. 235
Dobrée, Bonamy 819, 2713
Dobson, C. R. 236
Doederlein, Sue Warrick 1668
Dollerup, Cay 1174
Donaldson, Ian 237, 238, 820,
    1425, 1426, 1713, 2422
Donoghue, Denis 1175, 2098,
    2978
Donoughue, Bernard 239
Donovan, Robert Alan 821, 1176,
    1427, 1714, 1913, 2099
Doody, Margaret Anne 822,
    1715
Doody, Terrence 1177
Dooley, D. J. 823, 2979
Dooley, Roger B. 2284
Doughty, Oswald 240
Dowling, William C. 2100
Downey, James 241, 242
Downie, J. A. 2980
Downs, Brian W. 1716
Draper, John William 25
Drinker, Cecil K. 1914
Driskell, Leon V. 1428, 1915
Duckworth, Alistair M. 824
Dudden, F. Homes 1429
Dudley, Edward 243
Dudley, Fred Adair 26
Duman, Daniel 244
Dumas, D. Gilbert 2437
Duncan, Jeffrey L. 825
Dunham, William Huse, Jr. 245
Dunn, Richard J. 27, 1916
Durant, David 2505, 2646, 2647
Dussinger, John A. 826, 1717,

1718, 1718a, 1719, 1720, 1721,
    2101, 2506, 2507
Duthie, Elizabeth 2981
Dyson, A. E. 28, 1430, 2102, 2982
Dyson, Anne Jane 55

Eagleton, Terry 1722
Earle, Peter 1178
Eastman, Richard M. 827
Eaves, T. C. Duncan 1431, 1723,
    1724, 1725, 1726, 1727, 1728,
    2103, 2361
Eberlein, H. Donaldson 580
Eberwein, Robert 2791
Echeruo, Michael J. C. 828
Eddy, William A. 2983
Edwards, Averyl 2362
Edwards, Lee 1179
Edwards, Mary Jane 2333, 2334
Egan, James 1180
Ehlers, Leigh A. 2104, 2676, 2714
Ehrenpreis, Irvin 85, 829, 856,
    1432, 1433, 2792, 2984, 2985,
    2986, 2987, 2988, 2989
Einbond, Bernard L. 2793
Eitner, Lorenz 247
Ek, Grete 1434
Elder, Lucius W. 2990
Elliott, Robert C. 2991, 2992, 2993,
    2994, 2995
Elliott-Binns, L. E. 248
Ellis, Aytoun 249
Ellis, Havelock 2555
Ellis, Katherine 2696
Ellison, Lee Monroe 1917
Elkin, P. K. 830
Elton, G. R. 30
Emden, Cecil S. 2794
Emerson, Roger 250
Empson, William 1435
Emsley, Clive 251
Emslie, Macdonald 2508
England, Martha Winburn 2438
Epstein, Lynne 2648
Epstein, William H. 2395
Erämetsä, Erik 252
Erickson, James P. 2363, 2565
Erickson, Robert A. 1181, 1182,
    1729
Ermarth, Elizabeth Deeds 1183, 1730
Ernle, Lord 253
Erskine-Hill, Howard 254, 831
Esdaile, Arundell 31
Eskin, Stanley G. 2105
Evans, David L. 1436, 1918, 1919
Evans, Eric J. 255, 256

Evans, James E. 1437, 1438, 1920, 2106
Evans, Walter 2107
Eversole, Richard 2795
Ewald, William Bragg, Jr. 2996

Fabel, Robin 1921
Fabian, Bernhard 832, 2108
Fabricant, Carole 257, 2109, 2997
Fairchild, Hoxie Neale 258
Falk, Bernard 259
Falle, George 2923
Farber, Evan I. 20
Farouk, Marion O. 2439
Farrell, William J. 1439, 1440, 1731, 2110
Farringdon, Michael G. 1441, 1442
Faulkner, Peter 2288, 2289
Faurot, Ruth M. 2111
Fawcett, Mary Laughlin 2649
Fehr, Bernard 260
Felsenstein, Frank 1443
Ferenczi, Sandor 2998
Ferguson, Oliver W. 2509, 2510, 2999
Fiedler, Leslie A. 1732
Fiering, Norman S. 261
Fink, Zera S. 3000
Finley, Gerald 262
Firth, Charles H. 3001
Fischer, Michael 263
Fisher, Lois H. 264
Fisher, Marvin 2796
Fiske, Marjorie 457
Fitzgerald, Robert P. 3002, 3003, 3003a
Flanders, W. Austin 833, 1184, 1922
Flanders, Wallace A. 2440
Fleeman, J. D. 2756
Fleisher, David 2441
Flexner, Eleanor 2742
Flinn, Michael W. 265
Floud, Roderick 266
Fluchère, Henri 2112
Flynn, Carol Houlihan 1733
Fogle, Richard H. 2605
Folkenflik, Robert 834, 1444, 1445, 1734, 1923, 2797
Folsom, James K. 2305
Foord, Archibald S. 267, 2715
Fortescue, J. W. 268
Fortuna, James Louis, Jr. 1735
Foss, Michael 269

Foster, James R. 835, 836, 2342, 2697, 2698
Fothergill, Brian 270
Foucault, Michel 271
Foxon, David 837, 2396
Francis, C. J. 2113
Frank, Frederick S. 34, 1736, 2641
Franke, Wolfgang 1924
Frantz, R. W. 272
Fredman, Alice G. 1925, 2114
Freedman, William 1446, 1447, 2115, 2116
French, David P. 3004
Frese, Jerry 3005
Friedman, Arthur 838, 2511
Fritz, Paul S. 273, 274
Froe, Arie de 2117
Frye, Northrop 839
Frye, Roland Mushat 3006
Fulton, Henry L. 2639, 2798
Fulton, Richard D. 1363
Furbank, P. N. 2442
Furst, Lilian R. 2118
Fussell, G. E. 275, 276, 277
Fussell, Paul 840, 2799, 3007

Gaba, Phyllis 2800
Gadd, David 278
Galbraith, Lois Hall 841
Gallaway, Francis 279
Gallaway, W. F., Jr. 842, 2512
Ganzel, Dewey 1185
Garber, Frederick 843, 1737, 1738
Garmon, Gerald M. 35
Garrett, John 2650
Garrow, Scott 1926
Garver, Joseph 844
Garvey, James W. 2119
Gaskell, Philip 280
Gaskin, Bob 1186
Gassman, Byron 1927, 1928, 1929, 1930
Gaunt, William 281
Gawlick, Günter 282
Gay, Peter 283
Geering, R. G. 3008
Gemmett, Robert J. 2297, 2306, 2307, 2308
George, M. Dorothy 284, 285, 286, 287, 288
George, Margaret 2743
Gerber, Richard 1187
Giddey, Ernest 2309
Giddings, Robert 1448, 1931, 1932
Gifford, George E., Jr. 1188
Gignilliat, George Warren, Jr. 2415

Gilbert, Alan D. 289
Gilbert, Jack G. 3009
Gilboy, Elizabeth W. 291
Gill, James E. 3010, 3011, 3012
Gilley, Sheridan 292
Gillis, Christine Marsden 1739
Gilman, Sander L. 2622
Gilmore, Thomas B., Jr. 293
Gilmour, Robin 294
Gipson, Lawrence Henry 295
Girdler, Lew 1189
Glass, D. V. 296
Glock, Waldo S. 2364
Goad, Caroline 845
Godley, Alfred Denis 297
Gold, Alex, Jr. 2443
Gold, Joel J. 2801
Gold, Maxwell 3013
Goldberg, Homer 1449, 1450
Goldberg, M. A. 1190, 1933
Golden, Morris 298, 1451, 1451a,
  1740, 1741, 2120, 2513, 2514,
  2515, 2516, 2517, 2518, 2690,
  3014
Goldgar, Bertrand A. 846, 3015,
  3016, 3017
Goldknopf, David 847, 1191,
  1452, 1742
Goldsmith, M. M. 299
Goldstein, Laurence 1192
Göller, Karl Heinz 848
Gomme, George Laurence 300, 301,
  302
Goodin, George 2121
Goodwin, Albert 303
Goodyear, Louis E. 2802
Gopnik, Irwin 1743
Gordon, Ian A. 849
Gose, Elliott B., Jr. 2606
Gossman, Lionel 304
Gottfried, Leon 1453
Gove, Philip B. 36
Grabo, C. H. 2290
Graham, John 850
Graham, Kenneth W. 2310, 2311,
  2312, 2313, 2314, 2443a
Grange, Kathleen M. 2803
Grant, Aline 2651
Grant, Damian 1934, 1935
Grau, Joseph A. 2347
Grave, S. A. 305, 306
Graves, Lila 2122
Gray, Christopher W. 1193
Green, Martin 1194
Green, Mary Elizabeth 2519
Green, V. H. H. 307
Greenacre, Phyllis 3018

Greenberg, Janelle 308
Greene, Donald 309, 310, 311, 312,
  851, 2754, 2757, 2804, 2805, 2806,
  2807, 2808, 3019, 3020
Greene, J. Lee 1454
Greenstein, Susan 1744
Gregory, Allene 852, 2291, 2444,
  2572, 2582, 2699, 2744
Greif, Martin J. 1195
Greiner, Walter F. 853
Grennan, Margaret R. 3021
Griffin, Robert J. 2123
Griffith, Philip Mahone 1745, 1936
Grinnell, George 313
Gross, Gloria Sybil 2809
Gross, Harvey 2445
Grossvogel, David I. 2124
Grow, L. M. 2687
Grubb, Isabel 314
Grudin, Peter 2607
Grudis, Paul J. 2520
Grylls, Rosalie Glynn 2446
Guilhamet, Leon M. 854, 1746
Gury, Jacques 315
Guskin, Phyllis J. 3022
Guthrie, William B. 1455

Habakkuk, J. J. 316, 317, 318
Hackwood, Frederick W. 319
Hadfield, Charles 320
Hafter, Ronald 2125
Hagen, June Steffenson 2126
Hagstrum, Jean H. 321, 855, 1456,
  1747, 2127, 2810, 2811
Hahn, Emily 2365
Hahn, H. George 1196, 1358, 1359,
  1360
Hale, Will Taliaferro 2366
Halévy, Elie 322
Halewood, William H. 1197, 3023,
  3024, 3025
Hall, Basil 3026
Hall, Joan Joffe 2128
Hall, Michael L. 1457
Hall, Walter Phelps 323
Haller, William 324
Halsband, Robert 856, 857, 858
Hambridge, Roger A. 1937
Hames, Louise 1938
Hamilton, Bernice 325
Hamlyn, Hilda M. 326
Hammelmann, Hanns 327
Hammond, Barbara 328, 329, 330, 331
Hammond, Brean S. 1198
Hammond, Eugene R. 3027
Hammond, Lansing Jan der Heyden

2129
Hammond, T. L. 328, 329, 330, 331
Hannaford, Richard Gordon 1669
Hannay, David 332
Hans, Nicholas 333
Hansen, Marlene R. 2812
Hardwick, Elizabeth 1748
Hardy, Evelyn 3028
Hardy, J. P. 2813
Harfst, Betsy Perteit 2716
Harlan, Virginia 1199
Harp, Richard L. 2521
Harries, Elizabeth W. 2130
Harris, Jocelyn 1749, 1750
Harris, R. W. 334, 1200, 1458, 1751
Harrison, Bernard 1459
Harrison, John F. C. 335
Harrison, T. W. 336
Hart, Arthur Tindal 337
Hart, Francis Russell 859, 860, 861, 2814
Hart, Jeffrey 3029
Harth, Phillip 3030
Hartley, Lodwick 2042, 2043, 2044, 2131, 2132, 2133, 2134, 2135, 2815
Hartog, Curt 1201, 1202
Hartveit, Lars 1203, 1752
Hartwell, Ronald M. 338
Hartwig, Robert J. 1460
Harvey, A. D. 1753, 2447, 2702
Hassall, Anthony J. 1461, 1462, 1463, 1464, 1583, 1825, 3031
Hassler, Donald M. 339
Hastings, William T. 1204
Hatfield, Glenn W. 1465
Hauser, Arnold 340
Häusermann, Hans W. 1205
Havens, Munson Aldrich 2717
Havens, Raymond D. 2652, 2816
Havinden, M. S. 168
Hay, Douglas 341
Hay, John A. 2136
Hayden, Lucy K. 862
Hayman, John G. 342, 863
Hayter, Tony 343
Hazen, Allen T. 2704, 2718
Hearne, John 1206
Hecht, J. Jean 17, 344, 345
Heckscher, Eli F. 346
Heffernan, William 864
Heidler, Joseph B. 37
Heilman, Robert Bechtold 38, 865
Helgerson, Richard 2522

Helmick, E. T. 1939
Hemlow, Joyce 2367, 2368
Hemmings, F. W. J. 866
Henriques, Ursula 347
Herman, George 1466
Herrmann, Luke 348
Hersey, G. L. 349
Hewitt, Margaret 550
Hibbert, Christopher 350, 351
Hicks, John H. 2045
Higdon, David Leon 1119, 1207
Higgins, Ian 3032
Highsmith, James M. 1940
Hilbish, Florence 2700
Hill, Charles Jarvis 2556, 2557
Hill, Christopher 352, 1754
Hill, Rowland M. 1467
Hilles, Frederick W. 1468, 1755, 2817
Hilliard, Raymond F. 867, 2523
Hinnant, Charles H. 353
Hipple, Walter J., Jr. 354, 355
Hnatko, Eugene 2138, 2139
Hobson, J. G. S. 356
Hodgkin, John 2296
Hogle, Jerrold E. 868, 2448
Hogwood, Christopher 357
Holbrook, William C. 358
Holderness, B. A. 359
Holdsworth, William 360
Hole, Christina 361
Hollander, John 2397
Holland, Norman N. 869, 2140
Hollinsworth, T. H. 362
Holly, Grant 3033
Holmes, Geoffrey 363, 364
Holt, R. V. 365
Holtz, William V. 2141, 2142
Holzman, James M. 366
Hopkins, Robert H. 1469, 1941, 2524, 2525, 2526
Hopkinson, H. T. 1756
Horn, András 870
Horn, David Bayne 367, 368
Horn, Pamela 369
Hornbeak, Katherine G. 370, 1757
Horne, Thomas A. 371
Horner, Joyce M. 871
Horrell, Joseph 3034
Horsley, Lee Sousteng 3035
Hovey, Richard B. 2818
Howard, William J. 1208
Howard-Hill, T. H. 39
Howell, Wilbur Samuel 372
Howells, Coral Ann 872, 2608, 2653
Howes, Alan B. 2046, 2143
Howson, Gerald 373

Hudson, Kenneth 374
Hughes, E. 375, 376
Hughes, Edward 377, 378
Hughes, Helen Sard 873, 874,
    1758, 2144, 2682
Hughes, Leo 1470, 1759
Hughes, Mary Joe 379
Hughes, Peter 875, 876
Hume, Martin 877
Hume, Robert D. 878, 1209, 2315
Humiliata, Sister M. 380
Humphreys, A. R. 381, 382,
    1471, 1760, 1942
Hunt, John Dixon 383, 384
Hunt, Morton M. 385
Hunt, Russell A. 1472, 1761,
    2819
Hunter, J. Paul 879, 880, 881,
    1210, 1473, 1474, 1475, 2145
Hunter, Jean E. 386
Hunter, Kathryn 882
Hunting, Robert 2423, 2527,
    3036
Hussain, Imdad 2316
Hussey, Christopher 387, 388,
    389
Hutchens, Eleanor Newman 1476,
    1477

Illo, John 2398
Irving, William Henry 390
Irwin, George 2820
Irwin, Joseph James 2609
Irwin, Michael 1478
Irwin, W. R. 1479, 1480
Iser, Wolfgang 1481, 1943
Isles, Duncan 2047, 2593, 2594,
    2821
Itzkowitz, David 391
Itzoe, Linda V. 1762
Ivker, Barry 2399

Jaarsma, Richard J. 2528
Jack, Ian 2822
Jack, R. D. S. 1944
Jackson, H. J. 2146
Jackson, Holbrook 1945
Jackson, Wallace 1211
James, E. Anthony 1212, 1213
James, Overton Philip 2147
Jameson, Ted R. 392
Jarrett, David 393
Jarrett, Derek 394, 395
Jarrett, James L. 3037
Jarvis, Rupert C. 396, 1482

Jeffares, A. Norman 2529
Jefferson, D. W. 883, 2148, 2530
Jeffrey, David K. 1763, 1946, 1947,
    1948, 1949, 1950, 2369
Jemiety, Thomas 2823
Jenkins, Harold D. 2824
Jenkins, Owen 1483, 1764
Jenkins, Ralph E. 1214, 2623
Jensen, Gerard E. 1484
John, A. H. 397
Johnson, Abby A. 1215
Johnson, Clifford R. 884
Johnson, Clifford 1216
Johnson, Glen M. 1765
Johnson, James W. 398, 399, 400,
    3038
Johnson, Maurice 1485
Johnson, Reginald Brimley 401
Johnston, Denis 3039
Jones, B. M. 1486
Jones, Claude E. 41, 1487, 1951,
    1952
Jones, E. L. 402
Jones, Emrys 2825
Jones, Gareth 403
Jones, George Hilton 404
Jones, Kathleen 405
Jones, Louis Clark 406
Jones, Mary G. 407
Jones, R. Tudor 408
Joost, Nicholas 2826
Jordan, Robert M. 1488
Joughin, G. Louis 2581

Kahane, Claire 885
Kahrl, George 1953, 1954, 1955
Kallich, Martin 409, 2719, 2720,
    2827, 3040, 3041
Kalpakgian, Mitchell 1489
Kampf, Louis 410
Kaplan, Fred 1490, 1766
Karl, Frederick R. 886, 1217, 1218,
    1491, 1767, 1956, 2149
Karpman, Benjamin 3042, 3043
Kaufman, Pamela 887
Kaufman, Paul 411, 412, 413
Kaufmann, Emil 414
Kaul, A. N. 1492
Kaul, R. K. 2828
Kauvar, Elaine M. 2595
Kavanaugh, Thomas M. 1219
Kay, Donald 888, 1768
Kaye, F. B. 415
Kearful, Frank J. 889
Kearney, Anthony 1493, 1769, 1770,
    1771, 1772, 1773, 2829

Keech, James M. 890
Keener, Frederick M. 2830, 3044
Keesey, Donald 2924
Keevil, J. J. 416
Kelling, H. D. 3045, 3046, 3047
Kelly, Ann Cline 3048, 3049
Kelly, Gary D. 891, 892, 2292,
   2449, 2450, 2451, 2452, 2573,
   2574, 2583, 2654, 2745
Kelly, George Armstrong 417
Kelsall, M. M. 3050
Kemp, Betty 418
Kenney, William 2758, 2831
Kenny, Virginia C. 892a
Kent, Elizabeth Eaton 2531
Kerman, Sandra Lee 419
Kermode, Frank 1494, 1774
Kern, Jean B. 893
Kettle, Arnold 855, 894, 1220,
   1221
Ketton-Cremer, R. W. 2721
Khazoum, Violet 2150
Kiely, Robert 896, 2317, 2453,
   2610, 2655, 2722
Kievitt, Frank David 2677
Kilpatrick, Sarah 2370
Kimpel, Ben D. 1725, 1726, 1727,
   1728
King, Lester S. 420, 421, 422
Kinkead-Weekes, Mark 1775,
   1776, 1777
Kirby, Chester 423
Kirby, Paul F. 424, 2151
Kirk, Clara 2532
Kirk, John Foster 4
Kishler, Thomas C. 1495, 1496
Klein, Michael 897
Kliger, Samuel 425, 426, 3051
Kline, Judd 1957
Klotman, Phyllis R. 1778, 2152
Klukoff, Philip J. 42, 1958
Knapp, Lewis M. 1881, 1959,
   1960, 1961, 1962
Knight, Charles A. 1497, 1498,
   1499, 1779
Knopf, Maria 427
Knowles, A. S., Jr. 898
Knox, Norman 899
Kolb, Gwin J. 2832, 2833, 2834,
   2835, 2836, 2837, 2838
Konigsberg, Ira 1780
Kooiman-Van Middendorp, Gerarda
   Maria 900
Koonce, Howard L. 1222
Koppel, Gene S. 1500, 2153
Korkowski, Eugene 2154
Korshin, Paul J. 428, 901, 902,

903, 2839, 3052
Korte, Donald M. 1963
Köster, Patricia 2635, 2636
Kovačević, Ivanka 904
Kovacs, Anna-Maria 1781
Kraft, Quentin G. 1223
Kramer, Dale 2624
Kramnick, Isaac 905
Krause, J. T. 429
Kreissman, Bernard 1782
Krieger, Murray 906
Krier, William J. 1224
Kroeger, Frederick P. 2155
Kropf, Carl R. 907, 908, 1225,
   1501, 2454
Krutch, Joseph Wood 2840
Kuczynski, Ingrid 2455

LaCasce, Steward 3053, 3054, 3055
LaFrance, Marston 1502
Laird, John 1226, 2156
Lam, George L. 2723
Lamb, Jonathan 2157, 2158, 2159
Landa, Louis A. 430, 2160, 2841,
   2925, 2926, 3056, 3057, 3058,
   3059, 3060
Landor, Mikhail 2161
Landow, George P. 2162
Lang, Paul Henry 431
Langford, Paul 432
Lanham, Richard A. 2163
Lansbury, Coral 1782a
LaPrade, William Thomas 433, 434
Laqueur, Thomas W. 435
Larson, Kerry C. 1783
Lascelles, Mary 2759, 2842
Laski, Harold J. 436
Laslett, Peter 437
Lauren, Barbara 1784
Laurence-Anderson, Judith 1785
Laver, James 438, 439
Lavin, Henry St. C. 1503
Lawliss, Merritt 3061
Lawry, Jon S. 3062
Leavis, F. R. 3063
Leavis, Q. D. 440
Le Brocquy, Sybil 3064
Lee, Jae Num 3065
Leed, Jacob 1786
Lees-Milne, James 2318
LeFanu, William R. 441
Lefever, Charlotte 1787
LeGates, Marlene 442
Lehman, B. H. 2164
Lehmann, James H. 2533
Leigh, Agnes 443

Leinster-Mackay, D. P. 1227
Lenman, Bruce 444
Lenta, M. 1504
Lentin, A. 1505
Le Page, Peter 1506
Lerenbaum, Miriam 909, 1228
Lessenich, Rolf P. 445, 2456
Lesser, Simon O. 1788
Le Tellier, Robert Ignatius 910
Levett, Ada E. 1229
Levich, Marvin 3025
Levin, Gerald 1789
Levin, Harry 911
Levine, George R. 1507
Levy, Mervyn 446
Lewis, Michael 447
Lewis, Paul 912, 913, 914
Lewis, Wilmarth S. 2724, 2725,
   2726
Leyburn, Ellen Douglass 2843,
   2844, 3066, 3067, 3068, 3069
Lillywhite, Bryant 448
Lincoln, Anthony 449
Lindboe, Berit R. 1508
Lindley, Arthur 1790
Lindsay, Jack 450
Linebaugh, P. 451
Link, Frederick M. 2845
Lipking, Lawrence 452
Little, Anthony J. 453
Littlewood, S. R. 2584
Liu, Alan 2318a, 2845a
Lock, F. P. 3070
Locke, Don 2457
Lockhart, Donald M. 2846
Lockridge, Ernest H. 2165
Lockwood, Thomas 1509
Loesberg, Jonathan 1791
Loftis, John E. 1510
Lombardo, Agostino 2847
Longmire, Samuel E. 1511, 1512,
   1513, 1514
Longueil, Alfred E. 454
Lonsdale, Roger 2390
Louis, Frances Deutsch 3071
Lounsberry, Barbara 2166
Lovecraft, H. P. 915
Lovejoy, Arthur O. 455, 456
Loveridge, Mark 2167
Lovett, Robert W. 1613
Lowenthal, Leo 457
Luckett, Richard 357
Lutwack, Leonard 916
Lyles, Albert M. 458, 1792
Lynch, James J. 1515
Lyndenberg, Robin 917, 2611
Lyons, John O. 918

Lyons, N. J. 2558, 2559

Macafee, C. H. G. 2168
Macallister, Hamilton 1516
MacAndrew, Elizabeth 919, 1517
Macaree, David 1230, 1231
Macaulay, James 459
MacCarthy, B. G. 920, 921
MacCoby, Simon 460, 461
MacDonald, Robert H. 1232
MacDonald, Ruth K. 922
Macey, Samuel L. 923
Mack, Edward C. 1518, 1964
Mack, Maynard 1519
MacLaine, Allen H. 1233
MacLean, Kenneth 462, 924, 2169
MacLennan, Munro 2534
Maddox, James H , Jr. 1233a,
   1793
Madoff, Mark 925
Mahmoud, Fatma Moussa 2319, 2320,
   2848
Major, John Campbell 926
Malcolmson, Robert W. 463, 464
Malek, James S. 465
Malins, Edward 927
Malone, Kemp 2371
Mandel, Jerome 1520
Manheim, Leonard H. 1794
Manlove, C. N. 1234, 1521
Mantoux, Paul 466
Manuel, Frank E. 467
Manwaring, Elizabeth Wheeler 468
Manzalaoui, Mahmoud 2321, 2849
Marcus, G. J. 469, 470
Maresca, Thomas E. 928, 1522,
   3072
Margolis, John D. 2850
Marken, Jack W. 2424
Marshall, Dorothy 471, 472, 473,
   474
Marshall, Madeleine Forell 475
Marshall, Roderick 929
Martin, Robert Bernard 930
Martin, Terence 1235
Martz, Louis L. 1965, 1966, 2372
Maskell, Duke 2170
Mason, Philip 476
Mason, Shirlene 1236
Mathew, W. M. 477
Mathias, Peter 478
Matthews, William 930a
Maxfield, Ezra Kempton 1237
Maxwell, Leslie F. 43
May, Georges 931

May, James E. 2535
May, Keith M. 932
Mayhew, George P. 2927
Maynadier, Gustavus Howard
    2596
Maynard, Temple 2322, 2323
Mayo, Charles Herbert 479
Mayo, Robert D. 44, 933, 934,
    2656
Mayoux, Jean-Jacques 2171
McAdam, E. L., Jr. 2536, 2851
McAdoo, William 480
McBurney, William H. 45, 1238,
    2285, 2295, 2413
McCahill, Michael W. 481
McCarthy, John A. 482
McCloskey, Donald N. 266, 483
McClure, Ruth K. 484
McCormick, Donald 485
McCoy, Kathleen 1239
McCracken, David 2458, 2459,
    2460, 2537
McCracken, George 3073
McCrea, Brian 1523, 1524, 2852
McCullen, J. T., Jr. 935
McCullough, N. Verrle 936
McDonald, Daniel 2538
McDowell, Alfred 1525
McDowell, R. B. 3074
McElroy, David D. 486
McGlinchee, Claire 937
McGlynn, Paul D. 938, 2172,
    2173
McGuffie, Helen Louise 2760
McGuirk, Carol 939
McIntosh, Carey 940, 1795, 2853,
    2854
McIntyre, Clara F. 941, 2657,
    2658
McKee, John B. 942
McKee, William 2585
McKendrick, Neil 487
McKenzie, Alan T. 488, 943, 1526,
    1527
McKenzie, Gordon 3075
McKeown, Thomas 489
McKillop, Alan Dugald 490, 944,
    945, 1240, 1361, 1528, 1529,
    1796, 1797, 1798, 1799, 1800,
    1801, 1967, 2048, 2174, 2659
McLynn, F. J. 491
McManmon, John J. 3076
McMaster, Juliet 1241, 2175
McMullen, Lorraine 2335, 2336,
    2337
McNamara, Susan P. 1530
McNutt, Dan J. 46, 2298, 2601,
    2642, 2675, 2695, 2705
McVeagh, John 946, 1242, 1243,
    1968
Medley, D. J. 56
Megroz, Rudolf L. 1244
Mehrota, K. K. 2727
Mellown, Elgin W. 2176
Mendilow, A. A. 2177
Mercier, Vivian 3077
Merrett, Robert J. 1245, 1246,
    1531, 1532
Metscher, Thomas 3078
Mews, Hazel 947
Mezciems, Jenny 3079, 3080, 3081
Michie, J. A. 1247
Miles, Josephine 948
Miles, Peter 1969
Milic, Louis T. 949, 2178, 3082
Miller, Henry Knight 950, 1533,
    1534, 1535, 1536
Miller, Jacqueline T. 2461
Miller, Nancy K. 951, 1802, 2400
Miller, Stuart 952
Miller, Susan 1537
Minchinton, W. E. 492, 493
Mingay, G. E. 171, 494, 495, 496,
    497
Misenheimer, James B., Jr. 2855,
    2856
Mish, Charles C. 953, 954
Mitchell, B. R. 498
Mitchison, Rosalind 547
Modder, Montagu Frank 955
Moglen, Helene 2179, 2180
Mohler, Nora M. 3092
Monie, Willis J. 2857
Monk, Samuel H. 956, 3083
Monkman, Kenneth 2181
Monro, David Hector 2462
Monro, Hector 499
Montague, Edwine 2372
Monteser, Frederick 957
Moore, Catherine E. 1248, 1249
Moore, C. A. 958
Moore, John Brooks 3084
Moore, John Robert 1120, 1250,
    1251, 1252, 1253, 1803, 2858,
    3085, 3086
Moore, Robert Etheridge 500, 959,
    1538, 1539, 1804, 1970, 2859
Moran, Michael G. 2287
More, Paul Elmer 2324, 2373
Morgan, Bayard Quincy 48
Morgan, Charlotte E. 49, 960
Morgan, William Thomas 50
Morris, John N. 3087
Morrissey, L. J. 1362, 2403, 3088

Morton, Donald E. 1805
Moss, Harold Gene 1971
Moss, Roger B. 2182
Moynihan, Robert D. 1806
Muecke, D. C. 961, 1807
Muir, Edwin 2183
Mulford, Carla 1539a
Mullett, Charles F. 501
Munro, James S. 1808
Munro, John M. 3089
Munsche, P. B. 502, 503
Murray, Christopher 2539
Murray, E. B. 2660
Murry, John Middleton 3090
Musher, Daniel M. 1972
Musson, A. E. 504, 505
Myers, Mitzi 506, 2463, 2746
Myers, Walter 2184
Mylne, Vivienne 962

Namier, Lewis 507, 508, 509
Nangle, Benjamin Christie 51
Nänny, Max 2185
Napier, Elizabeth R. 1254, 1809
Nassar, Eugene Paul 1540
Nathan, Sabine 1541, 2540
Neale, R. S. 510
Needham, Gwendolyn B. 1093,
  1810, 2637, 2638
Needham, J. D. 1255
Nef, John U. 511
Nelson, Lowry, Jr. 963
Nemoianu, Virgil 1973
Neuberg, Victor 512
New, Melvyn 964, 2186, 2187,
  2188, 2189, 2190, 2191
Newell, A. G. 965
Newlin, Claude M. 966
Newton, Judith Lowder 2374,
  2375
Nicholson, Watson 1256
Nicolson, Marjorie Hope 513,
  3091, 3092
Niehus, Edward L. 1974
Nixon, Edna 2747
Noble, Yvonne 1811
Noel, Thomas 967
Norris, John M. 514
Norton, Rictor 968
Novak, Maximillian E. 243, 969,
  970, 971, 972, 973, 1121, 1257,
  1258, 1259, 1260, 1261, 1262,
  1263, 1264, 1265, 1266, 1267,
  1268, 1269, 1270, 1271, 1272,
  1273, 1274
Noxon, James 515

Noyes, Robert Gale 974, 975, 976

Oakman, Robert L. 1542
Oates, J. C. T. 2192
O'Brien, C. J. H. 1122
O'Flaherty, Patrick 2860
Okin, Susan Moller 516
Oliver, J. W. 2325
Olivier, Theo 1812
Olsen, Flemming 1543
Olshin, Toby 977, 1275, 2193, 2376,
  2409
O'Malley, C. D. 517
Onderwyzer, Gaby E. 2688
Orowitz, Milton 1975
Orr, Leonard 2861
Orwell, George 3093
Osborne, John W. 517a
Osland, Dianne 1544
Osler, Margaret J. 518
Ousby, Ian 978, 2464
Overman, Antoinette A. 2377
Overton, John H. 519
Owen, Joan Hildreth 520
Owen, John Beresford 521, 522
Oxley, Geoffrey Frederick 523
Oxley, Geoffrey W. 524

Pace, K. Claire 525
Pacey, Desmond 2338
Pagliaro, Harold E. 2862
Palmer, E. Taiwo 1545, 1546
Palmer, Eustace 1547
Palmer, Helen H. 55
Palmer, William J. 1813
Palomo, Dolores 2632, 3094
Pannill, Linda 1976
Pares, Richard 526, 527
Pargellis, Stanley 56
Parish, Charles 2194, 2195, 2196
Park, William 57, 979, 1548, 1549,
  1550, 1814, 1815, 1977, 2197
Parke, Catherine 980, 2863
Parker, Alexander A. 981, 1551
Parker, Alice 1978
Parker, Dorothy 1816
Parker, Geoffrey 732
Parker, George 1276
Parker, Gillian 897
Parker, Irene 528
Parkinson, C. Northcote 982
Parks, A. Franklin 2198
Parks, George B. 983
Parnell, Paul E. 984
Parreaux, André 1979, 2326, 2612

Parry-Jones, William   529
Paston, George   530
Paterson, Alice   531
Patterson, Emily H.   2378, 2379,
   2586
Patterson, Sylvia   985
Pattison, Robert   986
Patton, Julia   532
Paulson, Ronald   533, 534, 535,
   536, 537, 538, 539, 987, 988,
   989, 990, 1552, 1553, 1554,
   1555, 1556, 1980, 1981, 1982,
   1983, 2199, 2541, 3095
Pawson, Eric   540
Payne, Harry C.   541
Payne, William L.   1123
Peake, Charles   3096
Pearlman, E.   1277
Peck, H. Daniel   1278
Peck, Louis F.   2613
Penner, Allen R.   1557
Perl, Jeffrey M.   1558
Perry, Ruth   991
Pesta, John   2465
Peters, Dolores   1817
Peterson, Spiro   1279
Petrakis, Byron   2200
Petrie, Charles   542
Petrie, Graham   2201, 2202
Pevsner, Nikolaus   543
Philips, David   544
Phillips, Hugh   545
Phillips, M.   546
Phillipson, Nicholas T.   547
Philmus, Robert M.   3097
Philpot, Gordon   548
Pickering, Samuel F., Jr.   992,
   993, 994
Pierce, Charles E.   2864
Pierce, Robert B.   995
Pierre, Gerald J.   3098
Pierson, Robert C.   1818
Pinchbeck, Ivy   549, 550
Pinkus, Philip   3099
Piper, William Bowman   996, 1280,
   1984, 2203, 2204, 2205, 3100
Pitcher, Edward W.   44, 997,
   998
Plamenatz, John   2466
Plant, Marjorie   551
Platzner, Robert L.   878, 2625
Plumb, J. H.   487, 552, 553,
   554, 555, 556, 557, 558, 559,
   560
Pocock, J. G. A.   561
Politi, Jina   999
Poll, Max   3101

Pollard, Sidney   562
Pollin, Burton R.   2425, 2467, 2468,
   2469
Poovey, Mary   1559, 1819, 2661,
   2748
Popkin, Richard H.   563
Porritt, Annie G.   564
Porritt, Edward   564
Porte, Joel   1000
Porter, Roy   565, 2206
Posner, Roland   2207
Poston, Charles D.   1560
Potter, George Reuben   3102
Powers, Lyall H.   1561
Pratt, T. K.   1985
Praz, Mario   1001, 2614
Pressnell, L. S.   566
Preston, John   1002, 1281, 1562,
   1563, 1820, 2208
Preston, Thomas R.   1003, 1004,
   1986, 1987, 1988, 1989, 1990,
   2865
Preu, James A.   2470, 2471, 3103
Price, John Valdimir   567, 1004a,
   1564, 1991, 1992
Price, Julius Mendes   568
Price, Lawrence Marsden   1005, 2209
Price, Martin   1006, 1282, 1565,
   1821, 2210, 3104, 3105
Primer, Irwin   2472
Pringle, Patrick   1566
Privateer, Paul C.   2542
Probyn, Clive T.   2866, 3106, 3107,
   3108
Proctor, Mortimer R.   1007
Proper, Coenraad   1008
Pugh, Charles W.   1283
Punter, David   569, 1009, 1010, 1993
Putney, Rufus   1994, 2211, 2212
Puzon, Bridget   1995
Pyles, Thomas   2867

Quaintance, Richard E.   2728
Quennell, Peter   1011, 2213
Quinlan, Maurice J.   570, 2868, 3109,
   3110
Quintana, Ricardo   2490, 2543, 2544,
   2928, 3111, 3112, 3113, 3114,
   3115

Rabkin, Norman   1822
Rader, Ralph W.   1012, 1284
Radner, John B.   571, 1013, 3116
Radzinowicz, Leon   572, 1567
Raleigh, John Henry   1285

Ramsey, Roger   2626
Rather, L. J.   573
Rawson, C. J.   1568, 1569, 1570,
    1571, 1572, 1573, 1574, 3117
Ray, J. Karen   1286, 1823
Read, Herbert   1996, 2214
Reade, Aleyn Lyell   2869
Redwood, John   574
Reed, Kenneth T.   2870
Reed, Walter L.   1014, 1287, 1575,
    2215
Reichard, Hugh M.   2871, 3118,
    3119
Reichert, John F.   3120
Reid, B. L.   1576, 1824, 1997,
    2216
Reilly, Patrick   3121
Reiss, Edmund   3122
Relton, Frederic   519
Rembar, Charles   2401
Reynolds, Myra   575
Reynolds, W. Vaughan   2545, 2872
Ribble, Frederick G.   1577, 1578
Rice, C. Duncan   576
Richardson, Albert E.   577, 578,
    579, 580
Richetti, John J.   1016, 1288,
    1289, 2683
Richey, Russell E.   581
Richmond, H. W.   1017
Richmond, William K.   582
Richter, David H.   2217, 2873
Rieger, James Henry   2327
Riely, John C.   2729
Riggan, William   1018
Riley, Madeline   583
Rinehart, Hollis   1579, 1580, 1581
Ritcheson, Charles R.   584
Rivers, Isabel   585, 1019
Robert, Marthe   1020
Roberts, Bette B.   2590
Roberts, Donald R.   3123
Roberts, T. A.   586
Robins, Harry F.   1290
Robinson, Charles N.   1021
Robinson, E.   505
Robinson, Howard   587
Robinson, Roger   1582
Robson, Robert   588
Robson-Scott, W. D.   589
Rodgers, Betsy   590
Rodgers, James S.   2218
Rodino, Richard H.   2928a
Rodway, A. E.   1291, 2473
Roemer, Donald   2474
Rogal, Samuel J.   59, 591, 592,
    1022, 1292, 2730

Rogers, Deborah C.   1998
Rogers, Donald O.   2874
Rogers, Henry N., III   1293
Rogers, Katharine M.   60, 593,
    1023, 1294, 1583, 1825, 2339,
    2587, 2701
Rogers, Pat   50, 594, 595, 596,
    1023a, 1295, 1296, 1297, 1298,
    1299, 1584, 2219, 2220, 3124,
    3125, 3126, 3127
Rogers, Winfield H.   1024
Rohrberger, Mary   2221
Romberg, Bertil   1025, 1826
Romero, Christiane Zehl   2615
Ronan, Colin A.   597
Rosen, Frederick   2475, 2575
Rosen, George   598
Rosenberg, Edgar   1026
Rosenblum, Michael   599, 1999,
    2000, 2222, 2223
Rosenheim, Edward W., Jr.   2929,
    3128
Ross, Angus   2001, 3129
Ross, Ian Campbell   2002, 2003
Ross, John F.   1300, 3130, 3131
Røstvig, Maren-Sofie   600, 1585,
    1586
Roth, Martin   2224
Rothstein, Eric   601, 1027, 1587,
    1588, 2004, 2005, 2225, 2476,
    2477, 2546, 2875
Rousseau, George S.   602, 603, 604,
    605, 1028, 1827, 1882, 2006,
    2007, 2008, 2009, 2010, 2226,
    2227, 2547
Roussel, Roy   1828
Rubenstein, Jill   2380
Rudé, George   606, 607, 608, 609
Ruff, William   2662
Runte, Roseann   1029, 2011
Rupp, E. G.   224
Russell, H. K.   1030, 2228
Russell, Norma   2691
Ruthven, K. K.   1589
Ryan, Marjorie   2229
Ryley, Robert M.   3132
Rymer, Michael   2559, 2627

Saagpakk, Paul F.   1031
Sabor, Peter   1829
Sachs, Arieh   2876, 2877
Sacks, Sheldon   1032, 1590, 1830
Sadleir, Michael   2416
Sagarin, Edward   1301
Sale, William, Jr.   1670, 1831, 1832
Sallé, Jean Claude   2230

Salmon, David 610
Sampson, H. Grant 611, 612
Sams, Henry W. 3133
Samuel, Irene 3134
Sanderson, Michael 435, 613
Sankey, Margaret 1302
Saunders, John W. 614
Schackford, John B. 2231
Scher, Steven Paul 2232
Scheuermann, Mona 2343, 2417, 2478
Schilling, Bernard N. 1591
Schmitz, Robert M. 1833, 1872
Schnorrenberg, Barbara Brandon 62, 63, 64, 615
Schofield, Mary Anne 2566, 2567
Schofield, Robert E. 616
Schofield, Roger 617, 618
Schonhorn, Manuel 1303, 1304, 1305, 1306, 1592, 1593, 1594
Schorer, Mark 1306a
Schrock, Thomas S. 1306b
Schulz, Dieter 1033, 1034
Schulz, Max F. 619
Schwartz, Richard 619a, 2879, 2880, 2881, 2882
Sclater, William Lutley 2281
Scott, H. W. 2418
Scott, John 2328
Scott, Temple 2491
Scott, Tom 2012
Scott, Walter S. 620
Scott, William 2410
Scouten, Arthur H. 2883
Scrimgeour, Gary J. 1307
Scrivener, Michael H. 2479
Scrutton, Mary 1834, 2381
Scurr, Helen Margaret 2344
Seamon, R. G. 1595
Secord, Arthur W. 1308, 1309
Sedgwick, Eve 1035
Sedgwick, Romney 621, 2731
Seelye, John D. 3135
Seidel, Michael 1310, 2233, 3136
Seitz, Robert W. 2548
Séjourné, Philippe 2597
Sekora, John 622, 2013, 2014
Selby, Hopewell R. 3137
Sells, Arthur L. 2549
Seltzer, Alvin J. 2234
Semmel, Bernard 623
Sena, John F. 65, 2015, 2016, 2017, 2329, 3138, 3139
Sewall, Richard B. 2884, 2885
Sharrock, Roger 1835
Shaw, Margaret R. B. 2235
Sheehan, David 1596

Shepherd, T. B. 1036
Shepperson, Archibald Bolling 1037, 1597, 1836
Sherbo, Arthur 1038, 1311, 1598, 1599, 1837, 2018, 2236, 3140
Sherburn, George 1600, 1601, 1838, 1839, 2480, 2930, 3141
Sheriff, John K. 624
Sherman, Leona F. 869
Sherwin, Oscar 625, 2550
Sherwood, Irma Z. 1039
Shesgreen, Sean 1602, 1603
Shinagel, Michael 1312, 2402
Shohet, Linda 2340
Shroff, Homai J. 1040, 1840, 2019, 2237
Shugrue, Michael F. 33, 1041
Shuman, R. Baird 1841
Shumata, Natsuo 2238
Shyllon, Folarin 626
Sieber, Harry 1042
Siebert, Donald T. 2020, 3142
Siegel, June Sigler 1842
Sill, Geoffrey M. 1314, 1315, 1316
Simmons, Ernest J. 1043
Simms, J. G. 627
Simon, Irene 1604
Simonds, Bruce 628
Simonsuuri, Kirsti 629
Simpson, K. G. 2021, 2022
Sinfield, Mark 2239
Singer, Godfrey Frank 66, 1044
Singleton, Marvin R. 2240, 2241
Sirén, Oswald 630
Sitter, John 1045
Skilton, David 1046
Sklenicka, Carol J. 2886
Skydsgaard, Niels Jørgen 1317
Slagle, Kenneth Chester 1047
Slepian, B. 2403
Sloan, Kim 631
Sloman, Judith 1048, 1318
Small, Miriam Rossiter 2598
Smidt, Kristian 1843
Smith, D. Nichol 2755
Smith, Elton Edward 2481
Smith, Esther Greenwell 2481
Smith, Frank 632
Smith, Frederik N. 3142a
Smith, Horatio E. 2732
Smith, J. Oates 1605
Smith, Leroy W. 1319, 1606
Smith, Nelson C. 2663
Smith, Norah 633
Smith, Raymond 1607
Smith, Raymond J., Jr. 3143
Smith, Robert A. 634, 1608, 2733

Smith, Roland M. 2962, 3144
Smith, Sidonie 2360
Smith, Warren Hunting 1049
Smitten, Jeffrey R. 2242, 2243, 2244, 2887
Smyth, Charles 635
Snow, Kathleen R. 2245
Snow, Malinda 1320, 1321, 1609
Sokolyansky, Mark G. 1050, 1610, 2246
Solomon, Stanley J. 1051
Sossaman, Stephan 2404
Southworth, James G. 636
Spacks, Patricia Meyer 1052, 1053, 1054, 1055, 1322, 1611, 1844, 2247, 2382
Spadaccini, Nicholas 1323
Spearman, Diana 1056, 1612, 1845
Speck, Paul Surgi 2248
Speck, W. A. 637, 638, 1056a, 3145, 3146
Spector, Robert D. 67, 1883, 2023
Speer, Blanche C. 1613
Spencer, David G. 2628
Spilka, Mark 1614, 1615
Sprott, S. E. 639
Squires, Michael 1057
Stallbaumer, Virgil R. 2482, 2576, 2577
Stamm, James R. 1058
Stamm, Rudolf G. 1324
Stamper, Rexford 2483
Stanzel, Franz 1616
Starkie, Walter F. 1059
Starkman, Miriam 3147
Starr, George A. 1060, 1325, 1326, 1327, 1328
Starr, Nathan Comfort 2024
Stathis, James J. 2931
Stauffer, Donald A. 1060a
Staver, Frederick 640
Staves, Susan 641, 1061, 1062, 2383
Stebbins, Lucy Poate 2588
Stecher, Henry F. 2684
Stedmond, John M. 2249
Steele, F. M. 1063
Steele, Peter 3148
Steen, M. 2680
Steeves, Edna L. 1064
Steeves, Harrison R. 642, 1065
Stein, Jess M. 2734
Stein, William B. 1846
Stein, William Bysshe 1329
Stephanson, Raymond 1330, 1331, 1617

Stephens, John C., Jr. 1618
Sternbach, Robert 2888
Stevens, David Harrison 643
Stevenson, John 644
Stevenson, John Allen 1847
Stevenson, Lionel 1066
Stevick, Philip 68, 1067, 1068, 1619, 1620, 2025, 2026
Stewart, Douglas J. 645, 2405
Stewart, Jack F. 2250, 2251, 2252
Stewart, Keith 1069, 1621
Stitzel, Judith G. 1622
Stobie, Margaret 2253
Stock, R. D. 1070
Stoler, John A. 1124, 1363
Stone, Edward 3149
Stone, Jeanne C. Fawtier 648a
Stone, Lawrence 646, 647, 648, 648a
Storch, Rudolf F. 2484
Stout, Gardner D. 2254, 2255
Stowell, Helen Elizabeth 2384
Strange, Sallie Minter 1332
Strauss, Albrecht B. 2027
Streatfield, David C. 649
Streeter, Harold Wade 69, 1071
Stromberg, Roland N. 650
Stumpf, Thomas A. 1623
Styles, John 145
Suderman, Elmer F. 2889
Suits, Conrad 3150
Sullivan, E. E. 3150a
Summers, Montague 71, 1072, 1073, 2735
Summerson, John 651, 652
Sunstein, Emily W. 2749
Sutherland, James R. 1074, 1333, 1334, 1335
Sutherland, John H. 2293, 3151
Sutherland, Lucy 653, 654
Sutherland, W. O. S., Jr. 2551, 2890, 3152
Swados, Harvey 1336
Swann, George Rogers 1337, 1624, 1848
Swearingen, James E. 2256
Swigart, Ford H., Jr. 2664
Swingewood, Alan 1625
Sykes, Norman 655
Sypher, Wylie 1075, 2665

Tallman, Warren 3153
Tannenbaum, Earl 1624
Tarr, Sister Mary Muriel 1076
Tatar, Maria M. 2736

Tate, William E. 656
Taube, Myron 1338, 2406
Tave, Stuart M. 1077, 2257
Taylor, Anne Robinson 1339,
   1849
Taylor, Archer 2616
Taylor, Arthur J. 657
Taylor, Dick, Jr. 1627, 3154
Taylor, Douglas 658
Taylor, Houghton W. 1628
Taylor, John Tinnon 1078
Taylor, S. Ortiz 1079
Teerink, Herman 2932
Teissedou, Janie 2578
Ten Harmsel, Henrietta 1850
Ter-Abramova, V. G. 2579
Thacker, Christopher 1080
Thomas, D. S. 1629
Thomas, David 659
Thomas, Donald 2666
Thomas, Joel J. 2028
Thomas, P. D. G. 660
Thompson, Edward Palmer 661
Thompson, Harold William 2629
Thomson, David 2258
Thomson, J. E. P. 2259, 2260
Thomson, John 2667
Thornburg, Thomas 3155
Thornbury, E. Margaret 1630
Thorpe, Annette P. 3156
Thorslev, Peter L., Jr. 1081
Thorson, Connie Capers 1884
Thorson, James L. 2029
Tieje, Arthur J. 1082, 1083,
   1084
Tillotson, Geoffrey 2891, 2892,
   2893, 2894
Tillyard, E. M. W. 1085, 1086,
   1340, 1631
Tilton, John W. 3157
Timpe, Eugene F. 3158
Tinker, Chauncey Brewster 662,
   663, 664
Tobias, J. T. 665
Tobin, James E. 72, 2926
Todd, Dennis 3159
Todd, Janet 475, 1087, 1851,
   2407, 2739, 2750, 2751
Tomalin, Claire 2752
Tomarken, Edward 2895
Tomasson, Katherine 666
Tomkinson, W. S. 546
Tompkins, J. M. S. 1088, 2345
Tompson, Richard S. 667
Torchiana, Donald T. 3160
Torrance, Robert M. 1632
Towers, A. R. 1633, 2261
Tracy, Ann B. 1089

Tracy, Clarence R. 2262, 2896,
   2897, 3161
Traldi, Ila Dawson 3162
Traugott, John L. 1852, 2263, 3163,
   3164
Treadwell, J. M. 3165
Treadwell, Michael 3166
Treadwell, T. O. 2030
Trease, Geoffrey 668
Trevelyan, George M. 669, 670
Trickett, Rachel 671
Tripathi, P. D. 1090
Trumbach, Randolph 672
Tucker, Edward F. J. 1634
Tucker, Susie I. 673, 674
Turberville, A. S. 675, 676
Turner, Michael 677, 1091
Tuveson, Ernest 678, 679, 2264,
   3167, 3168
Tysdahl, B. J. 2485
Tyson, Gerald P. 2265

Uhrström, Wilhelm 1853
Ulanov, Barry 1635, 2266
Ulmer, Gregory L. 1854
Underwood, E. Ashworth 691, 2031
Underwood, Gary N. 2032
Uphaus, Robert W. 680, 1092, 1341,
   1636, 1855, 2033, 2267, 2268,
   2486, 2898, 3169
Utter, Robert P. 1093, 1856

Vaid, Sudesh 681, 1342, 1857
Vale, Edmund 682
Vance, John A. 3170
Van der Veen, H. R. S. 1094
Van der Voorde, Frans P. 1637
Van Ghent, Dorothy 1343, 1638,
   1858, 1859, 2269
Van Marter, Shirley 1860
Vann, Richard T. 683
Varma, Devendra P. 684, 1095,
   2617, 2668, 2737
Verbeek, E. 2899
Vereker, Charles 685
Vesterman, William 2900
Vichert, Gordon 686
Vickers, Brian 3171
Vincent, W. A. L. 687
Viner, Jacob 688
Voigt, Milton 2933
Voitle, Robert 2901, 2902
Von den Steinen, Karl 73
Vopat, James B. 1639, 2385
Voss-Clesly, Patricia 2386

Wagenknecht, Edward 2034
Wagoner, Mary 1884a, 2035, 2270
Wahba, Magdi 2330, 2903
Wain, John 2904
Walker, Robert G. 689, 2271,
  2905
Wall, Cecil 690, 691
Walters, John 692
Walton, J. K. 3172
Walton, James 1344, 2487
Walvin, James 693, 694, 695
Ward, H. G. 1862
Ward, W. R. 696, 697
Ward, William S. 74
Wardle, Ralph M. 2552, 2753
Wardroper, John 1096
Ware, Malcolm 2669, 2670, 2671
Wark, Robert R. 698
Warner, James H. 699
Warner, John M. 1640, 2036, 2037
Warner, William Beatty 1863
Warren, Leland E. 699a, 1641,
  1642, 1643, 2272, 2599
Wasiolek, Edward 3173
Wasserman, Earl R. 2906
Waterhouse, Ellis 700
Watkins, Walter B. C. 2273
Watson, George 52
Watson, Harold Francis 1097
Watson, J. Steven 701, 702
Watson, Tommy G. 1345
Watt, Ian 1098, 1099, 1100, 1125,
  1346, 1347, 1348, 1349, 1644,
  1645, 1646, 1864, 1865, 1866,
  2274, 2275
Weales, Gerald 2276
Wearmouth, R. F. 703
Webb, Beatrice 705, 706, 707
Webb, Robert Kiefer 704
Webb, Sidney 705, 706, 707
Webster, Grant T. 2038
Wedd, Annie F. 2562
Wedel, T. O. 3174
Weinbrot, Howard 1647, 2546,
  2907
Weinsheimer, Joel 2039, 2040
Weinstein, Arnold 1101, 1350,
  1648, 1867, 2277
Weissman, Judith 1649
Weitzman, Arthur J. 708, 1102,
  2908
Welch, Barbara A. 709
Wells, John Edwin 1650
Welsh, Alexander 1103
Wendt, Allan 1651, 1652, 1868
Wess, Robert V. 1653
West, Paul 2909

West, William A. 2041
Westerfield, Ray B. 710
Western, J. R. 711
Whibley, Leonard 2910
Whicher, George Frisbie 2568
Whinney, Margaret 712
Whitbourn, Christine J. 1104
White, Douglas H. 3175
White, Eugene 2387, 2388
White, F. Eugene 2278
White, Ian 2911
White, R. J. 713
Whitley, Alvin 2912
Whitley, Raymond K. 2408
Whitney, Lois 1105
Whitrow, Magda 75
Whittuck, C. A. 1106
Wicks, Ulrich 1107, 1108, 1109
Wiener, Harold S. L. 2331
Wiesenfarth, Joseph 1654
Wieten, Alida Alberdina Sibbellina
  2672
Wilding, Michael 3176
Wiles, Roy M. 714, 715, 716, 717,
  718, 719, 720, 721, 2913
Willard, Nedd 2914
Willcox, William B. 722
Willey, Basil 723
Williams, Aubrey 1655
Williams, Basil 724
Williams, E. Neville 725, 726, 727
Williams, Harold 3177
Williams, Ioan 76, 1110, 1111
Williams, Iolo A. 2492
Williams, J. David 3178
Williams, Kathleen 3179, 3180, 3181,
  3182
Williams, Murial Brittain 1656
Williams, Raymond 728
Williamson, Eugene 1657
Williamson, George 1112
Willis, Peter 384, 729
Wills, Antony 1869
Wilson, Angus 1870
Wilson, Bruce L. 730
Wilson, Charles 731, 732
Wilson, James R. 3183
Wilson, Mona 2692
Wilson, Stuart 1871
Wilson, W. Daniel 1113
Wilt, Judith 1872
Wimsatt, W. K. 2915, 2916
Winchcombe, George 2553
Winner, Anthony 1873
Winnett, A. R. 2917
Winstanley, D. A. 733, 734
Winton, Calhoun 3184

Wolf, Edward C. J. 1114
Wolff, Cynthia Griffin 1115, 1658, 1874, 2673
Wolff, Renate C. 1875
Wood, Carl 1659
Wood, James O. 3185
Wood, Theodore E. B. 735
Woodcock, George 1351, 1660, 2488, 2489
Woodforde, John 736
Woods, Charles B. 1661
Woods, Samuel H., Jr. 2221, 2493, 2494
Work, James A. 1662, 2279
Wright, Andrew 1663, 2280
Wright, Arnold 2281
Wright, H. Bunker 2685
Wright, Terence 1116
Wright, Walter Francis 1117

Wrigley, E. A. 737
Wynne, Edith J. 1664

Yates, Mary V. 1875a
Yeomans, W. E. 3186
Yolton, John W. 738
Young, Percy M. 739
Yoseloff, Thomas 2282

Zach, Wolfgang 1876
Zaller, Robert 740
Zimansky, Curt A. 3187
Zimmerman, Everett 1352, 1353, 1354, 1355, 3188
Zirker, Malvin R., Jr. 1665, 1666
Zucker, Paul 741